VERY BANGKOK

IN THE CITY OF THE SENSES

VERY BANGKOK

IN THE CITY OF THE SENSES

PHILIP CORNWEL-SMITH
AUTHOR & PHOTOGRAPHER

RIVER BOOKS

Dedication

I dedicate this book to the two personal mentors who've edited this book:

Consulting Editor: Marc Pachter
Editor: Alex Kerr

First published in Thailand in 2020 by
River Books Press Ltd.
396/1 Maharaj Road, Phraborommaharajawang
Bangkok 10200, Thailand Tel 66 2 2250139, 2259574
E-mail: order@riverbooksbk.com
www.riverbooksbk.com
@riverbooks riverbooksbk Riverbooksbk

2nd edition 2025.

Copyright collective work © River Books, 2020
Copyright text © Philip Cornwel-Smith, 2020
except preface © Lawrence Osborne, 2020
Photographic copyright as credited © Philip Cornwel-Smith 2020, or as indicated otherwise.

All rights reserved. No part of this book may be reproduced or transmitted in any form or by any means, electronic or including photocopy, recording or any other information storage and retrieval system, without prior permission in writing from the publisher.

Publisher: River Books Press Ltd., Bangkok, Thailand
EU Authorised Representative: Easy Access System Europe Oü, 16879218 - Mustamäe tee 50, 10621 Tallinn, Estonia, gpsr.requests@easproject.com

British Library Cataloguing-in-Publication Data.
A catalogue record for this book is available from the British Library

ISBN : 978-616-451-103-3

Publisher: Narisa Chakrabongse.
Consulting Editor: Marc Pachter
Editor: Alex Kerr
Researchers: Saran Mahasupap
Cover design: Xavier Comas of Cover Kitchen
Design: 1000 Ponies Co.,Ltd.; Ruetairat Nanta
Digital Image: DailyTouch
Production Supervision: Ruetairat Nanta

Printed and bound in Thailand by
Sirivatana Interprint Public Co., Ltd

page 2: An offering to monks at Wat Wachiratham Sathit.   **right: Pipes on a the street.**

Contents

FOREWORD
by Lawrence Osborne 6

INTRODUCTION 8
Witness 16

Senses

TIME 22
Timeline 23
Destiny 25

SMELL 26
Flower Culture 28

TASTE 30
Streetfood 32
Gastrothai 37

HEAT & DAMP 40
Se-waen 44

SPACE 48
Sanam Luang 51
Background City 53
Third Places 55
Green Space 57

DIRECTION 60
Centre Points 61
Wayfinding 62
Feng Shui 64

MOTION 66
Walking 68
Cycling 72
Custom Transit 75

BALANCE 78

LOOKING 80
Vertical Living 82
Larkitecture 88

COLOUR 90
Blossom Season 95

SACRED 97
Brahmin 98
Ratchaprasong Shrines 102
All in One 107
Muslim-Thais 108

SIXTH SENSE 112
Animist Shrines 118

TRANCE 120
Neo-Hindu 124

NIGHT 126
Partying 130

SANUK 133

LIBIDO 136
The Bangkok Noir 140
An LGBT Paradise? 143

TOUCH 146
Massage 149

PAIN 150
Local Heroes 151
Healing Hub 152
Pot Luck 154
Hell Park 155

SOUND 156
Birdsong 158
Bang-Pop! 162

SENSORS 164

Heart

THAINESS & THE CITY 170
Royal Presence 172
Krungthep or Bangkok? 178

INFLUENCE 180
Primate City 185
Sites of Dissent 187

BECOMING BANGKOKIAN 189
Mon 194
Indian-Thais 198

ROOTS 200
Isaan Travelogue 202
Regional Rites 207

STIR-FRY 210
From Jek to Thai-Jiin 214
Sino-Thai Identity 219

COMMUNITY 222
Roofless 229
Subcultures 230
Tin Town 234

MARKET 236
Talad Nat 239
Monohoods 242

YOUTH 247
Siam Square 250
T-Rap 253
Youth Protest Culture 257

CREATIVE CITY 258
Graffiti 267
Bangkoklyn 274

Face

MEMORY 278
Mind the Gaps 285
Retro and Nostalgia 288
Protukate 292

TOURIST TRAPPINGS 294
Slogans 297
Urban Explorers 299
Backpackers 302

PORTRAYALS 304
True Fiction 308
The Indecisive Moment 311
Cinematic Krungthep 312
Messy Aesthetic 314
Reality TV and Reality 318
Theories of Bangkok 321

FUTURES 324
Project Singapore 326
Bladerunneresque 332

APPENDICES
Acknowledgements 336
Bibliography 337
Notes & References 340
Photo Credits 347
Index 348

MAPS
Central Bangkok Map front flap
Greater Bangkok Map back flap

Foreword
by Lawrence Osborne
author of *Bangkok Days*, *The Forgiven* and *The Wet & the Dry*.

"Bangkok looks like it's been Photoshopped," Philip Cornwel-Smith writes in a chapter devoted to the subject of 'Colour.' "No pink could be that shocking, no gold that yellow. The glare of the sun dials up the brilliance, and casts deep blinding shadows." It would have been an apposite opening for this entire book, a brilliant and polychromatic look at Bangkok done in a way that no other writer has attempted. Consider the multitude of chapters and themes. There is a section called 'Flow' devoted to walking, cycling and 'Custom Transit.' There is one devoted to 'Roots' which considers Isaan migrant art and regional rites, and one given over to 'Sound' in which our writer mulls the questions of birdsong and Bang-Pop. From the strangeness of panoramas and Kudi Jeen to the nature of suffering and its assuagement through Healing Tubs and 'Body Collectors,' he turns Bangkok into a vast tapestry of meditations on the nature of cities.

Since writing *Very Thai* in 2005 Cornwel-Smith has become the city's preeminent mythographer in the English language. Who else but an outsider would be able to muster such an eternally-bemused concentration when trying to unravel the meanings of things which he didn't absorb unconsciously as a child? "By night," he writes in the same chapter on Colour, "the white-balance must be set to 'fluorescent'. " The city's signature hue, he tells us, is green, after the god Indra, while formal transit has "more jazzy stripes than Paul Smith socks." This makes for many a surprise.

So begins a charming and unexpected detour into the mythology and symbolism of colour, an element which we long-time residents see every day but which we either don't understand or cannot decode for ourselves. So it is with every chapter, whether it be on scent, taste, design, the nocturnal life, transport, flowers, the supernatural, or merely the perplexing enigmas of backpackers. The city is re-seen, re-imagined as a vast complex of signs which requires the informal encyclopedia which he has written.

I didn't know, for example, that Bangkok post-boxes are red because of the British, nor that coloured stacking chairs are an urban icon featured at the Thai pavilion of the 2017 Venice Biennale. I did know that black was the colour of Rahu, god of the eclipse, that the ubiquitous Bangkokian taste for "a yellowish alloy of gold" comes from the Chinese and that the days of week are associated with the colours of Vedic astrology. But I didn't know that Thais prefer the "mintier tones" of Fuji film over the "warmth of Kodak moments" or that in the late 20th century, "female officewear favoured synthetic dyes and dual-tone clashes as eye-popping as the chorus lines of folk music concerts." What one feels unconsciously, Cornwel-Smith puts into a fine and sensual prose that provides the reader with a little 'discovery'.

He is not afraid to speculate large. During the above-mentioned meditation on 'Flow,' he observes of the city's maddening movements in their constant (and confusing) ebb: "The commotion is not just on the surface. In an ancient creation myth, *thep* (angels) released the elixir of life by Churning the Sea of Milk. Krungthep's liveliness comes from constant churn; it reflects the fact that the city is structurally unstable at deeper levels. Things that most countries consider permanent, shift with surprising ease in Bangkok."

This is both fanciful and true, something again that one feels subconsciously, and yet it is not something that would occur to one automatically. *Very Bangkok* is filled with such bright gems, as if the writer had decided to deliberately imitate and evoke the glittering 'dragon-scale' ceramic armour of Wat Pho, with hundreds of little pieces assembled to form a whole. As it turns out, this is an ideal method for combining whimsy, erudition, a sensual precision of language and a deep

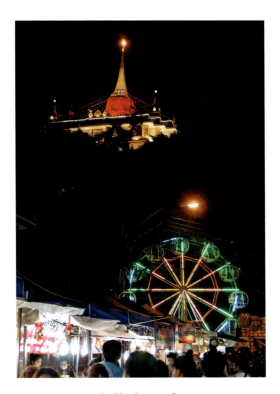

interest in Bangkok's almost-forgotten historical past. "Memory gaps," he writes in his section devoted to 'Memory', "are one cause of Bangkok's many mysteries, which get glossed over or spawn multiple theories." And this same chapter, subtitled "Remembering to forget," begins with this marvelous mini-paragraph: "The last Lao flute maker of Thonburi folds his wrinkled limbs under an anglepoise lamp and drills into a bamboo tube gripped by his feet."

Of all cities, Bangkok is perhaps the hardest to re-imagine in terms of its past, because so much of that past has been atomised by what Cornwel-Smith calls "auto-amnesia." We all know that old houses, sometimes beauties, are regularly demolished because they are thought to be inhabited by ghosts. But the malady is deeper even than that. Against this willful collective destruction of the past – which sits oddly with a professed love of 'Thainess' – it is possible that at this point only the written word can serve as a bastion. *Very Bangkok*, I think, sets out to be just that. And as such, a future reader, living in his or her air-conditioned nightmares, might well turn to it to find out what hand-made flutes, mangosteen-coloured taxis, street food and spirit doctors were all about.

left: **Polychromatic chimeras at Bangkok's most fantasmagorical temple, Wat Pariwat.**

right: **Golden Mount temple fair in Wat Saket at the Loy Krathong festival.**

Introduction
How does Bangkok sound, smell, taste, look, move and feel?

On the west bank of the river at Thonburi, the hubbub of Prannok Market funnels into a typical *soi* (lane) so tight its awnings almost touch. Motorbikes trundle through a path narrowed further by the shophouse residents putting out tables for selling portions of fish liver curry or packets of sweet squidgy bread. Wending past seafood restaurants, cheap apartments and a communal washing machine, the *soi* opens into a rare public space at the pier of Wat Rakhang. This ancient royal temple is named for its bells, which tinkle in the riverside breeze. There you can take in the most historic panorama of the Chao Phraya River. It's the prime vantage point to ponder the metropolis explored in this book.

A quarter millennium ago, the founder of today's Thai capital enjoyed this same view. The teak stilt house where Chao Phraya Chakri once lived still stands at the side of the temple. Through its trapezoid windows, he gazed east across the river from the short-lived capital of Thonburi to the Teochiu Chinese settlement at Bangkok. There in 1782, Chakri would found his new dynastic capital and rename it Krungthep, the City of Angels.

In place of the Teochiu seafarers' shrine – shifted downstream to today's Chinatown at Sampeng – Chakri built his golden-spired Grand Palace. Its crenellated walls were for two centuries fringed by the raft houses of an amphibious city pulsating with market trade. Today they're fringed by tourists, who make Bangkok the most visited city in the world.

The river is why this city exists. Silt-swollen waters deposited the alluvial delta on which it was built. Riverine trade was the reason it became a customs post and grew into a wealthy port. For centuries, Bangkokians lived above waterways that linked every citizen by boat and supported a water-based culture. It's an invented landscape, sculpted over eons. This stretch of river is actually a flood-widened canal, cut in 1542 to shorten the journey around the ear-shaped meanders of what are now Khlong's Bangkok Noi and Bangkok Yai – the canals of Little Bangkok and Big Bangkok.

The pontoon at Wat Rakhang Pier bobs in wash from the incessant boat traffic that ploughs back and forth. Cross-river ferries dodge commuter expressboats, hotel shuttles and longtail tour boats that dart down the remaining canals of this one-time 'water city.' After decades of car-biased planning had turned Bangkok's back on the waterways, the river is once again a fast way to move around this traffic-jammed city. Come nightfall, dinner cruisers bombard the old riverside with the bass of their open-air discos and their contours outlined in piped LEDs.

Upstream, cars shunt to a standstill along the Rama VIII Bridge, its suspension cables arrayed like a golden harp. Downstream looms the original Thonburi landmark, Wat Arun, the Temple of Dawn, where King Taksin founded a new Siamese capital in 1767 after the fall of Ayutthaya. Near its five slender towers, the first tunnel under the river links the new and old capitals through mass rapid transit into a hi-tech megalopolis.

The Chao Phraya just about remains a natural habitat. At temple piers, thrashing catfish gulp the pellets sprinkled by sightseers. A rising tide returns vegetal islets of water hyacinth back upstream, with white storks perched on the buoyant weed. A six-foot-long monitor lizard swims past, propelled by muscular tail-swishes. Its forked blue tongue darts out to taste the flavours of the mud-brown estuary.

These waters have witnessed the tides of history. In the 1893 Paknam Incident, French gunboats anchored here to threaten Siam, which narrowly averted colonisation. In 1951, the then prime minister swam to the riverbank from captivity aboard the navy's flagship, *RTNS Sri Ayudhya*, which was sunk by the army during one of Bangkok's many coups d'état. In 1976, demonstrators fled to this shore from a massacre at Thammasat University by swimming across its treacherous mainstream. This landscape of layered historic meaning is now being shorn of its diverse old communities and streamlined into a glorified monument park for mass tourism and national spectacle.

The river quietens after 10pm, but in peak hours it takes a momentous event to quell this aquatic hubbub. In 2002, no boats were allowed on the river one rush hour, so that an audience on the terrace of the Oriental Hotel could hear José Carreras sing arias in the black velvet air. In 2003, all traffic in the city centre, including on the river, was stopped for the APEC inter-governmental summit.

The river goes uncannily silent in auspicious years for the occasional Royal Barge Processions and rehearsals, for which Wat Rakhang has the clearest view. Eerie chants of boat songs sung by the naval rowers precede the flotilla of 55 gilded barges, with prows carved into mythical beasts: the *supannahong* swan, the *naga* serpent, Hanuman the monkey general astride a canon. Barge rehearsals are like a backstage reveal, minus the embroidered canopies, gold-piped scarlet tunics and the peacock feathers used by the cox to signal. With the oarsmen propelling the undecorated barges in sport-hued T-shirts, you can see the effort and structures that are obscured by costumed pageantry when the King rides the *Supannahong* to deliver robes to the monks of Wat Arun.

Surveying the scene from the Wat Rakhang pier is a giant statue of its legendary former abbot, Luang Phor Toh. Born when the city

above **A historic bend in the Chao Phraya River, with Rattanakosin Island to the right side beyond Phra Pinklao Bridge.**

Introduction   9

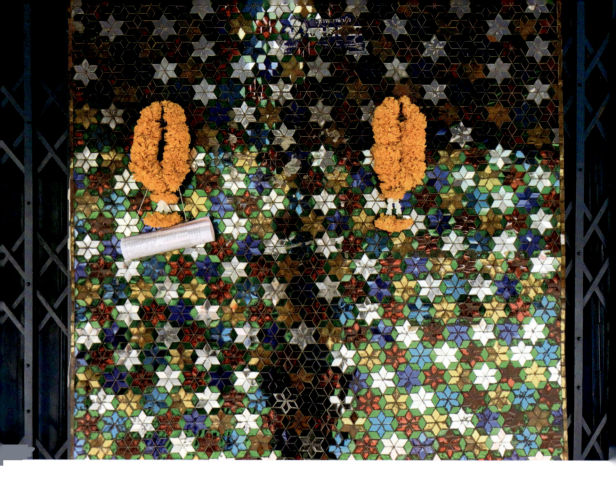

was six, Toh is renowned for advising kings and making Thailand's most prized amulets. While the intent of Buddhism is to overcome sensory urges, the contrarian Toh taught that sensory knowledge can be a source of insight.

For Bangkokians, nothing matters more than to 'gain face,' for the self, this city, or the nation. While a face mirror fuels the ego, Toh urged us to use a *krajok hok dan* – a six-panel mirror. As well as the front, it reflects less flatteringly from the back, the left, the right, below and above, so we get multi-faceted views of our true nature. Toh also paired each reflection to a sensory organ: eye, ear, nose, tongue, body, and heart-mind. To understand reality, we need all our faculties to perceive every angle. This book aims to be a *krajok hok dan* for Bangkok.

Inspiration for the cover comes from a Western version of a six-sided mirror: the kaleidoscope. Each time you shake or turn a kaleidoscope tube, the translucent shapes inside form a fresh pattern, only illuminated from within rather than reflected out. Bangkok is both a city of inward enlightenment, and of outward dazzle, but not straightforward reflection. That's why I've sought to provide a reflective guide.

Multiple perspectives are vital, because Bangkok is a story with an Official Version – plus many other versions that often lack voice. 'Thainess' is best understood as an ideology, a set of values about what should be, so using it as a description blurs distinctions between things considered proper to present, and improper things that should be hidden. This city's held in tenuous balance between its informal impulses and the forces of formality. But it's more nuanced than simply chaos versus order, for informal Bangkok has hidden order, while formal Bangkok is often a cause of the chaos.

This formal/informal juxtaposition is embodied by Luang Phor Toh. An advisor to kings, he's blessed with a memorial. To the public, he's a monk magician best known for exorcising Bangkok's infamously lovelorn ghost, Nang Nak, whose jealous spirit Toh then sealed in a jar and floated down canal. Nang Nak and Toh are worshipped at a less formal temple on that canal in what's now the suburb of Phrakhanong. The shrine there is profuse with offerings of dresses and dolls, plus mechanical devices for making merit with donated coins. Conscripts flock there for Nak's blessing, while fortune tellers read the devotees' moles, and gamblers rub powder into wood to divine lucky numbers for the lottery. So which is Bangkok's real character?

Wat Rakhang stands in Wang Lang, an area named for a long vanished palace that's now associated with its restaurants of fiery Southern Thai food. Southerners live in one the neighbouring enclaves, nearby migrants from the north, Isaan (northeast) and China, who each maintain ethnic traditions as subcultures under the national identity of 'Thainess.' Morning and evening, the area buzzes with markets and streetlife in an expression of how Bangkok's informal and formal cultures coexist.

Central to this dilemma is to gauge how 'Bangkokness' differs from 'Thainess.' This is a city with a split personality, a past life, and hidden histories. The capital is the epitome of Thainess – which it imposes on the indigenous cultures of the regions – and its antithesis, with urban qualities of its own. So much of what people see as typical Thainess is actually the Bangkok version. In that sense Thainess is Bangkokness.

To deduce what's going on, it helps to be specific about labels. Thais use the formal term, Krungthep, which is loaded with allusions to sacredness under its Hinduised origin myth. Its former name Bangkok was kept for international use. I mostly refer to Bangkok due to that foreign familiarity – and for another reason. As 'Bangkok' is a word from the indigenous culture, it feels better suited to discussing the streetlife, subcultures and everyday ways. 'Krungthep,' being the prestigious title, makes it hard to differentiate the city's informal lifestyle. When I refer to Krungthep, it's to explain the formal culture. Similarly, I refer mostly to 'Thailand' and 'Thai,' but use 'Siam' and 'Siamese' when explaining the pre-modern era.

Bangkok can't shake off some very stubborn reputations, whether lurid or precious. Those clichés get hardened by the hyper ways the city gets portrayed through exoticism or hagiography or innuendo. Over 30 years of living here, I've encountered many Bangkoks: formal and informal, traditional and indie, high society and slum. In a land that micro-manages how it's seen, this book treats those multiple angles as valid. *Very Bangkok*, like the intensifier 'very' in its name, brings undercurrents to the fore. Bangkok is all these things, but with added sugar, plus extra chilli. Bangkok is extremely *very*.

You can dip into *Very Bangkok* at any point, as its chapters deal with self-contained topics. In sequence, the book's three sections echo the stages of familiarity with a place. Upon first impression, Bangkok affects us on instinctual levels, so the first half of the book, SENSES, conveys our bodily experience of the city in the moment. Delving deeper reveals how the city works, so the core of the book, HEART, goes into the citizens' values, networks and lifestyles. In reflection upon the nature of this place, the closing section, FACE, unpacks how locals and outsiders interpret and represent Bangkok.

Senses

Bangkokians live with startling juxtapositions that outsiders struggle to process. Reconciling those contradictions is harder than re-stating clichéed judgments that Bangkok is chaotic, bizarre or inexplicably Oriental. Nor is all of it made clear by official Thainess, which is more a set of instructions on how to behave, rather

left: Garlands hang on a shophouse frontage near City Hall at Phra Nakhon.

right: An armada of tourist boats cruises towards their berth at River City.

left: **The canalside shrine to the famous ghost Mae Nak at Wat Mahabutr on Khlong Phrakhanong.**

right: **Graffiti with a cobra and a Chinese lion on a typical shophouse between Khlong Mahanak and Golden Mount.**

than a 'secret decoder ring' for Bangkokness. To 'read' what makes Bangkok unique, we need to make sense of our senses.

Aristotle defined the 'big five' senses: 'Smell,' 'Sound,' 'Touch,' 'Taste' and sight, which I've recast as the culturally engaged act of 'Looking.' Modernity, especially in 2-D screens, is overly visual, and heavily aural, but relegates other senses. Yet Thai culture relishes wider sensory input, which aids understanding of Bangkok through its spices, massage, herbalism, tonal speech and delight in heightened stimuli.

Surprisingly, we have as many as 21-33 senses, depending which receptors you count. Several vital ones reveal Thai cultural resonance, such as 'Colour,' 'Direction,' or 'Balance,' which studies find is the second sense that people most fear to lose. Bangkok has a constricted sense of 'Space' yet very fluid 'Motion.' If it seems like everything's going on at once; that's because when it comes to 'Time,' Bangkokians go by many clocks and calendars, as well as 'rubber time.' While the city's embrace of the 'Night' has much to do with cooler air, many feel pulled by Bangkok's most ecstatic sensibility: 'Libido.' All of this is modulated by a soothing attitude to 'Pain.' Often Thai actions boil down to climate, a wilting combo of 'Heat and Damp.'

Senses often shape beliefs. Buddhists hold that Dharma gets spread not just by scripture and murals, but also through sound by chiming bells, through scent by aromatic garlands, and through light by glinting mirror-tile mosaics. Luang Phor Toh's six-panel mirror adds a sixth sense: 'mind', which in Thai shares the word *jai* with 'heart.' Hundreds of phrases using *jai* show how Thais think with their 'heart-mind.'

Out-of-body sensing is part of life here, from kinship and face to karma and past lives, as featured in the 'Sacred' and supernatural 'Sixth Sense' chapters, as well as the surrender of the senses to others under 'Trance.' I also consider diverse perceptions of faith, from 'Muslim-Thai' to 'Neo-Hindu.' Technology now imposes digital 'Sensors,' but analogue Bangkok still revels in sensory authenticity.

Heart

Outsiders see apparent chaos, yet Thais order things by cultural levers. Rules aren't fixed, as even laws are subject to customs of hierarchy, beliefs, connections and situational morality. They tap a repertoire of mutually understood strategies that suit the 'sensitivity' of a given time and place. In 'Thainess and the City,' gritty Thai urban realness confronts an official ideology that is courtly, religious and rural.

A new chapter shows how the capital is run through 'Influence,' whether official or informal, and often erupts in a sense of crisis.

Residents show much ambivalence about their hometown, but it's so tolerant of outsiders that globalised expatriates and Asian diasporas delight in 'Becoming Bangkokian.' Its sprawling patchwork of urban villages often juxtapose several ethnic and religious groups, *tanaka*-powdered Burmese cheek by bearded Indian jowl. Many cities have ghettos, but Bangkok packs in four Little Indias, three

Portuguese barrios, two Tiny Tokyos, at least five Mon villages, umpteen Muslim medinas, and so many Chinatowns in a hybrid Sino-Thai culture that they get their own chapter, 'Stir-fry.' Meanwhile, 'Roots' shows how internal migrants maintain dual identities.

The heart of the Heart section is 'Community.' I consider what's home for each level of status, from mansion, *moo ban* (housing estate) and condominium down to shophouse, slum and the homeless. While the elite get the most attention in the media, it's the middle classes that shape today's shift from traditional 'way of life' to modern lifestyle. This plays out in the stalls and malls covered in 'Market,' which shows the drift from informal shopping to global online consumerism.

Within this seniority system, subcultures struggle to find space, whether the pursuits and protests of 'Youth,' or the worlds of art, music or invention. Bangkok's aspiration to be a 'Creative City' struggles with older impulses towards patronage and tradition.

Face

In this status city, being alert to 'saving face' almost qualifies as a sense. Saving Bangkok's face is a duty of all Thais, which makes the city receptive to Orientalist exoticism, but averse to its notoriety for sleaze. Visitors arrive with preconceived notions and marketed fantasies that don't match the reality – a disjoint that I explore in 'Tourist Trappings.' There is also a disconnect between that reality and the Thais' image of themselves. As the chapter 'Memory' relates, highly selective nostalgia, monuments and notions of heritage are contested by efforts to revive hidden local histories.

Bangkok had been a word-of-mouth city; in 'Portrayals,' I consider how it's becoming a known city. Global attention can flatter, but when the gaze turns critical, some claim that "foreigners can't understand Thainess." All that makes Bangkok a great subject for art, film, songs and books, with its own genre of 'Bangkok Noir' and dystopian science fiction that imagines a flooded Bangkok. Yet officials purge streetlife and nightlife to emulate sensible, antiseptic Singapore, recoiling from whatever entices the senses: markets, mess, noise, sex, alcohol and staying up late.

In conclusion, the 'Futures' chapter reviews the overarching themes of order and chaos through the lenses of planning, resilience and the city's main physical feature: the river.

The senses may help explain this place, but it still retains the capacity to surprise. The Bangkok Metropolitan Administration (BMA) brands this the 'City of Life,' while striving to remove too much unruly life from the streets – a mission that reflects the values of the elite. Bangkok's DNA is both to celebrate and subdue the sensory spark that gives it life.

A Book About Cities

This is also a book about cities, in which Bangkok is the subject. Thailand became majority urban the same year, 2012, that the world did, so cities are a hot topic. So many people have an interest in understanding how cities work, whether for architecture or design, business or tourism, services or security. Most cities are planned to functional need from 'objective' data, or are subject to ideology. Yet Bangkok feels like a mostly happy accident. It seems oblivious to Western aesthetics or systems you can measure – yet it became a world city anyway.

It may seem unlikely, but some urbanists see in Bangkok's accommodation of chaos a prototype of a larger world issue about how megacities might develop a 'messy urbanism.'

Its sprawl appalls planners, but its gift for flexibility and ability to morph offers potential coping mechanisms to intractable problems. Despite itself, somehow Bangkok works.

This is the first comprehensive book on contemporary Bangkok. It took a decade to write, during which the city transformed. Even more ructions – the Covid-19, the legalisation of cannabis, the youth-led protests against dictatorship, and the hobbled return of civilian democracy – have since required this fully updated second edition.

Witnessing this constant change, I have focused on the underlying reasons why Bangkok is this way. Even as the examples may change, Bangkok's internal dynamics stay consistent as it has morphed from backwater to ASEAN hub to the world's most visited city. Whatever upheavals occur, it will remain the ultimate city of the senses.

Translations

To interpret a foreign civilisation I must bridge chasms in custom and language. In the most forensic review of *Very Thai*, Mingkwan Charoennitniyom wrote her linguistics MA thesis on the myriad ways I'd transliterated 341 Thai terms. As an author, I was flattered; as an editor, I was mortified. It turns out that being inconsistent was helpful; one rigid methodology can't convey the context and intent. So in this book I've given Mingkwan more material, by going with whatever works.

In transliterating Thai spellings, I've largely repeated the *Very Thai* style, which favours flatter British/European sounds over twangier American vowels. However, I have tried to spell peoples' names as they do, and to spell place names the most common way found in search engines and Google Maps.

Where Things Are

This isn't a guidebook, but early chapters cover fundamentals like timeline, history, layout, orientation, climate, food and getting around. Sorting the city by sense and theme means that many generic topics don't have dedicated chapters. Some crop up in boxed text, such as markets, nightlife, art, film, music, fashion, gays, design, Chinatown, transit, backpackers, and many of Bangkok's ethnicities.

The book has two maps. In the era of online mapping, there's no point to include listings details, but it's helpful to point out where mentioned places are located. The maps also note some areas and communities that have an identity, but which aren't labelled as such on mainstream maps. The front cover fold covers the city centre, while the back cover fold spans the wider metropolis within the outer ringroad. The Greater Bangkok map is tilted with east at the top. That's for the practical reason that the places mentioned happened to be in a north-south swathe and the cover fold is wide not tall. We aren't used to seeing the city in that orientation, which jolts us from conventional perceptions.

Quotations and data come either from interviews with me, or publications that are listed under 'Sources.' I include a Bibliography and Acknowledgements of those who've helped this book come to fruition. The index has grouped subheadings. It also serves as a glossary of Thai terms, and contains some reference data, like dates of reigns and eras.

For further information, reviews, and news of talks and events, visit online at **www.verybangkok.co**, **Facebook.com/ VeryBangkok** and **Instagram/VeryBangkok**.

left: **A contemporary bamboo installation for a stage at EmQuartier mall.**

right: **A shadow puppet of the Kalapapruek 'tree of life' made to show today's lifestyle by artist Chusak Srikwan, shown at BACC.**

Witness

This book draws from a quarter-century of living in this city and studying it as my job. I'd arrived in Thailand in 1994 as a listing journalist on my way back to England, with a vague plan to move to Australia, where I'd spent the previous year. Yet within four days of visiting Bangkok, I was hired to set up its first city magazine, *Bangkok Metro*. Ever since, Bangkok has been my home and my subject.

Some expatriates come to Thailand to find a new identity. I was inadvertently reinvented by Bangkok. The Philip hired to start *Metro* was a different Philip than the sabbatical traveller who'd entered overland at Sungai Kolok. In the analogue era before Trip Advisor and social media, travellers trusted the visitor books of guesthouses. Well-thumbed, ball-pointed reviews portrayed Thailand and its notorious capital as "over touristy," "too Westernised," and "all trekked out," with nothing authentic left to discover. So rather than sightseeing, I tapped the country's fame for courses to learn life skills. These contributed to the 'cultural filter' I apply to my writing.

My first revelation was to study Vipassana meditation on a ten-day silent retreat at Wat Suan Mokkh, founded in the South by the reformist monk Buddhadasa Bhikkhu. Its 4 am-9 pm regimen reformatted habitual patterns to open a space for change – and I made breakthrough decisions in its wake. Not allowed to speak, I felt other senses intensify. I became present to each breath and footfall. I can't call myself a Buddhist, but the insights opened my senses and aligned my mind to Thailand.

My second revelation was to study traditional Thai massage at ITM in Chiang Mai. As with meditation, this everyday Thai skill reinforces sensory perception: touch, posture, breathing, intuition, temperature, pain, herbal scent. These two courses taught me that things with exotic Oriental mystique are knowable parts of the Thai mental furniture. By the time I reached Bangkok after seven weeks upcountry, I was beginning to 'read' Thai culture.

"Don't waste your time in Bangkok," advised fellow travellers. "Give it two days max." Back then, Bangkok was seen as the archetypal city gone wild: pollution, corruption, traffic, prostitution, piracy. Unplanned sprawl had squandered its 'Venice of the East' allure. Yet another massacre of protesters in 1992 was still a raw wound. Given low expectations, I found in Bangkok's popular culture a juicy, low-hanging fruit that was ripe for tasting.

"There's not enough going on in Bangkok," some mocked of the effort to compile *Metro* at a time when it was extremely difficult to find out information, when venue owners guarded their drink prices like state secrets. Yet within 15 weeks we launched a 100-page monthly magazine with over 1,000 listings. At one of our regular parties – having fun is the way to get

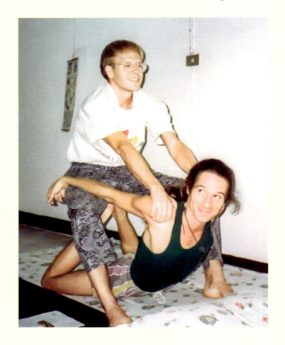

things done in Bangkok – a reader quipped that such a project wouldn't have been possible by an Old Hand familiar with the cultural and practical obstacles: "You didn't know it couldn't be done."

I'd learned listing journalism in London at *Time Out*, where I was deputy editor of the first *Time Out London* guidebook. It's a style of writing that demands getting every last detail, with a responsibility to the reader as a consumer. After eight years editing *Metro*, I rejoined *Time Out* as editor of its first *Time Out Bangkok City Guide*. What set Time Out apart from mainstream and backpacker guides, was their focus on young, creative urbanites who sought to engage with local scenes. Subcultures had been largely missing from guidebooks and not even considered by tourism promoters. Half the listings in *Time Out Bangkok* had never been in a guidebook, though those scenes are now staples for guides and tours.

As an editor, I got asked questions. I'd gained a knowledge of both pop and high culture, but was flummoxed by queries like: why do schoolgirls wear sailor suits and Chulalongkorn University footballers play in pink? Finding out became my next mission in writing the book *Very Thai: Everyday Popular Culture*. That, too, was the first book to cover many of its topics on the informal sector. By treating 'low' streetlife as culture, it became a cult sourcebook among a generation of young indie creatives, influencing many genres from art and design to events and advertising.

Very Thai took on a life of its own beyond my control. The physical book itself was curated by others as an exhibit in at least six exhibitions, and performed as a puppet in the performance piece *Wayang Buku*. Some creatives and academics have adopted 'VeryThai'

as a term for that genre of informal, improvised pop, to differentiate it from formal Thainess. As one Thai artist put it: "*Very Thai* coined the category."

It became apparent that as a documenter of Bangkok, and a longtime resident, I had to write about my adoptive hometown. Despite a plethora of guidebooks, these have dwindled into top-ten listicle format. Books on the city tackled either specific angles, or repeated predictable landmarks, without explaining the city's urbanism, with the focus always more about things 'Thai'. Instead, I'd come to view Bangkok as an urban organism with contradictory impulses: formal and informal. My approach is to accept that ambiguity, and to interpret what's going on beneath the orderliness and the chaos. In a link with *Very Thai*, its cousin *Very Bangkok* also presents many topics that haven't previously been covered for the general reader. My aim is to present a comprehensive portrait of contemporary Bangkok.

This book isn't a memoir, although it's mostly about the era I've experienced. I've drawn upon the unique access I've had as a correspondent, across the status thresholds, from slums via shophouses and subcultures through to high culture and royal audiences. I've attended events both famous and obscure. This book's widely ranging coverage comes from the good fortune of my breadth of exposure. My time here feels contemporary to me, like a 'long now'.

I've witnessed five phases, maybe six. I arrived while Thailand was swaggering as one of the Asian Tiger economies. When Bangkok's bad debts ignited the 1997 Asian Economic Crash, it was a time of hardship, but also of fruitful experiment with local resources. The third phase from 2000 saw those fresh ideas flourish through commercial design during the upbeat early years of Thaksin Shinawatra's premiership.

Opposition to Thaksin's wilful rule split the city, and country. Friends, families, communities and workplaces all divided between Yellow Shirts wearing the King's colour, and Red Shirts in the stripe of the flag that represents the 'people'. The protests expressed Thai inventiveness, but that became fraught through the 2006 coup and the massacre and arson of 2010. In a fifth phase, the 2014 coup then imposed authoritarian repression and censorship. The divisions darkened a mood that had been so carefree and optimistic. A sixth phase may have begun in 2020, with reactionaries having to share power with centrists.

In that boom era, the economy had been racing since the 1980s. Traditions were being tossed aside for modern imports and pirated fashions. Style was lurid, with office ladies in neon-hued outfits, business owners in shiny Versace shirts and *hi-so* (high society) dames in giant hair.

Architecture was just as loud and novelty-styled like a spaceship, castle or school bus. Malls were like theme parks, with cartoon-like attractions and rooftop waterparks with a volcano that 'erupted'. In the days when Ramkhamhaeng Road petered out into a rural lane, new highways were lined with boxlike soap-massage brothels, comedy cafés and all-in-one 'party

top left: **The author studying Thai massage in 1994, before deciding to settle in Bangkok.**

above: **Me at the still-burning Zen department store after the raid on the 2010 Red Shirt occupation of Ratchaprasong.** *Photo by Darkle*

Introduction 17

houses' with multiple venues, as traffic prevented bar-hopping. The wild nights of Patpong and partying till dawn were still in full swing. International-style bars were confined to Silom and few other spots, until a hundred theme-bars proliferated along RCA.

Before the BTS, and the empty first expressway viewed as too pricy, the infamous traffic jams deterred trying places far from home or work. No one would spend two hours going to Ekamai for fun. Lots of things couldn't be done here in 1994, like find a decent coffee, or bread and cheese. Bars only sold by the bottle; just beer, whisky and a few other spirits, with almost no cocktails or other drinks widely available before the arrival of Q Bar in 2000. Foreign films were dubbed into Thai and Thai films weren't subtitled in the stand-alone theatres, before the first multiplex opened. There was far less air-conditioning, with restaurants mainly in houses with garden seating. Around the corner of my downtown house, a canal-side village held cockfights, and arrayed fish to sun-dry on the side of the bridge. Elephants were a frequent site, begging on the street or foraging in empty lots off Ratchadaphisek Road.

Despite the construction, most streets looked alike, lined by shophouses. Buildings went up anywhere without much planning. Unfenced sites spewed cement dust and truck tyres shed clods of soil that dried and recirculated so that every day you could draw a finger through dust on an indoor table. The air was further fouled by leaded petrol, open burning, and continuing industry downtown. But it was an exciting time to witness a city being remodelled and a culture being remade. A democratic cultural opening since the 1992 massacre spurred a sense of progress, and enabled an Indie youth movement to flourish, though it has since retreated.

The country went into shock in 1997, when the collapse of the baht set off the 'Tom Yum Kung' Asian economic crisis. Firms shuttered, finance houses went bankrupt and unfinished ghost towers littered the landscape. The unemployed were absorbed by the informal sector. Many turned to driving an oversupply of taxis, just as traffic thinned and the BMA started building the BTS Skytrain. Middle classes flocked to buy and sell at 'car booth' sales, while at the Market of the Former Rich in a former Benz showroom in Soi Thonglor, nouveau pauvres sold Rolexes by weight.

It was a time of reflection and rethinking. Bangkok's most accomplished governor, Bhichit Rattakul, sealed construction sites, promoted community walking streets, and improved the environment. As imports couldn't be afforded, unemployed designers rediscovered indigenous assets like herbalism and weaving with water hyacinth from the river. As the economy recovered and Bangkok joined global trends in consumerism, tourism, and cultural commodification, Bangkok became renowned as a 'Design City'.

Experimental arts venues like About Cafe, Tadu, Project 304 and Patravadi Theatre spawned a new generation of creatives who are still cultural leaders. This flourishing of creative industries spurred government to get more open-minded, founding TCDC, BACC, Bangkok Fashion City, TK Park, Museum Siam and Creative Thailand. Though the seniority system's fear of critical thinking combats such initiatives, Bangkok lifestyle has continued globalising, with every label, foodstuff, trend and brand available. As the city trends towards international norms, corporate modernity reshapes the city's layout in exclusionary ways. A clean-up mentality is formalising the informal sector and removing much of the 'surprise' that had been a hallmark of the Bangkok street.

After witnessing and recording Bangkok's urban character so long, I realised that I was effectively compiling contemporary history. My background is studying history. At Sheffield University, I took World History. Instead of recounting the past through conventional ways of rulers and dates, or even economic and social history, this course probed far beyond, to the impacts from phenomena like inventions, disease, beliefs or crops that shape civilisations more profoundly

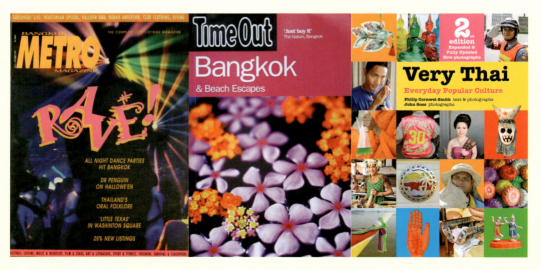

in the long run. Very Bangkok is like applying that multi-disciplinary approach to a city.

History is not nostalgia. The past was messier than its edited highlights. So I see Thainess as one thread of historical thought among a tapestry of narratives. Pull an ideological thread and that tapestry may keep its shape, or it may unravel. Now the internet enables us to find missing threads. So it brings earlier narratives of the past into question. Instead of history being restricted under labels like 'Great Men', dates, politics or economics, I grasped that history is shaped by subtler trends that include popular culture and social circles.

Mentors matter. I developed this book through two mentor-editors. I was lucky that Marc Pachter, a longtime director at the Smithsonian Institution in Washington DC, was so committed to this project. Marc was introduced by Charles Landry, the guru of the Creative Cities movement, who spoke here at TCDC. As consultant editor, Marc kept questioning my concepts until I'd distilled my ideas on each topic. He edited this book's update just before he passed away in 2024.

I learned much about the delicacy of writing about Asia from Alex Kerr, a Japanologist and fellow writer on Bangkok. He edited both *Very Thai* and *Very Bangkok*, helping me pare the drafts down to the core threads. Back at *Time Out* in 1989, my editor Hayden Williams, a trained criminologist, imparted ways of mulling evidence and motive in city-making, and the importance of ordinary people to culture and history. In many ways I'm a freelance contemporary historian. *Bangkok Metro*, *Time Out Bangkok*, *Very Thai* and now *Very Bangkok* have formed an eye-witness archive.

My status as an outsider is moot after 30 years of experience. Being so steeped in my adoptive city makes me a semi-insider. The book benefitted from detachment by being written partly outside the city, in Bali, which is near enough to Thai culture to see the Thainess of Bangkok more sharply.

Over the course of living in Bangkok and writing this portrait, time has changed me, and so has the involved process of writing it. By weighing Bangkok's place in the world I've come to ponder how Bangkok has changed me and how I sense the world.

left: **I edited *Metro* magazine, and *Time Out Bangkok* guide; and wrote *Very Thai*.**

above: **Spot me and Very Thai in this painting of the art scene by Navin Rawanchaikul.**

Introduction   19

Landsat satellite image of Greater Bangkok.

Time
A calendar and clock of your choice

8 am, noon, 6 pm and 8 pm: these hour-marks punctuate the Bangkok day. At 8 am and 6 pm sharp, Bangkokians stop what they're doing and stand. Across the city, pandemonium pauses while loudspeakered beeps count down to the playing of the National Anthem. Often accompanied by raising and lowering of the Thai flag, this ritual disciplines the day. A senator even proposed that all traffic stop for the anthem, which recurs at 6 pm. It's accompanied by patriotic video clips on TV, where later at 8 pm all channels broadcast the Royal News. The other landmark hour, the most popular one, is lunch, which is taken religiously at 12 noon.

Thais used to start the day not at midnight, but at dawn, with 12 hours of sunlight followed by 12 of dark. They still divide the clock into named sections: *chao* (6 am-11 pm), *tiang* (noon), *bai* (1-3 pm), *yen* (4-6 pm), *toom* (7-11 pm) and *dtee* (1-5 am). In this humidity, the practical intervals to get things done are early morning and early evening, known as *yen*, which means 'cool'.

Time has become a commodity to save or waste, give or spend, but in Bangkok has more relational flexibility than the rigid accuracy of the Greenwich Meridian, Date Line or Atomic Clock. People can pick auspicious moments from a range of divinations, whether Buddhist, Hindu, Chinese or folk beliefs, many detailed with illustrations in the *Phrommachat* almanac. Astrologers, Brahmins and monks calculate the date, hour and minute when to do any venture, from starting a business to holding a coup. Numerology, which favors the number nine, plays into time management, with such lucky moments as 9.09 am on the 9th of September.

Some days are decreed to be good for certain activities, while others are taboo. Hairdressers used to shut on Wednesdays as it was bad luck to cut hair on that day. You'd never have a funeral on a Friday, but Thursday, being a day of venerating teachers, is auspicious for cultural launches and art openings.

Thais mark three types of birthday. There's the day of the week that you were born on, which has a planetary god, a gem colour, and a Buddha posture. Letters in the Thai alphabet are allotted to each day, thereby limiting the choice of names. You can tell men called Mongkol or Nakorn were Friday born as their names in Thai script have no written vowels.

Then there's the date on which you were born, which is called a "birthday anniversary," differentiating it from the "birth day of the week."

left: **Lowering the flag at 6 pm, when the whole city stops to stand during the widely broadcasted National Anthem. The same drill happens at 8 am daily.**

right: **The giant clock atop the new rail terminus at Bangsue, Krung Thep Aphiwat Central Terminal, the biggest railway station in Southeast Asia. It has just one digit, the Thai numeral for nine, to honour King Rama IX.**
Photo courtesy of the State Railway of Thailand

Timeline

Early 1400s	Bangkok founded under Ayutthaya rule, as a multi-ethnic customs post.
1510	First European visitors (Portuguese).
1542	Canal shortens river from old course of Khlongs Bangkok Noi and Bangkok Yai.
1674	Portuguese settle at Samsen.
1688	Siege of Bangkok expels French from their fort and Western influence from Siam.
1700s	Settlements by Mon, Hokkien, Indians, Persians and other minorities.
1767	Ayutthaya destroyed. Phraya Taksin expels Burmese, crowned at Thonburi, which fills with multi-ethnic refugees and Teochiu migrants.
1782	King Taksin deposed and executed. Chao Phraya Chakri crowned as Phutthayotfah Chulalok (Rama I, d 1809), founded dynasty at Bangkok.
1809	King Phutthaloetla Naphalai (Rama II, d 1824).
1824	King Nangklao (Rama III). British colonise Burma, removing it as a threat.
1833	Treaty of Amity & Commerce with USA.
1851	King Mongkut (Rama IV, d. 1868).
1855	Bowring Treaty switched Bangkok from an entrepôt for Chinese junks into the European mercantile system.
1868	King Chulalongkorn (Rama V, d. 1910).
1872	Steamers from Swatow speed Teochiu influx.
1876-85	Abolition of Upparat (Deputy King) rank enables absolute monarchy.
1893	Paknam Incident. French gunboats on river force Siam to cede east bank of Mekong and western Cambodia.
1905	Slavery abolished, start of military conscription.
1910	King Vajiravudh (Rama VI, d. 1925). General strike by Bangkok's Chinese.
1911	Chinese Emperor overthown by Nationalists.
1925	King Prajadipok (Rama VII; abdicates 1935, d 1941).
1929	Great Depression wrecks finances.
1932	Revolution brings constitutional monarchy.
1933	Boworadej Rebellion fails to restore absolutism.
1935	King Rama VII abdicates. Ananda Mahidol crowned (Rama VIII, d. 1946).
1938-41	Phibun's Cultural Mandates enforce Thainess ideology. Siam renamed Thailand.
1941-45	World War II occupation by Japan, bombing by Allies.
1946	King Bhumibol Adulyadej (Rama IX, d. 2016), longest reign.
1947	Dictatorship ends brief period of democracy.
1951	Army defeats Navy coup, sinks the ship *Manhattan* in river.
1957	Sarit Thanarat's coup, militarised Development State, bureaucratic polity and royalist revival.
1966	Hosts Asian Games (and in 1970, 1978 & 1998)
1966-75	Treaty of Amity with US brings funding and Cold War military bases.
1967	ASEAN founded in the Bangkok Declaration.
1973	Massacre of protestors starts democratic era.
1975	Relations resume with China under Mao.
1976	Massacre of students ends in coup, dictatorship, demi-democracy and hyper-royalism.
1988	Electoral democracy, regional 'battlefields into markets' openness.
1991-2	Coup (1991) overthrown by protestors amid a massacre. Leads to democracy, open society.
1997	Asian economic crash starts in Bangkok, IMF bailout till 2001.
1999	BTS Skytrain opens first mass transit lines.
2001	Thaksin Shinawatra's electoral populism.
2003	Bangkok hosts APEC summit.
2005-14	Red-Yellow protests, coups in 2006, protestors killed in 2008, 2009 and 2010 amid arson.
2006	Suvarnabhumi Airport opens.
2011	Thaksin's sister Yingluck becomes PM and faces the Great Flood of Bangkok.
2012	Bangkok becomes the world's most visited city.
2014	Bangkok Shutdown protest. Coup by NCPO.
2015	ASEAN Economic Union begins.
2016	King Rama IX mourning period. King Vajira Klao (Vajiralongkorn, Rama X) ascends.
2019	King Rama X crowned. Junta-run election sees military parties govern, despite Pheu Thai and Future Forward coming 1st & 3rd.
2020-22	Ban on Future Forward Party sparks protests to reform state, monopolies and monarchy. Taboos broken, but protestors prosecuted. Cannabis decriminalised.
2023-24	Reformist Move Forward wins election, but barred from power, then dissolved for lese majeste. Thaksin returns from exile to prison hospital, royal pardon, lese majeste charge, and his daughter Paethongtan becoming PM for Pheu Thai.

Senses 23

While Thais do enjoy their birthday parties, the priority is to make merit by either donating to monks or releasing animals. At a longer timescale, they celebrate their turn in the 12-year astrological cycle. The big "birthday anniversaries" come at ages 12, 24, and so on, up to 108.

As for the year number, rulers have kept changing the counting system in a dizzying blend of calculations, resets and calendars both solar and lunar. Thus the auspicious official timing of something might not match the actual moment it occurred.

This raises the conundrum of Bangkok's age. Early rulers, in the Chinese way, often restarted their calendar at each reign. When the Chakri dynasty established Krungthep as the capital, the Siamese year was reset to the date of the ceremonial founding, at an astrologically-divined 6.54 am on 21 April 1782. But this timeline ignores that Bangkok as a town, is over twice as old, having being settled in the early 15th century.

Siam used a lunar calendar and had held Western notions of time at bay ever since the French were expelled from Siam at the 1688 Siege of Bangkok. Finally in 1888, King Rama V adopted a Thai version of the Gregorian solar calendar. Meanwhile, Bangkok kept a parallel lunar cycle for use in Buddhism, the tidal timing of floating markets, and full moon festivals like Loy Krathong.

Today, Thais use Christian Era year numbers for international convenience, but amongst themselves still number years by the Buddhist Era, 2020 CE being 2563 BE. Siam had historically counted from the start of Buddha worship (as Burmese still do), until Rama VI reset the Thai calendar to the death of the Buddha in 543 BC.

Once you've figured out how to count the years, you now face the question of when the year begins. This polyglot city marks not one but several New Years: International (January 1), Chinese (February), and Songkran, the traditional Thai New Year (April 13). Songkran had been a variable date, since it marked the sun passing through Aries, until King Rama VI fixed it at April 1. Then in 1941, the dictator Phibunsongkhram decreed New Year as January 1, and adjusted the Buddhist year-count to start then too. Later Songkran was fixed at April 13. If they don't like the time, Thais change it.

The generic calendar hung in homes and workplaces is crammed with smallprint about the several timing systems going on at once. Its big central digit is the Western Gregorian date, but it shares the complex layout with the Chinese lunar calendar, Buddhist dates and astrological cycles. For extra luck, it marks state lottery draws with a scribble in which you might discern a hint of the winning numbers. Thai Muslims pair this calendar with their own, and hang alongside it an additional clock set to Mecca Time.

Buddhism's ultimate lesson about time is to live in the moment. That's understandable given the fact that Hindu-Buddhist epochs, known as *kalpa*, are so inconceivably long. Each *kalpa* lasts 16,798,000 years, with more past *kalpas* than there are grains of sand in the Ganges. Faced with an endless expanse of time in which one could do anything, Bangkokians approach deadlines and appointments with what some call 'rubber time.' In contrast to the precision of ritual timings, this everyday lack of urgency draws from the rural roots of the

Destiny

Bangkok celebrates its birthday with more fanfare than it used to. By astrological reckoning, the Duang Meuang (city fortune) began at the 9th baht (an archaic increment) after dawn on the 10th day of the waxing moon of the sixth month in that Year of the Tiger, 1782. That's 06.45 am on 21 April.

The focus is Lak Meuang – the City Pillar erected at the moment of Krungthep's birth, yet go there and you'll find two pillars. Plus there are two foundational horoscopes. And Bangkok is a twin city, joined in 1972 with its predecessor, Thonburi. Bangkok's duality is built-in.

Legend has it that as the carved log of Javanese cassia was erected, four snakes slithered into the hole, joining the parchment horoscope. As the auspicious timing couldn't be altered, the serpents' sacrifice prompted King Rama IV to bury an improved Duang Meuang beneath a second city pillar in December 1852 and commissioned a statue of the city's guardian angel, Phra Siam Dhevathirat.

It was envisioned that a bridge to Thonburi would enhance the city's fortune, and the first span across the Chao Phraya, Saphan Phut, eventually opened on the 150th anniversary of the city's founding. That year, a coup abolished absolute rule. The new constitutional regime declared itself against superstition, yet the dimensions of the Democracy Monument reflect the numerology of the date 24 June 1932. Time is written into Bangkok's landmarks.

Duang Meuang "is a destiny that can't be altered," says astrologer Fongsanan Chamornchan. "It's like a person. You only have one fate once you're born." Yet Bangkok is looking forward to its 250th birthday. Perhaps destiny can be altered after all.

culture. Farming requires only about half of the year, with the rest given over to leisure, so what punctual visitors might decry as an idle waste of precious hours, Thais call 'empty time,' which should best be spent being happy.

Bangkok is a city of waiting patiently. Ordering by first-come-first-served seems a question of justice to Westerners, yet unjust to a people ranked by status. People queue-jump when cutting in front of a stranger who's considered "nobody," but shrink back to let a senior pass first. Big shots simply shouldn't have to wait behind others of low status. The powerful needn't worry about being late, because people will always wait for them. So the elite while away their hours in air-conditioned cars, rather than rush using other transit, ready to step out looking impeccable.

Scheduled events like film screenings can change at a few hours' notice, while venues may send e-invites out as late as the afternoon of an evening event. Group plans often divert at the last minute, swept by the whims of their circle. Bangkokians avoid formal dinner parties and favour shared dishes over plated courses due to unplannability – confirmed guests may not come at all, or could bring along extra friends.

Westerners anxiously check the time, worrying about critical paths, windows of opportunity, and the bucket list of things to do before you die. Bangkokians take an unrushed view, dwelling in the moment while anticipating fresh cycles of reincarnation. Something overdue may get done eventually, as the saying goes, "in the afternoon of your next life."

top left: **Traffic lights have countdowns for the green and red light changes. It seems to reduce stress.**

left **Motorcycle taxi drivers leave keys on makeshift boards showing the order of their rides.**

above: **The City Pillar marks a precise moment in time when the city was founded. A second pillar marks a revised date with a more auspicious horoscope. This was at a rite for Bangkok's birthday on April 21.**

Senses 25

Smell
Led by the nose

"The streets all smell of food," remarked my cousin Mark, when asked his impression of Bangkok. Foodies seek out the flavour and vibe of its streetfood, which perfumes many a *soi* (lane) with spice, herb and kaffir lime zest. Yet outdoor cooking has side-effects. Mark's abiding memories were of choking on atomised chilli acid and slipping on rancid washings from soup tubs. Sensory response is so personal, especially that trigger of memory: smell. Bangkok has a prize collection.

"When you arrive in Bangkok, first the heat hits you, then the smell. It's unmistakable, utterly unique, and quickly envelops you," food writer Kay Plunkett-Hogge says of her birthplace. "If someone created a scented Bangkok candle, its fragrance would probably be smoky incense, grilled pork, tuk-tuk fumes and sewage, with a top note of jasmine." Thai Perfume Runway has done just that, with frangrances of Sukhumvit, Zi Lom (Silom), Pak Klong (canal mouth, though referring to the flower market) and Bangkok By The Rain, which does have a top note of jasmine.

Bangkok really does smell of jasmine candles. Since the 1997 crash revived herbal lore and birthed a spa boom, aromatherapy spread until most every shop or venue has a lemongrass diffuser. Essential oils propel bodycare firms like Panpuri, Erb, Harnn and Thann. Karmakamet blossomed from a stall to boutiques with sense-quelling black interiors that perk your nasal sensitivity. Thai spas open your pores in a herbal sauna, scrub you with a fibrous, turmeric paste that smells like curry, then offer a choice of massage oils, often lavender, peppermint, *prai* or ylang-ylang, which in spa-talk means: 'relax', 'refresh', 'de-stress' or 'sensual.' You leave with a fragrant new coating against the noxious air outside.

Aromatherapy draws upon an old Thai culture of scent. Many healing balms include *prai*, a local root with medicinal properties and a soothing 'nose-feel.' Tinctures like the pink, rose-scented *nam yaa uthai* masked the dankness of water from a well or jar. Blessings of paste and holy water get their mystical lift from drops of rose-like *nam ob*, also used to mask the rot and formaldehyde at open-casket cremations, along with posies of shaved sandalwood.

Bangkok cooking delights in balancing not just flavours but smells. Cooks ply the olfactory scale from shrimp paste to lemongrass. They favour zingy fresh herbs over duller dry spices. It's also about covering bad smells; coriander root kills the gaminess of meat or fish. Eons before molecular cuisine, Thais thought to smoke desserts with a *tian ob* (scented candle), to impart a floral fumée to delicacies like a pandan custard so brain-meltingly delicious its named *leum gleun* – 'forgot I swallowed.'

Fragrancy implies modernity and status. A 1990s survey among many ethnicities found that Thais came out smelling by far the best, perhaps due to herbs in the diet, bathing two-to-three times a day, then dousing themselves in mentholated powder. Self-conscious cleanliness makes up for a less-sanitary past, when intimacy carried heath risk. So there's much judgement about people being *hom* (fragrant) or *men* (stinky).

Thais attune social values to smells, reading them with as much discernment as colour or sound. Thai culture promotes surface, but ranks aroma higher, as in the proverb: 'beautiful only in looks; unfragrant when kissing.' In this indirect culture, kissing needn't involve touch. The 'sniff kiss', an inhalation at the cheek, evolved from a check on hygiene (and a way to deal with tooth rot from chewing betel) into a token of family affection, as well as seduction. Paul Theroux noted a raunchier intake of pheromones: "As Calcutta smells of death and Bombay of money, Bangkok smells of sex, but this sexual aroma is mingled with the sharper whiffs of death and money."

Nasal sensitivity comes before racial or class sensitivity, especially at Nana's wild odourscape. When many a Western barhop, Arab tourist or Indian merchant boards the BTS at Nana, many Thais visibly recoil, even vacate an adjacent seat. The hoppiness of beer emanates from Nana's hostess bars, amid the cheap perfumes and ammonia from the heavy-duty cleaning. Nana's Little Arabia clouds the air with its fruity puffs from hookah pipes, ghee from curry houses and its trade in frankincense. Gulf visitors trail lingering clouds of argan, oud and myrrh that carry the mind to carpet souks.

You can still identify other specialist areas by the smell of their trades. Tha Tien's fishiness has top notes of camphor, as neighbouring Wat Pho preserves medicinal and massage lore. Stalls still array potions, powders and ointments, like soothing balms, *muaythai* liniment, and cool-heaty yellow oil. It's the same story at the apothecaries and amulet stalls of Tha Pra Chan. More addictive aromatic motes go airborne from the carpenters around Golden Mount and Prachanareumit Road. Buyers sniff-test to see if the lumber is truly teak.

In markets, the freshening chlorophyl from vegetables overlays the miasma from meat. Thewes plant market smells like a garden after the rain. Combining it all, Chatuchak Market adds the effluvium of pet shops, the staleness of vintage clothing, and the attic dust of antiques. At Pak Khlong Talad flower market the bouquets layer from genus upon genus of blooms, undercut by the foetor of leaves, stems and petals mulched underfoot by porters wheeling giant bunches of tuber roses.

Talad Noi smells of other oils and other herbs. Its Chinese pharmacies on Charoen Krung Road are a potpourri of star anise, roots and antler in wooden drawers or open sacks. Towards the river, the district cloys with petrol like a giant garage. The stacked axles, cogs and motor parts slick the *soi* with grease. Yet more spices – this time Indian – lend Pahurat the air of curry and chai. From here a cloth market extends along Sampeng Lane, shoppers inhaling the linty microfibres.

Strong smell is increasingly marginalised. Urbanites distanced from nature, fear its primal associations: animal instincts, sexuality, disease, the untamed wild. That desensitisation is partly why visitors relish Bangkok – for a shot of its heady realness. Yet it's forging an antiseptic future. Odours form 40% of complaints to the Pollution Control Division, so it hired 167 "smell assessors," who get 600 baht each time they're sent to identify and source each sample stench, from the dangerous to the merely malodorous.

Such is Bangkok's world-beating pollution that a headache can form at the airport and last days. The gaseous pall is due to the sheltered gulf location and the cool-season inversion of an upper layer of cold air trapping the sweltering mist of PM2.5 particles. Rot from the tropics' humidity is re-doubled

left: **A garland offering on the trunk of an elephant statue in a temple.**

above: **Tha Tien Market has for centuries been known for its dried fish.**

Senses 27

Flower Culture

Thailand is the Holland of the tropics. Most of its floriculture exports passes through Flower Market Thailand in Thonburi and Pak Khlong Talad market, where you can wade through thigh-high blooms.

This is a floral culture. Plant motifs interlace fractal *lai Thai* patterns in traditional art. Buddhist teachings use the life cycle of the lotus as a metaphor, and its forms bless many Bangkok things, from street signs and the city pillar to Bangkok Bank's logo. Many local women have floral names that carry symbolic meaning. The crown-shaped *dok rak* 'love flower' inspired the logo of Thai Airways, which presents premium customers with what's known as the 'Thai Airways Orchid'.

Streetside garland-threaders deconstruct blooms into petals, bracts and buds, then turn them into stylised floral shapes like the protective four-pointed flower *prachamyaam* found everywhere from the bolts on trucks to the route map of the MRT. Vendors also pin thistly amaranths into *phum* altar offerings shaped like the lotus buds that Buddhists offer as a metaphor for enlightenment.

Thailand's top flower designer, Sakul Intakul, applied this lore and his engineering training to the deconstruction of and reconfiguration of flower structures, his 'floritecture' influenced Asian flower design. Sakul also opened the world's first Museum of Floral Culture at a wooden mansion in Dusit. Its grounds show how Thai gardens were less about aesthetics than purpose: edible fruits and herbs; blossoms for floral art; auspicious placement of lucky plants; and aromatics grown for home, food and body. Garlands symbolically emanate the Dharma via their fragrance, which is for us to receive, but not take. "Do not sniff them," warns writer Natayada na Songkhla. "To do so will profane the garlands and make them useless as sacred offerings."

Sakul Intakul uses engineering to design floral art and founded the world's first Floral Art Museum in Bangkok.

by this being a sea-level swamp. Bangkok's aircon obsession is not just to cool, but to dehumidify, warding off mildew.

Much of the city air is unhealthy, says Green World Foundation, the worst being industrial suburbs like Bangna and Bang Khuntian, and traffic-clogged downtown, where half the residents have a respiratory illness. Another culprit is poor infrastructure. Bottlenecks cause cars and drivers to fume. Canals that can't be properly sluiced stagnate into foaming grey murk. Rancid refuse spills out of trash bags gnawed by rats. "The city dump was burning; there was a light red glow in the sky from the pyre," wrote Rattawut Lapcharoensap in a short story that portended a landfill fire in 2017 that caused evacuation of eastern suburbs. "I could still smell the putrid scent of tyres and plastic and garbage burning, the sour odour seeping through our windows."

Smell was what drove King Rama V to reform planning and move his court from the overcrowded Grand Palace to leafy Dusit. "I block my nose and my mouth with a handkerchief," he said. "After I have returned to the palace for a while, the stench still

hung in the air." It was so unhealthy that a British official deemed Siam a "death trap… not suitable for Western colonisation."

The Thai phrases "going to the rice fields" or "going to the pier" hint at earlier toilet customs – as shown in murals at Wat Suthat. Roads and waterways were also rimmed by pig sties, tanneries, seafood processing, limekilns and corpses left to rot. But the sanitising of Bangkok – from removing water stilt houses to installing crematoria and covering breasts – was often an aesthetic makeover aimed at instilling hygiene and a civic appearance, notes ML Chittawadi Chitrabongs: "More than a century later, Bangkok still has no public sewage system."

City drains get dumped with detritus, not least by food vendors. After the first rains, gangs of convicts are ordered down manholes to extract the black sludge by pulling knotted ropes through pipes. Bangkok has no public sewer mains; instead, the ordure fills septic tanks that get pumped out by *rot doot kee* – poop-sucking trucks.

Siamese Pooh-Bahs had turned their nose up at the price of sewer technology, claiming that "the best duty of the Sanitary Department is to maintain the roadways." Today's lack of public toilets dates from when early lavatories were actually removed because they detracted from the esteem of the new roads cutting through manky slums. We still have Thanon Sukhapibal (Sanitation Street), but polite names now grace Rotten Dog Disposal Forest Lane and, says Chittawadi, "Faeces Lane, where the Clean Work Company used to be, was changed to Changed Name Road. The traces of Bangkok's odours were expelled from street signs, although the sources of the smells might not have been dealt with."

Such a potholed city harbours mosquitos, so lanes get fogged with noxious clouds of insecticide that also contaminate ponds, frogs, birds, bees, kids. An invention in Khlong Toey slum had local motorbikes fitted with bug sprays to defeat dengue fever. Chemical fixes are so normal that one sickly couple found that their maid had helpfully been spraying their bed with Baygon.

"Bangkok has perhaps the widest range of smell of any city outside of India," posted Cameron Cooper, ex-founder of *Farang* magazine. "But one thing you can be guaranteed never to smell is burning toast." It's rarely served crunchy, though the artisanal movement has brought the homely scents of dough baking and coffee roasting.

Bourgeois Bangkok is veering away from ranker smells. Bland battery chicken has displaced gamey free-range *kai baan*. The funkier shrimp pastes and the ethyl jag of *maeng da* beetle have evaporated from menus. The area grows the world's best durian, the spike-cased ambrosial fruit that divides humanity. Like blue cheese or natto, it excites connoisseurs, whilst detractors liken it to athlete's foot. As in Singapore, it's banned from hotels and transit, but can come in denaturised forms: candied, cheesecake, paste or freeze-dried. The refurbishment of Tha Tien, a seafood market for 200 years, had dried fish and squid relegated inside, while the front shops can only sell seafood sealed in plastic.

When pongs are inescapable, Thais mask them. Envelopes, notebooks and tissues come perfumed as do *pha yen* cold towels. Householders hedge gardens with night jasmine. Garlands hung on car mirrors wave out molecules of jambu and jasmine, while the back shelf may have a sheaf of odour-eating pandanus leaves. Inhalers insert aromatics directly up nostrils, though herbal pellets and organic balms are giving way to synthetic fragrance, as with phenol air freshener and the saccharine vapour of additives piped into malls. Bangkokians put a scent barrier between them and the Big Smoke.

above: **Scents inspired by Bangkok include Pak Klong – 'canal mouth,' site of the flower market.**

right: **A canal-boat commuter shields lifts the splash guard and masks the smell with an inhaler.**

Senses 29

Taste
From streetfood to chic food

If there's one thing Thais and foreigners can agree on, it's that Bangkok cooks one of the great cuisines. For decades, foodies have flocked to what Thais call the "Kitchen of the World." It's a magnet for gourmet tourism, yet Bangkok's edge is not its peaks, but that its median average meals are so delicious. You can dine well at every level of price, class and setting; rarely face a bad meal; and savour each spoonful – often with real surprise. In a cuisine that sets out to tingle the senses, each meal is a privilege extended to all. Prices have risen, but are still so affordable and widely available that all can eat out most days, not just as a treat.

Thai culture is centred on food, and the food itself is highly cultured. The word for family, *khrob khrua*, means those covered by the kitchen. Before the word Sawasdee was imposed as a greeting, the Thai "*hello*" was *kin khao rue yang*: "eaten rice yet?" Face leads Thais to celebrate and negotiate while eating. Worship involves offering food. Dining is a social sacrament, where you each delve into a shared spread of dishes, according to hierarchy, and leave the last morsel in case anyone joins the table, which they often do.

Bangkok makes food an event. Only monks dine in quiet. Not only is the food stimulating; dining combines with other stimuli. Salty, oily *kub glaem* drinking food is served in nightclubs, music venues and karaoke dens. Group meals get ultra lively, while streetfood involves an environmental onslaught too. Food has become the prime draw of malls, while festivals are expected to offer specialities. Product launches and art openings get judged by their buffet and beverage. Fine dining had been the preserve of grand hotels, then posh restaurants with private rooms. Now dozens of tasting menus turn eating into an endurance joust in one-upmanship between foodies.

The Thai flavour profile arises from intensity, freshness and contrast. The cuisine is an orchestra of accents, which remain identifiable, yet somehow balance the five flavours: bitter, sour, salt, sweet and spicy. Its herbal vitality lifts Thai food from the dried spices of India and China, the pickles of Central Asia, the processed food of America or the blended sauces of Europe. Not only do aromatic leaves, unripe fruits and freshly pounded pastes thrill the tastebuds; they cure. Thais prize their food as medicinal, from invigorating enzymes and aromatherapy to the healing ability of herbs and rhizomes. Many marquee ingredients are intensifiers: kaffir lime, lemongrass, mint, three kinds of basil. Thais also ambush the palate with arresting effects: sweetened squid, chilli in cocktails, pork floss desserts, or fruit dipped in salt and dried chilli.

What gets marketed to the world as 'Thai food' is really the Siamese cuisine of the Central Plains, which wasn't homogenous, filtered through Bangkokian taste. Restaurants like The Local, showcase diverse recipes. Thais

left: **Chickens hang in a stall near Don Mueang, about to be made into *khao man kai*, a Hainanese influenced chicken rice dish.**

right: **Smoking with aromatic incense is one of the traditional cooking techniques practiced at R-Harn, which was awarded two Michelin stars for its exquisite take on royal Bangkok cuisine.** *Photo courtesy R-Harn*

go on weekend jaunts to sample and take home the delicacies of towns within a couple of hours' drive, whether *paet riew* (eight-stripe) fish at Chachoengsao, or the *pla tuu* mackerel in lotus stem soup at Amphawa.

Not all agree. "For a city with such a great reputation for food, Bangkok doesn't have much of these regional specialities," Suthorn Sukphisit writes in 'Bland Bangkok is most definitely not the food capital of the country.' "Even though many northerners live in Bangkok, we could barely find 10 *khao soi* eateries [serving] the classic Northern noodle dish. Chanthaburi's *liang* noodles can only be found in three shops. Bangkok isn't as open to different types of food as it likes to think it is. People can still be hesitant about trying new food." The capital took to *somtam*, but hasn't adopted other more bitter Isaan dishes or their unfamiliar vegetables.

Labelling food 'Thai' obscures not just its ethnic diversity, but the foreign and regional input to many recipes. 'Somtam Thai' is Isaan papaya salad made from New World ingredients brought by Portuguese, then Bangkokified with dried prawns. Most extreme is the nationalist noodle dish Pad Thai. "Noodles can hardly take claim as lying at the heart of my country's cuisines," says cooking instructor and writer, Kasma Loha-unchit. "For a dish to be so named in its own country clearly suggests an origin that isn't Thai."

That begs the question of Bangkok's unique contribution to Central Thai food, which is less in flavour, than in process. The capital so dominates its hinterland that it has generated its own tastes through trade and immigration, power dining and court arts. Rattanakosin family recipes brought a finesse to standard dishes. Bangkokians experiment with fusions and hone presentation, whether food carving, or nouvelle cuisine prepared by TV contestants for Iron Chef Thailand. Bangkok is the nexus of migrant settler food from upcountry and abroad, as well as outposts of international cuisines now earning stars from the Michelin Guide, with sponsorship by the Tourism Authority of Thailand (TAT). There are more Italian restaurants helmed by Italian chefs here than days in the year, and even more Japanese *izakaya* and ramen bars.

Thai culture is one of appropriation more than origination. The gateway was Ayutthaya, through which Portuguese traders brought the sweet pillowy bread that dominates bakeries, and the American ingredients used in *somtam*: papaya, peanuts and tomatoes. All Thai egg desserts – like the *foy thong* golden threads that bride and groom spoon each other at their nuptials – derive from Marie Guyomar de Pinha (Guimar), a half-Japanese Portuguese from Goa, who baked while confined after her husband, King Narai's Greek chief minister Constantin Phaulkon was assassinated in 1688.

Senses 31

Bangkok inherited the role of culinary blender. Fads turn to hybrids and become standard, most commonly Chinese stir-fry, but also Vietnamese pancakes and Malay sate. Some fusions horrify the outsider, notoriously sweetened sushi and ketchup on pizza. Several fusions have become modern classics. The restaurant chain of the fashion label Greyhound made spaghetti with dry chilli and salted fish. Tawandang German Brewery discovered that Schweinhaxe roast pork knuckle went well with seafood chilli dip. Big Mama's at Asoke serves green curry spaghetti steamed in a Chinese clay pot under a lid of pizza dough. What could be more Thai? "There's no single authentic Thai food," says Duangporn 'Bo' Songvisava of Bo.lan, a pioneer of Thai haute cuisine. "In the past, families cooked their own food, so their recipes varied, and were influenced by their ancestry." Streetfood arose from foreign and internal migrants: roti from Indians; pulled tea with condensed milk from Malays; *khanom jeen* fermented vermiccelli from the Mon; noodles, stir-fries, stews, rice porridge and so much else from the Chinese.

Dishes of smaller Chinese minorities, like Cantonese, remain closer to their original, whether roast duck or sweet and sour. But the dominant Teochiu group reshaped the Bangkok flavour profile. Their preference for mushroomy mellowness, accented with pickles and vinegar, explains the milder side to Bangkok meals, especially seen in steamed seafood and claypot prawns with glass noodles. Pig-leg stew and oyster omelet are little changed, while Thais have modified *khao tom* rice soup with a buffet of piquant nibbles. These dishes get laced with chilli, but Teochiu umami is an unspoken signature of Bangkok cuisine.

What's inarguably Bangkokian is *aharn chao wang*: food of palace royals. "The words 'royal Thai cuisine' convey some mystical feeling of Thai food being cooked differently. And that's exactly how the restaurants want you to feel," says Chef McDang, who was raised eating it in Sukhothai Palace with his great aunt Queen Rambhai Barni. The dishes only differ by ingredient quality, plus how they're prepared and served. "There are no extremes in flavours. Every detail is covered: the appropriate size of each item, masticatory safety, very balanced flavours and aesthetics. All fruits and vegetables have no pits, stones

Streetfood

Amid the global trend for streetfood, Bangkok has been the paragon. When CNN named its streetfood the World's Best in 2017, Thai authorities celebrated – and then, to shocked global headlines, vowed to remove streetfood from Bangkok.

"The BMA is working to get rid of the vendors from all 50 districts of Bangkok," said advisor Vallop Suwandee. Those evicted from swanky Thonglor, Ekamai, and Phrakhanong got just one month's notice with a total of 6,334 vendors ousted citywide by 2017. The BMA said it was due to complaints, without saying by whom, or why they outweighed the stall-grazing majority, not just vendors losing their livelihood, but low-income diners, and foodies Thai and foreign.

Insecurity of tenure is a Thai constant. Bangkok first got populated by herding ethnic communities around at whim. Vendor carts are wheeled echoes of the moveable prefabricated stilt houses. Streetfood owes its origins to marginal migrants subsisting on marginal pavements and in *sois*, but those commons have been decreed as public space to be reclaimed.

Streetfood is what the UN calls "intangible culture" (though *pad krapao* feels tangibly spicy). Its removal also has cultural motives. Most streetfood isn't indigenous, but was imported with earlier ethnic migrants, especially Chinese and Lao-Isaan. There'd been complaints about vendors being Burmese, Chinese or other migrants doing a job restricted to Thais. Also most of the fare, such as noodles, snacks or nibbles on a stick, is low-status food served by low-status people – often in front of high-status buildings.

To the hierarchy, foreigners awarding street food offends national face, by upending the "sky high, earth low" values of rank and status. The TAT met the outcry by announcing tidy, uniform showpiece streetfood stalls at tourist sites like Khao San, Chinatown and Bangkhuntian seafront. They missed the point that tourism and culinary quality are both side effects of the core need for affordable food.

"Streetfood makes all of the inner workings of Bangkok possible," says food blogger and writer Chawadee Nualkhair. "If the vendor is good enough, it brings all the classes together, sharing the same food." Auntie-cooked dishes fuel labourers, pennywise students and wealthy matrons who stop their Benz for noodles at a treasured stall. Bangkok's 'plastic-bag mums' grab takeaways from a nightmarket on the way home from work.

Planners seem oblivious that most housing stock was built with streetfood in mind. Thai kitchens used to be separate from the living space due to the flaming woks and charcoal smoke, and so the kitchenettes in tiny flats and condos only suit decanting streetfood. Removing streetfood at no notice creates an existential problem.

The BMA countered in 2017 by opening the first four 'Community Food Source' areas, but with room for fewer than half the original carts. One nightlife denizen feared his favourite crispy pork stall had gone, but found it in an old market hall nearby.

Vendors slunk back after previous purges, but that's hampered by regulations to improve pavements and restrict street vending to the registered poor. That would force higher quality streetfood into the scarcer shophouses or mall food courts, where some famous stalls have air-conditioned branches. Since the 2010s, food trucks have offerered tidier if pricier dishes than the mini-restaurants that vendors assemble from their cart, filling street and path with trestle tables and stools. Few disapprove of better hygiene, taxing vendors or clearer space to walk, but temporary stalls are actually a space-efficient way to meet demand at different times of day.

Foodies mourned when Chulalongkorn University moved Samyan Market and evicted Suan Luang's shophouses, often seen as the birthplace of modern Thai streetfood. Many of those vendors repopulated nearby Banthat Thong Road and Suan Luang Square. Post-Covid, with the shophouses repainted in retro hues, this home of streetfood reconstituted itself.

Overall, haphazardly, without tenure or strategy, Bangkok drifts towards the hawker centre model of Singapore, which houses local food in cheap, sterile halls. Chawadee warns that zoning may sap streetfood's seat-of-the-pants innovation and make it "an edible museum." At stake is a way of life and a sophisticated subculture of taste.

left: **Chinatown's most iconic street stall.**

above: ***Mee krob*** **is an old skool dish in a classic old town shophouse.**

top: **Dried squid on a food cart, waiting to be warmed over charcoal, then rolled through a mangle until made into pungent fibrous shreds.**

Senses 33

or peel, with the peel sometimes carved and attached to the fruit as decoration. When it comes to meat, there are no bones. Not even in the fish. Only later did I discover that the Thai mackerel actually has bones, as well as fins, and a tail too. Who knew?"

The many palaces indulged in friendly rivalry in cooks as with their musicians. "The court not only helped to establish and enhance Thailand's cultural identity, but has also served in highly specific ways to promote Thai cuisine," says the *Oxford Companion to Food*. "The royal kitchens have been a forcing house for the talents of Thai cooks, Kings of Thailand have written cookery books, and the category of royal cookery books has overlapped occasionally with another and exceptionally interesting category, which seems to be peculiar to Thailand, namely funeral cookbooks."

The first chef to gain a Michelin star for Thai food, Australian David Thompson, collected over 500 funeral cookbooks from upper-class households in researching his landmark books *Thai Food* and *Thai Streetfood*. "The development of Thai cuisine was clearly driven by those who did not have to cook or sully their hands with manual labour, otherwise they would not have demanded so much," says Thompson. "The result, however, was sublime."

As in Thai traditional arts, credit mostly goes to the patron. You see this in the rash of celebrity restaurateurs, and concepts based around nostalgia for 'grandma's' recipes (ML Terb, Never Ending Summer, Supanniga). Bangkok's first restaurants were patrician households that had their chefs cook for the public in dining rooms fronting their compounds in the well-to-do areas such as Silom/Sathorn (Thanying, Kalapapruek) and Sukhumvit (Klang Soi, Ton Krueng). Foodies also relish Old Town eateries like Khrua Apsorn in Samsen, or Khrua Aroy Aroy in Silom, where the dowdy décor is recast as retro and matters less than the cooking.

Pioneers who brought this food culture out into the open were MR Thanadsri Svasti in his Shell guide, his son McDang, and Suthorn Sukphisit, whose column on localised food cultures was edited by the late Bob Halliday, the gatekeeper for Thai food aficionados. A fluent Thai speaker, Bob wrote about those dishes and their creators with tender care under his *Bangkok Post* pseudonym, Ung Ang Talay. His respectful values spread through protégés like food writers Korakot 'Nym' Punlopraksa or Austin Bush.

This fossicking for lesser-known dishes coincided with a worldwide recoil towards local authenticity, popularised by CNN's Anthony Bourdain, whose 'Parts Unknown' made some parts of Bangkok less unknown. Mass exposure couldn't be avoided via guides, YouTube and social media in an age where everyone became a food critic.

Much of the best food will soon pass into legend. Recipes of one-dish specialists, like other craft wisdom, are jealously guarded and rarely disclosed beyond family. So the secrets often die with the inventor if, as at Jay Fai, the chef's children aren't willing to wield that wok over a stove for a lifetime, despite her winning a Michelin star.

We're at the tail end of a hand-labour, low-wage tradition, when Thai cuisine's challenge is to remain authentic, but keep innovating. Oral food history is being gathered, streetfood is entering the formal repertoire, chefs are launching branded sauces, and old-school restaurants like Khrua Apsorn and Kalapapruek have opened branches in malls. Much of this has been driven by outsiders. Besides Thompson, fellow author Andy Ricker earned a star for Pok Pok in New York, and former food writer Jarrett Wrisley opened Soul Food Mahanakorn, an *izakaya*-style eatery with variations on homely Thai staples like *pad krapao* with lamb. Suddenly, the articulate go-to guys for Thai taste included *farangs*.

"When someone presents himself as the spokesman of Thai cuisine it's like Osama bin Laden going to the Vatican and saying he is the high authority on Catholicism," said Bob

Halliday. "Politics is peace and love compared to what happens in the Thai cooking world." Nationalist fury that only Thais reared at grandma's apron strings can understand Thai food abated when confronted by the taste. "I came here to complain," a mandarin's wife told Thompson. "But I can't."

Thais are divided. Some Thai chefs revere Thompson's achievement. Others feel it's inauthentic and drowning in spice, but admit that someone like Thompson was needed to push Thai food forward. "Nahm was a real trailblazer," says Thaninthorn Chantrawan of Osha. "The Westerners in our dining scene led to the fine-dining direction. Presentation is another thing that's changed a lot because of foreigners serving Thai-influenced food."

In this acutely professionalisd scene, restaurateurs often mention in menus their small-scale suppliers – including a new breed of city rooftop farms, farmers' markets, and even their own farms. Chefs still rely on Khlong Toei Market, Talad Kon Lao in Wong Wien Yai and the farmer's organisation market Or Tor Gor, with some prime goods from the Royal Projects reducing the ongoing need for imports.

This artisanal boom is a reaction to the adulteration of Thai flavours from kitchen shortcuts like MSG, tofu from plastic tubes, and coconut milk from boxes, or making dishes from Mama instant noodles. Diners, more health aware, are wary of factory-farmed chicken and squid kept white by formaldehyde. One report found that half of Thai food labelled organic has more pesticides than is even allowed for normal veg.

The worst offence against Thai food's vaunted balance is over-sweetening, even of savoury dishes. The addictive high-fructose corn syrup in processed 'food' may have shifted the Thai palate to demand it that way. Cooks substitute pats of wholesome coconut sap with cheap, denatured cane sugar. A hotter climate means pricier limes, which affects countless dishes. "Where lime should be provided as a condiment, it often no longer is; you need to ask for some, and it comes in smaller slivers" says chef Napol Jantraget of 80/20. "Cooks try to substitute lime with tamarind, but it's just not the same." Tamarind is sour *and* sweet, upping the fructose, and cloying what should feel crisp, while tartness isn't quite the same using starfruit, *taling pling* or unripe mango. Many cheap restaurants use bottled 'lime juice', which is really citric acid, colouring, clouding agent and fragrance No 43002.

Foodies lament that the great streetfood cooks waste their talent on ever worse ingredients. To keep the price point affordable, cooks use the products of agribusiness, which in a vicious circle, corners food supply, so local markets lose out to wholesalers and hypermarkets, where many vendors now shop. The freehand flair of Thai food also faces an existential threat in standardisation. Recipes become internationalised. Chains impose their house style on branch chefs. Those not raised at auntie's apron strings rely on recipes. Pre-packaged ingredients from supermarkets

left: *Moo kata* (grilled pork with *suki* soup) is intended for social dining, seen here by Memorial Bridge.

above: Experimental, colour-coded food-on-a-stick in TCDC during Bangkok Design Week.

Senses 35

limit what's in each sachet. Thais are used to dipping into shared dishes that arrive at table without formal order. Now chefs construct tasting menus in courses to be eaten as directed.

As food is part of the country's face, officialdom keeps trying to standardise the Thai flavour profile, just as it froze Thai dance or Thai language. Thai Delicious is a million-dollar government scheme to control Thai food overseas. The agency standardises 'authentic' recipes, to be the basis of chef certification and ready-to-cook products for export. The Thai Delicious committee commissioned an 'e-Delicious machine', "an intelligent robot that measures smell and taste in food ingredients through sensor technology in order to measure taste like a food critic." Each recipe has an electronic conductivity signature, that with enough data will be able to identify any flavour defects. The 'authentic' signature is chosen from ten dishes sampled by 120 tasters, all drawn narrowly from unrepresentative Chulalongkorn University. A skeptical vendor, Thaweekiat Nimmalairatana, who'd been cooking for 25 of his 35 years, states the common wisdom: "I use my tongue to test if it's delicious or not."

It prompted a furious backlash, as did a junta plan to regulate Thai cooking at home and abroad, with the regimentation of a mess hall. "Standardisation is the enemy of Thai food," railed a *Bangkok Post* editorial. "The very notion that there is one way to cook a dish is laughable. Consider Thai massaman, which in 2012 was named by CNN as the No.1 dish in the entire world. Like dozens of popular Thai dishes, it's not traditional Thai. The curry originated in the Middle East and went through many iterations before the first bowl was cooked in Thailand. Every cook is proud of his or her massaman. Yet the one your mother made tastes just a bit different from the one cooked by the father across the street. Thai cooking is the only Thai traditional art that is still alive and thriving. That is because it is open to experiments which give each dish new meaning."

Thai food's laboratory remains the street and the kitchen, where innovation and tradition both rely on creativity. Personal flair is admired in chefs, but it's ingrained that authenticity can only come by cooks learning from elders whilst growing up. And cooking doesn't stop in the kitchen; it continues with each diner adjusting the flavour with condiments.

Thompson's mentor was the wife of a high official who lived in a palace. "Her cooking was instinctive; she disregarded cautious weighing and measuring, along with the dictates of any recipe, preferring to follow her own experience and taste," wrote Thompson. "I soon began to appreciate that hers was not a culinary bedlam, but a responsive and intimate way of cooking and seasoning. Thai cooking is at odds with the modern world, where speed and simplicity are paramount. It needs the cook's attention, it expects time and effort… and requires honed skills, but it rewards with sensational tastes."

left: **Bangkok has turned** *Mama* **packet noodles into a standard ingredient, seen here in a food court.**

above: **Bangkokians are getting plumper: an advertisement about diet on the Siam Skywalk.**

Gastrothai

The rule of Bangkok food used to be: the worse the decor the better the taste. Thai cuisine abroad had since the late 1980s gone from marginal to mainstream to global staple. But at home it was held back by restaurants for foreigners blanding out the flavours, and Thais refusing to pay more for Thai food in comfort, when it tasted better in dowdy old-school restaurants or at a stall in the street. Besides, Thais who could afford to dine out likely had a cook at home. Now the rule has inverted: while vendors struggle with eviction and serve poor ingredients to keep prices affordable, the top end has bloomed to join the best in the world, upping presentation and deconstructing recipes. As the city with the most restaurants in Asia's top 50, it's now a magnet for foodie tourism.

In boom-era 1990s Bangkok, fine dining had been limited to Frenchified silver service at Le Normandie, Le Banyan or Le Dalat. You can see *la problème*. Moneyed taste was stuck in the 1970s. *Hi-so* entertaining centred on hotels and banquets. Power dining meant private rooms for serving steak or shark's fin. In a face culture, ornate settings and obsequious service mattered. The new rich happily overpaid for prestige, which then meant foreign brands, and foreign food cooked by a foreign chef. Hotels were the only place to get decent cheese, coffee or cigars.

Hotels did innovate. The first designer eatery was Jesters at the Peninsula. Anantara's Biscotti introduced open kitchens and long tables. The Banyan Tree pioneered al fresco dining on a skyscraper rooftop at Vertigo. But hotels declined after the 2008 crash into corporate blahness. In a last hurrah, two Michelin-starred chefs pioneered Thai gastronomy at Nahm and molecular Thai at Kiin-Kiin.

Under-one-roof dining slid into malls, where neo-Thai eatery Paste or Michelin-starred Din Tai Fung chose to open amidst chain restaurants. Veteran restaurants like Kalapapruek spawned branches in malls and even food courts. The best mall food emerged from Greyhound, a fashion label spin-off that mastered eclectic Thai fusions and a pop take on Thai parfaits.

The baton of food innovation has passed since 2000 to stand-alone restaurants under a charismatic chef-patron, whose appearance is a face-giving event. Leaders included Hervé Frerard (Le Beaulieu) and a raft of Italians like Gianni Favro (Gianni's) and Paulo Vittaletti (Appia, Peppina). Now there's plenty of dish-explanation at hip eateries, from nose-to-tail meat at 100 Mahaseth to vegan burgers at Broccoli Revolution. "In Singapore or Hong Kong, seeing the chef is not that important," says Oliver Krammy of Water Library, which was solely a chef's table, a gustatory immersion for just ten diners a night. "But in Bangkok, the chef has to be there."

A foreign chef coming to their table appealed to the Thai elite, who've always imported expertise and treated cooking as menial. Asking to meet the cook in a Thai restaurant used to bewilder and embarrass all concerned – unless that chef had status for other reasons. "Too often, diners still get hung up on the nationality of their chef," says Nan Bunyasaranand of Franco-American Little Beast. "There was an outcry when David Thompson started cooking Thai food in Bangkok, and similarly, foreign chefs are expected to be the best at foreign food. When they see me, diners will go: 'This is the chef?'" At the other extreme, "someone graduates from a cooking school, puts on a sexy tank top and bakes a cake on YouTube. Thais love celebrities too much. If an actor opens a restaurant, then he or she is called a chef."

It only became acceptable for the affluent to study in culinary schools once Le Corden Bleu opened here in 2007, and thanks to TV cooking shows and the Korean food drama *Dae Jang Geum*. "Everyone wants to take shortcuts. People spend one million baht to go to cooking schools and they open a restaurant," laments Iron Chef judge Pongtawat 'Chef Ian Kittichai' Chalermkittichai, who began selling curry on the street and washed pots at the Waldorf in London.

The highest achievers spent years of apprenticeship under an exacting Alpha chef. Tee Kachonklin created La Table de Tee in 2011, aged just 26, after working at Roussillon in London. "I didn't care if I didn't get paid when I was a trainee," says Chef Worathon 'Tae' Udomchalotorn of Le Du. "I just knew I had to work

above: The nose-to-tail food fad suits Isaan food, as reimagined at 100 Mahaseth restaurant.

Senses 37

with Michelin restaurants to improve." Duangporn 'Bo' Songvisava, awarded Asia's best female chef in 2013, had worked at Nahm in London before founding Bo.lan with husband Dylan Jones as a new breed of edgy Thai restaurant.

Previously Bangkok only got glimpses of Michelin-calibre cookery in hotel promotions and the annual Bangkok Gourmet Festival, for a select social set who'd tasted such cuisines abroad. Food face reached its climax in the Epicurean Masters of the World, a wood-fired grill of vanities worthy of a Tom Wolfe novel, with million-baht meals hosted at the Dome, a neo-classical skyscraper topped by a gilded cupola. Stung by accusations of elitism, its second year saw the imported chefs helicoptered to a poverty-stricken location to give charity. "When the dining scene was a flat line, we might have been more excited by Chef Monsieur So-and-So from France," lamented *BK* in 'Tired Trends'. "But they show up with jet-lag, get lost in the Or Tor Kor market and usually cook up something that doesn't come close to the food that earned them their glorious stars."

What really put Bangkok on the gourmet map was the influx of chefs who'd made a big name abroad. Blue Elephant, a Thai-Belgian upmarket chain, upped its game for its Thai launch. "Thai people are really picky. If you can cook food in Thailand and people love it then I think you're the best chef in the world," says Chef Ian, who returned after success in several world cities, to helm a string of top restaurants, paired with innovative cocktails: Hyde & Seek, Namsaah Bottling Trust and Issaya Siamese Club. But he feels that for the scene to flourish, diners must show more respect. "Twenty percent don't even call if they don't show up for their reservation."

Eating may be Bangkok's social glue, but gastro-diplomacy is soft power. Cuisine became a tourist draw after Gaggan, with its degustation menu written in emojis, won Best Restaurant in the Asian Food Awards four years running. Gaggan Anand of

38 Taste

top left: **Michelin awarding stars to Bangkok restaurants has changed the fine dining scene, which now feels it must play with its recipes on multi-course tasting menus. This doll is displayed at the more traditional restaurant The Local.**

below left: **Bangkok is infamous for roving trolleys of deep fried insects. Now this protein of the future has been turned into haute cuisine at Insects in the Backyard at Chang Chui art centre.**

left: *Laab moo* [**pork spicy salad**] **in a cocktail, served at Eat Me! You inhale bacon aromas as you sip the chilli drink through ground roasted rice.**

Kolkata applied the molecular gastronomy he'd learned under Fernand Adria of the world's top rated El Bulli. Soon tasting menus became the norm, with Thai chefs keen to freeze-dry dessert, emulsify veg and turn soup into spheres. Now foodies now fly in with a schedule of meals booked at award-winners, then squeeze in farmers' markets, artisanal gin speakeasies, and late-night streetfood at Yaowarat.

You can see the change at Eat Me! Since 1998, this Australian restaurant by Darren Hausler was a regular drop-in for Bangkok creatives, gays, and fans of its art shows and cool music. But once it hired a top chef, Tim Butler and made the Asia Top 50, regulars can't get a table at short notice. Bangkok had never been a city where you needed to plan; great food was right there, but Southern Thai sensation Sorn now books out months ahead.

The world is also coming here to cook. Noticing Gaggan, foreign chefs saw Bangkok as a stage for the ambitious. Some like Jess Barnes built his reputation here through pop-up dinners and hip venues like Opposite. Famous chefs launched here under their own name, like Dutch Michelin-starred Henk Savelberg and the Sühring twins of Berlin, who wowed with their revelatory German *Neue Kuche*, while Joel Robuchon, who'd earned the most Michelin stars in history, opened here ahead of Michelin's arrival in 2017.

Some wonder whether Michelin, with its obsessions over French and Japanese precision, 'gets' Thai food's imprecision, since its first Bangkok stars went most to French food. Bangkok's forte is more playful, in a city where rice gets moulded as a teddy bear. At 80:20, Canada-trained Napol Jantraget has dishes combining four ways of cooking one ingredient, from a medley of eggplant to a rice dessert with fermented rice ice cream that tastes like blue cheese. And the city is most famed for food served outside of restaurants. As Southeast Asian chef Bobby Chinn points out: "If you fast forward to look at what's going to happen in the food world, it's moving to the street."

Yet just as Bangkok earned the world's respect for its streetfood, the authorities set about banishing it from downtown. "No one can compete with our street food," says Gaggan. "I hope that [Michelin] will understand our shophouses, too, as it's all about the same dedication." Michelin's first Bangkok guide awarded a star to shophouse legend Jay Fai, who cooks her succulent crab omelet wearing a beanie and ski goggles. Michelin and food pilgrims both recognise that haute cuisine can indeed be found in a plain shophouse open to the street – and open to the world.

Heat and Damp
Keeping cool in the world's hottest city

Bangkok teaches a lesson in humidity. Built in a swampy tropical delta, ringed by evaporating paddy and shrimp ponds, the city lies flat at sea level, in the torpid cleft between Indochina and its peninsula arm. Sheltered from bracing oceans, Bangkok is where air comes to wallow and put on weight. Thanks to technology, this is also a city of bracing indoor chill.

Bangkok's swelter creates particular effects. In the high humidity, crunchy foods soften, leather shoes mould and books turn a spotty yellow. One monsoon and recent cement stains with moss. Riding a motorcycle in a helmet is a torrid trial-by-fire, weaving past cars that act as radiators, whilst the 'wind in your face' feels like a hairdryer.

Bangkok is officially the world's 'hottest' city because its Tropical Savannah climate fluctuates so little from its high average. While desert towns shiver at night, and many hot cities vary over through the day and by season, Bangkok hovers mostly in the 30s°C with humidity averaging 80 percent and nights barely dipping to the mid-20s°C. Japanese and Westerners who cherish four distinct seasons often can't handle Bangkok's three phases of hot, hotter, and hot-and-wet.

Hot season gathers pace from February until May. Easing the slow roast, March winds enable kite-flying. Most cultures mark New Year at the most barren time, which here means Songkran, formerly an Equinox festival for many years fixed at 13-15th April. Pre-monsoon swelter peaks in May/June, with random downpours, often at night or in the morning, when the softening asphalt turns showers into oily steam.

The monsoon brings afternoon rains from June to October, peaking in September when it can drizzle and storm for days. The city goes on flood alert around the full and new moons of September and October, when the river's highest tides combine with the heaviest rainfall and run-off from the north. An hour's downpour is enough to cover shoes, two hours fills my *soi* to calf depth; twice a year the waters lap my door sill.

Given that floods are normal, the Venice of the East takes pride in its heritage as a 'water culture', even as rice growing and canals recede from prominence. Water still plays a crucial role in traditions and festivals, with beliefs in aquatic goddesses and the *naga* water serpent. When the sun is closest to Bangkok in mid-April, Thais spray each other on a nationwide scale at the Songkran Festival. It began as a polite dousing of Buddha images and elders' hands at a time when farmers had little to do, but has turned into a gigantic three-day water fight.

The extreme weather that gently shaped rural life now misshapes city life. Bangkok in the wet offers treacherous booby traps: doorways stranded beyond puddles; awnings swollen with rainfall that tip onto market-goers; cars splashing waves from flash floods over pavements. Even when all seems dry, an uneven paving slab tilts and spurts black water up your leg.

"Rain falls often here, but no one here wants it," says a migrant in Tadsanawadee's novel *Wall*. She feels that urbanites don't appreciate the gift of rain for food and regeneration, but comes to realise how rain can be a nuisance in modern life. Downpours jam roads and muss attire, while floods cause damage and disease. Diaries get thin during the monsoon, as few risk functions that rain might spoil.

Bangkok stories treat water as a metaphor. Living in a city drained of *nam jai* ('water of the heart': compassion), Paiwarin Khao-ngam's protagonist in the novel *Morning Song* revels in the communal water-throwing at Songkran. He says, "drenched to my very soul… that was truly one of my happiest days in Bangkok." By contrast, in Tew Bunnag's *Curtain of Rain*, set during the Great Flood of 2011, an English arrival felt the heat like "a clammy serpent caressing her skin, squeezing the water from every pore of her body." The Lao-Isaan lead in Apichatpong Weerasethakul's film *Mekong Hotel* speculates that the 2011 flood was "the tears of the Emerald Buddha, desperate to go home to Laos."

left: **Monsoon storm clouds burst over the city, with Wat Mahathat and the Grand Palace in the foreground.**

top: **Down pours the rain over the ceramic-inlaid** *chedi* **[stupas] of Wat Pho.**

above: **Up sprays water from BMA trucks in an effort to wash PM2.5 particles from the polluted air on Surawong Road.**

below: **Motorcycle drivers wait at the traffic lights of Ratchaprasong by sheltering under the shade of the Skytrain tracks.**

right: **At Songkran festival, Thais splash water during the hottest time of the year. An ad at Emporium.**

below right: **A tuk-tuk racing through floods on Ploenchit Road.**

You can sense the precise day when the rains stop. Moist winds from the Indian Ocean shift to blow cool and dry from China. The pall lifts and out bursts the energy of spring:, fresh, green and clear – a time to party.

Residents joke about the shortness of the so-called "cool season," which can last just the week around Christmas, or more rarely from November to February. One windy December morning in 1998 I shivered as a low of 15°C had a chill-factor of 9°C. Just once, never since.

Prized days in the centigrade teens see Bangkokians wrap up, if only for Instagram. Long sleeves appear under T-shirts, tights under skirts, and scarves under a Uniqlo puffer jackets. For a lark, some wear knitted panda hats with ear flaps that extend into mittens. Amid Christmas trees, Styrofoam snowmen and cashiers in Santa hats, Bangkok makes like a winter wonderland.

For that short interval, Bangkok can feel like a temperate city. Outdoor lifestyle thrives in the low-mid 20°s C. You can comfortably walk by day, and balmy velvet nights reel non-stop with fairs, festivals and beer gardens on every mall forecourt. Tap water, usually tepid, runs cold. People sleep with windows open, no air-con thrum in earshot. Foreigners wish it stayed that way all year, though many Thais miss the warmth, which returns soon enough.

We actually have two senses of thermoception – gauging heat and cold, and regulating body temperature. Visitors from temperate zones have thick blood and tight pores to keep warm, so they steam around town like pressure cookers. Tropical bodies cool by thinning blood and opening pores, so in air-con they over-chill. Our bodies take months to adjust and I've long since retuned to the Thai thermostat. While there's no official sense of 'aquaception,' humans, being mostly water, are hyper-sensitive to humidity. In this sultry sweatbox, we don't merely perspire – we drench.

Local ways to prevent overheating include the cool sensation from herbal balm, menthol inhalers or prickly heat powder after frequent cold showers, though Bangkok tapwater feels lukewarm, even hot from being in exposed pipes.

One can try to chill via the inside: ice in red wine, beer on the rocks, whole coconuts from the fridge. Pottery jars traditionally kept herbal drinks cool. At the hottest time of year, people eat *khao chae*, a Mon iced rice soup scented with candle smoke and jasmine. In contrast, Thai-Chinese avoid consuming anything cold as unhealthy. Instead, yin-yang principles hold that cooling foods like cucumber balance heaty foods such as durian.

Bangkok's longtime solution for personal climate change is the *pha yen* – a chilled damp towel that comes in a plastic sheath that you clap open with a satisfying 'pop'! Restaurants often provide a scented version that's automatically put on the bill. Street workers keep them in their Eskys of iced water. Tuk-tuk drivers often have one draped over their neck. Spas and hotels take *pha yen* to the next jasmine-scented level. A woman in national costume proffers a chilled white flannel upon a lacquer tray with sweet welcome drink and complimentary orchid. This ritual converts even the most heat-stroked, jet-lagged tourist to the charms of Bangkok.

Bangkokians used to dress down for the climate, but emulation of Western ways has led to the opposite. "With our black tailcoats, we resemble… the crows on the gilded eaves of the *wats* and we suffer terribly from the mid-day heat," wrote a Belgian advisor to King Rama V. Nevertheless, the elite and aspirational Thais adopted those coats to look *siwilai* (civilised).

Adoption of enclosing Western dress spread from the court to the masses in the 1940s, when the Leader, Field Marshal Phibun, decreed that Thais should wear uniforms or collared shirts with a long skirt or trousers – and not leave home without a hat. Those in traditional wraps wouldn't get served at government offices – and before long, at any shop or business in the city. The multi-pocketed safari suit and short-sleeved jacket-shirt became a climate-appropriate compromise for several decades, before suits became a workplace norm in the era of air-con. Men often wear undervests to stop their shirts sticking. Today, of course, foreigners dress less stuffily, and even some Thais wear shorts.

Guidebooks advise visitors to pack a smartish outfit to please officials. Yet many Westerners stubbornly dress in beachwear and react angrily to any resulting disdain from locals who feel their capital's being disrespected. "Bangkok is a real city. It's not a resort city just because it has a hot climate," points out Marc Pachter, director emeritus of the Smithsonian Institution. "It's only the vacationing Westerner who is bewildered by this. Nobody goes to Singapore and is surprised to see people in suits, yet here they are. In a business city, people wear suits. Not just plutocrats, but secretaries, sales staff and anyone in uniform. It has a lot to do with the extent that you take Bangkok seriously as a city."

For foreigners, some confusion about dress comes from extreme air conditioning. They shiver when they underdress for a mall or cinema that's kept at 20°C, rather than the comfy 25°C briefly imposed during a power shortage. Bangkokians constantly gripe about *bpen wat* – having feverish sniffles that are blamed on changing seasons and repeated thermal shocks between outdoors and in.

This is partly because in dank Bangkok, industrial air-conditioners must heat-exchange down to 10°C to condense the excess moisture, then re-heat that air, so mall-freeze is due to saving money on heating. As engineer Trevor Scott explains: "If this was not done, and the air simply cooled to 22°, we'd be working and shopping in low-cloud conditions."

Mall-freeze is also cultural. Convection vents cooled traditional buildings in a sustainable way, but they're considered low status and outdated. Air-conditioning is a

Se-wen

Bangkok can get too much. Over-stimulation and surprises make every day different. A city so rousing needs some anti-sensory antidote, and there's a place to decompress every few hundred metres: 7-Eleven.

This chain of convenience stores effectively provides sensory deprivation chambers. Inert inside, they offer artificially cool, dehumidified air, shadow-free brightness, synthetic non-scents, bland scripted greetings and no sense of place. What a relief!

Bangkokians relish the opportunity to feel cool – say wading through drifts at Snow Town fun park in Ekamai, downing vodka at -5°C in Bangkok Ice Bar, or seeing a movie in one of the infamously freezing cinemas. There they can don warm clothing and long-sleeved fashionwear. Residents stick up posters of waterfalls, alpine lakes or spring blossoms to feel a fresher mood.

Like malls and department stores, 7-Eleven is a sample of somewhere else. Many complain that it's cultural imperialism or modernity destroying Thai that ways. Yet *Se-wen*, as it's nicknamed, has become a Thai institution. Its insensible character is a dose of modernity, which appeals precisely because it's a break from the chaos outside. Going to *"Se-wen"* is like an asthmatic reaching for an inhaler. It's not natural air, but it gives the feel of a reprieve. Even *soi* dogs wait by the door to catch wafts of cool air.

What these stores really sell is packaging. Even supermarkets allow some contact with the goods. In convenience stores, not only does the food have palm oil and chemicals, but a plastic barrier prevents you from smelling, touching and often seeing what you buy. They come in smaller sizes to give an illusion of value, taking more resources and generating more waste.

We live in an era of dulled senses that distances us from nature and its primal associations: messy, wild, unclean. That desensitization, well advanced in other parts of the world, is partly why visitors relish Bangkok – for a shot of its visceral, heady realness. Yet it's emulating the most antiseptic, straightjacketed versions of modernity as we can see when the Singapore-style ban on durian in public places began creeping into Thai transit and hotels.

Developed economies realised too late that prioritising financial sense comes at the expense of every other sense. Yet the 7-Eleven and its identically analgesic rivals have been absorbed into Thai life. Their chill, antiseptic air is a reset for Bangkok's sensory onslaught, which resumes the moment the door jingle rings as you exit.

44   Heat & Damp

symbol of development, even luxury. Suits signal a prestigious white-collar job, and many staff are uniformed, so interiors are chilled to suit how they dress. It also enables the affluent to promenade in high fashion jackets. To cope, Thai men often wear long-sleeves that they can roll up outside, while women carry a shawl or sweater in their car. In a city that began largely topless, where working men still cool off by hitching up their shirts, air-con has created the retail genre of the "indoor jacket".

Bangkok novelists use seductive cool as a metaphor for status, notes Ellen Boccuzzi. In Tarin's 'Fake Beggar' newly middle-class Pimala hails a taxi, tired of waiting at a bus stop, "leaving the heat and crowds behind" and "moves to the centre of the seat in order to fully absorb the cool air from the front." Discomfited by fellow migrants on the street, Pimala can't help feeling guilt and "looks away, as if to evade the thought she had. But the cool air kept hitting her…"

Heat affects how Bangkokians position themselves. Upon entering a building, many recompose themselves at a stream of cool, dry air from a vent or fan. Similarly, the shade of a pole, or tree can dictate the odd angles that people stand outdoors. Open-air event-goers clump around the fans with spray nozzles to spritz the diners and partiers.

In Bangkok even Frank Sinatra wouldn't walk on 'The Sunny Side of the Street', and Thais always pick a shaded route. Rather than scale concrete footbridges with superheated handrails, they cross roads "underneath the flyover because it shields them from the sunlight," says a source in the Department of Public Works. "The problem of rain or strong sunlight can easily be solved by an umbrella, unlike the safety problem." A partial solution is covering the footbridges, which has extended into covered skywalks between malls, offices, hotels and station crossings. Similarly, boats tip to the side because few sit on the unshaded side; it's the same in buses, trains or parts of a room under direct sun. Drivers stay in lanes shaded by elevated roads or Skytrain, while bikes wait for traffic lights under any available shadow from a bridge.

Obsessed with pale skin, Bangkokians use umbrellas not just for rain, but as parasols. Oddly, this isn't much of a hat culture, so when caught in sunlight, Thais hold bags, papers, even shopping over their face. Women sitting sidesaddle on motorcycle taxis shield their face with a handbag. In rain, Bangkokians grab whatever's at hand to shelter, from bits of cardboard or banana leaf to scrunched plastic bags.

Climate affects transport too. Open-air tuk-tuks, *songtaew*, motorcycles and pedicabs are mostly used by low-status people, while buses and trains are demarcated by class between aircon and fan. "Sweat, heat and the press of crowds on lengthy journeys is the experience of traveling Thailand by train," says Kaewta Ketbungkan in Sompot

top left: **Ice houses are getting rarer, but this one in Talad Noi still sells ice blocks to vendors.**

left: **7-Eleven convenience stalls are everywhere. This one in Silom is fringed by stalls.**

above left: **Shophouses and blocks often have decorative grilles to filter out the sun's glare.**

above right: **Parasols are essential when renting bicycles in the green retreat of Chatuchak Park.**

Senses 45

Chidgasornpongse's documentary *Railway Sleepers*. Those with social clout go by air-conditioned car, taxi or deluxe van. Vehicles have various kinds of window shades, while their tinted windows are often illegally dark.

Foreigners often mock the *hi-so* Bangkokians who rarely leave air-con, but that's how they manage to avoid thermal shock. From home to car to work to shop to function to dinner to bar to bed, they float in a hermetically-sealed bubble of cool. Poorer Bangkokians mimic that to the extent they can, hanging out in air-con spaces. The slump of bus riders into the frames of open windows as they shunt for two-hours in a fume-blasted commute is a vivid measure of inequality.

Bangkok is a free preview of global warming. Occasional longer winters remind the elderly of the long misty cool seasons in the 1950s, before Bangkok became warmer than the Central Plains. The city's micro-climate – 2.5°C hotter by day, 8°C more at night – runs a feedback loop of pollution, notably from cars, cremations and outdoor burning. During the cool season, so many fine PM2.5 particles get trapped under 'cold air inversion' that on a few days Bangkok has the world's worst air.

"Bangkok is in fact getting hotter, and climate change needn't enter into the equation. The city is becoming an urban 'heat island'

below: **Climate Central's mapping of land elevations shows that by 2050 the area in red would flood, restoring the coastline from 1500 years ago.** *Map by Climate Central*

bottom: **A street worker covers up with a mask and arm sleeves, plus an umbrella for added shade.**

right: **In 2019 Bangkok had days as the world's most polluted city, as measured by PM2.5 particles. Many residents put on masks, inspiring the graffiti artist Headache Stencil to paint this commentary in On Nut.**

46   Heat & Damp

due mainly to its dearth of green areas," ran a *Nation* editorial. Just turn from baking Sathorn to tree-shaded Saladaeng to sense how trees make streets walkable.

What Bangkokians simmer in is not so much a kettle as a wok – a bowl hollowed by groundwater pumping, with the loose alluvial soils compacted under the weight of buildings. Much of downtown has negative altitude, keeping breezes weak and making Bangkok one of the cities most vulnerable to rising sea levels. The sinking land is compounded by the inability of the river to continue depositing silt on this flood plain.

The Chao Phraya's river basin drains half the country. That's a lot of water, which is why Thais used to build their houses on rafts or stilts that slope inwards to brace against the erosive eddies. They perched along the river and canals that drain the delta, adapting to the environment – in a way of life that barely survives in the remoter *khlongs* of Thonburi and Nonthaburi, where some still commute by boat. One reason the river and canals are so charming is that Bangkok was built to front the waterway, only later to face landward. In those houses on the river, water-cooled air convected through the floorboards to make life pleasant.

Chinese settlers then built the Chinese way in masonry on the ground, and later everyone adopted Western temperate architecture. Unfortunately, drainage never got rethought as canals were filled in or buried in pipes until the epic floods of 1995, when central Bangkok was spared by floodgates keeping areas like Bang Phlad inundated for three months. A lattice of giant mains moderated but didn't prevent the Great Flood of 2011, when the same Bangkok-first strategy directed water away from the centre so inner and outer suburbs endured knee-to-chest height waters.

This existential crisis prompts blunt solutions. Floodwalls line much of central Bangkok and while hemming in high tides, they haven't prevented the big floods. Walls also prevent riverine lifestyles, damage ecology and increase waves, whilst faster currents then undermine the walls. Plans to flood-proof the city's entire riverside risk severing communities, hotels and temples from their historic link to the water.

Other urban tidying exposes the city to more glare. Clearing vendors from pavements has the effect of removing shade from awnings

and umbrellas, while replacement of shophouses and their porches with set-back towers has opened up space, but also for sun and rain. In all these cases, the removal of trees and shade to display prestigious buildings comes from a craving to show face and modernity.

This lifestyle of chilled aircon interiors and denuded public space has snowballing consequences for architecture, planning, energy, traffic, and mass transit. Once it's accepted that Bangkok is a world city where people do serious business, wear high fashion, and pursue international lifestyles, even the sun and the rain and the water culture must bow to the quest for cool.

Space
Auspicious shapes and hidden patterns

Planners dream of zones and grids. They meet their match in Bangkok, an organic urban organism in which *sois* are cultural ecosystems. Hiking a terrain of potholes, concrete stumps and puddles – under canopies of canvas and strangled wires – makes pedestrians feel like urban explorers. Originally hacked out of the jungle, the city still works like a trail of forest clearings.

Clutter spreads through every kind of space, whether community, workplace or home. All that stuff gives a reassuring, lived-in feel, but in public spaces, the mess affects the city's image. Efforts to tidy don't resolve issues over who gets to use what space. Planning – or the lack of it – is hotly contested, going to the heart of differing values, power relations and the source of Bangkok's 'genius loci' – the talent of the place.

Ad hoc settlements of canals, roads and empty lots get branded today as encroachment, but was for centuries the norm. Management of space here still favours purge over pruning in efforts to empty plazas and open up vistas, along the Western model. Vendors and shacks face sudden eviction. Utility workers mutilate trees as if avenues were wilderness. But like vines entangling a rainforest, 'public space' soon gets re-colonised by traders or shacks.

Place is built into the Thai language, with its use of locational 'vector words' that privilege the front (*na*), which is also the word for 'face'. In English, 'space' implies a blank with potential content, while in the Thai hierarchy that allots everyone a slot, "space" is *neua tii* – 'meat of the place.' Bangkok has very meaty spaces. Packed with almost every national activity, it's the world's most primate city.

The centre is denser than most cities, but the suburbs sprawl even wider than LA, into six provinces: Samut Sakhon, Nakhon Pathom, Nonthaburi, Pathum Thani, Chachoengsao and Samut Prakan. Bangkok province is already large at 1,569 square kilometers, but the built-up connurbation is five times that, housing 16 million people. Greater Bangkok is a 'mega urban region,' like Hong Kong/Shenzhen/Guangdong.

Wags joke that Bangkok was built first and planned later. But for its first century, the format was clear. The walled city of Rattanakosin defended its royal and religious precincts, while outside arose a parallel city of ethnic enclaves and their trades.

Rattanakosin (Jewelled Isle of Indra) was created by canals. Its western side is an arc of 'river' that had originated as a canal cut in 1542 to shorten a meander in the Chao Phraya River. After 1782, the new capital gained moats to the east dug by prisoners of war, while Lao captives built the crenellated walls. Whitewashed fragments survive around the two remaining forts, Pom Phra Sumen and Pom Mahakan.

Like many Indic cities, Krungthep was laid out under Hindu-Buddhist cosmology as a 'mandala,' a sacred diagram centred upon the mythical Mount Meru. In addition, a mandala can be incorporated into the design of a building, or scaled up to a state. In the latter case, Thailand has been labelled a 'Galactic Polity,' in which provincial satellites revolve around the cosmological axis of Bangkok.

Each Thai kingdom's capital was centred on the throne. Given this premise, rather than rebuild Ayutthaya, King Taksin established Thonburi, translated as 'City of Treasures' or 'Money Town.' King Rama I then moved his seat across the river to Bangkok, renaming it Krungthep, and re-establishing the Ayutthayan linkage in its full honorific name.

Krungthep recreated Auytthaya's key buildings and island shape, which evokes a Brahmin conch shell. Both capitals centred on a Mount Meru temple (here Wat Suthat), with a three-spired temple within the Grand Palace of the King, plus a Wang Na ('Front Palace') of his Deputy King, a Wang Lang (a defensive 'Rear Palace'), and a Wat Mahathat for Buddha relics. Outside both moats rose a Golden Mount, and a version of a Khmer temple mountain (here realized as Wat Arun).

Cosmological planning diluted in the 20th century after King Rama V moved his court north in 1897-1901, from the cramped Grand Palace to the suburb of Dusit, laid out on a European grid. Linking them, Thanon Ratchadamnoen – the Royal Processional Avenue based on the Champs-Élysées – became Thailand's axis of power. He also built palaces for princes, many of which remain.

When lived in, the Grand Palace "was a town complete unto itself – a town of women, governed by women," wrote ML Chittawadi Chitrabongs. "The only man who lived there was the monarch himself. His residence was a walled palace contained within the inner city, which was itself walled within the Grand Palace, which was in the walled city of Bangkok."

Walls gave Old Bangkok its shape – and segregated its residents. Within the ramparts, the royal citadel was girdled by a precinct of nobles. Beyond that, the city's atomised character came from each ethnic group being allotted an area, known formally as *yaan* (neighbourhoods, especially old ones), though casually Thais talk of localities of a few streets as *taew* (rows). "The wall made people into citizens," writes PD Smith in *Cities*. It united them with a common identity and pride as "pockets of insolent power" against external threats. "It became a wall in the mind."

Gradually, the city encompassed more residents. A third canal girdle, Khlong Phadung Krung Kasem, brought Chinatown within the moat system in 1851. Development spread downriver along Bangkok's first paved road in 1862-4, Charoen Krung ('Capital Progress') to the port, upriver along Samsen Road, and west on Thanon Bamrungmeuang. As ever more roads radiated out, citizens who were used to being hemmed in suddenly faced no limits. Suburbs seeped past the Ratchadaphisek inner ring road, then highways, trains and elevated expressways played catchup as the peri-urban fringe chewed up paddy fields and plantations. Bangkok became what Paul Theroux called a "flattened anthill."

Greater Bangkok came to feel shapeless, with the Chao Phraya the sole topographical feature in a vast floodplain with no natural barriers. Its only hill, Golden Mount (Phu Khao Thong), was piled from soil dug from canals and collapsed before it could be encased as a giant stupa, so it was capped by the small stupa we see today. Nevertheless, it remained the

left: **There was no space for a football pitch in Khlong Toei, so CJ WORX fit in this make-do angled pitch, which got covered in** *Time* **magazine.** *Photo courtesy of CJ WORX & AP*

top: **Bangkok's 'population mountain' showing density data visualised using Mapbox's OpenStreetMap.** *Image from pudding.cool*

above: **City walls at Pom Phra Sumen fort.**

Senses 49

city's tallest point until the Dusit Thani tower in 1970. The first airport was built at the 'City Heights' (Don Mueang), at a giddy altitude of almost three metres.

After consuming the delta, Bangkok now eats itself. The sprawl has reached commuting limits, so developers fill in the gaps. Until the 2000s, the endless shophouses made most areas look alike. However, as land values soar, denser towers were built upon garden compounds or replaced earlier buildings, even the iconic Dusit Thani. An ever morphing skyline of distinctive towers now provides reference points for knowing where you are.

Urban growth exploded because the capital hogged the country's wealth and power. Reading the urban strata, you can see the inequality in who gets space. Around spacious elite havens, most people live in small homes. Slums are filled with farm folk who had to migrate here to advance. Bangkok's 'informal sector' use public areas because they've always lacked enough space.

Tightly packed communities are skirted by *thanon* (main roads) and fed by a few narrow *soi* (lanes, literally 'dividers'), branching into *trok* (alleys) and *sork* (dead-end 'elbow' spurs). *Soi* first referred to ditches bordering paddy fields and plantations, which is why they are so narrow and turn at 90° angles. Sandwiched between Sukhumvit and Phetchaburi Roads, the 'Green Route' (named for the trees visible over the wall-lined *sois*) zigzags 33 times in 3.5 kilometres.

In the absence of squares, *soi* and *sork* became a space to shop, work and play.

Similarly, *pak soi* (where lane mouths meet a road) are like floating markets at canal confluences, abuzz with petty traders as vehicles and people slip through the tumult.

The city crams 9 million vehicles and the occasional elephant into roads, designed for 1.5 million, that cover just 8 per cent of the built-up area – about half the ideal surface, a third that of Paris. That pattern recurs, or with new construction accessed via maze-like routes from a highway. In his Bangkok novel,

50   Space

The Windup Girl, Paolo Bacigalupi called such *sois* 'squeezeways.'

Such dense habitation explains the need for eating and socialising venues in public space. Increasingly, that informal streetlife is being corralled into gated malls and private complexes. Bangkokians have to maximise land use, because many sites lie idle. Abandoned sites still remain from the 1997 crash, most infamously Sathorn Unique (AKA the Ghost Tower), and 'Bangkok's Stonehenge' – the pilings for the aborted Hopewell railway beside the new Red Line.

The ad hoc growth was partly because mass transit wasn't put in first to act as a focus. As train lines belatedly reach the suburbs, denser construction is allowed within 500 metres of each station. When the Skytrain made it possible to peek over walls and shophouses built around the perimeter of lush compounds, the city was revealed as rather green. This alerted developers to an archipelago of gardens where they could plant towers.

Seeing from above how Bangkok is arranged is a recent privilege. Until the recent past, aerial photography was banned due to security, and for being higher than royal or religious sites. But in the mid-2000s that became moot, since we've gained bird's eye views first from skyscrapers with open-air rooftop bars, then from Google Earth and drones. Bangkok had been inaccurately charted before satellite mapping, which enabled impenetrable *trok* to be pinpointed by pixel.

Planners have always sought to simplify cities, whether through social engineering, martial avenues or numbered grids. Bangkok tried some of that rationalism in Dusit's boulevards or elevated transit. But it otherwise reflects the culture in its circuitous paths, multi-purpose spaces and constant revisions. Despite a centralising impulse, there's no coherent grouping of towers and functions. Nor could anyone accuse its numbered *sois* of clarity.

Bangkok is a palimpsest – a place where scraping off one layer to make room for another

Sanam Luang

Visitors often mistake Sanam Luang for a park, but this iconic open space is loaded with highly charged meaning, from reverence to nostalgia. Flanked by the Grand Palace, City Pillar, Wat Mahathat, the Supreme Court and the National Museum, it is Bangkok's most multi-layered space.

The royal citadel that King Rama I built upon the earlier Teochiu Chinese settlement of East Thonburi needed a royal cremation ground for erecting funeral Meru towers. The area was enlarged into an oval lawn on the European model by King Rama V, who added the northern half from the Front Palace of the Viceroy after he abolished that 'Deputy King' position.

After the 1932 revolution it was opened as a public event space under the name 'Sanam Luang' (royal field). Citizens flocked there for kite flying and religious festivals. On royal birthdays, the perimeter of tamarind trees is lit by fairy lights and fireworks are launched. For decades, it doubled as a space for streetwalkers and the homeless, who've since been driven out. In most years before 1983, it hosted the Weekend Market (before that went to Chatuchak).

Sanam Luang also gained notoriety as a political space. From the 1960s, it was a free speech site dubbed "hi-park" (from Hyde Park Corner). It witnessed massacres of demonstrators in 1973 and 1976, with lynchings from the trees. After hosting both Yellow and Red Shirt demos, the oval was cleared of vendors, vagrants and kite-fliers, then gated and landscaped. Meanwhile royal cremations have continued at the Pramane Ground, and in 2017 this hallowed space witnessed the tallest-ever Meru for King Bhumibol's farewell.

For decades, Sanam Luang was an open public space. An outdoor screening was typical public entertainment at events, as here for the display of the Buddha image from Wat Sothorn in Chachoengsao.

far left, left & near left: **City of levels: street with a 'lid' under Rama VIII Bridge; underground floors below the Rosewood Hotel on Ploenchit; the BTS and Skywalk beside that site.**

top: **A 'nail house' left when the rest of a plot was cleared except for this landowner or tenant, as seen at Ratchathewi.**

Senses 51

leaves traces of what came before. There's an aversion to disturbing an existing balance. So the past isn't fully wiped away, nor the relics well maintained, but augmented with new alleys and ad-hoc extensions. Many people enjoy this complexity, though it lacks harmonious beauty. Traces remain from all eras, but not in zones like Penang's heritage district. That messy layering can be due to a lack of interest in aesthetics, or disregard for 'un-Thai' patrimony of Western or Chinese origin. Fractured streetscapes also result from mixed ownership. Hold-outs who refuse to sell will leave 'nail houses' in otherwise cleared sites. That explains odd-shaped malls like Emporium. Terminal 21 was wedged between the MRT, a row of shophouses and remnants of the wooden Asoke Market that's been nibbled by each project. Lack of forethought also hampers future land use. At Asoke, the state failed to merge the MRT into the existing BTS, so they were later bridged by an escalator shed. In Hong Kong, it would be an integrated terminus, but this jury-rigged patchwork preserves the site's urban fossils.

Saladaeng junction has no fewer than seven layers of transport. The Skytrain passes over a flyover, above a Skywalk, the street, a subway underpass and two levels of MRT tunnels. Tha Phra's MRT interchange is just as multi-level and even crosses an ancient canal.

The Skytrain – by its fares, status and very nickname – elevates its riders above the bus-riding masses. It connects to malls and towers via Skywalks that are smarter and smoother than the hazard-strewn pavements below. The Skybridges linking Emporium, EmQuartier and EmSphere malls are landscaped with plants and benches to evoke New York's High Line.

Tiered spaces reinforce social tiers. Rich, middle and poor often live adjacent and may mingle in some public areas, but their worlds barely touch. Each class accesses separate overlapping grids, whether for work, shopping or socialising, with modes of transit for each class of passenger. The elite glide between air-conditioned spaces in luxury Alphard vans, which act as their mobile office, lounge and changing room, to emerge from their journey pristine, not bedraggled like those on public transport. Digital mapping has revealed a *hi-so*, hi-tech Foreground City superimposed upon the organic, low-tech Background City.

This remains a city of walls, both physical and psychological. Townhouses sit behind railings and gates. Shophouses get sealed with roller doors and caged balconies. Unlike American suburbia's open lawns or European doors opening onto piazzas, Bangkok prefers defensive enclosures, with broken glass atop walls. Exclusionary architecture reveals the limits of civic trust. Card-entry condo lifts and gated *moo ban* estates sift out the public. Firms use barriers or guards to shoo away any hoi-polloi sitting on their forecourts, which often

left: **Tha Phra interchange has six levels of transit, with MRT atop bridges.**

above: **'Location is everything'** - a BTS ad for The Line condo.

52　Space

Background City

City maps show the malls and ministries, stations and highways, but miss the granular detail of local Bangkok like the knots of stalls at *soi* mouths. The city operates on two different grids that overlap but don't interact. To see the hidden network it helps to use Depth Map, a visualisation of data about urban space by a pioneer firm in the science of cities, Space Syntax.

Planning professor Apiradee Kasemsook applied Depth Map to Bangkok. The accessible 'Foreground Grid' painted the rail, roads, malls and downtown areas in warm tones. It leaves blue the many minor, informal lanes, *taew*, slums and *moo ban* that were likewise ignored on pre-digital paper maps.

Zoom the Depth Map to short-journey range and out pop clumps of red. These are the 'Background Grid' of villagey sub-centres like Suan Plu, Chokchai 4 or Phetburi Soi 5 that don't appear on normal maps. They are linked through lanes, canals and paths traversed by foot or informal transit that barely connects to the formal Foreground transit. The orderly 'Foreground' hubs go by formal names, while 'Background' places get nicknames referring to landmarks known to locals and taxi drivers. Some are put in this book's maps.

Background Bangkok evolved organically through community and culture, while the more 'planned' Foreground Bangkok is created by business needs and political will. Depth Map reveals that Bangkok is not chaotic after all; it just has hidden layers of circuitry.

Depth Map enables us to zoom in to any scale and see the local lanes and informal community hubs within walking or motorbike distance of residential areas, which aren't marked on normal maps, but which play a vital role in the daily lives of Bangkokians. *Images from a paper by Apiradee Kasemsook*

have defensive landscaping. Malls and venues may deter through implicit dress-code.

Foreigners can be oblivious to the social rules of *kalatesa* (time-space), which govern what's appropriate to any situation, from manners to possessions. Indie film director Sopawan Boonimitra calls *kalatesa* "a temporal and spatial order that has been used as a form of social control. One has to behave according to the unwritten rules of space as well as time."

Kalatesa is most strict at spaces of seniority, whether palace or *wat*, shrine or statue. Bangkok has almost a thousand temples, some of them large enclosures of concentric walls, with cloisters holding *viharn*, chapels of the Buddha image and eight *sema* boundary stones delineating the consecrated ground of a *bot*, (ordination hall), which is reserved for monks.

Normal spaces may receive temporary reverence, say from a VIP at a wedding or a monk's blessing with white string around the perimeter. A regal visit can permanently raise the status of a place such as Yaowarat. Receiving a royal audience requires a dedicated throne and offering table, which may later get displayed at that site.

Thai architecture has always embodied social ranks. Stilt houses had floors with various levels; elders occupy raised platforms, as do monks in temples. When royal motorcades pass, police bar pedestrians from footbridges. Skyscrapers challenge this height taboo. Laws bar new structures in Rattanakosin from overlooking royal palaces and temples.

Walls in the mind have shifted to nationalism, with the state re-segmenting the city. Some districts are drawn around land use or communities, like Samphanthawong (Chinatown), Bangrak (international quarter) or Phrakhanong (an old village). Others border railways, waterways or roads that were canals. Bureaucrats have also subdivided old *yaan* to undermine their self-organisation. To manage the sprawl, Thonburi province was merged into Bangkok in 1972. The name 'Thonburi' now labels just a small district, though the right bank's still nicknamed 'Fang Thon' (Thonburi side).

Authoritarian attitudes also constrain 'social space': entertainments, youth venues or self-expression. The once wild nightlife is banned from areas near temples or schools, which is pretty much everywhere. Restriction's strongest on intellectual and political space. Protest space had been a carnivalesque feature of Bangkok life, with periodic mass occupation of rival sites of power. These have shifted from the old political centre of Ratchadamnoen to the consumer hub of Ratchaprasong. After the Red Shirt occupation of 2010, the BMA asked volunteers to scrub the site – literally and metaphorically – in a "Big Clean-up Day."

Bangkokians don't have much right to their own city. The play *Banglamerd* (Violated Place) was subtitled: 'A city I do not own.' Land ownership is ultra concentrated and priced out of most Thais' reach, so living units get smaller and more standardised: the four-metre-wide shophouse; the one-metre gap around a condo bed; micro balconies for air-con. In once limitless Bangkok, space is the new luxury.

Some planners hope satellite suburbs can create a looser city. Others envisage a denser core, with a ban on townhouses downtown, funnelling residents into towers, whilst bolstering outer hubs like Minburi. Decentralisation sends jobs and housing outward, which guts mixed communities of their multi-generational bonds. 'Air rights' have become so valuable that human-scale hoods are being replaced by stacked apartments for the affluent, most of whom aren't locals.

State agencies, *wats* and the Crown Property Bureau run vast holdings, while developers buy up 'land banks' of prime plots. Piecemeal construction is giving way to mega-projects that erase entire streetscapes. Like Central Park in Manhattan, Lumpini Park has been hemmed in by three giant complexes: Sindhorn Village to the north, Dusit Central Park to the South, and One Bangkok to the east, which cram 60,000 people into five skyscrapers, five hotels, three condos and two mall. Each has a small patch of park.

"Mega-projects with vast footprints inevitably kill much urban tissue," says cities expert Saskia Sassen, who notes that these exclusionary schemes de-urbanise the city. Grand from a distance, bland up close, such mega-projects favour chains over independent traders, and lack varied, human-scale social interaction. When vibrant spaces turn dull, it's a break with history. Distinctly Thai kinds of space disappear. The NCPO banned houses over water, which had been the original Bangkokian form of dwelling.

Bangkok is so at ease with impermanence, that it has categories of sites under temporary usage. Roving bazaars rent empty plots and the BMA's 'Pocket Park' program landscapes vacant lots for a while, such as Pathumwan Park on the site of what became Bangkok Art & Culture Centre (BACC).

"[*Kalatesa*] still prevails, particularly the way in which space is quite fragmented and there are no clear boundaries, as can still be seen in Thai mural paintings," says Sopawan Boonnimitra, who labels this spatial ambiguity using a term for social chameleon, *lak-ka-pid lak-ka-perd* ('sometimes shut, sometimes open'). "The different spaces can be presented in one painting with multiple narratives taking place simultaneously, which can be read in various ways." *Lak-ka-pid lak-ka-perd* also fits the multi-purpose districts that switch function throughout the day, with shifts of vendors making efficient use of limited space.

That optimum use of limited space is outside the law, so there's a parallel system of street traders paying 'rent' for this public space to corrupt officials, often organised by a mafia, so the traders remain prone to extortion or crackdowns. Informal colonisation of space has been quintessentially Bangkokian, but has come to be seen as encroachment.

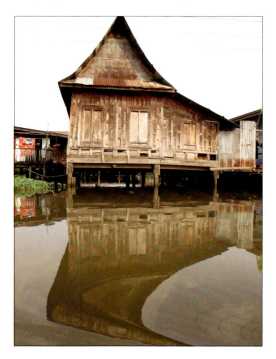

left: **Most wooden canal houses are in decay, as here on Khlong Om..**

right: **Open House bookshop-cum-venue in Central Embassy mall.**

Third Places

The soul of a city is its characteristic 'local', an informal gathering place where regulars bump into pals and trade gossip, such as the Barcelona bodega, Istanbul hammam, or Yangon tea shop. Bangkok's 'drop-in' is more diffuse: streetlife.

Bangkokians find cheer in their habitual stretch of stalls, shophouses and open-sided hangouts where Aunties recall your favoured foods. Every corner has a bench made of reclaimed wood, where *soi* habitués wile away uncounted hours. Quiet back-*sois* end up a communal space. In my sub-*soi*, a guard box and overlapping umbrella host impromptu *somtam*-and-whisky picnics for a motley bunch of maids, handymen and hawkers.

Ray Oldenburg coined a term for such havens: 'Third Places'. Home comes first, for family, privacy, security. Our second space is public, the realm of work, duty, status. In Third Places, community flourishes at ordinary venues that tolerate our unvarnished social selves.

To gain trust they must be a neutral ground where familiar folk swap tales without being too formal or fashionable, which discounts most institutions or cool spots. Third Places tend to be owner-run venues close to home that are bland, unbranded, or even grotty. That includes dodgy beer bars, karaoke lounges, and pubs where expats feel catharsis from shared humour. They tend to be levelling not pretentious. At dives – like Wong's Place or Speedy Grandma – you pluck your own beer from the fridge and the owner just tots up the empties.

"The *joie de vivre* cultures of the world are those in which Third Places are regarded as just as essential as home and work," Oldenburg wrote. That's true of Thais, who put social bonds before all else, often expressed through *sanuk* (group fun).

Bangkok is beloved for its simple, playful spaces to unwind, but is supervised by a righteous caste with a mission to instill propriety, discipline and duty. The crusade to formalise streetlife does more than tidy pavements – it removes the ecology of impromptu Third Places. That may be the intent.

"Social reformers as a rule, and planners all too commonly, ignore the importance of neutral ground and the kinds of relationships, interactions, and activities to which it plays host," Oldenburg adds. "Reformers have never liked seeing people hanging around... and assume that if people had better private areas they would not waste time in public ones." Such 'better private areas' need an expensive fashion quotient to be viable, which makes customers too self-conscious to relax. Cool season beer gardens on mall forecourts like Central World – once a commons of folding chairs and hawker food – now boast gated enclosures of white sofas.

As communities dissipate, 'locals' become less local. Havens can evolve out of shared interests, whether social clubs or board game cafés. Gyms fill that 'drop in' role, albeit with some posing. Gay bars, being a safe space for a marginal minority, have incentive to be welcoming. Galleries might seem pretentious, but with people involved in the arts scene so well acquainted, exhibition openings become a roving one-nighter Third Place, where bohemians can always bump into pals and unwind. Arty, well-educated types also drop into mixed-use centres such as BACC and TCDC. Open House, is a hybrid of eateries and meeting areas in a giant bookshop.

Probably most Third Places are bars, and prominent ones that have achieved 'local' cachet here include WTF and Smalls. There's no formula, but serving good coffee is a good start, given that the café has been a Third Place genre for centuries. With alcohol restricted to over-20s, coffee houses have become the default youth hangout, often integrated with co-working spaces.

Trendy So Thonglor tries hard to curate 'locals' for its condo-dwellers. Amid a glut of 'community malls,' a studiedly sociable one is named The Commons, while another calls itself The Third Place. Tellingly, its corner unit held a succession of failed venues, until Wine Republic removed the walls, and its humdrum terrace became a casual 'drop-in.' In the race to be rated top bar or hippest hangout in media top tens, being ranked in first place might be less sustaining than just being a friendly Third Place.

Senses 55

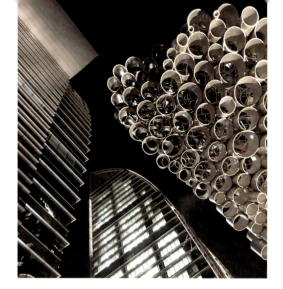

Since the Bangkok bicentennial of 1982, Rattanakosin has been gutted of its ministries, trades and residents, replacing the living heritage with spaces for tourists that showcase the official history. Popular urbanism hasn't been recognised in that heritage, so even unique old *yaan* have also been destroyed, a trend studied by Michael Herzfeld, who dubs it "spatial cleansing."

"Progress often means large, empty spaces," writes Herzfeld, who notes that many Thai planners impose Western notions of parks and plazas that don't suit local needs. "In Bangkok, it is possible to dream, as Mussolini did for Rome, of destructive relocations that would free up vast spaces… in which harmonious design would triumph over the messiness of markets and alleyways."

Bangkok lacks plazas or parks, while its sidewalks, where they exist, are obstructed. Seeking open spaces springs from 150 years ago, when Siam sought to be *siwilai* in Western eyes to avoid being colonised. Malls move messy stalls into tidy aisles indoors. Now corporations are privatising outdoor areas as 'Pseudo Public Spaces.' This includes semi-outdoor community malls like Tha Maharaj Pier or attractions such as Asiatique. Most are commercial event spaces, notably Siam Square and its adjacent malls.

You can laze in a park, but can't do all you wish in 'Pseudo Public Spaces,' which rarely provide free seating. Barriers impede your passage and guards whistle you into line. But commercial plazas do contrive festivities, such as Christmas trees to lure seasonal shoppers. Central World's vast forecourt also hosts official events like the New Year Countdown, but is now fenced in with bag searches so it won't be a protest site again. Its annual Krungthep Thara fairs showcase food from old *yaan*, thus co-opting potential visitors away from those real places.

While both the state and corporations try to use 'public' space for control, younger architects and entrepreneurs are creating new kinds of shared space. Individualistic lifestyles have broadened the social horizon beyond home and work into drop-ins termed 'Third Places,' though many cater to an educated arty echelon.

Bangkok's main Third Places are malls. Though commercial, they act as cool, neutral hangouts for non-shoppers too, especially youth with few spaces of their own. Thais seek out relationship-centred values, and treat their scarce open space as a community ecosystem, whether a cluttered street, a sleek mall or a social scene. Instead of a publicly-owned commons, Bangkokians get an earnest private mall called The Commons.

top left: **Public art in 'Ploenchit City.'**

top: **Buffet dining on the street at Soi Thonglor.**

above: **Ad hoc demarcation of space at Makkasan.**

top right: **When doves fly in Suan Santiphap (Peace Park).**

right: **The exclusive green space of the Royal Bangkok Sports Club in downtown.**

56   Space

Green Space

Bangkok's name evokes managed nature: water-village of plum olives. The wildness has thinned, save for pythons in canals and squirrels treating cables as tightropes. Concrete swallowed up the orchards of Silom, the rice swards of Sukhumvit, the plantations of what is now suburb. Yet nature remains in parks, empty lots and pockets of countryside.

There are still paddy fields at the peri-urban fringes, where bouncy plank bridges span canals slung with giant suspended fishing nets. In Nong Chok and Minburi districts, lanes with 'beware of cattle' signs come under the Country Roads administration. In the surviving arc of canals from Nonthaburi to Nakhon Pathom, plantations reached by canoe grow the world's best durian, but development blocks and contaminates the water flow.

Bangkok is mostly estuarine, but a spur of the capital province meets the sea in Bang Khuntian district. Off Rama II highway, a road leads past Bang Kradee Mon village to the capital's only fishing village, which breeds mussels on poles and raises shrimp in clay-grey ponds. Boardwalks lead walkers and cyclists through a low forest of mangroves towards the encroaching sea, where seafood restaurants teeter on stilts, sea-green to one side, leaf-green to the other.

From the air, Bangkok still looks somewhat green. Yet between 1994 and 2009, vegetated areas halved to just over 600 square kilometers, while the built-up area more than doubled. Since then many gardens and empty lots have been concreted. Just 1% of the BMA budget goes on green space, of which half is wages and a third is for the frequent changes of greenery in traffic median strips, leaving just 100 million baht for parks. Park area per head is a third of the global average (and a thirteenth of Kuala Lumpur's) at the size of a double bed, which the BMA's 25-year plan aims to expand to the area of a king-size bed.

Much of that average is from Bangkok's 'Green Lung'. Boats from Khlong Toei port slip between giant ships to an oasis of trees in Samut Prakan province named Bang Kra Jao – which fills a tear-shaped loop in the river. Since 1977, the state has protected its 1,900 hectares of plantations and farmsteads. Cyclists love exploring its lanes of Rajapruek trees and raised boardwalks over the irrigation canals to the floating market at Wat Baan Nampueng. You can't build higher than a coconut palm, and, though there's encroachment, some is sympathetic like the elevated guesthouse lofts of Bangkok Tree House.

Within this farmed greenery sits 'Middle Park' (Suan Si Nakhon Keun Kan), which gives botanical labels to each genus, like areca nut and sealing-wax palm. Its four dozen species of bird and the after-dusk pulse of fireflies signal the health of this retreat. A viewing tower offers peeks across the canopy to the tops of skyscrapers, ships and the four spires of Bhumibol Bridge.

Bangkok parks have serene names – Lumpini (Buddha's birthplace), Benjasiri (five blessings), Santiphap (peace) – but are far from peaceful. Post-dawn and pre-dusk, they throng with joggers, while *takraw* players acrobatically tap a woven rattan ball over a net. The din of loudspeakered announcements is drowned out by Techno from mass aerobics, where miked instructors bark directions.

The oldest park, Lumpini, was built in 1925 for an Expo that never happened, and still hosts the annual Thainess Festival and Red Cross Fair, plus Concerts In the Park on dry season Sundays. Early morning, retirees do ballroom dancing in the bandstand, practice t'ai chi or play chess on chequered terrazzo tables, while pouring jasmine tea. Joggers pass open-air gyms and lakes full of monitor lizards. As night falls, female freelancers stalk the east side, while gay men cruise the west.

Senses 57

Some state parks convert open land like Rama IX Park; others landscape different facilities, like the one around Rama VIII Bridge, Santichaiprakarn Park around Pom Phra Sumen fort or Romaneenart in the former prison. The lack of suitable sites is made plain by a new park filling two highway roundabouts near Suvarnabhumi Airport. In an improvised temporary patch, the BMA's Pocket Park scheme spruces up abandoned lots like Chalermla Park, which preserves graffiti from the Bukruk Festival. In one of the fiercest development fights, campaigners have secured a park in the plans for the State Railway's Makkasan depot.

Private benefactors also donate green space. The Crown Property is turning the former Royal Turf Club into King Rama IX Memorial Park and the canalside Pathumvanarak Park beside Central World. Chulalongkorn University built a small park in Siam Square and a bigger CU Centenary Park in Samyan, which has subterranean tanks for capturing water during floods. Megaprojects now have to incorporate greenery. There's a garden in One Bangkok, which was originally going to be the middle of a segmented park from Lumpini to Benjakitti, like the three merged parks that grace Chatuchak. But Benjakitti has been enlarged into the old Tobacco Monopoly, which has been terraformed into a vast wetland, with spectacular gantries wending through the treetops.

Park styles reflect the culture. Lumpini features naturalistic English landscaping, while others go for a formal French style, with hedges and paving. Benjakitti and Benjasiri Parks boast monumental signage, with expanses of concrete. Thai parks both replicate nature and contest it. "There is no Thai park style. It's like Thai food, a bit of everything," says Santi Opaspakornkij of the pressure group Big Trees. "Actually there *is* a rationale: the big bosses decide that each park must have a theme: for the elderly, for children, for cyclists, for dog walkers, for skateboarders, and so on. People complain if there isn't a park for their interests, so it's good that they listen, but it means many parks are ugly or not suitable for a variety of residents."

The scarcity and specialism of parks means that people must drive there, forcing parks to be partly car parks. The benefits of what the Japanese call 'tree bathing' are enormous to quality of life, so internationally the measure of green space has shifted from total area (with Bangkok figures padded by including private land), to measuring closeness of greenery to residents. Yet hardly any Bangkokians have a park within 15 minutes' stroll.

Most road trees aren't to grow a broad crown as in Singapore. Those on pavements or median strips get hacked in half by utility workers with no arborist skills, severing branches near wires and often leaving just a stump. That weakens trees and allows in disease, increasing the risk of falling branches. Top a tree three times and it will die. That's why most Bangkok trees live just 20-30 years and there are just four over 200 years old.

It's harder and costs more to maintain a tree than to plant saplings, which in this fertile soil take just

58 Space

six years to give shade. Only recently have developers like Singha Estate started to save old trees, instead of felling them. Typically, plots get totally cleared before sale, so even if a buyer had wanted old trees, its too late.

"That's farmer thinking, to clear a plot of its vegetation before growing a crop," says Oraya Sutabutr of Big Trees, which is now teaching tree husbandry to BMA crews. "That's so entrenched in the mindset of countries with jungle that people of every level think first to clear the land." Other cultural factors are feng shui beliefs against trees beside buildings, stopping messy leaf litter, and removing foliage that hides a building's 'face'.

"Developers have started paying a lot more attention to landscape design," says Pok Kobkongsanti of Trop Design. "It has become one of the best marketing tools." Concreted parts of the city now have trellises holding pot plants over bus stops and expressway pillars. Trees and vertical gardens get planted on stepped towers, with the EmQuartier having a five-storey faux 'waterfall' garden. Forestia in Bangna even incorporates a 'forest' with elevated boardwalk weaving between its towers.

Santi mentions how rich people who build a mansion ask a landscape architect what trees they should plant, and it's always the same answer: the mature trees that they'd cut down two years before. "There's actually an industry of transplanting mature trees ever since a developer offered 'instant mature trees'. The problem is that you can only transplant young trees; moving older ones often kills them. And now there aren't enough beautiful big trees available in the whole country in places like farms where they were bought up."

Until recently, the BMA could never employ a landscape architect for any of its parks or beautification schemes, because it couldn't legally employ professionals who don't have a registered association. So there is no understanding of botany, arborism or aesthetic use of public spaces to draw upon. To remedy this, an association was founded in 2019 by landscape architects including Yossapon Boonsom of Shma. He and others find it easiest to do independent projects with firms and organisations to provide beautiful green spaces that aren't top-down, but consult the locals wishes.

Greenery in Bangkok is put to work. Confining plants to pots makes them controllable and easily rearranged, whether in gardens, outside shops or for public display. In the trend for rooftop farms, Thammasat University has Asia's biggest. Bangkok's parks aren't intended to inspire awe at sublime nature, but had to be useful. The jungle wasn't quiet. Parks aren't meant to be quiet either.

above: Downtown towers ring the vast, newly terraformed wetlands of Benjakitti Forest Park and its aerial pathways.

far left: Electricity workers cut a tree in half.

left: Rice paddies in suburban Nong Chok.

Senses 59

Direction
The nine points of the compass

Lost in a taxi? Better give directions not a map. Compass points don't work. "The southeast side of Victory Monument" draws a blank because locals know it as "Saxophone" for the pub on that corner. Direction in Bangkok is relational to familiar landmarks: shops, shrines, trees. As landmarks disappear and new ones emerge, directions depend on the age of the person asked. Older Bangkokians still direct you to landmarks long gone, like Odeon Circle, a roundabout that younger folks know for its Chinatown Gate.

Today, GPS systems tell drivers where to turn, but this mazelike city went mostly uncharted until very recently. When I came to Bangkok, most roads looked identical, being lined with shophouses and lacking landmark towers or train stations. Getting around required local knowledge, due to Bangkok's weak history of mapping. Early Siamese charts left territory sketchy, with the focus on depicting temples and sites of power. They had sacred directional logic as elements in a mandala, a cosmic map still imprinted in many modern minds. As detailed below, directions depend on where you are in the social hierarchy.

The collectible Nancy Chandler's Map of Bangkok has a similarly relational, pictorial style. Since 1974, it has been drawn using highlighter pens and annotated with on-the-spot details about snacks and crafts, for which it's known as "The Market Map."

The first serious charting of Bangkok was as late as 1984, in Tanya Phonanan's *Bangkok Street Directory*, which was far from comprehensive. In the 1990s, German firms made thorough layouts of the centre, but locally-made maps still left blank most suburbs, sub-sois and old communities.

Only via satellite in the early 2000s did Bangkok's precise layout come to light. Google Street View then began imaging each road. Now visual mapping probes the narrower *sois* through crowd-sourced cartography and cyclists wobbling down paths with a GoPro strapped to their helmet. Once unknowable and impenetrable, Bangkok can now be tracked to back lanes where outsiders rarely reached. Technology is now decaying our inbuilt locational sense, towards knowing how to look things up.

Meanwhile, before Artificial Intelligence totally takes over, on-the-ground signage lacks systemic clarity and spelling, adding to Bangkok's sense of misdirection. Notices fail to appear at key turnings, and names on maps and brochures often fail to correspond to signs on the spot. Chatuchak Weekend Market is known as JJ after a less common spelling Jatujak, accessed by a station called Mo Chit but pronounced Morchit. Streets even have multiple signs with different spellings: Patpong is Pat Pong is Phat Phong. During Bangkok Design Week 2018, routes between venues were marked by luminous cutouts of cats, in the way people might leave a trail of string in the forest.

Languages are proliferating too. For ASEAN Union, Thailand set about making road signage bilingual with English script. Once Chinese became a third of all tourists, Chinese characters appeared on signage. Meanwhile Arabic signage is spreading outward from their hub at Nana.

In property ads, the names of fashionable areas are co-opted to upgrade neighbourhoods of lower status. Parts of Phrakhanong and Praditmanutham are getting rebranded as Ekamai. Condos buried deep in Tha Phra declare themselves as being "Sathorn" despite being miles beyond Sathorn Bridge.

Real estate follows the old rule: location, location, impersonation. Agents hire youths to dance in costumes with sign boards near the highway turnoff close to a new

left: **Temporary traffic flow during Skytrain piling at Charansanitwong Road.**

above: **In Bangkok, cars and trains drive on the left, but boats and walkers go on the right, as signed on bridges and stairs.**

Centre Points

Most city centres are obvious, agreed and signed as downtown, old town or Central Business District (CBD). Finding the middle of Bangkok depends on what you're doing and who you are. The port moved south from Sampeng to Bangrak to Khlong Toei. Shopping and entertainment went west from Yaowarat to Wang Burapha to Siam-Ratchaprasong to Thonglor. Nightlife zones hopped from Silom Surawong to RCA, Ratchada and Thonglor-Ekamai.

Rivalry of interest groups stymies attempts at an integrated plan. Business spread from Chinatown to Bangrak, but hopes foundered for coherent new CBDs at Ratchada, then Rama III, with plans for a Makkasan hub likely to end up another shard.

Meanwhile, a visualization of city data called Depth Map reveals that two massive sub-centres have arisen organically along broad stripes that form a giant 'L' north of the downtown: Phahonyothin-Don Mueang due north and Lat Phrao-Ramkhamhaeng to the east. It's not obvious from the street, nor recognised by planners, but has just evolved from public inclination. Having fragmented centres is typical of the Asian megalopolis and has been labeled 'Messy Urbanism'.

Even government's centre of gravity tilted north from Rattanakosin to Dusit to Chaengwattana. In a clue to where power lies, demonstrations focused on Sanam Luang and Democracy Monument in 1973, 1976, 1992 and 2005, then – despite sieges of Government House and Parliament – protest shifted to the retail hub of Ratchaprasong. Now dissent is moving online, as is media, entertainment, shopping, transit, socialising and sex. The new centre of Bangkok is your smartphone.

Senses 61

Wayfinding

Wayfinding in Bangkok is far from systemic, whether in naming, numbering, or spelling. Sometimes labels appear that aren't formally used, like the improved 2017 placards on the Saen Saeb canal piers, which label West as 'Old Town' and East as 'New Town'.

Most modern sois are numbered off the main roads they branch, but in addition to their road name, many acquire an extra name. Sathorn Soi 1 is also called Soi Atthakarnprasit, but informally known as Soi JUSMAG, after the American military centre on the corner. Older sois tend to have names and no number. These may express a landmark, family name or direction (Soi Langsuan, 'behind the park'), while oddities include 'Soi Pawit and Friends'.

Soi numbers should be odd to one side of the main road, even on the other, except when they aren't, as in my own *soi*, or when they form a grid. Often extra *sois* are later added in between, when they take a sub-*soi* number after a slash, like Silom Soi 2/1. Sukhumvit even had a Soi Zero slotted beneath an expressway before Soi 2, and further down between Sois 52 and 54, there's a Sukhumvit Soi Plus 1.

Then it gets complicated... Linked sois get at least two names; Thonglor Soi 10 is the same lane as Ekamai Soi 12, while the Japanese living around Sukhumvit Soi 49/4 are simultaneously on Soi 55/13. Adding to the confusion, building numbers might not match their order on the street, but reflect their order of construction. Likewise, buildings added in later get a slash and a unit number, like 49/22.

Residents frequently just make their own signs, which block pavements or stick out of poles at head height. Signage as advertising is rampant. Bangkok's community identities are giving way to corporate identities. BTS station signs are getting sponsored, often with a person pictured promoting a brand. The Chinese-style decoration of Wat Mangkon MRT Station in Chinatown is branded by Nescafé. This seems not just distracting but shameless, yet it reflects the affinity for personalised signage. When wayfinding is such hard work, no wonder Bangkokians prefer directions by something relatable.

above: Street signs have certain shapes. *Sois* get placards with *lai Thai* curly points at each end and a lotus bud finial on the pole. *Thanon* (roads) get deeper rectangular scrolls with lotus finials on the tips of the vertical rods at each side. *Khlong* signs are squarish like intersection signs, but with a bridge-like hump over the top.

below: Bus stops used to lack detail. After a schoolboy drew a colour-coded map of the Victory Monument bus interchange, the BMA came up with a huge unwieldy sign. Finally at Design Week 2018, the social enterprise Satarana made clear route signage that the BMA adopted.

condo development. In Santi Taepanich's 2005 documentary about Isaan migrants to Bangkok, *Crying Tiger*, wannabe comic Man touts for a seafood restaurant dressed as a fish. People respond to signage that's alive.

Mascots are big in Asia, and Bangkok's are especially friendly. The more authoritarian the sign, the cuter it is. The cartoon BTS guard wearing a traditional leg-wrap looks much more homey than the whistle-blasting guard on the platform. 'Ja Choei,' the fibreglass traffic cop modelled on genial actor Theeradej 'Ken' Wongpuapan, makes us smile on the side of the road. One notice I saw at a government office was adorned with a cute clip-art crocodile.

With traditional buildings, you can read much into the direction they face. Wooden houses tended to look north to avoid the sun. When Bangkok was a water city, most structures fronted onto canals or the river. A temple arch onto a narrow lane hints that this was originally the rear access, and that beyond it lies a waterway where the temple has a grander entrance. Within temples, the *bot* sanctuary faces east. Mosques often sit askew on their site as the mihrab must face Mecca. Where possible, Chinese shrines and mansions back onto raised land and face water, to optimise feng shui.

Thai culture is based around a map in the mind: a sacred diagram of the Hindu-Buddhist cosmos known as a mandala. King Rama I superimposed Rattanakosin Island with directional temples at auspicious positions taken from Ayutthaya's layout, as well as main, front and back palaces. Though the physical integrity of the mandala was burst by modernity, traces of the concept remain.

The cosmology that Siam inherited from the Khmers revolves around Mount Meru, the sacred mountain of the gods ringed by oceans and four continents. The Meru concept can be on any scale, from the costume of a king to Siam's regions being organised as *monthon* (mandala in Thai). And in the middle of Rattanakosin, Wat Suthat embodies Meru symbols, including the building at the south representing Jambu Dvipa, the southern continent where humans live.

Thai cosmology has a handbook, the 14th century *Tri Bhumi Katha*. It means 'The Three Planes of Existence': the physical, nether, and ethereal worlds. Studied in school, it underpins not just traditional arts and architecture, but also names and social relations. Just as Greek philosophy and Christianity unlock Western civilisation, Confucius guides the Chinese, and the *Mahabharata* embodies all things Indian, the *Tri Bhumi* is a key to Thainess.

Bangkok loves combining multiple systems. Wat Suthat is the fulcrum of Rattanakosin Island's royal mandala, but the city included a strip of Thonburi, so the centre of the early settlement that needed protection was actually beside the Grand Palace, where the Lak Meuang (City Pillar) stands. All distances in Bangkok were originally measured from the Lak Meuang, though 'Kilometer Zero' is now measured from Democracy Monument.

The Lak Meuang concept also blends two traditions in a typical Indo-Chinese mix. Tai tribal villages in Southern China placed

top left: **Direction using cute images is common. Here Art In Soi festival uses illuminated cats to show the way.**

top right: **Traffic police statues can't move, but look cute. Nicknamed 'Ja Choei,' they were modelled on actor Theeradej 'Ken' Wongpuapan.**

Senses 63

a pillar at the central crossroads. Similarly, a phallic symbol of Shiva was often erected in the middle of Khmer sanctuaries. Adding to the options, the Lak Meuang shrine holds not one but two city pillars, the second one modifying the city's fortune.

Every instance of a Meru design pulls its own directional force. The number nine is lucky here partly because a Meru mandala has nine directions: the eight compass points – and upwards. The nine-square cabalistic diagrams seen in tattoos, amulets and fortune telling are effectively a floorplan of this concept. For a 3-D model look at Wat Arun, with four cardinal towers and towering central *prang*. That parabolic shape – getting steeper as it rises – also corresponds to *sakdina*, Siam's ancient social scale in which people were ranked by points that escalated up with status. Though abolished, *sakdina* still moulds attitudes.

The Meru mindset reflects in the body, with the superiority of head over waist over feet. Positioning oneself in social and ritual situations requires an awareness of relative height and facing the correct direction. Offerings in vehicles are placed at its 'head' – the upper front part like a boat prow or motorcycle dashboard. Just as the head hosts each Thai's spirit, the King is often referred to as Phra Chao Yuu Hua – the God at my Head.

Mandalas exemplify the symbolism of the circle, cycles and spirals in Asian culture, whereas Western thinking is more linear, with notions of dialectic and progress along a timeline – a contrast proven in experiments. Instead of zero starting the sequence of numbers; the Thai word for zero, *soon*, means centre. The word for circle, *wong*, also applies to family and appears in surnames. The circle is not esoteric but embedded in mindsets and can be seen in daily life.

As this social gyroscope becomes second nature, the *manner* of directing should be polite. No finger pointing – unless you want a fight – just tips of the head to indicate "over there." Beckon a taxi or waiter with fingers politely downward, and the arm not too high. Wayfinding in Bangkok is not all about signs and maps, but social cues and who you are. Like everything Thai, direction should be indirect.

Feng Shui

Chinatown's maze of lanes has hidden directional principles that involve ancient beliefs, geomancy and theories of luck. Buildings have paraphernalia to counter bad luck, like wind chimes or faceted crystals on red cords of a certain length. shopkeepers post calligraphic amulets on lintels to ward off harm, flank frontages with lions, and place octagonal mirrors to ward off bad luck from junctions. A firm at the multi-way junction on Soi Phanu Rangsi erected a protective stone, engraved "Dare to Resist Evil."

Even Thais with no Chinese ancestry hire geomancers to divine the best feng shui for objects, buildings and their setting. Meaning 'Wind-Water', feng shui combines practical and supernatural concepts to arrange anything for luck, whether the auspicious rocks in front of Bangkok Bank in Silom or lucky plants at Government House. "Thais also have feng shui-like beliefs. We just don't know it," says feng shui master Visit Techakasem. "Even King Rama V once published his recommended plans for homes, based on our tropical weather."

In feng shui, an ideal settlement faces water, with hills rising securely behind, which in delta Bangkok meant a slight incline up the riverbank. Feng shui conceives of an axis up that slope being a symbolic dragon, with its 'head' being a waterside shrine. At Sampeng, Teochiu settlers made their dragon's 'head' the Lao Pun Thao Kong shrine, which is for blessing seafarers' journeys. Just behind that shrine, the Pei-ing School is the dragon's 'brain'.

The dragon's 'spine' led northwards up Trok Itsaranupharp – a quaint commercial lane, profuse with dried fish maw, toys, and spices. Further along the dragon, Talad Kao (Old Market) was founded at its 'belly', and further north, the Leng Buay la shrine's name means Dragon's Tail God.

As part of efforts to acculturate Chinese settlers, the state swivelled the south-north direction of

Sampeng's feng shui dragon to match Thai beliefs. The dragon was turned to face the water of Phadung Krung Kasem canal to the east, with its tail rising west towards the cosmological heights of then-walled Rattanakosin city. This was done through Rama V's redevelopment of Sampeng's dire living conditions.

Bursting with migrants, Sampeng had become a fire-prone slum that alarmed King Rama V on a visit to the new Charoen Krung Road. In 1891, he ordered masonry shophouses to be built along new firebreak roads with courtly names: Yaowarat (Crown Prince), Ratchawong (Royal Dynasty) and Mahachak (Great Chakra). Yaowarat was made the new east-west feng shui axis, undulating like a dragon's back. The belly moved from the Old Market to the New Market (Talad Mai). Later in 1999, the dragon gained a symbolic head, with the erection of a ceremonial gate at Odeon Circle. At Chinese New Year, Sino-Thais stand upon a plaque on the gate's threshold and bow in each compass direction.

This geomantic reorientation of Chinese into Sino-Thai was reinforced by the gate, named Soom Pratu Chaloemprakiat, being a Golden Jubilee Arch for King Rama IX. It also bears Chinese calligraphy by Princess Sirindhorn. The gate and dragon face east, like Thai *wats*, east being where the Buddha faced upon his enlightenment. The area's identifying nickname also shifted from the Chinese 'Sampeng' to the regal Thai 'Yaowarat', with the official district named Sampanthawong after a princely *wat*.

Now the MRT runs east-west through Chinatown, cutting across the original dragon's tail. Luckily, the station by Wat Mangkon (aka Leng Noi Yi or Dragon Lotus Temple), which has a dragon above its escalators, hasn't displaced the adjacent Charoen Chai community that makes paper offerings for funerals.

Chinatown has other gates too. On Ratchawong Road, an arch marks Soi Phalit Phon, where Sun Yat Sen orated. And in 2024, Chinatown got framed by a pair of Chinese entry gates along Charoenkrung, between Songwad Road and Khlong Ong Ang, to mark King Rama X's Sixth Cycle.

Sampeng's feng shui has changed, but an ancient directional marker survives: its sacred centre. Between Trok Chaiyaphum and Yaowaphanit Road, a path leads through a hidden covered courtyard flanked by a red opera stage and Sia Ung Kong Shrine. It honours the guardian spirit of Sampeng, Trok Por Lao Eia, who grants wishes and is nicknamed Thep ATM – 'cash-dispenser god'. South Chinese settlements used to have a protector shrine at their centre, and this was the Teochiu one for Sampeng. Thais call it San Jao Pho Lak Meuang (Shrine of the City Pillar Lord), as it is "like a city pillar, because this was among the earliest Chinese settlements here," explains historian Charoen Tanmaharan. Thep ATM is the secret heart of Sampeng.

left: **The old head of the 'Sampeng' dragon at Lao Pun Thao Kong Shrine and Pei-ing School**

above: **The new head of the 'Yaowarat' dragon at the Rama IX Jubilee Gate in Odeon Circle.**

Motion
Flow, change, and getting around

In this congested city, the fastest route from A to B might be via Q. My journey from home to publisher used to be fairly convoluted. I would zip on motorcycle taxi from sub-*soi* to BTS, and join the commuter crush for three stops. Back on street level, I braved the sidewalk slalom of pillars and utilities, until the pavement narrowed to single file over Elephant Head Bridge. I then ducked through a slum alley, under a veil of dangling tree roots, to a pier in Khlong Saen Saeb – the "Canal of a Hundred Thousand Stings." Five piers later, I clambered out by the Old City moat. From the seven-way junction at Saphan Phan Fah Lilas – "Sky Dance Bridge" – I hailed a tuk-tuk to the publishing house on the waterfront. Today I can take the subway to her door.

Bangkok works best when you surrender to its sense of flow. Few cities better fit the cliché of the Asian metropolis, teeming with activity in a cramped, disjointed maze. Yet Bangkok differs from Kolkata or Saigon in that its motion is uncannily calm. Aside from a few fatal cases of road rage, the calamitous traffic prompts just road irritation. Bangkokians don't confront their obstacles but weave around them with ingenuity and an elastic approach to rules. At South Ploenchit, there was no room for an expressway exit ramp, so they simply put in a hairpin U-turn from the speeding highway onto a side road. Incredibly, that U-turn also involves crossing a railway track. You can't make it up. Bangkok's flow is not the ease of the autobahn, nor a push through the crowd, but a bubbly stream around boulders.

There's pattern in this flow, drawn from the Central Plains water culture. Eons of coping with floodplains bequeathed an aquatic sense of balance still held in collective muscle memory. Calmly gliding through chaos also derives from social values. The Buddhist ideal of detachment treats conditions as impermanent, so not worth stress. The aversion to confrontation makes it hard to reform systemic flaws. Acting 'status appropriate' at all times means that laws and timeframes give way to what's called 'situational morality.' Squatter stalls keep trading and reckless motorists stay driving thanks to enforcers being considerate in exchange for gifts. Thai workflow draws upon cooperative ethics such as *long kaek*, a spirit of reciprocity from village life, and *tayoy*, in which each person does their own thing, and yet it all magically comes together.

The commotion is not just on the surface. In an ancient creation myth, *thep* (angels) released the elixir of life by Churning the Sea of Milk. Krungthep's liveliness comes from constant churn; it reflects the fact that the city is structurally unstable at deeper levels. Things that most countries consider permanent, shift with surprising ease in Bangkok. Institutions reinvent through frequent coups, constitutions and protest sieges. Trades long established in one place – such as electronics, amulets, and wood – suddenly up and move. Bar owners make a bar-strip into a scene, and when they've made back their money, they shutter it and reinvest elsewhere. Indie bazaars like the Train Market are especially itinerant. It's culturally consistent that the skyline morphs at a bewildering pace, because historically old wooden architecture was easily disassembled and re-erected. Prefab houses, prefab stalls, and prefab skyscrapers – it's basically the same process.

left: **Fast and Furious: crossing the road is a daring act in car-biased Bangkok. Here mall staff head home from Emporium, risking all.**

below left: **Wheelchair users have a hard enough time with Bangkok's broken pavements and high kerbs, but now they must slalom through pole-gates designed to keep vendor carts off the pavements.**

Sit at a pavement table long enough and you can see the streetscape morph during the day. While some Bangkok markets are held in permanent halls, most are periodic. Monthly, weekly or at certain times of day, their vendors cluster under canvas, then dissipate. Meanwhile, itinerant hawkers converge on opportune spots throughout the clock. This temporal flow has a long history from floating markets, although now city traders come not by boat but on wheels. At dusk, a fleet of vendors roll their storage chests out from a garage to compose a nightmarket at the kerb. A single trader slot may host different vendors in shifts: breakfast noodles, office wear for lunchtime shoppers, bagged dinners for working mums. Short-term leases force market owners to keep migrating. Market people – with no fixed business address and minimal stock – can respond instantly to fads and follow the buzz to the hot new hood. Unfettered by zoning, Bangkok keeps enterprise flowing.

The preferred Thai event format is "everything-going-on-at-once." The template for simultaneous activity is temple fairs, where people slip between sacred ritual and profane sideshows, competing entertainments and constant snacking. Modern events – whether indie festivals or corporate conventions – adopt that mode of weaving between rival attractions. Magnified to city scale, Bangkok's visitor appeal is not to focus on famous landmarks, but to flow through the constantly surprising spaces, sampling from its cornucopia.

These ambient impulses from the old water city are giving way to a rigid urbanism. Under American sway in the Cold War, the Development State policy favoured cars. They filled in most canals, ripped out the tram tracks and banned rickshaws. Expressways carved up the city, but the road area is just 8 per cent, half that of Paris. With too few secondary roads and *sois* that don't link up, one-way systems force local traffic to clog the arterial highways.

Because the city isn't fully accessible by road, it's ended up with layers of formal and informal transport systems that barely connect. Now mass-transit trains impose further layouts in the sky and underground. This disconnect accosts you at every turn. Trains fail to link with buses and boats. Cars own the few thunderous eight-lane highways, and hog the narrow *sois*, but can't access communities buried down pathways.

Lack of integration made Bangkok became the world's byword for bad traffic during the 1980s boom. It remains one of the most congested cities, ranking worst for the time

Senses 67

Walking

After the 1997 economic crash, neighbourhoods shut a road for a day to hold fairs. So totally had cars monopolised both the city that these "Walking Streets" felt subversive. Strollers kept glancing warily yet no vehicles mowed them down. Even now, permanently pedestrianising any road remains unlikely. Drivers rule.

The reasons are climate, class and culture. "We walk because we want to buy something or eat something, not because we want to walk," says Zcongklod Bangyikhan. "I think footpaths are part of Bangkok's character. Our footpaths are a market."[1]

That's a problem in this dense city. The junta's campaign to 'Reclaim Public Space' prioritised clearing the vendors who the BMA had long failed to manage. Furious complaints flare on social media, such as Saynostall, a Facebook page with the slogan: "Claim footpaths back for pedestrians... and condemn street vendors and those who support them."

Yet a survey ranked vendors as a lesser problem for walking than dangerous paving, motorbikes on footpaths, obstruction by signage, utilities or parking – and *sois* that lack any sidewalk at all. Streets newly cleared of markets languish desolate, devoid of walkers because their reason for going has gone.

"I love walking, but really, there is hardly a day that I can walk in peace," analyst Deunchalerm Khiewpan told *BK*. "The footpaths are bumpy and smell like urine. The hawkers are all over the place and motorcycle drivers seem to think the pavements are their streets." In 2019 a Japanese girl studying here caused a sensation by blocking bikers from riding on pavements, being treated as a hero by some, but assaulted by some infringers. The limited space for people to walk heightens the annoyance from people who block them, like dawdlers and people who push in front, most notoriously the so-called *manus pa*, literally "the auntie species."

Traversing Bangkok is hard for all, but nigh impossible for wheelchairs. "The reason you don't see disabled persons on the streets is not that they don't exist. It's because they can't get around easily," says Oraya Sutabutr of the pressure group Bangkok Sabai Walk. The world standard for a pedestrian path is that two wheelchairs can pass, yet here the chairbound can't go far, forcing them to use the road. Only new buildings have ramps, and most transit no access, although the BTS grudgingly installed lifts at some stations.

Universal access is slowly appearing. Bevelled kerbs and textured paths for the blind were laid in busy areas for the 1998 Asian Games, but they often zig-zagged around obstacles and some were abandoned after repaving. "Sidewalks with Braille blocks might seem useful," says Veth, a blind busker at Phra Chan pier, "but vendors tend to set up their stalls on them, so I end up bumping into or tripping over someone's stuff."

Broken sidewalks are an actual threat to life and limb. Murky floodwaters hide all manner of dangers, from spiky durian shells, to the unmarked open manhole into which a photographer friend dropped to his neck. Had a nearby woman not grabbed his hand, the suction could have pulled him under.

A bane of residents is loose paving slabs. One tipped an elderly friend onto the kerb, breaking her cheekbone. Another, pictured right, caused me a serious injury. The BMA blames vendors for unstable paving, but the culprit is mostly the drip-drip from gutters and aircon pipes upon too-thin, badly laid slabs.

Walking suffers from low status, but landscaping can make it attractive. Trendy night markets and 'pseudo public spaces' have boomed because they offer calm strolling. When the BTS opened there was no concept of linking transit to buildings. As malls, condos and institutions woke to the benefit, skywalks spread like spider legs from stations. Some are spotless beacons of luxury that host exhibitions, while murals adorn the mushroom-like shelters of the one spanning MBK, BACC and Siam Discovery.

"Skywalks decrease vehicle use. [Chidlom-Siam] skywalk transports 100,000 people a day," said Deputy Governor Teerachon Manomaiphiboon in 2011, when announcing an a 50 km network of Super Skywalks, since scaled back. "Bangkok is getting more and more crowded every day and the sidewalks just aren't enough."[4]

Overpasses are a bane that pander to the 30 percent who drive, while few drivers pause at zebra crossings. Socially, skywalks herd custom away from local shops into linked malls, via channels that segregate an elevated class walking in style above the lowly unkempt street. "People are the weakest vehicles. They should get the best treatment," says Khaisri Paksukcharern, a professor in planning. "Pedestrians should be at the centre of urbanism. And now we're moving them into the air where they won't have interaction with the urban fabric? It's all wrong." Solutions do exist. The Si Yaek Jaidee (Friendly Crossroads) project aims to apply principles of universal design to Ratchaprasong, including disabled access.

Bangkok's few pedestrianised areas tend to be isolated destinations where people can mill, but the BMA is gradually making it smoother to walk through the city. What makes European cities suit walkers is that their parks and promenades are linked by well-managed paths and greenery throughout. Walking in Bangkok advances not in leaps and bounds, but in stumbles and wary steps.

below: **Motorcycle taxi driver watching muaythai on TV while ferrying me.**

left: **Some wobbly paving slabs at Asoke and Lat Phrao stencilled with graphics from the game Minesweeper.**

above: **Choose your sidewalk hazard: this one at Ploenchit has a raised block, a jagged hole and a metal hook.**

lost idling, wasting a billion dollars a year just in fuel. Journeys are full of volatile encounters: touts, motorcades, roadblocks. *Soi* dogs are a constant hazard, and while elephants no longer beg on city streets, a viral video clip shows cars on the Bangna-Trad highway being overtaken by a speeding ostrich.

To cope with the disjoints between land and water, *soi* and highway, Bangkok devised informal, hand-tailored forms of transit so distinctive, that some have become symbols of the city: tuk-tuk, motorcycle taxi, longtail boat. The smaller the byway the more it depends on pick-up buses like *songtaews*, 'box cars' and motorbikes with trolley sidecars. Apps like Grab build upon this secondary system. Switching between formal and informal transit requires local know-how, and an ability to read Thai. The fastest way to cross Bangkok is often by multiple modes of transit.

The roads feel like canals that have never been paved. Obeying the laws of fluid dynamics, cars drift across lanes, pass on all sides within a hair's breadth, and turn in broad sloppy arcs. Transport expert Yanyong Boon-long studied how buses don't stick to a lane, but wend through traffic, speed along the outside lane, and slow to a trundle in mid-stream so passengers can hop on and off, rarely halting at the bus stop kerb. Markings direct cars to line up across the front of parking bays, handbrakes off. So trapped cars can get out, they get shunted back and forth like boats at a wharf.

Senses 69

below: **Luxury vans with tinted windows are the vehicle of choice for** *hi-so* **people, so they can change clothes and work between appointments, while always looking their best.**

right: **Wutthakat Skytrain station crosses an ancient canal, plied by longtail boats.**

below right: **Commuters catching a nap in traffic.**

Plans for a 'congestion charge' on the London model would price poorer drivers out of downtown. Harder problems are undisciplined driving and chaotic road conditions. Few push for driver training, or streamlining road layouts. Jams result from everyone going their own way.

Drivers feel liberated from social curbs on behaviour. Taxis and cars zip down the wrong lane to cut in – and clog a junction entirely. Vendors position at choke points like *soi* mouths precisely to snag passersby. Traffic police manually override phased traffic lights. Road blocks snare helmet-less bikers and wrong-lane drivers, while luxury cars seem to get waved through unhindered. Tailgating and veering without signal occurs with the confidence that karma steers life's wheel, though taxi drivers know that they also carry the karma of their passengers. It's not all fatalism; protective amulets give the gumption to take hair-raising risks.

Feral driving carries a cost – both in lives and 6 percent of GDP. Studies consistently show that Thailand has the world's most lethal traffic. At the hours when roads are empty, they turn into racetracks. Pedestrians contend with pavements being used by motorcyclists, whom drivers deride as *malaeng wan* (flies) for the way they swarm. Bus drivers often race to their depots due to company incentives for speed over safety or courtesy. Some of the erratic drivers are on *yaa baa*, a keep-awake amphetamine used by many on arduous shifts.

Officials and media push short crackdowns under slogans like "Seven Dangerous Days," which fail year after year. Each campaign comes with a gimmick, like free Brands Chicken Essence to stave off drowsiness.

Most crashes involve motorcycles, though that's partly due to their vulnerability. Road deaths also correlate to poor infrastructure, management and corruption. As Christopher Groskopf commented: "If you're in a country where everyone drives on the sidewalk and nobody stops at stop signs, you can be pretty sure the government isn't working right."

One instance of tackling a root cause is minivans (*rot tuu*, 'cabinet vehicles'). Designed for tourism, these passenger vans fill a void in commuter transit. The MRTA is among the world's biggest bus networks, with a Bus Rapid Transit (BRT) line, yet it doesn't reach many suburbs and housing estates, so vans link them with downtown. Cramped and impractical, with just one sliding door, vans have a horrendous safety record. In a notorious incident, a Mini driven by an under-age *hi-so* tipped a van of nine students off an elevated expressway. Now purpose-designed mini-buses are being brought in as safer substitutes.

Whatever the merits of pubic transport, cars remain a high status symbol. "There are almost twice as many vehicles per person in Bangkok than in Tokyo or Seoul, and about eight times as many as Shanghai," says planner Soithip Trisuddhi. "On top of that, the number of cars in the city continues to soar over 6 percent each year." In restaurants, affluent diners place their wallet and car key on the table, the logo on the fob facing up.

While commuters cram sweatily into buses and BTS, much of the road congestion is due to chauffeur-driven luxury vehicles that ensure the passenger has the composure required of rank. Many businessmen need a chauffeured car as a mobile office. The elite like being driven in luxury vans with names like Alphard or Wish, basking in leather swivel armchairs, inscrutable behind glass darker than the law allows. Teachers at international schools tell me that some spoiled Thai teenagers don't know how to cross the road because they've always been chauffeured. Owners of supercars like to be seen driving them, but hire a valet to park their Ferrari, for a fee, in the forecourt.

I've known some *hi-sos* who, without a flashy vehicle to make a grand entrance, hire a car and driver, due to the face-loss were they to roll up in a taxi.

Taxis have a host of problems. Taxi drivers often resist using the meter or refuse to take passengers, which infuriates those who live far from train or bus routes. One reason is that their base price hasn't risen since the advent of meters in 1992. Their overall fares are among the world's cheapest, aggravated by oversupply and the advent of hailing apps. One reason Grab does well here is that you can hail cars that don't look like taxis.

It took years for the middle class to feel that the speed of riding trains outweighed the shame of public transport. "It's safe to say our transport system shows the 'class' system," observes columnist Ploenpote Atthakor.

"Forget the electric rail system, MRT or BTS. They are simply off limits to the poor or those with meagre incomes." As a result, the BTS has from the start been a model of prestige and *siwilai*. Its pricing (higher than London's Tube) effectively excludes the poor, though some rode it on its launch as a family sightseeing jaunt.

The BTS was designed to link with two public transit stations, at Morchit and Ekamai, but as soon as it opened, access to the bus terminals became more, not less, difficult. Morchit provincial bus terminal was moved further out, while at Ekamai BTS, there's access from every direction except the neighbouring Eastern Bus Station.

For years, bus stops weren't integrated with stations. On the other hand, middle-class train commuters can walk direct to malls and towers via Skywalks and escalators. Developers now charge a premium for condos – named The Line or The Link – with bridges to stations. This stratification baffles foreigners who assume mass transit is for the masses.

The Skytrain was first planned for 1979, and the delay proved ruinous. Had the 1980s-90s boom growth followed transit lines, the city might not have sprouted random estates down inaccessible *sois*. Now playing catch-up, Bangkok had, along with Japan, pioneered mass transit in Asia. From 1888 to 1968, seven tram lines, covering 42 kilometres, served the whole city. They ran on electricity, but were nicknamed *rot ai* ('steam cars') due to

sweating in the packed interior. But the trams didn't keep pace with the expanding city. The early 20th century entrepreneur Nai Lert Sreshthaputra launched an omnibus service, with one displayed in the museum at his home Ban Nai Lert. The state later merged several bus companies into today's MRTA network. The Sarit dictatorship abolished the trams in the 1960s – with one trace of tram rail visible near the City Pillar – to make Bangkok a car-oriented city.

Mass transit hasn't yet changed the dynamics again, but digital mapping indicates that it could once all nine lines open. The journey to my publisher has already become streamlined with the opening of a nearby MRT station. But the train system is no panacea, since residents must still struggle to reach the stations from their homes buried deep in *sois*. Many have to rise pre-dawn to keep their commute under two hours.

Even fast trains can make for slow journeys when it takes so long to switch lines that don't join, while adjacent stations have different names and incompatible ticketing. New lines, rather than crisscross like a lattice, extend outwards like spokes to suburbs with too few interchanges. The underground MRT initially refused to integrate with the existing overground BTS and faced its porches away from BTS porches, forcing passengers to U-turn between them under the sun and rain. A universal ticketing card, Maengmoom (Spider), has been delayed for a decade while agencies wrangle. However, MRT lines do meet at Krung Thep Aphiwat Central Terminal, the hub of new fast rail lines crisscrossing ASEAN and linking to China.

Bangkok's transport maps reveal the jealous fiefdoms within the bureaucratic culture. Each operator's diagram excluded rival transit or showed it in diminished size. Rail maps excluded Expressboat and canal piers. Only in 2019 did an integrated transit map appear. There was a sensation when a schoolboy produced a comprehensive colour-coded bus map that clarified the official tangle. Since then, designers have made clear bus stop signage for the Bangkok Design Festival in 2019 that the BMA adopted.

The older, improvised transit patches these gaps in connectivity. Many deep-*soi* neighbourhoods were built around waterways, so the revival of boat transit has been extended to more *khlongs* like Banglamphu

Cycling

You can pinpoint when the middle class felt it socially safe to cycle. It was the moment in the late-2000s when the last poor people graduated to motorcycles from pedalling upright 'maid's bikes'. It also helped that cycling became hip worldwide. Suddenly, bicycles were everywhere, popping up in trendy venues. Cycle tracks opened like the one around Suvarnabhumi Airport. BACC and night markets spawned shops of expensive gear. Cycling offers a sense of possibility and quality-of-life. You can access more of Bangkok.

Some started riding because it was promoted through the magazine *a day*. "Status is deep in our culture. Many think we have to buy a bicycle as well as a car and a condo," says its editor Zcongklod Bangyikhan. "It starts from the trend of a prop to represent your lifestyle. We have to ride a bike that's as different as possible from that 'mama's bike' in model, price, clothing, everything." *A day*'s census of cycling in Bangkok found three groups. The biggest cycles for exercise. Another bikes for leisure or travel. The smallest is commuters.

As with other pursuits, the motivations are face and friends. Just as Thais hate to eat alone, they rarely ride alone. Posses in matching helmets and jerseys descend on brunches or gallery nights, in the same mode as other two-wheeled subcultures: tycoons cruising on Harleys, and indie Vespa riders in retro pilot goggles. The lifestyle involves bike customization, hip bodywear and belonging to a club with cachet, say Smile Riders or Fixed Gear is Not a Crime.

"We work on our bikes together, ride together, eat together, and basically live together, especially within our team," says Aran Kamonchan of Aran Bicicletta Cicli & Café. "Our beloved city wasn't designed with bicycles in mind. There are no rules to how people should ride in Bangkok and how motorists should share the road." Each Tuesday night, his club rides pursuit up the long "Local Road" beside Viphavadi Rangsit Highway – safely, of course. Unlike most road users, the new breed of cyclist is fastidious about having the correct lamps and reflectors.

Most trendy is the fixed-gear 'fixie', often seen as unsafe for lacking hand-brakes. "It forces you to be cautious and focused," says aficionado Wararat Puapairoj, pop star founder of Velayenn bike shop. "Lots of people think it's dangerous to ride a bike in Bangkok due to all the cars, but if you know your route, wear safety gear or ride in a group, it really isn't a problem."[2]

You see no thin-tyred racers, but you do see BMX trick bikes. "BMX is perfect for a city with crappy roads. It's easy to avoid obstacles and these bikes are made to be durable," says Varin Somprasong. He founded the Old School BMX community, who practise tricks at City Hall Plaza and Khao San Road. The best choice for uneven distance riding is the mountain bike – even though Bangkok has no mountains. But it does have the mangrove terrain of Bang Khuntian or Samut Prakan, and the bumpy trail by the cycle track under Ramintra Expressway.

Cycling has transformed how Thais see their city. For many years it was only foreign tourists who went on cycle tours with Co van Kessel and Spice Roads; now locals are exploring overlooked old *yaan* and creating advocates for heritage. Lack of car etiquette limits safe areas to cycle, but Old Town lanes make peaceful scenic routes.

"A bicycle is perfect for exploring the back streets. We are able to squeeze through very narrow lanes," writes journalist Peerawat Jariyasombat. "We went down one lane that can't be more than a metre wide to reach an enclave that few outsiders would ever venture into."

Cycling has shifted gear from subculture to mainstream with cycling maps appearing. Long-distance cycling has even become a mass sport. Firms use cycling for CSR credibility. Major roads are closed for annual Car Free Day when colour-coded riders form a giant Thai flag. In 2015, the future King Vajiralongkorn led the Bike For Mom and Bike For Dad massed rallies to honour King Bhumibol and Queen Sirikit.

Cycle lanes are increasing, but are often piecemeal and not thought through. Some lanes run along footpaths; others face steep ramps. Cycle lanes get invaded by motorists and make irresistible parking spaces. Cycling is a stated justification for the Landmark river promenade that is destroying many of the communities that cyclists want to go and see. Cycling routes are less like a network, than destinations to which you take your bike – by car – since they're mostly banned from mass transit.

Bangkok's *sois* have the potential to make a network of through-ways for bike commuters and ease access to mass transit. Four cycle networks will feed suburban stations in 2025. The status of wearing Lycra is already getting the BMA to upgrade road conditions. Drainage grates had been parallel with the kerb so bike wheels got caught in them. But the pressure groups had the clout to get the BMA to turn the gratings sideways. "A lot of people doubted if the phenomenal surge in popularity of cycling would last longer than the time an idle bike tyre could hold air," writes travel columnist Pongpet Mekloy. "Biking is here to stay."

left: An eccentric's bike with maximalist design, ridden at Saphan Khwai.

below: The car-free, ethnic Mon river island of Ko Kret island is a haven for cyclists.

below: **Pavements get clogged with obstacles to walking, such as vendors, food carts and motorcycles bypassing clogged traffic, as here at Ratchathewi.**

right: **Train carriages are like a village on wheels.**

far right: **Tuk-tuk drivers wait for rides at Nonthaburi river pier.**

and Phadung Krung Kasem. River and canal piers have been upgraded and are starting to be linked with rail, like Sanam Chai MRT opening beside Rajini Pier. Progressively, it's all being integrated.

When all else fails, there's one guaranteed way to arrive on time. "Life in Bangkok is fast," says Torpong 'Ball' Chantabubpha of indie band Scrubb. "People are used to flying somewhere on the back of a motorcycle taxi." The 3,000-plus *win motorsai* (bike ranks) cover the entire built-up area, within a five-minute ride of each planned mass transit station or pier – with a speed and efficiency that no other vehicle comes close to. *Win motorsai* have been regulated since Thaksin's time, and now ride-hailing apps are earning them recognition as a professional service. *Motorsai* endanger the knees, among other vital parts, but have become a city icon.

As the centre gets richer and more gentrified, a curious reversal has seen the affluent take up cycling as a hobby. Cycle paths and The Landmark embankment project along the river are for just that demographic, at the expense of the background grid of old riverside *yaan*.

The new breed of parks, curated markets and pedestrianised 'pseudo public spaces' has seen affluent Thais walk a lot more than they did.

The rise of more formal ordered transit now threatens to rid Bangkok of its informal flow. That fluidity had reconciled two opposites in Thai life: freedom and non-confrontation. Thai means 'free', and Thais cherish their autonomy, seeking advantage, defying rules and taking shortcuts. The vast informal sector refuses to be subdued and springs up whenever quashed. Unless the entire city is rebuilt, China-style, and formal transit imposed uniformly, Bangkok will remain a city of social bubbles, each with their tailor-made mode of transit. In this town, you are how you move.

Custom Transit

Riding in Bangkok's mascot, the *tuk-tuk*, you slide upon lurid cushions, hand gripping a curlicued chrome railing, while wobbling starburst lamps distract from the equally expressive driving. Every *tuk-tuk* is different. Built to order by rival firms, they share a shape, but vary in coachwork and personal touches, from bass speakers to novelty gearstick. Tourists love them, but the curving vinyl roofs afford a view of the road, not the sights. People hold the touting drivers in less affection, but few cars are cuter.

The *tuk-tuk* is the best known of Bangkok's handmade public transit, which is 'custom' in three ways. Their designs are custom-built by entrepreneurs to suit Bangkok's routes. Each vehicle is then customised to pop tastes and decked in folk offerings. And they plug into the customary ways of its ridership and the community that runs this offbeat system like a mobile village.

Highway buses can't fit down lanes, so commuters switch at *pak soi* onto nippier wheels. In some suburban *sois*, motorbikes bolt on a canopied trolley seating six. Pickup trucks turn into the *songtaew*, named for its 'two rows' of benches under a metal 'cap'. They dawdle along so as to cram in ever more riders, while latecomers cling onto the back entry ledge. In ones based on mini-pick ups – named *rot krabong* (box cars), or Subaru, after the brand – riders must fold under the low cap to reach the tiny benches.

Buses and river expressboats, too, are tailor made for this city. Their wooden floors are stronger and more durable than cheaper steel, plywood or plastic. In both, conductors have ticket tubes to store ticket rolls and change, using the metal lid to tear of tickets and clatter to alert you they're coming. Tellingly, this transit is all so cheap that most pay with coins.

The epitome of Bangkok's informal culture, such impromptu transit exists to fill the gaps in the formal system. The state has lately revamped some piers and bus stops, but its main role is putting a ceiling on fares. Just as price caps on rice impoverish farmers, earning just a few baht per ride prevent bus and boat operators from investing in hi-tech. Their solution is surprisingly efficient lo-tech. Superstructures of wood and canvas are easy to adapt and fix, with their array of pulleys, straps and clips. Any engineer can tinker with the motors. The longtail boat gets its name from a long propeller shaft that's attached to an engine from a pick-up truck, all of which can swivel through 180° and be lifted to avoid floating hazards.

Like wooden Thai architecture, custom transit is semi-open-air and retains a rural ambiance within urban life. *Songtaews* and *tuk-tuks* have roofs to shelter from sun or rain, with open sides that ventilate sweating bodies whilst keeping your hair unmussed. When monsoon rains blow in, open-sided transit has see-through tarpaulins to unfurl. In a concession to safety, *tuk-tuks* now have netting to stop passengers falling out the side. Drivers knot the string into patterns, such as a spider's web with a lurking toy spider.

Bangkokians feel pride at their swish electric trains, yet overlook the ingenuity of their informal transit, in which local initiative plugged unmet needs. Without state subsidy, these private startups flourished by being adaptive and responsive, earning staff and local loyalty. "Strangely, these are also technological breakthroughs of a different kind," says urbanist Yangyong Boon-long. "They were collectively designed

left: Canal boats were designed to allow access at any point along the side, as here at Mahanak Mosque. New rules to have one or two taller exits require less agility but are slower and less safe.

top right: Tiny 'box' car pickup buses, here in Phrakhanong.

lower right: A wire-guided ferry pontoon crossing Khlong Saen Saeb in Ramkhamhaeng area.

below right: Bangkok's buses are still handmade, with wooden floors and sash windows.

bottom right: Motorcycle taxi drivers have to make their own rank furniture and queue number boards, with improvised shelters.

and made by ordinary people. [To] understand how it works, the entire ecosystem of sociological factors must be viewed as part of the blueprint."

The 60-odd Chao Phraya Expressboats are custom built in wood to a unique shape using time-honoured craft. "The boat's design is one-of-a-kind, from the design to the boat builders, including materials... and the techniques passed on from generations," writes Rapeeat Ingkasit. "All originated from the Chao Phraya basin. Each boat has a unique 'signature'." Coachbuilt in three sizes – Orange Flag water bus, Yellow Flag commuter shuttles, and broader tourist craft – the Expressboats do at least four-70-minute round trips per day on the 35 km line from the port to Nonthaburi, with Saphan Taksin as Pier Zero.

"Driving the boat isn't difficult... it's the docking that needs practice to perfect," says a steersman of the wind, tide and current. As a boat nears the tyre-slung pier, the brown-armed steersman hops off to loop a hemp rope around a bollard so 50 passengers a minute can disgorge, then embark – with a nervous leap onto the open stern. Boarding has been made easier, but it'll never be accessible to wheelchairs. Between piers, the boats speed with thrilling pace, rising the wash of pleasure craft and dodging in front of tugs pulling barges that resemble water beetles. Expressboats have no brakes, so the steersman directs the captain using a code of beeps and toots on his whistle. These old boats are being replaced by toylike, enclosed electric catamarans that dull the experience.

The fastest way across town is the Saen Saeb Canal Boat. "I don't sell boat tickets, I sell time," says Chaowalit Metayaprapas, who initiated it as a social service. "If I can't build a subway, then I'll run the boats in a *'tube'*!" He's punning on London's underground 'Tube' and the Thai word for sewer, in a nod to the low status of canals. His idea was to board boats all along the side, as in trains. Riders stretch a foot to the gunwale, then hook the other leg into the hull, ducking under the canvas roof. As there's no need for an aisle, conductors in helmets collect fares by walking around the gunwales, from which rise tarpaulins against splashes from boat wakes. It's the passengers who pull up the tarps by tugging a pulley, then slacken it to let people step over the tarp at piers. Fun and sensually raw, this interactive transport relies on riders near pulleys to keep out the foetid spray. Sadly, while upgrading the piers, the authorities got the boats reshaped with an aisle and one exit midway, easing but slowing access.

With a gruff cough the boat meanders around submerged hazards and the pillars of humpbacked footbridges – but it offers one more surprise. At high tide the low-slung boat is too tall for the road bridges. Chaowalit hinged the windscreen and roof struts so the captain can push a lever and lower the entire roof, which brushes the pennants strung under each bridge. As the city refuses to adjust the bridges, it's the boat's very structure that bows.

Hubs where handmade transit gather become an archetypal Bangkok habitat. Certain *tuk-tuks* hang out at the same piers, markets and bus stops, often beside regular *win motorsai* (taxi ranks), *songtaews*, and bus terminus huts. *Samlor* (bicycle rickshaws) were banned from Bangkok in the 1960s, but in adjacent Nonthaburi *samlor* pedalers mill around with boatmen and tour touts. The densely parked, open-sided vehicles allow friendships and camaraderie to develop. It mirrors the way stall vendors, roving hawkers and security guards interact with shophouse dwellers and passers-by in local streets.

While bike taxi jockeys wait for their turn, they bond with their colleagues on the rank through banter and games like chequers, using bottle caps on a hand-chiselled board. Some knit fishing nets. "Sitting at street corners the drivers become privileged sources of local knowledge... but also provide a constant presence in the neighbourhood," wrote Claudio Sopranzetti in *Owners of the Map*. "City dwellers turn to them whenever they need something at their doorstep." Many run errands (paid), direct traffic (unpaid) and help with moving things, minding a stall, or even chasing thieves. Like policemen, they know the best local food. All these 'transit villagers' bind the social fabric.

The gulf between the international standard of mass transit and the adaptive local transit is now being addressed, with upgrades to piers, new bus routes and prospect of the universal Maengmoom Card being usable on buses and boats. Tellingly the few motorcycle taxi shelters are intended for customers, not the drivers, who wait on the benches they hammer from old planks – Bangkok's signature street furniture. Modernity and standardisation won't only change the vehicles but threatens this civic bonhomie. Digital ticketing leads to laying off bus conductors, who are often married to the driver.

Just as the state sought to extend canal boats to *khlongs* in Thonburi and Banglamphu, it is removing informal features that made them special. The boats are now getting fewer, with bigger chairs with aisles and single portals slowing and congesting each trip. The Expressboat operator also plans a new fleet of electric ferries.

As custom transit wanes, some of these vehicles get repurposed. *Tuk-tuks* take myriad guises, from vans to bars to hotel shuttles. Some itinerants have made homes out of an old bus, parked in Phutthamonthon or teak rice barges beached in riverside gardens. Bangkok's handmade transport, like its teak stilt houses, is turning into heritage.

Like street restaurants that fit into one cart or market stalls assembled out of a box, custom vehicles are paragons of collective innovation and show how Thais filter modernity. "Transient and impermanent they may seem, these [kinds of] transit enabled millions of people to have access to things they might not otherwise," says Yangyong. Yet unless Bangkok is rebuilt, its unique road and water layout will still need *soi* and *khlong* transit to feed its trains. In *How Buildings Learn*, Stuart Brand advocated for adaptive architecture. Bangkok is a lesson in 'How Transport Learns.'

Balance
The art of everyday grace

Bangkok knocks newcomers off balance. *Sois* with no sidewalks force feet to splay along V-shaped gutters. Guy cables threaten to garotte those who don't duck. Tourists stride boldly where this City of Angels fear to tread. Meanwhile, Thais nimbly avoid all the hazards.

We notice our sense of equilibrium more when it fails. Non-natives are apt to feel like a klutz – which doesn't go unnoticed by Thais, who dub an ungainly, stomping *farang* as a *yaksha*, or ogre. Thais make a point of being poised.

Bangkok's climate discourages exertion, prompting slow, gentle movement so brows don't bead in the heat. In a typical scene, women perch nonchalantly sidesaddle on taxi bikes, crossed ankles counterbalancing the raised arm shading her face with a handbag.

Thai culture hails balance as a virtue, exemplified in *muaythai*, dance, and worship. Notice how delicately a Thai wrist tilts to receive a garland. From Buddhism, mindfulness in the moment and a spirit of non-confrontation lead people to subtly dodge rather than lunge. School kids get taught *marayaa*t – formal etiquette that displays upbringing and inspires harmony.

Attuned to each person's relative status, a *wai* greeting is calibrated by the depth of bows, and height that their pressed hands are raised. At its pinnacle, the *wai* develops into the *kraab* – a prostration before an altar, teacher or royal that's precision bodily engineering. Less-limber foreigners find it a challenge to shift their centre of gravity as the body presses floor-wards upon knee, then hip, then elbow, whilst the wrists elevate into a *wai*. The sequence then reverses. It's a trial of balance.

Marayaat preserves how past Thais moved. That it was an aquatic past – when most Bangkokians lived on raft or boat – may explain their deftness in disembarking boats and treading planks over floodwater. Now landlubbers, Bangkokians inherited sea legs.

"Good people walk on tiptoe," says a proverb about the virtue of treading softly, as one does on creaking boards or a raft. Likewise, "good people" place things gently, and social juniors pass gifts with left fingertips touching right forearm in symbolic support. Servers pour drinks the same deferential way.

Choreograph *marayaat* and you get Thai dance. Traditional performance is an offering to the gods. Based on the *Ramakien* (the Thai version of the *Ramayana* epic), *khon* masked drama began in the court, and can be seen at Sala Chalermkrung theatre and the Thailand Cultural Centre. Even in tourist shows, Thai dance respects its ritual meaning, beginning with a balletic *wai khru* tribute to past masters.

Khon dancers embody non-human deities as they flow between climactic tableaux. They freeze in acrobatic poses, like a stop-motion animation of mural panels. When they move, they appear to float weightlessly, toes curled up, fingers bent back, spired crowns pointing heavenward.

Bangkok's most accomplished dancer, Pichet Klunchun, is lauded abroad, but has earned some local ire, because of his efforts to evolve this dance form in a contemporary way. The palace guards who originated *khon* focused on the energy of martial arts. Pichet's modern versions incorporate *qi* circling around each dance posture, revealing *khon*'s inner geometry and energetic

left: **In *khon* dance, a lift looks elegant but is very hard to do well.**

above: **Dancers practising in Lumpini Park in the Thainess Fair.**

below left: **Labourers need balance skills to carry loads in all kinds of awkward situations.**

below: **Martial artists begin each bout with a *wai khru* dance to honour their master.**

balance. To the *khon* manual's 59 set stances, Pichet's production 'Number 60,' adds fluid choreography.

Official stagings of *khon* can display the rigidity that rote learning and military diktat have introduced to Thai deportment. Authoritarianism has intensified the use of formal postures, in a literal nod to seniority. Standing for anthems, salutes by security guards, and stooping before superiors all require command of correct stance at risk of a public scolding.

Foreigners learn the Thai arts of balance and deference when they take up *muaythai* boxing. A century ago, regional styles like *muay* Chaiya or *muay* Khorat were codified into a Bangkok version as the national sport and labelled "Thai." The city hosts top arenas – Ratchadamnoen and New Lumpini Stadiums – and gyms where limbs get turned into lethal weapons. But before every bout, *muaythai* distils its leaps, sweeps and pirouettes into the *wai khru rum muay*, a respectful dance to venerate masters.

In more workaday contexts, labourers often play the foot-volleyball game of *takraw* on patches of ground at dusk. It's only doable by those with a honed knack for balance. Players swivel and scissor-kick the woven rattan ball across a net before landing on sprung feet like a cat.

Even the humblest of everyday gestures are infused with polite grace. Market-goers slip through crowds without bumping. Shop assistants appear silently at your shoulder, then proffer your purchase with the receipt, notes and coins stacked in a tidy pile. Balance is so expected that it comes as a shock to see a slump in how some locals carry themselves, whether hunched sitting, foot-dragging, or desultory service. These sloppier manners seem linked to consumerism, less agile physiques, and among the world's longest daily usage of smartphones.

Despite that creeping brusqueness, as a whole, Bangkokians remain averse to rushing, or pushiness. Most resist walking on escalators, and would rather miss a train than scramble their way in. The imperative is to maintain composure. It's not just a question of posture and movement, even one's mood must be kept in balance. Balance is a state of mind.

Looking
Seeing is not believing

In Bangkok, there's a lot to distract the eye. Trades, chores and pleasures take place in full public view. Exquisite in parts, sloppy en masse, the Thai capital challenges our notions of how a city should look.

Due to narrow lanes and hazards, it's harder to stroll here than on New York avenues or Parisian boulevards. You can't take in the vistas when the streetscapes and skylines are obscured by awnings, utilities and overhead railways. So we're drawn close to details. You can't help but notice odd things, like plastic effigies on shrines, the tousled knots of overhead wiring, and parking barriers made from a pole stuck in cement in an old tyre.

As Bangkokians aren't wont to wander the roasting streets, the city's most familiar vantage point is sat in shunting traffic. In 'Driving Bangkok,' photographer Wuthipol Uj started "indecisively documenting" the restricted views from vehicles: a roadside gallery of clipped hedges on red-and-white striped kerbs, and dozing bus riders framed by chrome sash windows. The *tuk-tuk* is loved for its fun quotient, but its canvas roof arches so low that tourists can see only road, wheels and feet, not the sights. So the boutique tour agency Expique commissioned their own fleet of tuk-tuks with translucent roofs.

Rooftop bars and the river offer relief from those constrictions; they're the city's most expansive spaces, where panoramas are finally possible. The Bangkok seen from high rises has a radically detached feel: a flooded forest of trunks – some shapely, some ugly – bristling randomly from an expanse of low structures. Viewpoints are among the first places visitors go to get their bearings. Vertiginous views from above have sprouted all over the centre, while IconSiam's multi-level decks have opened sweeping new vistas of the river.

Bangkok's undergrowth of umbrellas and tarpaulins get in the way of sightseeing, but have a practical rationale: shade. In this tropical climate, it's imperative to escape the sun. The glare makes it harsh to walk without sunglasses, hat or parasol. The rays can burn with short exposure, so street workers wear long sleeves and face masks to avoid sunburn. Narrow lanes restrict the amount of sky. Shophouses have a sheltered frontage with an awning that rolls down. Trees or overhead trellises of vines dapple many pavements with shadow. To shield diners from sun or rain, suspended vinyl banners are held in place by bottles of water on string tied to the corners.

Architecture used to face inwards, not out. The surviving wooden houses are dark inside, with small shuttered windows, broad eaves and a shady open-fronted space below. Modern structures tend to have cast-cement sunshades around windows and shelters jutting out over paths. A trademark of Bangkok's Brutalist architecture is its geometric sunshades, which have zigzags on Sampanthawong District Office, and parabolic curves on Srifuengfung Building at Rama IV Road.

Shophouses also run narrow and deep, derived from a Straits Chinese template that incorporated open-air courtyards, a feature not replicated in Bangkok's darker terraces. Older buildings lack picture windows, even if they overlook scenic views. Blocks are still being built that consign the best river or canal outlook to a stairwell. Given the demand for aircon and the rise in floor area costs, newer towers avoid balconies, while some have a few token slats to shield the floor-to-ceiling windows.

Suddenly a public who had always sought shade and ventilation is sealing themselves behind glass. Curtain walls spread from the Bauhaus to Chicago to Bangkok, starting with the Chokchai tower in 1978. Casings of blue-green glass hide the giganticness of Empire Tower and turn the riverfront CAT building into a green parabolic mirror.

Developers like the ease and sleekness of slotting together glass panels. But they waste a fortune in electricity bills and have intrinsic flaws: glazed walls fry the occupants, blind the neighbours with glare, and fool birds into butting the windows. Whereas Singapore's Changi Airport is an unassuming concrete box that houses refreshening gardens, Suvarnabhumi Airport is a grid of glass tubes that looks like a solar panel – and acts like one too. To cool its overheated staff and passengers, they had to install giant tarpaulins in the curved glazed ceilings, and give each immigration booth an indoor beach umbrella.

The ad hoc remedy to all this glass is to cover it up again. Condos have blinds constantly drawn. Tinted windows are a norm, whether in shops or cars, where many exceed legal darkening limits. Stickers garland lots of windows, leaving just a small aperture to peer through. Many cars have gauze filters suctioned to side windows and foil panels blocking the rear view. Perforated advertising stickers – which flatten our depth of vision – clad the entire length of buses, trains, and skyscrapers.

Bangkok light is dazzlingly harsh, with shadows correspondingly dark. The humidity lends a refractive quality that adds to the city's predilection for brilliant colours. Yet the predominant hue is grey, especially from stained concrete. On ultra smoggy days, Bangkok has had the worst city air in the world by PM2.5 particle count, which dulls golden-hour light into a sulphurous sepia. We see through a veil of soot, so on holidays when traffic subsides, we get an ocular shock from air clarity, like suddenly putting in contact lenses.

How we see is also conditioned by culture. Non-Asian views of Bangkok are still swayed by the Orientalist cliché of the East as exotic and passive. Many foreigners and Thais alike talk of 'Westernisation,' but this notably non-colonised land has modernised to its

top far left: **Mural by the top Thai graffiti artist Alex Face of his baby character.**

top left: **A *khon*-style mask worn by a dancer of Pichet Klunchun's avant-garde *khon* troupe, seen at Bangkok Theatre Festival.**

right: **In an ongoing beauty trend, some Thais see the world through 'big eye' contact lenses that make the eyes appear larger.**

Senses 81

Vertical Living

Sipping an overpriced cocktail at a skyscraper rooftop bar now heads the Bangkok bucket list. Every new tower seems to install a viewpoint. The Hilton and then IconSiam opened new cross-river panoramas, but less noticed vantage points include the Avani overlooking the Port, the Bangkok Marriott is close to the old town, and the So/ hotel overlooking Lumpini park from the bar named Hi-So, Thai slang for high society.

Bangkok rooftop bars entered global renown in *Hangover 2*, a Hollywood romp in which drunk tourists get plucked by a helicopter from the 68th floor open restaurant of The Dome. Named for its off-centre gilded cupola atop a non-symmetrical stack of neo-Grecian balustrades, it was designed by Rangsan Torsuwan, in a style labelled "exultant post-modernism, architectural pastiche in which styles are thrown together without any signs of restraint." He designed the similar Sathorn Unique nearby, which was left a ruin by the 1997 crash. Known as the Ghost Tower and in 2017 featured in a Thai ghost movie, *The Promise*, its 49 unfenced floors became a dare for 'urban explorers' to climb up illegally, until a Swede was found hung there. Now it's plastered with vast billboards.

Bangkok's first open-air skyscraper rooftop bar opened in 2001, when the Banyan Tree Hotel converted the narrow swooping roof of Tai Wah Tower II. With Moon Bar and Vertigo restaurant on raised decks at each end, it resembles Baron Munchhausen's flying galleon. The tower, which has a giant Chinese moon gate hole in the upper floors, also founded the annual Vertical Marathon in 2000. Runners take just over 6 minutes to race up the 1,093 steps.

Vertical living gets sold under literal brands like Vertic, Vertiq and The Vertical. At the luxury end, Le Raffiné Jambu Dvipa has a tiny pool on the balcony of each double-height apartment. One condo called '24' claims "a penthouse on every floor." At the low to medium end, it means cramped living in generic boxes that can't be adapted like Thai homes always could, let alone access streetlife. One compensation is the outlook, though Bangkokians ruefully expect to lose their view, because having one implies there's a space to build next door. Besides, Thai homes always shunned the sun and views. Deep balconies are only available in blocks from the 1970s-90s, while those with hot picture windows now curtain out the glare. In cheap flats, light seeps in past a tiny balcony filled by the aircon and laundry.

Verticalising Bangkok has much to do with land values. Few householders can resist the payday. Former landowners often take top floor apartments in towers they build, only some find they miss living in a house and later shift to the suburbs. Citing a loss of light and privacy, campaigns by neighbours against condos have been fought by the top cultural bureaucrat

82   Looking

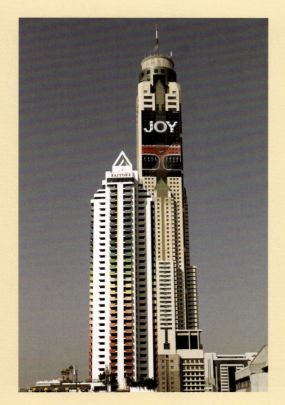

Chakrarot Chitrabongs of Plai Nern Palace on Rama IV and by National Artist Chakrabhand Posayakrit at his home-studio in Ekamai.

"Lower Silom is basically a condo slum," says photographer Manit Sriwanchphoom, who converted an old Thanon Pan shophouse into Kathmandu Gallery. "The construction of condos really destroys the view and environment, and causes even more pollution."

This seems like a break from the past, but architect Duangrit Bunnag sees a continuity. "I like the idea of shophouses. It's the Bangkok of 30-40 years ago. You do business on the ground floor, live on the second floor. Now, people live in a condo on top and the commercial space is at its foot, but its the same thing, really."

Bangkok's pivot from horizontal to vertical living is culturally awkward. The Rattanakosin Island Plan outlaws buildings higher than temples and palaces, though the 34-storey twin towers of Rattanakosin View mansion do overlook the Old Town. Recently, rooftop bars at Tha Tien look across, not down, at spires previously seen just from below.

The title of Bangkok's tallest shows how values have shifted. The earliest panoramas were photographed in 1865 by scaling the vertiginous steps of the original highest point, Wat Arun, looking across the river and palace to another *chedi* atop the Golden Mount. Little of the old town was visible above the flat deltascape of trees. By 1970, when just 25 buildings exceeded six storeys, mostly in Chinatown, the Dusit Thani hotel, regally named after a Thai heaven, rose 23 floors. Economic boom led to 120 high-rises by 1985, until in 2016 it boasted 1,731 high-rises including 252 skyscrapers. Bangkok had turned from garden city into a forest of concrete.

The first glass curtain-wall, cladding Chokchai Tower at Sukhumvit Soi 26 in 1981, heralded corporate sameness, but many architects went for novelty. Bangkok Bank took the 'tallest' crown by styling its 25 storeys to resemble a computer, followed by Baiyoke I in 1993 with rainbow stripes up its 42 floors.

The next tallest for two decades, Baiyoke II, thrust up 12,000 inches from Pratunam's sweaty thicket of clothing stalls. Hidden from any main road, it lacks frontage, forecourt and, forethought typical of cities like KL or Taipei, which made their world-record towers an elegant centrepiece. There will be more presence to the elliptical SuperTower, designed to rise 615 metres from a plaza behind the G building at Rama IX Road. More visible beside IconSiam would be the 459m Bangkok Observation Tower – a copycat of ones in Qatar and Guangzhou.

Few get to be tallest for long. That status was held from 2016-19 by Mahanakhon. Its German architect Ole Scheeren – of Beijing's two-legged CCTV tower fame – was inspired whilst co-curating the roving art project 'Cities on the Move' to embody Bangkok's part-built, part-eroded feel by 'eating into' its giant oblong with a spiral quarry of jutting pixellated boxes. Mahanakhon means Metropolis, evoking Fritz Lang's 1927 movie of that name, which foretold a vertical city of ground-bound proles and sky-dwelling angels. Thais see it more like a 314m-high game of Jenga. Its Skywalk offers a fully spherical panorama from the glass floor on level 78 that juts out 314 metres above a *soi* with wooden houses. Hierarchical Bangkok is looking down at its past and up at its future.

top left: The glass-floored Skywalk at Mahanakhon.

above: High rises loom behind Kudi Jeen community, seen from a Tha Tien rooftop bar.

top: Both Baiyoke towers were once the tallest in town. Baiyoke 2 held the title for longest, but Baiyoke 1 is better loved for its rainbow hues.

Senses 83

own shifting agenda. Proudly independent, Thailand has picked assorted systems from Asia and the West, a counterbalancing policy that has made Bangkok a mishmash. Stylistically, Bangkokians play magpie, plucking shiny trends from Korea, Japan, Italy or influencers anywhere.

Sight is the primary sense, but research shows that it dominates more in the West than the East, where scent and texture aren't so minor. The term 'Gaze,' comes from a French ideology whereby the viewer has power over the viewed. Some talk of Thailand as subject to the 'Western Imperial Gaze,' or the 'White Male Tourist Gaze.' Gaze is a useful tool, but a stereotyping one that renders the locals as impotent and lets other viewers off the hook.

Thais take charge of how others view them. This face-conscious land built soft power by projecting a beguiling image, having found over centuries that it's the one getting attention who has the lucrative power of leverage, while the 'gazer' can be fooled or willfully blind. Amid all the intra-ethnic gazing going on in Bangkok's fleshpots, it's worth pondering who is gazing more powerfully at whom.

Outsiders view Bangkok through various lenses. To Muslims, Bangkok can seem idolatrous in its attire and mixing of the sexes – yet they stay in its most brazen, sexually-mixed quarter, Nana. Muslims also comment how they're left unhassled here, without the constant profiling they sense in the West.

Chinese have long seen opportunity here, and been accepted, given similar looks and customs. Chinese journalist Jin Ni says they're fascinated at how Sino-Thais have acculturated, yet preserved traditions long since purged from the Maoist motherland. Chinese are the main foreign buyers of Thai condos, and estate agents report that Chinese buyers feel this is the part of Southeast Asia that feels least different. In the Chinese gaze, Bangkok is an easy first step abroad.

Neither ethnicities nor minorities are monolithic in what they find attractive or offensive, which derives as much from class tastes, beliefs and personal preference. Middlebrow people from any culture tend to enjoy the glittering spectacle and sensational aspects, while the bourgeois chase the chic and resist the mess. The broad-minded embrace Bangkok's perceived chaos as an inspiring charm, seeing beauty in imperfection, a perception contrary to the official Thai Gaze.

Bangkok appears as it does due to particular tastes. Both high and low culture revel in appetising variety. Maximalism has always been, and overwhelms graphics and décor today. Averse to fixed commitments, it's a sampling culture that favours funny novelty, vivid colour and accentuated presentation. The imperative of *saduak* (convenience) enables Bangkokians to graze a buffet of stimulation, whether a continuous procession of sales displays or clashing attractions in a fair.

Each level of Thai Gaze reflects relative status. Face culture is phrased as *naa-dtaa* – 'face-eyes.' Those of low status won't look higher ranks in the eye as it's impertinent, while staring is taboo. In nightclub shootings, staring has been cited as provocation by a culprit defending his honour. So when looking, don't peer too intently. Raised to calibrate behaviour with grace, Thais notice whilst averting the eyes. Demurely lowered eyelids are a leitmotif in Thai portraiture, partly for their elegant tilde shape, but also as a social signal. Soap operas exaggerate all this face-eye choreography, from doe-eyed good girl to glowering matron.

Bangkok is deemed beautiful for its modernity and prestigious highlights. Amid that status signalling, functional buildings are too low to matter, so much of city looks utilitarian, cheap and undesigned. Devoting most expense and quality to presentation has the downside of ensuring disappointment if you delve into substance. So when foreigners stare at the mess – or worse, praise low-status eyesores like street stalls or nightlife as precious – mortified officials rush to clean up the eyesore and declare that visitors come to see grand traditional culture, not bad things. To realists that seems like pretension or denial, but it's restoring the hierarchy's Thai Gaze.

Authenticity matters much to Westerners, who lament the lack of appreciation for indigenous wooden houses in the drive to make Bangkok look generically modern. Making the capital look like other cities has in fact been integral to how Thais conceive their state. Replicating Ayutthaya, and so indirectly the architecture of Angkor, underpins the *devaraja* legitimacy. Erecting Italian palazzos on Frenchified boulevards was instrumental in staving off colonisation by appearing already *siwilai* (civilised). Reshaping the city on car-focused American plans expressed Sarit's 'Development State'. Even cleaning up Rattanakosin into a museum island isn't about restoring the past, with its crowded streetlife, but emulating the open vistas of heritage districts in Paris or Rome.

Most capitals have some consistency of style, while the most celebrated are visually coherent. Fragmented Bangkok is the wardrobe of a fashionista who serially adopts new looks. That applies across the culture, from design to art. For centuries, Southeast Asian elites have appropriated cultural imports to signal prestige. Access to foreign luxuries and technology has been a way to position the powerful above their indigenous peoples. Now the middle classes, too, differentiate themselves from the poor by the trappings of an international lifestyle.

Suddenly, an intellectual trend decrees 'cultural appropriation' to be offensive, yet cultural borrowing has been the norm in all civilisations – and Bangkok is ultra-eclectic. Creative cross-fertilisation mirrors the instinct for genetic diversity; memes mimic genes. Thai dance is typical of tribal codes of dress that mark identity, yet are themselves hybrid. Bangkok's dance canon, from *khon* to *likay*, involves movements and costumes appropriated from other cultures, be they Indian, Khmer, Malay or Burmese. From craft masters to today's art schools, teaching is about

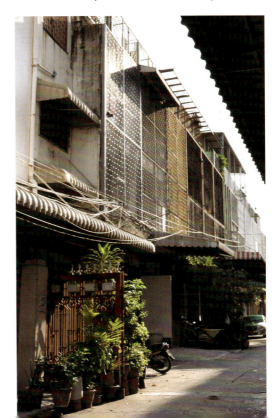

top left: The Skytrain gliding high through the skyscrapers at Sathorn.

right: *Sois* of shophouses use awnings and grilles to shield from the sun.

applying traditional templates, so creativity turns to riffing on imported novelty. Rather than simply copy the Japanese motor-rickshaw, Bangkok's version of the *tuk-tuk* is an iconic design adapted to local needs and tastes, showing cultural borrowing on its own terms.

Imitation is a proverbial form of flattery, and thus a diplomatic tool. Thais don't borrow from just anyone, but from the prevailing powers of the day. The first Siamese ambassador went to France wearing a Persian gown, a Brahmin hat and a Javanese *kris* dagger; today diplomats wear a Western suit. That Persian gown is still worn at state rituals and university graduations. Engaged in the Chinese junk trade, King Rama III applied porcelain gables and Moon Gates to temples as a nod to China. National costume features the *jongraben* leg wrap, akin to the Indian dhoti, with black shoes and long white socks, topped with either a puff-sleeved Edwardian blouse, or the official white jacket, which was based on Prussian naval uniform. Cultural appropriation is core to the Bangkok look.

Bangkok's archetypal hybrid is the Chakri Maha Prasat Throne Hall in the Grand Palace. The initial British neo-Renaissance design was too foreign for the ex-regent Chuang Bunnag, who swapped its planned triple-domed roof for three spires adapted from a late-Ayutthaya temple. Its nickname, "Farang with a Thai Hat," spells out who's on top. Ever since, countless modern structures have been dressed with Thai roofs and porches, often clipped on without regard even to Thai design principles; the token Thai motif says all it needs to.

Hybrids often lack the original rationale. I used to work in the turret of a neo-Gothic townhouse complex, where a cathedral-style rose-window faced onto its carpark. Greco-Roman motifs get tacked onto lowly shophouses and lofty skyscrapers like The Dome. With porticos placed off-centre, or Doric columns that rise three stories but support no weight, they flout the rules of Greek architecture.

People used to Renaissance perspective's linear rules forget that the fixed disappearing point is a Western invention from scientific ways of looking. By contrast, Chinese ink paintings used swirling mist to telescope scale between bridges and pine-tufted mountains. Thais have their own rules of proportion, seen in murals and neo-traditional paintings, where perspective is more to show social rather than physical distance. Important things get foregrounded higher in the composition, regardless of their geographical position.

Thai perspective also arises from the cramped quarters having few panoramas. Bangkok was carved out of forest, then densely settled, with major buildings walled off. Murals are like constellations, where buildings float with multiple sides visible, so your viewing position keeps shifting.

The West and China aligned avenues and squares upon pivotal structures, whereas key Bangkok buildings were placed according to cosmological position, and rarely as the locus of a street plan. So in discovering Bangkok's treasures hidden behind other buildings, there's surprise in their slow-reveal. In the old town, only outer Ratchadamnoen Avenue feels like a processional route that ends in a focal point: the dome of Ananta Samakhom Throne Hall – and that was designed by Italians.

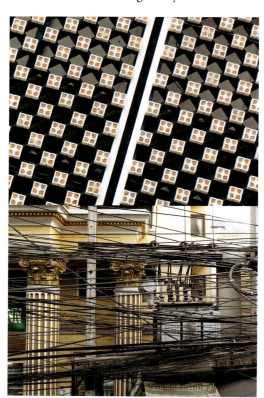

top: **Sun grilles and concrete mouldings are 'Mid-Century Modern' styles, seen at Narai Hotel.**

above: **Skeins of wires mask most city views.**

right & far right: **A hybrid Bangkok style infused Thai design into this Madonna shrine at Calvary Church and an Imam's mimbul at Tonson Mosque.**

Artifice has always been part of Thai city making. Thai ideals of beauty tend towards fantasy because palace and temple design employ the décor of Buddhist cosmology. Siam imported many forms – bell-shaped *chedis* from Sri Lanka, tiered roofs with corner finials from China – then stylised them with Indian foliated ornament into abstract lines that entwine across surfaces. Collectively they're called *lai thai* (Thai patterns). Motifs include fabulous chimeric beasts from the Himaphan Forest of Mount Meru. If it all seems unreal, that's because it conjures up unseen realms of existence.

The city's most coherent architectural element is the abode not of humans but deities: temple and palace roofs. These delicate shelters float unattainably above the humdrum fray. Like the spire on a dancer's crown, they're more connected to the heavens than the earth. As the head is sacred, so are the uppermost part of buildings, but there are also practical reasons. Across Southeast Asia, rooflines are the architectural signature or the basic building unit: the *sala* – a pavilion of pillars and raised floor that might not have walls, in which the roof is the identifier of tribe, status or belief.

The architecture of Thai commoners was always highly functional. Teak now seems rarified, but until the 1960s it was plentiful and prized as resistant to floods and bugs. Form followed function in stilt houses. The exposed structure looks exquisite when carpenters peg panels onto poles with tapering proportions for steadiness in floods; less so in shophouses cast in crude ferroconcrete with their blue and yellow utility pipes in full view.

Shophouses invest all their looks in the frontage, while the sides of each row – often at odd angles – reveal crude construction with random windows. Many mid-sized buildings are not designed in a unified way, but have shophouse frames stacked ever higher, indicated by the beams and pillars being picked out in a contrasting paint to the walls.

All societies have gone through periods of ugliness in the transition to modernity. Until recently, utilitarian eyesores were thrown up with no expectation of competing with the treasures of old. The straggling wires, grimy pipes, and rattling compressors that disfigure frontages used to signal that newly industrialising Bangkok had electricity, fresh water and air-conditioning. Lately, shophouses have been brought into the heritage bracket as part of the acceptance of the Chinese

contribution to modern Bangkok. As in Singapore or China, preserving the past often means purging and rebuilding fake Asia as a themed attraction, whether the faux warehouses of Asiatique The Riverfront or the mock-Chinatown façades of Wat Mangkon MRT station.

Younger Thais literate in art history savour the distinctive lightness of Bangkok's concrete Brutalism. Modernism is undervalued and at risk of demolition partly due to it being associated with the People's Party era, which adopted Modernism as a deliberate break with tradition. Thainess ideologues rebut the aesthetic that modernity can be beautiful, let alone worth preserving as heritage. That's why we lost hybrid masterpieces as vital as the Dusit Thani and Siam-Intercontinental hotels, the latter by a pupil of Frank Lloyd Wright. There's a nationalist view that considers only pure Thai-style buildings as having worth, not hybrid-Thai buildings. Hence the shrug at people erasing traces of past eras that aren't part of the Thainess narrative, but anger whenever someone without status uses Thai sacred forms in contemporary design.

"In London you have new landmarks every decade. We only have beautiful things from a long time ago that are traditional, but beautiful modern landmarks: no," notes Zcongklod Bangyikhan, former editor of *a day* magazine. "Government buildings have criteria that we need to pay the least for it, so it is more function than design." The rise of the Thai design industry in the 2000s, and access to sources online, has since raised the quality of ordinary buildings, especially interiors, but to a rather bland international sameness.

Senses **87**

Larkitecture

Thai designers favour toonish character products. Bangkok buildings, too, can smile. The skyline is like a row of mascots resembling toys or animals, boats or beer barrels. In a city that resists the serious, architects get to have a lark; call it Larkitecture.

The genre's master, Sumet Jumsai, made the Grand Pacific hotel (1988) evoke a cruise liner and *The Nation* newspaper HQ a circuit board in Cubist style. Sadly, UOB ruined his 'Robot Building,' which had bolt-like ears, heavy-lidded 'eyes', antennae and a paned grin of blue-glass teeth.

Excitement about modernity inspired many boom-era edifices. In 1982, Krisda Arunwongse na Ayuthaya (elected Bangkok Governor 1992-96) made the Bangkok Bank HQ resemble a computer.

"Seemingly a compendium of all possible architectural styles, modern Bangkok defies easy categorisation... with more than a hint of Disneyland," wrote John Hoskin in *Bangkok by Design*. "Concerned architects talk, only partially in jest, about 'Architectural Identity Disaster Syndrome'."

Yet it's culturally consistent with the riotous hodge-podge of old Bangkok. Its palaces, temples and houses were imbued with symbolism, such as boat-shaped bases to temples and pulpits, or *chofa* finials of a *naga* or swan. The multi-colour *prangs* that W Somerset Maugham called "monstrous vegetables" were a vivid version of Hindu towers, while other forms related to Buddhist tales or Thai cosmology. King Rama II styled the base of Wat Yannawa's *chedi* (stupa) as a sailing junk to honour trade with China. So Thais are used to buildings as signals for something else.

Traditional forms incorporated elements from abroad, like the broken Chinese porcelain used as mosaic on Wat Pho and Wat Arun. Their quirky detailing of deities and chimeras is taken to extremes at Wat Pariwat, where the china-mosaic effigies include a shark-headed man, Picachu, superheroes, warriors, and geniuses like Shakespeare and Einstein.

To identify what's specifically Bangkok style, we must look beyond Siamese forms, which had Indian, Chinese and eclectic roots. Architecture is the most political art – its scale, appearance and materials impact everyone. It makes a public statement about power and ownership. Adapting anything sacred can only be done by those with prestige; businesses that use temple shapes get lambasted for sacrilege. So contemporary architects have taken two paths: riffing on elements that abstractly hint at Thainess, or playing with imported novelty.

The neo-traditional arts movement birthed in Bangkok distills selected motifs. Several towers slope like trapezoid Thai cabinets, such as Sathorn City Tower, La Maison, and both the former and reincarnated Dusit Thani hotels. Pointy protrusions are an abstract allusion to *chedis* at Tri Devakul's black-spiked Tridhos City Marina and Robert Boughey's gold-tipped Siam Commercial Bank HQ. The roof of the now-gone Siam-Intercontinental Hotel resembled a royal hat, replaced by Siam Paragon, which is envisaged as a faceted gem. Park Ventures Ecoplex and the Rosewood Hotel each evoke the *wai* gesture and greet each other across Ploenchit Road.

Bangkok even made Brutalism fun. The now lost Scala cinema was a pirouette of parabolic curves. Sunshades on the Narai hotel are patterned with auspicious *prachamyaam* flowers. The frontage of the Nightingale-Olympic Department Store, in the textile district, feels like concrete embroidery. Bangkok's playful modernism has become a fetish of retro aficionados.

The Thai taste for cute can be seen as a passive response to harsh social relations. Cute also softens harsh edges, as in the golden crown atop Terminal 21 or the coloured sticks on the pointy site at the Sumet-designed S31. Delight in novelty theming results in Wang Dek (Child's Palace), made to look like Lego blocks, and Tawandang German Brewery having a vaulted roof styled on a beer barrel.

All these threads of symbolism, character and novelty come together in one form that's typically Thai, and could only have been built in Bangkok: buildings shaped like elephants. Erawan Museum is within the body of a three-headed pachyderm, while the Elephant Building at Phahonyothin Soi 26 is a stylised version, with three grey towers bridged across the top, which looks like a letter M, were it not for the jutting 'ears', cantilevered 'tusks' and 'tail' protruding down its rump, which contains a condominium. Landmarks like these bring Bangkok's skyline alive.

88   Looking

A blog about condos, called Realist, divides Bangkok tower styles into categories: 'Simply Modern,' 'Timeless' (like neo-classical 98 Wireless), 'Ornamental' (swoopy Laviq) and 'Futuristic' (Q-shaped Ideo Q). They didn't mention the most infamous trait: novelty. Bangkok's most distinctive modern buildings are the themed gimmicks done during the 1980s and 1990s boom.

In a historic shift, Bangkok is tidying up its clutter, sparking joy in many residents and visitors, but appalling fans of vernacular architecture. Mass tourism demands more space, while locals too want a photo-friendly setting. Bangkokians also take pride in an unimpaired vista of Rattanakosin to rank alongside the world's great riverscapes.

Crucially these landmarks must be viewable from a distance. Chalerm Thai cinema, a pop culture icon, was torn down to reveal the tower of Wat Ratchanadda. Half of Tha Tien's ornate shophouses were demolished to show off Wat Pho. The mid-century hybrid National Theatre is at risk because some want to see the traditional dance school's Bunditpattanasilpa Hall from Sanam Luang. Standalone landmarks look more enticing in tourism brochures, especially when as artfully lit as the Grand Palace under its impeccable new illumination. Rattanakosin's ordinary buildings must now be repainted a uniform shade of creamy-yellow. Editing heritage from a multi-cultural bazaar to mono-cultural memorials makes it easier to read a city, and to manage crowds, but also to illustrate the official history.

How we see the modern city is also being modified. Elevated trains, roads and SkyWalks open previously unseen vistas, whilst boxing many roads into a concrete netherworld. As multi-level transit bifurcates the streetscape into high and low zones, a new trend in split-view architecture has one design for street level and another for the upper parts. At Noble Ploenchit, a curved frontage fits below the BTS station, while above the tower rises in a boxy grid. Next door, the Rosewood hotel is blank below the BTS platform level, whereupon it branches into its design based on *wai*-ing hands.

In the low zone of the pavement, vendors are being banned from main roads, utilities streamlined, and the tousled wires moved from over-burdened poles into buried ducts.

As obstacles get removed, our views zoom from macro close-up to wide-angle. People can now go boulevarding unimpeded, see more sky, and take in what the entire street looks like.

Tidy sidewalks lend a Singaporean élan to the gleaming statement towers of Ploenchit City. Elsewhere, we can't help but notice that the clutter had shielded us from a lot of shoddy construction that may have looked better obscured. The ancient market that spanned Saphan Hok bridge was erased to turn Khlong Ong Ang into a showpiece. It's pleasant to find a broad waterside swathe of the old town to stroll through. But most of its canalside structures range from plain to unsightly. It also slices out a section of Sampeng Lane Market, a covered street stuffed with textiles and accessories that has been a continuous bazaar all of Krungthep's existence. Letting in direct daylight changes the atmosphere utterly.

That contrast helps us notice Bangkok's underlying, contradictory taste. The urban fabric is woven with exquisite traditional symbols, eclectic appropriation of imports and improvised practical solutions. Cleaning away the sensuous jumble of clutter reveals older layers of hybrids. As Zcongklod remarks: "Bangkok's pattern is no pattern."

left: **Thailand is often accused of copying foreign things deemed impressive. But it can be done with a wink. Bangkok Pearl is uncannily like London's Gherkin, only here the phallic shape has been squished and paired with two ball-like structures at the base.**

above: **Few places on the planet are more consumed with selfies. Instagram data reveals that compared to other countries, Bangkokians have a distinct way of posing for selfies. Their heads are more tilted, eyes more open, and posture gazes upwards, all in seeming deference.**

Senses 89

Colour
Somewhere inside the rainbow

Bangkok looks like it's been Photoshopped. No pink could be that shocking, no gold that yellow. The glare of the sun dials up the brilliance, and casts deep blinding shadows. Thais like the polychromatic, from iridescent silk to candy-coloured shophouses. Even the curries are known by their colour: red, yellow, orange, or green. By night, the white balance must be set to 'fluorescent'.

Hue sets a mood, not just aesthetic, but also social. Bangkok's brightness matches the extrovert Thai personality. While the psychedelic streetlife gives an anything-goes impression, colour is loaded with meaning when seen through Bangkok's cultural prism.

Thai colour choice draws upon beliefs, taboos and tribal allegiance. Bangkok has its own signature colour, green, drawn from the hue of the city's patron god, Indra. That's one reason the Emerald Buddha (actually made of jadeite) is so treasured by Bangkok. The BMA uses green for its trucks and insignia.

Bangkok's traffic may be grim, but the view out the window is kaleidoscopic. While London has Black Cabs, New York the Big Yellow Taxi and Singapore a fleet of silver, Bangkok taxis, as though to match the wandering fruit carts, are sprayed in shades of mangosteen, guava, banana, rambutan or butterfly pea. Each shade identifies a taxi firm that stencils their logo on the side. Green-and-yellow signals an owner-driver cab.

Motorcycle taxi drivers' vests used to differ by each *soi*, but by 2003 were standardised by district into a few solid hues, and then in 2015 to citywide "emergency orange." Not to be outshone, in 2017 city buses kept their old paint-jobs of red-and-cream, blue-and-white or orange, but had their fronts re-painted to match the new zones named B, Y, G or R for blue, yellow, green or red.

Informal transit has more jazzy stripes than Paul Smith socks. Tuk-tuks revel in gleaming chrome and bubblegum-pastel seats. *Songtaew* pickup buses and trucks bear auspicious flower patterns, metal plaques of gods, and pastoral sketches in gaudy enamel. Minivans may be silver, but their interiors dazzle with shiny nylon curtains and two-tone moulded ceilings. Tour coaches are mobile graffiti walls, their sculpted bodywork painted with manga, folk scenes or death metal schlock.

Street design has its trademark tints. Road signs must be blue. Post boxes and hydrants copy the British red. Motorcycle taxi shelters appear in powder pink. Benches come in painted concrete or covered in corporate ad stickers at Siam Square.

Folk art objects used to enchant with their naïve decorations done in crude paints. Their successors, ink-jet vinyl banners, scream with futuristic intensity. Shophouse interiors feature posters of tulips, alps and waterfalls. Their Technicolor verve goes beyond kitsch postcards into the hyperreal visions in films like *Inception*.

Coloured stacking chairs have become an icon of Bangkok. They were exhibited in installations at Bed Supperclub in its heyday and represented the city in 'Krungthep Bangkok', Somboon Hormtientong's Thai pavilion at the 2017 Venice Biennale.

A major influence is immigrant Chinese bringing their brash ornament into business and construction. They now are the arbiters of lifestyle taste. During the later decades of the 20th century, female officewear favoured synthetic dyes and dual-tone clashes as eye-popping as the chorus lines of folk music concerts. The frocks of *hi-so* ladies became so outrageous that *Thailand Tatler* magazine held Worst Dressed of the Year awards. Since then, the rise of Thai designers has mellowed local fashion, but Thai silk still shimmers with iridescent hues.

When photography meant film, Thais preferred Fuji's mintier tones over the warmth of Kodak moments. At dowdy old studios around Banglamphu and Tha Pra Chan, arrays of photographs show how grandees and graduates liked to sit for the portraits seen in homes, shops and Chinese shrines. Men in white suits and matrons in blinding silk asked for Soviet soft-focus on their blushed cheeks, offset by sashes and medals in Lego-colours. Now the power is in the hands of smartphone owners, who swipe to accentuating filters of their choice.

"Bangkok was found to be the most visually unique city," found an international survey that sorted 4,000 Instagrams. Bangkok was a real outlier in its preference for intense and cooler shades (green, blue, shadow) 40% of the time, compared to 25% in say Berlin. Thai images shun natural shades and prefer their green to be lurid more than merely leafy. Bangkok Instagrams avoid middle tones and cluster towards the brighter edges of the spectrum. In terms of filters, they exaggerate global trends: popular filters are more popular than the norm, unpopular ones less so, and subtler filters barely feature at all.

Artificial hues catch the eye, but a second glance reveals earth tones from the original city. Creamy temple walls, clay tiles, timber stained a subtle russet – these remnants survive in patches, often coupled with surviving greenery. Unrelenting construction has removed the canopy of trees that once blended a garden city into the wooded delta horizon. Culturally as in Instagram, Bangkok has flattened its mid-tones and upped the saturation.

The colours stand out partly because Bangkok's backdrop is one giant smudge of bleached plastic and stained concrete. Certain cities reflect the hue of their materials, whether yellow London brick, grey Edinburgh granite or pink Marrakech stucco. Bangkok went for concrete.

Concrete now suits the vogue for minimalism. Fleeing from the maximalism of popular taste, the elite retreat into plain bunkers of design, which predominate in the posher hotels, bars and restaurants. Upscale malls such as Gaysorn Plaza, Central Embassy, and EmQuartier – all share severe neutrals, unadorned geometry and expressionless facades.

left: Shophouses often come with bold colour schemes, from red-and-white chequerboard tyre repair shops to the blue-and-white stripes of this chain of opticians.

right: Bangkok taxis look like an assortment of candy, as each taxi firm or taxi cooperative is distinguished by a different colour livery. These tend to be bright solid colours – no metallics or neutrals, which are the favoured hues of Bangkok drivers for their personal cars. Taxis with green-and-yellow two-tone bodywork indicate that the taxi is owned by its independent driver, and so they tend to be older vehicles than the late-model fleets of company taxis.

Here, seven taxi door panels are arranged to show another kind of Bangkok colour coding. Under Thailand's Hindu-influenced cosmology, each day of the week has a colour, which relates to an astronomical body, which is ruled by a deity: yellow for Monday (the Moon); pink for Tuesday (Mars); green for Wednesday (Mercury); orange for Thursday (Venus); Blue for Friday (Jupiter); Purple for Saturday (Saturn); and Red for Sunday (the Sun). This auspicious colour coding is found in all kinds of contexts around town, from royal insignia and the political colours to the choices of people about what clothes to wear that day.

In the old days, muddy canals and faded teak were a smudge, in which gold provided a flash of brilliance. Today, gold remains a defining colour of Bangkok, thanks to gold-leafed *chedis*, shrines and statuary. Among several countries claiming to be the mythic 'Golden Land', Thailand used one version of that name, Suvarnabhumi, for Bangkok's airport. As temple spires get lost amid the concrete, modern structures acquired gold paint: the peaks of the green-glazed SCB Plaza, the flange on Jambu Dvipa condo, and the crowning buttresses of Q House Lumpini. Most notoriously, The Dome is known for its golden cupola atop a neo-classical skyscraper. When the harp-shaped Rama VIII suspension bridge was considered too bland, it gained a gilded obelisk and gilded railings. Bangkok can't have too much gold.

Under Chinese influence, Bangkokians value a more yellowish alloy of gold, such as you see on sale in the shops in Yaowarat. They use that yellow gold in shiny re-gilding, rather than maintain the burnished patina of old gold.

Gold combines with ceramic glaze and glass mosaic in traditional design. Of all Thai dance costuming, the brightest outfits are Bangkok based. The characters of *khon* masked dance are colour-coded according to Hindu mythology.

Likay folk opera, which began in Rattanakosin, employs paste gems to accentuate gaudy outfits against backdrops in luminous paint – all the better to be seen under coloured fluorescent tube lighting at outdoor temple fairs.

Colour is a cipher in Thai belief. *Wats* have their own colour template, from the saffron robes of monks and white robes of *mae chee* (nuns) to the architecture. Mirror-tile on exterior walls and gateways glint and reflect, the idea being that they disseminate the Dharma through light. The tiled roofs of green rectangles fringed with orange derive from cloth tenting on royal barges. Many *wats* from the early 19th century are clad in colourful shards of imported Chinese ceramics. The effect on Wat Pho and Wat Arun is like multicoloured dragon scales. When the latter was badly restored in 2017 its 3-D effect was lost along with so much of its Benjarong porcelain that tourists unwittingly now refer to it as the "White Temple."

Shrines brighten the dullest of streets. Each deity is believed to want offerings of a specific hue, such as red or green soda. For major gods, everything should match, with incense, candles, flowers and the supplicant's clothes in all red for Trimurti or all black for Rahu.

Historically, colours were restrained by taboos and by access to pigments and lustrous materials like gems or silk. Only certain ranks could wear restricted colours, such as purple or gold. Farmers were limited to natural dyes, which explains the natural tones of textiles, such as indigo *moh hom* farming wear. Once the more exclusive pigments became socially accessible and affordable, all Thais aspired to blast colour to the max. Pop culture and chemical technology intensify those hues, as colouring once done in lacquer and ceramics gain a new lustre in acrylic and Day-Glo.

Another phenomenon is the tradition of 'day colours'. Under Vedic astrology, each day takes on the god and gem ascribed to a celestial body. There are actually eight 'days': Monday (Moon, yellow pearl), Tuesday (Mars, pink garnet), Wednesday day (Mercury, emerald green), Wednesday night (Eclipses, black), Thursday (Venus, orange topaz), Friday (Neptune, blue sapphire), Saturday (Saturn, amethyst purple) and Sunday (Sun, ruby red). Rahu, the god of Wednesday night who causes eclipses by eating the sun or moon, has his own cult. Many Thais believed he caused the economic crash in 1997. That year, during an eclipse, the prime minister's wife worshipped the god with the nine black

above: Thai Tone is a range of paint created by designer Pairoj Pittayamatee, who drew the tints from real-life colours found in Thai buildings and objects.

left: In a Pecha Kucha talk in TCDC, Ploy Mallikamas was the first to map the hues of Bangkok streets. Later TCDC mapped swatches of Charoen Krung for Bangkok Design Week.

far left: Sartorial street taste can be incredibly bold and lively, as spotted in the Than Guay Salak festival beside Wat Benchamabophit.

Senses 93

offerings. Shrines to Rahu's cult include the Hindu shrine at Huai Khwang and a pharmacy in Thanon Phra Chan – Moon God Street.

The day colours enable you to read meaning into traditional designs, such as royal insignia or the sacred triple scarves tied around sacred pillars and trees. During King Bhumibol's Golden Jubilee year of 2006, millions of Thais wore the colour of his Monday birth, yellow.

Royalist protestors became known as Yellow Shirts by literally wearing their allegiance on their sleeves. In riposte, the populist Red Shirt protestors were inspired by the national flag. In the flag, red stands for nation (or people), white for religion, and blue for monarchy (after the Friday birth of King Rama VI, who introduced this flag). Few capitals display their flag more pervasively than Bangkok, where the *trai rong* (tricolour) is in almost constant sight. Later, the Bangkok Shutdown protestors (largely Yellows) appropriated all three stripes of the national flag for their outfits and whistles.

Political colours got even more complex. Troops in khaki were dubbed "Green Shirts", subdivided into "Mangoes" (yellow inside) or "Watermelon Soldiers" (red inside). Black-clad militias among the protestors were branded "Men-in-Black". A disenchanted group, to defuse or confuse the tribalism, called themselves "Multicolour Shirts", and were dubbed "Salim" after the candied fruit parfait. In fact, they wore white shirts, and later shirts of any hue. It got so confusing that people put charts on Facebook to explain the splintering spectrum of political loyalties.

When yellow became too politicised, royalists adopted pink as King Bhumibol was born in Massachusetts at an hour that was already Tuesday in Bangkok. Pink had long been linked with Tuesday-born King Chulalongkorn, and the university named after him. Its varsity football team in matches played against Thammasat University wears a soccer strip of pastel pink.

"When you are obsessed with colours as students, then it's likely you will practice cronyism as a grown up," notes columnist Ploenpote Atthakor on how political science graduates from Chula and Thammasat are known as 'black lions' and 'red lions' respectively when they join the Interior Ministry. "Such a tradition makes some people think it's okay to see 'otherness' in those from different institutes… the promotion of interior officials depended greatly on the colour of the 'lion'."

After the 2014 coup banned political activity, colours began to lose their partisan stigma. Then for over a year after King Bhumibol died on 13 October 2016 the capital plunged into a sea of black. Buildings were swathed in black and white cloth. Colour faded from magazines, ads and homepages. Many shops used greys for displays, bags and even their signage. Overnight, this polychrome city turned monochrome.

As it turned out, the colour restriction inspired creativity. Formerly, Thais had owned few clothes in the unlucky hue of Rahu. Suddenly, office ladies had to turn up for work in a little black cocktail dress. Football fans could at least wear the pied strips of Germany or Newcastle United. Soon every shop mannequin donned black and white outfits. Those unable to afford a new wardrobe were initially scolded on social media, then allowed to pin a black ribbon. It sparked a revival of clothes-dyers, who pedalled around sois with tins of black dye.

Fashionistas evolved a mourning ensemble that melded style with respect. Matrons who'd competed in vivid silk formalwear, now appeared in ankle-length, long-sleeved, high-necked couture of finest black fabric, offset by pearls with a silver diamond brooch in the shape of the late King's numeral nine. After the cremation, Bangkokians were urged to wear "polite colours" in a long, slow return to normalcy. "Lifestyle gurus have come up with their own ideas of what polite, just-out-of-mourning Pantone colours one should adopt," columnist Atiya Achakulwisut remarked. Only in Bangkok could black be so colourful.

above: **The Chulalongkorn University colour is pink because it's named for a king born on a Tuesday.**

Blossom Season

Every hot season, Bangkok bursts into bloom, when flowering trees colour parks, roads and gardens. Lumpini Park alone spans the spectrum: from the shocking purple orchid tree (*chong-kho*), through delicate mauve Thai bungor (*salao*), wispy red Flame Tree, and orange-flowered copper pod, to yellow sprays of Burmese rosewood petals.

Thais could have their own *Hanami* – the festival of viewing cherry blossom (*sakura*) that has swept across Japan each spring for over a thousand years. "Thailand actually has a lot more variety [of flowering trees] than Japan with their *sakura*" says botanist Yongyuth Chanyarak. "If only we knew how to make people appreciate it better."

Thais travel to Chiang Mai to view the Wild Himalayan cherry erupt in boughs of pink in mid-January. Now Bangkokians are becoming aware of their own mini-*hanami*. Pink trumpet trees (*chomphu pantip*) flank the Chatuchak and Suan Rot Fai Parks and Kasetsart University's Kamphaeng Saen campus in Nakhon Pathom, which sprout clouds of pink in mid-April. Photographers love to snap their sweetheart posing amid the carpet of blooms on the grass. Similarly, while tours go to sunflower fields in Saraburi, Bangkok has a field of them by Satree Witthaya 2 School on Kaset-Nawamin Road that open their petals in March.

Bangkok had a vast green canopy that has been hacked into fragments. Still, there are concentrations of certain blossoming species. Flame trees ignite, April to May, down Ratchadamri Road and Khlong Phadung Krung Kasem. It took the embassies along Witthayu Road to save its stately raintrees (*jamjuree*), planted by the philanthropist Nai Lert. Their crimson rake-like stamens flutter from August to February. The best interlocking canopy of giant raintrees lines the public grounds of Chulalongkorn University, which names its Jamjuree Building and Jamjuree Gallery in its honour.

The median strips of Bangkok highways are usually the domain of pruned bushes and tired saplings, with many ripped out for overhead trains. But some have mature avenues of flowering greenery, notably the glorious frangipanis bisecting Charoen Rat Road. As frangipani were named *lanthom*, and sounded like the Thai for sadness, they were planted in funerary *wats* and considered unlucky. Later the tree was renamed *leelawadee*, so now all can enjoy its playful waxy blooms of pink or white.

Coloured petals attract pollinators by day, but after dark white-flowered shrubs and trees – jasmine (*mali*), champak, bulletwood (*pikul*) – become fragrant and use their petals for nighttime pollination. The popular Chinese box trees (*dok gaew*) – fully grown or clipped into hedges – erupt most months with diamond-shaped petals that smell of almond.

Most dramatic are the golden shower trees (*ratchapruek*), which cascade with tiny round yellow petals. Also called *dok khoon*, this cassia is designated the National Tree, because it symbolises both Buddhism and royalty, being the hue of the Buddhist flag and the day colour of Kings Rama IX and Rama X. Its bright yellow chandeliers bloom profusely through April. Santichaiprakarn Park wreaths its old fort in this blossom, while thousands of saplings run the length of the eponymous ringroad, Thanon Ratchapruek.

The peak period of efflorescence is March, the windiest month, when trees distribute their seeds. Aerodynamic seed pods have such self-propelled, auto-germinating ingenuity that Yongyuth calls them "the most technically advanced spaceship."

top: The *ratchapruek* 'Golden Shower' cassia tree is the national tree and blooms in April.

above: Red flame trees still line the Phadung Krung Kasem canal.

Sacred
Organised belief

"Welcome to Buddhaland!" proclaim billboards at Suvarnabhumi Airport, where the luggage hall is lined with temple murals and travellers pay homage to a gilded Buddha shrine. At check-in, stand statues of *yaksha* giants; in Departures, painted sculptures of deities pulling a *naga* serpent depict the Churning of the Sea of Milk. In a land where nine in ten are Buddhist, Suvarnabhumi is a religious showcase.

How faith is actually practised can be seen in the taxi ride to town. A Buddha image sits on the dashboard, often accompanied by figures of a great King, a Hindu god or a Chinese deity. Amulets rest over the speed dial, while multicoloured scarves bind the steering column. Drivers have magical tattoos; patriotic flag stickers frame the windows. The expressway to town passes several mosques and a couple of churches. Arrival in Bangkok reveals a city of various beliefs, that venerates the nation and a semi-divine King.

The City of Angels is one of the world's 'thin places' – a Celtic term for locations where the gap between heaven and earth so narrows that the divine animates the mundane. At dawn, monks pad barefoot on the gritty streets to receive alms. Householders make offering to the spirit house on their land.

In a thin place, spirituality isn't confined, but filters daily life. Bangkok has so many ways to pray: thousands of *wat* (temples), countless shrines, and a sacred spot on each vehicle or plot of land. The talismans and coloured scarves tied around trees are just the outward signs of a vast occult subculture, from consulting a fortune teller to casting spells.

One reason for Bangkok's friendly reputation is the tolerance of diverse beliefs. This long history is clear from the crucifixes and crescents atop many river landmarks. Religious minorities are most visible in the arc from the old International Quarter of Bangrak through to Sukhumvit. Closer than any *wat* to my home are 15 churches, six mosques, a Sikh Gurdwara, two Hindu temples, seven Hindu statues at Ratchaprasong, an altar to Prince Chumphorn, a spirit tree decked in dresses, and Tubtim Shrine's garden of phallic fertility offerings.

Buddhism's reputation for coexistence with other beliefs has lately taken a knock in some countries, but in the national slogan, 'Religions' is plural. Bangkok keeps to the Middle Way, hosting a huge range of faiths. The syncretic local beliefs are more receptive to inclusive religions than to monotheism, as we can see in the role of Hinduism, and the low conversion rate to Christianity. Tolerance worked due to allowing religious freedom within enclaves as long as they conform to the broad Thai umbrella. Sub-sects also mix well. Sunnis flock to Nana's 'Soi Arab,' which is owned by an Ismaili Shi'a family. Seventh Day Adventists co-run the Vegetarian Association buffet nights with Sikhs.

Thai Buddhism uses heightened sensation to impart its ultimate goal, which is to extinguish the craving for that very sensuality. The Dharma is a set of mental tools to end suffering; the method is to quench desire through self-mastery. While good works are "Applied Buddhism" within daily life, Thais extol monks for doing hardcore denial of worldly things on their behalf. Ordination is a vow to obey 227 precepts, many being denials of sensory desires.

People perhaps feel a need for eclectic beliefs, because the national school of Buddhism, Theravada, is so strict.

left: **A Sino-Thai boy dresses as the Buddha in a procession at the Hokkien Vegetarian Festival.**

above: **Twin boys with top-knots pray before the pre-dawn tonsure-cutting ceremony at Devasathan.**

Brahmin

Bangkok's smallest ethnic and religious minority wields huge cultural influence. In an ancient tradition, Siam's hereditary line of Brahmin priests conducts rites for court, city and commoner. Led by the Phra Maharajakhru Asdacharya, Bangkok's 15-20 remaining Brahmin priests earn a palace retainer. They crown kings, and officiate at the City Pillar, and royal cremations.

For the public who offer donations, Brahmin priests bless weddings, homes and new businesses ventures, as well as installing spirit houses. To the sound of conch-shell horns and hand-held drums, Brahmins scatter flowers over a table laden with pig's heads, boiled eggs and fruit speared with sticks of incense. For all of these rites they divine astrological timings.

Myth holds that the Indian Brahmin caste was created from Brahma's mouth to instruct mankind. Predating Hinduism, Brahmanism's scripture, the Vedas, offers secular guidance, too, from administration to medicine to yoga. Brahmins Indianised Southeast Asia nearly two millennia ago. When Ayutthaya conquered Angkor the Siamese brought back Angkorean Brahmins and appropriated the Khmer belief in a *devaraja* (god-king).

After the Burmese destroyed Ayutthaya, King Taksin replenished the priesthood with recruits from India. So did King Rama I, who built them a Devasathan (place of the gods) in the centre of Rattanakosin. Its iconic Giant Swing represents Mount Meru, the symbolic hub of the universe.

Brahmanism faced decline with the end of absolute monarchy. King Rama VII cancelled the annual swing rite in 1935 as too dangerous, and its empty, 25-metre-high frame was replaced in 2005. Many Brahmin ceremonies weren't held for decades until some were revived, such as the Royal Barge Procession on special occasions, and the Royal Ploughing Ceremony each May, when Brahmins predict the harvest from the foods chosen by a pair of Brahmin bulls.

An ancient song played at the Royal Ploughing Ceremony, the 'Ballad of Lady Naga', shows how patriarchal Brahminism merged with Thai matriarchal animism. In India, Brahmanism prevailed over Buddhism, but here, despite theological contradictions, they became symbiotic. At any event with a Brahmin ceremony, their rites will be preceded by chanting from Buddhist monks. A convention also arose that Brahmin priests first ordain as a Buddhist monk.

above: **A Brahmin priest conducts the blessing of a business, in this case the Museum of Floral Culture.**

left: **Brahmin elders accompany the top Agriculture bureaucrat, in Brahmin robe and hat, during the Royal Ploughing Ceremony on Sanam Luang in May.**

top right: **A Bangkok governor joins a Brahmin to tie a sacred scarf to the Giant Swing, after it was restored.**

Adopted from Sri Lanka many centuries ago, Theravada means 'Teaching of the Elders' and offers orthodoxy and meditation as the path to Nirvana, which only a few perfect individuals can achieve. In the other Theravada lands of Cambodia, Laos, Burma and Sri Lanka, recent civil wars have enabled Bangkok to assert itself as the Theravada metropolis.

The earliest Buddhist influence here, fifteen hundred years ago, was the Buddhist school that called itself Mahayana (Great Vehicle), based on its belief in saint-like bodhisattvas – enlightened beings who forwent Buddhahood to help others. Chinese immigration revived Mahayana, though the similarities have enabled Sino-Thais to embrace Theravada too.

The 'Asian tiger' boom years of the 1980s and 1990s saw a more open expression of Chinese-Thai beliefs, leading to a boom in the worship of the Bodhisattva of Compassion, in his female incarnation Guan Yin (Kwan Im in Thai). A giant shrine in Chokchai 4, Lad Prao, shows her with a thousand arms. Even Theravada *wats* and home altars can have a statue of her in white flowing robes. "Bangkok is such a lonely and dangerous place, and people don't trust one another anymore," says Charoen Wongpiyachetchai, a Christian who likens Gwan Yin to the Madonna. "Mother Goddess Gwan Yin makes me feel protected." *Wats* also memorialise iconic recent monks in statues of bronze or lifelike wax with bristly hair, and sell miniatures to devotees in a kind of sanctification that created bodhisattvas and made lucky Daoist deities out of ancient Chinese generals.

Many rituals have an element of social networking, from weddings and funerals to ministers making offerings at a shrine upon starting a job. Blessings of a new building or the launch of a project such as filming a movie, held at an auspicious timing, involve a Brahmin ritual with pig's heads and conch-blowing, followed by chanting from an odd-number of monks. The lead monk then splashes holy water and ties white *sai sin* thread from a Buddha image around the property like esoteric energy wiring.

Popular Thai Buddhism is fragmented even within its Theravada mainstream. Leaders have never been able to impose one doctrine or liturgy. The devout follow favourite monks, whose loyalties and teachings pass down through lineages of masters. Teachers carry an aura of sacredness – whether from school to masters

Today's busy Brahmanical calendar is handled by a dwindling number of priests. Brahmin extended families have declined from 80 in the 1920s to eight. When officiating, they wear white *rajapataen* suits, gowns and pointed hats, but are otherwise free to dress how they like, marry and pursue a career – though they can't eat beef, nor cut their hair, which is gathered into a bun. Ever fewer sons ordain (*dhavichat*, being 'twice born'), which can only be done at the 15-day Brahmin lunar New Year around December. "I used to wish [my father] were a businessman so that I wouldn't have to take on this duty," reflects management graduate Pakorn Wutthipram. "But since nothing can be done, I'll try to do my best."

Pakorn studied on an Indian state scholarship at Deem University near Chennai, the home of Brahminism. So did Sisada Rangsibrahmanakul, who ordained at 18, but became a video game programmer. "For me, ordination was like a natural progression," he said. "like entering adulthood."

Another age threshold is marked by a Brahmanical hair belief: topknots (*juk*). Each January Devasathan holds a pre-dawn tonsure-cutting ceremony that transits a child (typically at 7, 9, 11 or 13) into adolescence. Peer pressure now makes this non-fashion hairstyle quite rare. *Juk* also show how Brahmanism merged with indigenous beliefs. As with the white Brahmin wrist strings that Thais believe bind the *khwan* (life essence) from straying during illness, sleep or stress, they came to believe that a *juk* likewise binds the *khwan*. In a sense, Brahmins are Thai society's topknot, a tiny top caste who bind a modern Buddhist Kingdom to its ancient soul.

Senses 99

below: **A Bangkokian ordains for a month at Wat Pathumwan.**

below right: **A sculpture at Suvarnabhumi Airport shows the Churning of the Ocean of Milk myth.**

right: **Multiple busts of King Rama IX at Chang Chui art centre, showing the revered monarch in military uniform, coronation crown, monk's robes, jubilee regalia and an international suit.**

of arts, crafts and esoteric shamanism. Followers recharge this crucial relationship at least annually when they pay homage in *wai khru* ('worship guru') ceremonies.

With the monastic bureaucracy divided by rival groups, charismatic monks found cults that appeal to niche congregations. The ascetic Santi Asoke group run vegetarian restaurants and promote recycling. It became politicised through its adherent Chamlong Srimeuang, who became Bangkok governor and later a Yellow Shirt protest leader.

Most dramatically, the Dhammakaya sect appeals to urbanites by choreographing mass spectacles with thousands of monks and white-dressed laity collecting funds. "The problem of Dhammakaya is not so much what it teaches – very few Buddhist temples in Thailand do not cash in on superstition – but its gigantic size, extensive reach and its grand ambition," says Buddhism campaigner Sanitsuda Ekachai. "Its rise to prominence stems from the clergy's failure to speak to the middle class and respond to their needs." In 2015, its then-leader conveyed a message from the afterlife of Steve Jobs, before claims of links to Thaksin led the junta to besiege its temple in the northern suburbs, which looks like a flying saucer.

What's sacred keeps changing. The 1990s boom ushered in deification of King Rama V, lately joined by veneration of King Rama IV, both as icons of Thai development. It also became trendy to pray to Trimurti (the god who combines Brahma, Vishnu and Shiva). In the 2000s came cults of the 'Living Arahant' (an enlightened Buddhist monk); Pi Siew, a Chinese lion-like talisman; the Jatukam Ramathep amulet; then *luk thep* sanctified child dolls.

People outside the traditional rural and court audience of official Buddhism find sympathetic deities in the Hindu pantheon. Thus, artists venerate Ganesha; women, gays and *katoeys* are drawn to Kali and Uma Devi; and businesspeople worship Lakshmi for prosperity. Earth Mothers recur in Kwan Im, Nang Kwak (the beckoning lady), and the logo of the Democrat Party, Mae Thoranee, who wrings floods from her hair to wash away the demon Mara.

In reaction, purists try to remove the accretion of folk beliefs and superstitions. In 2017, the junta put a ban on *wats* selling amulets. The urge to rationalise the irrational leads to pundits calling Thai religion 'syncretic', a mix of parts to disentangle, rather than accepting the tangle as the religion. For clarity it's tempting to deconstruct bits of popular religion into categories like 'Hindu influence' or 'spirit worship.' Yet to ordinary Thais, all of it combined is 'Buddhism' – a reflection of their multifaceted identity.

Many surveys find Thailand is among the world's most pious countries, at 98% of the population calling themselves religious. One reason is that belief is embedded in Thai identity. "People think someone who doesn't have religion is not civilised," explains Nasa Saze, a Thai Buddhist who went to a Catholic school. "Thais will answer quickly without thinking that they are (mostly) Buddhists… but they aren't really into it. Many have their mixed beliefs… they don't study too deep about religion."

By bringing belief into everything, they bring everything into belief. Wat Takian in Nonthaburi is known for its Transformer guardians and basement of shrines where you enter via a tiger's mouth. At Wat Pariwat, the main Buddha image is supported by a statue

of David Beckham, while mosaic guardian sculptures include Pikachu, Batman and a pistol-toting Che Guevara.

"Thailand might not be as religious as you think: no legal enforcement of any aspect of Buddhism; alcohol is widely consumed; cheating is widespread; the majority rarely go to the *wat* if at all," says translator Suttichart Denpreuktham. He reckons the pious image comes from religious education and eclectic Buddhist festivals. Formerly a government propagandist, he says that Thai religiosity "has more to do with nationalism rather than philosophical aspects of religion."

'Religion' is one of the three official pillars of Thainess, along with 'Nation' and 'Monarchy.' Although never designated in any constitution as the state religion, Buddhism is protected and sponsored by the king. Portraits of the royal family beam from ceremonial arches and shrines both inside and outside buildings, with vast decals covering a façade. Families of Brahmin priests, resident in Siam for centuries, conduct royal rituals. Festivals re-enact the divine roles of royalty within Buddhist and Brahmin rites, from the annual Royal Ploughing Ceremony ahead of the rice-planting season to the Royal Barge Processions.

Bangkok Kingship entwines two religious concepts of monarchy: Dhammaraja from the Sukhothai era (1248-1438), and Devaraja from the Ayutthaya era (1350-1767). Drawn from Buddhism, a Dhammaraja is a 'righteous king' who performs good works. That resonates in royal development projects, donations during crises, and support of modernity, exemplified by Kings Rama IV, V, VI, and IX.

Ayutthaya adopted Hindu Devaraja 'divine kingship' from the Khmer Empire, along with sacred design elements and the *rajasap* court language broadcast nightly on the Royal News. The godlike ruler Prince Rama of the city Ayodhaya (an avatar of Vishnu), rides Vishnu's mount, the man-bird Garuda, the emblem that heads all state documents, as well as royal vehicles. The monarchy lends prestige to places or ventures labelled 'Under Royal Patronage,' or displaying the Garuda crest of the Royal Warrant.

The royal court dance, *khon,* is a performative offering, and its blessed masks are sacrosanct. *Khon* relates Rama's tale, *Ramakien*. In 2016, the Culture Ministry protested a tourism video of Rama's adversary, the demon king Thotsakan, cooking a pudding, because his godlike status demands more dignity. In the *Ramakien*, the top demon can't die on stage, just as justice isn't seen to be done to top-level offenders.

The nation-state has tried very hard to sacralise itself. Few Thai things are more worshipped than the national flag, which is raised at 8 am and lowered at 6 pm with great solemnity to the strains of the National Anthem, while the public stands to attention and soldiers salute.

Nationalism has led to a state version of Buddhism. "Recent times have seen the rise and dominance of… 'Bangkok' Buddhism, a homogenised form of the religion promoted vigorously… by a succession of governments in order to buttress political authority," writes Sophorntavy Vorng.

The monumental Buddhist complex in the Western suburbs called Putthamonthon was built by the Phibunsongkram dictatorship

Ratchaprasong Shrines

Several growing phenomena meet at Ratchaprasong intersection: highways, Skytrains, shopping and Hinduism. The crossroads of Thanons Ratchadamri, Ploenchit and Rama I earned the materialist label Ratchaprasong Shopping Square, because it's ringed with high-end malls. It also receives pilgrims to its six Hindu shrines. What started as an impromptu local rite became a must-do for Asian tourists. Maps on walkways under the confluence of BTS lines make it easy to do the circuit. In a borrowing from Buddhism, Thais walk it clockwise.

Start with the most important, Than Tao Maha Brahma, nicknamed the Erawan Shrine because it's the spirit house for the previous Erawan hotel built on this site. Accidents that plagued its construction ceased on 9 November 1956 after a soothsayer Rear Admiral Luang Suwicharnpat advised that a shrine to Brahma the Creator be erected to placate the spirits of the land. Devotees still celebrate that day as the shrine's birthday. Foundations were laid at the 'wrong' time and without asking 'permission' to use the name of Erawan, three-headed elephant mount of the city's presiding deity Indra. Ever since the shrine has become a go-to god for Asian luck-seekers, leading Uighurs to bomb it in 2015 because gets Chinese visitors.

Near-identical Brahma shrines appear throughout the city. This one matters so much because its cross roads location makes it a kind of city pillar for the capital's downtown. As at the real city pillar, Lak Meuang, those with granted wishes return to offer thanks by commissioning traditional dancers to perform, which they do over fifty times a day. Karma costs B260 for two dancers, B710 for eight. A foundation donates the shrine's huge proceeds to charity.

All that concentrated power overwhelmed the neighbours, who counterbalanced with other Hindu deities. Erawan was kept in check by the green-skinned Indra Shrine next door at his namesake mall, Amarin Plaza. Trumping everyone, on the corner opposite Erawan the former World Trade Center erected the Trimurti Shrine, the combo of Hinduism's holy trinity: Brahma, Shiva, Vishnu. The same mall also erected a Ganesha Shrine. Across the road, the adjacent Big C mall installed a gold-domed shrine to Uma Devi. At the corner facing Erawan, Gaysorn Plaza luxury mall venerates the goddess of wealth, in a Lakshmi Shrine on the roof. Come the Divali Festival, Hindus invite Lakshmi, Vishnu's consort, into their homes with lamps to bring prosperity.

Along Ploenchit Road, the Intercontinental Bangkok Hotel displays a stylised Vishnu Statue on a decorative plinth. Depicted riding on Garuda's shoulders, it has since acquired a working altar. In addition, the Garuda Royal Warrant emblazons the Police Hospital. And next door the Police Headquarters has another Vishnu Shrine, this time riding the multi-headed *naga* serpent.

In a shock on 21 March 2006, an apparently insane man smashed the Erawan Brahma with a sledgehammer, though we don't know if he'd been commissioned, as bystanders beat him to death. Afterwards, devotees continued to venerate the boarded-up empty shelter. As to rumours that someone powerful had his amulet cast into the replacement, or obtained part of the original statue for himself, ask Brahma.

The Ratchaprasong cosmology changed again in 2007 when Central moved the Trimurti Shrine to be beside Ganesha. Trimurti had meanwhile become a hybrid deity for Bangkok youth. This three-god combination, might not specifically be a god of love, but since 2003 thousands of young devotees worship the shrine daily in the search for a partner, especially a foreign mate. To sense the power, flexibility and endurance of Thai Hinduism, turn up at the most auspicious time, 9.30 pm on Thursdays. Masses of young Bangkokians dressed in red bring red roses, red candles and red incense to utter mantras at the altar. As a way of bringing together like-minded lonesome romantics, it sure beats speed-dating.

top left: The Erawan Shrine to Brahma, seen from the Skywalk.

above: A devotee makes red offerings to the Trimurti Shrine, believed to be a 'god of love.'

to host a world conference for the 2500th anniversary of Buddha's Enlightenment in 1957. A later dictator, Sarit Thanarat, turned the management of monks into a giant bureaucracy under a supreme Sangha Council. It was led by a 100-year-old Supreme Patriarch, who was succeeded by the abbot of Wat Ratchabophit at a sprightly 89.

While the national motto says the state defends all 'Religions' in plural, Buddhism is the de facto faith in all but name. That's less of a barrier to Taoist Chinese than to Muslim Malays. Each time the constitution is rewritten (averaging every five years) activist monks try and fail, to enshrine Theravada as the National Religion.

The current reformist zeal responds to the spiralling materialism after the economic booms and crashes since the 1980s, which brought social divisions into open revolt. Actually, religious revivals aren't new. Bangkok's founding brought on a bout of puritanism, since the fall of Ayutthaya was blamed on decadence.

Another spurt of fervour responded to the prudish disapproval of Western missionaries during the reign of King Rama IV. That's when Siamese started to wear high-collared, long-sleeved shirts. Missionaries were appreciated for the technology they brought, and since then generations of top families educate their children in missionary schools to this day.

While priest-teachers haven't been allowed to indoctrinate the kids in Bible studies, they instilled notions of sin. Many of today's elite went to the likes of Mater Dei, St Gabriel's, Bangkok Christian College or Assumption University, which explains some of their moral assumptions.

Thai monks are not all the same. They used to be split between town and country orders, and that divergent outlook survived a major reform by Prince Mongkut before he became King Rama IV. While spending the reign of his younger half-brother as a monk, he found that popular religion was based on handed-down tradition and deviated from scripture.

King Mongkut commissioned a new definitive scripture, then founded the monastic order of Thammayut, literally "yoked to Dharma." He had himself and others re-ordained under reformed rules, akin to a born-again Buddhism. Thai monks remain split between the Thammayut, who dominate the Bangkok establishment, and the majority order of Mahanikaya. This mirrors many modern dilemmas between purity and pluralism.

above: **On a canal near Taling Chan, Wat Kor has spray-can murals by two French graffiti artists.**

The pessimistic fear that Buddhism needs saving from decline is inbuilt to the religion's own law of impermanence. Moreover, the Thai fad for amulets originates from votive tablets buried beneath stupas to be unearthed as time-capsules which would re-propagate the Dharma should Buddhism fade.

Tellingly, the fetish for amulets has grown as the number of monks fell from 6 to 1.5 million between 2000 and 2010. Most ordinates robe-up for just a few days, some for the month that jobs allow, even fewer for the full three-month Rains Retreat. The memorisation of scripture bores the social media generation, while the shaving of head and eyebrows disrupts their fashion identity. Some wonder if it's the best use of their son's time, but it does earn merit for the mother, who can't ordain.

Female monks are prominent in Myanmar, but the Thai order died out centuries ago. Any *wat* visit shows that older women are the main congregation, yet the Sangha elders refuse to re-establish the female monkhood. So *wats* remain, in Sanitsuda's phrase, a "feudal patriarchy." Women may only take some vows as white-robed *mae chi* nuns of lesser status. Disenchanted women pursue Buddhism in other ways. Some lean towards Mahayana and venerate Kwan Im; many meditate in retreats led by a monk, *mae chi*, or New Age guru.

It's not easy being an urban monk, gathering alms on hazardous roads as ever fewer devotees rise early to donate food. Condominium dwellers are physically removed from that duty, which is kept up by street-level market-goers. But even they give less than before. They've seen monks wielding smartphones and getting out of luxury cars, so may assume no alms are needed. Trust in monks has also been eroded by sex and money scandals, as well as a decline in younger monks' scholarship.

Enter any *wat* and you can't miss commerce. It starts outside the gate with displays of cellophaned orange buckets of monk offerings. Inside the gilded gates, fundraising booths entreat the faithful to pour wax into a candle mould, sign a roof tile, or clip banknotes onto a 'money tree'. Abbots manage vast amounts of property and cultural patrimony without training or supervision. Donating money or goods "makes merit." It's like spiritual savings deposits to overcome karmic debts of yourself or others to reduce suffering in the next life.

"Monks and devout Thai Buddhists are not the victims of the trappings of a material world but often the greatest purveyors of stuff," says Buddhism expert Justin McDaniel. Money has been a source of many monastic scandals. Most notoriously, a monk was pictured luxuriating in a private jet. A candidate for Supreme Patriarch was sidelined due partly to the museum of antique Mercedes-Benz cars at his temple. Other disgraced monks have been caught dealing drugs, taking lovers or fathering children.

Bangkokians atone for their consumer lifestyle with bursts of renunciation, encouraged by the state. One of today's go-to monks, Phra Prayuth Payutto, calls this "sense-restraint". Often, the abstemious go without alcohol during Buddhist holidays, while the 'Rains Retreat' from July to October has gone from being a time of monastic study to a 'Buddhist Lent' for lay folk. Perhaps half of Thais forego beef despite eating pork, rationalising that it's wrong to kill bigger animals. The Sino-Thai Vegetarian festival in October is more about denying sensual pleasure to the tongue than it is about celebrating vegetables.

"Attachment to sensuality conduces to family love, to diligence and energy," said monk-philosopher Buddhadasa Bhikkhu. "People then go off in search of pleasure – in the form of colours and shapes, sounds, odours, tastes and tactile objects – which is what keeps them going. Even merit making in order to go to heaven has its origins simply in a wish based on sensuality. Taken together, all the trouble and chaos in the world has its origin in sensuality." Taking such views as their cue, bourgeois puritans blame the trouble and chaos of Bangkok on its sensuality. The self-described City of Angels is going through its latest fit of righteousness. If Sin City seems less lively of

104 Sacred

right: The artist Pannaphan Yodmanee paints concrete in mural style, with subversive commentary. In *Ruin 5* she has a 'Last Supper' style array of religious figures, including Buddha, Krishna and Kwan Im as well as Jesus. Seen here at 1Projects Gallery.

below left: Cute ceramic dolls of monks and *mae chi* (nuns) in a uniforms shop in Phra Nakhon.

late, that's partly due to moralist curbs on its streetlife, nightlife and sexlife. Moral panic also explains the crusades against "tastes and tactile objects," from alcohol and tobacco to spaghetti-strap tops.

In the past, folk Buddhism was less purist and more practical. Temples used to be community centres, hosting schools, clinics, sports and entertainment. Many temple schools remain, but secular society has moved on. Now, most Bangkokians rarely go to the *wat* except perhaps on major holidays, funerals, and *ngan wat* (temple festivals).

On the main Buddhist full-moon festivals, devotees conduct candlelit processions around temples. On such nights, Wat Pathumwan, overlooked by malls, attracts younger fashionistas who post selfies in glamorous outfits. It's also favoured for *hi-so* ordinations. "This is truly a wat for city people," says Art, a teacher who meditates at its Vipassana centre with in-laws who run a beauty clinic nearby.

Faced with modern tastes and Dhammakaya's innovations in spectacle, the state invents new ways to herd the flock. They promote Visakha Bucha as the Buddhist Day to rival the global fame of Christmas or Ramadan. Now a Visakha festival lasts a week, full of exhibitions, conferences and broadcast sermons. A procession accompanies a relic or Buddha image to Sanam Luang as a focus for pilgrims.

Since the 2000s, they've urged Thais to mark Western New Year's Eve in midnight meditation at a *wat*, and over a million do. To similar success, January 1 became a day to tour an auspicious nine sacred sites in the old town, including a church and the Jao Phor Seua (Chinese Tiger Shrine). Here, a secular foreign party has turned into a rite of righteousness.

Another extension of puritan attitudes is the campaign to clamp down on uses of Buddhist imagery which are deemed disrespectful. Photographers can't resist snapping orange-robed novices, while hotels stage alms giving as a spectacle. "Please don't look at me as a toy of culture," pleads monk Phra Kovit Khemananda. Posters across tourist areas warn that "Disrespecting Buddha is wrong by law." One activist group, knowingbuddha.org, warns against putting a Buddha image in the middle of a table, or inappropriate depictions, from tattoos to Buddha Bar decor.

It's illegal to export any Buddha image, not differentiating national treasures from copies cast in pink resin. As Buddha images and amulets can't technically be 'sold', their 'price' is a 'rent'. As any visit to Tha Phra Chan or other amulet markets confirms, there's a vast informal business of temples, amulet markets, monks and occultists. The NCPO junta banned *wats* from selling religious objects, alongside purges on activities like alcohol and premarital sex, as being regarded as Buddhist defilements.

This revival of religious zeal responds to fears of social decay. "Do not believe in traditions simply because they have been handed down for many generations," states knowingbuddha.org. At issue is the future of the informal culture and syncretic folk Buddhism. "Religious arts and cultural aspects will be organised to mobilise the society," reads the mission statement of the Culture Ministry, which seeks to foster "immunity" against sin. "Young people will be encouraged to be ordained and study morality during a summer vacation. Support will also be given to Islamic morality studies."

This bureaucratic guard of tradition sees itself as a bulwark against the practice of the

wider public whom they regard as uneducated. "They [bureaucrats] belong to a profession which used to be very influential but which is being rapidly marginalised as the society becomes richer, more commercial, and more open – and they have nostalgia of an idealised past," wrote columnist Chang Noi. "The results have been both hilarious and tragic."

Appointees of this caste who consider themselves *khon dee* (Good People) dominate organisations like the Thai Health Foundation (TCH). Rich with funding from 'sin taxes' on alcohol and tobacco, TCH uses sponsorship to turn almost every youth, arts or community event into a platform to preach morality. In this light, the eviction of street markets and informal culture becomes a moral crusade.

"Many Thai… still believe in spirits and don't have *panya* (wisdom)," a TCH official, Yok, told writer Daena Aki Funahashi. "This is the problem. If you don't have mental immunity… you are just like a *khwai* (buffalo) who lives only to gratify its senses… At TCH, we try to educate the masses, but they don't listen!"

"Mental immunity" and *panya* crop up in slogans and are crucial to a prevalent Bangkok mindset. According to traditional cosmology, the Dhammaraja king at the top of the pinnacle has a panoramic vision of existence, and vision grows narrower the lower you go. Therefore, the Good People in the upper hierarchy have enough *panya* to be specialists – in, say, health or bureaucracy – while those of lower status with little *panya*, languish in ignorance. Good Governance requires 'Good People'. Full stop.

This is a form of karmic fundamentalism, counters critic Paisarn Likhitpreechakul. Thainess "is underpinned and its social order buttressed by a sort of karma theology, turning Buddhism on its head," he says. "The Buddha would immediately recognise Thailand as a modern variation of the Brahmanistic caste society which he rigorously criticised," Paisarn continues. "Other laws don't matter. No need for social justice or human rights, because those who are underprivileged are so because they are karmically inferior and lazy – nothing to do with our economic and social system." Historian Thongchai Winichakul, calls the Good People idea one of the "spells" under which Thailand is run.

Such attitudes puzzle outsiders who perceive Buddhism as a pacifist, harmonious philosophy rather than as a religion with social baggage. That international image was partly cultivated by foreigners. who adopted choice bits of the doctrine, especially meditation.

The first people to set about the simplification of religious identities were proponents of the British Empire. A transcendent image of Buddhism and Hinduism emerged from the Interfaith Movement of the late 19th century. Ever since, rinsed versions of Eastern religion have appealed to secular foreigners who seek spiritualism. The accompanying focus on gurus has led to the celebrity status of the Dalai Lama and Thich Nhat Hanh.

Meditation tourists have flocked here for silent retreats since the 1980s backpacker wave. They tend to enjoy the ritual as culture, but baulk at believing the liturgy. In a parallel phenomenon, middle-class Bangkokians also began to go on meditation retreats rather than frequent the *wat*. That distillation of Buddhism into a practical method for modern living has circled back. It now influences the way urbanites idealise their faith as a science, shorn of its superstition.

Those who study meditation in Bangkok, Thai and foreign alike, often prefer the retreats that talk in lay terms. The Vipassana insight meditation they learn is not the concentration meditation (Samadhi) that Thais historically did. The pioneering centre of Vipassana is Wat Mahathat, off Sanam Luang, where a monk named Ake Asapa revolutionised Thai meditation. After World War II, he invited two Burmese monks, adepts of the 'New Burmese Method.' Their techniques of mindful sitting and walking have since become Thailand's main form of meditation. Many Bangkokians also follow Burmese spiritual leader SN Goenka, whose Vipassana style also spread worldwide.

Many white-collar Bangkokians traipse down South to do the silent 10-day retreat at the hermitage of Buddhadasa Bhikkhu, a modernist monk who energised urban Thais with his notions of Buddhist economics. Along with Ajahn Chah, who emerged from the austere Thai tradition of Forest Monks, to be championed as pure by modern Thais weary of monastic scandals.

Bangkok hosts frequent exhibitions on Buddhism in malls, museums, and festivals. Most go for a minimalist 'edutainment' approach full of abstract special effects and slogans, but devoid of how Thais practice their faith, with older folk traditions being portrayed as impure, even un-Thai.

Many wats remove the artefacts of messy worship outdoors. You can still pray before the Buddha images, but candles, lotus and incense are banished to small altars outside, thereby lowering the fire risk while keeping the *wat* tidy and clean. This 'thin place' remains enchanting, but at times can feel a thinner experience.

All in One

Bangkok, ever the exuberant hybrid, counters the puritst trend in Buddhism. Lek Viriyahbhun, a Sino-Thai banker and industrialist, was an ecumenical philanthropist who sought "to introduce Asian traditions and cultures... to instruct those who have been lost in scientific prosperity, which causes them to be materialist and worldly-minded." Near Pattaya, his ornate Sanctuary of Truth is a temple to all religions being about one truth. At Muang Boran (Ancient City) near Bangkok, he reconstituted a theme park of Thai landmarks at in the shape of the country. It bedazzles with sculptures of every imaginable Thai, Hindu or Chinese deity – as well as some you can't imagine, like the Ananada Fish of the Cosmic Ocean.

Within Greater Bangkok, Lek built the Erawan Museum inside the body of a three-headed, three-storey bronze elephant. Under a stained-glass ceiling, you climb a staircase of teak and Baroque mosaic to a lift up one of the rear legs. Inside the elephant's back, Lek's Buddha statue collection sits in alcoves lining the altar beneath a heavenly mural, where you can contemplate the Middle Way. In Bangkok, that means allowing space for every belief and diverse ways of worship, just in case.

left: **Maximalist styles of Buddha and Rahu images at Wat Khun Chan in Thonburi.**

above: **The new minimalist meditation retreat style at Suan Mokkh Bangkok at Chatuchak Park.**

above: **The three-headed elephantine Erawan Museum.**

Senses 107

Muslim-Thais

The expressway from Suvarnabhumi Airport reveals a sub-culture few expect of 'Buddhist' Bangkok: a series of mosques from Thailand's biggest religious minority. The road crosses a suburban crescent of Malay-Thais arcing from east to north around communities in the city centre from all over the Islamic world. Minarets share the Chao Phraya riverbank with chedis and some church spires all the way upstream to Ayutthaya. Onion domes dot Bangkok's longest canal, Khlong Saen Saeb, between the old town at Mahanak and the new town of Minburi, while quaint Shi'a chapels stud old Thonburi. Bangkok is not just the world's main Theravada Buddhist metropolis, but also one of the biggest Muslim cities in mainland Southeast Asia.

Headcounts are elusive. Most surveys put Muslims at about 5% of Thai citizens, but they have the highest birthrate in a land of declining population. Thailand's Islamic Committee cites 8%, and the Foreign Ministry claims 12%. Bangkok city has around 500-600,000 Muslims. As the conurbation spreads into provinces where many Muslims live, the Greater Bangkok total would be higher. There are also residents who are registered upcountry, the 12% of tourists who are Muslim, and long-stay visitors from the diasporas.

Bangkok has always been part-Muslim without much tension – and their presence is getting more visible. Since the late-1990s, Thai-Muslims have held such posts as foreign minister, parliament speaker, interior minister, army chief and coup leader, as well as a Thai head of ASEAN. In 1998, Thailand joined the Organisation of the Islamic Conference.

The capital has Thailand's most liberal Muslims, mainly dressed the same as other modern Thais. There's also social and ethnic depth. Certain city enclaves cherish their historical lore, like the Cham silk weavers of Baan Khrua who worked with Jim Thompson, or the Mesjid Jawa community founded by the gardeners brought from Java by King Rama V. In peri-urban Nong Chok and Minburi, some Muslims have become wealthy landlords as their fields sprout factories or housing. Yet parts of that area still feel like languid Malay *kampongs*, where farmers in batik sarongs raise songbirds in elaborate cages and tend to their paddy, cattle, and cantilevered fishing nets.

Muslims lived here before it was the capital. Makassars fleeing their abortive coup in Ayutthaya settled at the area still called Makkasan. Refugees from ruined Ayutthaya moored their houseboats near Thonburi's oldest mosque, Kudi Tonson, which dates from 1689, or became the only Muslims living inside newly walled Rattanakosin at Masayid Chakrabongse Mosque, first built in 1779. In an early Bangkok needing more people, Muslims became a fifth of the city.

Kudi Tonson was Shi'a, since Persians had arrived even earlier than the Chinese, during the Sukhothai era. Later they helped govern from the time of Ayutthaya's King Narai. Descendants of the 16th-century trader Sheik Achmad Qomi produce ministers and leaders to this day through the Achmadchula family and its Buddhist branch, the Bunnag clan. Persians also influenced Thai style, from the pointed windows of Wat Chong Nonsi to the translucent gown worn by Brahmin priests and by graduates when receiving their degree.

The Chularatchamontri (or Sheikul Islam) is the formal leader of all Thai Muslims. The rank was inherited by

108 Sacred

the Achmadchula line until 1932, since when he's been chosen from the 99 per cent Sunni majority. As most Muslim immigrants came from the South or Southeast Asia, their moderate Sufi customs were absorbed with Siamese ways into a hybrid subculture.

The Southeast Asian tendency to prefer human relationships over doctrine means they celebrate Mawlid on Muhammed's birthday, a festival banned in Saudi Arabia as an idolatrous innovation of the 11th century. Royalty opens the Ngan Mawlid Klang festival at the Chularatchamontri's compound, which showcases arts, fashions and foods, and sells clocks to show Mecca time.

Siamese traditions were porous. The Central Thai dance form Lakhon Chatri – performed as an offering at both the City Pillar and Erawan Shrine – has Malay roots. Southern Thai festivals feature Manohra dance and Nang Talung shadow puppetry, which both came from India via Java and Malayu. *Likay* folk opera was born in Rattanakosin's Pom Mahakan community. Based upon Malay chanting, with Burman costume, *likay* opens with an *ork khaek* (Muslim Prologue) by a man in an embroidered black vest and *topi* cap.

You can track the phases of Thai Islam through the design of Bangkok mosques. Initially, they had to conform to Siamese rules. Thonburi's ornate Shi'a 'mosques' take the term *kadi* or *kudi* (as in Kudi Jeen community) from the Thai *kuti* monk residence. At Bang Luang Mosque, the gable has Sino-Thai floral patterns, while the imam's golden carved *mimbul* (pulpit) looks like a Rattanakosin window.

Globalised trade after 1855 brought in foreign styles. Some applied forms from their homelands – such as the tiered roof of Jawa Mosque – but most referenced big Muslim powers, hence the Mughal onion domes, Ottoman minarets or Arabian forms seen by Hajjis in Mecca. Most in vogue was European taste, as in the Malay-Renaissance fusions at Sai Kong Din Mosque or the timber merchant mosque at Bang Or. A neo-classical Mosque in Sampeng served Chinese Muslims from Central Asia. Dawoody Bohra family from Gujarat confected the Seifi Mosque (aka Tuek Khao), in the Venetian Gothic style seen at Government House.

"During the reign of King Rama V, Muslims from several countries became Thai people who were proud to Muslim, rather than being attached to their own ethnic concern," says professor Adis Idris Raksamani. "Thai became the medium of communication between ethnic groups. With the idea of *ikwat* (brotherhood), Muslims in Bangkok from several ethnic groups related to each other as a network."

The green of Islam is dusky like desert shrubs in the Middle East, but in the tropics it turned turquoise, as at the multi-ethnic Haroon Mosque. Sited by the French Embassy and the Customs House, Haroon

top left: The congregation at Haroon Mosque during Ramadan.

left: The gable of Kudi Khao in Thonburi is in hybrid Sino-Thai style.

top: T-shirts showing the identification of Bangkok Muslims with Thainess.

Senses 109

was founded by a French sailor convert, whose descendant is an elder there. It's the only place where the imam preaches the *khutba* not just in Arabic or Thai, but in English. The onion-domed hall still welcomes Muslim traders, especially from the Indian subcontinent. At Ramadan feasts on mats downstairs, the congregants sport an array of bright Malay *niqabs*, orange Pakistani beards, white Arab robes, blue Tuareg turbans, taupe shalwar-kameez from India and vivid Nigerian prints.

During the era that Thai nationalism enforced assimilation, Islam in the wider sense went through a revolution in countries that were colonised. Mosques became neutrally modern with revivalist touches, like the filigree windows on the rebuilt Chakrabongse Mosque.

In 1926, a Cham from Ban Khrua, Direk Kulsiriwad, pioneered Thai Islamic reform. Inspired by the movement of pure, scientific Islam from Egypt, he sought to purge it of corruptions from colonial and Ottoman rule. Direk advocated translating the Koran into Thai, and challenged the authority of *ulemas* (theologians) and the Chularatchamontri. "Muslims in Bangkok have turned to the basics of their religion rather than to local traditional beliefs," adds Adis. "The new style represents the identity of global Islamic culture rather than any particular ethnic culture." Thus many ornate old mosques get replaced by ones devoid of decoration. Others use abstract geometry to expresses Islamic ideas, such as the Brutalist forms of Thailand Islamic Centre in Khlong Tan, or the parabolic curves of Darul-Aeihasan Mosque in Bang Phlad.

At quaint old *surao* (Muslim chapels) in Thonburi you'll hear wistful anecdotes of pride in settling here so long. Talking to worshippers in a modern mosque at Phrakhanong can entail earnest discussion of transnational Islam, with admonitions to convert. "You're very lucky to find us all here at Ramadan," said one Thai with a long beard and a forehead callus from repeated prayer-prostration. "Normally we're spread out all over the world. I will put you in touch with good Englishmen like yourself who've become our brothers. We have many good friends in Dewsbury."

Localised traditions are being lost regionwide, from Kelantan to Java. "The dress code adopted by the 're-islamicised' persons in Thailand copies the fashions of Kuala Lumpur," writes Michel Gilquin in *The Muslims of Thailand*. "For want of an Islamic-Thai ethos, and given the numerical weight of Yawi speakers and southerners... the Malay world provides their models."

The editor of the indie youth zine *Roti-Mataba*, Davud Lawang, spots a trend: "Muslim Thais are forming their own sub-culture. You will see more and more teenagers dressed in the Islamic orthodox way." Reader Farida was moved to become a contributor. "The stories made me feel comfortable being a Muslim," she says. "I used to be too shy to wear the *hijab*. Now I hardly remove it."

Some new-generation Thai Muslims find answers in the global *um'ma* of believers. Given the separatism in the Deep South, this alarms defenders of Thai harmony. Some websites have been shut for fear of conflict. In 2019, Bangkok universities were told to monitor Muslim students, provoking a public outcry.

Loyal Muslims feel nervous at calls to make Buddhism the state religion, while the new Parliament design is a mandala under a *chedi*. Most took the establishment side in the political division and appreciate the monarchy being patron of all religions. King Bhumibol is revered for sponsoring Mawlid, development projects, and translation of the Koran as *Algura-aan*.

Bangkok's Muslims are still rather conservative. They earn slightly lower income than Buddhists, but there's no job discrimination; rather that's due to Muslims favouring traditional education and lifestyle. Their *yaan* remain mostly houses, many wooden, as it's easier for neighbours to keep an eye on behaviour in the *soi* than in the corridors of tower blocks. That low profile means scant coverage in the wider culture.

"Thai movies hardly contain any Muslim characters," writes film expert Kong Rithdee, who lives in the Haroon community. "But at every screening we'll see Muslims smiling happily veiled and skullcapped and

far left: **Songbird keeping is a Malay hobby, seen in Khlong Tan.**

left: **The Nonthaburi band Baby Arabia, playing at BACC – and a wedding party near you.**

bottom left: **Pulled tea vendors from Pattani, in Chatuchak Market.**

sometimes hand in hand with Buddhist Thais, in an MV of the anthem." With director Panu Aree, Kong has written documentaries on Thai Muslims, with *Khaek: In Between* on current identity, and *Baby Arabia*, about a band from Nonthaburi, who infuse weddings and mosque fairs with ululating vocals over churning riffs. Their horror feature, The Cursed Land, explored how Khlong Saen Saeb was dug and settled by Malay captives from the Deep South.

Khaek is an ambiguous label that lumps Muslims with Hindus, Sikhs and Malays. A Hokkien word for 'guest', *khaek* honours those settlers, just as Muslims extend hospitality as an article of faith. But 'guest' also implies outsider, and *khaek* gets used as a pejorative. The official term 'Thai-Muslim' stresses religious difference, whilst obscuring ethnic identity. Malaysia, Singapore and Indonesia push multiculturalism, with public holidays for minority festive days, but Thais have gone for assimilation, with no national holiday on Eid.

"Thailand's nation-state construct leaves virtually no room for the Malays," writes journalist Don Pathan. I've heard one Bangkokian whisper about his family's historic status in the South, while another was puzzled that his roots were Malay. Faint are the traces of those brought here after defeats of Patani's ancient city state, which had previously been the Hindu kingdom of Langkasuka. Patani was finally annexed in 1906 and its rulers rehoused in Banglamphu. Ever since, its palladiums, the Seri Negara and Seri Patani canons, have stood in front of the Defence Ministry. Bangkok Museums barely touch Muslim history, although some like Museum Siam and Rattanakosin Exhibition Hall mention specific old communities.

The umbrella of Thainess omits minority histories, but it does enable people to move forward in practical ways. Quietly, Bangkok has become a major world hub of halal. The annual Bangkok Food Fair has a vast halal hall. It's not just the *roti* and biriyani stalls. Pork aside, 70% of Thai food has the halal diamond logo to reach local and export markets. A Bangkok firm has devised the most effective halal-production monitoring system, which draws people from the Middle East for training and is "a decade ahead of any system from Malaysia."

Thai hotels design for Muslim tourism, with facilities like prayer room, halal kitchen and a separate pool for women. Market-goers delight in the acrobatic tea-and-coffee juggling of the *chaa chak* (pulled tea) vendors in Pattani costume. The OTOP scheme (One Tambon One Product) marketed village (*tambon*) crafts with professional quality. Then came OMOP (One Masayid One Product, a Muslim scheme using local crafts to empower women.

The Nana clan – Hanafite Sunnis from Gujarat – created a destination for Muslim visitors in their Nana estate at Sukhumvit Sois 3-5. Known as 'Little Arabia', it teems with Egyptian restaurateurs, Nigerian shoe shops, and emporiums selling frankincense and musk. Rich Gulf families often stay at Nana for its Bumrungrad Hospital, which cornered a market in medical tourism by catering to Muslim needs, with waiting areas resembling Bedouin tents.

A visitor from Jakarta to the Haroon community marvelled at how well-kept and welcoming it is. "We have two Hindu families here, and Chinese too," says Sakharin, a mosque committee member, while setting the stage for an Arabic band. "It's all fine, no conflict." On the Hajj day of goat sacrifice, relatives enter the *kubor* (graveyard) to spread garlands and petal carpets upon the raised earthen mounds, in a ritual evocative of Thai and Hindu flower culture. Bangkok has shown how ethnic and religious diversity can be transcended through shared sensibility. "Our cultures are fused because we came from the same roots," says Southern pundit Rattiya Salae. "We used to be Hindu together; what's the point of quarrelling with one another now?"

Senses 111

Sixth Sense
Being animist, fearing the supernatural

Down a blackened *soi*, off an even blacker canal in the old town, a clunky projector beams an outdoor movie to three old men and a dog. The film isn't in their honour, but for the resident of a mirror-tiled shrine, who gazes at the screen – as well as up, down and across the canal – with each of his four faces. The statue's spirit had granted a wish. Now in a rite known as *kae bon*, the lucky guy was repaying his vow with an old romantic comedy.

Same deal at the spirit house on each plot in the city, where citizens entreat the guardian of the land, Phra Phum Jao Thii, to bring fortune, a lover or some such luck. Beyond the standard daily payoff for protection – a garland, betel set and glass of green drink – some wishes extract a higher cost. Bangkok's busiest sacred site, the Erawan Shrine, is the spirit house erected to placate demons who caused death during construction of the previous Erawan Hotel in 1956. Human dancers get paid to perform by those who return with wishes granted. A friend's neighbour did *kae bon* by dancing naked at 3 am before her spirit house after a lottery win.

Untold millions of effigies populate this city, whose citizens have a relationship to them all, from lacquered statues of gods to plastic models of their servants. Beneath the modern tastes and Buddhist-Hindu values, Bangkok is animist. Supernatural beings (*phii*) dwell in trees, water and other natural features, but also buildings and bridges. Animism also animates objects – usually likenesses and symbols of the spirit – via holy blessings or *sayasaat* (black magic). Believed to be watching, those spirits are capricious.

An intuitive 'sixth sense' imparting power over material and spiritual realms has always excited mankind. Rationalists and doctrinaire Buddhists condemn it as a hallucination, but animists act on that premise, so it has real consequences. It matters that drivers take their hands off the wheel to *wai* the Erawan Shrine as they turn that busy corner. Thai religion is eclectic, even contradictory, for a practical reason.

Bangkokians wield a bewildering range of spiritual solutions, based more on need and relationships than dogma. Theravada is the moral benchmark and unifying thread, but even that splices with choice bits of Hindu, Brahmin, Chinese and Mahayana religions. The state credo is already multi-faceted, but overlays a far more ancient and still evolving pantheon of nature spirits, ghosts and ghouls.

To make sense of these beliefs, rationalists seek to disentangle the parts, rather than accept the tangle as the religion. They call Thai faith syncretic or hybrid, but those labels don't capture its vitality. Instead, think of it as a "repertoire" of spiritual practises, says Justin McDaniel, who sorts it not by creed, but by lineages of masters, whose followers act like "fanclubs."

Each cult might be national, regional or within a clique. Spiritual fans buy the holy merchandise, pin up the posters, and dress up for events at the *wat* or shrine. And like music fans, they can be fickle. Cultists juggle their gurus and fetishes as the supernatural scene keeps morphing. Voodoo dolls made of bound string were a creepy fad, which faded once cute copies turned up as key fobs. After a charismatic master dies, his line may wane while others intensify.

Animism's strength is its lack of consistency. An oral lore that responds to phenomena, it helps manage life's travails. Believers seek confidence from a lucky charm, a sympathetic ear via a medium, or advantage through a spell.

It's less of a religion and more a way of life. Making offerings is as routine as paying bills or feeding the cat.

To engage with things you can't see, you must amp up your other senses. Amulets are made to be felt, whether sculptural, embossed or tattooed. Shamans press gateway points on the body, like the third eye, nape or lumbar spine. Elixirs of herbs and animal oils bewitch through scent. Possession causes people to retch, contort and speak in an alien voice.

The white *sai sin* strings seen on wrists help corral the 32 personal angels (*kwan*) we are born with in case of ailments when they stray. Tied by a monk or spirit doctor, *sai sin* show how Buddhism and animism blend. Other kinds of *phii* that pass through permeable souls may disturb the *kwan*. It's like the Buddhist notion that we get on better with those of similar karmic debt. "Often people feel unstable with a spirit because their levels clash," explains Ajarn Kiaow, a tattoo master in Bang Phra. He claims that meditation can lift you to the spirit's level and strengthen the mind against demons.

Bangkok's spirit world reflects its sensory one. In daily life, Thais need luck, protection or help – so they turn to heavies with 'dark influence.' Bad spirits extort gifts like garlands as effectively as human mafia demand 'tea money' from vendors. Bar owners give oranges to their Chinese floor shrines, and whisky to officials on their rounds.

Just as big people get minions to do tasks, ordinary folk can recruit spirits. "You don't take care of them; they won't take care of you. Stuff will go missing. You'll fall ill," explains Watcharapol 'Jack' Fukijdee, host of a phone-in show, Ghost Radio on The Shock FM. "It's all about beckoning angels to take care of you."

Commissioning a charm or curse may lure others to do your bidding, like turning someone into an lover by plying them with a philtre. Traders symbolically lure customers by dangling a tiny fishtrap from the ceiling or enshrining a statue of the Beckoning Lady, Nang Kwak. Animism is empowerment for less effort.

From the menu of occult options, Bangkokians favour fortune tellers (*mor doo*). Costumed in leopardskin fabric and clashing colours, they sit at tables or on mats at renowned sites like Wat Mahabutr or beside the Huay Khwang Hindu shrine. In the basement market of Centrepoint Charoen Krung, a mage views palms and a crystal ball in a gypsy tent swathed with spangled red gauze. High-society prefers a more discreet setting such as the astrology booths in the Montien Hotel. But if their predictions upset the powerful, they can face a bad fate.

Soothsaying techniques run from reading tarot to reading moles. Seers consult the prediction tables in the *Phrommachat* manuals, which are illustrated like medieval fables. Even within each method, say numerology, *mor doo* glide between local and foreign traditions.

left: **A scary ghots set at a haunted house sideshow in a temple fair at Wat In.**

right: **An illuminated Thai spirit house at a Chinese shrine in Khlong San.**

above: **Offerings at the main spirit house in Siam Square have the cute character of the area's young clientèle.**

Senses 113

Astrology, to most of the world, means either the 12-monthly Western star signs or the Chinese 12-yearly animal horoscope. Thai astrologers mix both of those, along with Indian weekday cycles and indigenous divination in a blend of lunar, solar and planetary systems. If one forecast is unfavourable, there's another to try. Supplicants are invariably told to make an offering, because masters can't accept a fee, just a donation of a figure ending in a lucky nine.

Gauging what divinities want is like pandering to those with seniority; spirit temperaments and tastes reflect human foibles. Flattery works, as in the mantra uttered to each deity, and offerings of miniature servants. Spirits want to be entertained, hence the figurines of dancers and musicians on most shrines. For *kae bon*, besides film shows, a spirit can be treated to being a guest at a human party. At the shrine to Chuchok, a hideous beggar spirit with a gorgeous wife, devotees give thanks for granted wishes by commissioning Coyote dancers to gyrate in hotpants.

Bangkok spirit houses must keep pace with upgrades in human accommodation – or else the spirit might enter the better property and do poltergeisty mischief. One in Sathorn Soi 1 takes the form of a classical mansion. As the only Thai city with ultra modern towers, Bangkok's getting postmodern spirit houses of opulent marble, geometric glass, or minimalist chic. Spirit house effigies declined from ceramic to cheap plastic under industrialisation, but urbanites are now buying finely-costumed dolls for *hi-so* shrines. Bangkok's land spirits, like their transient human lodgers, are becoming middle class.

Well, not all of them; indigenous spirits remain marginalised like traditional human folk. When spirit houses come in pairs they're called *phra phum chao thii*, showing how folk and Indic traditions meld together. A higher masonry temple on a pedestal enshrines the gilded figure of Phra Phum, which is Sanskrit for 'Deity of the Land.' In a lower house of wood with six stilts dwells an elderly couple embodying *chao thii*, the ethnic Tai term for 'Lord of the Place.' Phra Phum's mansion gets modernised with the materialism of high status people. The folksy stilt house stays unchanged, echoing the admonitions to peasants not to live above their status. The gulf between classes is hardwired not just into karma, but also into animism.

Thai spirits, like Thai humans, love to snack, and they're believed to eat for the duration that the incense burns. From basic rice and water, offering cuisine rises through bananas and bottles of Yakult to gelatinous desserts sprinkled with grated coconut. Stallholders in Pak Khlong Talad Flower Market sell packs of betel quids to suit the bygone tastes of ancient spirits; altars to King Rama V receive cigars and shots of cognac, his known favourites. The Soi Nai Lert shrine to Chao Mae Tubtim (Lady Ruby) acquires strings of pearls and red-tipped *palad khik* penis charms.

far left: **A *luk thep* sacred doll, seen in a fortune telling shop in a market. It's the cutest form of the *kumarn thong* (golden boy) spirit assistant.**

left: **An effigy of *kumarn thong* rendered in a scarier way than usual, like its original form as a roasted foetus.**

top right: **The filth ghost Phii Kraseu, whose trailing innards have been portrayed as plastic tubing in this display at Warehouse 30.**

"Red Fanta is far and away the most popular," says Chatgaew, an offerings vendor. "One Fanta will get you ten wishes." Colour coding affects many spiritual decisions, from the hue of a spirit house to the scarves tied around its pillar. Red liquid is oft seen as a polite substitute for blood sacrifice, but can be paired with green Fanta. The green is more likely linked to Indra or the planetary colour of Wednesday. Or such offerings may just be a cute gift. "Angels want fruit and Fanta and other nice things," says Ghost Radio DJ Jack.

The same spirit can manifest as a deity or a demon. Traders invite Kumarn Thong (Golden Boy) to possess a child doll with bags of gold and silver. He's a genteel version of the *luk krok* – a child slave spirit made by roasting a human foetus, as was done by the hero of the 17th-century epic *Khun Chang Khun Paen*. It's not just literary history; in 2010, some 2,002 aborted foetuses smuggled from clinics were found in a Bangkok *wat*. A distressing sight, they remain potent tools of *mor phii* (spirit doctors) like the now-imprisoned fake novice Naen Ae who grilled them for politicians. "Some *mor phii* like to have ghosts around," explains Mill, a medium of the god Vishnu. "It destabilises things, so it attracts customers to solve problems, which is good for business."

For refined Bangkokians, 'child slave ghosts' are déclassé, but in 2016 celebrities led the craze for a cute update known as *luk thep*, or 'child angel,' in which the spirit is invited into a mass-produced doll. Blessed with *yantras* on their forehead, the life-sized plastic babies cost thousands of baht and require pampering with designer outfits and food at restaurants. Neta Grill offered a Luk Thep buffet at children's prices, while Thai Smile airline sold tickets and food for the "spiritualised" dolls, but insisted they take window seats and buckle-up.

Luk thep reveal the fragility of this transitional era. They emerged in the aftermath of the 2014 coup, while the 2006 coup set off a craze for amulets of the deity Jatukham Ramathep. In planes above Bangkok, monks blessed Jatukham amulets, which had mushroomed from a Southern obscurity into a national craze, from special editions for millionaires to 79-baht plastic medallions daubed with neon paint.

Tha Phra Chan Amulet Market offers the latest styles, such as figurines inlaid with blobs of coloured glass, a chubby version of Nang Kwak, or cutesy deities moulded in glittery

resin. The community of dealers and collectors shoot the breeze as they peer through loupes to check the authenticity and details they've read about in occult magazines and websites. The trade has grown from old town markets to occupy whole floors of suburban malls like Pantip Plaza Ngamwongwan.

The wildest range of fetish objects line the path to Chatuchak Weekend Market from Saphan Kwai BTS. Mixed in with antique statues and bric-a-brac, lurk jackets bearing *yantra* diagrams, spirit knives with handles of antler, and natural oddities like meteorites or gnarled vines carved into auspicious beasts.

The supernatural is a factor in why Thailand has the world's most dangerous roads. Traffic laws and consideration of other road users pale beside karmic fate, which infers that accidents only happen to those who deserve it. Since rules, patrols and news report fail to curb reckless driving, drivers use protective amulets as spiritual road insurance. It's been shown that shrines at danger spots are more effective than warning signs. At Pathum Thani's Si Yaek Roy Sop (Hundred Corpse Crossroads), drivers pay touts at the traffic lights to go over and drape a garland at the shrine.

Most Bangkokians fear ghosts, and many claim to have seen them. Famous ghosts include the children and nannies who play in the pavilion of Silpakorn University from

Senses 115

when it was a palace garden, and the "red lift" in Thammasat University where students were murdered by rightists in the 1976 massacre.

Places of death make all humans uneasy, but the vividness of Thai spirit belief makes hauntings a practical concern and a real estate risk. Silom is the CBD, yet its middle stretch remains undeveloped because buildings erected on parts of its old Chinese and Western cemeteries have failed or gone unlet. Similarly, Bangkokians prefer modern buildings and furniture over preserving heritage and antiques for the reason that old stuff is likely haunted.

There are over a hundred genres of *phii*, mostly unreincarnated spirits stuck in the hierarchy of Buddhist heavens and hells. The most malevolent are ghosts of the violently killed. *Phii* are often used as a socialisation lesson for children, who are still raised with warnings that ghosts will jog your arm if you carry a knife pointing forwards, or water ghosts will pull you under if you swim alone.

Placating benign spirits so they don't become vengeful is a matter of daily precautions through offerings, prayers, amulets or necromancy. Exorcising requires a monk or a *mor phii* to coax out the spirit with good magic. Even Bangkok's British Club did it in the 1990s.

However, Bangkok's most famous exorcism was that conducted by the renowned monk Luang Phor Toh of the superstar ghost Nang Nak, who terrorised the village of Phrakhanong (now in the city) nearly two centuries ago. This female ghost tale has since been dramatized many times for cinema and TV.

Animism contributes to Thailand's soft power. TCDC and other creatives laud animism as an undervalued source of Thai ingenuity. Bangkok ghost movies are a hit across Asia. Some have even been remade by Hollywood, such as *Shutter*, about apparitions in photos. The supernatural shares a lot with pop in its fads, fans and spinoffs. In turn, it infuses popular culture, from lucky 9s in car plates to a *hi-so* Nang Kwak with Birkin bag and Jackie O shades.

However, animism's downsides can ignite contention. When a turtle had an operation to remove over 900 coins tossed into its pond for long life, social media railed at the ritual abuse of nature, such as trapping and releasing eels or birds. "It doesn't matter that [it] makes little sense and is illogical. They are products of our mindset stemming from our animistic belief system," writes journalist Wasant Techawongtham. "[Animism] has its own logic and at one time served as a guide post for society. Instead, the system has been bastardised just as our belief in Buddhism has been bastardised. The culprit is materialism. All the above practices are not parts of Buddhism, and yet they have found support among large numbers of monks."

There's no denying the money swilling around temples, cults and amulets. But the transactional nature of Thai spiritual practices is inseparable from the ancient offering culture. "Monks and devout Thai Buddhists are not the victims of the trappings of a material world but often the greatest purveyors of stuff," McDaniel points out. "Rarely are things ever removed from shrines; abundance is valued. Piles of stuff show how much a shrine is honoured."

Ridding altars of their stuff is a rather Puritan impulse. In the past, Christian missionaries dissed Thai faith as idolatry. As a result, in seeking to be *siwilai*, high officials trained in Christian schools have for over a century adopted that disdain. Similar zeal urges anti-globalists to save 'authentic' faith from materialism.

Bangkok certainly tests modernity's effects on belief. Animism just kept on riffing with technology, with digital fortune telling and lucky phone numbers. Charismatic monks now mass produce their amulets. Like many religions facing change, mainstream Buddhism has become defensive. Those ashamed of the paranormal rail at its defilements in the "anti-ignorance" Facebook and YouTube group called 'FuckGhost'.

Reformists reject animism as detracting from Buddhism's scientific rigour. "There are beliefs involving magical artefacts and secret procedures… beliefs that on rising one must pronounce a mystical formula over water and then wash one's face in it," said the modernist monk Buddhadasa Bhikkhu, who turned many middle class against superstition. "This sort of thing is completely irrational. Many people professing to be Buddhists cling to these beliefs as well and so have it both ways."

People, of course, want it both ways. Upgrading karma takes several lifetimes. Animism tempts with shortcuts. It's also a coping strategy for precarious Bangkok life, whether saving a marriage or launching a firm. "When the financial stakes are higher, there is a greater need to rely on supernatural powers," says Professor Suwanna Satha-anand. "The need is even greater when the rules of the game are not clear."

The rules of Thai power have always been unclear, so politicians often consult fortune tellers. Generals purportedly saw the Burmese blind dwarf astrologer E Thi about timing a coup. News pops up of influential figures burning salt as a curse. New ministers pray at shrines on their first day at work; each regime reconfigures plants and objects at Government House, whilst denying it's for geomancy.

Throughout Bangkok's protest battles, both sides resorted to black magic. Yellow Shirt leader Sondhi Limthongkul was reported to have placed used sanitary napkins around the equestrian statue of King Rama V allegedly to counteract spells that blocked it from emitting energy. Red Shirts donated blood that was poured, in a mock-Brahmin rite, on the gates of Government House. The stockade of the Red Shirt encampment near my house had a giant phallic charm to repel any siege. When it was raided by soldiers, arson burnt out Zen department store, which observers later noticed was the only building at Ratchaprasong without a spirit house.

Animism can also be a force for good. Local beliefs bond communities together, while animism helps preserve urban ecology by protecting trees. Residents of Sukhumvit Soi 28 saved a big old pink trumpet tree by tying sacred scarves around it as monks do to stave off deforestation.

The supernatural can sit uneasily with sanitised Thainess, though selected spirits do get promoted. Hanging dresses in haunted trees for the wood nymph *nang takian* at sites like Khlong San Market gets criticised as backward. Yet the goddesses of rice (Mae Phosop), water (Mae Khongka) and transport (Mae Yanang) are acceptable faces of folk belief.

Bangkok even has official animism. Statues of four spirits guard the phallic City Pillar. To the three original spirits (Phra Lak Meuang, Phra Seua Meuang and Phra Song Meuang), King Rama IV later added the presiding national spirit, Phra Siam Devathiraj. On the Pillar's April 21 anniversary, officials present *bai sri* offerings of folded banana leaf, which the public pulls apart so as to take bits of leaf as lucky charms for their home altars. Whether the spirit is formal or informal, you can never make too many offerings.

top left: **Devotees at the shrine to Nang Nak rub** *takian* **wood to discern lottery numbers, and relay it live online by phone.**

above: **A fortune teller in Bangrak Market uses indigenous mythic archetypes, as well as foreign divination.**

Senses 117

Animist Shrines

The higher status the sacred site, the more homogenous its style. Yet the irrepressible world of animist Bangkok keeps surprising with its outlandish shrines and even wilder offerings. There's a vast pantheon of Thai spirits, but each encounter is particular to a place, with its own origin tale and folksy charm.

SNAKE SHRINE

Near Holland Beer house on Rama II highway, devotees at a shrine offer plates of eggs draped with rubber snakes. A construction worker dreamt that a pregnant snake asked for a week's delay in building the road. The foreman dismissed his warning, but diggers then unearthed masses of dead snakes. Soon accidents befell the area and road workers mysteriously died, until a medium advised making a shrine and the mayhem stopped. Now people pray for luck at its altar of snake statues and woman effigies. Giant wooden cobras decked in strings of pearls flank full-size mannequins of parents and children dressed with snake crowns, who look even creepier than the serpents.

CHAO MAE TUBTIM SHRINE

Women hoping to conceive take penis carvings down a *soi* near Ploenchit BTS to this fertility shrine, dedicated to Chao Mae Tubtim (Mother Ruby). It was erected in the 1920s by the tycoon Nai Lert Sreshthaputra to placate the spirit in the old ficus tree in the grounds of his mansion. When word spread that Mae Tubtim granted a woman's wish to fall pregnant, the grounds attracted phallic offerings in stone and hardwood, many bound with multicoloured scarves. Either stylised or lifelike, some shafts lie cradled in the buttress roots of the tree; others stand upright, forming a penile fence. Devotees also bring the deity combs, pearl necklaces, and bunches of lotus and jasmine.

Thais worship phallic amulets (*palad khik*) for many kinds of abundance and protection. Some men sling them on strings around their waist, or dangle them from belts; male or female traders put them in shop tills. Not all approve. Bangkok has a history of trying to purge penis charms, with King Rama I expelling all phallic offerings from Rattanakosin *wats*. Historian David Wyatt noticed that no record exists where they went. Thais don't destroy old offerings, but place them under a sacred ficus tree. He surmises the *palad khik* were canoed along the main canal out of town and dumped at this tree, where the penis cult kept going. Since tourists discovered this and another phallic altar in a Krabi cave, penis carvings have been disappearing from both shrines. Whether they're stolen, or removed to save face, you can bet the penises will pop up again.

CHUCHOK SHRINE

Old men who snag comelier maidens than they deserve may identify with a shrine in the northern suburbs. Those seeking wealth and a hot lover can emulate an earlier lottery winner and go to Baan Chuchok on Ruam Pattana Road with a troupe of Coyote dancers. The bikini-clad women gyrate as an offering to the bearded, potbellied effigies.

Chuchok was a hideous old Brahmin beggar during the Buddha's past life as Prince Vessandorn. While Chuchok was away to make money, his riches earned from past good deeds were spent by a friend, who repaid Chuchok with his beautiful daughter.

"I own the most Chuchok statues in the world, over 5,000," said the shrinekeeper, Kung Kannika, in her daywear of spangly makeup, crown of flowers and diaphanous gown of clashing prints. "My house is full of money. All my Chuchok sculptures wear gold." Depicted with a begging bowl, the main effigies are draped in jewels, amulets or garlands of banknotes. In a cautionary tale, the hedonist Chuchok grew greedy until his gluttonous stomach exploded. Kung devoted her life to Chuchok after he granted her wish to recover from kidney disease. She also earned fame from her clinic of breast augmentation through vigorous mammary kneading. "My legal name is Madam Boob-slap na Songkla. My occupation is boob-slapping, face-slapping and bitch-slapping."

She also caters to gays and *katoey* pageant contestants. "This statue is homosexual," she says, pointing out a Chuchok with whitened skin and long black eyelashes. "Look at his rouged cheeks. You can tell he's a third sex."

A hundred-plus visitors per day pose for photos with Chuchok, their right hand raised and left palm upturned. "Of course this sculpture is real; there's no need to use some scientific scanner on him. You can just feel it," says Kung, who kisses the protruding chin of one tattooed, eighty-year-old statue that she calls Horny Daddy. "He's passionate about giving me money."

NANG NAK
Conscripts and would-be mothers make the pilgrimage to Wat Mahabutr for its canalside shrine of Bangkok's superstar ghost, Nang Nak. She's often named Mae Nak Phrakhanong after the village she haunted two centuries ago, which is now an inner suburb.

In the gallery of Thai ghosts, most feared are wraiths of pregnant women and the stillborn. This prototype of love is so jealous, it's lethal. Nak and her baby died in childbirth while her husband Mak was away at war. Upon his return their ghosts fooled him that they were still alive. Once Mak eventually noticed her malign powers and fled, she terrorised Phrakhanong until exorcised by Bangkok's most revered real-life ghostbuster monk, Somdet Toh.

Nak's shrine is busiest ahead of twice-monthly lottery draws and the annual military draft. Devotees slip letters of their wishes between the holy coloured scarves that gird three auspicious, hand-blackened *takian* trees. They offer dresses, cosmetics, guns and toys to gilded effigies of Mak, a shaggy-wigged Nak and two plastic dolls of her baby. They didn't replace the old baby that had been worn by the touch of devotees, just added a new one.

Nang Nak is no obscure oddity. She's attained fame in the phantasmagoria of Thai belief, alongside powerful gods and deities. Relatable as a totem of motherly protection, Nak happens to share pronunciation with the mythical *naga* serpent, which is one of the main indigenous deities of this region.

An occult magazine bears her name; countless films and TV series recount her tale, and the highest grossing Thai movie, *Pee Mak Phrakhanong*, was a spoof from her husband's perspective. Somdet Toh is revered in his own right as a master in folk Buddhism, whose portrait empowers amulets and statues. The *Jinpanjara Katha* chant he used to quell Nak has become a meme, available in print, encased in holy water or recorded as a downloadable ringtone.

EKAMAI TREE SHRINE
Dresses hung from the wizened boughs of an old tree indicate the presence of a wood nymph (*nang mai*), as seen at the mouth of Soi Suan Plu and in Khlongsan Market. Each tree shrine differs, but typically has a mannequin effigy in a shelter as well as offerings of dresses, shoes and accessories. The tree spirit cults show how animism reveres the natural world, for instance in protecting valuable resources. In the city, such beliefs resonate with rural migrants and traditionalists alienated by modern development. Among nymphs specific to certain flora, *nang takian* haunts *takian* (ironwood) trees, whose waterproof lumber is prized for boat hulls.

left **Serpentine effigies at the Snake Shrine on Rama II Road.**

top: **A cute doll effigy of Nang Nak and her stillborn baby, wearing other offerings.**

above: **Traditional Thai dresses hung in a tree indicate the presence of *nang mai*, the tree nymph who's known as *nang takian* when she's haunting a precious *takian* tree.**

Trance
Surrendering your senses to another being

Down a suburban On Nut sub-soi, a man writhes possessed by the millipede tattooed on his arm by Ajarn Neng, who dispels the trance with a sharp blow of air. In a shophouse off Wong Wien Yai roundabout, a pirouetting woman in white robes collapses before the tiger-print throne of a medium called Mill, who channels consoling words from Vishnu.

In many ordinary-looking neighbourhoods, you can find a *tamnak* (house of spirits) where people go to enter into trance. This vast occult subculture encompasses mediums, shamans and a middle-class cult of worshipping Hindu deities. Conducted mostly beneath the mainstream radar, it is obscure due to both widespread disapproval, and the confidentiality surrounding getting possessed. It's a grave act to surrender your sensory perception to that of a spectre.

In a city that retains animist beliefs, the bold go beyond propitiating spirits through offerings to more direct contact. *Raang song* (mediums) speak in the tongues of their adoptive beings. They may summon a known deceased person, but usually call upon a generic deity or historical figure using telltale postures and props. One female medium channelling King Taksin, struts with his black brimmed hat and sword. A Kwan Im seer swans in her billowy white gown and pursed-lips smile.

"My body has been used a lot by spirits, so anyone can come through – but they have to ask Vishnu first," says Mill of his principal spirit, who appears when Mill dons an embroidered gold cloak and mitre. "Vishnu's voice is deeper than mine; the Ruessi is very frail and I suddenly look old." He also channels King Rama V or Ganesha. One doubter sent seven spirits through Mill in an hour to test his veracity by asking financial advice. "Now Vishnu is not a human; he doesn't know the bank names, so Vishnu just said it's the colour: yellow. So the man went to Krungsri." That bank's logo is indeed yellow.

Devotees, too, can slip into trance. Involuntarily they take on the attributes of that soul, expressed through mannerisms, convulsions and interpretive dance. Many faint upon coming out of trance. Others bring them round by stroking their ears, then support their wobbly walk back.

Spirits apparently can only enter souls deemed 'permeable' – mostly assumed to be feminine, which is why most mediums are women, gays or *katoey* (also called 'Third Sex'). Buddhist ordination is believed to make a male soul impermeable, as can deep meditation. Monks are drafted in to quell spirits and exorcise ghosts – a bit like a crucifix repels vampires.

Males who can't channel spirits can instead follow a darker path as shamans who command spirits, whether by imbuing amulets, concocting love philtres, or activating the spell of a tattoo with a single hidden dot. "I don't get possessed by a spirit," says tattoo master Ajarn Kiaow at his wooden *tamnak* in Tha Phra. "I enable and prepare the person to receive a spirit and summon a spirit that wants to occupy that person." Kiaow can also subdue anyone reacting strongly to a spirit because his body energy is stronger. Each time one goes into fits or rictus postures, he can match the spirit's movements and tamp down the energy, usually by touching the head, arms and body, finishing by sliding his palm down their spine.

"I have 450 followers after only four years. I must *krob khru* [initiate] each one individually," says Kiaow, whose annual *wai khru* ceremony filled the *soi* to his wooden house with followers between 7 am and 3 am the next morning. "It takes a toll on the body."

Some holy men turn from Dharma to the dark side as a *mor phii*. By manipulating spirits they provide occult services. In an occult den, the supplicants contort into

left: **A woman entering trance under a medium channelling Trimurti.**

below: **The medium Ajarn Mill performing *krob khru* using a mask of a multi-face Ruessi hermit.**

demonic grimace expressions, eyes rolled back, to incantations in the shaman's menacing growl.

Social welfare is scarce, so Bangkokians may turn to the occult for personal crises or psychological problems. A woman at Ajarn Kiaow's kept slipping between histrionic fits and catatonic trance, as her tales of marital grief unfolded. Those who can't get through the system may seek out figures with influence – be that a powerful person or a potent spirit. Unrequited love may switch to devotion with a smear of *nam mun phrai* – a love philtre made from the chin fat of cadavers.

With such spells and curses being cast around, people seek protection, whether from amulets or counter-spells. A tattooed person in peril utters a mantra to activate the spell of the spirit protecting his skin. That moment of trance in a crisis provides a clarity that might

Senses 121

khom script) on her left shoulder from Noo Kanphai, a master based in Nonthaburi who now charges superstar prices. Thai starlets and their fans copied her, while white-collar workers also now sport traditional tattoos. *Sak yant*'s graphic strength appeals to design-savvy millennials as an ethnic niche in the global tattoo boom.

Posters warn tourists against getting tattoos of the Buddha, a depiction some Thais view as disrespectful. Buddhism is ultimately about self-control – the opposite of letting one's soul be manipulated by a spirit or shaman. Despite such disapproval, dedicated magazines and websites cover the supernatural, from exorcisms to spectral phenomena. Advertisements include accessories for the pro ghost handler, while the cover is often an advertorial for a spirit master. Fortune telling is accepted by most Thais, while mediums are more underground and tap into ancient cultural roots.

Bangkok mediums favour Hindu deities, reflecting their high status and the presence of Indian temples. This cult is most visible at the Navaratri Festival held each October when tens of thousands of devotees gather around the Hindu Temple in the Silom business district. However, mediums also channel indigenous spirits – for instance, enacting the Golden Boy's playful antics. At Lanna festivals in Bangkok, *katoey* mediums go into trance during the *fon phii* – a spirit dance accompanied by a Mon traditional band, just as experienced at shrines in the north.

The Chinese trance tradition is milder here than at Hokkien shrines in the South. The Phuket Vegetarian Festival features trials that can't be felt under trance, like scaling ladders of blades, walking on hot coals, or piercing both cheeks with multiple swords. That festival in Bangkok has much less mortification, but in the back room of a Hainanese shrine in Dusit stands a spirit chair where a medium sits on nail spikes.

Bangkok is home to hundreds of *tamnak*, which are typically a timber house where the guru lives above a shrine room painted red. *Tamnaks* draw a stream of devotees, often at night, with an influx of inducted followers at annual *wai khru*. *Tamnaks* are magpie nests of devotional objects. Besides standard images of the Buddha and royalty, you find Hindu, Chinese, and animist objects, plus enshrined keepsakes, like a Sai Baba calendar or a Chiang Mai panda souvenir. Supplicants pass tiger statues guarding the door, and crouch before the

save the day. For similar reasons, I saw one medium give another a dog pelt. "The dog is a vehicle for a high spirit so when somebody casts a black spell the dog skin protects him," one explained. "He writes the name of the person who does black magic on it so that the spell rebounds."

The revival of *sak yant* began in the 1990s with the *wai khru* in early March of the late tattoo master of Wat Bang Phra, just west of Bangkok in Nakhon Chaisi. Publicised as 'The Tattoo Festival,' it draws venturesome foreigners to the thrill of seeing massed trance. Mantras preached from the outdoor stage trigger many of the throng to roar or lunge into the actions of the beings depicted on their bodies – a pouncing tiger, slithering snake, doddering *reussi* – then maniacally rush the stage. Rows of soldiers grab the writhing, growling disciples and calm them by lifting them up and stroking their ears while monks spray holy water from hoses. They wander back dazed with no recollection, apt to erupt again if a mantra awakens one of their tattoo spells.

A spate of exhibitions and books has brought fame here and abroad to tattoo masters like Ajarn Neng. But submitting to a guru's spell is not a light decision. It may open a window of wisdom, as claimed, but can also seem like a cult.

Bangkok's middle class used to scorn *sak yant* as a superstitious protection for those in risky or low-status jobs. That changed when Angelina Jolie got a *haa taew* (five columns of mystical

medium's throne, decked in hermit style with leopardprint cloth. Half the room is taken by a stepped altar of painted masks and incense-smoked effigies decked in dusty scarves. Cloth *yantra* diagrams twirl from the ceiling, while the walls heave with animist illustrations and photos of the medium with spirit masters and VIP devotees. In the back room of one *tamnak*, I spied a gold-leafed human skull and a desiccated foetus for conjuring a boy-ghost assistant.

At a typical *tamnak* near Rama VIII Bridge, the resident guru Phor Trimurti has channelled Trimurti, the trinity of Shiva-Vishnu-Bramha, nightly at 9.19 pm since 1995, except on Buddhist holy days. His wife receives the Trimata spirit of their wives: Uma Devi, Lakshmi, Saraswati. At their *wai khru* each March, followers clad in white carry a Hindu effigy through the auspiciously decorated lanes, dancing and tossing petals to recorded Indian music and a live *phiphat* band. The next morning, after offering food to Buddhist monks and the deity, Phor Trimurti conducts a *krob khru*. Swathed in gnarled *rudraksha* beads, he daubs each follower's forehead in red, and holds over their head a mask of Ngoh the jungle spirit, or other mystical figures. They shudder, scream and jerk their hands into sacred mudras or claw-like gestures. A smattering of holy water calms their convulsions before Trimata's blessing sends them into another fit. "It gives people confidence," one devotee explains. "When infused by the spirit they feel they can achieve what they want."

As with any in-group scene, spirit handling became a circuit, then a commercial industry. Some *tamnak* sell paraphernalia, though other shops stock accoutrements for the Hindu spiritual lifestyle. Disciples open new *tamnaks* and lineages emerge that rival established others. "They always seem to war with each other," notes Ton, who worked one such shop. "When you have a *wai khru* they gather all their followers. But they all talk bad about the *tamnak* of another master. They say here we are more clean, more powerful, more lucky."

Like Bangkok art dealers who hand out their own leaflets at a rival gallery's opening, some mediums visiting rival *wai khru* often dance with Martha Graham flounce, introduce themselves and hand out invitations graced with their portrait. "We call it *samakhom khon song* (channelling society) and I don't like it," says Mill, whose business supplies *bai sri* offerings of folded banana leaf in shapes like giant *naga* serpents. "When they greet you, they invite you to their *wai khru* and then you have to go. And give them money– 100 baht up to 1,000." So the circuit turns into a pyramid donation scheme.

"*Tamnak* come and go. It's a trend," adds Mill, noting that people learned they can make money out of it, but that fake mediums who don't practice meditation or observe Buddhist rules will fail. "I teach my followers to channel by using meditation as a base, followed by Buddhist rules, plus techniques of tuning between spirits and our bodily elements of water, soil, fire and wind."

Overall, many believe, while sceptics suspect a scam, and some just feel it's gone too far. Costumed trance dancing can seem more cabaret than cabalism; channelling at times descends into chatting. Mass entrancement has been diagnosed as 'group imagination.' But you can never be too sure, as Kiaow points out: "When the hermit mask goes over your head, then you are under the protection of Ruessi, who can shield you against things you cannot see."

top left: **Tattoo master Ajarn Kiaow calms an entranced devotee using holy water.**

above: **A tattooed devotee of Ajarn Kiaow *wais* after being entranced by a spirit in his tattoos.**

Senses 123

Neo-Hindu

Each October, thousands of Bangkokians carry Hindu statues from their home altars to Silom's South Indian temple to be recharged with spiritual energy. They hold the effigies aloft at processions during the nine-night Navaratri Festival. It culminates with the presiding deity, Maha Uma Devi, and other gods being pulled in golden mobile shrines around the block. It's rare for city roads to be closed to cars, but then Ganesha is known as the Remover of Obstacles.

The senses are bombarded into an altered state from being jostled for hours amid disciples careening in rapture. Literally miles worth of garlands mask heady notes of incense, free curry and betel quid lime. Ears disorient through constant bell trills, speaking in tongues, and "om shakti om" loudspeakered on a loop for 12 hours. The white clothing of adherents gets spattered with holy water, milk from smashed coconuts, and red powder cast by the priests, who wear peacock feathers upon a metal *kavadi* canopy hooked into their flesh. Bursting the spell, rubbish trucks sweep up the no-longer-sacred trash, as believers head home, leaving the hardcore to meditate beyond midnight.

Navaratri opens the mind's eye to Bangkok's neo-Hindu subculture. Besides serving Indian-Thais, the city's Hindu temples draw Thai Buddhists, adding a new layer to their ancient observance of Brahmanical rites. "The sudden surge in the Hindu gods' popularity is based on a purely Thai adaptation of the original Hindu beliefs into the modern Thai environment and culture," says mythology expert Komkrit Uitekkeng. Wat Khaek also enshrines statues of Buddha and Kwan Im, so it draws Thai and Chinese luck-seekers, as does the Ganesha shrine at Huai Khwang, which is flanked by fortune tellers.

"It's not bad to mix Hindu gods, Buddhist mantras and traditional belief; that is the Thai way, but it is not truly Hindu," says Max, a migrant from Isaan who formally changed his religion to Hindu, and his name to Tintrinai, which means Third Eye of Durga. "If I want the true Hindu way I would go to India. In my blood I am Buddhist. I still worship Hindu gods, but I'm open to all gods, as they are all really one thing."

The trance at Wat Khaek derives from it being a Tamil temple, since Southern India escaped the northern purge of mysticism by Mughal Muslim overlords. This is a glimpse of the world's oldest unbroken religious tradition. A mile away – but a world apart in decorum – the same festival's marked at Wat Wisanu, by northern Uttar Pradeshis conducting genteel tribute in saris, suits or *salwar kameez* outfits. "The spirit possession is a South Indian culture. Northern Hindus don't approve of that," says Pok Chelsea, a society hairdresser who's penned books on Ganesha and Shiva. Pok reckons Thais are getting more orthodox. "The Sivaratri in January is very authentic. The royal Brahmins are from Varanasi and their clothing and rituals are just like I saw there."

The neo-Hindu trance cult appeals to many of the marginalised, especially women, the creative and the young. Navaratri is the main festival of Shaktism, which favours a feisty goddess over patriarchy, as heard in its chant "Om shakti om." The characterful gods of the Hindu pantheon – which relate to activities and professions – offer a personal bond to diverse urbanites who find state Buddhism too dry.

Accoutrements for the Hindu lifestyle are sold by shops like Om Santoshi in Thanon Pan. "I worship different gods for love, for education, for success. I pray to Lakshmi for riches, for love to Krishna and Radha," says owner Yanisa. "I can worship them by myself at home. And they are real."

Artists are responsible for the spread of Ganesha images throughout Bangkok, since he's the emblem of both the Fine Arts Department and Silpakorn University. Mistreated by his father Shiva, Ganesha went through life with literary talents and physical struggles (an elephant's head, a broken tusk) that marked him out as different. No wonder he resonates with creatives, gays and misfits. "Firms like Work Point Entertainment have had Ganesha shrines installed on their premises," writes journalist Manote Tripathi. "This new interest in the spiritual life culminated in a Ganesha sculpture contest, which drew a staggering 196 entries."

Scores of temporary shrines at Navaratri feature carpets of petal mosaic; the most dramatic have gay attendants and floral offerings like hotel lobby arrangements. Even at 'straight' shrines, *katoeys* possessed by the demon goddess Kali cavort then tremble in *mudra* postures, baring the whites of their eyes, tongues distending to their chin.

Besides having souls permeable to spirits, many of the 'Third Sex' identify with Hindu avatars who have multiple states of being, can change gender, or unite male and female energies. They worship the statue of Ardhanarishvara at Sukhumvit Road near Soi 25, with halves of Shiva and his wife Parvati joined down the middle, like a famous costume routine of Bangkok's Calypso Cabaret.

Bangkok's Hindu shift has a millenarian fervour. "If you talk to Thais about the disasters since 2000 – floods, earthquakes, tsunamis – many will tell you it's about a major change in the world. The end of an era which will purge the Bad People," confides Mill. "More spirits are using human souls to get things done. I know it's the coming of a new avatar of Vishnu, his tenth. That's why so many are learning about how to be a Good Person, so they'll survive when the wipeout happens."

top left: **A neo-Hindu ritual underway in a festival at a *tamnak* near Wat Ratchatiwat.**

top: **A devotee at the Navaratri Festival in Silom performs purifying mortification by skewering his cheeks.**

left: **A trans medium of Kali doing mortification by dousing a bunch of flaming candles at Navaratri Festival near Wat Khaek.**

Senses 125

Night
What goes on after dark

The balmy night is one of the Bangkok's most sensual experiences. More fun seems to happen in the dark, from plucking blooms in the Flower Market to supping booze in speakeasy bars – and whatever else transpires after hours.

The blinding day is so harsh that sundown resets life back to normality. Early evening is the city's optimum time, with a brisker pace and a busier feel. The cooler air enables more outdoor activity and draws both residents and tourists out onto the streets to enjoy nocturnal pleasures. Walking becomes a pleasant activity; residents mingle on their doorsteps or at neighbourhood hangouts. After work and commuting, urbanites liven up.

Dinner is taken early by most Thais, partly a habit from pre-electric times, but also to make good use of time with colleagues or friends while waiting for the rush hour to subside. As dusk falls the streets fill with market food for eating on the spot or bagging to take home. The more affluent relax in garden restaurants, feast on seafood in breezy riverside eateries, or toast sundowners at the dozens of rooftop bars. In the cool season, forecourts fill with beer gardens, typically with live bands on a stage. "When people have been rushing through breakfast and working through lunch, dinner becomes the meal of leisure, of relaxation… for many, the first proper meal of the day," commented writer Natayada na Songkhla. "Night, then, is a time when friends get together and families reconvene."

For blue-collar Bangkokians, however, work doesn't end at dusk. Much of the infrastructure gets built or maintained on night shift. In pre-aircon times, indoor work was focused on the cool night hours, even in the royal court. Flexibility of labour lets city chores be scheduled outside the hot, congested hours.

Bangkok has a reputation of being a city that never sleeps. Since the 1960s, it has profitably colluded in its cliché as a non-stop party. However, leaders lost such face from the international Sin City image of their sacred capital that they launched a puritanical backlash. Since the early 2000s, social order campaigns have curtailed the anything-goes scene of the 1980s-90s, when ravers fuelled on Johnny Black would dance till dawn at after-hours parties in dive bars, suburban hotels or obscure locations.

This is the seedy demimonde mythologised in the noir genre of Bangkok novels. Its debauchery had become a mass-media brand by the time of the movie *Hangover 2*. Now debauchery has become commodity. You can join Hangover night drinking tours of the film's Bangkok settings, after getting a temporary Mike Tyson facial tattoo.

Prohibitionists had so tamed bar-going that in 2015 they attempted to ban all alcohol over New Year. Already for years a campaign has encouraged young Thais to see in the New Year whilst meditating. Sitting cross-legged at countdown isn't what most revellers do, but some party animals do head to the temple that night. Nightlife thrives, and *sanuk* animates the evening, but the bar scene has mellowed from wild to mild.

Things still open very late or very early – and some round the clock – but the tone is less hedonistic, more domestic. Instead of clubs, convenience stores are the new all-night venue, with many a 7-Eleven open 24/7. "In Bangkok, if you don't sleep (or can't), the city stays up with you," writes journalist Manta Klangboonkrong. "You can do your grocery shopping anytime of the night, rummage around a library, get a bag of tacos and even tuck into a dim sum breakfast at an ungodly early hour."

Fewer vehicles after 'rush-hour' doesn't always mean lighter traffic. Malls are at their busiest between dusk and 10pm closing, which pours shoppers and staff into a late-night traffic jam. Lines of empty taxis hog the side of bar strips, seizing up Nana, Silom, Thonglor, and even the Ratchada ringroad. Municipal water tankers inch along the 'fast lane', hosing the foliage on median strips. Cars squeeze past areas coned-off by utility crews digging up storm drains that are covered by day with massive steel plates.

The traffic changes form. Buses and commuter cars ebb, leaving taxis and tuk-tuks to rule the roads. Leisure cyclists emerge in timid convoys, enjoying the cool and lower risk as they exercise and socialise. All brace for the nightly invasion of giants. Thailand's radial highways clog with tailbacks of trucks that are only allowed into the city at 10pm. On arteries like Sathorn, the ten-wheelers rumble by, gears crunching, pneumatics wheezing, auspicious metal imagery of gods glinting in the headlights.

River traffic also switches after early evening from its workaday transit of longtails and expressboats, though tugs still pull cargo barges around the clock. With sunset come the cocktail cruises, some on luxury teak barges. At River City, coach tourists and office party groups board giant cruisers that can hold as many as 500 passengers apiece. Cruiser decor gets ever wilder, with flashing light displays and swooping lines picked out in pink neon. One disco boat has a superstructure resembling a Batman mask, while *Bangkok Island* is a steel barge converted into an indy party venue, providing a curated option for club-goers. Their lights and reverberating music shatter the peace of the riverside, but after they pass, calm descends again upon the black waters.

River cruises usually turn at Rama VIII bridge, whose illuminated tower and suspension cables resemble an enormous harp. Downstream they turn, and often stop, at Asiatique. Redeveloped around heritage warehouses of the East Asiatic Company, this huge attraction inherited many vendors and Joe Louis Thai Puppet Show from the much-loved but evicted Suan Lum Night Bazaar. With a Ferris wheel, and Calypso Cabaret's ladyboy floorshow,

left: **Temple fair fun at Wat In, Dusit.**

above: **Soi Cowboy's neon go-go bar strip.**

Senses 127

it became Bangkok's biggest pedestrian zone and started a trend for promenading space.

Day tourism gives way to night tourism. It's no longer just those gaudy riverboats gliding past spotlit chedis and churches. Best Bangkok Tours runs motorcycle trips, which include an evening convoy through historic lanes and quirky nightlife. The professional drivers don't drink so the passengers can.

The cool night and quieter streets also draw bicycle clubs for locals and bicycle tours for visitors. "To ride through [Sampeng] after dark is to see it from a totally different perspective," reports Peerawat Jariyasombat. "During daylight, this area is bustling with porters pushing trolleys and motorcycles weaving between all the shoppers. So it is quite remarkable how easily we can roam along *trok* that even pedestrians normally find too densely packed for comfort."

Nightfall allows us to see city details without so much clutter and grime. Eyesores fade into shadow, but vignettes are lit up against the darkness. Fluorescents turn each open shophouse into a living diorama framed in black. As Natayada says: "Bangkok feels much more human a city at night simply because there doesn't seem as much of it to take in."

Browsing night markets remains one of the city's great passions. Though vendors were evicted from bazaars at Silom and Nana, hawkers still set-up impromptu stalls for bar-goers. Meanwhile, suburban night markets thrive, from Ramkhamhaeng Road stalls for students to Huai Khwang Market's stalls supplying lingerie to the night workforce of Ratchadaphisek Road. By day, the area's an office hub of white collars; come nightfall, it's known for loosened collars. Neon signage reveals it as a hotbed of massage parlours and party houses, for youth, gays, or Asian businessmen.

Perhaps the most enchanting night sight is the flower market at Pak Khlong Talad, held in the cool dark hours because blossoms would wilt in the sun. A common stop on nighttime tours, it's also a popular place to extend an evening after bar closing time, wading thigh-deep through bouquets of orchid, rose and lotus.

Many prefer sightseeing through this shadowy filter, when landmarks get spotlit and dim street lights render the city romantic. At festival time coloured fluorescent tubes light the route to temple fairs, while fairy lights spangle trees and outline the details on buildings. Ratchadamnoen Avenue looks majestic under arc lamps, from the crenellations and spires of the Grand Palace, past the soaring wings of Democracy Monument, while Golden Mount's burnished cone hovers high in the dark sky. Up the avenue, the white marble of Ananta Samakhom Throne Hall is easy to spot from downtown towers. Every guidebook lauds the skyscraper rooftop bars, where it's a treat to swig sundowner cocktails while the firmament purples. Spread out below, traceries of lights twinkle in urban constellations.

The inaugural Bangkok Design Week in 2018 showed a new way of exploring the potential of the night. A string of lighting installations drew attention to unsung backstreet details of Talad Noi, from modernist architecture to ancient stucco walls. Most magically, the pool in the courtyard of the 250-year-old Fujian mansion So Heng Tai reflected its ornate gate. But the young Thais photographing the installation might be afraid to return there on a normal night without that special lighting.

Middle or upper-class Thais are brought up to harbour fears about the night and the kind of people who inhabit it. Though lists circulate of dangerous *sois* and footbridges, the streets are remarkably safe at night for a city this big, although on stretches of highway in the weekend early hours, *dek waen* (boy racers) on illegally customised bikes, can be a genuine danger.

Thais, in general, are possessed by a folkloric dread of the dark. In collective memory, within the lifetime of elders, it was literally a jungle out there. Darkness was full of threat: animals, bandits, ghosts. The involvement in nightlife of 'dark influence' – gangsters running prostitution, gambling or drugs – has kept this primal fear alive in the subconscious. Even a place as loved as Lumpini Park flips after nine from joggers to streetwalkers: callgirls to the east, moneyboys to the West.

A new cast of fearsome characters stars in the night shift. Security guards, stationed at every valuable building and compound, play lead roles, along with officers doing the rounds of venues that get to bend rules like opening late, playing music or dancing without a license. Since the 2003 rise in the drinking age to 20 and the 2006 bombings, clubs began to hire bouncers.

The pantheon of once-spooky Thai ghosts has branched out into entertainment. An award-winning ad for Sylvania lamps shows generic ghosts appearing in the light to Bangkokians who act blasé, but as soon as night falls, the ghosts make them scream. You can see them appear in haunted houses – that is, costumed actors in sideshows at temple fairs. Braver souls go actual ghost spotting. DJ Kapol Thongphlub hosted a weekly radio and TV show called The Shock, broadcasting from reputed haunts in Bangkok.

Some spirits need night-time attention. Rahu, the god who eats the sun or moon, should be placated with black offerings, as is done at Huai Khwang Hindu Shrine. One lunar eclipse, a friend wearing black set up a black altar in my garden, and as totality neared, lit black incense and candles, flanked by Pepsi, Guinness, black bean jelly, black chicken and Marmite.

The moon matters much to Thais, who also follow a lunar calendar. It's easy to loose track of the moon's phases amid the urban glare, but full moons mark several enchanting festivals. At the three Buddhist public holidays of Makha Bucha (February), Visakha Bucha (May) and Asalha Bucha (July), devotees circumambulate each temple and Buddhist site under the full moon with lotus bud, incense and candle. And as full moon pulls the November tide high, the Loy Krathong festival sees Bangkokians release millions of illuminated banana leaf floats on the city's waterways.

At festival times, Thais traditionally combined serenity with *sanuk* at temple fairs – the original format of Bangkok nightlife. Contemporary Bangkok struggles to reconcile a new urge to social control with modern temptations of the night, branding good people bad because they like to party. Raucous festivals were specifically about managed transgression, yet even temple fairs are attacked for the profanity of their shows.

Nightclubbing too gets tarred with that brush. In the early 2000s, Thaksin's interior minister Purachai Piemsomboon ran a Social Order Campaign that permanently tamed Bangkok's freewheeling nightlife. Raids detained bar-goers for hours while their pee was tested for drugs, inviting media to film the mostly innocent punters. The raids subsided, but crackdowns flared again with ensuing regimes, such is the power of the self-appointed cultural guardians. The same moralism drives the policing of women's clothing and patrols of love hotels.

Billed as a 'War on Dark Influence,' the raids targeted bar owners who paid off police to keep trading after legal hours. Edicts for ever-earlier closing fuel that black economy, since the new limits of midnight for bars and 1pm for nightclubs are unrealistically early and deprive venues of their 1-3 am peak revenue time. Ad Carabao's immortalised the interior minister in his song 'Purachai Curfew', lamenting the impact on a million incomes nationwide.

Moral crusades are heavy on night-time activity, yet rarely touch the lucrative prostitution operators. After-midnight roadblocks see police shine torches into taxis, from which random foreigners have been illegally forced to get out and take a pee test.

Prohibitionists are now in charge of regulating alcohol, further demonising nightlife. Venues demand to see ID and foreigners technically should carry their passports while nightclubbing. Bans on alcohol promotion damaged not just magazine income, but event sponsorship, with the cool-season delight of beer gardens almost outlawed. Social media went into shock when celebrities were prosecuted for being photographed with identifiable drink labels. Suddenly, anyone posting a pic of partying with a bottled beer could be arrested.

left: **The Old Town's night-time quietude, in a *soi* at Tha Tien facing Wat Pho.**

right: **A modern float with sparklers and palm leaf at Loy Krathong festival.**

All this is out of sync with how the citizens actually live. "Because Bangkokians have an urban lifestyle, working too late, coming home late, we have to hang out late," says Zcongklod Bangyikhan. "In the provinces, they turn off the lights at 9-10 pm and go home to sleep. In this way Bangkok is different from other Thai cities."

As Bangkok's size and population grew, so did its need for an after-work drink, a party place and a Saturday night out. In town planning, nightlife wasn't considered at all, just assumed to evolve – and it did spectacularly. Despite crackdowns, the authorities can barely contain its ebullience with early closures, narrow zoning and a higher drinking age of 20.

Student quarters worldwide – from Shibuya in Tokyo to Schwabing in Munich – are the liveliest parts of a city. Not in Bangkok, where bars are banned near *wats* or schools, even universities. That's why the youth magnet of Siam Square is hectic by day, uncannily hushed by night.

Night-time leisure is yet another aspect of Bangkok in which the restriction of public space funnels everyone into corporate spaces. Malls hog many evening options, from cinemas to bowling to concerts. They even house most of the gyms. Malls open later in Bangkok than most places, typically till 10 pm, with periodic Midnight Sales. Open House bookshop at Central Embassy, with its seating and restaurants, draws bookish denizens till nearly bedtime.

Barcelonians can amble Las Ramblas and Veronese visit the amphitheatre, but Bangkok lacks an evening promenade. Sanam Luang once sufficed, but has been fenced off recently. Creating promenades is a must-do mission in city making, encouraged by successes like Singapore's Marina Bay. Banned from bars, teens mass at the new breed of indie night markets, while hipsters stroll at artier markets and river venues like Jam Factory, or Lhong 1919. Bangkok's night-market instincts are now finding a sophisticated indoor-outdoor format.

The Bangkok night is irrepressible. Soon after street-trader clearances, back spring bars in vendor carts and converted tuk-tuks, with vodka Red Bull in a bucket. Bangkokians like their designer bars and malls, but Thai sociality bubbles most naturally on the street. In the words of music critic Chanun Poomsawai: "Bangkok to me is like that one friend I can text at 2 in the morning, knowing that they'd still be awake and up for a bit of mischief."

Partying

My name is Bangkok and I'm a reformed partyholic. Once known for nightlife addiction with a taste for go-go bars, I was a city that never slept, but now I'm going to bed earlier.

Many Thais still seethe at that Sin City notoriety, as captured in the long-banned song 'One Night in Bangkok'. A big night out is now more likely to involve artisanal cocktails at a designer lounge like Siwilai, Soho House or Bangkok Social Club. The all-night benders have been curbed by a two-decade purge enforced by all regimes since the 'Purachai Curfew' of 2001, named for Thaksin's interior minister as part of a 'war on dark influence'. Since then, clubbers and bar owners have gone through raids, bans, zoning, age limits, price hikes, drug tests, ID checks, shorter hours, drink ad bans, holy-day closures and clearance of street bars. *Sanuk* of course found other outlets, like skyscraper rooftop bars, all-white raves and pool parties, where it's the customers not hostesses who are in bikinis.

Flashy bars around Sois Thonglor and Ekamai, compete in opulence, mixologists and trends like craft beer or artisanal gin. Laid-back hostelries have sprung up in Soi Suan Plu (Smalls, Junker) and Sathorn Sois 10-12, while a hipster invasion is gentrifying the old town and Chinatown. That started in Soi Nana, with Tep Bar, Teens of Thailand and its sister bar Asia Today, which give Chinese doughnuts free with its cocktails made from foraged ingredients like wild honey.

Before nightlife zoning focused bigger venues, short-lived bar strips flared up all over the city, from vintage Old Town shophouses to suburban

plazas. As late as 2005, official publicity was still fixated on the declining fleshpots of Patpong, saying it was "full of go-go bars, bar beers and stimulating places," a decade after inventive 'partypreneurs' had created new kinds of nightlife: novelty pubs, indie art bars and giant 'partyhouses': one-stop venues with disco, karaoke, restaurant, live music pub and private rooms.

Mainstream pubs paired food with live music for pals sharing whisky bottles kept behind the bar. Thai and expat trendies hung around bar strips like Silom Soi 4 and Royal City Avenue (RCA), which burst like a supernova with over 100 wackily themed bars before condensing into a few mega clubs like Route 66. House music fans sucked lollypops while dancing till dawn at raves held in adhoc locations, from an unfinished expressway to an atrium in a hospital.

Revellers have seen dizzying changes. Exposure to global trends is now instant, with a constant influx of clubers from East and West. Condos have replaced gaudy big-box dance pubs, which have retreated to the Ratchadaphisek ringroad, Pradit Manutham, Lad Prao and beyond.

Taste also turned from clubs like the spaceship-shaped Phoebus, where thousands rubbed shoulders, to small saloons with a rarified clientele, such as Iron Balls, which distills its own gin. Debutante daughters and don't-you-know-who-my-Dad-is sons of influential figures used to flaunt their status at broad spectrum clubs like Brit Pub, but today's more sophisticated equivalents express their social standing through exclusivity. Now sharp-dressed locals gain entry to so-called speakeasys by 'secret' entrances, through a photo booth or by picking the right door number in a wall of lockers.

Novelty themes remain the way to draw custom from fickle Bangkokians. Among the first international style clubs, Bed Supperclub had combined fine dining and art installations into a club that drew star DJs under the creative direction of Sanya Souvarnaphouma. Another transformative figure, Australian Ashley Sutton designed many outlandish venues after conceiving Iron Fairies as a Victorian foundry with hidden rooms. Sanya and Sutton collaborated in two landmark venues: Maggie Choo's (like a Suzy Wong's pawn shop) and Sing Sing Theatre (evoking a Shanghai cabaret).

Pressure on venues by police led to one-nighter theme-parties that shifted venue, as directed by their charismatic impresarios. Pongsuang 'Note' Kunprasop drew a design and fashion crowd to Dudesweet, Lady Soma's Club Soma was more indie, while Ark Saroj and Jojo Goldenmountain hosted camp extravaganzas at Trasher. Regulation and the increase in partiers has forced those one-nighters into formal venues with a strict door policy, but can't suppress the *sanuk* of their devoted tribes.

In the past, bouncers never dared eject anyone in fear of who their powerful family or friends might be. But the enforcing of age restrictions familiarised young Bangkokians to a doorway drill. Bouncers suddenly

left: **Informal street bars often appear at Nana, serving cocktails by the bucket till the early hours.**

above: **A town for swingers: high-end fun at the Sino-themed Sing Sing Theatre.**

Senses 131

left & lower left: Pool parties like this one at So/ hotel start by day and splash into the night. *Photos courtesy of So/ Hotel*

below left: Smalls is famed for its music, pours, and tastemaker clientele. *Photo by owner David Jacobson*

below right: A wild theme party. *Photo by Trasher*

unseen. Often a rich host (or clique of friends) will rent an apartment for a night or weekend for celebrating through the night and into after-parties, then pay for a maid to clean up. Inevitably this may have resulted in other group activities that could be enjoyed in bedrooms, on sofas or up against kitchen counters. Tabloid news was aghast as raids on condos exposed Thais engaging in consenting sex in private. Meanwhile tycoons run multi-storey brothels untouched.

With nightlife getting expensive, exclusive and extortionate for ever shorter time periods, people sought their after-hours kicks through something free in the palm of their hands: smartphones. "A lot of nightlife just went online," says Chardchakaj Waikawee, a photographer who documents youth culture. "If you want sex you no longer need to spend thousands of baht over many nights in bars trying to pull; you just hook up via an app."

Given that nightlife is also happening outside of licenced venues – in pools, saunas, houses and specially rented apartments – police attention is shifting from bar raids to home raids and random roadblocks, hauling passengers at random from cars and taxis to pee in a drug-test cup. Some now avoid driving near nightlife areas, fearing the trauma and rumours of extortion. Nightlife venues are dwindling, and it remains to be seen where Bangkokians will go to party.

Sin City had been overdue a sober reckoning, but the pendulum swung too far. Then semi-legal ganja reduced demand for alcohol. New rules in 2023 extended club closing to 4am in some zones, amid outcry by moralists, but most bars still face a capricious negotiation with local officers. Realists regard nightlife as a pressure valve that allows youth to let off steam. Besides, just as water finds its level, alcohol finds its outlets, substances find their market, and libido finds its release.

had powers and used them to screen-out not just underage kids but also riffraff and those they didn't like the look of, like older Western males. A city without effective door policies soon sprouted red velvet ropes where punters might need to queue or plead – and pay escalating entry fees. The shareholders, DJs and PR hosts have such wide circles, and favoured regulars, that those who have to pay could be a minority.

Bangkok always used to stay up late, with a favourite dive being Wong's Bar. Early closing of course led to the late-night scene going underground. The affluent used to host their friends by hiring one of the karaoke rooms or private lounges that ringed the balconies of big clubs, where they could be seen to gain face. Being denied a full-night's revelry spurred many fun-seekers to gather in private parties in houses or condos. Young professionals now have downtown condos, where their friends can hang out till late, drink whatever they want, or take illicit substances

Sanuk
Group fun

Centuries before the ice-bucket challenge became a brief global meme, Bangkokians were throwing buckets of water at each other every April to mark Songkran, the Thai New Year. Songkran is formally to bless elders and Buddha images by sprinkling water, but at the hottest time of year, it's informally a raucous nationwide water fight. Now Thailand is asking UNESCO to make its Songkran water-throwing an intangible Cultural Heritage. When water thrown at motorcyclists leads to deaths each year, Songkran feels less laudable, but the festival is irrepressible because it's a moment of national catharsis when order is upturned and you can throw water at anyone, even at police or elders. Songkran is the ultimate expression of *sanuk* – the Thai sensibility for group fun.

Bangkok is more entertaining than most cities, bursting with jollity and startling sights. Humour (*talok*) is a Bangkokian trait: the language fizzes with articulate wordplay, comedy is clownishly slapstick, and toonish mascots lighten everyday tasks. For *talok* to become *sanuk* requires making that humour sociable, which can include what's posted by friends on social media. Thais are amongst Instagram's heaviest users, not just to show face, but to spread *sanuk*.

Bangkok structures things to facilitate *sanuk*. Even the most serious of activities gets turned into a festival or fair, as browsing stalls and nibbling treats with friends is especially *sanuk*. To draw locals to events and promotions, it's essential to provide amusing interactive sets and chatty hosts, while Bangkok advertising wins awards for its imaginative wit. Company trips are non-stop games.

Venues cater specifically to *sanuk*. MK Suki restaurants enable group-cooking at the table, then the staff boost the jollity by dancing actions to MK's novelty song. Tawandang German Brewery's hundreds of staff dance to their own song, too, in a 2000-seat hall geared to throngs of colleagues and friends, who go wild under roving spotlights while cabarets fuel the fun with dancing candelabras or Godzilla descending over the audience on a wire.

above: **Frolickers fly in from Asia and beyond to join Thais in getting wet at the Songkran water festival. Pictured is** *It's Raining Men* **(enamel on acrylic) by Daniel Monfort Gil, from** *Our World* **at Serindia Gallery.**

Senses 133

You can hear *sanuk* from far away; up close it can deafen. Shrieky giggles emanate from gaggles of friends who act-out fast-paced monologues, and play-up with anything to hand used as props – the kind of larks that foreigners might do at a private party, but which Thais revel in while sober in public space. When group fun erupts in contexts like fine dining, not all Thais appreciate it, but would rarely intervene to quell *sanuk*, as doing so could enrage the revellers. *Sanuk* is part of the Thai sense of freedom.

Bewildered foreigners marvel at the spectacle but may wonder what the joke is. Introverts can struggle with it as 'compulsory fun.' The dynamic is uniquely Thai. *Sanuk* is not high culture but springs from folk ways. Hard tasks on the farm were made easier if group work became fun. The word for work, *ngan*, also means festival, and while 'party' in English can mean a work party, *sanuk* is not just about cooperation, but is an expression of release from having to constantly calibrate behaviour to whatever is status appropriate.

"It's the energy of the group. You can be yourself with those you trust, so you don't need to pretend to be someone else," says Beer, an office worker. "That's why you make jokes, dress up, act things out. Many Thais are good storytellers. We fill in the background, often doing actions and impersonations. Gossip is *sanuk*, because you add other stories to it as well. We always find additional information about a third person, not always in a bad way, though envious people can turn it into a drama."

This storytelling is truly ancient. It's a living oral tradition. Siam mostly wasn't a literary culture, with knowledge passed on by masters, monks or elders. These often took the form of dramatised narratives, focused on stereotypes rather than on abstract principles. Those moral epics always get leavened with vignettes by comics, the *sanuk* interludes that have become the mainstay of Thai entertainment.

University here has its bookish side, but also teaches social graces through oral culture. As well as *marayaat* (genteel manners), *sanuk* is practiced on campus, field trips and in *rup nong* (induction of first-year *freshies*). *Freshies* make up songs and accompanying poses, while seniors choreograph routines to perform on graduation day. Hazing can be brutal, but is mostly silly games that bond peer groups for life through endurance trials of fun. Graduates apply that outgoing, cheery personality to presenter-focused TV and online videos that, even if newsy, are just as full of comic asides, cartoonish graphics and musical cues to laugh.

"Word of mouth is one character of Thai society," Beer says. "You don't know the origin of your reference, which has a drawback as it can be unreliable. People often don't question what they hear, just accept it until someone's critical and asks for the source." Being critical is shunned because, well, it's not *sanuk*.

Wanting to make light of things grim extends to cremations. Mourners don't want grievers to suffer and so inject fun into the funeral. By gathering, cooking together and volunteering help they unleash that group spirit, which extends into drinking, shows and often gambling. Wealthy families stage movies, plays or dance. Royal cremations provide traditional entertainment for crowds to enjoy, but at that high level, it is a spectacle to marvel at, rather than being truly *sanuk*.

Foreigners can feel disconcerted at finding their own festivals so earnestly celebrated by Thais. Come Chinese New Year, even non-Sino-Thais can be seen posing in cheongsams and munching Chinese delicacies. At Halloween, street vendors wear glittery devil horns, while Buddhist Thais dress up in costume and make-up for parties citywide.

left: Find out how hard it is to be Super Duper Happy in the Factory of Happiness. A Christmas interactive display at Amarin Plaza.

right: Having group fun. Members of the Bangkok Swing dance club after a massed dance in a lane at Kudi Jeen community during the Art In Soi festival.

below: Make way for the costume-dressed celebrity Mae Baan Mee Nuad (Housewife with a Moustache).

"You have to accept that we Thais want to become acceptable, more civilised, so we don't only practise our culture, we accept other influences as well," says a Thai who had just bought a reindeer sweater. "We may not celebrate Christmas in the right way, like going to midnight mass, but we understand why you celebrate it and adopt it to our society. We sing Christmas songs, we decorate everywhere." That's not just in malls that play 'Jingle Bells' on a loop, but also in schools and offices.

Workplace *sanuk* is an efficiency technique not taught at Harvard Business School. Many firms are run like a village. I've seen a next-day shipment being met only because staff had called in friends to work through the night with fried chicken, *somtam* and whisky. They meet targets through fun incentives: workplace high-jinks, cutesy premiums, group karaoke, and company jaunts. The West has water-cooler conversations; Thai workers gossip over *khanom* (sweets). "Our office has a table just for *khanom*," says architect Kwanchai Atthikomprasit. "Staff gather there through the day to nibble. And if people know you went somewhere that weekend and didn't bring back a delicacy to share, that's a problem."

Sanuk underpins Bangkok's seeming chaos, yet isn't anarchic, and operates within certain bounds. Festivals evolved as managed transgression, upending norms, when folk could flirt and mock others in staged *lamtad* banter. Even a military takeover enforces jollity amid all the purging and censorship. The 2014 junta dictated that it would 'return happiness to the people,' instilling duty through a novelty song, free movies and festivals of Thainess.

In stressful, fast-moving Bangkok, *sanuk* might seem like a coping strategy, yet it's more of a group-minded approach to life. Urban living ups the opportunities for fun. Young people increasingly stay independently downtown, away from their suburban family, so they can see friends at will. "Bangkok is very competitive, but some people find that a fun, interesting challenge," says Beer. "Living this lifestyle in Bangkok is *sanuk*."

Senses 135

Libido
Sin City meets Prim City

The men's magazine *Details* once paid a journalist to circumflirt the world to have sex. The catch was, he wasn't allowed to pay. He scored in Osaka, Mumbai, Moscow, Istanbul and Berlin, but the only place he failed to complete his mission was Bangkok. Declining gay advances, he found Thai women too guarded. Bangkok's unbuttoned a lot since then. But when I recounted that tale to a German making a documentary about dating cultures in 2011, he exclaimed: "I found the exact same thing! I thought it would be easy in Bangkok, but no."

If the journalist had paid, it might have been a different story. Outside observers can't help but contrast Bangkok's prudish airs with its bawdy reputation and what Ross King calls its "libidinal landscape" of brothels, bars and steameries. Gay-friendliness, and the prominence of convincing transsexuals dubbed 'ladyboys' add spice to the cliché of 'Sin City.' Yet it could as easily be dubbed 'Prim City.'

Hand-holding is rare, and kissing taboo as Thais eschew public displays of emotion. Certainly you would never hear catcalls. Courting is cautious, with informal chaperones and circles of friends to impress before getting to first base – which in Bangkok might be a "sniff kiss" not quite touching a cheek. Males as much as females publicly conform to a conservative hierarchy that has a uniform slot for everyone, though many find their own niche in private. Under this politeness regime, those anticipating spiciness in bed may find that, as Thitipol Panyalimpanun puts it: "there's an image of an ideal Thai to be sexually passive."

In old-style communities of extended families, aunties knew everyone else's business. Couples paired off locally and young. As Bangkok modernised it grew looser. Condos and 'third places' (outside of home and work) provide anonymity to play away from the elders' gaze. Now the city plugs into global trends and networks, bringing foreigners and more assertive courting cultures.

Beyond parental control, the Internet in some ways acts as a modern matchmaker, facilitating liaisons in a franker sexual discourse, from sexting and nelfies to Tinder and camsex. Startlingly, subcultures of Thais risk open-air sex and upload the pictures, while there's been an uptick in flashing on public transport. It's like generations of repression being shed with their clothes. But the stakes rise as Bangkokians get richer and more people have 'good names' to lose. Thais take a matter-of-fact view of bodily functions and urges, but the social implications mean that the most protected body part is face.

"Thailand put itself into this struggle by positioning itself as a noble society," says Thitipol. Since the Culture Ministry was re-founded in 2001, with a mission to protect Thainess, it has played auntie in a non-stop moral panic. Bourgeois propriety upholds a standard of *siwilai* Thainess that is freighted with notions of sin brought by Christian missionaries over a century ago.

Official scolds tend to go after easy targets, such as female clothing. Guides and cultural primers warn foreigners to dress demurely, but visitors counter that they see Bangkok women wearing hot pants and miniskirts. Society looks down on working girls dressing in denim cut-offs and lacy tops, but happily lets posh girls flaunt skimpy designer outfits. One arm of state decries sleeveless spaghetti-straps, while another arm of state is promoting Thai fashion with bared shoulders.

The contradiction is resolved by social sanction on selected scapegoats. The actress Chotiros 'Amy' Suriyawong, was lambasted for going to an award ceremony in a "publicity-grabbing dress" typical of Oscar gowns, allegedly without undies. She lost roles and her university, Thammasat, ordered her to make a public apology and read books to blind kids as a community service.

Meanwhile, all around blares sexualised commerce. Billboards and platform ads flaunt bared skin, both female and increasingly male. Sex shops are banned, but dildos are openly displayed in street markets and touts in certain areas whisper "DVD sex" to passers by.

Sales stands are routinely staffed by 'pretties' – buxom, attractive ladies groomed in micro-mini uniforms, often with 'big-eye' contact lenses. Authorities have clamped down on pretties pouring alcoholic drinks at festivals and promotional stalls at restaurants. But at malls and events, pretties fawn titillatingly over shoppers with the bored endurance of karaoke hostesses. 'Coyote dancers' (named after the movie *Coyote Ugly*), are women wearing extremely revealing clothes, who dance provocatively. They have migrated from gyrating at men's clubs to product launches, and even to temple fairs. Bangkok motor shows don't just have skimpy models draping their booty over the boot; they stage full-on coyote dancing – and this has become a subculture with a huge following on YouTube.

Mainstream entertainment gets just as saucy. "It doesn't matter if you play like the Scorpions or are terrible as hell," says columnist Tulsathit Taptim. "The first thing a pub-owner is interested in is near-nudity in your show. Every band now has to employ sexy singers who are not afraid to appear all but naked." For decades, comedy cafés and variety shows alternated slapstick routines with parades of women bearing numbers for patrons to select. A contestant in 'Thailand's Got Talent' who painted using her bare breasts drew indignation from the show's female judge, who herself had years earlier posed for a magazine cover dressed only in paint. Glossy monthlies routinely tease with female and male nudity, yet film is subject to censorship; digital masking obscures flesh, cigarettes and beer labels.

"Like any other country, we have a humorous side, a ridiculous side, a perverted side, a dark side that many people often sweep under the carpet, or camouflage," says columnist Usnisa Sukhsvasti. "If you look at the local daily tabloids, these are the real sides of Thainess that you will see… There was a much-publicised story about a private party held in a Thai spa where the dress code was 'towel or nothing' – male guests opted for the towel, while the girls went for the latter."

In a piece of Bangkok folklore, the owner of Hi Class massage and five other parlours on Ratchadaphisek, Chuvit Kamolvisit, was arrested in 2003 for paying officers to violently evict a market at Sukhumvit Soi 10. Angry that he had paid huge bribes to be protected from the law, only to get into legal trouble anyway, he divulged the policemen's names in his VIP ledgers.

left: Every combination of gender is embraced in this Thai insurance ad at the busiest MRT station.

top: Passing the time between liaisons in a *katoey* (trans female) bar at Nana.

Senses 137

right: **A viral quote from a military prime minister.**

below: **Offerings at a bar in Patpong.**

far right: **The same PM lambasted the rapper Lamyai for her twerking.**

below right: **A 'somtam vendor' at Hua Lamphong Station, getting ready for a night's trade pounding pestle in mortar.**

London has Soho, Tokyo Roppongi, Hamburg the Reeperbahn. Singapore had Bugis Street, now Geylang. Bangkok offers a much broader range of red lights: Patpong, Nana, Ratchada, Thantawan, Thaniya, Saphan Kwai, New Phetchaburi, Maitreechit, Soi Cowboy, Sukhumvit Sois 3, 4, 5, 7, 8, 10, 11, 12, 22, 23, 24, 33… There's even home delivery. Touts in Patpong still proffer menus listing "pussy ping-pong, pussy write pen, pussy razor cut paper." But the street of dwindling go-go bars lacks the edge from when *The Deer Hunter* was filmed amid the chrome poles of Mississippi Queen. Like other bar strips aimed at foreigners in Nana and Soi Cowboy, Patpong has become a novelty sideshow. Coaches decant middlebrow tourists into its market of souvenirs. Families peer through semi-curtained doors at girls in bikinis and stack heels slouching on the dance poles or doing the bored 'Bangkok shuffle.' Inside, the captain pesters punters to buy drinks for the hostess trying to share your barstool.

Onlookers tend to blame poverty and foreigners exploiting locals. Meanwhile, anecdotes of gold-diggers, drugged drinks, and scams have been grist to Bangkok noir novels and expat chat threads in ThaiVisa.com (rebranded ASEAN Now). A reviewer notes that noir author James Newman's contention, "that the foreign johns are the greater victims in the sordid death-sex-life-dance that moves along the streets of downtown Bangkok, may not be palatable nor agreeable to all readers."

Different standards apply to the johns. Disapproval tends to gloss over wealthy businessmen using high-class escorts who operate out of discreet joints with classical pillars, whereas those frequenting the streetside hostess bars are seen as low-class losers, amid much scorn about gulfs in age, income and culture. Photojournalist Nick Nostitz went undercover with those who succumbed to "nightlife addiction." They'd typically lodge in digs around Soi Ngam Duphli. The lure of the chase proved too strong for many. Oil firms repeatedly tried to rehabilitate a genius of that industry, but he kept relapsing. Nostitz found "Bangkok's twilight zone… a sexual underground where people get sucked in, changed, moulded, and eventually spat out."

It pains many Thais to admit that many women, men and *katoey* sell sex here. There aren't official figures for sex workers, partly

"A pimp is better than a politician. The whole system is corrupt," Chuvit declared. "Even if I'm a pimp I can do something for this country." After hosting anti-corruption phone-in shows, he formed the Love Thailand Party, stood twice for city governor and got elected as an MP on a platform of cleaning up sleaze.

"Thai society clearly has its own definition of sexual nobleness," says Thitipol. "While sex toys, pornography and prostitution are illegal, if you ask an honest man… nobody goes to *ab ob nuat* (bathing and massage) parlours for backaches, but for sexual services." Other countries do have a bigger flesh trade, yet the mud sticks to Bangkok like candle wax to a pole dancer.

"We want the sex industry gone," declared then tourism minister Kobkarn Wattanawarangul in 2016. "Tourists don't come to Thailand for such a thing; they come here for our beautiful culture." At the same time, the industry is visibly vast, its income prized, its social roots deep. And everyone knows where to find the bawdy houses.

because they earn so much for the economy. Numbers vary wildly, but Havocscope's black market research counts 250,000, who earn $6.4 billion, or five per cent of GDP. Most are internal or regional migrants. While trafficking remains a problem, NGOs have been instrumental in improving Bangkok's flesh trade, which is now largely voluntary, with less harsh conditions.

When the BTS stops at Nana, you notice that a lot of the men getting on and off are entwined with a bar girl, and you can see other passengers recoil. But Bangkok night workers can earn merit though supporting family and temples. "No one wants to work in this business, but it's fast and easy money," admits a former sex-worker from Maha Sarakham who earned five times the minimum wage per night. 'Sideline girls' are a recent trend where middle-class girls sell their spare time online in order to afford luxuries like the latest handbag. Sex workers drift into the sex trade, whether through circumstances, friends or profit, but often because it's easy. Not all want to be 'rescued.'

Cases of slavery and degradation are rare in Thailand, says former UNESCO trafficking expert David Feingold, who compares the lurid hype with the Victorian prurient interest in redeeming fallen women. Sensationalism funnels funds to NGOs that are perhaps less about anti-trafficking than about anti-prostitution.

"We have now reached a point in history where there are more women in the Thai sex industry being abused by anti-trafficking practices than there are women exploited by traffickers," says sex work reformer Chantawipa Apisuk. Her charity Empower safeguards sex worker rights and offers training for alternative work. Empower also runs a Sex Museum in Nonthaburi, while its Patpong office displays tantalising tools of the trade, and has chrome poles on its danceable meeting table. Empower's *Bad Girls Dictionary* acts as a phrasebook to deal with questions like "Where do you come from?" The answer: "We think you expect us to come from abusive (bad), poor (backwards) or uneducated (stupid), rural (naive) families." Among its confidence-building definitions are: Bad girls: "Any woman who behaves or thinks outside the space society maps out for women."

Sex: "Something most people want to do, but also want to stop other people doing; a private activity with yourself or one or two or ten other people; sometimes just five minutes of our 8-hour working shift."

Bangkok's prostitution subculture was documented for 37 years in the notoriously blasé Nite Owl column by Bernard Trink, a Gonzo journalist who the female Nightprowler blogger Barbara Woolsey dubbed the "hardest working man on the commercial coitus beat." His favourite bar, Thai Heaven on Phetchaburi Road, had 200 girls, which he said felt like "being crushed by 400 breasts." Trink disliked brothels where the women can't choose, but revelled in the horseplay of bars, where the go-goers become adept at playing pool and Connect 4. "None of them knew how to give a massage, but after they finished squeezing you, you couldn't stand up for days!" he said. "It was sex. They played the game, and I couldn't argue." However, 'family' readers did argue with Trink's unapologetic mentions of the 'flying tuk-tuk,' which was cranked down

Senses 139

from a Patong bar ceiling with a couple tuk-tukking on the back seat.

Trink-era Bangkok ranks with Weimar Berlin, fin-de-siècle Paris and Warholian New York as one of history's wild Bacchanals. Although the sex trade keeps pumping, it stopped being the city's zeitgeist by 2003 when the *Bangkok Post* shut down the Nite Owl column.

Bangkok's fleshpots made news in the 1960s, when high demand met ready supply at the dawn of mass media. US forces fighting the American War in Indochina sent the GIs here for Rest 'n' Recreation. Go-go bars opened in the air crew hangout of Patpong, massage parlours began to flank New Phetchaburi Road, and ships docked in Pattaya, turning a Bangkok weekending beach into Asia's most notorious red-light resort. Drawing migrants from Isaan, Pattaya remains what Michael LaPalme calls "Somtam and Gomorrah."

In 1975, when the exit of US troops was expected to bring economic collapse, tourism took up the slack. Westerners tend to blame the West for the sex trade due to colonial guilt, letting off the hook the protected local infrastructure of pimps and procurers, not to mention the investors and landlords. Yet *farang* sex tourism has been estimated at just five per cent of total prostitution in Thailand. It's well-documented vulgarity deflects attention from the far larger, more discreet industry that services Thais and other Asians.

The flesh trade began long before the GIs. Prostitution obviously pre-existed, but was turned into an industry by a different influx of single males: the hundreds of thousands of Chinese who've settled here since the mid-19th century. Only a minority of sojourners found local wives before Chinese women were allowed to emigrate after 1911. So entrepreneurs catered to their natural

The Bangkok Noir

The city has its own literary genre, the 'Bangkok Novel' – and, no surprise, it's noir. Crime stories about its seething underbelly make top-selling 'airport reads'. Most revolve around white expat guys and prostitution, with noir providing a moody fictional tool to shine a detective's torch on the shadow economy of vice.

Noir authors meet periodically at the Check Inn 99 pub, with such stalwarts as Tom Vater, James Newman and Dean Barrett, whose arch "poetic tragedies" include *Skytrain to Murder* and *The Go-Go Dancer Who Stole My Viagra*. The marquee name is John Burdett. His bestsellers *Bangkok 8* and *Bangkok Tattoo* weave local context into the plots and characterisation of his half-Thai cop hero Sonchai Jitpleecheep.

The scene's prolific sage, Christopher G Moore, wrote a series about private investigator Vincent Calvino, which is peppered with asides about Thai culture. Those not into hardboiled genre fiction can access Moore's insights through his essays, whether on politics, society or AI, via his blog and books like *Rooms*, about how humanity has literally boxed itself in. Moore also edited the compilation *Bangkok Noir*, with a story by the main Thai noir author, the late police general Vasit Dejkhunjorn.

Noir also lends itself to film and art. Colin Cotterill is famed for his Lao coroner novels, but began as a cartoonist whose scabrous Man Farang panels appeared in *Metro* magazine.

The scene's visual signature is the luridly hued paintings by Chris Coles of red light districts, sex workers, johns and wider Bangkok lowlifes. A Hollywood producer, Coles compares his expressionistic work to that of artists documenting earlier demimondes: Henri Toulouse-Lautrec in Paris or Georg Grosz in Weimar Berlin. "It's such a rich subject matter, but no local artists are painting it," he laments. "This scene will surely disappear and with no trace unless people depict it."

urges. Johns went to the wharves of Sampeng for a roll in the floating brothel boats, versions of which docked in Pratunam's canal until the 1980s. Newspaper cartoons in the 1920s mocked the locals' lack of interest in Thai dance compared to Chinatown's erotic cabarets. Sampeng had green lanterns outside lanes of '50-*satang* brothels' half a century before Patpong became a red-light district. Its Sino-Thai owner, Udom Patpongpanit, was reputedly an OSS (CIA) asset, and leased the private street to go-go bars, airline offices, expat drinking dens and the covert Air America operation, according to the Patpong Museum.

The brothel towers erected in Ratchadaphisek's new Chinatown often focus on *ob ab nuad* (soap-steam massage baths). These 'soaplands' are one cause of Bangkok sinking due to their illegal pumping of groundwater. It was Japanese occupiers in the early 1940s who slipped Japan's bathhouse subculture into Southeast Asia. Yet these Asian origins of the sex trade went underreported as prostitution was legal until 1960, when it became a hobbyhorse of salacious reporting and moralisers.

Paid sex is deeply embedded in Thai customs. The world's oldest profession is much less formal here, where the biggest bordellos also function as restaurants. Taking clients to high-class hostess lounges is integral to business networking. Groups of lads visiting a brothel has long been a standard way to lose one's virginity when any marriageable woman should be chaste. Such taboos remain common precisely because traditionalists object to the increase in sex before marriage.

Hi-So marriage is often an alliance of families. Courting can hinge on relative status and the bride price. For Sino-Thais that may be bullion and bricks of banknotes. At Thai weddings, guests leave an envelope of money. Exchanging vows is legally simple and can done at home in the morning, but receptions are a huge societal deal with grandiose hotel banquets that can gut family savings.

Siam used to admire polygamy, with the ability to afford multiple households being a proof of male status. Like collecting slaves and war captives, polygamy was partly due to population being scarcer than land and so more prized. As Thailand modernised, polygamy was banned, and extended family and multiple wives gave way to nuclear monogamy.

When Rama VI ceased the royal harem in the 1920s, his plays promoted an ideal of romantic individualism. The Thainess cultural mandates of the 1940s then promoted nuclear families and insisted that traditionally unisex Thai names be more feminine or masculine.

By the 1990s the size of Bangkok families had shrunk to Western norms. Population growth and AIDS were both curbed, thanks to the promotion of condoms and vasectomies by Meechai Viravaidhya. Meechai was nicknamed Mr Condom, and condoms were known as a 'Meechai.' Nevertheless, the family structure and ageing demographics fail to mesh with lingering playboy values.

Male sexual privilege is widely taken for granted, but with changing accents. "Chinese-Thai men usually described themselves as 'responsible' family men in contrast to 'irresponsible' working-class Thai men who 'lay eggs' everywhere, but do not support the family," found researcher Jiemin Bao. "Being a successful breadwinner – a key symbol of

left: Chris Coles is a rare artist who documents the Bangkok Noir. This lurid scene is 'Boystown,' but Coles paints all: girls, pimps, johns, big shots.

right: Fancy a 'Book Blind Date'? Write in a book and wrap it your way with a note, then choose one that you like. At LIT Festival, Museum Siam.

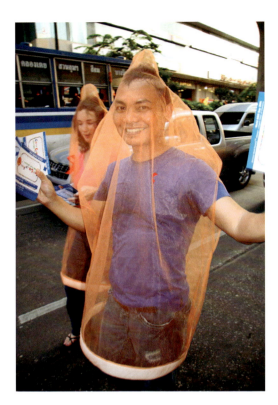

middle-class respectability – delineated the boundary between Chinese and Thai."

Below the surface, family dynamics keep roiling. A significant number of apartments are bought to house a *mia noi* (minor wife). Many claim that Thai wives favour their men seeing prostitutes rather than taking a *mia noi*. Both public and police treat domestic violence as a private matter, with *tob-joob* (slap 'n' kiss) as common as *wais* in prime-time soap operas known as *nam nao* – "foul waters."

Soaps perpetuate cliches. The male role model is genteel, righteous Rama, unlike macho *nakleng* (ruffians). It's deemed normal for a *jao chu* (philanderer) to be 'led astray' by the glamour and cleavage of a *nang rai* (bad girl). Meanwhile, the politely pretty 'good girl' waits virtuously at home under protection of her parents. Classy gays are slowly being written in, but the media often mocks the volatile *katoey* as a clown. Meanwhile, lesbians tend to adopt butch-femme roles as *tom* and *dee*.

"Boy Meets Girl, Boy Rapes Girl, Boy Marries Girl. The premise is so common in Thailand's popular primetime melodramas it could be called a national twist on the universal romantic plot line," ran an AP report "Thai soaps trigger outcry over romanticizing rape."

Producers cite ratings and the needs of plot. "There clearly is a problem here," says Nitipan Wiprawit, a campaigner on harassment. "The station reports rape as a crime during the day and broadcasts it as entertainment at night."

This is rooted in a tradition that frowns on female sexuality. Thais distinguish between *khom-kheun* (criminal rape) and *blum* – the 'wrestling' of non-consenting sex to win-over a resistant woman, which is pivotal to the TV drama *Power of Shadows*. "In theatrical terms, it was an act of love," said the producer Arunosha Bhanupan. "It wasn't rape. It was more romantic, because they were in love." A survey of youths found that more than 20 percent found rape scenes their favourite part of soaps and deem it acceptable.

Thailand has the world's second highest rate of teen pregnancy. "Morality in love has significantly decreased. People are less concerned about maintaining a long-term relationship," says Napaporn Trivitwareegune. "Teens and even grown-ups, would rather be free from commitment and responsibility. There's an attitude that as long as you're not married, it's OK [to cheat], which is just sad." This trend for having one or more *gik* – a friend-with-benefits – has been boosted by the popularity of apps. Today that *Details* journalist would be able to complete his mission by swiping right on Tinder.

Libertines are locked in a battle with last-ditch traditionalism. In 2015 the Health Ministry faced outrage from moralists for putting condom machines in high schools and colleges. The same year, the BMA planned to distribute three million condoms ahead of St Valentine's Day, which, as in Muslim countries, has become a lightning rod for religious nationalists.

"Available information suggests that 83 percent of Thai teenagers plan to have sex on Valentine's Day," calculated Sin Suesuan of the Moral Promotion Centre. Those amorous youths clasping roses are emulating their elders, who spend 1.5 billion baht on Bangkok's Valentine's Day economy.

"Valentine's Day has been dubbed, unofficially and cynically, as the 'National Day for Losing Virginity,' especially among teenagers, who make it an occasion to kick off a sexual relationship," notes journalist Kanokporn Chanasongkram. "The situation is similar to the romantic full-moon day of Loy Krathong. But with a teenager's hormonal surge, it might as well be any other day."

In the past, social mores loosened at festivals so the young could court. Temple fairs still host amuseuments, where lovebirds can snuggle in Ferris wheel gondolas. The romantically candle-lit Loy Krathong rite used to come after youths emerged from their rainy season monk's ordination as full men. Now on full-moon night, gangs of boy racers cruise around with their *dek sakoi* (trophy girls) riding pillion.

Today, prim Bangkok values have inverted the role of festivals from being an escape-valve into a platform to preach righteousness and punish naughtiness. The water-throwing at the Thai new year, Songkran, used to be an upside-down time when juniors could douse seniors. Now Songkran gets zoned off and the crowds policed, with bans on the aromatic paste that gets smeared amid the flirting. Indeed, the main drive is preventing girls from getting wet T-shirts. When the Culture Minister condemned three young women for dancing topless on upended bins amid the revellers in Silom, social media lit up with screenshots of the Culture Ministry homepage banner: a painting of Songkran's seven mythical goddesses cavorting topless.

At those festivals, police conduct vigils at short-time hotels in case young couples get the wrong idea. Tucked off main roads, 'love motels' do a brisk trade all year, especially for their fantasy rooms. Peep Inn 2 has a boxing ring bed, as does Banana State, which offers a Star Wars suite for light-sabre duels. A metaphor for Bangkok's morals, love motels are called *man root*, which means 'pull curtain', after the car-port drape that shields your car from scrutiny.

In an unprecedentedly open move, a bill was put to parliament in 2024 to legalise sex toys and non-exploitative pornography. The idea was to accept reality, reduce the hypocrisy and support healthy adult sexuality through clear regulation rather than the risky illegal trade. Its vote didn't pass, but public opinion is shifting that way.

"Sexuality both is and isn't taboo in Thailand. It is taboo only when it's inconvenient or causes embarrassment (real or perceived)," says Kaewmala, who wrote the blog 'Thai Sex Talk'. "Thais like to think that we are a conservative and proper society when we really aren't – at least behind closed doors."

left: **Safe sex promoters in Silom Road during one of the occasional Bangkok gay festivals.**

right: **All June, Pride is marked with commercial, social, activist and official celebrations, as at Samyan Mitrtown mall.**

An LGBT Paradise?

When Thailand became the third Asian country to legalise equal marriage in 2024, Government House was awash with rainbow flags. The prime minister and Bangkok governor have joined LGBT events. Pride month in June is now a huge commercial festival. But is this a queer paradise?

The Asia Equality index had ranked Thailand first in friendliness but 5th in laws, though now there are fewer rights issues to settle. A Thai NIDA poll found that 93% accepted LGBT friends or colleagues, and 91% as relatives. Thai bakers would not refuse to ice a gay wedding cake.

Tolerance doesn't mean full acceptance, but while homophobic violence is low, stereotyping is ingrained. Buddhist doctrine defines a third gender, known here by the ancient term *katoey*. So non-binary Thais do have a place in the hierarchy, though it's a lowly one.

The Thai ideal of genteel male manners gets misread by outsiders as effeminacy, since Thai society is surprisingly macho. The prevalence of queeny antics may be a reaction to that militaristic hyper-masculinity. Tops used to get called *man* or *real man*, and bisexuals *seua bai* (bisexual tigers) for their impressive appetites. Similarly, lesbians often adopt the roles of butch *tom* or girlier *dee* (from 'la-*dy*').

Thai sexual playfulness results from Buddhist Thais treating private life as a personal freedom. As saving face is so vital, Thais rarely pry, and outing is rare in politics or social life. Scandal only arises when peccadillos become public. Few Buddhist Thais would disown an LGBT child, though it's more fraught for Muslim Thais.

Because LGBT have multiple identities, many are drawn to Hinduism's pantheon of diverse gods. [*See* Sacred: Neo-Hindu] Winners of the Hero Award for LGBT advocates get a statuette shaped

as Ardhanarishvara, a Hindu deity who combines Shiva with his wife Parvati (Uma Devi). Some *katoey* make offerings at the pink-blue statue of the god at the mouth of Sukhumvit Soi 23.

This karmic society doesn't seek to change others, but to adjust oneself. While allowing *katoey* teens to get hormone treatment alarms some, a startling number of schoolboys present with effeminate flamboyance, banding with fellow *katoey* to form networks as they mature, overseen by 'mother' mentors bracing them for a tough life. For decades, *katoey* were branded 'mentally ill' by army conscription rules. They could work only in lowly trades, such as beauty or prostitution. Some made it as drag stars, either in tourist fantasias like Calypso or Mambo cabarets, or in bawdy bar shows. Now *katoey* work in any profession, from bureaucrat to nurse. Khru Lily is a respected Siam Square English tutor who fills lecture halls with eager students.

Bangkok's camp sense of *sanuk* is a happy fit with the gleeful sensibility of *katoey*, yet in comedy, TV and film, *katoey* still get mocked as unstable or untrustworthy novelties. Among positive terms like 'Second Kind of Woman' or 'Angels in Disguise' lurk insults such as *toot* (from the film *Tootsie*). Lurid foreign caricatures of the *ladyboy*, derived from the sex-trade, are also rejected by those embracing 'trans' as a kinder epithet.

Thai sexual definitions have waned with the 21st century spread of global LGBTQI+ labels. *Kathoey* has narrowed to mean just transwomen and the queeny, while *gay* went from a synonym for *kathoey* to a straighter-acting identity that appeals to middle-class professionals.

Gay visibility here was boosted by migrants, as villages were more accepting than the bourgeois capital's majority Sino-Thais, whose LBGT often aren't fully out, saying "I think my family knows, but we don't talk about it." The UK gay magazine *Attitude* launched its first foreign version here in 2011, but initially they found few out Thai couples to profile, though nowadays many more are open.

The pioneer of Thai LGBT rights was the lesbian Anjaree Group, and *tom-dee* couples are very visible. Their scene has a magazine, *Tom-Act*, and the Lesla group's monthly "mother of all parties," dancing to the band Mister Sister. Among influencers, Punnatha 'Kwang' Pathikorn styles her *tom* look like hair-dyed K-pop star G-Dragon. "I've now got lots of foreign friends, especially in Asia," she told *BK*. "Some people contact me for advice as their country doesn't accept gay relationships. Some companies contacted me to sell their products on my Instagram account. My girlfriend is also harassed by some of my followers. They're just jealous of her."

The 2019 general election was a watershed. Several parties fielded LGBT candidates, one ripping open his suit to reveal a rainbow-striped chest, while the Muan Chon Party nominated a *katoey* for Prime Minister. Thailand's first out-LGBT MPs were elected (all for the Future Forward party), two of them gay and two trans, who included Tanwarin 'Golf' Sukkhapisit, a filmmaker (*Insects in the Backyard*) who'd earlier been elected president of the Thai film director's association.

As LGBT went mainstream, they've gained more positive, sympthetic portrayals in media and entertainment. Thailand gained a world-leading soft power in production of BL, the 'Boy's Love' genre of cartoons and filmed series of male-male romances, aimed more at young women than gays. Queer art has mushroomed since the 2010s. While female nudes got scarcer, male and trans nudes have grown brazenly widespread, whether in public exhibitions or LGBT spaces like Pulse, and Oat Montien's Bodhisattva Gallery. Oat embodies an unapologetic trend in homoerotica, alongside artists Maitree Siriboon, Ark Saroj, Anuwat Apimukmongkon, Harit Srikao and Baphoboy.

In academia, Thai gender studies has flourished. LGBT academics include two transgenders: Prempreeda Pramoj na Ayuthaya and Kathawut 'Kath' Kangpiboon. Kath was sacked by Thammasat University for using a penis-shaped lipstick, but got her job back by court order.

In 2018, Museum Siam held an unprecedented exhibition, *Gender Illumination*, documenting life stories with exhibits including a trans dilator dildo and gay porn magazines lent by the Rainbow Archives of Thai LGBT publications. On 22 November that year, the cream of Southeast Asia's gay world converged on BACC for Spectrosynthesis II – Asia's biggest-ever show of LGBT art, following an earlier exhibition in Taiwan. The same night, the Bangkok-based advocacy alliance, Apcom (Asia-Pacific Coalition on Male Sexual Health) bestowed its annual Hero Awards for community courage. Within Asia, such diversity could only flourish here.

Gays can cavort without fear in Bangkok, where venues are just out of public view, while saunas have blank frontages. As Thai-Asian oriented discos in Lamsalee or Ratchada, like Fake Club, have faded, the scene has refocused on Silom. Since the 1970s, Silom Soi 4 has drawn foreign and cosmopolitan Thai gays. It greets more than twinks, with bars for muscle bears (Beef, Hugs) and drag (Stranger, Bipolar). Many migrate to Silom Soi 2, a totally gay *soi*, where its distinct bars and DJ Station club have merged into a two-level circuit under a roof. GOD (Guys on Display) raves on till later. The LGBT-friendly clinic Pulse even has a bar-gallery with a dark room!

There are other scattered bars, and a swish penthouse drag club Heals, run by drag superstar, Pangina Heals. Born Pan-Pan Narkprasert, s/he is a 'waaking' champion who pursues drag as an art form and found global fame as co-host of RuPaul's DragRace Thailand.

The notorious gay sex trade that was located on Surawong Road and 'Soi Twilight' had to relocate its go-go bars to Patpong Soi 2 and Silom Soi 4. That 'moneyboy' scene has declined into a tourist curio amid the advent of hookups via app. There's ease and less risk of losing face in swiping an app than in going to a bar. Grindr and Asian apps like Blued have hastened the demise of mainstream gay venues too. Meanwhile, the Internet has also given hope, information and connection to the isolated.

Gay Westerners have for decades flocked here for holidays or a new home, and since the budget airline era, gay Asians do likewise. LGBT are loyal return visitors. TAT awoke to the 'Pink Baht' and ran a same-sex tourist campaign, 'Go Thai, Be Free', even depicting a lesbian 'wedding' before legalisation.

LGBT visitors are mostly male, and snide remarks about older gay *farang* being 'sexpats' does apply to a minority from any ethnicity, but not the majority. Bangkok is a saucy playground, but also a sympatico setting to live long-term, stay part-year or retire to. Thai respect for elders includes gay silver foxes.

Bangkok truly is paradise to LGBT from less tolerant societies. Thai marriage equality sparked online disgust and fear from Muslim neighbours and South Korean Christians, showing why sexual minorities find Bangkok a respite or a refuge.

Asian gays visibly swan around malls, galleries, cafes and Chatuchak Market. Many party in local Thai venues. At Songkran and New Year, thousands flaunt their abs at Asia's biggest G-Circuit festivals, with days of dancing and pool parties. For them, Bangkok is not just a safe place, but a stage.

"I'm a misfit, but I still feel safe in [this Buddhist-Hindu] culture," says Nuh Peace, a Thai 'post-gender' drag artiste, whose face is a powdered map of graphic symbols. "Even if they hate you, they're not going to punch you or arrest you. They're going to be nice to you. In any other religion, if you are queer or different, you're out. But Bangkok accepts you how you are."

"I'm a misfit, but I still feel safe in [this Buddhist-Hindu] culture," says Nuh Peace, a Thai 'post-gender' drag artiste, whose face is a powdered map of graphic symbols. "Even if they hate you, they're not going to punch you or arrest you. They're going to be nice to you. In any other religion, if you are queer or different, you're out. But Bangkok accepts you how you are."

left: **Drag artist Pangina Heals, co-host of RuPaul's Drag Race Thailand, had earlier found fame by hosting the Sunday night gay party at Maggie Choo's.** *Photo courtesy Pangina Heals*

below left: **Several LGBT stood for election in 2019, and four became MPs.**

below right: **The gender exhibition at Museum Siam asked visitors to draw their gender identity.**

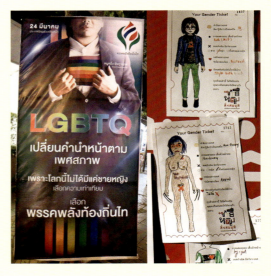

Touch
Tactile experiences, public and private

Bangkok feels uncomfortable. The humidity makes your clothes cling. Locals pre-empt that by wearing undervests and slathering themselves in talc. Bangkok sprawls at the middle of a sweaty delta. Its fine delta silt, joined by soot and other pollution, dusts the city. Increasingly residents wear masks to avoid ingesting the airborne molecules. The air here has palpable presence, as if with the pressure of more than one atmosphere.

Bangkok also looks uncomfortable, given all the craggy concrete, cushionless seats and glossy tile. Seeing a surface has been proven to set off our haptic and motor senses even if we don't come in physical contact. Run your palm along a railing, and your skin may be nicked by hidden barbs. The strong security culture makes itself felt in windows grilles, gates of die-cut steel and walls topped with jagged glass. Most Bangkok exteriors yell "don't touch!"

The city has a particular history of how to sit. Though its design industry has growing repute, there isn't much history of indigenous furniture that wasn't ritual. Chairs, chests and beds were an imported feature, originally from China, later the West. Instead the Siamese had wooden platforms of different heights, which were basically floors, elevated higher or lower. Younger and lower-status Bangkokians will still happily sit on the floor, often beside a sofa that never gets used. There may be or may not be a mat of reed or squishy plastic weave, perhaps an embroidered pad wadded with kapok seed fibres. Often people on public benches and chairs, sit cross-legged atop the seat, with their shoes placed on the ground in front.

Even with today's modern furniture, chairs frequently aren't padded but continue the hard-seat theme. Colonial-era armchairs, made of teak with low backward-tilted seats, require a heave to get out of – but are popular again in retro bars. Contemporary Thai designs for recliners or chairs favour conceptual curves over the contours of the body. Even when there are cushions, they tend to be in geometric shapes: cylindrical bolsters, boxy pillows, triangular backrests. It may seem unergonomic, but sitting awkwardly has given Thais fine posture.

The erstwhile teak carpentry of Bangkok is giving way to factory-made synthetics, like flat-packed veneered chipboard and flimsy

plastic chests. Silk often turns out to be Rayon; Patpong's souvenir 'wood carvings' are moulded from resin. Research shows that humans feel happier when they hold authentic textures, with their natural aroma, ambient temperature and solid heft. So Bangkok's retro trend is more than aesthetic; it's haptic and happy.

This is a rare metropolis where much is still handmade. Sticky-rice baskets and garlands of folded petals humanise the city by conveying a depth of manual care. Bangkok is blessed that TCDC hosts one of the world's first Material Connexion libraries of innovative materials, where designers can leaf through sample swatches. Its Thai materials draw on a long history of weaving, folding and reconstructing forms from nature.

You can find intriguing textures outside TCDC too. The street is an informal library of found and recycled components, from bobbled textiles to banana leaf wraps. Innovations often employ unlikely materials, like designer Saran Yen Panya's turning stackable crates into chairs. The incidental landscaping of *sois* is an assemblage of pocked laterite, basketry and tendrils of forest liana.

Among the most inventive tactile objects are the sculpted wooden massage tools found in markets. Their nodules, probes and scrapers are integral to Bangkok's prowess at bodywork. After the 1997 crash, Thailand pioneered the global spa industry. Now it's an everyday regimen to receive acupressure in the countless spas or reflexology parlours.

Yet Bangkok is touchy about touching. This most intimate sense takes Thai indirectness beyond a precarious threshold. Bangkokians shrink from incidental contact, unless it's a trusted commitment – as among family, friends or lovers – or a professional job. So unyielding is the taboo of touching, that masseurs, like hairdressers, will *wai* you for permission to contact your sacred body. Traditional Thai

top left: **This modern city still has handmade objects. Here is a carrying device for drinks in a bag.**

left: **Street furniture made from re-used wood is a common if uncomfortable sight.**

above: **Migrants from upcountry farms are a big if marginal part of Bangkok. Some crafts toys and decorations from natural materials, like this couple on Phetchaburi Road.**

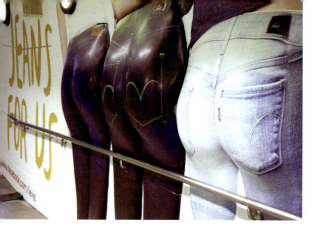

massage avoids much touching of skin, by pressing meridian lines through clothing.

In most cases, flesh should only be pressed in private. Public displays of affection break a taboo, though they're increasingly seen. Thais don't shake hands unless in a Western context. They greet at more than arm's length; the only palms being pressed are your own which are brought together in a prayer-like *wai*.

Bangkok is cramped, yet strangers maintain a polite distance – even if that is only five millimetres. No matter how crowded it gets, Thais glide through without brushing. It's partly poise, but also not wishing to impose. Touts pester once, rarely twice, and anyone grabbing your arm is almost surely not Thai, but in Nana could be a Kazakh hooker, or in Silom a Chinese DVD dealer.

Bangkokians can be touchy-feely among trusted pals of the same gender. Friends drape shoulders, grip forearms and entwine pinkies. Mates josh with *muaythai* moves. Toddlers get swept up by gleeful waiters and neighbourhood aunties. Kids bundle into group fun with an absence of personal space that accustoms teens in Siam Square cafés to happily share a chair.

Thai public touching is mainly same-sex. Soaps and movies show how close boy can almost-but-not-quite touch girl. At least on camera. Thais make dark assumptions about a woman seen holding a foreign man's hand. In 1996, I drew gasps from colleagues when reporting the first time I'd seen a Thai girl and boyfriend hold hands in Siam Center. That's since become frequent, but is still not the norm. More often, the girl gets the boy to carry her handbag.

On the street, vendors and motorcycle taxi drivers share a casual intimacy. They give mutual neck rubs, pick each others nits, or doze with their head in a colleague's lap. The most confronting aspect of riding a motorcycle taxi is proximity. You can't avoid contact with the driver – cupping thighs-to-hips, chest to back.

In contrast, the West has become so detached from the psychological need for touch that the term 'bromance' had to be invented to justify inseparable mateship, while adult males dare not hug a child for fear of accusation. "What Bangkok offered to the ageing human was a culture of complete physicality," Lawrence Osborne wrote in *Bangkok Days*. "It was tactile, humans pressing against each other in healing heat: the massage, the bath, the foot therapy, the handjob, you name it."

'Physicality', can be a polite word for sex. A five billion-dollar chunk of the economy engages in the sex industry. Bangkok provides many an innovative venue, such as the No-Hands Restaurant, where spoon-feeding by hostesses frees up the customer's fingers. However, the spa boom is finally wrenching massage back from 'happy endings' to its original healing purpose.

"It's a city of hard edges", a Thai colleague warned me soon after arrival, "but with a soft heart." Touch, and before you know it, Bangkok touches you.

top left: **Advertising that touches you. A 3-D jeans ad at Sukhumvit MRT.**

above: **Massage tools are a useful craft sold from markets and at shops in Tha Tien, near Wat Pho.**

Massage

She starts at the sole, with a prayer, asking *kwam metta* (compassion) to let her touch. Rocking her bodyweight, the kneeling masseuse presses thumb, wrist or elbow up the body from the feet, working along the energy meridians. Such is the way Thais heal with the hands.

Most Thai masseurs trained in Bangkok's own style of bodywork: *nuad paen boran* – 'ancient massage'; with the most famous school located in the temple of the reclining Buddha, Wat Pho. It was effectively Siam's first 'university', and is a UNESCO-listed store of *phum panya* (traditional wisdom). Displays include wall-mounted tablets depicting energy meridians and gnome-sized sculpture of Ruessi Dutton, sages contorted in 'self-massage', or 'hermit yoga'.

The northern massage style is stretchier and, like Lanna people, gentler. In Bangkok's more assertive method, thumbs jab each acupressure point with a flourish, then double-handed twists jerk the joints to a satisfying crack. The latest trend is *tok sen* – tapping the points with a mallet and probe, which requires special skill. If it hurts, that's your fault due to tension, and, if necessary, they'll even walk on your back.

Spas and massage parlours are one of Bangkok's mystery businesses, with so many outlets – at least ten in my *soi* – you wonder how they profit. Signs saying just 'Massage' tend to be the unclothed version involving a soapy bath and a 'happy end', but those saying 'Thai Massage' are often legitimate. Masseurs subsist on piece rate plus tips, so they often tout for custom from the doorstep. Some customers may be tempted to pick the best looking, but patrons who seek healing over pampering prefer experienced masters. The most savvy advocate the skill of blind masseurs, who possess a heightened sense of touch.

Bangkok massage has spread across the globe and foreigners come here to learn the art. Although the International Massage Organisation decreed that Thai massage can't be registered as unique as it blends Chinese, Indian and local methods, Thai massage has been added to UNESCO's intangible cultural heritage. Fusion is the national forte, so that's like saying Thai food or dance are no more than their imported elements. In truth, food and massage are both highly sensual Thai gifts to the world.

top: Oriental Spa led the global wellness trend.

above: Public massage in a National Stadium fair.

Senses 149

Pain
Suffering and hell parks, caring and ganja

People come to Bangkok specifically to have their pain soothed. It's a special talent of the place, achieved through the power of touch in massage, the insight of Buddhism in meditaion, and the care of its hi-tech hospitals. The city is famous as a good-value pioneer in medical tourism, but another way to soothe pain is drawing visitors: the legalisation of marijuana.

In Bangkok, you also get confronted by the matter-of-fact Thai way with pain. In, *Thai Rath* newspaper, I once counted 22 pictures of corpses. Most showed crimes or accidents, plus open-coffin shots of late VIPs. Today, the media show less gore, and pixellate the face, but still expose the blood and flesh, leaving little to the horrified imagination. "If you watch Workpoint News on YouTube it shows all the most spectacular crashes," said *Bangkok Noir* novellist John Burdett. "They even give you the wheel odds, e.g. '18-wheeler versus Honda moped'."

"It's pure sensationalism," says Anucha Thirakanont, an expert in communications at Thammasat. "We don't like it, but it sells more copies." While that's true, tabloids in most nations shield gruesome images, yet here they flourish throughout the culture. Although it's confronting to see front-page pictures of a friend's disturbing death scene, readers have a very direct sense of grief and mortality. Bangkok has museums of pain, murals of pain, sculpture gardens of pain. Bodily harm is a Buddhist learning opportunity.

The award-winning Thai movie *Malila* showed monks contemplating a corpse as an advanced meditation on impermanence. Pain, death and grief just happen; the Buddhist way to eliminate suffering is to observe sensations with detachment then let them go. Bangkok's temptations are the ultimate challenge. "If we examine any person who has sunk into dereliction, we always find that it has come about through his clinging fast to some desirable sense object," wrote the philosopher-monk, Buddhadasa Bhikkhu. "They are well disguised as sweet, tasty, fragrant, alluring things, beautiful things, melodious things." As the Buddha himself said: "the enjoyment of sensual pleasure is the womb of pain."

Bangkok is often cited as being remarkably safe to stroll at night, even for lone women. But there's a disjoint between how safe you feel and how at risk some people are. In the *Economist*'s 2017 safety survey of 60 cities, it came 12th from bottom on a list of the world's least safe major cities. Much of that is due to accidents, while random mugging seems rare. We feel safe partly because the victims of the many shootings, gang fights or business conflicts tend to know their assailant. The Thai cocooning of emotion results in few unbiased channels to dissolve disputes, so they can erupt into violence. Media frequently reports assassination hits against businesspeople, environmentalists or heirs. Land disputes often get resolved through hired muscle.

left: Wat Khlong Toei Nai, like many crematorium temples, has a skeleton to greet mourners.

right: Volunteers fom Poh Teck Tung help fight a fire deep in the lanes of Chinatown.

The Thai media is full of lurid crime reports that rarely get coverage in English, although gun crime is as high as in the US. Many firearms are kept in cars, which emerge in road-rage incidents, while guards at gold shops are clearly armed. Guns are one legacy from past civil conflicts, a formerly lawless frontier, and millions of ex-soldiers with combat training.

Buddhism's unflinching focus on suffering has a flip side: compassion. Yet this medical tourism hub, with top private hospitals and cheap universal healthcare, does not have a state ambulance service. Picking up the pieces – literally – are private ambulances and charity services, Poh Teck Tung and Ruamkatanyu, whose racing pickups are the first on the scene of any accident or disaster. These ambulance volunteers are true altruists in doing their gruesome work on behalf of the public.

A Thai ethic is to show composure in the face of suffering. Upon an injury, notice the impassive practicality and lack of howls, flails or crying; likewise at funerals. Westerners can be puzzled if Thais laugh when someone gets hurt, misreading their effort to relieve tension. Thais typically rush to help, despite their aversion to taking on somebody else's karma. A New Yorker who fainted on a BTS platform was impressed to find half a dozen Thais tending to him.

Yet if 'face' is at stake, reactions get fierce. The idealised Thai male is genteel and placid, yet Thai masculinity can be macho. Besides *muaythai* being the most lethal martial art, male groups bristle with a jocular braggadocio, and an honour code can spark fights at the slightest violation. The public has grown weary at 'little emperor' incidents by entitled sons of the rich brandishing their inherited don't-you-know-who-my-dad-is line. The most dangerous injury you can do to yourself in Bangkok is step on the wrong person's toe.

One disturbing sidelight on Bangkok life can be seen in *nam nao* ('dirty water', slang for soap operas). *Nam nao* depict hurrumphing men and sneering women, mostly posh, in scenes of tantrums, hair-pulling, face-slaps

Local Heroes

A rite of passage for Bangkok reporters is to ride one night with the 'body collectors'. Incredibly, there's no public ambulance service, besides those of a few private hospitals. So the city relies upon the volunteer ambulance services of two Thai-Chinese charities. They got the body-collecting nickname in the 1990s, because their pick-up truck crews raced each other to arrive first on the scene. Photo journalist Philip Blenkinsop recalled, in his book *The Cars that Ate Bangkok*, how he sat in the back of one of their pickups with a victim's brains nestling on a newspaper in his lap.

This voluntary goodwill service originated in the efforts of Chinese settlers to improve life in their new city. Some early tycoons used their good fortune to found Siam's first charities. They began with Tien Fah Hospital, which still offers traditional Chinese medicine in the clinics beside its shrine to Kwan Im (the goddess of compassion), the doctors making their diagnosis over fortifying cups of Chinese tea.

The Tejapaibul family, bankers who built what's now Central World, created Poh Teck Tung Foundation. Based at the shrine of that name in Phlabphlachai, Chinatown, it provided a decent burial for Chinese settlers who died alone and penniless. They've since expanded to provide emergency care for accidents, fires or disasters. Later a similar charity, Ruamkatanyu, provides ambulances. At their base in Wat Hualumphong, you can donate towards coffins for the impoverished.

Thailand gets global praise for its universal health care, which was initiated by Thaksin Shinawatra. Yet it discomfits the patronage system, which prefers to see the plight of the poor alleviated by generosity from above. Chinese settlers were outside that feudal setup, so the destitute had to rely on self-help and the kindness of kin and clan. Sino-Thai charities turned that mutual help into a social service for all.

Today their ambulances are getting higher specs, more high tech, and volunteer paramedics patrol public events. When a fire raged in a *yaan* near my house, the first responders were these brave, selfless fellows, always ready to help.

Healing Hub

Several million foreigners a year come annually to Bangkok to heal. Out of the global medical tourism industry, Thailand accounts for a world-leading 40%. More than one million alone go to Bumrungrad Hospital, which has some of the world's most advanced equipment and patient technology.

The consumer campaigner famed for *Super-size Me*, Morgan Spurlock, found that a colonoscopy here, including flights and hospitality, cost a third of US treatment. Foreign travel to Bangkok hospitals is more than merely cheap, or enticingly packaged with idyllic recuperation holidays. It is efficiently modern, with very short waits to use the latest equipment. New laws to charge medical tourists highter rates, reflect concern that profiting from foreign patients diverts resources from Thai health.

Many specialists at international hospitals like Samitivej are impressively patient-centred and alert to laypeople having researched their ailments online. However, some old-school practitioners tend to be more doctor-centred. The profession has huge social prestige and is a favoured career among middle class and up. This breeds imperious attitudes and such doctors treat patients' questions or suggestions with indignation as a loss of face. Their status – and role of many as pharmaceutical salesmen – can cower patients into being afraid to get a second opinion. However, today patient empowerment via internet or alternative medicine threatens their position, though it remains one of the most prestigious professions.

Doctors here notoriously over prescribe. Hospitals tend to demand payment before handing over medicines including some you may not need. But that's what the patients expect. A history of herbalism based on rebalancing elements within the body gave rise to the expectation that there must be a potion for any ailment. Moreover, medicines are notoriously easy to get in Bangkok, even those which elsewhere would be prescription drugs. Pharmacies are plentiful, and residents know that the best value medicines are found in the row of competitive drug stores near each major hospital.

Perception of illness as imbalance also helps explain why the health of Bangkokians seems so delicate. Most common is the malaise *bpen wat* – sniffly, feverish "under the weather" symptoms linked to seasonal shift, or going in and out of air-conditioning. What may seem like hypochondria might be the Thais seeking to rebalance their systems.

Dentists would surely testify to the low Thai pain threshold, which explains why healing here gets such compassionate coddling. Doctors and dentists at clinics like Thantakit are skilled at minimising pain during their procedures. Nursing is marked by an acute attention to patient feelings. Instead of retreading standard pleasantries, doctors and nurses come across as personally interested in what ails you. That by itself will bring millions to the city.

left: A skeletal promotion for a private hospital reaches out to its customer base at Emporium mall.

right: **Death Café**, at Kit Mai Buddhist centre in Aree, urges you to rethink how to spend your limited time alive. Among its installations is a coffin you can test. Just knock on the lid to let the staff know when you want to get out.

below: **Impromptu hand basins outside shops are one legacy of the Covid-19 pandemic.**

and rape. You can see the soap histrionics rub off onto ordinary people. The capital has the country's worse figures for domestic abuse and family-related suicide. Yet the general public and police reaction is: "Don't interfere in a matter of husband and wife."

The topic became unavoidable in 2013 with the murder of Olympic marksman Jakkrit Panichpatikum, allegedly commissioned in self-defense by his repeatedly battered wife. "It was evident that people were rooting for the couple to reunite like in a happy ending of

a movie instead of realistically fixing the root cause," reported the *Bangkok Post*. It also noted a survey of men in which a third regarded wives as property, 44.8% admitted to assault when they were drunk, 42.4% had forced their partner to have sex, and 14% viewed male violence as showing love because he was jealous.

"Love hurts, as we teach our children, or it's not love," says film reviewer Kong Rithdee about a real-life fight over a man between two gangs of women led by a soap actress and her rival. "This is what Thai soap fans call a classic *dak tob*, a slap-ambush… you need to ensure that your gang, your network, your clique, your club, is more powerful than that of your rival's."

This endorsed *hi-so* braggadocio is emulated by a lower stratum whom the privileged disdain: *dek chang* (vocational students). Thailand desperately needs more technicians but doesn't give them status. *Dek chang* are often poor, troubled youths, who assert their dignity through fights over their school's honour. As codes of family and faith corrode, they join gangs and apply the seniority system to the bottom of the hierarchy, as they never touch university students.

In 2015, Bangkok endured over 1,000 cases of violence by students who made their own weapons. Starting in the mid-1970s, *dek chang* feuds drifted from theft of collegiate emblems to vicious public affrays. They've pushed people from buses or shot at passing vans. In 2001, 300 rampaging students from three colleges damaged dozens of vehicles, lit a fire and fought with knives, bars, home-made guns and ping-pong bombs. Stray bullets from student battles have killed passers-by; one even went through my neighbour's roof and hit the bed.

Senses 153

left: **Siriraj Hospital has six teaching museums that have become macabre tourist sights. On show are these Siamese twins, with offerings to their spirits.**

below: **One of the many 'medical cannabis' dispensaries that light up the Bangkok night since the legalisation of marijuana.**

double-down on the militarism and force brawlers into cadet training. "Even if there is three months' training, it won't change how we are when we go back to school," says Abhisit Sa-in, 17, of Samut Prakan Technical College. "We are always ready to rip each other apart."

In schools, corporal punishment is outlawed, but still gets inflicted on pupils. One teacher was so angry that a girl's hairstyle was longer than the regulation bob that she scissored her hair and severed an ear lobe.

Initiation rites into adulthood instil social submission upon pain of punishment or even ostracism, whether among military conscripts, gangs, or university 'freshies'. Most years there's a fatality. At a Bangkok art university, I saw seniors order a freshie to lie face down wearing

Band-aid ideas to staunch the bloodletting include merging rival schools, closing non-reformable ones, or banning uniforms. Some students already travel in plain clothes so they aren't identifiable. A standard response is to

Pot luck

Bangkok woke up in June 2022 to find marijuana was no longer illegal in the land infamous for Thai Sticks – hollow tubes of ganja beloved of hippies and GI soldiers. In the 2019 election, the Bhumjai Thai Party had made cannabis legalisation their price for enabling the junta leaders to keep power. The old guard seemed to disapprove yet agreed.

A huge industry arose instantly. Hemp leaf logos grace food, body and clothing products, sold in shops, malls and convenience stores. Ganja had historically been used in Thai remedies and in cooking to impart umami flavour. Those health benefits of cannabinol (CBD oil) had been the stated aim of the law, but it oddly lacked tax or regulations, so police couldn't stop ganja containing the narcotic THC compound from being sold for recreation.

Thousands of weed shops opened to sell bongs, edibles and buds from all over the world, treating smokers like wine or cigar connoisseurs. Some dispensaries resemble clubs or have smoking rooms. Thais call it ganja, but most dispensaries use English terms like 420, Green, Puff or Mary Jane, often in fun names like Starbuds, Coughing Apes, High Got You, Ministry of High, Your HighNess or Never Not High. Some use local riffs on spliffs: Sukhumweed on Sukhumvit, Sala Dank on Saladaeng or THC: Thonglor Hemp Club.

Toking in public was banned, but the aroma lingers city-wide. The black market also flog buds from street stalls. Despite brands like 'Bangkok Cannabis Souvenir',

airlines warn fliers that carrying pot to certain lands remains a capital crime.

Due to over-saturation, many suppliers will fade like smoke as specialists, some foreign, take over the joint. Some Thais want weed recriminalised; others call for regulation. Yet draft rules are stricter than for alcohol, which is worse for health and behaviour. Meanwhile, alcohol duties and rules were relaxed "for tourism," though it was pot that drew visitor growth. Tellingly, pot had reduced sales of alcohol, which is run by monopolies that also outlaw indie breweries and distillers. At stake are huge industries, jobs, investments and the national reputation. Perhaps it all has less to do with medicine, beer or pot, than another drug: money.

just his underwear in the rain, and to worm along the courtyard without his hands touching the concrete that cut his flesh. Lying face-down and shirtless with hands tied behind the back has also been used for subduing gangs or protestors. Recently, a series of conscripts have died in unexplained punishments.

The justice system is notoriously harsh. Warren Fellowes' memoir *The Damage Done*, made infamous his 12-year ordeal inside the 'Bangkok Hilton', Bang Kwang Prison near Nonthaburi Pier. It fuelled a subculture of expats and backpackers visiting prisoners who lack in-country support. Today, the British Women's Club still organise weekly visits. Stung by the reputation, Bang Kwang has instituted some reform and hadn't conducted executions for so long it was considered lapsed. In 2017, Thonburi Remand Prison became the first jail in the world to implement the humane Nelson Mandela Rules, but execution has since resumed.

Meanwhile, Sook Station is the world's first prison-themed hostel where you can literally spend a night on bunks behind bars in a tiny cell, having had your mugshot taken in a striped uniform. Inspired by *The Shawshank Redemption*, owner Sittichai Chaivoraprug says: "Prison experiences don't have to be scary."[10]

Jail scares the well-connected less, because they can usually get bail and avoid conviction, unlike those without status. The most notorious evaders of justice involve reckless driving, from the Red Bull heir who ran over a policeman in his Ferrari, to an under-age *hi-so* girl whose speeding car shunted a van of students off an elevated highway, and who shirked even her community service sentence. Some Thais believe that the privileged get away with crimes due to merit earned in past lives, but will face elaborate tortures in the next. Bangkok would make a great topic for *CSI*, except that each puzzling case would fizzle out without an ending.

Covid-19 never had an ending here either. Hand sanitiser, plastic screens and wash basins remain in public areas. Officialdom still advises mask-wearing in civic spaces and transport, but plenty are happy to comply. Some say masks feel reassuring, compassionate and a way to fit in – and relieve having to smile so much. Bangkok was the first place outside China to get Covid, but already had a culture of wearing masks. Thais had supplies due to the cool season smog and the habit of wearing a mask when being *bpen wat* – having a cold or flu. Masking-up is a way Thais show they care.

Hell Park

Bangkok has little public sculpture, but its most common form of sculpture parks depict the tortures of hell. Buddhist cosmology has four levels of hells, some drawn with relish in the lower panels of Bangkok temple murals. The most creative tortures, however, are sculpted in concrete at Buddhist theme parks like Wat Phut Udom in Lamlukka.

It's a family day out for instilling good behaviour. Do something wrong and you could face scorching heat in Pratapana or chilling fate in the Hell of Shivering Tongue (Utpala). The Death King, Phya Yom, may haul the fallen to Hells of Swelling (Arbuda) or Shrinking (Nirarbuda), or to laceration in Kalasutra, the Hell of Black Wire.

Meanwhile rote-learning schoolchildren daily endure an earthly preview of Samjiva: the Hell of Constant Repetition. Thanks to karma, 'good people' can of course watch these images of suffering with a clear conscience.

top & above: **Tableaux of tortures in hell spur believers to avoid these sin-specific punishments.**

Senses 155

Sound
Hearing the Bangkokophony

Many visit Bangkok on a whistle-stop tour; residents wish it could be a stop-whistle tour. Incessant blasts by guards on their whistles shred peace of mind. Expressboats employ specific whistles to signal direction to the captain, but most blasts by traffic attendants lack any system. Whistling is a status trip, a sign of being in charge: directing a car, halting traffic, warning walkers. Whistles are just the crest of a sonic tidal wave. Nerves judder at the traffic, drills and mechanical clangour. Ears bleed at the volume of TVs. Among the sources of noise pollution, whistles have become the battleground: a tool of protestors in the Bangkok Shutdown, and the cause of protests by the pressure group Quiet Bangkok.

Beneath that bedlam, a quieter Bangkok emits grace notes. The city offers surprising aural delicacy, from Buddhist sermons on taxi radio to a wealth of birdsong. Then there's the plangent local language with its tones and compound vowels. Thais are raised to speak and tread softly. In crises they rarely shout. Drivers don't hoot their horns. And faced with the constant racket, few raise voices in complaint. Bangkok is a duet of whispers and cement mixers.

There's a musicality to daily life. Monks chant at dusk. Students collecting for charity chant in the ancient form of call-and-response to the rhythm of tapping sticks. Bangkok hosts ululating singers of central and Isaan folk styles, but also refined *phiphat* court music, *likay*'s mannered folk operatics, and its own pop-rock genres of *luuk krung* ('capital kids' pop) and indie. Everpresent are open-air cover bands and the tinkle-tonkle of hotel and restaurant musicians. Pervading public spaces like stations and supermarkets at certain periods everyone is reached by piped, patriotic songs.

Noise is present countrywide – pestle thuds mortar in kitchens – but Bangkokians are noticeably louder than upcountry folk. This could come from the capital's Chinese quotient. Many expressions of Chinese culture were suppressed and faded, but not the belief in making noise. In feng shui, noise has a positive connotation of liveliness, flourishing and appreciation – and chasing away ghosts. The Chinese tendency to holler and verbalise enjoyment has passed into Bangkok habit, though Sino-Thais have absorbed the Thai trait to soft-talk when appropriate. The combined result is far mellower than the contrasting mainland tourist cacophony, which prompts massive outcry through social media.

In personal interaction, most Bangkokians speak softly with enough breathy emphasis that you notice their polite spoken manners. Gangs of friends, however, may shatter the air. The Thai personality is rather outgoing, and fulfilled through *sanuk*, a sensibility for group fun that fuels nights out singing, partying or watching TV sport with a bunch of mates. Among Bangkok's happiest times are getting carried away at live music venues such as Tawandang.

As the city gets more sophisticated, gleeful shrieks can jar at venues with more decorum. Consideration for strangers is not the priority

when boisterousness is a means to bolster group identity. *Sanuk* can feel compulsory, as at the exuberant Songkran Festival water-throwing. Comedies lacking in wit strive for laughs by overdubbing drum clatters and 'boing' noises. Some groups use sound as their trademark: bikers rev their customised bikes; *katoeys* relish squealling banter; macho dudes josh in *guu-mung* 'guy talk.' Acting loud may betray a lack of influence; those with power stay quiet. Thai leaders hold their voice in reserve, so that when they finally speak, all listen and try to parse the coded implications.

Noise escalates because social inhibitions stop it being curbed. *Kreng jai* is the pressure not to complain so as to spare the offender's feelings, but also to avoid backlash. Try quelling a late-night party or karaoke caterwauling; the reaction can be violent. When friends complained of illegal construction noise till 2am, the influential developer demanded their identities from the police. A resident of a new condo who complained about temple bell-ringing at night became the target of an online witch-hunt, raising the dilemma over noise into an emotive headline issue.

Excessive noise hurts our hearing and disturbs the emotions. Over 70 decibels are unhealthy and beyond 80, tempers flare. Traffic pressure points like Lad Prao Road exceed 85 decibels, the threshold of physical ear damage. A whistle hits 120 decibels. Like roadies inured to concert speakers, affected people grow deaf to certain frequencies and keep turning up the dial to levels they find audible. To tolerate such physical and mental harm, people must be cowed by its source, be nonchalant about avoidable din, or embrace noise as a choice.

"Asians today love loud noises," says Oraya Sutrabutr, founder of Quiet Bangkok. "It means they're having fun or getting attention, a sign of insecurity. Also, there's a lack of sensitivity or respect for public, shared domains, that you shouldn't violate." Beyond immediate circles of family, friends and colleagues comes what Suchada Tangtongtavy calls the "selfish circle" – the impersonal realm of strangers with no link or rank, who don't merit consideration.

In public space, the most selfish noise comes from businesses out-yelling their competitors. Shops may have giant speakers outside to relay their sale. Roving trucks talk-up their wares via loudspeaker as they troll the *sois* at 8am on a Sunday. Sales pitches are inescapable, from

left: **Multicolour loudspeakers are a new feature of tuk-tuks.**

bottom: **Measuring noise pollution on the street.**

below: **Installation for hearing noisescapes in *The Hidden Sound of BKK*, by Nithiphat Hoisangthong, part of the 'Live the City' exhibition in BACC.**

giant LED screens with penetratingly dense audio to pairs of MCs at events or mall promotions, who never pause their microphoned chatter. In supermarkets, motion sets off audiovisual displays, while in-store radio stations hard-sell shoppers their discount toothpaste. Ad volume impinges most in confined spaces like trains, which was campaigned against by the People Who Love Quiet Club, claiming "Somebody is getting rich at the expense of our right to peace and quiet."

Such an overlapping soundscape was normalised at the temple fair. Sideshows, stages and films go on simultaneously with blasts of techno when the Ferris wheel turns, and

Birdsong

The dawn chorus erupts with chirps, fluttering whirrs and abrupt random honks. Few know that this city is one of the world's major birding sites. On a single-week's visit here, birder Hanno Stamm identified 85 species, including Dollarbirds, Yellow Vented Bulbuls, and the Greater Racket-tailed Drongo.

The Bangkok Wild Watch 2014 survey found that 22 native and nine migrant bird species inhabit the main downtown greensward, Lumpini Park. It also recorded a forest dweller – Thick-billed Green Pigeons – along with the rare Ashy Drone and Javan Pond Heron.

Bangkok may seem to be an unlikely nest, but it was built in a vast, nourishing wetland. The immediate surrounds of the upper Thai Gulf are one of the world's most unsung, yet vital, birding zones. Here in 2007, ornithologists found a Large-billed Reed Warbler, a species whose warble had gone unheard in 129 years.

Every cool season, millions of migratory birds fly from northern climes to feeding and mating grounds in Bangkok. Oddly, Siberian swifts only gather in two locations, Lumpini Park and Patpong, where patrons dodge droppings as they bar-hop. Experts assume insects may have originally drawn this annual frenzy from October to March. Even Skytrain noise and cutting their favoured trees hasn't diverted the birds from their perches.

Other birds thrive in this modern environment. And not just the pigeons in one of the city's few plazas around the Giant Swing. Facing the wooded peninsula of Bang Kra Jao, Bangchak Oil Company runs the Bangchak Bird-watching Club, where enthusiasts can view the habitat around the oil refinery.

One drawback to siting Suvarnabhumi Airport at low-lying Cobra Swamp (Nong Ngu Hao) was the risk of jets sucking up the local wildfowl. Its Bird Control Unit tries to keep the airport's water devoid of life-forms, to deter herons and cranes, as well as reducing nearby flocks. Nevertheless, not far away near Lad Krabang Industrial Estate you can spot owls, egrets, and mynahs at Putkao Bird Sanctuary. Cormorants arrive in the rainy season, while most Open-billed Storks fly north in summer. Storks also nest upriver in Pathum Thani at Wat Pailom and at a stork colony in rice fields at Lumlukka, visited on Spice Roads cycle tours. Others go birding at Bang Phra Non-hunting Area.

With big game virtually exterminated in the Thai wild – lower Isaan once was second only to the African savannah in large mammals – binoculars focus on birds, with birders joining organised trips such as those by Nature Trails. Birds still find places to survive around the city's ponds and empty lots, but the loss of green gaps may intensify with a mooted tax on unused land. Many species are threatened, which is aggravated by feral cats and kids with wooden slingshots.

Bangkokians also enjoy birdsong by caging the singers. Fanciers and breeders peruse bird markets like Chatuchak. Older *yaan* – especially of Malay Muslims – fringe their verandahs and awnings with graceful rattan cages, shaded by coloured cloth shades and slung from an ornamental hook. Hopping inside, mynahs and barred doves bring music to the ears of residents and judges in cooing contests.

While Lumpini Park air quality declines, the redevelopment of Makkasan swamp threatens to ruin the city's largest central wetland. The adjacent district of Din Daeng, one of the most polluted areas, was where a firm made the CD 'Bangkok Birds: Field Recordings'. Bangkok's dawn chorus might end up just an app.

an amped-up abbot preaching Dharma over the fairground fun. That's now the norm. Walking along a bar strip like RCA or Silom Soi 4 is to pass through a patchwork of clashing songs from the outdoor sound systems of rival bars. Bangkok nightlife is generally too loud for easy conversation. In suburban strips like Ratchada or Lamsalee, the blasting *sam-cha* techno can literally vibrate your viscera.

Bangkok's format is such that life is lived openly in the streets. The public must contend with the banter of bike taxi boys, and the hubbub around hawkers, as woks clatter and liquidisers whirr. Passers-by get this in stereo, because open-fronted shophouses expose all to machining in workshops and the full domestic chorus: TV, toddlers, nagging. It's like Bangkok is gathered in one giant kitchen with the family over-talking each other.

This sonic soup keeps recirculating due to Bangkok's particular architecture. Early Bangkok was made of absorbent materials – wood, thatch,

clay – with further dampening by greenery. Then came the Chinese and their shophouse format. Brick walls with jutting masonry rose on both sides, causing the racket to reverberate. It's no surprise that the loudest clashpoints tend to be areas like Pratunam and Saphan Kwai, where shophouses rise several floors with sound-trap balconies. Magnifying the effect, their security grilles cause distortion at higher sound pressures, which abound from the metallic traffic.

Many of these noise traps were further enclosed when elevated transport brought in hard pillars and broad strips of concrete that box in roads like Ramkhamhaeng or Charansanitwong. Skytrain stations almost touch the buildings lining Sukhumvit and Silom.

The current replacement of shophouses by set-back towers with landscaped forecourts may diminish streetlife, but it does let some of the din escape. Overhead Skywalks further trap the sound at street level, yet provide a hushed space above the pandemonium.

The open fronts of shophouses invite street tumult inside. Even when shutting up shop, roller doors or concertina grills make a rattle. Construction tends to leave pillars and beams exposed, multiplying the reflective surfaces. Floors are tile or terrazzo, sometimes wood, never carpet. Walls are thin enough to hear through. Bangkok's multi-storey shophouses lack the inner air-well of original Chinese design, or walls around stairwells, so sound travels throughout.

Bangkokians go in for sparse decoration with hard chairs and minimal soft furnishings. Many windows go uncovered, or have hard closures such as shutters or louvres rather than curtains. Walls are largely bare, even in restaurants or bars, which rarely have linings or acoustic baffles, though a few use panels of egg-boxes. Tep Bar is lauded for hosting *ranat ek* musicians in a heritage shophouse, but they're surprisingly loud.

All these specific sounds in particular places amount to an aural signature, what composer R Murray Shafer labelled a "soundscape." Bangkok rings with its own take on modernity: a chorus of rasping tuk-tuks, exploding transformers, and the Green Music stalls that emanate Thai-style Electone ditties played on a loop in spas.

left: **Cranes nesting in Lumlukka are among Bangkok's many bird colonies.**

top: **Conch horns being blown in a Brahmin rite.**

above: **Bells for you to ring on Golden Mount.**

However, some distinctive street sounds are beginning to fade. The clapping of conductors' ticket tubes, and handmade chimes heralding each kind of vendor could be exhibits in the online Museum of Endangered Sounds.

"The internationalism of urban design has resulted not only in some visual but also aural sameness," notes sound artist Hildegard Westerkamp. There is no uniqueness to the gurgles of espresso makers, the synthetic pings of electronics, or the ding-dong of the door to 7-Eleven. Schafer calls this the "bad breath" of high-rise buildings.

Noise isn't a new problem. At the turn of the 20th century, the whine from sawmills along the Thonburi bank drove residents out of Charoen Krung Road. That road remains buffeted by daytime traffic, but despite an influx of nightspots, is remarkably quiet after rush hour. Further into the old town, the roads get almost deserted. Within each *taew*, residents rise and go to bed early. In suburbia, *sois* turn so quiet that many are reticent to walk at night. The only sound is often the barks of *soi* dogs, or the put-put of a Honda Dream wending through lanes as placid as those in Vientiane, Laos. Despite the aural onslaught during the day on Bangkok's main roads and construction sites, the city is quieter on average.

What happened to amplify everyday hubbub to ear-threatening pitch was, literally, amplifiers. The advent of cheap radios and speakers in the 1970s was an easy way to boast of electrification, and show status by increasing the volume of one's voice. This tumult is partly the soundtrack to progress, as Bangkok rushed to be developed.

Bangkokians don't recognise noise as a problem partly because it has accompanied wealth and progress. Fines haven't increased since a 1956 law charging offenders a paltry 100 baht. So there's no incentive for easy fixes like servicing the belching buses, enforcing mufflers on motorbikes or covering the engines of longtail boats that reverberate off every riverside wall.

Under soft-spoken etiquette, making noise is a means to impose. The state does this by controlling the airwaves through licenses and their own channels, as well as broadcasts that must be carried on all media. A network of loudspeakers relays official orders in neighbourhoods, and civic updates in parks. When those speakers play the national anthem everywhere at 8am and 6pm, the song brings Bangkok to a halt.

Protestors have made noise their trademark. Yellow Shirt demonstrators tired of clapping their hands at rallies, so they invented plastic hand-shaped clappers, which they shook with less effort but to more effect. The Red Shirts responded with foot-shaped clappers. Then during the 2013-14 Bangkok Shutdown, protestors against Yingluck Shinawatra's government styled themselves "whistle-blowers." Thousands of them blew flag-coloured whistles in unison at daily demos for months until a coup. Then all protest was silenced.

Now noise is the subject of protest. When King Bhumibol criticised excessive noise in his 2004 Birthday speech, people responded. Zoning of bars away from quiet areas dates from that time. Roadside noise began to be monitored by foam-covered mics and awareness of noise pollution grew. By the late 2000s, civil society took notice that noise is no longer a sign of modernity. Whistling guards became the first target of the Quiet Bangkok movement, who persuaded many building owners to have their guards direct cars using white gloves and flashing red batons.

But a truly Quiet Bangkok remains elusive. The 'Green Lung' of Bang Krajao, and the few parks do offer respite, but not always. Mass aerobics, music players and official loudspeakers prevent any natural peace. Nor are temples the sanctuary one presumes.

Wats were always a hub of community; today they hold schools and events, while above the clatter of everyday activity, the grounds ring with broadcast sermons. Dedicated seekers of quiet escape to meditation retreats and spas.

Awareness of the need for quiet spaces has been a boost for the arts. Galleries and museums are growing in both number and youth interest. Major libraries have opened at TCDC, BACC, the City Library in Ratchadamnoen and the riverside Bank of Thailand.

Acoustics too are improving. Overloud pubs tend to be the older, cruder ones, whilst trendy venues take pride in their quality of sound. Galleries increasingly feature aural art. Meanwhile the blind buskers outside add their tunes to Bangkok's concerto of the street.

opposite left & right: **Thai protestors make distinctive sounds. Yellow Shirts made labour-saving hand-clappers, then later blew whistles and wore flag colours in the Bangkok Shutdown. Red Shirts adopted the clapper in the taboo form of waving a foot at their opponents.**

above: **The property developer Noble turned the patterns of its condos' designs into readable notation, which a program then turns into noise, to create what Noble calls the 'sound of architecture.'**

left: **Tep bar has a loud *ranat-ek* band as its neo-traditional concept.**

Senses **161**

Bang-Pop!

Every city has its soundtrack. Some create a signature music: Merseybeat, Seattle grunge, Chicago house. Bangkok's own genres, ever since *luk krung* (kids of the capital), offer aural massage. This polite pop is soothing, non-threatening, music-academy playing, with a romantic message. "Think Soi Thonglor: dress shirt, white European car, no dirt under the fingernails," says rock star Hugo, aka Chulachak Chakrabongse. "I call the sound 'Bangkok Clean' – two words that don't belong together."

There's evident talent, but it's stifled. "All the bars play the same music," says Norasate Mudkong, aka DJ Seed, an indie music pioneer. "It's understandable that people aren't open to new things when they don't get any variety." Spaces to experiment like Adhere are rare. Musicians get told what to play, both by business owners and the audience. Requests for the same old songs turn bands into cover bands, concerts into karaoke.

Key to the city's musical profile is that Thais love to sing along, which energises variety halls like Tawandang German Brewery. To holler the chorus, they must know the song, whether 'Hotel California' or catchy standards by '90s divas like Christina or Mai.

"I felt ashamed singing other people's songs," admits Jessada 'Gap' Teerapinan, singer of the legendary ska band T-Bone, who began the city's ska-reggae scene. "We'll never play reggae as well as Jamaican people. It's not our roots. We decided to only play our own music. We also refused to do requests."

Few artists stand apart. T-Bone rose during the 1990s indie wave when, from among new labels and garage recordings, Bakery Music nurtured the indie sound. It spans from Goth eccentrics like Rik via punkish rock to singer-songwriters on jangly guitar. Bakery settled on a loungey jazz-funk vibe exemplified by POP and Groove Riders.

The sound of an era eventually becomes a time capsule; now Bakery bands are veterans doing reunion concerts. "Gen X was Modern Dog," says Bakery founder Kamol 'Sukie' Clapp of his top signing. "Gen Y was Bodyslam, Big Ass and Silly Fools – which I call ThaiNuMetal – the last time we had a sound that crossed all barriers, but that was ten years ago. Generation Me has yet to have a sound. This has to do with Millennials growing up with the Internet." Bangkok's musical gatekeepers have gone.

In analogue times, the capital had a lead over provincial kids in access to music trends. Now that gap has closed, Bangkok's musical trademarks will lessen. "The key thing is the accent you sing in," says Hugo, whose blend of Thai country rock, bluegrass and lyrical craft earned a contract with Jay-Z. Unusually, he sings in both Thai and English. "The moment there's any hint of a country accent – whichever region – it ceases to be a Bangkok record.

The only unifying Bangkok sound would be a certain effeteness that could be expected from any capital."

At the postwar dawn of pop, Suntaraporn Band created what became Bangkok Standards – tremulous ballads that still seem compulsory at nostalgic events, and drove the plot of the hit movie *Tears of the Black Tiger*. Suntaraporn hitched Big Band brass to local crooning, which accentuated the uneasy pairing of Thai tones and Western tunes.

From the 1960s, *luk krung* applied Thai melody to Western dancehall, later adding the rhumba, foxtrot and cha-cha-cha. These cross-pollinated to form Sam Cha (three chas), the insistent beat used in surprising ways, from Carabao's bluesy rock to the Thai techno that blasts from suburban bars.

Sam cha also propels the churning drive of *luk thung*, the central plains folk music named for "kids of the fields." Isaan folk rap, *molam*, also adopted Latin, brass and surf rock. Based on regional song traditions, these folk genres have the widest national appeal, fueled by ribald lyrics that lament rural and migrant hardship. Within Bangkok, folk music was confined to AM radio and migrant venues like Isaan Toerd Toeng in Pinklao. Then just as the 1997 economic crash revived indigenous arts, folk debuted on FM radio. Heard in taxis, it gained middle-class fans, who gave it ironic cachet as *choei* – a retro cheesiness. Today, *molam/luk thung* have merged, with infusions of rap, electro and K-Pop.

Carabao's bluesy style began in the 1970s political rebellions, which birthed the plaintive genre Songs For Life. This became a lifestyle seen in pubs like Raintree or Tawandang, which is fading as 'October Generation' fans leave middle age.

"The 1980s was when Thai music was really born: Thai composed, Thai produced, Thai sung," says Vasu

Sangsingkaew, a diplomat who sang in the boyband The Palace and as an Elvis impersonator. "There was still some influence from the West, but we twisted it and made it our own." That slick, sentimental Bangkok template was honed by Asanee and Wasan Chotikul, who solved how to match Thai tones with rock refrains. Thongchai 'Bird' Mcintyre perfected this at the label Grammy, which with RS matched model-celebrity-actor-singers to a corporate songwriting stable, akin to New York's Brill Building.

"Writing songs in Thai is very hard, like playing jigsaw," says Tul Waitoonkiat of indie band Apartment Khunpa. "Thai language is already musical. Each word has a fixed tone and not all can fit to a ready-made melody." This can sound 'off', so the musicality varies less and lyrics take priority. "Thai vocals are mixed twice as loud as guitar, bass and drums, whereas Western rock or pop treat the vocal as an instrument."

Today's musical sugar vapour that wafts through malls, bars and phones, draws ideas from anywhere, not least K-Pop. "It's upbeat, snappy and memorable, just like the city itself," says music reviewer Chanun Poomsawai. "We're partial to pretty melodies and recognisable lyrics. That's probably why bossanova covers of pop hits are such a mainstay."

Several Thais joined K-Pop bands, starting with Nichkhun of 2PM. Lisa Manoban, of BlackPink, went solo and became the first Thai global megastar, with the heft to close Yaowarat Road to shoot a video.

The public prefers live bands over discos or DJs, so the city has a huge number of music venues, including restaurants and outdoor events. Most nightclubs have a stage for bands, with dancefloors covered in tall tables, around which people do expressive actions rather than boogie. They're there for *sanuk* and won't tolerate earnest mumblecore art-rock. "Thai songs in general do not allow abstract lyrics," Tul adds. "It can be heavy metal to EDM – as long as the song is about love, Bangkok people enjoy it. Bangkokians dance to the lyrics, not the rhythm."

left: Star singer Hugo combines many Bangkok pop traits: country-blues fusion sounds, half-Thai heritage, and singing in Thai and English. In his band is fellow star, synth-pop muso Jay Montonn.

top: A mini-concert in a mall by Phrae, a star from the music reality TV contest *Academy Fantasia*.

above: Carabao folk rock band, as toys in Wat Nam Pueng Floating Market.

Sensors
Feeling Digital

Beep, beep, beeeeeep goes the security gate at stations, malls and offices. These noises are merely the most audible of the electric sensors that are making Bangkok digitally compliant. The chaos is ripe for algorithms to sort, manage and predict. Harnessing tech to Thai ingenuity, the state hopes, could help lift the country from the middle-income trap before its ageing population sucks up any gains in productivity. While apps enhance some Thai social traits, the power of computing to standardise and subdue marks a fundamental wrench in Thai life. Gating by sensors could sap the city of its impromptu, easy-going character. Yet most of the digital disruption is keenly embraced.

People in Thailand spend more time on the Internet than in any other nation, 9.38 hours a day, and the most online via mobile phone, 4.56 hours. With so many waking hours glued to a screen, they can't help but text while they dawdle, face-down, along paths and stairs. Kasetsart University devoted half a pavement to a lane for students who scroll while they stroll. Bangkok has more Facebook profiles than any place on earth at about double its population. That's about 3 profiles per user, who have a formal profile, one for a fun persona, and often a commercial page. Thais were pioneers of selling things on Facebook, rather like opening a street stall.

Networking technology turbocharged the city's obsession with social connections. Compared to the world average, Thais have many more Facebook friends. The country is the world's 6th fastest growing Internet culture and one of the topmost in the social app LINE. Thais leave one of the clearest digital footprints, which the state is actively logging, demanding in 2019 that shops and cafés track their customers' online usage.

In this relationship culture, impersonal technology often isn't allowed to prevail over personal whim. The classic test case of how Bangkok handles technology is traffic lights. Successive attempts to program them automatically have failed because humans crave power over the switch. For decades sensors have been able to sync traffic light timings to the weight of optimum vehicle flow, yet police in their sentry boxes insist on overriding the phasing of traffic lights beyond their immediate view. They have a theory to 'empty' each road in turn, however thin the density, while the other lanes pile up. Police are even reputed to shunt jams into a rival district. Most importantly, manual switches let motorcades whizz through unimpeded.

Navigating Bangkok's jams became easier through sensors. Overhead LED signage indicates alternative routes as green, amber or red. Apps like Grab overcame the bane of Bangkok taxis refusing rides or avoiding the meter. GPS dashboard mapping often helps, but lacks precision. Varied name spellings send drivers the wrong way. It went viral when GPS guided an SUV down an ever-narrowing lane until the wheels slipped astride a concrete path over a Nonthaburi khlong.

The inventor of Thailand's first electronic taxi dispatch system and a GIS map of the electrical grid, Visit Hirankitti, also patented a Thai-style DIY sensor during Bangkok's most existential crisis: the Great Flood of 2011. Volunteers could send flood depth data from each sensor – made cheaply of plastic pipe, float, and string – via an app to crowdsource a 3-D online map of the floodwaters.

Flood isn't the only catastrophe that might be helped by new sensors. Bangkok suddenly has a 10% chance of an earthquake of 5.9 on the Richter Scale, according to geologist Panya Charusiri. Vulcanologists recently discovered that the Ongkarak active fault runs for 30 km to Bangkok's northeast. It's minor, but like most Thai faults tend to be shallow, making quakes cause more damage. Panya warns it last rumbled in a 2.5 magnitude temblor 50 years ago, and "could happen today or any time over the next 2,500 years." Buildings with foundations that don't reach through the sediment to bedrock would tip in the same way as a stick after being wiggled in wet sand.

New technology is transforming the city. The glare from LED billboards removes mystique from night-time streets and riverscapes. Waiters increasingly order on e-tablets. Motion-detector ads accost supermarket shoppers with perky sales patter. Office workers and condo-dwellers are used to card-scan access, and now stored-value cards are spreading from train passes into smart ID cards to pay bills and receive services. Museums are installing touch-screen displays, often tailored to Instagram – another app in which Thais are world leaders.

All this has conditioned people to surrender their data, location and opinions, which in turn is enticing the state to become more tech-savvy. The junta aims for a cashless society, launching a nationwide e-banking scheme called PromptPay, while other corporations start their own e-payment schemes. They proposed making vendors use QR codes to eliminate cash (and tax-avoidance), starting with the biggest target, Chatuchak Weekend Market. Visas have been made easier for inward investment in ten future-focused industries – all part of efforts to prepare for the info-based fourth industrial revolution, hence the name of the project: Thailand 4.0.

Bureaucrats seem to prefer Thailand 0.4. The only people who still send faxes are Thai ministries. Forms in government offices tend to be faint photocopies of an original once pounded out on one of the manual typewriters still lurking in many an office. One crucial form has half a line for 'address' but a whole line labelled 'date' – then over the page another whole line for 'month' and 'year.' The entire three-page form could be streamlined onto one side of A4. Or, just imagine, an app. Fondness for paper and rubber stamps means that data needs refilling on countless forms, each page requiring a signature. Government offices burgeon with wads of documents clamped by bulldog clips and stacked like bricks into protective walls.

Red tape is finally getting a snip, however. Any venture requires filling several of Thailand's 700,000 licensing forms, which a reform panel aims to simplify to a mere 1,000. "Each law repealed or merged is estimated to save around one billion baht," says the minister responsible, Kobsak Pootrakool. When forms do go online, they rarely work with all browsers. Even so, programming and e-commerce are among the trades being made easier for startups. Within one year, 2017, Thailand shot from 48th to 26th in the World Bank's Ease of Doing Business Index.

Officials have wised up to digital sensing as a tool to control. Habits of hand-scribbled ledgers and looking the other way are succumbing to hi-tech surveillance and cold-eyed duty. Computerisation is finally

far left: **Wi-fi from the finger of a deity in the logo of the Digital Economy and Society Ministry.**

left: **Downloading data while dressed as angels, surveilled by the digital Big Brother.**

Senses **165**

catching up with Bangkok's sketchier characters: visa overstayers, criminals on the lam, English teachers without a degree. The leader of the Dark Web and the world's biggest arms smuggler, Viktor Bout, were both caught here. But the highest tech still can't nab the highest crooks, whether bid-rigging contractors or scam-devising inspectors.

Thai laws had always been unrealistically strict to balance the public's lenient niceness, but under relentless enforcement, those harsh rules could unleash a security state. This strictness is starting to crimp daily life. Bars install scan gates and bouncers demand age-proof even of those decades older than 20. Scans and pat-downs at rock concerts result in loose trousers as hundreds of forbidden belts are removed and wrapped around railings at the entrance. Police checkpoints patrol so many roads at night that they had to be reduced in 2015 so traffic could flow.

This fetish for checking reveals a wide mistrust in the public by a hyper-sensitive establishment that submits the entire society to systems of control. Censor bots track suspect words in social media, with even Facebook 'likes' for posts considered as dissent being prosecuted as crimes. The junta made each new SIM card require fingerprints and facial scans.

The vetting also extends to foreigners. Immigration webcams have snapped airport arrivals since 2005. Visa runs got harder once immigration linked up its systems, and serial re-entry ceased in 2016 under the policy of "good guys in, bad guys out." Then in 2019, a 1979 law for tracking refugees was applied to all non-Thais, who had to report returning home even after one night away. Formerly an off-grid haven where misfits could disappear, Bangkok now monitors everything so no one can hide.

Foreign residents with work permits must submit to annual x-rays, blood tests and questions about where they hang out. Inspectors at Nana and Asoke were caught extorting 'fines' from foreigners for not carrying passports. Behind this is a general concern about the prevalence of faked IDs, which is now being tackled. Bangkok's notoriety in falsifying passports for traffickers has been reduced. Getting a pirated student card or driving licence from stalls on Khao San Road faces tighter checks. Buying fake ID used to be a lark for tourists; now sensors can nab the rascals for fraud.

A smart ID card for citizens was first planned under Thaksin in the early 2000s, with gold cards issued for the 30-Baht health scheme. In that early period, state computerisation was done with a customer-service mindset. Then, after successive coups, the emphasis switched to national security.

Sensor gateways became a permanent fixture at malls and MRT stations after the New Year's Eve 2007 bombings around the city, several exploding at the Ratchaprasong countdown. It was unclear who did it, but the main beneficiary was the security apparatus.

166 Sensors

Other bombings followed, and each had the effect of submitting the citizenry to a higher level of suspicion, scan and search.

After the 2015 Erawan Shrine bombing, the torch-and-salute bag ritual extended to the BTS. The guard peers into the top of each bag with a torch that must have magical powers of detection, then spends half of the two-second inspection giving a salute. Actual, rather than ritual, rummaging through bags only happens at official events with dignitaries, or else only to poorer Thais and tourists hauling luggage. At posher venues, high status 'good people' get waved through with a black plastic wand.

A similar escalation occurred with CCTV, which had been limited to traffic snarls until the 2007 explosions. Through the period of Red Shirt and Yellow Shirt protests, CCTVs spread from intersections to 7-Eleven and mass transit to the point that by 2012 the city had 200,000 cameras: one per 41 residents.

Despite the threats to privacy, never have Bangkokians been more engaged with the world and across social barriers, thanks to apps. Digital tracking and cashless payments undermine informal trading, yet provide new incentives to continue evading authority. Expect phone-free zones and discounts for cash.

Philosopher Paul Virilions sees urban life as caught between two parallel worlds: the realm of the senses at a physical location – and the electromagnetic network via devices at unlimited distance. The survival of the informal culture is at stake. Bangkok is turning from a handmade culture into a handheld culture. But the Thais have shown over and over a skill in adapting outside innovations and making them their own. Time will tell if digitisation poses an existential threat to the sensory experience of Bangkok – or gives it new flavour.

In a scandal dubbed 'CCTVgate' in 2011, photos and a video of empty CCTV boxes went viral. The BMA admitted that 1,300 dummy cameras were empty, and 9,000 more weren't wired up to electricity. The public was incensed that crimes in front of 'blind' cameras yielded no footage, or were blurred from not being cleaned. Wags asked for a sensor to see where the budget went.

Bangkokians now live in a digital fishbowl. To Thais from close-knit communities, the intrusion on privacy feels familiar – like nosy neighbours or mums who hound kids to text their every move – so few oppose it. Most assume that CCTVs deter crime, yet in London, with 14 people per lens, they solve only 3% of cases. Cameras tend to be clumped in locations that are high-profile or *hi-so*, rather than high-risk. "There are more areas at risk than just downtown," says designer Nitipol Temprim. "I do feel BMA just installs the cameras for rich people, to show they are taking care of them."

middle: **Electromagnetic pollution could be heard as sounds via headsets at BACC, by German artist Christina Kubisch:** "Some are very poetic, like barber lamps and MRT screens," but mostly Bangkok's EM signature is high beeps and deep nervous drones. "I've never heard such intense signals before."

top left: **CCTV cameras are everywhere in Bangkok, but not all of them have a camera in the box.**

above: **Beeping gates are the norm in stations and malls, but with the little actual screening of bags, perhaps from fear of antagonising customers.**

Senses 167

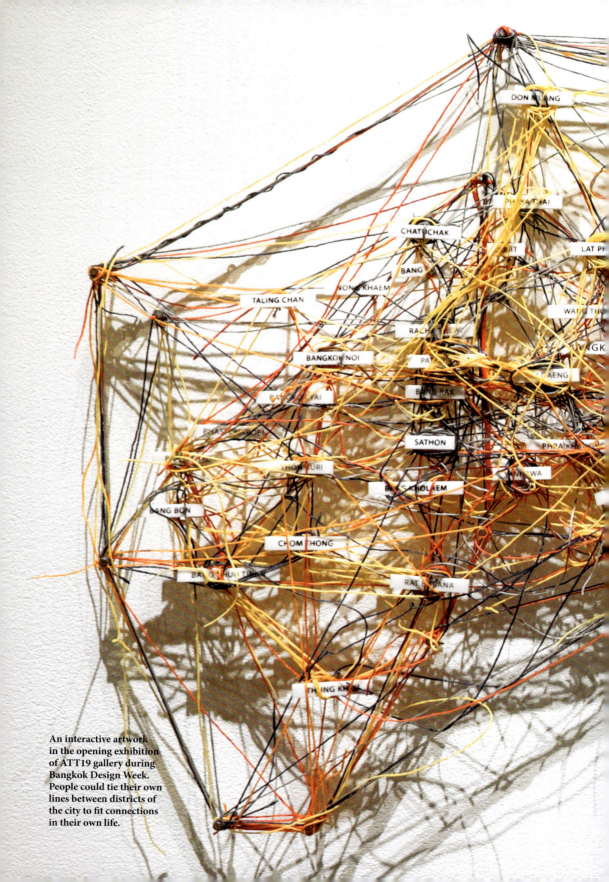

An interactive artwork in the opening exhibition of ATT19 gallery during Bangkok Design Week. People could tie their own lines between districts of the city to fit connections in their own life.

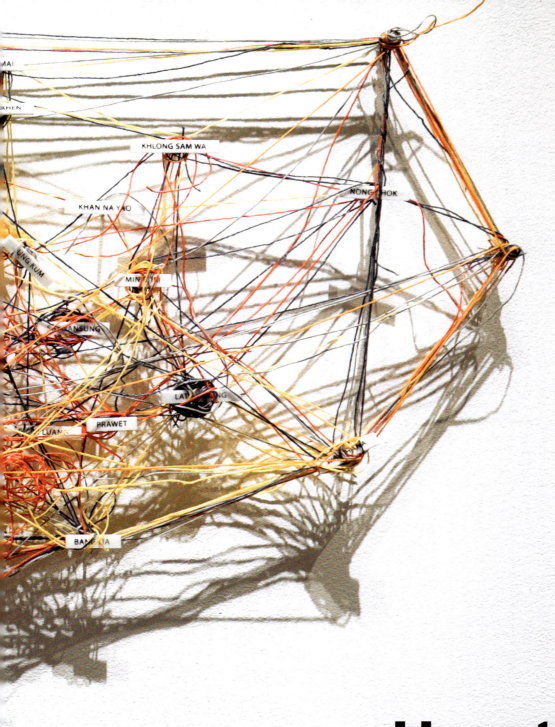

Heart

Thainess and the City
Seeking an urban identity

Bangkok is the centre of the universe. Not on every map, perhaps, but the Old Town is a mandala – a physical and mental map of the Hindu/Buddhist cosmos under the *chakravatin*, the Universal King. Today's capital inherits that mindset. Those closer to power gain more status, lending Bangkokians an aura over the Thai world. Its formal title, which Guinness records as the world's longest place name (see box), reads like a resume of sacred credentials.

Many capitals flaunt a superiority complex – think Paris – but Bangkok considers itself a fount of superlatives: City of Angels, dynastic seat, uncolonised capital. Since 2012 the world's most visited city, it is rivalled as a regional hub only by Singapore. Many consider this the leading city of Buddhism. Bangkok-centricity is not just in the Thai mind, but hardwired into the infrastructure as the most primate city on the planet.

Beyond national pride in Thai exceptionalism from the rest of the world, Bangkokians often assert their exceptionalism within Thailand, whether in education, taste, success, discipline or political judgment. For nearly a quarter millennium, the country has revolved around what the capital wants. Yet there's little celebration of Bangkok as an urban phenomenon. The city's sense of its own identity is cramped by how strongly Bangkokians identify with Nation. Some compare its fervour for Thainess to *Juche* in North Korea.

The term 'Thai' is a paradox: it is both a description of what is, and a prescription of what should be. When outsiders see the messy reality and reach for an adjective, they assume 'Thai' embodies popular values like *mai pen rai* (never mind) and the four Siamese Ss: *sanuk* (fun), *sabai* (ease), *saduak* (convenience) and *saeb* (intense flavour). Yet as the label of the national identity, 'Thai,' is taken as an imperative to overcome those undisciplined traits and perform the gracious cultural ideal, in line with social pressure and several lists of instructions by the state.

Thainess is part delight, part duty. It is best understood as a social contract of nation-building. In a well-documented history, its ideology has changed with the times, revising stances on Sino-Thais and modernity. Early elements include King Rama V's concept of *siwilai* (being civilised), King Rama VI's nationalism, and the codification of heritage by his brother Prince Damrong Rajanubhab, dubbed the 'Father of Thai History.'

In the 1930s and 40s, the 'Leader,' dictator Field Marshal Phibunsongkram, distilled Thainess into a 'National Culture' under the martial influence of German Kultur, Italian Fascism and Japanese Bushido. His 12 Cultural Mandates changed the country's name and steer policy to this day. The ideologue Luang Vichit-Vadhakan instilled the format of modern Thainess through new 'traditional' dances, moralistic plays and the patriotic songs still broadcast at festival times.

Royalist nationalism galvanised under the 1957-63 militarist regime of Field Marshal Sarit Thanarat, with a revival of noblesse oblige articulated by the aristocratic politician-polymath MR Kukrit Pramoj. King Bhumibol embodied Thai virtues for a devoted public during his 70-year reign. In the 1980s, General Prem Tinsulanond's premiership instituted a National Culture Commission, spectacular pageantry and the National Identity Board, which after the 1997 crash decreed five Thai virtues to obey and 12 un-Thai values to avoid. Similar strictures followed the 2014 coup, with children tested on memorising the junta's 12 Core Values. This penchant for numbered lists echoes Buddhism's itemised ethics like the Four Noble Truths and Eightfold Path.

"Strangely enough, the self-proclaimed heralds of whatever constitutes 'Thainess' are all from Bangkok, dictating to the rest of the country what 'Thainess' is supposed to be," says pundit Saksith Saiyasombut. This poses a conundrum. Official Thainess distils an essence of Bangkokness, yet Bangkok clearly violates tenets of Thainess.

The fantastical imagery in Thainess festivals or the Songkran new year parades prompts cognitive dissonance, given the looming skyscrapers and elevated trains. This 'auto-orientalist' mythology is partly for tourism, but also for internal reinforcement. Since the mid-19th century, Bangkok has sought to embody two contrary legitimacies: a long, glorious history, centred on court and pastoral tradition – and also that it's up to date. Where modernity appears in Thainess promotions, it's shown as national development, contemporary architecture as a hi-tech bauble, and city people as generic Thais. Only lately have shophouses been embraced as nostalgic settings, built by nobles, as an extension of the genteel Rattanakosin nostalgia. There's no coherent framing of bus commuters or condo dwellers as urbanites, yet Bangkok is part of a vast megalopolis and the country became majority urban in 2012, the same year as the planet.

"Bangkok culture is not represented in the official culture," says documentary filmmaker Ing K. "Meanwhile organic Thai culture, including the urban and especially the intellectual, is discouraged." Whilst Bangkok contains migrants and traits from all over the country, it plainly differs from provincial Thailand by almost every measure. It's a world apart from even the surrounding Central Plains. Thainess does not equate to tradition, and the multifarious traditions of the regions are being relentlessly subsumed into Bangkok's uniform Thainess. Yet this chaotic megalopolis violates that genteel national self-image. It's as if citizens feel proud about the capital's national qualities, but ambivalent, or perhaps realistic, about the city's own character.

A Thai friend who asked why so many *farang* move to Bangkok was incredulous when told they love its freedom and ease of living. Though middle class, he cited the Thai perception of the city as harsh and difficult to live in. A survey found that many would live upcountry if their job was available there. Given such an outlook, it's not surprising that few champion Bangkok as a model of development, yet some contrarian urbanists see its resilience and informal sector as a way of managing chaotic Asian megalopolises.

left: **The walled city-within-a-city of the Grand Palace. Above the crenellations soar the gilded and ceramic spires of Wat Phra Kaew (Temple of the Emerald Buddha).**

right: **'Country of Bangkok'** by Prakit Kobkijwattana **about the capital's mindset, and the mooted Kra Canal across the peninsula, seen at WTF.** *Photo by Christopher Wise of WTF*

Heart 171

Royal Presence

Could any city be more royalist than Bangkok? Reminders of "the highest institution" appear in every building, street and media, in song, on clothing, fluttering upon flags. Thais speak of matters monarchical in the courtly language of *ratchasap*. They receive degree certificates from the royal patron of their university. Subjects prostrate before the royals in audiences, and genuflect to their pictures, and those of past kings, who are credited with guiding the nation since the first Thai state at Sukhothai. Tributes to royalty recur in anthems, on the nightly royal news, before every show, in professional vows, in religious rites, and at festivities and one-off events. The ideal of Thai deportment is the etiquette of the court.

Krungthep is Thailand's dynastic seat. In Asia, capitals tend to relocate upon changes of ruling house. After the fall of Ayutthaya, King Taksin re-founded Siam at Thonburi. Before Taksin could start a lineage, King Rama I acquired the throne, and established his Chakri dynasty in Bangkok. Its honorific name, beginning Krungthep, declares it as another incarnation of Ayodhya, sacred city of Rama from the *Ramayana* epic. King Rama VI later applied the Roman numeral style to retitle his ancestors Rama in reference to the hero.

Kings Rama I and II were originally named after Buddha images (Phra Buddha Yotfa Chulalok and Phra Buddha Loetla Naphalai) that embody the Dhammaraja notion of righteous, responsive Buddhist kingship. Rama, an avatar of Vishnu, embodies the Devaraja concept of divine Hindu kingship, inheriting absolutism from Angkor that places the crown "above politics" and protected by law from criticism. The Thai crown combines these Buddhist and Hindu cosmologies, with other influences: the modernity of European courts; Chinese imperial regalia; Russian Czarist uniform; Persian crown, gown and slippers; and the Tai ethnic custom of the fatherly chieftain. Tributes to King Bhumibol often bear the words 'Father' or 'Dad'. Attributed all these qualities, Thai rulers are termed the Chakravartin – the Universal King.

Each Chakri king built or rebuilt palaces, several within the Grand Palace and Dusit Palace. Dozens of other princely mansions included: Wang Chakrabongse (Prince Chula), Wang Bangkhunprom (Prince Paribatra), Wang Varadis (Prince Damrong Rajanubhab) and Ban Plainern (Prince Naris). Kings also founded royal temples, indicated in their full name by the suffix Rajaworawihan, where their ashes are kept, notably at Wat Pho, Wat Bowonniwet and the Chakri shrines of Wat Ratchabophit.

The city was for the first 150 years built and run by the Chakris. Each year, King Rama V unveiled a new "Birthday Bridge", ornate spans across Rattanakosin canals. In the modern era, kings have initiated or commissioned many of the city's landmarks, districts, and infrastructure works: canals, roads, bridges, schools,

172 Thainess & The City

hospitals, railways, highways, expressways, parks. Now each Chakri king has been dedicated a river bridge, a highway and a memorial statue.

Many other roads, parks, hospitals, schools, institutes, railways, museums and monuments were either commissioned by royalty, named in their honour, or mark regal events such as jubilees. The 2nd stage Expressway is named Si Rat ('Glorious Reign') and the Skytrain is formally the 'Elevated Train in Commemoration of HM the King's 6th Cycle Birthday'.

Descendants' titles dilute with each generation – from Mom Chao to Mom Ratchawong (M.R.) to Mom Luang (M. L.) to the suffix na Ayutthaya. Aristocratic families still hold enormous sway. Several have raised high achievers in arts, media and administration, besides the publisher of this book. The Nakhon Sawan family: aviator Prince Paribatra, artist Marsi Chumbhot-Pantip and Bangkok governor Sukhumbhand Paribatra. The Pramoj family: two prime minister brothers, polymath Kukrit and conductor Seni, whose son Kamron founded *Image* magazine, and transgender academic Prempreeda. The Svasti family: horticulturist Pimsai Amranand, photographer Ping Amranand, chef/writer McDang, environmentalists Oy and Non Kanchanavanit, filmmaker Ing K and artist Jakkai Siributr.

Bangkok royalism stands apart from other Asian crowns and the 'bicycling monarchies' of Europe in its personal connection to the public. Its inviolability makes defamation jailable under the lese majeste law, with cases spiking after the 2006 and 2014 coups.

The King is referred to as the 'royal lord at our head', and his subjects 'the dust beneath his feet'. King Bhumibol Adulyadej The Great was especially revered for his good works and *baramee* (righteous charisma). At his rare public audiences, millions of teary devotees wearing his birthday colour of yellow called themselves 'Yellow Dust'. As one at his diamond jubilee put it: "I didn't come to see him; I came so he could see us."

The annual calendar marks several royal holidays: Chakri Day (April 6), Coronation Day (May 4), Queen Suthida's Birthday (June 3), King Vajiralongkorn's Birthday (July 28), Queen Sirikit's Birthday (August 12), the Memorial Days of Kings Bhumibol (October 13) and Chulalongkorn (October 23), and Father's Day (King Bhumibol's birthday, December 5). Around those dates portraits cover the sides of skyscrapers and decorations turn bridges into *soom pratu* ceremonial arches.

Regal ceremonies stopped by the 1932 Revolution have been revived following the regime of Sarit Thanarat, such as the Royal Ploughing Ceremony in May. Premier Prem Tinsulanonda oversaw the 1982 bicentennial of Bangkok and the Chakri dynasty. Ever since, royal anniversaries have been marked by elaborate celebrations, often lasting two years, including major anniversaries of the King, Queen and senior royals. On auspicious occasions like jubilees and the 2019 coronation of King Rama X, the king rides in the Royal Barge Procession, a flotilla of over 50 longboats elaborately carved with symbolism.

The most spectacular pageantry attends royal cremations. For over a year after King Bhumibol passed on 13 October 2016, the city was plunged into mourning, with his subjects wearing black, and monochrome shrines at every public building. His funeral would surpass that of King Rama V, under the tallest Meru crematorium on Sanam Luang at 50.49 metres, clad in symbolism and exquisite sculptures of mythical creatures from the Himaphan Forest as well as his beloved dog Khun Thong Daeng. Nowhere else on the planet, even London, matches the pageantry of Bangkok.

left: **The coronation land procession of King Rama X, in front of the Grand Palace.**

below: **Royal barge rowers sing 'boat songs' in the Winter Fair, before Ananta Samakhom Throne Hall.**

"Thais aren't like Westerners where they have New York pride or Liverpool pride. We don't have that strong city-based identity," says pundit Voranai Vanichaka. "There's no rivalry. It is understood that Bangkok is the centre of the Thai universe." Yet some rural migrants now skip Bangkok for the growing provincial conurbations of Khorat, Khon Kaen, Udon Thani, Had Yai or Chiang Mai. Developing to the capital's unplanned template, tier-two cities have breached Bangkok's former monopoly on Thai urbanism.

In fact, Thainess has always been centred on towns. Bangkok and Ayutthaya were not just mandalas, but city-states from the Tai tribal tradition of *meuang* – fortified towns that were a seat of power, with a market and professions. Settlements all over the Mekong basin bear variants of the word *meuang*, which remains the Thai term for the capital district of a province and, informally, for the country as Meuang Thai. If anything, old Siam was a network of towns and city states.

Phra Nakhon Sri Ayutthaya was the longest-lasting and most glorious Thai capital, thriving from 1350 to 1767. Lauded as a seat of court, controlling vast territories and conducting wars, it was also a teeming metropolis of trade and industry. Thai and foreign sources mention professionals like merchants, officials and lawyers. Beyond agriculture, its ethnic enclaves specialised in production of everyday goods. "Most of the neighbourhoods were named after the products that were made or sold there, reflecting pride in the city's production and commerce," note Chris Baker and Pasuk Phongpaichit, who calculate that 40-60 percent of Siamese then lived in towns.

Ayutthaya peaked around 1700 at around a million people, possibly the world's biggest city at the time and greater than Europe's biggest metropole, London. Its ruins are extolled as a World Heritage Site, yet the national narrative plays down this astonishing urbanism, so as to boost the rise of Krungthep, which took over 150 years to exceed Ayutthaya's size. Instead it diverted its legitimacy to claims of lineage from ancient Sukhothai. King Mongkut reported finding the Ramkhamhaeng Stele in Sukhothai, which bears an inscription extolling that city-state's happiness under its Dhammaraja (righteous king).

Ayutthaya's loss cast a pall over the Thai psyche. Anger at that cataclysm still falls mainly on the villain through anti-Burmese

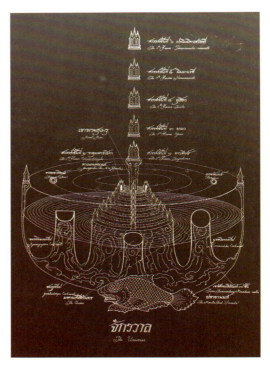

films and museum displays. Blame also fell on the supposed moral decline of Ayutthaya, prompting a purge of superstition upon the founding of Bangkok. Worldwide, most traditional cultures denigrate cities as impure, and there's a sense of that in Bangkok, though in the Thai moralists' mind, Good People of karmic quality are associated with closeness to the centre of the mandala.

Unlike other mandalic cities – which are either ruins like Angkor or desacralised like Mandalay or Beijing's Forbidden City – Bangkok remains uniquely active as a sacred site. The king, officials and Brahmin priests perform that cosmology through rituals in the court calendar like the Royal Ploughing Ceremony or Changing the robes of the Emerald Buddha. Some still regard all Thai land as royal, and in 2018 the vast landholdings of the Crown Property Bureau were transferred from the royal insitution to Rama X's personal name.

We see the mandala in the city's official motto: "City of angels, built by angels, central city of governance, brilliant temples and palaces, the capital of Thailand." The public chose it in 2011 from a shortlist proposed by a jury that declared: "We are looking for something that values the best of our cultural treasures." The approved self image – ruling, royal, religious – overlooks secular assets like its river,

food or trade. "Built by angels" refers to the commissioning deity, not to the labour who constructed the place. In this sense, Thais revere Krungthep as one gigantic offering.

To explain the cityness of Bangkok also requires acknowledging the role of non-Thais in its making. Academia began that process in the 1970s, and it reached museums when the first Thaksin administration opened Museum Siam. Though there's still no museum of Bangkok city, early urbanism also gets coverage in the BMA's district museums like the Bangkokian Museum in a bourgeois household. The Chinese-Thai, who dominate the urban fabric and the middle class, got belated recognition at the Chinatown Heritage Centre, where dioramas show the origin in Yaowarat of such metropolitan pastimes as dining, shopping and nights 'out on the town.' But in The Rattanakosin Exhibition Hall, the ethnic *yaan* are couched as quaint relics of festivals and food, rather than as a defining format of how the city was structured.

"Traditional popular urbanism was never proclaimed – it just was," says sociologist Marc Askew. Bangkok inherited from Ayutthaya two characteristics: being atomised and amphibious. Both were 'water cities,' an East Asian urban form often dubbed 'Venice of the East.' Except that unlike Venice, most residents lived not on drained land, but over the water in stilt houses, boats or bamboo raft huts, linked along the waterways to create floating precincts dubbed "riverside ribbon urbanism."

Minorities were controlled by confining them to self-managed enclaves. Bangkok remains a patchwork of 'urban hamlets' fed by dead-end *sois*, rather than an interconnected lattice. Unlike the ghettos of foreign cities, the entire conurbation was compartmentalised.

"Bangkok was not perceived as a distinct urban phenomenon, but as a type of extreme densification of rural habitation," explains architect ML Chittawadi Chitrabongs. Housing, production and trade kept a village quality. Temples were the focus of health, schooling, and entertainments. "While Rama V was enthusiastic about importing objects of modernity, he did not introduce an alternative way of life to Bangkok's inhabitants."

As part of modernisation, reformers have targeted 'dense rural habitation' as backward. Surviving 'riverside ribbon urbanism' was erased as canals were filled in, floating houses banned, and wooden homes cleared for concrete construction. After a century as a backwater, Bangkok took off as a hybrid metropolis in a largely free-market experiment, with unplanned development and disconnected transit. It's been the main gateway to what's new in the world. Understanding Bangkok is key to understanding Thai modernity.

For most of Bangkok's history, residents haven't much identified with the city as a whole entity, clinging to their immediate *taew* lanes or ethnic networks, until the nationalist era broke down local organisation and switched the citizen's fealty to country. Identifying as a metropolitan is extremely recent and is most expressed by young advocates of urbanism who grew up under democracy.

The result is a city dominated by corporations, towers and suburban sprawl – ways of living that divorced Bangkok from both its own roots and from the provinces. At times, the capital can seem like a bubble that's oblivious to its own behaviour. "Encountering Bangkok for the first time was a culture shock," recalls Chiranan Pitpreecha, who arrived from the south and

far left: Mural of Thai riverine life at Wat Arun.

above: Mount Meru in Thai cosmology, from an exhibit in Museum Siam.

left: The last site of early Rattanakosin urbanism was destroyed by the BMA at Mahakan Fort, despite campaigns to save that heritage.

Heart   175

above: **Seeing Bangkok through Thai-tinted spectacles. Spotted at the Bangkok Shutdown protest.**

below right: ***Way*** **magazine had an issue about the Bangkokian self-image.**

became a SEA Write Award winning author. "Being from Trang, Bangkok was like self-contained world that had never been affected by outside suffering. People just lived their lives regardless of the situation in rural areas."

Dominance by Bangkok is a core issue in Thailand's social and political tensions. The heavily urban Yellow Shirts mocked the largely rural origins of the Red Shirts, whose occupation of downtown shopping districts was meant and felt as an invasion of urban icons. A divisive event in framing Bangkokians' sense of home was the feeling of being under attack by arson during the eviction of the Redshirt encampment in 2010, followed by an emotive clean-up by volunteers. It was an incident that made some other residents question if the city really belonged to them.

"Many Bangkokians still think that there is some underdeveloped wild savage hinterland beyond the city borders, and look with weariness and condescension to the rest of the country," says Saksith Saiyasombut. "There really is a belief that this city has its own set of rules and laws. A saying has it that Thailand has never been colonised by anybody, except by Bangkok. Look at that satirical Facebook page 'Prathet Krungthep' – 'Country of Bangkok'."

To migrants under the spell of Bangkok equating to modernity, moving to the capital was viewed as a necessary step to advance their career or make enough money to see out their later life back home. "One day I saw a *likay* actor, who had played the part of a king," recalls comedian Teng Terdterng. "He was fishing with a net. I realised I didn't want to be a poor actor like him. I wanted a good future, so I went to Bangkok."

Settlers have a different stake in Bangkok than those born in the city. First or even second generations treat the capital in practical, transactional terms. Wistfully they regard 'home' as their provincial origin, to which they send remittances. "I love to talk with those people who don't feel they are Bangkokian – like those in the low-ranking service sector," says Pitch Pongsawat, who wrote a manifesto for a liveable Bangkok, *Meuang Gin Khon* (The City is Eating Us). "They have double identities and that's how Bangkok is shaped."

That divided loyalty surfaces with the exodus upcountry at Songkran. It's like the holiday hordes moving around Indonesia at Ramadan, or China at Lunar New Year. Media romanticises the millions of Bangkok residents enduring day-long traffic jams to spend Thai New Year with family. It tugs the heartstrings, but makes the city feel oddly empty. "My family has been here since the early Bangkok period," Pitch adds. "I feel like a Bangkokian really only when we have Songkran and I have no other place to *glap ban* – return home."

Bangkokians came from all over the country, region and world, but their stories have formerly been omitted from most mainstream histories in favour of the national narrative. Their roots are usually glossed over as 'ethnic colour,' omitting painful specifics. That tension remains palpable in attention to accent, manners and skin colour. Sojourners didn't know if they'd return to their homelands, while captives didn't want to dwell on why they came, so they suppressed local histories and built fresh futures as Thai.

This has made the city's inhabitants warm-hearted, resilient and keen on raising status. At times of adversity like floods the sense of community togetherness is palpable. As Ing K writes: "Bangkok is quintessentially Thai precisely because of the excuses made for it by its resigned and indulgent inhabitants, some of whom are actually quite proud of their city's unlivable reputation, which they believe to be a glorious reflection of their own toughness."

All this makes Bangkok hard to define. Current theories of urbanism reduce everything to class or power relations, and dismiss the factors intrinsic to place, culture and belief that animate Bangkok. Its shapeless structure emerged from a jumble of meanings, some official, some personal, some mystical. It's unfashionable to admit the impact of individuals, but the capital might never be here were it not for Kings Taksin and Rama I. The city's fabric and mindset were altered on the initiatives of Kings Rama V, VI and IX, as well as through the uniformity from Phibun Songkram and the 'Development State' ethos of Sarit Thanarat.

The Western model of what a city should be makes Asian megalopolises seem distorted byproducts of modernity, whereas they are local solutions to dense living. "The city in the non-West is often disregarded as a phenomenon in its own right, with its own distinctive history, traditions, rhythms, meanings and senses of place," writes Annette Hamilton in *Wonderful, Terrible: Everyday Life in Bangkok*. Bangkok's incoherence to Western eyes is precisely why sci-fi writers style it as a possible guide to handling an untidy apocalyptic future.

"Wonderful, terrible" are many residents' feelings about Bangkok. A top tourism draw, it scores low in quality of life (124th in the 2003 Mercer rankings). Thai praise for the city tends to come tempered with lament, especially for traffic than no one gets used to. "Bangkok is unique, one of the few places that has everything. The juxtaposition of random subjects is amazing," says illustrator Tripuck Supawattana. "Our urban lifestyle is chaotic, confusing and full of social inequalities. It sounds negative but it's also a charm. I love this city for its diversity, but also hate it. Sometimes it's just too much."

Despite its centrality, Bangkok shows weak civic spirit. The reasons are partly physical, from the poor construction of buildings and paths to the incoherent overall look. The urbanist Jan Gehl has shown how humane towns require human scale, easy walkability, and neighbourly interaction. Old *yaan* do have some of that, and the city is getting more public spaces, but it remains dominated by cars. If it's difficult even to stroll round the corner, residents are bound to care less about what they don't know personally.

"I feel some harmony that we belong to Thainess, and Thainess belongs to us. But we don't feel we belong to Bangkok. Bangkok doesn't belong to us," says travel writer Zcongklod Bangkyikhan. "The community sense is very poor compared to any other province, where the local people can decide something as a group. We don't have a voice.

We cannot do anything. So Bangkok is a city we stay in, but are not involved with much. In every direction, Bangkok is guided by business or officials in a way that people cannot stop."

That fatalism comes partly from residents having so little clout. Upgrading the quality of life is thwarted by top-down impositions and the rejection of bottom-up initiatives and representative organisations. The gulf between high and low, the lack of a middle ground, manifests as much here as elsewhere in this book.

Nation-building has smothered loyalty to any rival grouping that's bigger than community level, whether region, ethnicity or political party. As globalisation falters and corporations out-scale nations, many foresee a renewed rise of the city state. While the mayors of Berlin or Bogotá can become international figures, Bangkok governors aren't allowed much rein.

This isn't so unusual. Anti-cosmopolitanism is a trait of Brexit, Islamic State or Trump's attacks on 'sanctuary cities.' Cities may produce wealth and new ways of living, but they upset hierarchy and taint the purity of tradition. Cities thrive on foreign trade, immigrants, luxuries, entertainments, intermarriage, cultural exchange, tolerance of unorthodox beliefs and behaviours. "In harbouring foreigners and cosmopolitans is where cities get complicated in the emotional lives of nations," notes Marc Pachter, director-at-large of the Smithsonian. "Nativists are not just barbarians at the gates, but people

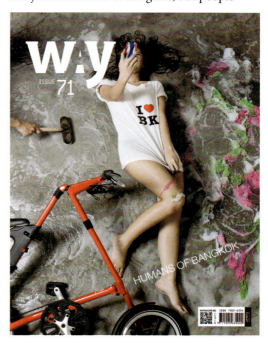

Heart 177

who cling in an uncomplicated way to their feeling as being French, or Indian or Thai. Cities like Bangkok complicate that. The city, especially the capital, is the nexus of nationalist confusion about what makes a nation great."

What makes Bangkok great may not be 'purity,' but being so gleefully hybrid. Its peoples are a model of ethnic integration, its cuisine an exquisite fusion, its tradition a blend of India, China, Mon, Khmer and much else. Modern Bangkok jostles Thai wooden homes, Chinese shophouses, Italianate palaces, suburban American houses and globalised hi-tech.

The BMA is trying to emulate Singapore in its purging of streetlife, clutter and informal trade. Even the progressive governor Chadchart Sittipunt insisted in 2024 that street vending owould be phased out in the long run. But officials haven't learned how Singapore preserves its urban heritage. Pursuing development but feeling ambivalent about a cosmopolitan lifestyle has led Bangkokians to underappreciate their city identity.

The sensibility of many new-generation Bangkokians no longers accepts the separation of high-and-low culture, city and countryside. Their enthusiasm for everyday pop and retro style, is predicated on embracing the hybrid as legitimate. City-born rather than farm-raised, these hipsters support rooftop gardening. Literate in global trends these citizens are receptive to new kinds of city living, from third places to co-working spaces, and are targeted by advertising as 'urbanistas' with downtown lifestyles. While few champion Bangkok as a model of development, some contrarian urbanists see its resilience and informal sector as a way of managing chaotic Asian megalopolises.

Everyday life in Bangkok may be tough, but it's a warm struggle shared with others in a genial way. As foreign repeat visitors relish, it's the city's informality that enables people to be themselves. If 'Krungthep' expresses the divine side of a city for angels where humans must do their duty, 'Bangkok' is the humane city of communities and streetlife, where the lack of coherence is a relief, even a liberation. Like everything Thai, this city is a duality, even a multiplicity. "There is no identifiable image of Bangkok," says Voranai. "There's the thing that we want to be: 'hub this' or 'hub that'. Logically, there's the thing that we are: 'a big mess'. Emotionally, I love Bangkok in spite of the big mess."

Krungthep or Bangkok?

Imagine if this book were called 'Very Krungthep'. The name that Thais call their capital – translated as 'City of Angels' – conveys local parlance, propriety and sacredness. Thais like long titles and short nicknames. Adding 'Mahanakhon' (metropolis) gives the formal version, Krung Thep Mahanakhon, which gets abbreviated to KTM (pronounced Kor Tor Mor), the acronym of Bangkok Metropolitan Administration. Short versions are needed, because the full honorific title is the world's longest place name at 64 syllables:

Krungthepmahanakhon bowornrattanakosin mahintarayutthaya mahadilok popnopparat ratcha-thaniburirom udomratchanniwet mahasathan amornpiman avatarnsathit sakkhathatthiya visnukarprasit.

"Great city of angels, the supreme repository of the divine jewels, the supreme unconquerable land of the immortal divinity (Indra) endowed with the nine noble gems, the delightful capital city abounding in royal palaces, which resemble heavenly paradises for the reincarnated deities, commissioned by Indra for Vishnukam to create."

This one-word origin myth defines the place as divine, but omits the city's informality and variety. Relabelling can't erase the original mould, however, just as most still name Ho Chi Minh City as Saigon. Krungthep is an accolade, a talisman, a declaration of faith – yet the city brand is Bangkok™. It's air and banking codes are BKK, its city magazine *BK*, its earliest districts called Bangkok Yai and Bangkok Noi. Residents have gained the label 'Bangkokian'. Krungthep can't shake off its alter ego Bangkok.

Punchy and easier to say, Bangkok remains the city's international name. This Ayutthaya-era trading post got its tag from Bang Makok – Water-village of Plum Olives – or possibly Bang Koh: Island Hamlet.

178 Thainess & The City

King Taksin's reign recast it as East Thonburi, then after 1782 King Rama I bestowed his new dynastic seat as 'Rattanakosin' – Indra's Jewelled Isle, the jewel being the 'Emerald Buddha', enshrined since 1784 within its namesake temple Wat Phra Kaew, in the Grand Palace. Over time, the old town citadel became 'Phra Nakhon' (Holy City) and then gained its full current title.

Names propel power, especially to those who speak mantras as magic. Thais often change name to gain luck, status, even health. Tracing historical figures is hard since they were known by titles they were besowed. Suriwong Road and Ban Somdet Chao Phraya subdistrict are both named after titles of King Rama V's regent, whose birth name was Chuang Bunnag. Across Asia, new regimes tend to shift the location of the name of their capital.

Thai actually has four terms for town, which illuminate how Bangkokians see their city: as a capital (*krung*), a realm (*nakhon*), a model abode (*thani*), and a hometown (*meuang*). The first three occur in the full name, with Sanskrit roots. *Krung* came via Khmer. *Nakhon* is how Thais say *nagara,* which implies a leader's personal domain. *Thani* is a literary term for habitation. The hotel Dusit Thani (Heavenly Abode) was named after a miniature town built at Phyathai Palace by King Rama VI, which modelled a potential Siamese democracy, with an assembly, civic amenities and a newspaper.

Missing from Krungthep's full name, *meuang* is the less formal indigenous Tai term. Across the Mekong basin, towns and former city states have names with variants of *meuang*. Northern 'Thais' call themselves Khon Meuang (People of the Towns) and their language Kham Meuang – 'Words of the Towns'. Thai provincial capitals centre on a Meuang district, some of which centre on a Lak Meuang (City Pillar).

Duality runs through this ambiguous culture, providing options. Krungthep's Lak Meuang has a second City Pillar that was installed to give the city a second horoscope based on an adjusted foundation date. Until the late 1800s a Deputy King, a viceroy with almost as many powers as the king, mirrored Prince Rama's loyal brother Lakshmana in Thailand's version of the *Ramayana* epic. Bangkok has since 1972 incorporated the previous capital Thonburi.

The country, too, has dual identity. Siam was renamed Thailand by Phibun in 1938. Siam was used more by foreigners than locals, who felt 'Tai'. Chinese called it Siem, while Khmer, Cham and Pagan empires knew it as *syama* ('swarthy' in Sanskrit). Few took up a campign to reinstate Siam led by historian Charnvit Kasemsiri, claiming it's "more ethnically inclusive," and that "Siam needs saving from Thailand."

Even 'Thai' has duality. The Phibun dictatorship re-spelled the nationality 'Thai' differently to the ethnicity 'Tai', adding a Y in Thai script and an H in English. As with the capital, a Tai term for realm (*ban-meuang* or town-village) gave way to formal titles: *chart* and *prathet*.

Nation is 'chart', which meant 'birth' or 'lifetime', implying a common birthplace and bloodline, as heard in the National Anthem: "the blood and flesh of the Thai race." The political state, 'Phrathet Thai' (Thai territory), draws from *desa* (Sanskrit for area), as do other redrawn states like Bangladesh. Listen how Thais declare "Phrathet Thai" and "Chart Thai" with patriotism, but say the casual nickname "Meuang Thai" softly with affection.

In metaphor for this cultural duality, spirit houses often come in a pair. Krungthep is like the higher, masonry, Hindu-style temple, while Bangkok is the lower, wooden, indigenous house. As the city gets richer and modernised, the urban-style spirit temple must get upgraded to match its grander building, with many now stylish steel or glass. Meanwhile, the folk spirit house is never upgraded to be *siwilai* – a metaphor for rural culture that's kept restrained in traditional stasis.

Something similar happens in conservation. State plans that impose National Culture monuments over informal popular heritage led critics to revive 'Bangkok' as a term for the subculture of ordinary communities. As Marc Askew put it, those conflicts over preservation or demolition "are a conflict between readings of the city itself – between 'Krungthep', the aestheticised abstract heritage paradigm, as against 'Bangkok', a city of the *yaan* and common people."

Modern Thais do say 'Bangkok' and 'Siam' casually and use them as the names of brands, Bangkok and Siam lend a different flavour to Krungthep or Thailand. Siam conjures visions of imperial, multi-ethnic tradition. Bangkok conveys the villagey sides of its character. The words appear in names of venues and locations like Siam Square or the show Siam Niramit, Bangkok Noi or the Bangkokian Museum. While 'Bangkok' is understood by all as the city; mention 'Siam', and most Thais will think you're going shopping.

top left: The full honorific name of Krungthep is a common device on T-shirts.

left: This tuk-tuk is in the 'Bangkokian' livery of branded souvenirs by Emporium mall.

Heart 179

Influence
Who gets to run Bangkok?

Bangkok is infamous for chaos, so we wonder who's really in charge. Its frequent sense of crisis also sparks bursts of order, with purges, censorship and 22 coups d'état – 9 failing, 13 prevailing. Yet despite the cycles of chaos-order-chaos, somehow most things work.

Recurring crises favour the forces of order, however much extra chaos they cause by overthrowing 'rule of law' for 'rule by law.' This norm is so arbitrary that law, precedent and legitimacy are now malleable concepts, with 21 constitutions since 1932. Governance reflects a Thai ideal of doing whatever you want.

'Thai' means 'free' – and this stirs both national and personal pride. Foreigners relish the everyday liberty found here, even under dictatorship, though some mistakenly assume that anything goes. In fact, liberty is curbed by hierarchy. Behind the messy surface operates a finely calibrated seniority system.

This country is famed for its flexibility, whether with diplomacy, immigration or its culture of localised imports. Lately, in the face of unprecedented change, the system's been unusually rigid. Modernisation wrenches all countries, but is especially fraught in a rare land that didn't have its ancient beliefs diluted by colonialism. Countries that had to fight for independence gained a clear common cause, whereas Thai national identity was imposed from above. That imbalance has led to decades of Thais tussling over rival visions for their country: top-down or bottom-up.

You can see this in the architecture – at seats of power, sites of protest and monuments to each side. Bangkok is not just the setting for power plays, but its citizens play lead roles. The academic Anek Laothamatas coined a well-known saying that provincial majorities elect the government, only to be overthrown by the Bangkok minority. Ultimately, protest movements have been either for or against bringing another class into the system. Increasingly, though, the rift is generational and about reform of the system itself.

This is part of a broader shift in society, culture and business. Similar dynamics play out over school uniforms, conscription or modernising traditional arts. Entrepreneurs chafe at monopolies that dominate trades. Communities resist redevelopment. When grievances boiled up in the past, they used to get smoothed over; now the internet enables all Thais to hear about it and have their say.

Governance of Bangkok cannot be easily disentangled from that national political jostling. On paper, the capital province is run by the Bangkok Metropolitan Administration

(BMA), with its elected Governor and assembly, plus 97,000 staff, from planners and cleaners to teachers and *tetsakit* (inspectors). In practise, this metropolis straddling seven provinces can't be run by any single authority. Instead, several sources of power and influence act in concert, rivalry, or their own interests. Ultimately, grandees find ways to steer Bangkok to benefit national players.

City Hall sits at the heart of the original Bangkok Mandala. It flanks the north side of Lan Meuang (City Square), with the Brahmin's Devastan Shrine headquarters on the east side, and to the south the Brahmin Giant Swing and the Mount Meru temple of Wat Suthat. Facing the swing, the full name of Krungthep is inscribed in marble. Among the city's various hubs, this civic centre is also the sacred centre.

Behind City Hall's colonnade of pointed arches, its courtyard was based on Stockholm City Hall. Its functions are split with a complex in Din Daeng, where the whole BMA will move, to leave the old City Hall as a museum. As when ministries moved out, that will take custom from the area's old restaurants and shops, further hollowing out the old town.

Bangkok governors lack enough power to build a legacy. The capital is too vital to statists to be granted autonomy. Ministries ensnare almost every BMA responsibility: Transport directs its roads; Interior runs the police; Education overrules its schools; Irrigation co-manages floods; Defence commands the river. The 2014-2023 military regime even suspended city planning to force through contested issues like evictions of communities.

The first gubernatorial election was held during a democratic interlude in 1975, but the victor was removed after the 1976 coup.

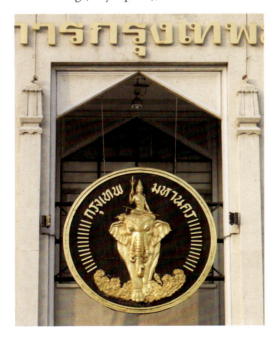

top left: **The parliament, sits on military land in a sacred mandala design.**

above: **At the Democracy Monument, the left sign says: "Democracy for what?"**
Photo Boony Narksakul

left: **The insignia of the Bangkok Metropolitan Administration (BMA) on City Hall, showing the city's patron deity Indra riding the elephant Erawan.**

Heart   181

Since elections resumed in 1985, governors have been the Buddhist vegan ascetic general Chamlong Sriuang, suave modernist architect Krisda Arunwongse na Ayutthaya, eco-aware son of a party boss Bhichit Rattakul, brusque autocrat cook Samak Sudaravej, genial manager Apirak Kosayodhin, and royal academic Sukhumbhand Paripatra. The NCPO installed Pol Gen Aswin Kwanmuang, but the cycle of needing public endorsement resumed.

In 2022, record numbers of voters chose Chadchart Sittipunt, an ex-transport minister detained by the junta for "attitude adjustment." Memes cast him as an everyday superhero, walking barefoot in shorts with a plastic bag. His first act was let the public submit problems via the Traffy Fondue app that entered the to-do list for each department, whether potholes, burst pipes or snakes in a school.

Party manifestos based on voters' wishes contradict the patronage system that has prevailed since tribal times. When electors switch parties and follow personalities more than policy, that's less about celebrity than about the nature of Thai leadership. This paternalistic society extols *baramee* (righteous charisma) in a patron, typically alpha-male, whose entourage prioritise his *na-ta* (literally 'face eyes'). Anyone gaining popularity for achievements risks their wrath for not attributing the credit upwards.

Thai power is a zero-sum game, though factions of *phu yai* (big figures) keep shifting. Whispers say that 150 clans run it all, some of them 'new money.' Scions of 'good families' glide into key roles in politics, business, military and officialdom – even in the arts. "In some countries, it's all about what is done," wrote *Nation* editor Tulsathit Taptim. "In Thailand, it's all about who does it."

They ran what Fred Riggs famously dubbed the 'bureaucratic polity.' That oligopoly has weakened, but its patrician mindset persists, as seen in public moralising. For centuries, low-paid officials were hired to farm taxation and monopolies for state quotas, beyond which they had the right to exploit their position. Echoes of that recur when officials seek 'brown envelopes,' whether petty 'tea money' or cuts of major contracts. Many Thais accept it as a normal cost of getting things done.

The bureaucratic culture also pervades large firms. Public relations is less about a firm's products than gaining face for the boss. Offices can be mini-fiefdoms, with much

below: **City officials with a T-shirt saying 'work, work work', and a bag made of an old election poster of Bangkok Governor Chdchart Sitipunt.**

right: **In the Bangkok Shutdown protest's Art Lane market, stalls sold T-shirts saying '*Khon Dee*' (Good People) in gold.**

pandering to bosses, who repay that *bun khun* social debt by patronising employee events like weddings or funerals. The mostly Sino-Thai middle class aspires to the lifestyle of the new-rich '*hi-so*,' who excel at the face-eyes game.

Elites from that bubble are used to privileged treatment from brandishing their status symbols, and can erupt when feeling slighted. A young TV host had a notorious road rage incident when his BMW Mini hit a motorcyclist.' After punching the biker in the face, the host forced him to *graab* or prostrate to his dented Mini. Social media exploded with the hashtag #graabmycar.

The Bangkok middle class used to be seen as apolitical – but that's partly pragmatism about advancement and protection under patronage networks. They are also cautious due to protestors dying in 1973, 1976, 1992, and 2008-10. Since 2008, objectors have been subjected to 'lawfare,' with fines, prison and bans from office or suffrage. Parties with mass appeal get stymied from governing or implementing their policies. Some got ousted by military or judicial coups. Since 1998, over 120 parties have been disbanded, removing fresh leaders from shaping Thailand's future.

Unsurprisingly, citizens with fewer connections seek a voice though elected representatives, who are increasingly driven by policy platforms. But laws only work when

obeyed and enforced, while some laws seem vaguely drafted as if intended for selective use. The news reports a flow of high status people flouting the rules but rarely getting punished – so what might have been a deterrent instead fuels a sense of injustice at double standards.

The Thai political impasse is over contested notions of legitimacy: electoral rights versus moral duty backed by righteous force. Under *Triphum* cosmology, power emanates from a hierarchy based on karmic merit accrued over past lives. At its peak, the universal king has the widest insight, while breadth of understanding declines with each social level.

When pundits reach for metaphors from the *Ramakien* epic, that's literally the historic Thai model of moral rulership inherited by Ayutthaya from the Angkorean Khmer Empire. The king is named for the Hindu royal hero Rama. His peerless attributes interplay with those of the regal demon Thotsakan, devoted brother Lakshman, chaste wife Sita, and loyal monkey general Hanuman – who all mirror traditionalist social roles.

Anyone doubting the currency of such stereotypes should notice how ministry emblems depict Indic mythology. The BMA's logo depicts the city's spiritual founder, Indra, astride the elephant Erawan. It's believed that such deifications activate through performance, whether of Brahmin rites or Khon masked court drama, hence the strictness over depictions of mythical beings.

"In old Thai culture, power is unified and indivisible… because the king is an incarnation of god. Division of powers is a Western idea," wrote historian Nidhi Eoseewong about a Thai 'Cultural Constitution,' which endures, unlike written constitutions. "Power of any kind is not be trusted unless there is some counterbalance… First, through Buddhism, which laid down standards…Second and more widely used was to call on influence… The Thai common people can survive in the space created by the counterbalancing of authority and influence. Sometimes they call on authority to counter influence, and sometimes vice versa."

Conservatives often infer that *khon dee* (good people) deserve to decide things as their high social status reflects a karmic superiority. This *khon dee* discourse de-legitimises politicians and elections as inherently corrupt, while challengers of traditional authority simply 'don't understand.' Fatalists often shrug that politics is just struggles between the elite factions – and that protestors are hired or misled by deceptive 'bad people.'

The constitution defines Thailand as a 'Democracy with the King as Head of State.' Traditionalists have argued for nearly a century that the Thai public are not yet ready for democracy. Instead they advocate 'Thai style democracy' as a guided benevolence with the public interest represented by the guardianship of a virtuous monarch, whereas politicians divisively pursue self-interest. Many Yellow Shirt royalist protestors against Thaksin Shinawatra's premiership were also civil society liberals with anti-capitalist sympathies who saw in King Bhumibol's Sufficiency Economy Theory an alternative model for development. Coupled with calls for unity and Buddhist ethics, those principles can be heard emanating from every kind of institution, industry and profession.

This belief finds physical form in the new parliament building. The previous National Assembly of 1974, Sapha Hin-on (Marble Parliament), was an emphatically horizontal structure in Modernist concrete, with glazed galleries showing openness and contemporary art. The abstract sculpture at its entrance was replaced after the 1976 coup with a statue of Rama VII, the king who signed the People's Party charter of 1932 that brought in constitutional democracy. That parliament was demolished in 2021. Its site and the Ananta Samakhom Throne Hall, which housed the first parliament, have since been reintegrated into the King's palace, Amphorn Sathan.

The new parliament – the world's biggest – opened in 2021. Called Sappaya Saphasathan, this mandalic Meru mountain of a building evokes Borobudur, the Buddhist monument in Java. Based on the Triphum (the Buddhist 'Three Worlds' of Heavens, Earth and Hells), its design by Teerapol Niyom is emphatically vertical, with a Democracy Museum at the 'worldly' ground level. A gilded 'sun' chamber for MPs to the north and silvered 'moon' senate to the south both have symbolism of cooling *khwan* (spirit energy). Above them, the monarch presides over the State Ceremonial Hall, beneath a gold, chedi-like spire enshrining an image of Phra Siam Devathiraj, Siam's guardian deity.

Secularists criticise the religious styling and the subordination of democracy to Dharma. To traditionalists, that's the point. "The problem of social and political conflicts among people at present is due to moral degeneration," declares the Guide to Parliament. "People do not only have different opinions in society and different views of politics but also face moral problems and decay. Therefore, the New Parliament Building would be 'Sappaya' of the nation, or the 'place for doing good deeds,' which is the realm of wisdom, the center of all spirits of the nation, the sacred place, and the epitome of morality, ethics and good governance."

A former Australian Ambassador, David Wise, contends that the classic three branches of government – legislature, electorate and judiciary – in Thailand are actually five, because, "the monarchy and military continue, at times, to play a refereeing role."

The military is highly visible and controls 1.8 million acres of land. The Royal Thai Air Force has half of Don Mueang Airport. Royal Thai Navy bases flank the river. The Royal Thai Army occupies swathes of Bangkhen, Dusit and Phyathai districts north of Victory Monument, a bayonet-shaped cenotaph for the fallen. At 842,000 men, it's the world's 15th biggest army. While the US gets by with 231 generals, the Thai army has over 1,700.

As in Myanmar, the armed forces regard themselves as national saviours, yet here they do many development projects. They also run businesses, two TV and 245 radio stations, 37 golf courses, six hotels, a boxing stadium and a racecourse. Security guards are often veterans. Most families have had servicemen, though well-connected sons often avoid conscription. The internal security aparatus has set up mass organisations, while key civilians in firms and institutions are steeped in the security mindset from elite courses in the psychological warfare department of the National Defence College, as reported in the news in 2023. These varied social relationships help explain why the military gets granted such leeway.

Yet all those powers still lack full control. They must contend with rival influences, such as patronage networks, powerful families, entrenched bureaucracies, protest movements, 'influential figures' (mafias), and the 'hidden hands' that nobody dares name. Thaksin held a crackdown against 'dark influence' in underground trades in 2001. When the junta did a similar purge in 2016, a poll found only 12 per cent thought it could be eradicated, and 82 percent dared not report mafia.

Crucially, Thai corporations have had seats at the top table since General Sarit allied soldiers with Sino-Thai tycoons in the 1950s. A select circle of bank, food, drink, retail, real estate and industrial logos recur as sponsors of state projects and social campaigns.

left: "Eating the country." A display at BACC from the Museum of Thai Corruption.

right: **Prince Chumporn Shrine at the old Armed Forces Preparatory School (now One Bangkok).**

Primate City

Bangkok is so hard to manage because it tries to do too much. When one giant conurbation dwarfs a country's secondary towns, it's known as a 'Primate City'. Bangkok's more primate than any other world city. While most countries base some key things outside the capital, Bangkok is the epicentre of all national life: royalty, religion, government, military, business, banking, property, media, arts, entertainment, shopping and all forms of transit.

The numbers are extreme by global levels. With 17% of the population, Bangkok makes 26% of GDP, but takes 72% of public spending. It surely takes a similar gulp of private investment, tourist spending and the black economy. Many functions require large spaces, such as 26 palaces, 32 universities, 88 golf-driving ranges and nearly 900 temple compounds.

ROYAL SEAT
Cosmologically, the Thai capital is where the King sits. Several palaces, such as Amorn Sathan, Chitralada, Sukhothai, Sra Pathum, Chakri Bongkot and the Grand Palace cover huge city blocks, plus royal piers and 20 former palaces with new uses.

ADMINISTRATIVE CAPITAL
Decentralisation has moved bureaucracies to the suburbs (but not upcountry) like the huge Government Complex on Chaengwattana Road, the new Parliament in Kiakkai. Soon the BMA will outgrow City Hall. Historic ministry buildings remain intact for museums. The main prisons are also here.

MILITARY BASE
The armed forces have vast installations in the city. The navy rules the river with its HQ, dockyards, glitzy conference centre, Navy Club and royal barge sheds plus a signals base in Sathorn. The army's King's Guard holds swathes of northern Bangkok filled with barracks, tanks, a stadium, and command centres. The air force has half of Don Mueang Airport.

SPIRITUAL AUTHORITY
Thai Buddhism is run from the Old Town's symbolic mandala. There are two Buddhist universities, Putthamonthon Dhamma Park, and around 900 *wats*. Wats have larger sanctuaries than most churches or mosques, due to historic roles as a community hub, school, hospital and festival ground.

EDUCATIONAL SHOWPIECE
The city's 32 universities are mostly in the suburbs, but the elite city campuses include Chulalongkorn, Thammasat, Silpakorn, Srinakharinwirot and Bangkok Uni. Prestige private schools like Vajiravudh, Mater Dei, Debsirin, Bangkok Christian College and 96 international schools have big grounds.

COMMERCIAL & FINANCIAL HEART
Much industry moved to the Eastern Seaboard, but factories still ring the capital, which has the main markets, banks and corporate HQs. Several malls and Chatuchak Market are among the world's biggest of their kind. Most Thai trade fairs and conferences are held at its MICE facilities: Impact, BITEC and the rebuilt Queen Sirikit Centre.

TOURISM & MEDICAL HOST
The world's most visited city since 2013, Bangkok has 90,000 hotel rooms. It's also a world medical tourism pioneer, with massive private hospitals. Most Thai medical training is done in Bangkok, especially at Siriraj, the world's 4th biggest hospital.

LOGISTICS HUB
Fulcrum of the country's road, rail, air and river traffic, Bangkok conveys 95% of Thai import-export. It retains a port and two oil refineries, although most containers go to Laem Chabang in Chonburi. It has two airports: Suvarnabhumi is one of the world's biggest by area and a regional hub, while Don Mueang is the world's busiest budget airport.

ENTERTAINMENT VENUE
Bangkok claims almost all the TV and radio stations, film and music studios, internet firms, ad agencies, design houses, architects, theatres, galleries, dance troupes, concert halls, opera companies and orchestras, though art galleries and creativity centres have provincial outposts. Amid scant facilities for community fitness, there's room for the most space-consuming prestige sports, with a horse-racing track, 18 golf courses, 88 driving ranges, two polo clubs and over 30 stadiums.

INTERNATIONAL AGENCY HQ
Being a Cold War outpost drew NGOs and agencies like UN ESCAP, UNESCO, ILO and SEAMEO-SPAFA. The US Embassy is its third biggest embassy in the world, after Baghdad and Cairo, with half of its staff covering non-Thai matters and several compounds, including the joint military command JUSMAG.

left: **Yellow Shirt supporters put roses and ribbons on tanks that were occuping Government House after the 2006 military coup.**

right: **Ratsadorn protestors at Siam shine phone torches to show they are *ta sawang* – seeing clearly how the country is run.**
Photo Vinai Dithajohn

In labelling this system, besides 'Thai-style democracy' or 'bureaucratic polity,' pundits talk of 'dictatorship,' 'demi-democracy,' 'neo-absolutism,' 'democracy with feudal characteristics' and a new term coined by Thitinan Pongsudhirak: 'custodial democracy.'

"Some like to state that democracy is not compatible with Thai culture," Nidhi wrote. "I'd like to point out that dictatorship is not compatible with Thai culture either, because it allows those with power (both authority and influence) to do harm. A coup is a form of influence that destroys almost all institutions of authority except the monarchy, courts, and the oversight of the great world powers. That is why protest signs have to be written in English."

In crises, protests have occupied areas for days or months. Despite some violence, mostly by the state, these demos felt carnivalesque. Each group created signature graphics, props and costumes. The anti-Thaksin Yellow Shirts waved hand-clappers. After the 2006 coup, the Thaksinite Red Shirts responded with foot-shaped clappers. The PDRC 'Bangkok Shutdown' campaign blew whistles with flag colours to usher in the 2014 coup. Then young Ratsadorn protesters brandished *The Hunger Games*' three-finger-salute and floated rubber ducks on blue water cannon sprays. Such artefacts of Thai protest are now being archived, at museums in South Korea and the Netherlands, and in the young historian Anon Chawalawan's Museum of Popular History.

The mostly-provincial Red Shirts were often denigrated in Bangkok as "uneducated buffalo," despite their political awareness. That can't be said of the Ratsadorn, which is full of graduates, professionals and even *khon dee*. Their associated party, Move Forward, won the 2023 election by sweeping Bangkok and the wealthiest, best-educated regions.

The seniority system bristled at Ratsadorn's egalitarian goals, its anti-monopoly policies and its impertinent youth. Daringly, Ratsadorn broached the ultimate taboo. On 10 August 2020, it issued a ten-point plan to modernise the monarchy in line with constitutional monarchies abroad. That watershed moment triggered hundreds of lèse-majeste cases, but exposed the issue to ongoing scrutiny. To royalists, this was a kind of blasphemy.

Ratsadorn insists that "reform ≠ revolution," yet courts ruled that elected MPs adjusting the lèse-majeste law equates to overthrow, so they dissolved Move Forward and banned its leaders for ten years, despite their 14.2 million vote mandate. Contrastingly, coup plotters, who actually do overthow the state, never get punished. Officials raised in the Cold War associate protest with that era of Communist insurgency, and many nationalists are anti-globalisation. Many worry that reform would undermine things they hold dear.

Pundits ponder whether the Red Shirt revolt of 2010 marked "the end of deference?" Ironically, military rule that later imposed deference for a decade had the opposite effect of accelerating the young to a 'post-deference' stance, focused on the future.

Whatever happens, the mystique has faded. Many Thais ask others when they became *ta sawang* ('eyes brightened') – suddenly aware of how the country is truly run. The phrase came from an incident in 2008, but people each have their own moment of revelation, which can be emotionally painful and socially wrenching.

The cultural constitution evolves through paradox. Thaksin ended his exile in 2023, via prison hospital, to see his daughter Paetongtarn become premier for Pheu Thai, oddly allied with 'Yellow' parties. His royal pardon was offset by a lese majeste charge. The the cycle of chaos and order keeps churning, but with Deep State ploys ever more revealed.

Sites of dissent

Mapping where Bangkokians demonstrate says a lot about each group's cause and class. Thai constitutionalism was declared on 24 June 1932 at Royal Plaza in front of Dusit Palace by the People's Party, an elite cadre of nationalist officials. Theirs was the first of several revolts by ever-broader classes seeking inclusion in the power structure.

The plaque marking the spot was unaccountably replaced in 2017 by a royalist plaque, which only made the original more famous. Copies spread on memes, pins, T-shirts and coasters. Its lettering was turned into a font used on posters and books.

The People's Party unveiled the Democracy Monument in the middle of the royal processional route on 24 June 1940. Designed in Art Deco style to numerology of the revolution date, it has four 24-metre-high wings (for the four forces) with bas reliefs by Silpa Bhirasri depicting citizens, soldiers and officials. In the centre, a folding book of the constitution sits elevated upon a pedestal tray.

The educated upper-middle class, mainly Sino-Thai, rallied there in 1973, only to get massacred by the dictatorship, who left power after King Rama IX intervened. The 14th October 1973 Memorial stands nearby. When those dictators returned, students protested at Sanam Luang. On 6th October 1976, they were slaughtered by ultra-nationalists around Thammasat University, where a memorial stands.

In "Black May" 1992, the broader middle class won their "mobile phone revolution" against a junta, but only after another army massacre at Democracy Monument, also quelled by King Bhumibol.

In 2006 the 'October Generation' split. The nationalist Yellow Shirts called for a royally-appointed premier to replace elected Thaksin Shinawatra. Amid the global 'occupy' trend, they siezed the royal ground Sanam Luang, Ratchadamnoen Avenue and nearby Government House, plus also new centres of corporate power: the tourism gateways of the airports and the retail heart at Ratchaprasong.

The Red Shirt rebels of 2008-10 were maligned as peasant "buffalos" by Yellow Shirts, and called themselves *phrai* (serfs), but mostly were egalitarian Octobrists plus the pick-up-truck-owning working class wanting a say. Mirroring the Yellows, the Reds colonised Ratchadamnoen – as 'Ratthadamnoen' (People's Procession) – and the posh downtown, before violent dispersal by the military amid much arson. The Yellows' Bangkok Shutdown protests in 2013-14 re-occupied similar areas (plus TV stations), calling successfully for a coup.

The 2020-22 Ratsadorn Movement likewise rallied at Democracy Movement, Sanam Luang and Ratchaprasong, calling it Ratsadornprasong (Citizen's Wishes), prompting the junta to shield the Grand Palace with a wall of shipping containers. The junta then limited protest to zones like Lan Meuang, which led to short 'flash mobs' at cause-specific sites like courts, Victory Monument or Police HQ.

As the contested issues became more cultural – whether ecology, LGBT or uniforms – the highly educated Ratsadorn held events at galleries, theatres, the youth hub of Siam and especially the plaza of Bangkok Art & Culture Centre (BACC).

Wherever demos take place, the situation remains circular and unresolved. Like Democracy Monument's location on a roundabout in a highway, democracy remains an obstacle for authoritarians, yet tantalisingly out of reach to the public.

Becoming Bangkokian
Decoding the city's DNA

Wend through Ban Somdet Chao Phraya community in Thonburi and the capital's ethnic variety pops out at every turn. In this block behind the Sikh shrine at Ban Khaek, hamlets of Lao, Mon, and central Thai craftsfolk live in neighbouring knots of *sois* with Hokkien Chinese, whose crossroads of shophouses have offerings at a red pillar, from a South China village tradition. Nearby Nurulmubeen Mosque and graveyard are tended by descendants of Malay silversmiths, brought here from Satun 150 years ago by a noble of the Bunnag clan with Persian genes. These peoples all live compatibly within one square kilometre, within a city born of migrants, within a land of 72 ethnicities – now all hyphenated 'Thai-'.

Polyglot Bangkok prides itself on hosting people of any origin. Its scores of ethnic urban villages are living museums that draw tourist, expat and local curiosity. Yet their diversity is now dissolving into the mainstream. This peaceful absorption of minorities is a model success in this era of migration crises. Bangkok avoided most of the racial chauvinism and communal violence that's plagued several ASEAN neighbours. Bangkok's Muslims live calmly among other beliefs, despite a Malay insurgency in Thailand's Deep South. Ever since Chinese gangs were pacified a century ago, huge efforts have built social harmony.

"Unlike the West, where race and ethnicity can often result in riots and lynching, and all sorts of discrimination, this isn't really an issue," writes columnist Voranai Vanijaka. "There's no Lao Pride Parade. No Malay Affirmative Action Group. The trouble in the Deep South is political, where ethnicity and religion are used as tools. But other than that, the central authority has done a great job through the years, of melting everyone into the Thai identity. The difference is in social class, divided by wealth, rather than ethnicity."

Thailand's in a region with widely varied DNA, creed and lingo. Yet it has long been touted as homogenous. The CIA *World Factbook* ranks it the 8th most mono-ethnic country at 97% Thai, but it's not that simple. Other counts put Thais at 77%, with many sub-groups. Around four in ten citizens are kinds of Lao, yet since 1905, census categories have excluded Lao, so they can only pick 'Thai.' Another two fifths have at least some Chinese genes. Historian Sujit Wongthes described the result as "Jek bon Lao" (Chinese on Lao), while northern Tai expert Vithi Phanichphant, himself part Chinese, describes Bangkokians as the "Hinduised Chinese."

In Bangkok province, out of 6.9 million residents in the 2010 census, half were Chinese-Thai, with the rest being: Thais of various kinds 3.14 million; Indian-Thai 207,000, Westerners 140,000; Japanese 70,000; other East Asian 70,000; Africans 35,000 and Arabs 35,000. Uncountable numbers come and go from upcountry, so no one knows precisely how many live here, not least since the city spills into six other provinces. Such a mix has been true for centuries, with intermarriage widespread.

Tracking the Y chromosome reveals that the core DNA in any population remains the original stock, however much modified by later arrivals. Genetics is like coffee. Steep a pot of Mon-Khmer robusta beans for 1500 years, add Tai arabica for 800 years, pour in Chinese milk for 700 years, strain it through a Malay-style filter, spike with Indian spice or Western whisky for 500 years – and it remains a type of coffee. In this case rebranded *kafae Thai*.

left: **An installation by Mon artist Sornchai Phongsa to show the migrant dream of an identity card. At BACC in Bangkok Art Biennale.**

above: **A sign at The Market mall expresses the aspiration of many bus-riding, taxi-driving migrants.**

Heart 189

The same is true for values. "The specific characteristics of the first group able to effect a viable society are crucial for the later social and cultural geography of the area, no matter how tiny," found Wilbur Zelinsky, who named that the Doctrine of First Effective Settlement. Bangkok's first effective settlers were multi-ethnic. Its character's still plural, despite nationalist assertions of Thai purity.

Assimilation has gone in phases: natural, then forced, then a -Thai hyphenation that acknowledges roots. Old Siam was like the Austro-Hungarian Empire: a pan-ethnic, shape-shifting territory under a 'Universal King' who accrued prestige the more minorities over whom he ruled. Bangkok was its Vienna – the cosmopolitan imperial seat. Integration happened through centuries of interaction.

During the nation-building era, forced assimilation fused a singular identity. Bangkok, as the immigrant gateway, was the crucible for this melting pot. Compulsory 'Thainess' bonded the regions and acculturated the influx from China, India and beyond. Cultural differentiation was banned, even noting Thais as Southern or Northern, under the blanket phrase still used constantly: "All Thais."

Reflecting the worldwide multi-culturalism trend, assimilation is now more negotiable. Internal migrants brought their local values, while minorities called for recognition. Once ethnicity felt less of a threat, their heritage came to be treated as historical curios. Many now hyphenate Thai- with their race, like Thai-Indian, and some feel multiple identities. Bangkok is like a 'stir-fry': a Thai cooking style of Chinese origin that leaves each ingredient distinct.

Aliens can be Bangkokian too. With globalisation, half a million expatriates add a transnational vibe to what's flowered into a world city. Though few long-stayers become citizens, many feel a sense of belonging to their adoptive town.

Migration never stops. Newcomers are handled at arm's length, with reluctance to integrate the 2.2 million unregistered non-Thais, many of them in Bangkok. Although this used to be a safe harbour, refugees and émigrés now often get sent back. Trafficked workers, mainly Burmese and Khmer, often face discrimination and struggle to get the right papers. Thai-born Mon artist Sornchai Phongsa was stateless until shortly before he starred in the Bangkok Art Biennale. His installation showed undocumented Mon labourers praying to an image of a thumbprint from their yearned-for identity card.

Bangkok managed diversity by cantonment. Enclaves retained their own ways within *taew* of narrow lanes, which shielded their social structure from modernity. They brought skills or were allotted specialist trades, creating 'mono-hoods' that became their contributions to city life. This inadvertently led to natural

left: **Dreaming of a condo called Wish in 'Midtown.'**

below: **Many taxi drivers come from a network of certain rural provinces.**

right: **"Ugly but true,"** says Rakchart Wong-arthichart of his viral map about how **"nationalistic education"** leads **"half of inner Bangkokians"** (aka **'Thailand'**) to view other regions and neighbours.

assimilation as other Bangkokians went to other ethnic *yaan* for things they needed.

Each minority was self-governing under an appointed noble title. Mon were led by the Chao Phraya Mahayotha, Lao by captive Vientiane princes, and Chinese by the Phraya Chodoek Ratchasetthi, a rank inherited by Hokkiens until the more numerous Teochiu and Hakka got their turn. Meanwhile, French and Portuguese bishops vied over Catholic primacy. The only title to survive the 1932 Revolution was the Chularatchamontri, still the nominal head of all Thai Muslims. Until the modern era, he wasn't from the Sunni majority, but a Shi'a from the lineage of a Persian sheik whose family ran much of the Siamese bureaucracy for centuries. Their descendants who converted to Buddhism, the Bunnag family, still produce many social leaders.

The status of diasporas reflected how they arrived, whether they were invited, granted refuge, or held captive. Thonburi and Bangkok arose out of Ayutthaya's depopulation. Refugees floated their raft-houses downstream to safer moorings near pre-existing communities of Mon in Thonburi or Portuguese in Samsen. Cham Muslims from Cambodia were bestowed land at Ban Khrua by King Rama I for helping to repel the Burmese – a grant that later saved them from eviction for an expressway.

Until the past century, Southeast Asia was thinly populated with distinct tribes scattered along rivers amid forested wilderness. Land was plentiful, but labour scarce, so wars were fought to acquire peoples. Entire villages were hauled to Bangkok, put to work, then allowed to settle along canals they'd dug. Stigma still shadows ethnicities whose ancestors were brought as slaves from upcountry, or worse, as war captives from raids in Patani (modern-day Pattani province), Cambodia or Vientiane.

Chinese coolies were shipped in as much-needed labour in Thonburi, through much of the Rattanakosin period. Although most arrived destitute on junks or steamers, they were never slaves, and worked their way from the margins to the core of Bangkok society. Many a community from Bangkok's dawn survives, such as Talad Noi, where Hokkien were allocated that swampy margin beyond the Teochiu town of Sampeng.

Enclaves occur even when not mandated. Western cynics snipe at expatriates for clustering

in downtown bubbles and joining national clubs. Yet they're being as authentic as any other minority, who find that being among their own kind is vital for well-being, whether sharing support, humour or comfort foods. Country-focused venues, film screenings or festivals are among Bangkok's most valued cultural platforms.

Indian Punjabis who fled Partition have stuck together, even moving en masse within the city from Ban Khaek to later enclaves like Nana or Pahurat's Little India. Indians also marry within their communities, or to a spouse from India. As with Muslims and Chinese, Indian-Thais are sub-divided between sects or place of origin and live in their own enclaves.

Heart 191

Cambodia and Vietnam was applied to every non-Thai, who had to report their address whenever returning home, even after one night away. Outcry about the imposition and impracticality obscured the fact that corralling foreigners has been policy for all the city's history. Ever wary of foreign takeover, Bangkok keeps non-Thais off-balance.

Natural assimilation might be deeper, but in Siam's loosely structured society, self-contained communities had low incentive to blend in. Given the ambiguous allegiances of Indians, Muslims and Chinese, completing a united identity took force. "Most minorities did not want to assimilate as they were happy to maintain their identity and beliefs," wrote art collector Disaphol Chansiri in *The Chinese Émigrés of Thailand*. "Prior to 1932, …most ethnic Chinese maintained their Chinese citizenship [or] identified themselves as Chinese even if they were born in Thailand."

Chinese sojourners – who were all-male until women were allowed to leave China in 1912 – aimed to return home, even if they married Thais and had *luk jiin* – half-Chinese kids. They juggled other loyalties: to their ancestral home, *sae* (clan), dialect group, *ang yi* (secret society) and network overseas. Plus they ran the economy and sent a fifth of its earnings home. By the early 1930s, Thai-Teochiu alone accounted for 10 percent of all global remittances to China.

The tipping point for forced assimilation came in 1910. To protest a poll tax, the Chinese stopped the city for days with a general strike. *Ang yi* threatened strikebreakers and troops rode the tram to Yannawa's docks to quell the riots. This alarm came amid a royal succession and Sun Yat Sen making three trips to Sampeng to raise funds for a nationalist revolution in China. The Emperor was overthrown in 1911, a year before the new Thai king quashed an attempted coup. The stakes were high.

In an effective ultimatum, Siam said those who renounced Chinese nationalism could stay if they committed to becoming fully Thai. Soon followed laws on nationality and family names, which Thai commoners also lacked. In a typical Thai hybrid, the Chinese could mix in their given name, *sae* and lucky words into multisyllabic surnames that are today a quick way to identify a Sino-Thai. Likewise, you can often tell Indian or Muslim Thai surnames from the Hindu or Arabic parts of the name. This transition took decades to complete.

The parcelling continues today. Ratchada-phisek and Chong Nonsi attract the Fourth Wave of Chinese immigrants, who no longer come from China's southern seaboard, but from inland provinces. Mini-Myanmars spring up, with Burmans in Ratchathewi, Shan in Yannawa, or 'New Mon' labour in nearby Mahachai.

Foreigners are still cantoned. Expats and retirees can only buy condo units, not land, nor majority-own their own business. In addition, immigration rules for 'aliens' keep shifting. Since the early 2000s, every foreigner has had to re-register every 90 days, even if they have a work permit. Then in 2019, a 1979 law to deal with the refugees from

In a break from its multi-racial history, Thai nationality was based upon racial purity. Minorities who had not seemed that foreign in Siam, were suddenly "the others within." King Rama VI published a pamphlet labelling the Chinese 'The Jews of the Orient.' Between 1932 and 1975, most Chinese schools and newspapers were shut, secret societies outlawed, and printing in characters banned. It was also hard for Bangkok's Thai-Bharat Lodge, the émigré base for Indian independence from the British. Enforcement of Central Thai language restricted ethnic and provincial dialects to home and business. Location names were Thai-ified, with even Sampeng Lane, the heart of Chinatown, gaining the nondescript sign: Soi Wanit 1.

Enamoured by racial theories of 1930s Europe and Japan, the dictator Phibun and his ideologue Luang Vichit-Vadhakan, passed cultural mandates for a uniform identity within a racially defined new country, Prathet Thai (Thailand). A new National Anthem was written to start with the words: "the blood and flesh of the Thai race."

Both Westerners and Thais tend to paint Thai nationalism as a defence against the Western colonial encroachment that defined the borders, but its immediate imperative was to absorb millions of Chinese. Many authors of Thai nationalism – including Phibun, Vichit-Vadhakan and Kukrit Pramoj – had some Chinese ancestry, and so knew from the heart what terms might work.

It was painful at times. The benign nickname for Chinese, *jek* (uncle), turned into a shameful pejorative if they didn't conform to Thai manners, while Chinese-Thai schoolchildren were mocked for their accent or look even as late at the 1980s. So for an easier life, they integrated. "Fourth-generation Chinese were unheard of," according to a widely agreed paradigm by anthropologist William Skinner, "because all great-grandchildren of Chinese immigrants had merged with Thai society."

The novel *Letters from Thailand* by Botan shocked Thais by its frank portrayal of this process. When a migrant character resists assimilation, his Bangkok-born daughter tells him: "It's not something you decide to do. It happens in the normal course of things." Later in the book, her father concedes: "I could not shelter them from the thousands of experiences which made them another people, another race. There are so many of us here, yet the Thai have won – the Chinese have turned into Thai."

Most Sino-Thais arrived destitute, as the saying goes, "with just a mat and a pot," then pulled themselves up to the heights of society. "Psychologically, most of the Chinese in Thailand see their ancestors as coming from peasant stock," *The Encyclopaedia* of *the Chinese Overseas* quotes a young Sino-Thai professional. "So believing in a culture is an upgrading for them."

Thai-Jiin (Sino-Thais) feel gratitude for being given the chance to flourish more easily here than in China. The Hainan-born media mogul Sondhi Limthongkul refused to make one last return visit to China: "Living 50 years under royal aegis, loving Thailand more than some native Thais, she said that Thailand was her home and she did not want ever to leave the country. Today her children have thrived in Thai society." It was Sondhi – leader of the Yellow Shirt movement against Thaksin Shinawatra (a fourth-generation Sino-Thai) – who coined the term 'Sino-Thai patriot.'

top left: **A 'White Asian Look' has replaced the half-*farang* look as hip.**

left: **Star Nadech Kugimiya was taken as half-Japanese, his adoptive dad's origin, but is Thai-Austrian. Seen here on *Praew* magazine.**

above: **Not many foreign residents can become Thai, but anyone can become Bangkokian and feel that this city is their home.**

Mon

In festive tents down *sois* of old wooden houses, Mon maidens in frilly costume sit in rows; at their feet hand-sized wooden discs stand on their narrow edge. Wearing Mon-style capes, larking youths banter with the girls and take turns to toss their own disc so it bowls over their sweetheart's one. Lasting into the night, this courting game of *saba* has varied rules in several Mon neighbourhoods of Phra Pradaeng at Songkran, the Mon New Year held a week later than Thai Songkran. Since unmarried males and females didn't traditionally mix, the game enables a coy inspection at polite distance of hands, eyes, mouth and agility – amid much teasing.

Some *saba* players also compete in the Mr & Miss Songkran contest at the district office by the river promenade. Next day, the winners lead the grand procession on ornate floats, while the public throws water at each other.

The Mon minority blends seamlessly into Thai life, sharing much in looks, lifestyle and Theravada faith. Mon also maintain traditions and timber houses in enclaves that feel like pockets of old Siam. One in Thonburi dates from before Ayutthaya fell, on a canal still called Khlong Mon. You can tell Mon *wats* by the gilded goose statues on poles and banners of centipedes.

Wistfully named Mon-Raman, after their lost kingdom of Ramanayadesa, these 'Old Mon' were refugees. Pushed out in waves by Burmans via today's Mon State, they were welcomed by Siam. Many served the state, gained high rank or married up. Mon queens gave birth to Kings Rama II and Rama V.

The 'New Mon' fled here during Myanmar's dictatorship, and lately keep coming for work. Like other low-status economic migrants, they're handled warily with bureaucratic barriers. Officials laud Mon traditions, but stop New Mon in places like the nearby Mahachai seafood port from joining Old Mon festivities or holding those same rites.

Even older were the 'Original Mon' who first settled what's now Thailand. Mahayana Buddhists, the Mon spread from Manipur in India across Burma and 1500 years ago overlapped with Khmers in today's Thai territory. Nearby Nakhon Pathom was founded a millennium ago as the capital of a Mon empire called Dvaravati, as retold in the Mon museum at Ratchaburi.

Bangkok's best known Mon village is Ko Kret, a car-free river island famous for its tilted whitewashed *chedi* and etched Mon pots in the shape of a lotus-bud. It had been isolated from change, but today hordes of tourists and weekending Bangkokians cram its narrow paths, browsing the packaged foods and trinkets. Its museum of earthenware was wrecked in the Great Flood of 2011, while the last kilns churn out gaudy souvenirs. Mon residents now number just nine.

By authentic contrast in Bang Kradee, off the Rama II Road to Mahachai, around five thousand Mon villagers often wear sarongs and *thanaka* bark face powder. You still see toddlers with topknots, ankle bells and amulets strung around the waist. "We are Thai-Mon, different from other Thais and from Mon State in Burma," says Thawatpong Monda, 32, who has led a revival of Mon culture. "I turned my collection of Mon artifacts and instruments into a museum to show other villagers how to preserve their crafts."

Several folk 'museums' at lived-in houses instruct visitors and Mon children in the crafts of reed mat weaving, palm crafts, dessert making, musical instruments, *saba*, costume, mosquito whisks and cradle knitting. A photo gallery captures the feeling at festival time. The village marks full moon with early morning rites, when the community shows its vitality, with all in costume, sharing food and conducting ceremonies.

"At Songkran we do a Mon *khao chae* with rice in chilled jasmine water and seven dishes – one for each Songkran goddess," adds Thawatpong, who used to be called Somchai. "HRH Princess Sirindhorn bestowed me with a new name. Thawatpong means Guardian of Ancestry. That's my mission."

left: At the Mon Songkran in Phra Phradaeng, young Mon in traditional garb flirt in the disc-kicking game called *saba*.

top & above: In Bang Kradee, heritage guru Thawatpong Monda makes the Mon iced jasmine rice dish *khao chae* **and Mon kid's top-knots can be seen at local festivals.**

When King Bhumibol passed away in 2016, the Thai-Chinese Chamber of Commerce, Teochiu Association and United Chinese Clans Association held a tribute in Yaowarat called 'Beloved King of the Chinese Community.' "I think as ethnic Chinese we will be forever grateful to the King who cared about our well-being and treated us equally," said Ma Chongxian, a restaurateur and Kuomintang exile, who had joined prayer vigils for King Bhumibol. "I think he should be credited with the fact that we don't feel like we are a minority group here and we share the sense of security living in this nation."

Assimilation hasn't always prevailed. The Mon, Lao, Chinese and other Buddhist groups have integrated more smoothly than have Hindus, Muslims, Christians or secular *farang*, with the highest barriers being their beliefs and physical dissimilarities. The 1940s Cultural Mandates about wearing modern clothes were intended to unify, but a ban (since rescinded) on the sarongs and caps of Muslim-Thais only alienated the second biggest minority, who also intermarried less.

Ethnic enclaves seem like a benign attraction today, but for decades their diversity was seen as a barrier to unity. *Yaan* like Ban Somdet Chao Phraya had their boundaries redrawn and the local leadership replaced by state bureaucrats. Since the 1970s, communities and academics (often outspoken Sino-Thais) have called for ethnic recognition, buoyed by a global trend to champion the indigenous, not least for reasons of tourism. By the 2000s, ethnicity wasn't seen as a threat and the National Narrative began to accept minority heritage and neo-Chinese pride, as long as it professes loyalty to the state. Gen X and Millennials rekindled interest in the roots their parents and grandparents had stifled. Now the multi-racial enclave of Kudi Jeen – with its legacies of Portuguese, Chinese, Mon and Shi'a Muslim – is being conserved as a project for Bangkok's 250th anniversary.

Thais constantly change masks to be "status appropriate" in the hierarchy, so given the plural society of Bangkok, it's second-nature to hold multiple ethnic identities. 'All Thais' is fragmenting into hyphen-Thai categories: Thai-Jiin, Thai-Isaan, Thai-Indian. Thai-Muslim differs by being a religious tag, as separatism in provinces near Malaysia makes it sensitive to admit most are ethnic Malays. Besides, Bangkok's Muslims come from half a dozen

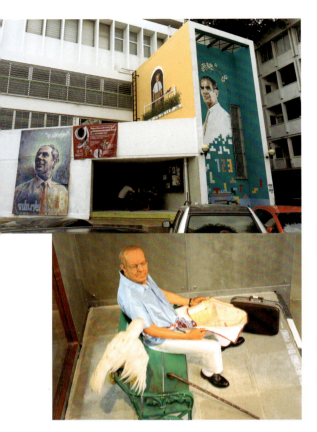

lands, to which many maintain links, replenishing their cultural distinctions. Thai-Indians never dropped links to India, while Sino-Thais are rekindling their links to China and their diaspora.

Assimilation isn't one-way; the host culture also changes through the process. Identification with Thainess is more intense in Bangkok than in provinces where indigenous ways hold stronger. Assimilation within Bangkok is also eased by having the shared umbrella of modern lifestyle. Since most Chinese settlers chose Bangkok, the capital has ended up with much of its population having paler Sinified features quite distinct from regional Thai looks.

Intermarriage is key to assimilation, though that's wrenching for Indians and believers in monotheistic religions. Weddings reveal ethnic patterns. Some *farang* marrying Buddhists do dress up in Thai silk regalia for the monks' blessing and the pouring of holy water from a conch shell over the couple's garlanded hands. Sino-Thais do that too, but when both spouses are Han the betrothal can be ritually Chinese, with lucky red styling and a dowry of gold bars. I've been to receptions where the band, food and seating were divided between Thai and Chinese. Muslims insist a Buddhist spouse converts, but the receptions tend to have a parallel set of waiters serving halal food and drink. It's a delicate dual identity.

"I feel some inner conflict because my mum's side is Muslim and my dad's side is Buddhist," says a head-scarfed lady in *Humans of Bangkok*. "I give full spirit when attending ceremonies from both sides… I just know that if I upset my mum and dad, they become sad. And I will soon be sad too. So, I choose to get along with both religions, but have my own belief in life."

Thai-Western offspring known as *luk khrueng* (half-kids) often waver between their heritages. *Luk khreung* are popular in Bangkok, and often hired as models or entertainers. Many have a good education abroad or at international schools, and get plum jobs. But like Thais who study overseas, they're semi-outsiders with a stark choice: immerse in the Thai world; live in Bangkok's international circles; or handle the stress of multiple identity. For individualist *luk khrueng* raised in egalitarian environments, submission to hierarchy can be a deal-breaker.

"As long as you truly understand both cultures you can move in both worlds – you also have a unique view of knowing and understanding both culture which is an advantage," says Kamol Sukosol Clapp, a half-American who co-founded Bakery Music and the band Pru. "One thing I find interesting is that all wealthy Thais are sending their kids to international schools or abroad, and these kids are growing up *farang*. This is a tiny minority, but it's a bunch of *farang*-attitude Thais who'll be running the country – it's gonna be interesting."

Mindset is a higher hurdle to integration than looks, though integration is easier for east Asians. So varied are Bangkok genes that visitors from ASEAN often get mistaken for Thais. Bangkokians also prize certain features from Northeast Asia or the West, seen in the taste for pale skin and plastic surgery for eyelid folds, nasal bridges and pointy chins.

Being Bangkokian is more malleable than becoming Thai. The city's so popular with expats, sojourners and frequent visitors precisely because it welcomes a floating population of unassimilated people, who are mostly left free to be themselves. Few expats become citizens, but thousands stay Bangkokian for decades, or often for life.

top far left: **The Italian 'father of Thai modern art' Corrado Feroci is revered at Silpakorn University, as Silpa Bhirasri.**

lower far left: **Disappeared expat Jim Thompson seen at the Art Centre in his famous house. Sculpture by Navin Rawanchaikul.**

left: **A sideshow at the British-run Ploenchit Fair.**

below: **French food vendor Samuel Montassier makes** *yum woonsen* **in Yaowarat.**

Expatriates aren't all Westerners; the majority here are Asian – and always were. This isn't recent; for centuries, hiring foreign expertise was a strategy across Southeast Asia, so that indigenous subjects couldn't threaten the rulers' power over imported luxuries, technology and know-how. Ayutthaya had a Greek prime minister, a Japanese general, and Dutch cannon-makers. For three centuries, the Persian Bunnag clan helped run Siam, and still produces leaders, including a recent foreign minister. King Rama V modernised Siam by getting a Dane to found the army, a Belgian as advisor and a Briton, Henry Alabaster, to lay the first road, Chaoren Krung. Italians built palaces and landmarks in the early 20th century. In recent decades, the Japanese paid for cultural facilities. Outsiders still play a role in the Thai system.

Foreign consultants and compradors pale beside the long role of Chinese in tax farming and running state monopolies or concessions. Similarly, Chinese coolies were imported rather than Siamese farmers re-deployed into new urban new trades, as it wouldn't disturb the feudal social contract, *sakdina*, which echoes in today's patron-client expectations. Professions remain more accessible to Sino-Thais – as Chinese always dealt with money and trade – than to indigenous farmers, who dealt more in kind.

It's a courting game. Playing-off various economic suitors is how Bangkok engages with geopolitics – and with diverse settlers. Powers who want a piece of the action are allowed leeway, but not if they push too far. Bangkok then smiles at a rival power, and adopts their fashions as a new layer in the city's strata of taste.

"Fetishism of the foreign commodity is indeed one of the distinctive characteristics of Thai identity," according to the 'Xenomania' exhibition at Museum Siam. "We Thais often value prestigious foreign objects more than we value our own culture, but on the other hand, we can be strongly nationalistic, particularly when we encounter non-Thais."

We see this counterbalancing over centuries. Ayutthaya kicked out the French, but closed only to Europe, whilst still inviting Asians. When Chinese merchant lords got ensconced in Rattanakosin, the court found alternatives in trading with colonial powers, and then played off the French and the British. On the losing side in 1945, Thailand was saved from

punishment by America, which in turn became overbearing in the Cold War, so Thais turned to Japan for industrialisation. After the 1997 crash, the IMF got too pushy, and Thailand returned to China's orbit, later off-set with fresh invitations for Japan and Korea to the investment dance.

"Have you ever noticed that the objects of Siam's fascination only come from the great nations?" said a panel at 'Xenomania.' "Our forebears also took pleasure in keeping up with the latest trends from Cambodia, China, and even Persia. Our taste for trends coming from the world's high civilisations is a reflection of our desire to show the global public that we are also part of this modern world."

Those strategic machinations affect how foreigners fit into society. The wish to be *siwilai* also explains the cooler reception to migrants from upcountry or less prestigious lands. It's not about cultural compatibility, witness Bangkok's jarring juxtapositions. Successful settlers bring attributes that flatter Bangkok's face.

Later arrivals have established colourful quarters across the city, keeping its aggregate style. Gulf families buy myrrh and puff on shishas in Nana's Soi Arab. *Chaebol* managers from Seoul eat *bibimbap* in Sukhumvit Plaza's Korea Town, opposite the Manhattan Hotel where the first Korean visitors stayed. Japanese croon karaoke in the mini-Ginzas of Thaniya and around Thonglor's J-Avenue.

This ambiguous city feels at ease with extended impermanence. It's not just internal migrants and diasporas who flow in and out. Sojourners have been a 'Bangkok type' for centuries, residing till the trade winds changed or working enough years to return with savings and prestige. Local tolerance enables other ways of being, so it's a haven for social misfits, from bohemian artists to the gay diaspora. An echelon of settlers fleeing the West are Asiaphile 'Easties,' who feel that Asia is their spiritual home. Fellow Easties in hippyish idylls across the region also tend to regard Bangkok as their simpatico metropolis.

All these migrants must deal with erratic visa rules in order to stay. The advent of cheap flights and internet has only boosted the shuttling of professionals, creatives and digital nomads who find themselves sticking here, or coming back to settle in this most receptive of cities. Outsiders from anywhere with the wits and patience can become Bangkokian.

Indian-Thais

Some of Siam's earliest migrants came from India. Millennia ago, they put the Indo into Indo-China, which underpins much that's 'Thai': language, architecture, the *wai* and beliefs, from Buddhism and Brahmanism to Vedic astrology and *The Ramayana* epic's role in statecraft. Thais worship at Hindu shrines, but detach their ancient cultural debt from contemporary Indians, show little interest in India itself, and in some cases feel averse to their food and ways. Consequential in business, this minority are considered Thai, but also a puzzle.

The Indian-Thais are 200,000 strong, but their main public presence is tailoring. You can't walk through Nana or Bangrak without an Indian tailor offering a suit, two shirts, a second pair of trousers and a free kimono – all made-to-measure within 24 hours. Indian-Thais own most tailor shops, and have a loyal following. A friend from Sydney only gets his suits from Jit Malhotra, the Sikh tailor of Siam Emporium, who's got records of his lengthening waist size going back over 20 years.

At the west end of Chinatown, a "Little India" emerged as Pahurat's textile market in the 1930s. It got a boost when the state suppressed traditional clothing, itself derived from Indian wrap designs. Suddenly Punjabi Sikhs and Hindus – who'd learned tailoring from their British colonists, and had just fled here from Partition – sewed up the compulsory new market for fitted Western outfits. Many an Indian-owned hotel, condo or chainstore was built upon bolts of cloth.

Rajawongse Tailors in Nana is named for the street in Chinatown where many Indian-Thais began their ascent. While Chinese spread from crowded Sampeng, Punjabis moved out as a group from there and from Ban Khaek in Thonburi to the then-cheap suburb of Sukhumvit, where many made a fortune in real estate.

Bangkok has two kinds of Sikh. Those with blue turbans have a gold-domed Gurdwara in Pahurat, while Namdharis, with a white hair wrap, worship at a Gurdwara on Asoke Road. Sikhs first settled at Ban Khaek in Thonburi, now marked by a Sikh gateway. They also went into medicine and due to their heritage as warriors, became trusted guards or hotel doormen. Along with Seventh Day Adventists, Sikhs are stalwarts of the Bangkok Vegetarian Association.

Other migrants from the subcontinent have their own enclaves. King Rama I granted Brahmins land in the sacred centre of Rattanakosin at the Devasathan temple and Giant Swing, a symbol of Shiva creating the world. Around the corner stands the Dev Mandir temple and school of Punjabi Hindus. At its celebration of Krishna's birthday, the blue baby deity appears via animation, crawling on TV monitors around the altar hall.

Bangrak has another hub, where South Asians run Bangkok's world-class jewellery trade. Dawoodi Bohras from Gujarat settled there, with their Nana family founding Nana *sois* in Talad Noi and Sukhumvit. In Lower Silom live Muslim Indians and Pakistanis from Sindh, as well as Tamils who arrived with British firms. Tamils hold a wild trance procession at Navaratri each October at their Maha Uma Devi temple. By contrast, paler northern Uttar Pradeshis focus on their Vishnu temple in nearby Yannawa, where Navaratri is a genteel rite with devotees in suits and saris.

Unlike the Chinese isolated from Red China, Indian-Thais kept links to India, where many still trade, source a spouse, or send their kids to study. They marry and socialise mainly among themselves. Highly educated, typically at international schools or in India, they are probably the wealthiest Bangkok ethnicity. Inter-married families gradually established associations and places to worship.

English-speaking Indians make ideal compradors. The Sikh Narula family led the way in gaining concessions for international brands like Replay. They also created labels like Chaps and Jaspal, which partnered with Karl Lagerfeld. Rachvin and Surin Narula brought in Thailand's first internet café, Cyberia, then founded a location agency for foreign films.

Typically fluent in English, Indian-Thais network through business clubs, embassies and Chambers of Commerce, while their youth likes to party at *hi-so* and expat venues. Promoters bring in Bollywood movies, Bhangra drummers, Delhi DJs and traditional performers through both the Indian Cultural Centre and organisers like Gaurav Sehgal, who runs the hip Indian restaurant Indus. The annual Festival of Music and Dance was founded in 1998 by JS Oberoi. He is one of several Indian-Thai publishers in English, the language of the glossy community magazine, *Marsala*.

Many Indian-Thais have been bestowed state honours, and some have gained celebrity, like Varin Sachdev and Athip Nana. Yet there's been just one Indian-Thai lead in a Bangkok film. Their position as citizens is ambiguous. In the nationalist era when Sino-Thais were suppressed, it was likewise taboo to express Indianness. Thais also felt uneasy about Indian resistance to the British Raj being headquartered at Bangkok's Thai-Bharat Lodge. You still hear the hurtful Thai saying: "if you see a snake and an Indian, kill the Indian first." Due to origin and skin colour they get lumped in with Malays, Indonesians and Muslims as *khaek*, meaning 'guest' – which implies welcome, yet non-belonging. As tax auditor Vorasa Srichaikul says: "I don't know any person of Indian heritage who is comfortable with the word *khaek*."

At the other end of the scale, poor Indians without permits hawk peanuts at bar strips, or fried bananas around Nang Loeng. In 2016 the community was incensed by the *Thai Rath* newspaper headline: "Crackdown on nut-selling Khaek: sell fabric, give loans, act like mafia, stay long time." Many feel hurt at such discrimination given how much their ethnicity has contributed. "How can they still get away with such generalisations?" asks Maynica Sachdev. "Indians cover a wide range of professions from doctors, lawyers, engineers, hoteliers to social workers like myself. This country is my first home and will always be."

top left: **An expat from Delhi celebrates the Divali festival with candles at her home.**

left: **A mural about the Indian-Thais by Navin Rawanchaikul drew leaders of the community to the launch in Warehouse 30 of Khaek Pai Krai Ma (Guests Who Come and Go). Many saw themselves or their elders in the murals in a landmark exhibition that recognised the long Indian contribution to Bangkok and Thailand.**

Roots
Finding Thailand in Bangkok

"The best thing about Bangkok is that it's located right next door to Thailand," Ambassador Ralph Boyce told his new US Embassy staff. "I recommend you go there sometime." As in other centralised states, the Thai capital differs radically from its hinterland, which Thais call *ban-nok* – literally 'home outside', a more separating term than the translation 'upcountry'. That doesn't make Bangkok any less Thai, but shows who's central and who's peripheral to the national story.

Urbanites who stay in their air-con bubble – or only visit resorts that replicate Bangkok taste, like Hua Hin or Khao Yai – seem not to appreciate how much the countryside has modernised. Cultural and tourism promotions project a rural idyll with a passive peasantry maintaining tradition. Villages and provincial cities have developed to the point where moving to the capital is no longer the only hope to advance, yet Bangkokian presumptions about provincial people lag behind the new reality.

Meanwhile, Millennial Thais raised after the nation-building era are exploring their own city and finding that *ban-nok* is right next door within the city too. Waves of internal migrants infused the informal sector with rural ways, from village organisation through to farmhouse recipes and folklore. Children gambolling in top-knots feature in public imagery of Thainess, but have disappeared from the capital – except you can find them for real in the city's migrant shanties and enclaves of ethnic Mon. Northern communities here do life-extension rituals, where an elderly or ailing person sits under a cone of three poles garlanded with offerings of banana and popped rice.

When I arrived in 1994, certain districts were known for their regional character, as provincial arrivals were recent, the influx starting with industrialisation in the 1960s and declining after the 1997 crash. Dusit had a Lanna flavour, Ramkhamhaeng felt Southern, and Isaan was in the air at Saphan Kwai,

Khlong Toei, Pinklao, Soi Lassalle in Bangna or Soi Rangnam near Victory Monument. An 'Isaan Bangkok' themed issue at *Metro* magazine in 2002 would be harder now. "Isaan people are no longer in certain areas; we are everywhere," says Tanyaporn Singchalee, from Ubon. "We go wherever there is a job to earn a living."

Migrants often put down roots near their work or where transport dropped them. That's why *molam* music clubs popped up around Mo Chit Northeastern Bus Station, and many Southerners settled around the old train terminal at Bangkok Noi. This also made it easier to travel back home for family, holidays or to help with the harvest.

Kinship bonds shape *baan-nok* Bangkok. Workers often end up here by invitation or suggestion from family, friends or neighbours who made their fortune here, or fibbed that they did to save face. Many stay in the same place, eat at the same stalls, and frequent the same services. The village feeling of Bangkok's *taew* and streetlife was only partly created here. Often neighbours migrated as a group, bringing the tendrils of village relationships that go back generations. Ask a taxi driver where they're from and most will say Roi-et, Ubon, Khorat, Kalasin, or Udon Thani. That's because taxi firms typically recruit through the grapevine of particular localities.

Provincial groups establish clubs, enlist sports teams, observe rituals and run fairs. Institutions draw provincial followers too. Certain temples always appoint abbots from a certain region: Southerners to Wat Rachathiwat in Dusit; northerners to Wat Benchamabophit. In sports like football or volleyball, the players from teams named for a province often live in Bangkok, fly to 'home' matches upcountry, yet when they stay home to play 'away' to Bangkok teams, get 'home-away-from-home' support from migrant fans. Ramkhamhaeng University taught so many Southerners that the area drew others from the Peninsula to trade or to meet for fish liver curry, chatting in their rapid-fire dialect. Even in Bangkok prisons, convicts from the same province tend to bond and eat together.

The easiest way for outsiders and Thais who live downtown to access ethnic *yaan* is through their food. Sampling specialities is a compulsion for Bangkokians, who graze the many food fairs of renowned regional recipes, and buy packaged helpings to share with family or colleagues. Food courts and night

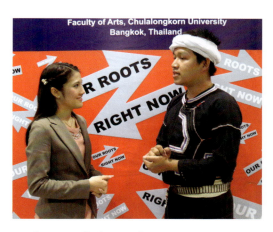

markets usually have at least one purveyor from each region: Isaan *somtam*, Central *namphrik* dip, Malay biriyani, Northern *sai oua* spiral sausage, maybe even Southern turmeric roast chicken flattened between bamboo sticks. Stalls along Rama IX Road advertise their Isaan province of origin, ready for the closing-time influx of staff from the RCA bar strip – a nightly hometown reunion after work.

Folk venues are a casualty of urban cleansing. After the 2014 coup, the BMA evicted several old markets, plus tens of thousands of street vendors, many of them providing cheap tastes of home to migrants. Redevelopment has pushed out Southern eateries from Ratchathewi, Lanna stalls from Langsuan and *molam* pubs from Sukhumvit. It's a worldwide phenomenon that when enclaves empty, the last trace is restaurants, like bagel shops in London's East End. With fewer regulars, local stalls and

left: **Villagers recruited from the provinces to dress as idealised peasants for the 2015 Thainess Festival, in the parade from National Stadium to Lumpini Park.**

above: **Our Roots Right Now: a symposium about ethnic minority rights.**

below: **The now-closed Hua Lamphong Station was the longtime gateway – and route home – for rural migrants.**

Isaan Travelogue

An Isaan guy called Man puts on a cute fish suit each night to work as a tout for a thousand-seat suburban seafood restaurant. He is among four Isaan migrants portrayed in the documentary *Crying Tiger*. We see Man get promoted to acting as a fall-guy in drag for a comedy troupe, while a *molam* crooner, Pornsak Songsang, tells why he has stayed in the same dingy short-time lodgings since his first night in Bangkok 20 years before: it's a reminder of his dream, widely held, to go back to the farm.

Isaan and Bangkok feel like separate countries, quipped Isaan's only SEAWrite Award winner, in 1978, Lao Khamhom (aka Khamsing Srinawk). Demeaned as *choei* (unsophisticated), northeasterners have found an unlikely outlet for their tales through the arts.

The influx of Isaan farmers was as epochal to Bangkok as the Great Northward Migration of blacks was to Philadelphia or New York. Culture-wise, both brought their soulfood and songs of woe from field to factory. "Isaan natives are like people of African descent," said comedian Thongchai Prasongsanti. "We're both discriminated against over race and colour, but what we have in common is a love of music and the ability to work hard." Like blues floated up the Mississippi to Chicago, *molam* trucked down the Friendship Highway from the Khorat Plateau. And just as blues gave rise to urban genres like rap and house, *molam* has morphed into racy rap.

That Chinese sojourners prospered and Isaan migrants languished led to attitudes that Sino-Thais work hard and study, while the Isaan are lazy, uneducated 'buffalos'. "We are coming to look for a job. Don't say we are lazy," sung Pong Prida in her musical riposte 'Klap Baan' (Return Home). "When it's time to plant rice, all of the Isaan people will go home... We are Isaan; we still care about our home and rice fields."

Yet adversity can spur success. Since Isaan's burst of political might in the early 2000s, its culture has leapfrogged the Thai mainstream into prominence abroad in art, film, food, music and fashion. No other Thai music comes close to *molam*'s global appeal. The second Thai restaurant to earn a Michelin star was Somtam Der. Tony Jaa was Thailand's sole global film star, Nakadia its only famous DJ, headlining at European festivals, and Rojjana 'Yui' Phetkanha its first supermodel to go 'inter'. The top arts achiever is Apichatpong Weerasethakul, a triple Cannes prize-winning auteur/artist with the world's top critics voting three of his films in the top 37 of the 21st century.

"So far as I know, Bangkok has yet to give birth to a great novelist, poet, playwright, philosopher, architect, or social thinker," observed Benedict Anderson. "It is Khon Kaen, not Bangkok, that gave birth to Apichatpong, who is internationally regarded as among the very top world directors. You might have expected that an artist of this calibre would be the object of immense pride by a bourgeoisie always anxious to show its international credentials. But no."

Feisty originals like badboy rocker Sek Lo-so don't conform to bland Bangkok pop, with its politesse and *hi-so* surnames. That's precisely why Isaan so appeals to many *farang*, who prefer the earthy Isaan wit.

Isaan arts are steeped in ribald vernacular lore that is authentic and easily grasped, yet shunned as backward by some Bangkok arbiters who misread the themes and audience. Many Bangkokians need subtitles, as ever more Isaan films get acted in Lao. In another disjoint, Isaan arts favour melancholic realism, while Bangkokians prefer fanciful beauty.

Isaan's mass migration to Bangkok in the 1980s and '90s is a story that demanded telling. Paiwarin Khao-Ngam launched 'migrant lit' with his 1995 poem 'Banana Tree Horse', which won the SEAWrite Award. The organic toy stands for innocence lost in Bangkok. "Although I've been in the city for over twenty years, I still have the foundation of a *khon ban-nok* (bumpkin)," he says. "I am the person who communicates between different worlds."

In a watershed moment, when the economy crashed in 1997, *molam* and the Central folk music *luk thung* gained access to FM radio. Hearing Isaan vocals in taxis and stalls helped accustom Bangkokians to Isaan's dialect, ways and outlook. The frugal, nostalgic post-crash aesthetic, and the need for local ingenuity, brought Isaan's rustic culture some overdue interest from designers seeking goods with a *genius loci* – that elusive 'spirit of the place'. Isaan *choei* acquired a 'good bad taste' cachet, with fashionistas wearing items made from *pha khao ma* loincloth. Ribald Isaan humour helped many Thai advertisements win ad awards at Cannes.

Just when *molam* live music clubs were driven out of downtown by rent hikes in the 2000s, retro *molam* was repackaged by Bangkok DJ Maft Sai as a World Music. He gathered master players to form The Paradise Bangkok Molam International Band, which tours the world. At his party nights and Studio Lam bar, this pulsating music appeals to foreigners and even attracts hip Thais who'd never go to grungy *molam* clubs like Pinklao's Isaan Terd Terng.

Bangkok needed to be told that Isaan is a source of quality. TCDC opened in 2005 with 'Isaan Retrospective: Deprivation, Creativity & Design,' an exhibition about how much Bangkok relies on Isaan skills. Of the first 70 Thais trained in Japanese high cuisine for embassy chefs worldwide, 56 came from Isaan, while Sukhumvit's Japanese restaurants had 192 Isaan chefs. Provocatively, to enter the TCDC show you had to step on photos of Isaan faces.

Living in town changes the migrant too. City life ends up more complex, harsh and expensive. Exposure to new influences often changes the settlers' taste and sophistication to an urban persona. Homesickness leads to romanticisation, but upon return, leavers find their village has also changed, and relationships evolved without them. Besides, the lack of rural development that drove them to Bangkok persists and makes it hard to progress in a career outside the capital. In the phrase of Isaan literature expert Ellen Boccuzzi: "Bangkok-bound migrants are ultimately bound by Bangkok."

Artist Maitree Siriboon depicts a full arc of the Isaan migrant journey through photographic tableaux and Lao-style glass-mosaic scenes. His alter ego, 'Isan Boy Soi 4', primps himself in a *pha khao ma* as a vessel of desire for older *farang* men in Bangkok bar strips like Silom Soi 4. Then comes the awkward return: the brash Soi 4 boy posing in silver shorts amid rustic vistas that turn from treasured memory to fashion backdrop, painting albino buffalos in rainbow hues. Maitree articulates an elegy for how to be Isaan, Thai, Bangkokian, international, an artist and himself, all in the same identity.

left: Paradise Bangkok Molam International Band is a supergroup formed by DJ Maft Sai.

above: A *molam* busker with puppets and *naga*-style *phin* on Chaengwattana Road.

top: Isan Boy Dream: artist Maitree Siriboon made photographs based on his urban migrant life, seen in the series *Isan Boy Soi 4* about a country lad in city nightlife, who returns to the farm with urban tastes.

below: **A Thainess festival brings rural crafts to Lumpini Park, like this teak-leaf Lanna temple.**

right: **Saucy cross-dressing humour is a fixture at Isaan Tawandang music pub in Khlong Tan.**

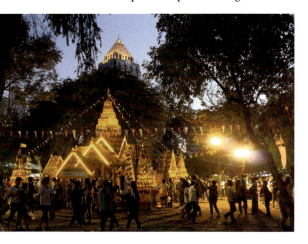

cookshops struggle, but restaurants from a former Isaan enclave remain at Soi Rangnam.

"In the past, if you wanted to eat *somtam*, you'd hide under the table and eat it, because Bangkok people would look down on you," said former Deputy Prime Minister Prachuab Chaiyasarn. Isaan streetfood eventually so beguiled the middle class that *somtam* spread citywide. My soi has five Isaan outlets, including a cart, a branch of the mall chain Have A Zeed, and the hi-so Café Chilli serving a Sino-Isaan fusion of *larb* dim sum. Interest in authentic provincial food has soared, with workaday delicacies repackaged as exotic to urban foodies. The Lanna restaurant Gedhawa offers herbal delicacies in what resembles a Lampang crafts shop, while Supanniga has a rare menu of dishes from Chanthaburi's unsung East Coast fare. The latest regional cuisine to get the gourmet treatment is Southern, pioneered by Supaksorn 'Ice' Jongsiri, who helmed the traditional restaurant Baan Ice and the innovative, Michelin-starred Sorn. The Thai ploughman's lunch has leapt from the frying pan into the sous-vide.

A Bangkokian hobby is to venture out on day trips to country markets to sample and bring back delicacies. Food historian Suthorn Sukphisit warns that provincial kitchens are losing their rarer dishes as Bangkokians impose their safe, sweet taste through reviews and social media posts. Such culinary colonisation is most apparent where stalls from all over the country are arranged by region at Central Embassy's luxury food court Eat Thai! and at the kitschily themed IconSiam, where vendors in straw hats ladle soup from vats in boats moored in the mall's faux canal.

Appreciation of provincial food contrasts with the tensions between capital and countryside that play out on TV. "I love to watch differences in soap operas between the Bangkok-based Channel 3 and the upcountry dramas on Channel 7," says urbanist Pitch Pongsawat. "The issue is not just about the image, but the self-moralisation of Bangkokians via Channel 3 and how Channel 7 makes fun of the Bangkok people." Advertising habitually casts dark-skinned upcountry Thais as subservient to actors with light complexions. One notorious ad on the BTS even said: "This seat is reserved for people with pale skin."

Bangkok's air of superiority begins to co-opt migrants too. Remoteness from the centre of power automatically lowers status. One sportsman who had played for his country found condescension from Isaan Bangkokians so mocking of his skintone and 'bumpkin' accent that he moved back to Nong Bua Lamphu province. Meanwhile, rural youth increasingly skirt Bangkok and head to places with less discrimination, like Isaan's modernising cities, tourist resorts, or the northern capital of Chiang Mai, where Isaan artists like Mit Jai-In and Apichatpong Weerasethakul moved.

Bangkokians tend to say ethnicity is a non-issue, or that "all Thais are equal." Yet Thai language and the tenets of Thainess enforce unequal distinctions. There is a Cultural Map in which findings from the World Values Survey plot countries on axes of values, from survival to self-expression, and traditional to secular. Thailand averages in the moderate middle of that graph, except that since 2007 its scores have moved further into the extreme fifth on all questions of race, like not wanting other ethnicities immigrating or living next door.

Stereotypes shape many Bangkokian decisions, whether employment, rentals, pricing, or who to sit beside. Differentiating peoples can lead to racism. Yet in this culture based on face and karma, physical differences carry moral weight. Despite tolerating diversity, Bangkokians tend to rate people based on ethnicity, birthplace, build, skintone, grooming, and facial features. That's why firms here insist on job applications bearing a photograph.

The seniority system echoes the ancient Sakdina social points ratings, based on how many rice bales you were entitled to. Siamese were ranked Siamese on a steep curve, with *amartya* (nobles) high and the least points for *phrai* (serfs), slaves then captives. Bangkokians talk with pride about abolishing slavery in 1905, while banishing from memory (and schoolbooks) values that were still alive while the elders of today's elders were young. Chinese immigrants might have included coolies, but they never bore that Sakdina stigma. The Red Shirts sparked fury when they couched their struggle as *amartya* vs *phrai*, as if Bangkok was still feudal. In a defence of 'Thai-Style Democracy,' Seri Wongmontha, who co-led the 2013-14 Bangkok Shutdown protest against the Reds, proclaimed that "300,000 votes in Bangkok are votes of quality and are better than 15,000,000 votes in the provinces which lack quality."

The political divide has an ethnic tinge. Southerners, Thai-Chinese and central Bangkokians are largely Yellow; the North, Isaan and outer Bangkok are broadly Red; while the Malay Deep South has a separatist insurgency. Electoral maps reveal consistent fault-lines, which match the lines on a British atlas from 1850 – just before Thai nationalism began. Land on that map labelled 'Siamese' voted yellow, areas marked 'Lao' voted red, and 'Patani' was in 'Malaya.' While opinions vary, Thais of all stripes want more insider status and fly the tricolour with nationalistic pride.

So they can advance, citizens must speak Central Thai well and adopt Bangkok ways. It's as if being indigenous isn't considered Thai enough. The nub of this conundrum lies in how the authors of Thai nationalism based Thainess not on roots, but ideology, yet labelled this blend a pure race. "We had always been told there was just one kind of Thai," says professor Vithi Phanichphant, who helped revive northern traditions based on Tai tribal research. "The government did not want people to know about their ethnicity; they wanted a unified, centralised, Thailand. We used to see signs saying 'This area is free from local dialect.' We were supposed to speak Central Thai only."

A typical national survey puts Central and Isaan at 30% each, plus 11% Northern, 7% Southern, 11% Chinese, 6% Muslim, and 3.4% Khmer. Such figures confusingly mismatch region and ethnicity, because of taboos in counting Malay, Lao or part-Chinese origins, the latter two each often estimated at around 40%. In the 1990s, Bangkokians still referred to both Isaan and northerners as broadly 'Lao.'

Vithi notes how the name 'Lanna' was "cooked up" in 1996 to promote Chiang Mai's 700th anniversary.

During the 1930s-40s dictatorship of Phibun Songkhram, ideologues devised an expansionist history, which seeded notions of racial superiority that still inflect hyper-nationalism. School books still repeat their tale that Tai tribes migrated from the Altais, where Mongolia meets Kazakhstan, which has been debunked by historians like Charnvit Kasetsiri, who found zero evidence there of Thai ways. Instead, Tai tribes spread from between Yunnan and north Vietnam as far west as Assam, and south into a future-Siam, which had for 1500 years been the area where Mon overlapped with Khmer. Wherever they roved, the Tai peacefully blended in.

These tensions may be less about ethnicity than power. "In a world driven by diversity, this Thainess mantra is the conservatives' insistence on holding on to their cultural stranglehold, the domain of homogeneity, obedience and compliance," wrote columnist Kong Rithdee. "And the Thainess in question isn't even about race or origin; it's about who's ready to subscribe to the official prescription. In this case, middle-class Chinese-Thai in the affluent parts of Bangkok are more 'Thai' than, say, Malay-Muslims in the far South or rural northeasterners, who both speak rapid-fire dialect, sour melodies to the standard ear, and who may harbour impossible dreams that Bangkok will never fulfill."

Underlying attitudes come from Thailand straddling quite contrary civilisations. Central Thais are patriarchal, white-rice-eating formal Buddhists with Brahmin hierarchy, showing Khmer and Chinese influence in language and culture. They've dwelt on plains in a centralised state under a semi-divine universal monarch.

Bangkok projects that onto Lanna and upper Isaan, which were matrilineal, sticky rice-eating followers of folk Buddhism and *naga* serpent belief. They lived loyal to accessible chieftains in valley principalities with links to the Silk Road. Different again, the Southern peninsula hosted Hindu and Muslim empires where Siam met the Malay world. Its port-states linked seafarers from India, Persia, Rome and China.

In *Siam Mapped*, Thongchai Winichakul showed how Thailand wasn't defined by its culture or people. Rather it was a "geo-space" – the gap between the borders of European colonies, into which Bangkok projected the backstory of a unitary Thai state with capitals at Sukhothai, then Ayutthaya. Ethnicity is a tool in the perennial quest for legitimacy by whoever takes power in Bangkok. After the Redshirt uprising of 2010, the state began to refer possessively to Isaan as 'Thai-Isaan' and Lanna as 'Lanna-Thai.' Bangkok's fantastical cultural show, Siam Niramit, even re-brands Lanna as 'North Siam.'

Tourist promotions talk-up the native diversity, whilst the state denies indigenous rights. At a conference in 2016, Thailand claimed to accept 62 ethnic groups under their preferred names, despite really validating just a dozen. "The formal recognition of minorities would be very progressive if it were actually true," wrote Peerasit Kamnuansilpa and John Draper. The delegates cited ethnic identities like 'Thai Malay', 'Thai Lao' and 'Northern Khmer', whereas officials insist upon the non-ethnic labels 'Thai-Islam', 'Thai-Isaan' or Northeastern Thai. "Thailand is therefore somewhat unique in its recognition of ethnic communities internationally before actually recognising them within the country."

Such initiatives spring from a global trend to recognise indigenous culture, fuelled by new data: genetic tracking, digital mapping, oral histories. The de-colonising movement is usually directed at the West, but integrating diverse peoples under secular, militarist nationalism was typical of post-colonial nation-building across the region. "We were not a colony, but we were colonised," says Vithi. "We colonised ourselves."

In another incentive, minority culture is a new source of money, whether for tourism, commercial design or repurposing heritage for leisure. The yearning to recover some identity as a hyphen-Thai minority has ended up as a commodity.

Some country migrants reconstitute elements from their regional calendar, from re-enactments of Southern ghost rituals and Northern nail dance to concerts of *molam* music. These may not be as customary as upcountry, but satisfy pangs of yearning by settlers who say the refrain: "*kit-teung ban*" – miss home.

The state, too, re-edits indigenous cultures in showcases like the annual Thainess Fair at Lumpini Park. Charming and fun, it's ostensibly for tourism, but this cherry-picked jamboree of national harmony aims at bridging the regional rifts. It's a retread of the Constitution Fairs of the 1930s-50s (held on the old National Day of 24 June), which instilled National Culture through festivity and beauty contests. Lumpini Park's pond hosts a floating market of the Central Plains. Children ride bronze Isaan water buffalo. At plywood cutouts of Phrae teak mansions, Lanna musicians in indigo farm-wear pluck the plaintive *pin* mandolin. Head-scarved Narathiwat women sell batik, Chinese exhibit lanterns. With models of provincial sights, it unites the nation as a backdrop for selfies.

left: **Northern dance star Waewdao Sirisook performs Lanna Dream, a spoof on the Lanna myth.**

Regional Rites

Moving to the capital divides family and community, a separation most keenly felt at festive times of togetherness. Ahead of the Songkran holiday in mid-April, an exodus of Bangkokians heads to their hometown to celebrate the Thai New Year. But that's the longest stretch of public holiday, and employees get scarce leave, so it's hard for Bangkok residents to join relatives at other key dates in the calendar. Informal workers can be flexible, which is one reason why Isaan migrants make more journeys back. Meanwhile, settlers from the North and South have re-created in Bangkok some regional events of deep meaning.

In the North, early April is a season of folk festivals, including 'life extension' rituals, which Wat Benchamabophit hosts in Dusit, Bangkok. A temple hall hosts two pyramids made from three decorated bamboos swathed in offerings of betel nut, coconut and cotton pom-poms. Elders take turns to sit underneath, whilst connected to well-wishers by sacred white *sai sin* thread.

Wat 'Ben' (aka the Marble Temple) has been linked to northern monks since a past era when Dusit had a Lanna enclave. In 1964, a charismatic abbot decided to host Tham Guay Salak, a festival held each September to encourage monks to persevere in their studies to the end of Phansa – the Buddhist Rainy Season Retreat.

After a costumed procession, a mass ordination enables time-restricted Bangkok males to fulfill a shorter Phansa retreat. Tents for each Lanna province display their own styles of 'offering trees' – draped in die-cut paper, banknotes and household goods. Northerners take turns to present monks with bamboo baskets of supplies, and a prayer form for writing their ancestors' names. Crowds then mill around a *gad mua* (northern market of groundsheets under umbrellas), with vendors selling northern herbs and delicacies, like spirals

top: Fon Nan dancers at the Tham Guay Salak festival in Wat Ben.

above: Hercules beetle fighting at Wat Wachiratham Sathit.

Heart 207

of *sai oua* sausage. Fairground sideshows line the canal towards a stage where Lanna singers croon till dusk.

On other September Saturdays, less formal Tham Guay Salak take place at northern-style wats like Wat Wachiratham Sathit in Sukhumvit Soi 101/1. It has a Lanna cultural school, where dancers prepare for the procession and for performing rounds of *fon phii* spirit trance dance, wearing long scarves and twirling brass nail extensions. Each province has a stage, including Nan, where a dancer of *fon nan*, dressed in a hand-spun *pha sin* tube skirt, bends backwards so far that she can pick up donated banknotes on the dais using just her teeth. Meanwhile cheeky vocalists trade repartee over sonorous melodies on the three-stringed *sor*.

In a corner, boys cheer their dads' sportive hobby: Hercules Bbeetle wrestling. They twirl foil goads to spur the males to use their antlers to knock their rival off a log, under which they can scent a female who gets to mate with the winner. Such folk pastimes feel a world away from Bangkok – and for homesick revellers that's the point.

"Like Northern Thais, Southerners in Bangkok live in a mental ghetto," admits Takerng 'Be' Pattanopas, an artist from Phattalung. "Both hold culturally specific ceremonies at temples where the abbot comes from their region. Unlike the Northern events, Southern festivals aren't publicised as spectacles for the general public." That's because each Southern rite occurs at temples linked into particular provincial networks. Wat Ratchathiwat draws those from Surat Thani and Nakhon Si Thammarat, while Wat Dusitaram hosts many Songkhla and Phattalung natives.

On the last day of Buddhist Lent each October, Surat Thani province holds the Chak Phra procession, in which people pull boats laden with Buddha images. The Surat community around Samsen re-enact that rite at the nearby royal temple, Wat Rachathiwat. After donating alms to 99 monks, devotees pull a Buddha image's carriage, which is shaped like a *naga* serpent, around the local roads.

Earlier in October, that wat marks Sart Deuan Sib (Tenth Month Autumn Festival), a family bonding rite that delivers merit to ancestors, especially the recently departed. "I feel so sad for *khon pak tai* (Southerners) who can't go home at this time," laments one mournful young man attending with his mother. They placed a relative's portrait and ornate urn with others on one of the altars in the stilt space below the wooden *viharn*. Once the monks stop eating at noon, congregants scramble through the food offerings, carrying out dishes of curry for families and friends to eat amid clearings on the floor.

The festival is also called Ching Pret, because the participants make merit for greedy people whose karmic penance is to languish starving as a tall *phii pret* ghost. A *pret's* pinhole mouth is so tiny it can apparently only eat *laa*, a dessert matted from filaments of sugary batter, made by vendors in the temple grounds. While ancestor rites take place in the *viharn*, spirit rites must happen outside the sacred precinct. Trays of nine delicacies including *laa* get offered to *pret* at an altar by the river. In the surrounding trees, human effigies twist from nooses, their clothes spattered with red paint. It may resemble the set of a Thai ghost movie, but to believers it is all too real.

In the *ching pret* rites at Wat Dusitaram in Prannok, an area famous for Southern food, the gathering of offerings to eat turns into a dramatic stampede. At the stroke of noon, kids leap in for the choice items, as a scrum of adults wade through the scattered foodstuffs for edible scraps.

By night, temple festivals turn into fairs, which are rare chances to see traditional arts. Wat Dusitaram is linked to Phattalung, so it presents that province's art of *nang talung* – shadow puppetry in which the *talung* (narrator-puppeteer) retells epic tales spiced by topical

satire. Shadow puppets also feature at *ching pret* held in Wat Phitchaya, along with the Malay-influenced bird-dance *manohra*. Traditional dance and puppetry is barely supported anywhere in Bangkok besides privately sponsored festivals. Performing those arts in their authentic ritual context means that much more to migrants' collective identity.

"I've noticed all through my long time living in Bangkok that Isaan people are not culturally strong like the Southerners or Northerners," says Tanyaporn Singchalee, a food expert from Ubon. "In rituals we mix into the Central Thai style. We see ourselves as adaptive to whatever is the local culture, except in what we eat and what we speak, but we are not socially exclusive."[1]

There's little Isaan cultural infrastructure in Bangkok, though general venues do host northeastern performers, especially of *molam* folk music. "To make a big festival in Bangkok is difficult; it's much easier to travel home," explains Worathep Akkabootra, an arts writer with the pen name Can Dan Isaan. He lives in an Isaan enclave near Siriraj Hospital where there's a small *sala* (pavilion), but he's never seen activities there as he goes home to Khon Kaen for major festivals. "Some ceremonies you have to do at home, like making merit for your grandparents while they teach you how to do the rituals. Migrants wouldn't like to bring their elders to Bangkok to do that."

Many Isaan people who work in labour or informal retail return seasonally to help at family farms. It's no coincidence that rural work times coincide with festivals, like the Rocket Festivals to summon monsoon rains for planting, or the Kathin festivals to donate robes to monks after Phansa, which is around the first rice harvest. Work and play go together in Thailand, and both share the same word, *ngan*, which expresses communal effort. It takes a lot of commitment to journey home or to hire performers and chefs from far regions to the capital – but it brings great joy.

Re-creating village ritual in Bangkok demonstrates an identity with tradition that Bangkokians can rarely muster for their own city. "There are associations in Bangkok for people from each region, and many provinces also, but I've never heard of a Bangkok Association upcountry," says Wimonsiri Hemtanon of the Southerner Association. "If you ever see one, let me know!"

far left top & above: **Ching Pret festival at Wat Rachatiwat, making merit for ancestors in the** *wat* **and for** *pret* **ghosts on the river bank.**

far left below: **A vendor at Wat Rachatiwat sells** *laa*, **a sweet given as offerings.**

above: **A devotee blesses his offerings in Ching Pret rites at Wat Dusitaram.**

left: **At the stroke of noon, a stampede erupts to eat food offered to spirits at Wat Dusitaram.**

Heart 209

Stir-fry
How Chinese is Bangkok?

The world knows *pad thai* as the country's signature dish, but look at this most Bangkokian of recipes. Tofu and bean shoots, spring onion and noodles – these are Chinese ingredients stir-fried in a Chinese wok with local tamarind and dried prawn to make a kind of noodle that Thai patriots could call their own. In a nation-building project, it's telling that the food chosen as the national dish was not indigenous, but a Chinese fusion labelled Thai.

Pad thai was invented at a pivot in Thai history, when natural assimilation of 'aliens' switched to forced assimilation. The dish – launched by 1940s leader Phibunsongkhram – symbolised the blending of diversity into uniform Thai citizens. Most Thai-Jiin (Sino-Thais) express pride in becoming Thai. Yet Chineseness is so vivid and resurgent here that claims of full assimilation seem premature. Stir-frying retains the sensory tang of each ingredient. The Thai-Chinese kept their tang. They're as Thai as *pad thai*.

The world has about 60 million 'Overseas Chinese,' a term that raises questions of allegiance. Thailand has the biggest chunk: 6 million, or 9-plus million if counting mixed-blood *luk jiin* (children of China). Around 3.5 million Thai-Jiin dwell in Bangkok, where two in three residents have Han genes. They are well integrated, but retain enough rituals, business methods and other traits to comprise a Sino-Thai hybrid subculture.

Bangkok can't help but exude Chineseness, since the Chinese built most of it – and lived at this customs post before it became the capital. Pioneers set the tone of the settlement forever after, in both genetics and culture. Leaf through magazines, glance at billboards, scan the room at society events, channel-hop the soaps, note the faces of fashion models – the images, and the image-makers, are overwhelmingly Thai-Jiin.

Bangkok's default building format is the Southern Chinese shophouse that its diaspora spread across Southeast Asia. In most shophouses, a Chinese spirit shrine sits on the floor; on the front are posted a Chinese paper amulet and daubed a Buddhist monk's paste blessing. Many a business or condo displays both a Buddha and ceramic figures of the Three Sages, Hok Lok Siew. Thailand acculturated its Chinese immigrants more smoothly than elsewhere in Southeast Asia, with the assimilation more like a merger. The Chinese became part Thai, while the Thais absorbed something Sino.

Just as there is no generic Thai, Bangkok's Chinese aren't homogenous either. Today's economy, accent and food gained much diversity from the dialect groups of Southern Han, who came in three waves to escape unrest or famine. Over half are Teochiu (54%) from a hardscrabble enclave around Swatow in Guangdong, at the time disdained by the more powerful Cantonese (6%) and wealthier Hokkien from Fujian province (6%) as fisherfolk and alleged pirates without high culture. Their fierce rivalry with more established Hokkien settlers sparked power struggles in Thonburi and early Bangkok. Hokkien were the insiders in Ayutthaya, but under half-Teochiu King Taksin, an influx of Teochiu populated East Thonburi, only to be evicted downstream to Sampeng by the new pro-Hokkien Rattanakosin regime.

Steamer links with Swatow from 1872 enabled the mass migration that fuelled Bangkok's modernising drive. Aboard lines like the Chino-Siam Steam Navigation Company, this Second Wave included Hakka (16%). Lacking their own province, this precarious and divided minority has spawned game-changing leaders, from China's Sun Yat Sen and Deng Xiao Ping to Singapore's Lee Kuan Yew and Thaksin Shinawatra, who visited his ancestral village whilst Thai premier.

Dialect has declined, but physically shaped the city. Many specialist districts derive from the trade monopolies run by dialect groups: Teochiu (rice mills, pawn shops, traditional medicine); Hokkien (rubber, engines); Hakka (leather, tailoring); Cantonese (machinery). Among the Third Wave in the 1920s-49, late-arriving Hainanese (12%) had to live on the outskirts and got left with retail, restaurants, hotels and media – then minor trades that fortuitously boomed. Among Hainanese VIPs are Red Bull's Yoovidhaya family, the Patpongpanich landlords of the Patpong red light district, and Central Department Store's Chirathivat lineage.

The diaspora gravitated to places speaking their home dialect, where they could trust spoken business contracts through networks of family, village or *sae* (clan). That's why Bangkok snowballed as the main haven for Teochiu. "It has been said that you could almost conduct a cabinet meeting in Bangkok in Teochiu,"
quipped Lee Hsien Loong, a Hakka Prime Minister of Singapore. Teochiu remained the language of Bangkok business during the suppression of Chinese culture. In the 1990s, a photographer for a corporate brochure was stunned when the board switched from pleasantries in Thai to conclave in Teochiu the moment the boardroom door shut. At the prestigious Thammasat University, students half-jokingly dubbed it "the world's biggest Teochiu university."

It was like that from the start. When the Teochiu and their Lao Pun Thao Kong shrine were moved from the East Thonburi site of the future Grand Palace, they effectively formed a parallel Teochiu town at Sampeng that managed practical needs outside the walls. The governing mandala of Rattanakosin and commercial acumen of Chinatown made a complimentary pair. "The number of Chinese living there was greater than the number of Siamese," wrote Malcolm Smith, Queen Saovabha's physician from 1905-19.

"The Chinese were the shopkeepers and merchants, and nearly all the trade of the city was in their hands. The Siamese on the other hand were the administrators, men drawn from every rank, whose whole existence centred around the court, each one dependent for his living upon the man above him [in] a giant pyramid, on the summit of which sat the king."

left: **Chinese lion dancers in Bangkok often now hail from Isaan.**

above: **A Sino-Thai family release birds from a cage to make merit.**

left: **Ia Sae coffee shop has moved a couple of times over its many decades in Sampeng, but always caters to its customer base of quiet elder males nursing their glasses of** *oliang* **coffee and watching the world pass by.**

right: **An ancestor shrine in what is now the café My Grandparents' House, on the river in Khlong San, one of Bangkok's 'other' Chinatowns.**

Both urban centres were sacred entities, whether laid out to Thai cosmology or feng shui geomancy. Rattanakosin was centered on its Lak Meuang (City Pillar); Sampeng was centered on its own city pillar shrine under the guardian spirit Tok Por Lao Eia. After about a century, those parallel settlements merged, with Chinese and Western urbanism prevailing citywide, even within the sacred walls, all under the identity of Thainess.

"Bangkok was essentially a Chinese city. Almost every visitor or resident has commented on this," writes historian Michael Smithies of the era before mass migration from the provinces. "But one thing that has changed is the status of the Chinese… in 1960, most servants were Chinese; now the Sino-Thai, if rich enough, have Thai, or, if failing such means, Lao or Burmese servants." Taxi drivers today mostly hail from Isaan, but the most elderly are relics from when it was a Chinese trade. Sino-Thais are getting back into driving now that hailing apps offer smart private cars.

After professions restricted to Siamese – military, bureaucracy, police – were opened to Sino-Thais in the 1970s, many became administrators in that pyramid. Most Thai Prime Ministers have some Chinese ancestry. "Chinese immigrants are generally highly respected in Thailand, partly because many of the king's senior advisers and officials have Chinese origins," says Chen Mingquan, 54, a Bangkok-born trader and historian of Sampeng. "And we are usually perceived as the most capable and diligent people in Thailand."

Bangkok's development gets labelled by default as Westernisation, and both Thais and Sino-Chinese have diluted their differences through both adopting some Western ways. Yet globalisation has been a Chinese process too, having exported their mercantilism for centuries via tea horse and junk, shophouse and Baidu. As across Southeast Asia, Chinese traders have reshaped Bangkok through the Chinese Way of Business.

To say that the Chinese have influenced Bangkok business and built its middle class understates a tsunami. Sino-Thai entrepreneurs of the boomer generation played the state monopoly concession game to found corporations that have minted billionaires and millions of jobs. The Teochiu father of Chang Beer baron Charoen Sirivadhanabhakdi fried oyster omelettes on a stall outside Lao Pun Thao Kong Shrine. Working his way up the drinks trade, Charoen created a whisky monopoly, parlayed the Carlsberg franchise into the Beer Chang giant, and became the 'Mergers & Acquisition King' of ASEAN to turn his ThaiBev conglomerate into one of Thailand's marquee brands. The owner of enough land to cover two provinces, he was bestowed an honorific name by the crown. Thaksin Shinawatra is fourth generation, yet no-one could miss the Shin in his family and corporate names. One wag spoke of his cabinet that their faces were each "a map of China."

Chinese strategy is present on every street corner. Bangkokians can't move without passing several 7-Elevens. That tactic comes from the fact that the Thai franchiser, CP All, is run by the head of the Thai Go Association, Korsak Chairasmisak. In Korsak's office, guests sit at a Go board, by the rules of which the winner smothers the competition. Gating each road with 7-Elevens stifles rival mom 'n' pop shops and convenience stores. The surplus of underused malls makes sense when you see them as game counters. The Central Group favours prime corners, while The Mall Group masses in clusters, but both must consolidate positions and open new fronts by placing outlier counters like Central Rama IX, Paradise Park or IconSiam. Bangkok is a giant board for the Game of Go.

The most potent strategy for getting ahead is *guanxi* – a connections culture that arose out of clan houses and dialect groups. The Chinese founded Bangkok's first associations, which ran from devout shrine organisations to less virtuous *ang yi* (secret societies). At the turn of the 20th century, *ang yi* turf wars erupted into fighting over their protection rackets. Before their suppression, *ang yi* ran the pawnbrokers, casinos, opium dens, and the trafficking of labour using 'loan tickets.'

There can be a fine line between trust and cronies, gifts and bribes, connections and corruption. The term for mafia godfathers is '*sia*' after a Chinese word. Gamblers use the Chinese '*huay*' for lottery and '*suay*' for periodic bribe. 'Tea money' is a Thai euphemism for bribery, after the cha served during a payoff.

Entertaining is also geared to *guanxi*, hence the private rooms in bars, discos, restaurants, karaokes and member's clubs. Bangkok's vast flesh trade is usually blamed on the visible GIs and sex tourism, but long before it had been Chinatown that had commercialised sex to service the countless young single male Chinese migrants. Though prostitution was made illegal in 1960, their business model spread to Patpong, Saphan Kwai and to the new Chinatown on Ratchadaphisek, where the customers are Asian businessmen, many going in groups after dining nearby. The first Bangkok restaurants were also Chinese, so multi-course Chinese feasts at round tables became standard for wedding banquets and business deals. Dining, Chinese style, is diplomacy. In Thaksin's famous advice: "never eat alone."

Bangkok grew a gold-plated infrastructure to support *guanxi*, from golf, associations and charity boards to the inter-family diplomacy at weddings and funerals. Education gains skills and kudos, but also peer contacts in useful sectors. The *hi-so* circuit is a branch of Sino-Thai business. *Hi-so* socialites gain prominence through ostentatious display via couture wardrobe, launch parties and grand entrances to make a media splash. Entrepreneurs who aren't yet famous join group photos with VIPs until they're a noticed somebody.

Dialect and other networks have mostly formalised into business networking. From Chambers of Commerce and trade associations to charity galas and advisory boards, Thai-Chinese remain committed to committees.

Reciprocity is a virtue in Confucian conduct. Aside from family and duty to ruler, that means mutual aid. As Chinese sojourners were outside the Thai *bunkhun* feudal system, and lacked family and sometimes even fellow villagers, they depended on reciprocal help, which evolved into Thailand's first charities and social services. The pioneer was Tien Fah Hospital, which still dispenses herbs on Yaowarat. Another is the Poh Teck Tung volunteer ambulance service, with its temple base at Phlabphlachai.

The Chinese way of being has philosophical rigour, whether Taoist, Confucian, Communist or Mahayana Buddhist – and that's a delicate issue under Thainess. "Thailand's Confucianism never affects beyond middle-class overseas Chinese and even that is quite thin due to most immigrants here being largely uneducated," posts Suppanut Jonjitaree on Quora. "Although old Thailand was under the practical influence of China, Thai elites never liked to adopt Confucianism as state ideology as it would eliminate their attempt to monopolise legitimacy [by] aristocratic divine right. This is also why Thailand didn't have a civil service before copying it from British India, while Vietnam had it long before it became a French colony."

Nonetheless, Confucian ethics emerge through legalism, moralism and self-improvement. "Thai elites treated education and knowledge as something to control like

left: **Dumnam diving school is located in the courtyard of So Heng Tai, a two-century-old Fujian style Hokkien mansion in Talad Noi.**

right: **Former leaders of a Chinese association pictured in the rafters of a traditional Teochiu building.**

below: **Today's Mandarin influence seen in the hip Ba Hao in Soi Nana, which serves herbal cocktails in soup bowls.**

From Jek to Thai-Jiin

Naming identity is a fateful act. Thai has many terms for Chinese, depending on era or class, from *jao sua* (merchant lord) to *jek*, a name for coolie labour from a Min Chinese term for uncle. The idea of one monolithic 'Chinese' ethnicity is a modern invention. Bangkok received five main dialect groups of Han, all rivals – Teochiu, Hokkien, Hakka, Cantonese and Hailam (Hainanese) – plus lately from Yunnan and northern China.

"In our Teochiu dialect, we never call ourselves *jiin* or *jek* as the Thai call us, nor do we ever call them 'Thai'," says cultural expert Kasian Tejapira. His immigrant father used Teochiu names drawn from dynasty, dialect group or clan, and knew Bangkok as 'Mang-Kok' in the land of 'Tsien-lo' (a blend of Sukhothai and Lavo/Lopburi). "For us the Thai are Huan Nang." Huan Nang refers to any tribes southwest of the Middle Kingdom.

Chinese had dwelt here so long they weren't regarded by Siamese as foreign – that is, until Sun Yat Sen went pamphleteering in Sampeng to fund a nationalist revolution in 'China.' That gave Thai nationalism an 'other' to define itself against. *Jek* became derogatory for those who didn't adopt Thai manners. Most assimilated as *Thai-Jiin* (Sino-Thai). Colloquial nicknames are a way to sense how history felt through the overlapping phases and four immigrant waves of Chinese in Bangkok.

KHUN CHANG ERA (13th Century-1767)

Early settlers were Hokkien with status, most arriving by invitation or for trade, plus Teochiu buying rice for their less fertile land. An archetype was the rich, bland old merchant Chang from the folk epic *Khun Chang Khun Paen*. During the Ayutthaya era, Teochiu traders lived on the eastern bank at Bangkok, facing Taksin's capital of Thonburi Sri Mahasamut (Ocean Money Town) with the custom's post and Hokkien shrine. *Legacy*: Hokkien Kuan Un Keng Shrine at Kudi Jeen.

JIIN LUANG ERA (1767-1782)

In the First Wave of mass immigration, the half-Teochiu King Taksin recruited many Teochiu to populate Thonburi. Those with privileges and rank rose to be *jiin luang* (court Chinese). *Legacy*: Taksin's Wang Derm palace.

JAO SUA ERA (1782-1855)

Early Bangkok favoured Hokkien again, but ongoing Teochiu immigration turned the city more than half-Chinese. *Jao sua* ran the tributary junk trade via Guangdong, which peaked under the "King of Trade," Rama III (nicknamed 'Jao Sua' by Rama II), then was ended by the 1855 Bowring Treaty favouring colonial powers. *Legacies*: Fujian mansion at Dum Nam; Wat Yannawa junk-shaped chedi; Rama III era Sino-Thai *wats* with mosaic from Chinese porcelain.

JEK ERA (1855-1949)

Second Wave of mass immigration of poor all-male *jek* (uncle) coolies fleeing war, famine and crisis. Teochiu

outnumber rival dialect groups, which each ran their own trade monopolies. From the first steamer link with Swatow in 1872 solo male sojourners kept links with China and the diaspora, took manual jobs, married locals and did well, some earning titles, but keeping their Chinese culture intact until the 2010s. *Legacies*: Songwad Road godowns; Pei-ing School; Tang To Kang Gold Shop; Lhong 1919.

LUK JIIN ERA (1910s–1970s)
Acculturated half-Thai offspring known as *luk jiin* (Children of China) prospered under 'Thai' nationality laws and de-linked from Red China. Thai suppression of clan, dialect, culture, schools, newspapers and *ang yi* (secret societies) meant each generation spoke more Thai, less Sino dialect. The 1911 Revolution let women leave China, enabling all-Chinese families in the The Third Wave of migrants (1920s-49). Late arriving Hainanese went into retail and hospitality as Yaowarat became the entertainment area. *Legacies*: Sun Yat Sen gate; Yaowarat's art deco; Blue Elephant.

THAI-JIIN ERA (since 1970s)
Thai-speaking, demonstratively patriotic Sino-Thais dominate business, media, academia, and governance, as well as protest. They re-assert cultural distinctiveness in monuments, museums and festivals, and restoring old Chinatown, with 'neo-*jek*' pride, whilst expressing loyalty to Thailand. *Legacies*: Chokchai 4 Kwan Im Shrine; Chinatown Heritage Centre; Bangkok Bank HQ; Central malls.

MANDARIN ERA (since 1999)
Resumed links to China brought trade, investment, mass Chinese tourism, and a 'Fourth Wave' from inland China to new Chinatowns, as at Huai Khwang. Diasporic bonds grow via social media, with the culture and language filter now being generic Mandarin. Many Sino-Thai like to say they're "*Khon Thai mii chuesai jiin*" (Thai with Chinese blood). Legacies: Chinatown Gate; Confucius Institutes in 23 universities, China Cultural Centre.

Brahmins in India," Suppanut adds. That can't stop the Sino middle class from pursuing education for status and *guanxi*. As a result, Sino-Thais dominate the intelligentsia, literati and political class, as well as both students and faculty in universities. In the schism over political rights, the heavily Sino-Thai Yellows cited their education credentials.

"In family or business, the Sino-Thai tend to stress Confucian beliefs such as filial piety, diligence and thriftiness," says Liang Chua Morita. Many hold family meetings over Sunday lunch, less now at home, more at round tables in hotels or restaurants like Chandrphen. There the patriarch can steer the family's business ventures, hound kids about their grades, and badger Number One Son on prospects for a marriage alliance. "However, in politics, religion or social demeanour, they emphasise loyalty to the King, believe in accumulating merit and emulate polite Thai posture and speech." Those manners set Sino-Thais apart from mainland Chinese, as can be seen in their social media complaints about Chinese tourists and Fourth Wave immigrants. But even if Chineseness is restricted to private life and business, that's still a huge swathe of Bangkok life.

Those most discomfited by the freewheeling Sin City image tend to be the Sino middle class. From their ranks come most of the self-appointed moral guardians, alcohol temperance enforcers, and civic crusaders. That's partly bourgeois propriety, but Confucianism puts utmost store on reputation, since each generation is a vessel for the family's good name. Impropriety risks that lineage, as does homosexuality, which is slowly overcoming its taboo of not providing descendants to worship ancestors.

The Siamese way was the opposite of purist, whereas China has been harsh on impurity, from the First Emperor to the Cultural Revolution. Citing the model of Chinese opera hero Judge Bao, Sino-Thais lead crusades on corruption. The China-Singapore model of cleansing the streets comes at the expense of the informal culture, which ironically derives much from migrant Chinese who traded there.

Despite their reverence for parents and ancestors, Chinese migrants have since the earliest arrivals adopted Thai cremation, held monk chants in Theravada *wats*, and shifted ancestor rituals towards Thai merit making. Today, some sweep ancestor graves on Thai public holidays, not just Qing Ming Day.

Chinese New Year isn't a public holiday but many businesses close for a week and employees citywide get a bonus in a red *ang pao* envelope.

"Chinese-Thais and Thai-Thais and Lao-Thais are pretty much alike," says Voranai Vanijaka. "We believe in ghosts. We make offerings to any gods and spirits that are available. We adhere to social structure. We exercise tribal, clan and network connections." These traditions are syncretic, animistic and involve food offerings. Thai spirit houses have a parallel in Chinese shrines to the house god placed on the ground at the rear of homes, businesses and venues, and with the big shrines found in market halls.

Both Thai and Chinese mark the 1st and 15th nights of the lunar calendar, have the same 12-year zodiac, turn banknotes into decorative offerings, and revere the Buddha. Differences between Thai Theravada and Chinese Mahayana Buddhism have narrowed, with Chinese holding worship, weddings, funerals and ordinations in *wats*, where Thais revere statues of real ancestral people and pray to altars of Kuan In (Kwan Im in Thai), the multi-armed Boddhisatva of compassion, who has become a Bangkok cult, with giant shrines at Tien Fah Hospital in Yaowarat and Chokchai 4 in Lad Prao. Princess Sirindhorn spoke at the Asia Society in Hong Kong about how her family conducts some Chinese rites, such as ancestor veneration at Lunar New Year.

While Sino-Thais have adapted their rites to their new home, they aren't steeped in the indigenous heritage and approach Buddhism with a different emphasis. Many Sino-Thais are drawn to growth in disciplined 'scientific' meditation held at 'secular' retreats. Traditional Buddhism had a court and rural character, but lacked relatability to city people. Urban Chinese were instead rooted in the Mahayana Buddhist mode of venerating historical figures, so they revere King Rama V as the Great Moderniser. Many worship Zheng He (Cheng Ho) – China's eunuch explorer who may have visited Siam in 1410 – in the form of Sam Po Kong, the wise old man of the Triple Gem (Buddha, Dharma, Sangha). Sino-Thais make merit in the 7th lunar month at temples linked to Sam Po Kong, like Wat Kalayanamit, which the Hokkien Kalayanamit clan built in the Sino-hybrid style of King Rama III.

Each new year, Chinese pray to the Taoist god of wealth, Caishen (Chai Sing Ia), whose image spread across phones and shops in a craze begun in 2019 by Lalisa 'Lisa' Manoban, a Thai rapper in the K-pop band Blackpink. "Since I changed my display picture to this image, lots of money has been flowing to me," claimed a viral tweet by @Honey_beigr, which was retweeted 13,000 times. Now solo, Lisa is Thailand's biggest ever international star.

All these beliefs combine in an amalgam of cultural integration that hangs in most homes and workplaces. The Sino-Thai almanac calendar integrates Thai, Chinese and local beliefs into a divination format drawn from ancient China. Into the Western months squeeze two lunar schedules, Buddha days, lottery clues, folk taboos and Chinese rites. Bangkokians of all kinds can read the calendar for their own subculture's schedule.

"As far as Bangkok is concerned, the result of this successful assimilation has been the steady decline, virtually the disappearance, of anything purely Thai," wrote William Warren, the doyen of expat authors. "Official committees (often themselves largely composed of Sino-Thais) can coin new expressions like *ekkalak Thai* (Thai identity), issue publications stressing 'Thai' characteristics and generally strive to promote such concepts, but they have little relevance to what you see and experience all around you in Bangkok."

Sino traits are subtle yet so pervasive they feel normal until you view the city from upcountry or compare its past. An exhibition of early photographs, *Unseen Siam*, flashed back to Thai streetscapes and faces so much darker and more indigenous before the migrant influx.

Beyond genes and business, the Chinese have changed Bangkok culture. They do most of the wealth creation, innovation and speculation, deciding what factories produce, what shops stock, which imports enter. In entertainment, it's largely they who choose the models, direct the movies or flaunt the trends. Sino-Thai taste sets the style and tone of city living, not least in food.

Sino-Thai disseminate their look through their ownership of media, entertainment and advertising. Celebrities are predominantly porcelain cheeked *muay* (Chinese girls) and round-jawed *tae* (handsome) sons of Sino-Thai families, rather more than the square jaws and *piew dum* ('black' skin) of Isaan folk. This is not just a narrow niche promoting its own;

right: **A Teochiu resident of Sampeng.**

216   Stir-fry

Sino-Thai looks and success are role models for provincials with aspiration.

Bookshops reveal how the middle class draws outlooks from Chinese texts like the Tao, Lao Tzu's *Art of War*, and *The Romance of Three Kingdoms*, a saga localised here as *Sam Kok*, through novels, TV dramas, cartoons and guides to living or business. Some employers even hire using *ngo heng* (facial analysis), and ethnic Thais optimise feng shui.

Amid this fusion culture, rigid templates quash non-conformity in design, temples, dance, music, art or any other cultural expression. A uniform Thai style was imposed because the capital's artisans were no longer indigenous but almost all Chinese. They applied techniques and beliefs from China that affected countless decorative decisions. The fact we know of the Sino-Thai muralist Khrua In-khong, who painted at Wat Bowonniwet and Wat Borom Niwat, is a break with the norm of craftsmen being been anonymous.

In response, manuals of approved Thai style imposed forms that are collectively called *lai thai* – Thai patterns. Like *pad thai*, anything bearing the adjective Thai is not a pure national tradition, but a hybrid of modernity, imports and a local variant, just as *muaythai* is a Bangkok fusion of southern and northeastern martial arts with the Queensberry Rules. *Lai thai* manuals kept Chinese workmen in line, but also diminished vernacular folk styles in favour of elite symbolism, which was prestigious and easier to standardise. Whenever creative expression gets chastised as un-Thai, it's an echo of how far Thainess is a response to Chineseness.

Sino hybrids raise a dilemma for the National Culture. As the Chinese influenced Thainess whilst becoming Thai, then Thainess isn't as fixed or pure as proclaimed. But if these hybrids apply only to Sino-Thais, then they must be a subculture distinct from other Thais. And if that hybrid affects primarily Bangkok, then culture is not uniform countrywide. At least one of the 'All Thais' taboos – cultural purity, ethnic unity, or national homogeneity – can't fit reality. You just can't dodge the Chinesish-ness of Bangkok.

"The Chinese in Thailand are neither identical to the Chinese in China (nor to other overseas Chinese) nor to the Thai," says Liang Chua Morita. "Chinese culture in Thailand, especially religion, has always been in a state of change, as has its Thai counterpart." Pressure and enthusiasm for unity obscures the fact that Sino-Thais are a coherent subculture.

Self-identifying as Thai patriots, Sino-Thais lack the clarity and label of diaspora brethren, such as the Sino-Filipino 'Mestizo'; Sino-Indian 'Chindian'; or Sino-Malay 'Peranakan', 'Baba-Nyonya' and 'Straits Chinese' of Singapore, Malaysia and Java. After generations of not being allowed separateness, Sino-Thais don't seek their own label, raising the question as to whether a subculture has to identify as distinct to qualify.

One clue is that this self-hidden hybrid subculture has a territory, a population and an identity that's disarmingly obvious: namely 'Bangkok.' Another possibility might be that modern 'Thai' identity fits Sino-Thais more snugly than the diverse indigenous groups. As a nation-building ideology and test of loyalty, Thainess was partly an imperative to absorb so many Chinese. Written largely by part-Chinese, Thainess imposed court manners and Western trappings to appear *siwilai*, while spurning native ways, which are still looked down upon or exoticised, and got replaced by National Culture. It's worth pondering whether this least ideological of cultures would have come up with such a rigid ideology as Thainess without Chinese influence.

Bangkok is less an epitome of Thai culture than a bubble of Sino-Thai hybrid subculture. It has always had a Sinified ethnic composition, bolstered by four waves of immigration, and compounded by their descendants rising to power in every facet of life, culture, taste and belief. In making themselves Thai, they have infused Thainess with Chineseness – and that stir-fry has become the national benchmark. The greatest indirect impact of Sino-Thais has been to revise what it means to be Thai.

Sino-Thai Identity

If Sino-Thai cultural confidence can be measured in gates, it has risen fourfold since the 1990s. There had been just one small arch in memory of Sun Yat Sen's fundraising visits. Then in 1999, China's President Jiang Zemin opened a ceremonial gate at Odeon Circle, which was deemed the eye of a symbolic dragon that snaked along Yaowarat Road and realigned Chinatown's feng shui towards the palace. Bearing calligraphy by Princess Sirindhorn, it was a breakthrough in acknowledging Thai-Chineseness as a distinct entity under Thainess.

The gate commemorated the 72nd birthday of King Rama IX. To mark the same 5th cycle birthday of his son Kign Rama X, Sino-Thai donors erected two further gates in 2025. They bracket Charoen Krung Road at each end of Chinatown: near Odeon and Khlong Ong Ang.

Another icon of Chinese revival was the restoration of a pier across the river in Khlong San's little Chinatown. The galleried warehouses flank a shrine to Mazu, goddess of seafarers. Its grand opening in 2017 as the arts complex Lhong 1919 saw the Sino-Thai elite in silk shirts and cheongsams, proudly expressing their roots. Sadly the complex closed and will be converted into a hotel or spa.

Several strands of the immigrant story converge at Lhong 1919. The name comes from the Teochiu term for 'steamer port', which was bought in 1919 by the Wanglee family. Their restored traditional mansion stands next door amid weeping willows. Many poor Teochiu began their Bangkok life at their pier. Sojourners sent so many earnings back to China that the Wanglees made a fortune from handling remittances and founded Nakornthon Bank. The family then diversified into insurance and the archetypal Sino-Thai middleman industry of milling rice. They epitomised the diaspora trade network by keeping bases in Hong Kong, Canton, Singapore and Saigon. Such clans rose to business leadership, but between the 1920s and 1980s, it had been wise to keep the ethnic aspect quiet.

The reassertion of Chinese cultural confidence since the 1980s comes under the umbrella of Thainess. New museums detail Sino-Thai history, festivals celebrate Sino-Thai culture, and traders rebuild links with China. What they have most wanted was recognition. "There is a cultural revolution under way," wrote columnist Chang Noi. "The official version of Thai culture simply blotted out the Chinese immigrants, their large numbers, their extraordinary history, their big contribution to modern Thailand. They are not trying to dig out a 'Chinese' identity. They want to redefine 'Thai culture' as something more like the melting pot which it really is."

The cultural coming out was the conversion of Chinese New Year (Trud Jiin) from a private event into a citywide festival. Unlike in most of ASEAN, it has never been a Thai public holiday. Yet Bangkokians had to stock up as the city used to shut down for ten days until the 1997 crash, which released the economy from the grip of Chinese family firms. As residents and business moved out, Chinatown too transformed, from a workplace into a leisure space and lately a gentrifying hipster enclave.

A Trud Jiin food fair that began off Yaowarat Road in 1994 grew phenomenally under a Sinophile royal patron whose portrait is framed in countless shops there. "If it weren't for the support of HRH Princess Maha Chakri Sirindhorn... and that of the TAT, we wouldn't have managed to make Chinese New Year as big an event as it is today," says Visit Limprana, president of the Thai-Chinese Traders Association. After the 2002 Trud Jiin parade was led by a local son in a silk suit, finance minister Somkid Jatusripitak, it became a mass event with historical displays and live performance. Chinatown had been a forbidding maze to access, but now hosts thousands of revellers at the Mid-Autumn lantern festival. As a mine of streetfood, it also draws foodies.

"There is a saying: 'Chinese or Thai, we are all brothers'," said former prime minister Anand Panyarachun upon its inauguration. "Being of Hakka origin from my mother's side, I may be of the fourth generation, yet I am considered completely Thai. Some Chinese traditions are still practised... Naturally these familiar practises have been integrated into Thai lifestyle. It is not false to say that the Chinese-Thai play a major role in business. But to consider further, they are Thai."

left: "What is Chinese in Thailand?" ask performers from Shanghai to the audience at Low Fat Art Fest in Lhong 1919.

above: A sculpture of Sino-Thai guardians as 'Siamese twins' by Komgrit Tepthian, in front of the new Chinatown gate on Charoen Krung Road.

left: **Murals of benefactors and leading Sino-Thai personalities line the pagoda at the Kwan Im Shrine in Lat Phrao.**

right: **In the 2000s it became socially acceptable for Sino-Thai politicians to portray their Chineseness on election posters, an ethnic 'coming out' that has continued across party lines.**

below: **A Sino-Thai looks through lucky red glasses at a lantern festival in Chinatown's Yaowarat Road.**

In the mid-2000s, news mogul Sondhi Limthongkul published *Da Jia Hao*, a Sinophile magazine that encouraged young Sino-Thais to celebrate Chineseness whilst giving loyalty to their adoptive land. It was prominently sold at youth festivals where a new indie echelon was starting to explore, photograph and write about the origins that their parents had quashed in the pursuit of integration. Features lauded Sino-Thai fusions and the 'New J Generation' of *jeh* (vegetarian) Sino-Thais, who follow the Hokkien Vegetarian festival each October. One issue matched famous Sino-Thais to faces of Xian's terracotta warriors. Another, headlined "Some Muey and Some Dtii" (Some Sino Chicks & Sino Guys), proclaimed: "Now, it's hip to be Chinese."

"It's good for the younger generation to be exposed to aspects of traditional Chinese culture which they rarely get a chance to see nowadays," says Visit, a second-generation Teochiu spice trader. One such Thai-Teochiu youth, Pop, was so curious about his ancestry that he created the first tours of Chinatown. Historians tracking the community's hidden history drew on his research, since he always knows where *ngiew* (Chinese opera) is being performed at which obscure stage.

Recall recedes with each generation. That's gets acute as analogue ways become incomprehensible to the globalised digital mindset. When I arrived, Bangkok's archetypal immigrant Chinese granny in perm and pyjamas barely uttered Thai, while her bicultural daughter spoke Teochiu in the shophouse, Thai at the office. Now the Sino-Thai granddaughter thinks in Thai and knows barely enough Chinese to venerate ancestors at Qing Ming. And if she speaks Chinese it is from learning Mandarin in simplified script as an important world language. "This is a communication problem in every Chinese family," says antiquarian book collector Paisarn Piamettawat, who says he feels Thai, and lives as a Thai, but that Chinese remains his subculture.

Chinese immigrants became Thai during a century when China was beset by civil wars, colonisation and misfortune. Reassertions of Sino-Thai pride have mirrored the revival of China back into the region's hegemon. Calls to acknowledge the Chinese contribution to Thailand date from when premier Kukrit Pramoj visited Mao in 1975 to restore relations, an event documented in Kukrit's Heritage Home museum. Cementing that amity, Deng Xiao Ping made a state visit in 1978, when he presented robes at the ordination of the future King Rama X. A year later, Deng handed China's very first Foreign Investment Certificate 001 to Dhanin Chearavanont of the Sino-Thai conglomerate CP, which remains one of China's biggest investors.

Links with the Chinese diaspora raise spectres. At about 60 million wordwide, the 'Overseas Chinese' are the size of Thailand. Sun Yat Sen called them "the mother of the Chinese Revolution." After Chinese president Jiang Zemin opened the Chinatown Gate, eyebrows raised when he met privately with Sino-Thai business leaders. When the Thai-Chinese Chamber of Commerce hosted the 3rd World Chinese Entrepreneurs Convention in 1995, Michael Vatikiotis reported, China's ambassador broke a taboo, "which was to call openly on all Chinese to work towards the unity of China." Xi Jinping has used the phrase: "realisation of the China Dream is the ultimate vision of China's sons and daughters within the country and overseas." Some feel disquiet, but historian Kasian Tejapira sees China-Thai *guanxi* connections as "a kind of cultural capital and ethnic capital that will help Thailand grow in the region."

Bangkok was an early recipient of Confucius Institutes in 2007. While the Goethe Institute or Alliance Française are casual venues, Confucius Institutes are strategically embedded in universities. Thai students thus get acquainted with Mandarin, calligraphy and selected Confucian values through lectures like 'Ethnic Groups in China and Religious Harmony'. Some parents send their offspring to study Chinese in China, while Beijing tells Chinese schools abroad to offer "patriotic education." The mainland's 'Birthright Programme' gives overseas Chinese aged 12-18 a grounding in their ancestry by paying them to attend a two-week 'Root-Seeking Camp'.

Fascination with China fits a world trend. The diaspora has preserved elements of old China that the Cultural Revolution destroyed at home: a living tradition. Hong Kong and Taiwan enshrined some aspects, but are losing old lifestyles, character and settings. Yet Sampeng, like Penang, preserves a fraying ecosystem of Chinese urban heritage, from gables to godowns, amulets to accents. Popularity may spoil Chinatown, however. Luan Rit community was well restored, but the themed redevelopments of Woeng Nakhon Kasem and a prominent block at the east end of Yaowarat risk the loss of authentic shops, restaurants and charm.

Thailand has lately become the biggest destination for mainland tourists, hosting nine million in 2024. Many discovered Bangkok through China's highest grossing movie, *Lost in Thailand*. Their sheer numbers and notoriety for noise and brusque behaviour often chafes with soft-spoken Bangkokian manners, showing just how integrated Sino-Thais have become. Mainland Chinese feel they're visiting a foreign place, noticing the Sino-Thais' acculturated ways, and some surviving cultural relics eroded in China like *ngiew* Chinese opera in both Teochiu and Hainan versions.

New Chinatowns near Chong Nonsi or the Chinese Embassy on Ratchadaphisek Road, brim with long-stayers from inland provinces. This Fourth Wave of immigrants resembles the phase of sojourners before the 1930s, in that they earn money on extended stays, then pivot elsewhere or head home. Some work in jobs like retail that are legally reserved for Thais.

Now that China's resurgent, its ancient sophistication once again beckons as a tool of soft power. In the 80s, came Cantopop and martial arts TV shows from Hong Kong, which popularised nicknames like Tae. Then China sent acrobats and lion dancers, pandas and Xian Terrracotta Warriors. Now Thai-Jiin connect with Chinese and fellow diasporites through Chinese digital gateways

like Alibaba, Baidu or Blued, where many cite their ethnicity as Thai-Chinese rather than just Thai. How they identify and what they've been called has gone through many phases.

Eventually, their immigrant heritage entered state institutions, notably Museum Siam, which opened in 2007. "We Chinese were here from the very start, as far back as the Ming dynasty. That's 650 years ago," said a panel in its first permanent exhibition. "Even today the Chinese community is a vital and prosperous part of Bangkok."

The Chinatown Heritage Centre then opened at Wat Trimitr, in the new *mondop* (pavilion) housing the world's biggest solid gold Buddha. It's an edited narrative of how Chinese became loyal Thais, focusing on the harmonious result rather than the rocks in the road. You walk through dioramas, from junks moored at a Sampeng wharf, via its sanitary re-planning by King Rama V to the mid-20th century 'Golden Age', when Yaowarat Road hosted Bangkok's early tall buildings, department stores and pop culture. Audio-visuals then immerse you in today's Instagrammable markets and festivals. As at the Kuan Im Shrine in Lat Phrao, it concludes with murals showing 'Thais of Chinese descent' venerating royal patrons.

Recognising the Chinese part of the melting pot came about once the state was content that *luk-jiin* were now loyal locals. Sino-Thai patriots are indeed the new establishment, with a nuanced complex identity. Thais now flock to Chinatown festivities via Wat Mangkon's dragon-themed MRT station, which has morphed into one of Bangkok's themed attractions.

Community
'Way of life' yields to 'lifestyle'

Above the whine of rotary saws from the carpenters behind Golden Mount, a metal tapping is the audible guide to finding Baan Baat, the last community that still forges monks bowls by hand. Like many old *yaan*, it's reached only by foot or by bike down gaps between rows of shophouses. In a winding lane blackened by the soot from domestic foundries, residents sit outside their workshops on low wooden stools. Using hooked hammers, they beat the bowls over a knob-headed prong that's been stuck in the ground for lifetimes.

"It used to be that every house did this all day, and you would wake up to endless 'ping, ping, ping,'" says craftswoman Pranee Sutdis. "Now there's are only a few and it's not so noisy." These foundries passed down family lines since their ancestors fled the fall of Ayutthaya. Some gave up, but the remainder have successors in this most sustainable of Bangkok's 'urban craft villages.' A newcomer joined them, because the bowls command a premium price as objet d'art, given their complex process. "There are at least 13 major stages and about 21 in all," says Hiran, a craftsman who crouches at an open coke furnace to forge an alloy of copper, tin and gold. His sister Mayuree smooths the zip-like joins between the eight metal strips, which symbolise Buddhism's Eightfold Noble Path.

Each April 16, the community hosts *wai khru* – worship to their craft's master. His statue wields a hammer beside an altar that enshrines a pair of wooden bellows like those still in use. They go on to party with music and *likay* folk opera.

Fellow-feeling is a Bangkok trait, enabled by interaction taking place outdoors. The streetlife and open-fronted shophouses put private social life on full public display, making informal community a visitor's first and abiding impression of "village Bangkok."

The civic quilt retains urban hamlets that made the city a patchwork of close-knit clans. Ancient *yaan* evolved from bonds of kin, craft

left: **Old wooden shophouses in the still vibrant Hokkien Chinese** *yaan* **of Talad Noi.**

below: **Baan Baat, where descendants of refugees from Ayutthaya's fall still make monk's bowls, and worship a shrine of old wooden forge bellows.**

or faith, and remain intimate knots of identity. Behind a crust of highway shophouses, a tracery of narrow *soi* and narrower *trok* embeds their folk character. These urban landscapes are also mindscapes of ritual, lineage and memory.

But sense of belonging has become less rooted in place or genes. Identity has spread to other affinities: career, peer group, Thainess, brands. Extended blood relations are atomising into nuclear families. Socially diverse neighbourhoods are re-sorting by class into generic condos, gated estates or gentrified lanes. In a new migration, bonding has gone online. The like-minded who live in distant suburbs link up via app and mass transit. They gather at 'Third Places' – venues that aren't home, or work, but host common pursuits, in a voluntary community of subcultures. Globalised 'lifestyle' ousts unique 'ways of life.'

Terminology reveals shifting values. *Yaan* is a written word for area, but most evokes old enclaves, whereas *taew* is the spoken word for small vicinities. One *yaan* might have several *chumchon*, an official label for communities, often of distinct race and religion. It's a huge achievement that Bangkok's multi-ethnic *yaan* get along so well. "We have Catholics, Buddhists and Muslims living here and we always look out for each other," says Surachai Sukson, 36, who works in downtown but lives in the *yaan* of his birth, Kudi Jeen. "If we run out of food, we can go to our neighbours, and if they do they can come to us."

Chumchon could mean any community, but can feel tainted. It evokes nostalgia for bygone conviviality, but also whiffs of lower status and social problems. "The word *chumchon* is a little vague – it doesn't necessarily mean poor or run-down, doesn't necessarily mean illegal," says an Asian Coalition for Housing Rights report. *Chumchon* of unmodernised wooden homes get dissed in Thai with the English epithet *slum*. This applies to shacks that line rail tracks at Nana as well as tidy lanes of timber houses that still dot the CBD, as at Soi Phiphat, behind Bangkok Bank's HQ.

State regulations can put existing *chumchon* outside the law, so officials label canal-side shanties as squatters, and refer to *chumchon bukruk* (trespassing communities). To counter this, NGOs defend them as *chumchon bukberk* (pioneering communities), which harks back to when pre-fabricated stilt houses were moved to empty sites like riverbanks. All can agree upon *chumchon ae-ut* (crowded community). Bangkok sure is crowded. Though the density of downtown has decreased by a quarter in recent decades, there remain 690 teeming slums. Many begun as temporary labour camps, like Khlong Toei slum in 1962, which today houses 100,000 people. Another term conveys the closeness: *chumchon trok* (path communities).

Living in open-fronted homes just one-to-three metres apart, as if in adjoining rooms, ensures close-knit bonds. Being too narrow for traffic, *trok* become a social arena, where geezers banter from their doorsteps and kids wobble past on bicycles with a friend stood upon the rear wheel hub. Grannies chat while they fold banana leaf parcels of squidgy rice dessert.

Heart 223

Each old *yaan* is an urban organism evolved around its trade. Flower porters in Pak Khlong Talad trundle bouquets around market halls by cool of night. Plantation farmers at the city fringes still live, lark and paddle on the canals that nourish their crops.

A strong community was considered to need three pillars known collectively as *boworn*, namely: *baan* (house), *wat* and *rongrian* (school), the word combining the pronunciation of their initials b-w-r. Although *wats* are losing their role as social hub, *boworn* persists through temple schools, good works, and rites as seen at Bang Kradee, where villagers cook vats of delicacies to share. There's also a fourth community institution: the market – the heart of work and socialising. To the rest of the city, a *yaan* was known for its trade, from hi-fi decks in Ban Mo to hi-lo dice in Tha Tien.

Banglamphu is known for Khao San Road, backpackers and a wave of 1960s youth culture, but sustains six *chumchon trok*, including Mon and two sets of Muslims. They all get along and care for the area using informal rules, posting notices in open spaces, schools and places of worship. "Some residents identify themselves with the traces of high culture as their ancestors worked as servants of the palaces," writes Wimonrat Issarathumnoon. "'Great' and 'little' traditions of urban life existed in harmony, reflected spatially in the coexistence of the royal citadel and its surrounding *yaan*."

As modernity intrudes, mutual support can wane. Impersonal ventures move in, families get more cramped and youngsters venture out. "If you have a chance to upgrade your life, you would take your family to live in better place, like a *moo baan* (housing estate) or a government flat," says Anirut Apidech. He works near Nang Loeng and has noticed the *yaan*'s viability erode. "This is one factor why communities are losing their identity."

It's the tension of change versus tradition, personal versus collective. There's little sentiment to preserve an earlier, poorer stage of development, when you can aspire to a condo called Aspire. Riches might even afford a mansion in a *moo ban* called The Rich.

Take a typical migrant couple who became Bangkokian. Like other arrivals from their Central Plains farming district, they first stayed at a shared house in Lat Phrao Soi 1 near the Northern Bus Terminal. The man went into business with his brother-in-law, while the wife wove blankets in a factory at Soi Sena Nikhom, where they got their own home. It was one of many shacks pressed together on stilts, linked by planks raised over murky standing water. They saved up to build a wooden house in a suburban plot and to educate their kids at private schools. In turn, their children got professional jobs and built a smart concrete house for their parents. Mutual help, striving for security, repaying elders – it's the life arc of millions who've realised the 'Bangkok Dream.'

Community feeling persists in the suburbs, too. Neighbours often move as a group. "Many of us came from other provinces, so we brought that character of country people to Bangkok," says Anirut, whose family moved from Ayutthaya. His *moo ban* dates from the 1980s, when Ramintra was the peri-urban frontier with paddy fields. Back then, landowning companies sold plots to anyone to build what they like, so it's a mix of poor and middle-class people, who spread word about that cheap land through their networks. "This is the old way of *moo ban*. People know each other. We respect neighbours as our family. I call the corner shop owner auntie, not by her name. We help each other, like when we have a wedding or ordination or funeral. If something happens, we tackle the problem together, or we help the staff from the BMA."

Moo ban means 'group of houses' and was the Thai term for 'hamlet.' Bangkok housing estates used to be run like rural hamlets, by a

above: **Mon residents of Bang Kradee make food for monks in the local tradition of *boworn*.**

right: **On the road to Bang Kradee stands a gated housing estate called The Rich.**

224 Community

phuyai ban (village elder) under a subdistrict's *kamnan* (village head). Informal *moo ban* now elect a committee and president, but still with a cooperative spirit.

Very different are formal *moo ban*, which are privately run tract housing projects. Branded with grandiose names, they're built and run rigidly like condominiums, with the body corporate being a legal entity that hires contractors from the compulsory residents' fees. Many buy 'off-plan' before construction through mall promotions by a developer that builds identical houses, with a better road and amenities, all gated and guarded. The gardens, drives and walls cause a structural separation between residents, who drive in and out. Many don't know their neighbours, or even wish to, so fights flare over parking or noise.

"Compared to the old way of *moo ban*, where the mums talk every day, and the dads share beers at the corner, you don't have any connection," says Anirut of tract housing. "They may say 'hi' sometimes, but their kids play with their own friends from different schools, not with the kids next door. Working parents come home late and just mind their own business."

Private *moo ban* and condos have sprucer facilities – gym, pool, function room – but are less convivial than older ones, where event *salas* get donated by district officials or politicians. That sociability comes from the migrants' rural upbringing. Their city-born offspring may know each other, but can feel awkward at group festivities, not knowing what to do.

Modernity has made life more secure, so the need to cooperate wanes. In an ethic called *long khaek* (gather invitees), villagers would pool efforts to defend against marauders, harvest each field and move prefabricated teak houses. Even in Bangkok, evicted *chumchon* may have to dismantle their own homes. Street workers also infuse this spirit with *jai dtem roi* ('full-hundred heart') commitment, whether *motorsai* drivers directing traffic, vendors minding a neighbour's stuff, or masseuses massaging each other.

A test of *long khaek* was the Great Flood of 2011. Communities came to blows, when some got spared while others were inundated. Yet submerged estates also came together with ingenious ideas to solve crises, like impromptu rafts made from barrels and bicycle power.

Informal institutions also spring from this altruism where there's a lack of formal services.

In the absence of public ambulances, two charities rush converted pickup trucks to crashes and emergencies. Motorcycle taxi ranks double as conscientious traffic managers, messengers, deliverers and handymen – aside from their trade being a patch for failures in public transport. The self-help radio station Ruam Duay Chuay Kan (Help Each Other Together) has shifted into social media as a new way to get voluntary help on local problems.

Such inclusive places nurture what Jane Jacobs, the pioneer of 'living cities', called 'public characters,' eccentrics who take on a social responsibility, or mission to entertain. Bangkok seems to specialise in geezers who dance while directing traffic, and gas deliverymen who dress in superhero costumes just to make people smile.

That easy-going helpfulness was ruptured by the political schism. Families and neighbours split so vehemently over Thaksin that group events and social media became minefields of righteous shaming. Ironically, the Red Shirt, Yellow Shirt and Shutdown protests were facilitated by *long khaek*. Thousands of the demonstrators set up villages on major crossroads. Volunteers, some paid, erected shelters, seating and stages, serviced by free kitchens, bathrooms, first aid and guard patrols. Run like temple festivals with live shows and shrines, they had joy in fellowship – until events turned deadly.

During the 2009-10 unrest, protests spread into residential areas. Tenants bandied to defend their blocks in Din Daeng, while at Bon Kai, neighbours fought on Rama IV Road. In the aftermath, instead of reconciliation, social classes are disentangling as the poor get removed from downtown.

Bangkok society has gone from collective to atomised existence. Individualist lands with nuclear families had longer to adjust. Extended family cultures like here have rebuilt the urban fabric faster than their values, opening gulfs between neighbours and generations. Informal influence still works through Thai social circuitry – the circles (*wong*) and strings (*sen*) of personal networks – but as status becomes more about money than rank, Bangkok is getting stratified by economic class.

Bangkok ranks a lowly 133rd in Mercer's 2019 worldwide *Quality of Living Survey* and 46th in the *World Happiness Report* 2018. That's partly due to the survey's basket of goods being weighted to expats, but subsisting here is getting harder. Global surveys tick only generic boxes and can't quantify casual character or the way that informal trade and reciprocity enhances ordinary life here. Despite rising prices, almost all Bangkokians can eat out daily, go socialising and meet core needs, near home, at affordable cost.

Climate is also a factor in the sociability of Bangkokians. Community flourished before air-conditioning. When most buildings were open for ventilation, indoor-outdoor living was the accessible norm. Now homes, shops, workplaces and even festival venues are designed as chilled, exclusive sanctums. Communing visibly in the open is increasingly reserved for the poor, whose airless rooms push them to interact with passersby at streetside hangouts, crooning karaoke in lounges without walls. It's become a mark of prestige that whether you're home or out, you stay indoors.

"Condo dwellers don't sit out front of their shop, chatting to passers by, they don't even necessarily know who their neighbours are. They leave in the morning, come home after dinner, maybe spend an hour in their air-con gym," writes Monruedee Jansuttipan in *BK*. "They don't get their clothes fixed at the local street tailor, don't buy their new brush from the guy with the handcart, they drive to their mall. It means a day will come when all you find is a row of fancy condos, but nowhere to shop, eat or get your watch fixed."

Apartment living has gone through the same trajectory, from porous to sealed. From the 1960s-90s, towers adapted the fan-cooled, indoor-outdoor living of houses in gardens. Low-rise blocks, often named 'Court,' had few flats per floor. Deep balconies front and back let breezes flow through plants and over expanses of hardwood parquet. Fitted kitchens often had a balcony section for Thai wok and brazier cooking. Blocks of smaller units got cross-ventilation from louvres onto open-air light balconies, often around a light-well that was later capped with a lantern roof. Tenants decorated those common areas with plants, fish ponds and statuary, even benches. Such sociable, climate-appropriate flats are adored by expatriates and retro fans, but not by those wanting status. Many of the remaining courts languish amid poor maintenance and a weak resale market, or get torn down.

Consumer lifestyle leads condominiums to follow identical templates. Unless you splurge half a million dollars on a duplex penthouse with balcony pool, you get a metre or two around the bed, sofa and kitchenette counter. Most new condos seal you off from the street and the elements via card-access lobbies and air-con, with micro-balconies for compressors, while there's no cross-ventilation to the windowless corridor, where nobody would hang out.

Newer housing stock is not designed for extended family. Nor do most of their tiny, unvented kitchens enable Thai-style cooking, which drives people to eat out. One condo near Lumpini crams all internal functions behind a sliding wall, so you can access the wardrobe or the cooker, but not both at once.

As empty lots fill up, developers' 'land banks' join plots until there's enough room for a condo or mall. Bangkok has always been rebuilding, but usually squeezed new between old, so you could read history amid the jumble. Since the 2010s, entire streetscapes get levelled. Samyan community – beloved for its food and student hangouts – was razed for hi-tech offices plus, in a social contribution, a park that stores floodwater.

Affluent communities, too, make way for mega projects. TV host Korakot 'Nym' Punlopraksa filmed the process as her neighbours' garden villas and teak houses came down in 2010, along with a market and famous restaurants. "I built this little house to last my lifetime and have lived here for 55 years," Boonliang Koomklong, 81, told Nym. "Suddenly at this age, my life has to change beyond my preparation. Where can I go?" Soi Langsuan's village lanes made way for Sindhorn Village, a mega-project of park-view condos, flanked by what's dubbed a 'community mall.' Hoardings around the superblock showed a flawless young woman strolling a woodland alone, with the slogan: "Better Community."

For the upwardly mobile, having gym membership and swipe card access does seem a better community. But speculation may not match residential needs. Many towers target investors – largely Chinese diaspora Millennials – who resell or rent out their unit, or stay there only part-time. In 2019, Thailand had 450,000 empty homes worth US$22.5 billion, with 65,000 units added the year before, most of them in Bangkok.

Condos initially went up before of mass transit; now they're built around projected stations. Rail expansion to historic quarters raises the stakes for hitherto unperturbed *yaan*, as you can build higher around stations, and rent hikes drive old-timers out. The Orange Line will disturb Samsen, where genteel schools, plant market, temple festivals and wooden cottages evoke a different city and era, like rummaging in Bangkok's attic.

Swathes of old Bangkok survive partly because the Crown Property Bureau (CPB) had for decades held rents below market rate. Ownership of the city lies in few hands, often held or sold off by aristocratic estates. Other vast landholdings – city, state, *wats* – had let tenants and squatters stay whilst the capital sprawled. Among private owners, my landlady is one who upholds a fading ethic of not raising rents on sitting tenants. Once both land prices and building density soared, compassionate coexistence reverted to mass relocations.

Temples retain vast holdings of land over which abbots have absolute, unaccountable

left: **Le Raffiné Jambhu Dvipa – a luxury condo of double-floor apartments named after the realm of humans near Mount Meru in the Thai cosmology.**

right: **Construction workers rest at a condo construction site in Pathumwan. Note the handmade benches of the motorcycle taxi drivers' rank below.**

Heart 227

control. Many *wats* built shophouses – and so can take them away. Headlines recount temples ousting *yaan*, whether on the banks of Khlong Lat Phrao or Wat Yannawa's historic, boat-shaped terraces of Soi Wanglee. Its tenants had supported Wat Yannawa when it fell on hard times decades ago, but during an eviction battle in 2007, residents told me that demolition began whilst they slept inside.

"This country does not have laws that genuinely recognise community rights," notes reporter Ploenpote Atthakor. "It is disastrous when abbots pursue materialism and turn a blind eye to wider communities' place in the social landscape. Many abbots forget that the land they own, in some cases, was given to their temples by these locals' ancestors."

A wife of King Rama V bought land at Wat Kalayanamitr so its rents could support the temple, and later her descendants donated that land. Since 2003, the temple terminated their tenancies, took the residents to court and demolished their houses, along with dozens of listed monuments. In their place rose pavilions of Thai, Hindu and Chinese statuary, where the idea is for tour groups to buy offerings. Many saw that *yaan* as a slum, yet it was famed for its dessert maker, its fighting fish breeding, and its melodious wooden *ruen krueng* – a traditional music conservatory.

No fewer than 29 *yaan* were ousted for the junta's river promenade plan in 2017, erasing centuries of habitation along 7 km of both banks. "The officers called five communities to gather together, and they got us to sign the eviction papers. We had less than a minute to read through everything," recalls Supharat Pothisuwan, 42, of Kiakkai Pier community. "They gave us one day to move out before they would tear the house down. We had been living here for three generations. We felt numb and hopeless, but… life goes on even though we are just small people." Those signing could get a flat nearby or on the city fringes. At Wat Soi Thong community, Prakij Thamniam, 56, upon being told to demolish his own four-generation house, moved his family back to their ancestral hometown out East, declaring: "There is nothing left for us in Bangkok."

Uprooting ancient settlements expunges a sense of place and continuity, even proof of presence. Stilt houses on riverbanks remind us of how Bangkokians lived. That's the problem. Authentic *yaan* embarrass the upper echelon's self-image as up-to-date. Folksy *yaan* are seen rarely as heritage, rather as relics or a mess that devalues prime real estate.

As the legal system only recognises private ownership not ancestral rights, informal *yaan* got stranded when goodwill evaporated amid the land grab. Not all those served eviction notices agree to leave. Protests flare as vulnerable communities flummox owners and officials by saying that this is their city too.

The 1990s-2000s democratic era saw bottom-up views championing the *khon rakya* (grassroots), a term that has broadened from rural poor to anyone disadvantaged in the world's third most unequal country. The NCPO junta tried to replace the word 'grassroots' with 'low-income individual' on grounds that the word creates class divisions. Many middle class see themselves as better educated and making more contribution to urban society, while some Facebook pages blame slums and street workers. Labour that the city needs often ends up in worker camps as squatters get removed from railways, roads and canals.

The test case of tenure, at Pom Mahakan fort's *yaan*, ended in 2018, when the BMA smashed the timbers of the last authentic homes dating from Early Rattanakosin. Every conservation and civil society body appealed against a park replacing the multi-generation residents and the museum they founded. This last, best stand of historical presence had spiralled into a test of bureaucratic honour. If such a vital and viable *yaan* couldn't be saved, many more will surely be swept away.

The old town's role has been contested ever since the 1982 Bicentennial. It boils down to divergent views on history and identity. Marc Askew frames this as "a conflict between readings of the city itself, between 'Krungthep', the aestheticised abstract heritage paradigm, as against 'Bangkok', a city of the *yaan* and common people." Krungthep is the dream, Bangkok is the root.

Bangkok used to be remarkable for being a world city with a vibrant historic centre. Yet the Rattanakosin Island Plan to create a monument park mandates removing residents and ministries, so beloved old restaurants must turn from local custom to tourist taste. "In Tha Tien, it's really now only just the traders and my family," said Narisa Chakrabongse. At the BangkokEdge festival she held around her ancestral Chakrabongse House and Museum Siam, a panel on how *yaan* can survive asked: 'How to live with granddad's heritage?'

Thais view society in terms of familial duties. Benevolent elders and teachers get revered as fatherly or motherly figures; mature people as uncles or aunties; friends, peers or cousins as *phi-nong* (older-younger siblings), and the immature as *dek* (kids). Community cohesion has much to do with prioritising relationships over abstract ideals. Everyone having a place explains the tolerance for gays and misfits, even villains, since karma is the ultimate operating system.

The state is also run like kinship. Officials bond as if in private clubs; indeed many belong to the Royal Bangkok Sports Club. Administration has swollen into a web of agencies and bureaucratic firms, where jobs are valuable sinecures with influence. That so-called 'Bureaucratic Polity' remains the bastion of communitarian values, enforced through hierarchy, dogma and dress code. Civil servants are so insulated through benefits like unsackability, pension and health provision that they live five years longer than those under public health care.

The norm is to allocate resources not to the public, but to a trusted in-group, whether voters, clique or kin. Some may scorn motorcycle taxi drivers as gangs or swarming hawkers as mafia, but their defensive organisation arises from their precarious livelihood and experience of being extorted.

Lately, public spiritedness is shifting from informal kindness to formal state services, NGO projects, and corporate social responsibility. Conservatives fear that fraying traditions are no longer instinctual, but need enforcement, so children must now learn the '12 Core Values' at school. The belated inclusion of old *yaan* in museums only hastens their drift into the

Roofless

Passers by marvel at the graffiti over Ratchathewi's Hua Chang Bridge and other downtown walls, which resembles engineering mind maps. The annotated diagrams about infrastructure, haircuts and ephemera are "whatever you imagine them to be," says sixty-something Samer Peerachai, who studied arts at technical collage and worked in community development at Nong Chok. Living under that bridge since his wife left with their baby, the savant says of his technical graffiti: "I just write my emotions out."

Bangkokians without a bed soared from 2,500 to 4,000 between 2011 and 2017, due to poverty, family rejection (for debts, mental troubles, HIV or infirmity) and evictions. A fifth of them used to doss in Phra Nakhon. The Mirror Foundation fed them weekly from a pig-shaped food truck on the plaza of City Hall. Embarrassed, the BMA stopped the feeding and expelled the itinerants. Only 40 can stay in the Big House shelter in Bangkok Noi. Most simply now camp on the raised, dry platforms under BTS bridges around the city, and like Samer, make a living by gleaning trash. Issarachon Foundation reckon that rehabilitating them all back into the community would cost just 500 baht per head.

left: **A homeless man lives on his porter's trolley.**

top: **Mirror Foundation feeds the homeless from its pig-like food truck.**

above: **Mathematical savant graffiti at Ratchathewi by Samer Peerachai, who ended up in the Bangkok Art Biennale.**

Subcultures

Community does not equate to tradition. There are other ways of communal bonding than custom, locality or ancestry. It could be a community of common interest, or the shared life-experience of a sexual minority. The most established non-local grouping is peer group bonds from student years, perhaps the loyalest non-family cohort in a Thai life.

As the city's living quarters atomise, studio apartments disconnect downtown individuals from their elders in the suburbs or cramped *yaan*. Close-knit communities can impose narrow values, and limit potential, but having one's own space while young enables a new generation to find their own friendships, pursuits and lovers, free of prying.

Loosed from generations of attachment to place, the young hop between neighbourhoods hyped as 'in' by condo marketers who flatter this yuppy generation as 'urbanistas.' Bangkok hasn't before had such a phenomenon of relishing urbanism for its own sake. The clientèle of artisanal coffee houses, curated night markets, and wakeboard surfing clubs are experimenting with fresh ways of being Thai in town.

Bangkok is widely noted as a city of reinvention among foreigners. Countless Asiaphile 'Easties,' who feel alienated by the West, come here to pursue a new path in life, and bond with expatriates and locals with similar outlook.

Yet Bangkok's growing anonymity makes it possible for Thais to reinvent themselves – or add a parallel identity. This is especially true of upcountry migrants, but also of contrarian misfits and those from lowly backgrounds making a splash.

This globalised city offers an escape for cosmopolitans who feel trapped by parochial mindsets, but feel more

affinity among counterparts with the same interests than with their place of origin. Bangkok has subcultures and international networks that offer cosmopolitans the liberation to join communities they choose.

Residents of old *yaan* likewise bond in non-traditional ways online or via interests like sport or dressing up for cosplay gatherings. Charismatic Instagram influencers – with dedicated followings in the hundreds of thousands – are the self-anointed village heads of Virtual Bangkok.

past tense. We are witnessing the tail-end of traditional Bangkok.

The middle class, aspiring to be *siwilai*, increasingly regards those still living communal lives as undeveloped. "I cannot go to Na Ram [Ramkhamhaeng street market], it's so scary!" exclaims Amara, a law MA, in *Status City*, a study of middle-class Bangkok. "It's very likely that you'll lose stuff there. And the people there are… I don't mean anything by it, but they're just scary." A film by the acclaimed director Pen-Ek Ratanaruang shows a *hi-so* girl cowering from a working guy who's merely offering to fix her broken-down car.

The city embodies such fears in the elevated Skywalks, the guards at privately-owned 'public spaces' and the defensive architecture that puts barriers between pavement and gated towers where once shophouses were open to all. "Social

well-being and psychological health depend upon community," writes Ray Oldenburg on how mixed societies get sifted into demographic silos. "Most [modern] residential areas have been designed to protect people from community rather than connect them to it."

Social engineering has been a hallmark of the Thainess project, with standardisation to dilute local allegiances. Cultural mandates since the 1940s still micro-manage everyday activities. In the Mana-Manee school books issued after the 1976 coup, the centre of community is not *boworn* but the state's district office. Lately, zoning to ban alcohol near *wats* and schools makes *taew* less lively. Now the mutual informal economy is being dismantled. Formalising the informal sector funnels all that dispersed mutual exchange into housing, malls or chains owned by

One camp that's huddling outside of family norms is LGBT. Their rainbow of genders finds mutual support and expression in gay, lesbian and *katoey* venues, where they're no longer a minority, or scenes where they're prominent. An overlapping group, fashion scenesters, twirl through their own diary of launches, catwalk shows and themed parties. The designers, stylists and models are mostly a tight-knit coterie of decades' standing, who mix closely with their customer base: the *hi-so* nouveau riches.

Hi-so arose out of a need for inclusion, as most self-made Sino-Thais weren't part of the old-money polite society. Since the Asian Tiger boom years, achievers could get noticed through proximity at launches for Porsche watches or Clinique wrinkle-remover. Aspiring business owners turned product launches into ostentatious parties for their own echelon, enabling PR for all who make an entrance. The most outrageously coiffed and gowned get photographed for *hi-so* magazines and websites in a feedback cycle of prestige that gets accounted annually in the *Thailand Tatler Society 500*. As socialites re-circulate at the same events, *hi-sos* form a community of shared ambition.

Intellectuals and *lo-so* arty types mingle in a scene of gallery openings, film screenings, indie concerts and alternative festivals. Several art residencies receive foreign artists into a shared home, as at Tentacles in the N22 art enclave, off Narathiwat Soi 22. In a city insensitive to aesthetics, the art community – along with writers and designers – can feel like a tribe of initiates who sense things so deeply it hurts. Theirs is a community of introverts.

Alternative notions of community are rarely seen as legitimate, so bohemians get edged out wherever they perch. One 'art colony' has turned Chinatown's Soi Nana into a core of the Creative District. A few designers and artists had lived for years in its lanes, where herbal medicinal aromas emanated from wooden shuttered shophouses. When steep rent hikes caused the closure of Cho Why gallery in 2018, it heralded the tipping point when artists started to get priced out by bigger players. It's arguable which community is more vulnerable: the traditional *yaan* or the outsider artists.

a few corporations – effectively an extractive mono-culture.

Amid Thailand's 'transformation crisis', living heritage satisfies a yearning for simpler times. After the 1997 crash, attention turned to overlooked cultural assets. Handmade goods were sold at 'Walking Street' fairs in *yaan* that closed a road for those days. Many prize craft communities for being holdouts of 'local wisdom.' But craft is static and poorly paid. Inheriting the family trade can mean flipping a wok of the same ingredients non-stop each day for the rest of your life. Vicarious traditionalism is well meant, but treating community as something unusual to visit only underlines that the craft has gone from staple to curio. It's the urban equivalent of the elite preaching that the picturesque peasantry shouldn't abandon the rice culture for modern lifestyle.

If vulnerable *yaan* aren't protected, heedless redevelopment may leave little authentic to save. Heritage cachet and new convenience will lure outsiders to move in, drawn by the character they themselves then dilute. To avoid that happening to Kudi Jeen, the progressive Urban Design & Development Centre (UddC) has got the BMA to limit condos to near the Gold Line, leaving the houses intact.

Saving old *yaan* entails turning community into a commodity. As with folk music and retro, Bangkokians adopt things *choei* (outdated) only once they get modernised and lose stigma.

above: **Portraits from the legendary indie bar Gig Groceries by Jesper Haynes, shown at Moose.**
Photo Jesper Haynes

below: **One of Bangkok's climate-friendly old apartments with balconies, Siri Wireless.**

right: **Ads for *moo ban* housing on Ratchapruek Road, which cuts through the last intact canalscape.**

Community tourism has grown since the mid-2000s into an attraction for those who seek authenticity. Airbnb offers 'Experiences,' like cycle rides with locals. Contemporary arts now infuse festivals like Art In Soi, where Kudi Jeen hosts installations and performance amid its laneways and unused warehouses, turning *yaan* into a creative venue.

Nang Loeng has all the potential elements: famous community, prized desserts; elegant market hall; Chinese shrine; oldest wooden cinema; and last *lakhon chatri* dance stage. Inspired by the markets of glass and ironwork King Rama V saw in Europe, Nang Loeng is Bangkok's Covent Garden – and must likewise convert to tourism as local custom dwindles. But nothing's sure. The market was restored, but not yet the cinema.

"We don't get to participate whenever there are changes," says Nang Loeng community leader Suwanna Walploy-ngam. "We have no money and no power to negotiate. Information and news are also limited. They care more about GDP than cultural values… so it disappears with the old world."

Suwanna presented Nang Loeng's *lakhon chatri* at Appear, a fair to raise awareness of old *yaan*, held at the posh Sukhothai Hotel. "I don't want Bangkok to be without a soul," says the organiser, Achariya Thamparipattra of Hivesters, a social enterprise that's matched six communities with a local hotel each, to provide guest experiences that support the *yaan*. Motivated by the eviction of Mahakan Fort, Achariya drew on her MA in luxury branding from Paris to preserve craft enclaves.

Sadly, there's no common policy across branches of government. Pak Khlong Talad flower market, was evicted from its main site, supposedly for tourism and traffic motives, regardless of the traders' urban ecosystem. "You can build a new marketplace in an instant," noted Supitcha Tovivich, chair of the Community Act Network of the Association of Siamese Architects. "But to re-create a neighbourhood in the community sense – that takes decades."

When the Creative District encouraged tours of Charoen Krung, activist Walailak Songsiri predicted more development and fewer people. "Do you actually have real human life for them to see or are you just lying to yourself?" she said. "I dare to say Bangkok is dead. It has actually been dead already since a long time ago. Without humans, it cannot be a city."

That sounds alarmist, but it's a global trend. Urbanist Pitch Pongsawat tracked the pattern of how *sois* lose key buildings, then liveliness, then food security for its ordinary folk. That reduces the sensory experience that makes Bangkok so prized. As travel writer Samantha Gillison put it: "The way to kill a complex city is to chase out all the poor people – and their food."

'Domicide' (erasing neighbourhoods) used to happen in war, but became a modernising policy in Asia. Bangkok's evictions are milder than those in Phnom Penh or the extreme 'urbicide' (wiping whole cityscapes) in Beijing or Delhi. The compromise and compensation here stems from active resistance, but also from patience by bureaucrats, so relocations can take decades. That's why Bangkok's juxtapositions of eras, classes and lifestyles still co-exist.

Social upheaval has been the historical norm. Some *yaan* began with refugees from the urbicide of Ayutthaya. Early on, the city swelled with relocated villages or war captives, who were told where to stay, what to make and who to obey. That feudal system faded amid a vast influx of Chinese, whose trading culture revolved around shophouses, streetlife and *guanxi* networks. Industrialisation spurred a surge of factory and service labour from upcountry. Relocating Tha Phra Chan traders to distant Bang Bua Thong is mellow by comparison, but consistent.

That long history of having to resettle, restart trade and reinvent identity has bred an ability to cope and accept a new normal. Several woodworking *yaan* were sent in the 1980s to Prachanaruemit, which soon felt like an ancestral carpentry village. Historic *yaan* might fade, but migrants establish fresh ones, like the Burmese at Ratchathewi, or the Chinese in Huai Khwang. In some buildings or *sois*, community accrues through incomers already being friends. My own *soi* has built a community for 30 years that shares activities and repairs. That amity gets replenished as the tenants can choose who moves in.

Aligning Bangkok with the global system challenges presumptions of what community means. While this entrepôt has always had foreign enclaves, it's now a base of country-hopping metropolitans who don't see nation as a barrier. That trend has brought artisanal coffee and vegan salads to Bangkok, but has also turned once-unique cities worldwide into interchangeable preserves of a lifestyle typified by *Kinfolk* magazine.

When young people with fresh ideas lease empty spaces in rundown areas, it gets criticised as gentrification rather than renewal. Eviction isn't the only displacement; bohemians moving into *yaan* like Charoen Krung, Aree or Samsen inadvertently put pressure on social cohesion. Neglected areas of cities are cheap and so attract artists' studios, which can spark the gentrification cycle: artsy venues, then designer boutiques, which start out-pricing both long-timers and artists, before corporate chains and redevelopers bland-out the former charms.

For society not to stagnate, it needs outward-minded creatives, such as the young cadre of environmental urbanists who are championing rooftop gardens, distributing surplus food, or saving big trees. At the same time, it's hard for the patronage system to conceive that top-down decisions might be a source of mediocrity, let alone to accept that consulting communities can lead to better results. Landscape architects with a public mission, such as Yossapon Boonsom, have begun to get the BMA's park program to consult with locals and incorporate their wishes.

While art colonies are tiny and fragile, the idea of creative collectives has gone viral via co-working spaces, which encourage cross-fertilisation. Now co-housing offers collective living – as at the Parsuke Cohousing Project and the Arsom Silp Institute of the Arts' co-housing condo in Lat Phrao Soi 39 – but the format faces legal and mortgage rigidities.

"We can choose our neighbours and remove fences to get a lot more spaces," says award-winning community architect Patama Roonrakwit. She co-founded TEN House, which has common facilities and private units designed through workshops to each owner's taste, needs and budget. She sees building new co-housing communities as compatible for the lower middle class, as it fits in with Thai ways of shared living and helpfulness.

Despite the changes, Bangkok's collision of eras, ethnicities and affinities induces a feeling of connection. Most areas retain improvised streetlife, while gentrification is mild so far. The affluent can gorge on every luxury and cuisine in superlative venues, while ordinary folk can get basic needs met in convivial surrounds. The contrasting mishmash is what wins resident and visitor affection.

Bangkok is rebuilding, and its people relocating, at an ever faster churn. Constant destabilisation keeps Bangkokians nimble. That precariousness strengthens the persistence of community grit around the de-cluttered pockets of glitz. *Yaan* are urban ecosystems, where familial roots and trading tendrils evolve organically. That breeds resilience. So if an urban village gets uprooted, or a new enclave formed, it can draw on collective values and adaptive ingenuity. In Bangkok, community tenuously, tenaciously, tenderly endures.

Tin Town

Cooking With Poo may not be a delectable cookbook title, but it has put the whiffy Khlong Toei slum on the world's culinary map. Khun Poo, whose means Crab, lives in the portside ghetto, but transcended its cycle of poverty, alienation, addiction and violence. While a vendor, Poo was encouraged to teach cooking by Anji Barker, an Australian who moved into the slum to found the NGO Helping Hands. At its Second Chance used clothes shop and Munjai (Confidence) Café, kids can learn skills to overcome being stereotyped. "I love teaching and I want people in the slum to have a job," says Poo, whose class now gets booked a month ahead.

Poo's class begins at Talad Khlong Toei, Bangkok's biggest downtown fresh market and the slum's public face – a reminder of how much the city relies upon its most marginalised. Round-the-clock, teams of chatty fishmongers cleave innards from carp, while Shan butchers with balletic grace slice whole pigs into pan-ready cuts in minutes flat. Through the mud, porters haul produce from trucks to stall and then off to the customers' tuk-tuks and refrigerated hotel vans.

Earnest cycling tours and street photographers venture deeper. Cynics diss that as 'slum porn,' but witnessing Bangkok's underbelly stirs the conscience. Beyond the soccer stadium of Port FC, the roads narrow into shadowy lanes then unsafe dead-end paths, where visitors are advised to bring an escort by day and to avoid by night. Kids play with broken toys amid the discarded syringes of spaced-out single parents, as grannies in old-fashioned camisole blouses sell vegetables to feed the family.

Residents dub their liminal community a city ("Nakhon Khlong Toei") or even a continent ("Thaweep Khlong Toei"); indeed, they're Antarctica to the condo-owners of south Sukhumvit who don't like their district name being Khlong Toei. At its heart, a grid of lanes clamp around unsluiced inlets called The Locks. The bleakest favelas skirt the docks, refinery and railway. Space is wherever you can find it. Ramshackle huts teeter on stilts over the stagnant canals, huddle under expressways, or spill right up to the rails. Khlong Toei means 'Pandanus Palm Canal', but the reality is less fragrant: an olfactory overdose, soured by the refinery's chemicals, sweetened by burning meth.

Slum life is grim, yet well organised, run like a hamlet in Isaan. Given the city's neglect, each slum depends on the effectiveness of their *loong pratan* ('uncle leader'). They announce news over loudspeakers – the fire watch roster, reminders to vaccinate – and assemble residents at the football-cum-basketball yard for merit making. "Khlong Toei people like to help each other, the opposite of snobbish rich kids," runs a line by 19TYGER x H3NRI, one of the slum's outspoken rap bands.

The surprising liveability of slums like Khlong Toei comes from village values of self-reliance, ad-hoc solutions, solidarity and sheer persistence. Residents build their own tiny houses of found materials, a colourful patchwork of scrap and election boards, with furniture home-made from shipping crates. Households craft knick-knacks from used cans or bottles, while seamstresses darn clothes at sidewalk treadle machines. Informal workers who keep the city ticking – vendors, drivers, maids, guards – live among its 100,000 densely-pressed souls.

Infused by their rural roots, slum-dwellers keep up traditions more than the bourgeoisie. At Wats Khlong Toei Nai (inner) and Nok (outer), locals dance around the *bot* at ordinations and trudge anti-clockwise at cremations. Nowhere in town will you see more kids with top-knots. Tying a lock of hair gathers a child's 32 *khwan* (bodily spirits), whose waywardness causes illness – a hint at how much slum kids get sick. Others turn to Kasem, a *medium* who does faith healing at his red home-shrine.

"When you get up in the morning it often feels like a village, and you can smell washing powder as children are getting dressed in white shirts for school," says Anji. "By eleven o'clock it gets really hot, it's smelly, there's sewage and rubbish everywhere and you can just

see the depressed looks on the elderly. There are a lot of disabled and sick people sitting outside their houses. Then by evening there's a lot of fighting and yelling... people hitting tin walls."

Thai slums aren't as extreme as those that blight Jakarta or Manila. Close-knit neighbours don't tend to steal from each other. Yet to maintain harmony they may socially accept people who push pills. For several NGOs, drugs is the prime concern, along with shelter and schooling. Two have been mythologised through the undaunted character of their figureheads, dubbed Father Theresa and Slum Angel.

Father Joe Maier, an American priest to the Catholics who ran the slaughterhouse, founded the Mercy Centre. Filmed in Jeanne Hallacy's documentary *Mercy*, it provides schooling, micro-credit and practical help. Pupils who've left for good careers often return to help their own grassroots. Father Joe pens homily-style articles in the *Bangkok Post*, prompting expats to donate, volunteer or adopt orphans.

The 'guardian angel' of Khlong Toei, Duang Prateep, was a local girl evicted from her slum in 1974, who became an educator and created Thailand's first slum foundation from the winnings of her Magsasay Prize, Southeast Asia's Nobel. Visitors can see videos and get shown round its many projects, from nutrition and deaf schooling to women's welfare and dealing with chemical fire victims at the Port.

It was Khlong Toei Port's need for stevedores in 1962 that birthed the city's biggest and oldest slum. Other shanties soon clotted around the railway at Makkasan, near factories in Bangkapi, wherever hired labour. Suspected arson has ousted several slums from prime real estate, but depite fires ahead of port extensions, Khlong Toei slum survived.

Shanty dwellers have progressively been rehoused, often willingly. "I'm happy here," says Tui, 37, while buying packet noodles at a corner shop by a football pitch. A burly day labourer, he rents a shack for a thousand baht a month. "There's not much crime, but I'd prefer to move out. I'm afraid of fire and I don't want my children to get into drugs."

Authoritarian rule sides more with tidiness and developers, expelling slums to blocks far from their livelihoods. Evictions soared after the 2014 coup, with canal encroachers wiped from Khlong Lat Phrao. Democratic rule tends to upgrade slums with drainage, paving and plumbing under schemes like Ban Mangkon. A model success at Bang Bu kept the folk together, whilst landscaping the canal as public space. Fires gives landowners the right to retake a property, so burnt-out slum-dwellers and NGOs race to re-squat the site, negating the rare chance to plan. Yet a fire in downtown Suan Plu resulted in rehousing on site in a safe, healthy mix of dwelling styles.

"Khlong Toei is so tough. There are so many special interests," says an expert in slum rehousing. Local mafias object to the vulnerable getting stronger, politicians oppose rival initiatives, loan sharks loathe micro-credit, pill dealers rely on its demand for *yaa baa* and its supply of runners willing to risk all for some cash. Even well-meaning NGOs would have to confront their raison d'être. "Lots of people stand to lose if Khlong Toei becomes an upgraded community integrated with the rest of the city."

Plans from 2019 aim to turn two-thirds of the port area into a "smart community" and "business city" mega-project for mixed use, such as river tourism, by 2035. About 13,000 households would be rehoused into towers nearby, or plots of land in Minburi. That would atomise social life, separate workers from their work, and make it hard to store carts, or make the goods and food they sell.

The end of Khlong Toei slum would extract the taproot of Village Bangkok – yet still leave 690 slums. The cycle continues. Thailand has been registering roughly three million foreign migrant labourers, a plurality of them lodging in Bangkok, many in temporary labour camps. These cubicles of sun-baked corrugated tin – often stacked double with elevated gantries – have been moved out of the construction or demolition sites, where infants used to toddle amid the debris. Their crews shuttle to and from work standing in the back of trucks. Tin towns are now more prevalent in the suburbs. In distant Khlong Samwa district, outside labour makes up eighty percent of the Kaeb Moo (Pork Crackling) community. Bangkok always keeps its marginal people at the margins.

far left & above: In the daytime, slums are mostly inhabited by women and children.

near left: Shacks squatting at the railside in Khlong Toei port.

Market
From stall to mall to app

This city known for markets is turning into a city known for malls. Both indoor and outdoor shopping flourish in this supremely capitalist capital, which panders to anyone's fancy, with malls that offer celebrities as your personal shopper, plus assistants to carry your bags. Even mall-blessed Singaporeans fly here for long weekends to stock up on bargain clothing at Platinum Mall and crafted homewares at Chatuchak Weekend Market, as the savings pay for their trip. With each class defining themselves through consumption, what's most on display in this citywide 'shop window' is Bangkok society itself.

We may be hitting peak retail. A 2015 count found 31 major malls on a rail line with just 25 stations, just as street vending got pushed from the main roads, and shophouses get replaced by towers. Despite the rise of online shopping, this remains a world-class marketropolis.

Nevertheless there's still a *talad* (open-air market) for every trade, from amulets to antiques, DJ decks to dried fish. Hawkers busy the pavements like in no other world city, and turn any occasion into a sale. Temple rites spawn fairgrounds. Indie festivals treat designer stalls like art installations. Trade Fairs aren't just for wholesale buyers; but offload last season's lines on public days. In addition, vendor subcultures build community bonds. Napoleon called England a 'Nation of Shopkeepers;' well, Thailand is a 'Nation of Stallholders.'

Trade spirals through Bangkok's DNA. The customs post of Bang Makok grew into an entrepôt with a market for each ethnicity's speciality trade. Commerce began in this swampy delta with floating markets (*talad nam*), which spread onto land in wooden pier arcades (*talad bok*), where amphibious Thai vending met Chinese mercantilism. Sampeng was the port and market hub for a century, retaining many bazaars as time capsules from the era when each street had a speciality.

Commerce prospered within Rattanakosin's walls, too, at Tha Tien, then Banglamphu. Markets filled the route to Chinatown via Pak Khlong Talad's produce halls, Lang Krasuang military outlets, Ban Mo's electronics backstreets and Pahurat's Little India. And that's just the market core; strings of street traders link countless *talad* in a citywide lattice of retail.

Markets always contributed much of the city's chaos. In a response that still reverberates, the dictator Phibunsongkhram applied his orderliness policy to trade. He turned temple fairs into markets to disseminate modern products. He herded old town vendors into Pak Khlong Talad seafood market, to form a central food wholesaler. And in 1948, Phibun founded the Weekend Market. It filled the newly civic space of Sanam Luang – with intervals at Saranrom Park (1949-57) and the Defence Ministry (1957-8) – until moving to State Railway land in Chatuchak in 1982, to make way for the Bangkok Bicentennial celebrations.

Chatuchak grew into the world's biggest market of its kind with around 12,000 stalls attracting a quarter of a million people each weekend. Chatuchak got a boost in the 2000s from the Thai design boom, but creative items spread elsewhere. Controversial sections also declined; the looting of heritage sites made trading antiquities risky; animal rights activism purged the pet section of rare species, cockfights and caged songbirds, before a fire in 2014 imolated thousands of its anmials. Chatuchak's content is now more predictable. The traders' after-market party vibe depleted too, with Viva bar an echo of that carefree era.

Chatuchak is torn between the wild market spirit and the tidy mall mindset. Attempts to enclose all or part of it have failed since first proposed in 1995. The outdoor character has prevailed, with vehicles banned, but the stalls have been hemmed in by hulking concrete blocks that are not fully let with stalls. Instead, their forecourts are colonised by traders of bric-a-brac, such is the need to be near the customer.

In a climate that deters exertion, strong social values of *saduak* (convenience) and *krengjai* (consideration) make things easy – or, as many Thais admit, lazy. You see this habit when taxis and buses halt at the exact spot a passenger hails, regardless of blocking traffic. This explains the constricted paths in markets, and the intention behind why wares jut out to slow down passers-by. The hubbub shields those sampling goods without being too obvious, which is doubly true for knickers, or illicit wares like knock-off Viagra. But vendors do get to know regulars, building trust. Some even exchange faulty fakes.

Bangkokians also like shops to come to them. Mobile shops prioritise the relationship with potential buyers over consideration of pedestrians or road users.

Bearing the shopper's burden takes its toll on the roving pedlar, who in blistering sun has to haul around rattan chairs or charcoal braziers. From age 15 to 45, Umpai Promporn has lugged 70 kg of plastic tubs for 12 hours a day. "In order to survive in this job, you need a fighter's mindset. You also have to be patient. I work in the heat, the cold and the rain. It was very hard during the floods," says Umpai, whose 20% commissions have built him a house in Kalasin province. "The flexible hours mean I have the freedom to rest when I'm tired and eat when I'm hungry. I like what I do, and I do it well."

Roving pedlars seem the freest agents, but conform to hidden patterns. Many work for a wholesaler boss. Their quirky shirt or straw hat is a uniform. Like any sales force, they're allocated a territory, ply a rival patch at their peril, and face the wrath of *tetsakit* (municipal inspectors). "We have to be quick runners,

left: On Khao San Road, some shops will buy from and sell goods to the area's backpackers.

above: Chinese-Thai shopkeepers keep the city supplied, from shops like this in a Chinatown lane.

Heart 237

below: **Patpong Night Market stalls get set up in precise sychronisation with whistles.**

bottom: **An entire noodle restaurant packed into a trolley in a paragon of efficient design.**

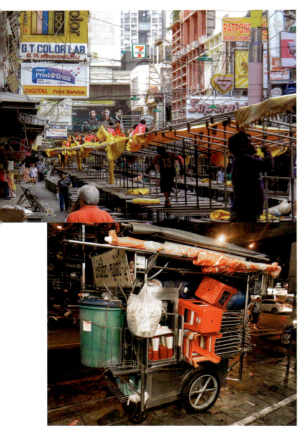

Market folk live, work, and sleep out of sync with white collar workers. "Every day I wake at 5 am to prepare the ingredients," says Nuanla-or Sripila, who sells fried bananas on Convent Road. "I come here at 7 am and start cooking. I'm sold out by around 3-4 pm. Every couple of days, I go by tuk-tuk to buy my ingredients at Khlong Toei Market." Khlong Toei is busiest at 3-4 am, when morning traders buy and prepare their goods, then sell them, before going to bed in daylight. Night vendors rise late, prep in the afternoon then sell till late evening. Perhaps a million Bangkokians work such odd hours, each shift re-infusing the city's streetlife around the clock.

Managing supply, prep and stock takes skill, strung out between pre-dawn market, production-lines at home, and a tiny sales space. Vendors fit their entire shop into a pushcart, which is a lesson in efficient design. Hawkernomics used to require everything to fit in a boat so as to float between house, piers and markets. In the late 2000s, designers took notice of these ad-hoc innovations and TCDC held an exhibition on the ingenuity of push carts. Stalls whizz by on the road, with motorbike sidecars packed with stools, woks, tubs, bottles, folding tables, gas tanks and ice box – all tessellated like puzzle pieces.

At Patpong Night Market, like most markets, the vendors' battered metal chests the size of a kitchen table are stacked in lock-up garages. Vendors heave them into rows down the private road, assemble scaffolds and stand upon the long plywood trestles ready for the 5pm whistle. At that signal, they all flop yellow canopies over the tubular frame within minutes, in a finely calibrated drill. Reversed after midnight and repeated six nights a week, Bangkok's re-packable markets are a model of informal precision.

so they don't catch us when they are out on patrol," says Charoen 'Ang' Rungreung. He sells boxed meals along Silom Road with six relatives, in a vest uniform they designed. "We don't have a proper stall because it is so old-fashioned to just sit and sell stuff. Instead, we directly approach the customers. Call it a guerrilla selling strategy."

Street trading may look chaotic, but it's allocated to the nearest square inch and priced to the exact *satang* (penny). Many bazaars are run by the Markets Organisation of Thailand, the BMA, private enterprises or as spinoffs from malls. Vendors tailor their wares to specific customers over an agreed schedule, inside marked slots. In prime spots, vendors rotate through multiple shifts with finely tuned changeovers. Many vend part-time around family or other jobs. *Talad nat* (appointment markets) repeat at set times, whether by daily, weekly, monthly or annual schedules.

The traders themselves form subcultures. Old markets were bound into their *yaan*. They sold the wares of local trades and supplied the community or ethnic enclave with its traditional foods, goods and ritual paraphernalia. Many are fading. "It was once a close-knit community where people knew one another," says Chaivuth, who's lived and sold tea leaves for over 60 years at Pak Khlong Talad, which has been turned into touristy Yodpiman Riverwalk. As decentralisation removed residents and workers from Rattanakosin, he has seen those ties loosen. MRT stations here and at Chinatown have hastened the city's oldest markets' slide from authentic workaday use into tourist traps.

Talad Nat

Bangkok's stallscape may appear a free-for-all, but vendors occupy set sites at specific times to suit the needs of that period. *Talad nat* (appointment markets) repeat by day or night shift, office lunchtimes, weekend, month, season or year. In prime spots, vendors rotate through the time slots with finely tuned changeovers.

Talad nat are windows on subcultures. Tailored to niche customers at optimum hours and low prices (typically ending in 9), they respond to changing taste and suit Bangkokians' attention span. Traditional markets barely alter, which charms tourists and heritage buffs, but can bore faddish locals.

NIGHT MARKETS
Whole streets sprout stalls after dark. Phetchaburi Soi 5 serves the area's cheap student dorms. For a kilometre flanking Ramkhamhaeng University, Talad Na Ram caters to students and a suburban hinterland. Almost as long, Talad Huai Khwang sells gear for the nightlife workers of Ratchadaphisek, from revealing gowns to wigs and plastic crowns. Talad Saphan Phut 2 (moved from the Bangkok side of Memorial Bridge to the Thonburi side), is a hangout for low-income youth.

WEEKLY MARKETS
Talad Chatuchak famously draws 200,000 visitors between each Friday night and Sunday dusk, but it has another weekly rhythm. Each Wednesday it fills with wholesale plants and trees. Wat Suan Kaew teems with weekend treasure hunters sifting through its donated second-hand goods. Talad Rot Fai (Railway Market) and its retro hipster rivals run each weekend night. Floating markets used to be held at high tides around new or full moon, but at touristy ones close to Bangkok, they're now weekend attractions.

SEASONAL & ANNUAL
Traditional festivals and *ngan wat* (temple fairs) always set up fairground stalls. Curated hipster sales like Great Outdoor Market and Art Box recur a few times through the dry season, while annual music festivals – Noise Market, Big Mountain and Wonderfruit – design themed markets for artistic goods.

WORKDAY MARKETS
Week-day lunchtimes see food, housewares, cosmetics and budget officewear sold around corporate towers, famously Silom's Talad Soi Lalaisap beside Bangkok Bank, and Talad Loong Perm (Uncle Perm) behind Thai Airways' HQ, which like the nearby Jay Loong store brims with 'duty free' brought in by air crew. Prannok Market, by Siriraj pier, catches Thonburi-bound commuters and visitors to Siriraj Hospital.

FOOD MARKETS BY MEAL
Different food vendors relay according to meal: *oliang* coffee and doughnut carts at breakfast give way to lunchtime noodle stands, then curry tray tables at dinner, *khao tom* buffets for midnight feasts, and 3 am fuel food for those on nightshift. Mobile restaurants unpack for certain mealtimes, while fixed markets like Chokchai 4 are common at commuter nodes, where staff serve at tables under awnings or pack take-aways for *mae tung plastik* – 'plastic bag mothers' on their way home from work.

Beliefs matter deeply to traders. On their cart or display case, traders place garlands, *yantra* diagrams and talismans, especially *nang kwak* (beckoning ladies) or *palad khik* (phallus charms). Some pat their display with the first banknotes earned that day. Of Chinatown's two adjacent fresh markets, Talad Mai (New Market) flourishes partly due to its lucky shrine, while Talad Kao (Old Market) is losing custom due to its road being broadened. "Making it wider could cause money to flow or fly away," a feng shui expert explained to historian Suthorn Sukphisit. "A narrow, constricted path like Talad Mai prevents money from being able to go anywhere."

As *yaan* dissolve, one bond is to trade together. Vendors, en masse, form urban villages. Despite rivalries, they support one another, bring family along, and socialise over food, drink or games, while some watch TV on their phones. This sociability extends to the mall, which has taken over the role of meeting point, eating place and entertainment hub. Malls are platforms for group togetherness, where urbanites can express their modernity in a space that's air-conditioned, so their look is more composed.

At first glance, Bangkok has too many malls, but each has its own target market, aimed at a particular class. *Phudee* grandees and *hi-so* arrivistes prefer the minimalist, thinly-peopled luxury of Gaysorn and Central Embassy. Mid- to upper-middle class remain loyal to Central Chidlom, Emporium and its twin EmQuartier. Siam Paragon has tourist presence, and a world-class aquarium, while its sibling on the Khlong San riverside, IconSiam, is mostly for sightseers. Affluent youth gravitate to Zen, Siam Center and Siam Discovery, the latter two winning awards for their artistic design. The broad middle frequent Esplanade, Amarin, Seacon Square, Paradise Park, and branches of Central and The Mall Group, with its youth hanging out at SiamSquareOne and Terminal 21. Lower middle class scour for bargains at MBK, Union Mall, Robinson, and Imperial World. The poor rely on *talad nat* markets, and splash out on a family trip to budget hypermarkets: Carrefour, Tesco-Lotus, Big C.

In Siam Paragon, Bangkok got its flagship mall, which links to four others and the main BTS interchange at Siam. A popular meeting place with Instagrammable lobby, it has uneven custom, with most crowds in the cinema, middle-brow chains, and the basement's dining zone. "We have figured out Siam Paragon," quipped *Guru* magazine. "It's a place where rich people go to fashion shows, middle class people go to eat and working class people go to escape from the heat. But we're still not quite sure who shops there."

Paragon innovated by selling investment condominiums in the promotional space and putting car showrooms on the technology floor, but not just any cars; we're talking Maserati and McLaren. To show off the valet-parked Mercs and luxury vans, the front of the car park has a spangled blue epoxy floor that glitters. But as Paragon is frequented by middle-class strollers, true elites promenade in Emporium, where a gloved attendant proffers supermarket trolleys that are painted gold.

Bangkok's haute-materialism had begun in the late 19th century with aristocrats appropriating European fashions to prove they were civilised. As the elite's cosmological legitimacy began to fade, they projected rank through luxury goods, which let money become the path to prestige. Industrialisation wrought a class of Sino-Thai nouveau riche known as *hi-so*, who ensured that their shopping was seen to be done. Magazines filled their front pages with photos of *hi-so* partygoers posing at product launches. Unlike in the West, where 'exclusivity' means restricted access, these events are held on a mall concourse, merely roped off in pens so all can see who's been invited.

The old hierarchy lacked a place for white-collar metropolitans and the lower-middle class, so those in-between groups pursued a way of being Thai in town: mass consumerism. They differentiate themselves from the masses by aspiring to that tantalising *hi-so* lifestyle.

right: **At Bangkok's most gilded mall, Emporium, a gloved attendant hands a gold-plated shopping trolley to a gold-braceletted shopper at the luxury Food Hall.**

below left: **Bunny ears were the theme of the moment at an iconic mall that has been ranked as the most Instagrammed place on the planet: Siam Paragon.**

"Middle class Thais don't have traditional culture," says cities expert Pitch Pongsawat. "Their identity is constructed: by consumerism, by media, by themselves."

Malls get maligned as anodyne, but their bland placelessness acts as a blank canvas for 'urbanistas' to invest in a hip identity, which might be rungs higher than their true background. One branded item can transform a basic outfit bought from *talad nat* markets or budget malls. A Twitter influencer was scorned by social media when he posted his state discount card for low-income people after years of posting selfies with pricy accessories. He pleaded that using his looks to hawk branded goods was a precarious job earning minimal cash to pay bills. Posing as a jet-setter had been too convincing.

A prime preoccupation of youth is *dern len* (play walking) in hip places like Siam Square or Talad Rotfai (Train) Night Market to graze on food, take photos, or buy cute accoutrements. Terminal 21 mall caters to *dern len* by selling trinkets and affordable fashion amid selfie-props like a London bus. Even the toilets are themed, so you can pee in what looks like a tube train or Zen garden.

In a break with seniority, middle-class culture is propelled by youth trends. The first pop culture district was Wang Burapha, where the early department store, Nightingale Olympic, still has stock from the time when rock was young. The fashion scene moved east to Ratchaprasong, which remains the heart of retail. Where today stand the budget malls Big C and Market, teens clamoured to ride Bangkok's first escalator at the Japanese store Thai Daimaru that opened in 1964, dine at the Wimpy hamburger joint, stroll the boutiques in Ratchadamri Arcade and lining Soi Kesorn (today's Gaysorn Plaza). Nearby Siam Square was opened in 1970 and became the heart of youth fashion in 1973 with the launch of Siam Center.

Malls metastasized during the 1980s-1997 Asian Tiger boom, with the gargantuan World Trade Centre (remodelled as CentralWorld) and suburban Goliaths like Seacon Square and Fashion Island, which both opened in 1995 as the 3rd and 5th biggest malls on the planet. The 1997 crash burst that bubble for a while. Anti-materialism became a cause for radical bohemians, puritan Buddhists and defenders of tradition, who advocated the Sufficiency Economy. An official code of Thainess railed against "living above one's status," but Bangkok intensified its pursuit of status objects.

"The greatest new social change ushered in was the new political philosophy of Thaksin," wrote Brian McGrath. "Thaksin made shopping a national duty at all levels of society." Stoking domestic demand has continued whoever's in power. Bangkok usurped Singapore's Orchard Road with 'Ratchaprasong Shopping Street.' Rival mall chains compete to attract elite foreign brands, whilst the twice-yearly Thailand Grand Sale hawks the capital as one giant discount market.

Monohoods

Bangkok has dozens of quarters devoted to a speciality trade. They derive from settler skills, whether wrought metal, chiselled wood, wove baskets or baked desserts. These often began as ethnic enclaves, like the Satun gold leaf pounders in Banglamphu or the Cham silk weavers in Ban Khrua whom Jim Thompson hired.

The Chinese handled so much commerce that Sampeng became, like Hanoi's 36 Streets, a lattice of one-trade *sois*. Each dialect group cornered a sector. Before the 1997 crash opened up the economy, you'd cross town for one particular widget. Traffic congestion was a factor in Chinatown's decline, but now its MRT station has put at risk the fragile core of Chinese cultural crafts around Soi Plaeng Nam.

Demand and standardisation requires bigger production and distribution, so experts diversify or die, while bland one-stop-shops service mass tastes. Yet the monohood idea continues in specialist malls, with Fortune Town full of tiny shops competing in digital goods, cameras and hi-fi. Browsing a row of rival shops keeps prices low, service eager and merchants keen to stand out with better goods, though some brazenly copy or collude like cartels.

Foodies love to sample delicacies from knots of rival vendors: Southern Thai in Prannok, chicken rice in Pratunam, and from day-trips to get river fish from Chachoengsao, or palm sugar treats from Amphawa.

Malls have illusory 'choice' among chains, so it's fun to get all variants in one place. "This is where people go looking for anything related to sports," says Canteen Malakanok, who's run Parrot Sporting for 30 years near National Stadium. Ekkachai Jaruesilp, frets that his shop lease is up: "We don't know when Chula [University] is going to take the land back. It's sad that developers tear down old communities instead of trying to preserve them."

Craft villages tenuously survive with fewer makers, like the bronze bowl forge at Bang Bu. Since the old town prison became a museum, the shops on Thanon Mahachai selling basketry woven by prisoners have dwindled to three, with rattan now an imported material and the market narrowed to new year hampers and decor items. "Who will take over the shop?" ponders Sunanta Suapattakul, shopkeeper of Yuphadee Wanich. "Our children all have good careers in companies."

Viable trades can reconvene at a more sustainable location. Wholesale veg vacated Pak Khlong Talad to Or Tor Kor and Talad Thai. Plant nurseries decline at Thewes and Ekamai but flourish at Chatuchak and Bang Bua Thong. Carpenters of various old *yaan* had been relocated from the old town to Prachanaruemit, where teak gateways brand the mono-hood anew. "They have everything here so I can finish all my shopping in one day," says customer Uthumporn Hengsirisakul. "Prices are good because they have to compete."

There is solidarity at Wood Street. "We have a rule to let customers pick the shop. We even share work sometimes when we can't deliver a big order on time," says Daeng Meeyod, 63, owner of Daeng Kan Chang for 30 years. "Our work is all handmade, very detailed and made to the highest standards. We're actually the most expensive, but we're the best." In a globalising city of increasingly generic goods, Bangkok's monohoods provide niche products with a personal touch.

above: A playful take on monohood goods in the guide *aLoud Bangkok*.

top right: A typical *pak soi* scene at the entrance to Sathupradit Market.

Retail also diffused from the centre. Suburbanites found that they could hang out locally at such complexes as Mega Bangna or WestGate in Bangyai. Thai malls conform to Reilly's Law of Retail Gravitation, that shoppers frequent the largest mall they can reach with ease. The spread of condominiums led to the trend for small, semi-outdoor 'community malls.' Meanwhile, convenience store chains like 7-Eleven displaced the friendly mom 'n' pop general stores.

Part of why the capital's so unlike the hinterland is that it had housed almost all bourgeois Thais, to the point that 'Bangkok' is a shorthand term for 'middle-class.' So they felt miffed when the former peasantry aspired to their lifestyle, buying pickups, dining at MK Suki and asserting their voice. Lately a boom in provincial cities is spawning an upcountry middle class who go to their own malls on the model of Bangkok. Worldwide, the democratising of luxury goods has diluted the cachet of formerly exclusive brands, but in Bangkok it diluted the cachet of formerly exclusive people. It's harder to tell status if anyone can buy a fake 'Louis Vuitton' bag.

America's proverbial 1% own half of that country's assets, but 46.5% of Thailand's wealth belongs to just 0.1%, who all live in Bangkok. However, most people here don't couch that differential in terms of economic justice, but by Thai values of rank, prestige or karma for being a 'good person.' "Thailand is not characterised by a class system… It is more of a status conscious system," wrote columnist Thanong Khanthong. "Any Thais, from whatever background or race, can rise to the cream of society." Social position is relative to each situation, and so status rises with age and can shift due to job, income or qualifications. That fluidity depends on where you start, privileging surname, connections and patronage.

There's no escaping the moral connotations of having *thana* ('financial status'). Symbols of *thana* – car, clothing, jewellery, a villa in Thana City estate – get collectively nicknamed with the English word 'furniture.'

"*Furniture* can open a lot of doors, and can get you respect and status," one shopper told Sophorntavy Vorng in her study, *Status City*. "Like wearing a badge saying, 'I can afford this.' It's kind of tacky, but it's true." So a market has emerged for *hi-so* to borrow their IWC Pilot Chronograph or rent their Dior

dress. Students have been known to sell sex for a Birkin bag. The most brazen bling gets dissed as *krer* (stained), so prestige is moving back to preferential service, from privilege card memberships to concierge bank branches, styled like airline VIP lounges with free drinks and bank tellers literally kneeling at the customers' feet.

Some elites get too used to brandishing their *furniture*. A young TV host Acharanat Ariyaritwikol won notoriety for road rage when his BMW Mini collided with a motorcycle. After repeatedly punching the biker in the face, the host forced him to *graab* (prostrate) on the road to his dented Mini, sparking online outrage and the hashtag #graabmycar.

As the middle-class taxpayers wield more clout, they mimic elite attitudes. 'Thai People Against Street Vendors' is one of the anti-hawker Facebook pages, getting 20 times more 'likes' than the 'Support Thai Street Vendors' page. It calls for a boycott, fines for shoppers, and condemnation of pro-vending advocates. Krisadakorn Puangput posted this about the litter at Huai Khwang Night Market: "While many people are so proud of street vendors and regard them as the identity and beauty of Bangkok, if they are so mesmerising why don't you place them in front of your house?"

Who hawks what where – and for how much – depends on competing powers. The pavement is a blur of jurisdictions: the landowner; a sub-letting lease-holder; the shop that gets blocked; the BMA's inspectorate; the police; the boss of any vendor group; and gangsters who protect that patch, having carved up public space into fiefs. Some stalls persist for years, even generations, in a symbiotic relationship with the shophouses they front, sustaining streetlife on both sides of each path.

above: **At events, so-called 'pretties' present goods like Shark energy drink.**

left: **Thai fashion label Fly Now III is famous for its fantasy animal mannequins.**

below right: **Online shopping is denting the retail malls.**

bottom right: **A vendor on the Skytrain with a tray of rice desserts in folded banana leaf.**

Many Bangkokians feel attached to vendor culture, but want it to be more orderly.

"I'm worried that the permission for street stands might be revoked in the near future," says Convent Road banana vendor Nuanla-or. "We all have our names registered at the district office, yet the authority is pretty strict. The sanitation unit comes quite often, municipal officials too. Sometimes we have to pay them a little something like a 'cleaning fee,' but I don't want to talk about it. It's sensitive."

In Bangkok's freewheeling hawkernomics, the law is a late intruder, so regulations act less as a rule than an extractive tool. Notoriously, hired thugs smashed up stalls at disputed sites in Sukhumvit Soi 10 and the original Train Market. "With law enforcement nearly non-existent… people with influence moved in to collect 'rent,'" writes journalist Wasant Techawongtham. "These could be *thetsakit*, or men in uniform or, as we learned from news reports, city councillors."

Often sub-letters co-opt lots of stalls to re-let at many times the contractual rate. Rent inflation can make stalls as pricy as a shop, only without air-con or good utilities. Many lessees charge 'key money' to take over their market stall or shophouse, which is effectively paying off the debt of someone's failed business before you can rent a tenancy. Affordability drives vendors to colonise public space, where their pleas to earn a livelihood confront those for walkable pavements.

"Reclaiming public space," was the rationale of the NCPO junta's crackdown on informal enterprises, with tens of thousands of vendors evicted. Earlier governors had been flexible, but Sukhumbhand Paribatra used troops in evicting Chinatown's 40-year-old Flashlight Market, against resistance by its 2,300 vendors. Many of Bangkok's estimated 300,000 hawkers then joined forces in the Network of Thai Street Vendors for Sustainable Development, which has negotiated with some success.

Lax enforcement has led many vendors to assume rights they didn't have. The BMA even evicted 16,000 stalls that had licenses in the 600-plus legal zones. New rules limit a stall to two square metres, leaving a metre width for pedestrians, on penalty of a 2,000 baht fine. "It felt like we were struck like lightning," said Nimit Kaewkrajang, who had legally cooked noodles at Lat Phrao junction since 1984. Another legal noodle vendor being forced out with his seven staff after 20 years, Banyat Sanguansittikul, doesn't know what else to do. Farming's no longer an option and a replacement site offered in Pinklao is unfeasibly far away.

Hawkers migrate to any open area, whether forecourts, parks, bridges or walkways, but this crackdown feels like a pivot point, mirrored in many Asian cities. Downtown and tourist areas have so many competing needs for ever more valuable space, so prime areas will likely stay more formalised. Other measures against the informal sector like cashless transactions and shifting markets onto private land like mall forecourts enable tighter control and broader taxation.

Bangkok's format of tiny stalls and shoplets has acted as a petri dish for young creatives. After all, the Chang Beer tycoon, Charoen Sirivadhanabhakdi, is the son of a food vendor. This multi-pronged campaign against the informal sector funnels spending that was widely spread towards a few corporate behemoths, whilst removing competition from thousands of family businesses and making it harder for startups.

"Street vending is not just a lifestyle but a cultural phenomenon that cannot be made to disappear at the whim of the powers-that-be," wrote columnist Wasant Techawongtham. "Most of us in Bangkok depend on street vendors for food and affordable goods. Without them city living would not be possible for the majority of low-income people; in fact, the city could not have been developed to the degree that it has."

Street market habits don't cease when Bangkokians enter air-conditioning. Malls launch with broad empty concourses, but they soon get cluttered with sales booths, promotional stands and penned zones of discount clothes. Then aisles clog with rummage boxes and till counters get festooned with knick-knacks. The market impulse moves indoors, stopping the flow with racks, bins and mannequins. MBK got so taken over by stalls that this cramped market format became the mall's permanent character.

Bangkok's addiction to ever-bigger malls bucks a global trend, where physical stores are going out of business as online shopping takes their trade. Digital retail is another way to bring the shop to the customer. Delivery avoids schleps through debilitating traffic, but inefficient shipment may add to the congestion. Malls are turning into social and dining centers, but that role is also going virtual, through social media and food delivery.

Online retail is dominated by foreign apps like Lazada or 11 Street, which threaten to suck up spending that previously went to countless thousands of independent stallholders, shops and even the major chains. They could gut a vast sector of the economy and countless livelihoods. Thailand lags in the technical prowess to devise competitive apps and e-platforms.

Meanwhile, like stalls in the street, social media has become colonised by freelance hawkers. Instagram influencers promote their preferred products, while scantily clad models flog lotions and gimmicks. Ordinary people buy stock, promote it on Facebook, LINE or Twitter, then upload postal receipts to instill confidence. It's a wild frontier, and several celebrities got in trouble for advocating untested body products.

One appeal of hawking via social media is the personal contact. Unlike with corporate malls or anonymous e-commerce tick-boxes, customers can chat with sellers, who often sit on their floor stuffing envelopes with product. It's a flashback to the familial intimacy of the shophouse and the market auntie who knows your regular order.

In a reverse of the social scale, middle-class Bangkokians are becoming stall traders, selling upscale wares as part of the makers' movement. As brands and malls become samey, curated night markets offer a sociable and select way to shop, and be noticed by your peers buying just the right statement goods.

Whatever the retail venue, Thai identity is shaped by where you shop and what you're seen buying. Bangkok is more than a market economy; it's a market culture.

Youth
Seniority, fame and fights over hair

Bangkok gets most of its energy from the old. The vibrant streetlife comes less from skateboarders or street-corner dudes busting out dance moves, than from informal trades run by "aunties" or "uncles." Elders speak loudest, make the decisions and guide taste. While juvenile delinquents do brawl and race bikes, hellraising is more the domain of *nakleng*, the muscle of hierarchical mafias. Nightclubs for youth get curbed, and are barred to teens, while there's less restraint on the raunchier nightlife that's aimed at mature men.

Young Thais had long been unpolitical. Most Red and Yellow Shirt protestors of 2005-2014 were veteran 1970s students. Then the seniority-minded coup of 2014 sparked a backlash led by the disaffected youth.

Developing Asia frets about getting rich before it gets old, but Thailand dawdles in response to its ageing society. By 2040, just half of Thais will be of working age and elders will outnumber youth 8:3. So Thais must get more productive just to stand still. A scarce resource can gain leverage, but reformers talk of empowering youth precisely because that's not how the gerontocracy thinks.

Within living memory of today's elders, Bangkok was a fully traditional society. Modernity intrudes, but core values – karma, seniority, emulating masters – all steer youth to retread patterns of the past. In the West, parents and grandparents often subsidise their kids'. Here, young adults must subsidise their parents so much that it's hard to pursue their own path. Ageism in the West consigns over-50s to the scrapheap, whereas Bangkok practices ageism against the young.

Tradition relies on uncritical transmission of old ways through rote learning, rather than critical thinking to find fresh ideas. *Dek* (children) became *phu yai* (adults, literally 'big people') not via a freewheeling interval discovering themselves, but by conforming to social initiations (ordination, conscription, student hazing, marriage) in a cycle of supposed harmony. Modern pressures to loosen that grip provoke vehement backlash; after all, today's old expect payback for their own earlier sacrifices.

Far into adulthood, *wairoon* (teenagers) still get controlled through their hair, whether in school, monkhood or military. Youth is all about hair, from body hair that signals sex hormones to the styling of coifs to align with the fashion and music of their emergent identity. Grooming is so core to Thainess that unapproved hairstyles (or clothing) get scolded as if threatening national security.

In cultural notices about how to behave, children are shown wearing topknots. A rarely-seen relic, that ancient hairstyle was thought to bind the soul's 32 wayward *khwan* (spirits) via a scalp shaved except for one, two or three patches of long locks that get tied into buns or pigtails. Childhood ended with the cutting of topknots, girls at 11, boys at 13. Dozens still get sheared before dawn in a rite each January at the Brahmin Devasathan temple, their severed topknots dropping onto a lotus leaf cupped in their lap.

Monkhood requires the shaving of not just scalp, but eyebrows. Men were not deemed 'ripe' or marriageable until ordained, often

left: **Cosplayers gather at Japan Festa in Siam Square.** above: **Schoolboy busking Isaan music near Siam.**

at 20. The seasonal farming that allowed for a three-month monkhood during the rains retreat has declined upcountry, while in Bangkok, taking the robe is largely a parent-placating gesture lasting just a few days, often put-off due to study or earning money. Job contracts allow a one month ordination, and over a year for conscription, which enforces a crew-cut, a style that in 2017 was further shortened to have fully shaved sides.

The annual lottery for military service is a cliffhanger for males of 20 who didn't do cadet training at school. The draw can be delayed due to study or sporting prowess, with some exemptions like being transsexual. In 2015, the Thai-German heartthrob Mario Maurer submitted to the bare-chested exam and picked the black dot, but many *hi-so* boys seem to avoid the whole draw, let alone pick the dreaded red dot of conscription. The 18 months lost from a conscript's career is less about learning skills than doing drills. Scandals often erupt over conscripts becoming servants to officers.

Elders, who feel it did themselves no harm, bristle at criticism by the young, who "haven't yet bathed in hot water" (are immature). "The (over-)zealous control of students' head, hair, face, dress and more, is all about prohibition," writes blogger Kaewmala. "Perhaps these people are oblivious to the new reality. Today's Thai youth are rushing headlong into the 21st century, only to be pulled back by the hair."

Adolescent subcultures, as George Melly put it, "revolt into style." Not here. *Wairoon* can't break the Thainess mould, so they adopt foreign pop style (and hair) – mod fringe, punk mohawk, emo spikes – but without the original's rebellious tone. Death-metal Thais are more sweet than scary, hiphop gangstas rap politely, and 'indie' kids are not so independent. The fad for Japanese cosplay (costume play) is giggly, without the bleak Japanese *otaku* (isolated nerds). The late-2010s saw the franchising of idol bands, with BNK48 copying Japan's AKB48, as identically did Jakarta's JKT48 and Shanghai's SNH48. Even during the indie movement (1994-2010), Bangkok pop has excelled at costume play.

Thai teen tribes flower during democracy, but wilt under authoritarian rule. Youth culture here is curiously un-modern, perhaps because it favours fads over fundamentals. Youths face serious issues, from bullying to lack of recreation, yet their few advocates get suppressed. Most teens bear their burdens as meekly as their subculture plumage.

Youth movements require spaces and time, which are not just lacking, but deliberately curtailed. Besides hours spent in commutes to class, kids are expected to run errands and provide company to elders. State and family discipline instil duty, but the school system so fails to prepare pupils for university entrance exams that pupils must spend their salad days stuck with tutors. There's little left over for hobbies, play or personal growth – and few venues for exercise or self-expression.

"Youth culture is inexpressive and bland because it's still under surveillance of school, parents or state," says Saran Mahasupap, editor of Thai slang for Apple's Siri. While the West embraces youth lingo, Thai gatekeepers resist anything not bestowed from above. Even the idiom for cutesy fawning for approval, *ab baew*, was rebuked by an elder statesman for being coined by juniors. "In Thai tradition, children need to be obedient, as in the saying 'follow adults and dogs won't bite you.'"

Uproar greeted a tweet by Suthita Chanachaisuwan, 19, a singer and Thammasat student: "*Heng suai* [lousy] country. In 50 or even a 1,000 years, it won't become developed. Shoot me! We can't even make buses and vans come on time…. I would be willing to work hard and pay higher taxes if daily welfare would improve." This stung guardians of Thainess, who condemned her as ungrateful.

Suthida had gained fame by placing second in Thailand's version of *The Voice*, and her nickname is 'Image'. Polls of youth reveal that the prime career ambition is celebrity. What seems like a flimsy dream may be rather practical. Ordinary entrants to the workplace have their prospects blunted by cronies with connections and the eviscerating grind of the seniority system. The informal economy is precarious. So teens such as Image seek a shortcut to success through fame in Bangkok's celebrity industrial complex.

A production line of singer-dancer-actor-models has kept talent studios busy since the 1980s. Many parents take their babies to model agents, then enter toddlers into pageants. Malls at weekends mix promotional sales with star-turns by kids, from B-boy spins to K-Pop routines. Classical dance roles used to be assigned to body type – lithe hero, spry monkey – but that's harder as kids grow plump on junk food and sedentary lifestyles.

Reality TV widened the paths to stardom. An aerialist from Cirque du Soleil, Rajanikara Kaewdee, won Thailand's Got Talent and put his winnings into a studio where young Thais can learn to twirl upside down on red ribbons. The genres and Reality TV formats are not homegrown. Teen taste drives the economies that most influence Thais: Korea, Japan, Britain, the States. Pop culture is soft power, but seniors doesn't like empowering youth in shaping Thailand's image.

Soft power reflects hard power. Western rock captivated *wairoon* during the American ascendance from the 1960s to the 2000s. When economic heft seeped from West to East, indie rock lost ground to the softer pop of Japan, Korea and China. Comparisons of Siam Square to Harajuku in Tokyo predate the cosplay boom. In the early 2000s, its lanes witnessed weekend promenades by 'fruits' – teens in outlandish outfits who recorded and spread their looks via cute photostickers.

The photography studio CHEEZE On Street took teen modelling aspirations to agent-level through its catalogues of street fashion snaps and talent events. Bangkokians then became extreme exponents of the selfie. Now girlfriends have their boyfriends photograph their begowned postures at hip locales.

Fads imported by the public flit by; fads imported by the state get stuck. Schools enforce a century-old imported style: boys dressed like Scouts and girls in sailor suits and bob hair. Uniforms must be worn outside, too, as it represents the honour of the school.

Regimentation doesn't stop at childhood. This is one of only five countries where undergraduates must wear strict uniform. Though faculties differ and some universities like Silpakorn allow creativity, even private ones like Bangkok Uni comply. While socially levelling, uniform shows the militarisation of Thai life – plus it's lucrative for designated outfitters. But dressing adults in schoolwear has unforeseen effects: a Japanese poll ranked them as the world's sexiest student uniforms.

Teens try to subvert the rules. Stalls stock blouses sized XXXS, which lift the bust and flash the navel. Hemlines creep above the knee. Boys with shaven crewcuts can gel the 5 cm top into a quiff or peak. Regulation belts don't fit the diversity of people, so teens fasten the long end at the back with a bulldog clip. Girls choose flowery coloured clips, while boys use big black bulldog clamps to slim their knapsacks. It's like the whole culture is bound in a standardised belt that youth find their own way to tighten.

Youth culture appears more prominent than it is because the BTS centres on Siam Square. Its warren of *sois* and arcades, became a teen hub in the 1970s, and since the 2000s it's been where people went to seek the pulse of young Thailand. Yet lower-status teens feel out of place among the affluent students and fashionistas, lacking the right pose or the cash to dress '*in-trend.*' After the burning of Siam Theatre's arcade in 2010, the landlord,

left: Breakdancing on the MBK/BACC Skywalk.

above: Only five countries compel undergraduates to wear uniform, seen here at Silpakorn University.

Heart 249

Siam Square

"I am Siam" read posters of a skateboarder claiming his domain. Styled after art by Gilbert & George, this series of youth imagery in Siam Centre mall struck a chord. *Dek Siam* (Siam Kids) identify that Siam Square's maze of boutiques, venues and cafés really is their realm in a city with scarce room for youth – even if the area actually bans skateboarding.

"Siam Square is like nowhere else. It has a feel and atmosphere that you can't get from malls," says Premsiri Tarasantisuk, 29, shopkeeper of Pony Stone. "Most of the stuff comes from young designers or small brands so you can be sure your shirt won't be mass produced." Its flexible formats – from 2x2 metre booth to shophouse to Siam Centre boutique – have been petri dishes in which start-ups with minimal capital could grow a business with *sanuk* names like Burger Queen, bad.outfit.today or Kinky for Homosapiens. Many top creatives fledged here, from Whitespace Gallery and the shop-turned-art-hotel Reflections to the clothiers Issue, AbNormal and It's Happened to be a Closet.

Siam Square is not an open square, but a grid of sois built over a slum in 1970 by Chulalongkorn University, to tap income from its affluent students. Three iconic cinemas (Siam, Lido and Scala) then drew *mod* kids from Ratchaprasong and took off. Later came the British Council, Hard Rock Café and tutoring schools by DaVance, The Brain and transgender educator Khru Lily.

By the time its BTS central station opened in 1999, 'Siam' was so iconic it had its own media, websites and radio station. Riding the boom in Thai pop culture, it alerted Asian and Western trend-spotters to where Thai youth tribes happily mixed. "It's very Shibuya," says Pim Sukhahuta, a fashion designer with Sretsis, name-checking the nexus of Tokyo pop. "There are a lot of places hanging off the trends."

It peaked with the 2007 film *Love of Siam*. Not only was it set there, but *wairoon* accepted the daring gay subplot because it declared a wider liberation: meek *khun noo* (little mice) daring to express themselves in their own urban space. "All in my generation love Siam," says Pasaraporn Mongkolrueangrawi, a returnee since junior high. "It's a place that holds special memories, especially for those who went on a date here."

In its free zine, *You Are Here*, a girl called Air wrote: "No other places could compare. It has surpassed the state of being a 'place' to a 'community.'" It's heart in the 2000s was Centerpoint, a plaza with a stage ringed by stalls intended as a 'safe space,' where *dek point* (Centrepoint kids) were protected by *roon yai* – older boys wielding seniority. Although *dek point* dressed up only at Centerpoint, moralists feared a slippery slope to debauchery and forced its closure. Two efforts to relocate Centerpoint failed.

The spell had burst. Rent hikes soon priced out the cheap shoplets that were its lifeblood. Lifestyle change doomed cinemas and photo studios. Its safe reputation was harmed by Red Shirt and Yellow Shirt protest occupations, during which teens got used to suburban hangouts like Tawanna and Union Mall. Amid the 2010 crackdown on Red Shirts, arson of the Siam Theatre block saw it replaced by a mall, Siam-One, styled as a ramp to the BTS rather than to nurture a scene. A few survivors like Inter restaurant and the music shops DoReMi and DJ Siam have also since faded.

"Siam Square is no longer the epicenter of youth; it's become a hub for young professionals," reflects Saran Mahasupap, who's spent most of his life there, while studying at its Triam Udom School, doing a BA and MA at Chulalongkorn, then working from his laptop at its Starbucks. "The only youth heritage left there is tutoring schools."

Just 15 percent of Siam denizens were adults in the 2000s; now students are diluted by tourists, who outnumber *wairoon* in MBK mall's shoplets. Chulalongkorn has institutionalised the whole area, erecting tall buildings and two parks, one in Siam, another in Samyan, once a student hood of dorms, stalls and *manga* rental shops. Chula demolished the sublime Scala cinema, but made Lido a youth arts venue, opened Siam-Ganesha Theatre and made Samyan MitrTown mall a hub for youth, LGBT and art film fans. Siam's Saturday concerts are now bigger than at Centerpoint, but more formal.

London's Covent Garden still trades on soft power from the post-punk creative seedbed that it sold out to chainstores. Now Bangkok sells Siam's youthful identity just as it dulls its teen buzz. Pop culture tourism is a thing, from clubbers to foodies. Yet when young visitors seek out their Thai counterparts they find Bangkok stifling its own Harajuku, in the same way it promotes streetfood whilst evicting its curbside cooks. Siam's former flowering of informal youth expression has been corralled into what's approved. One street fashion promotion featured telling signage that declared, no longer "I am Siam," but "I am Siam-ish."

Chulalongkorn University, hiked the rents and redeveloped arcades into malls. Pennywise teens drifted to nearby Suan Luang Square or suburban hubs, like Union Mall in Lat Phrao.

Pitch Pongsawat, who teaches urbanism at Chula, assigned students to note the diversity of people in city locales. Almost all chose places around Siam. "*Everyone* goes to Paragon," reasoned one student, while Pitch pointed out that "everyone" might exclude the majority. "If I walked into the malls, the fancy people would look at me strangely," Kwan Khetpratum, a 20-year-old docker from Khlong Toei, said in an article on inequality. "I've never even thought of going there."

Poorer Thais also avoid *hi-so* bars, while young bourgeois, especially sheltered young women, view club scenes outside their circle as "scary." The cute-obsessed fans of saccharine Thai pop known as *luk krung* (city kids), contrast with fans of alt rock, who tend to have rural roots and affect an outsider stance. The latter's refuge was the Saphan Phut night market, until it was evicted by the junta in 2016. Now Saphan Phut 2 Night Market, over the bridge in Thonburi, reeks of the orderliness that the scruffy youth were escaping.

Hardscrabble youth find solace in *lo-so* defiance. They're fans of 'badboy' and 'badgirl' singers, like the band Lo-So, whose anthem 'Mai Dai Pai Pantip' is a rousing twin of Elvis Costello's 'I don't want to go to Chelsea.' Its maverick leader Sek Lo-So riles polite society, but to factory workers in peri-urban zones like Bang Pu, he's their guitar hero.

Lacking their own venues, *lo-so* youth forge their identity on the fly. Many zip on their mopeds to suburban night-markets that grew out of a bike accessory flea market at Ratchada. Most such bazaars are short-lived, while the Railway Market on Srinakharin Road got touristy, but still offers used clothes, free bands and outdoor bars.

Other informal hangouts include *luuk thung* shows at temple fairs and concerts held on open ground, like the car park of Big C hypermarket on Ramkhamhaeng Road. There in 2017, the singer Lamyai drew notoriety for singing Techno folk songs while twerking in a gold bikini. After getting scolded by the junta leader, she scaled back her "nine level" twerking to just three thrusts at a time. Then just 18, Lamyai drew sympathy for having supported her family since her preteens, a not-untypical burden.

Across the world, student districts are vibrant into the night, like Schwabing in Munich or Fitzroy in Melbourne. But Thai laws ban bars near places of education, so after 8 pm Siam Square and other campus areas fall flat. Innovation needs a critical mass of young people to cross-fertilise ideas, but that requires vibrant nightlife, as Singapore research found.

"The music scene suffers because the authorities are too afraid of letting teenagers in," says Nita 'Amp' Dickinson, co-founder of dance-music venues Café Democ, Club Culture and Culture One festival. "In many Western societies, teenagers are only barred from buying alcohol, but not from clubs. Here, they have to wait until they are 20. It's too late for them to build a musical identity by then as most clubs just play the same old pop or covers."

Similarly, cinemas and bowling rinks are confined to malls, and priced more as a treat. Internet cafés were put under curfew over fears about video games, which just sent gaming onto smartphones, while board game cafés have only nerd appeal. Movie fare is tame, with 20+ ratings on a censorship scale that extends to soap operas, though TV is also losing its sway over shaping new adults.

"Youth culture has no epicenter anymore. The new space to fulfill youth identity is online," texts Saran, noting how social media is affordable for poorer kids. Due to online games, dating apps and streaming, many teen venues become unviable. "Instagram is a simple space to share their looks and it's easy to become famous there. The number of ♥s is way more important than acceptance in real life."

above left: "**I am Siam**": A Siam Center slogan shows how youth identify with Siam Square.

above: "**I am Siam-ish**": A promotion at Siam Center hints at the ambiguity in Thai fashion and identity.

Defenders of "family values" fear their authority eroded by *dek mee panha* – problem kids. Today's elders, raised under dictatorship, prescribe duty, not resources for arts, hobbies, or fitness. "Our government has never put teenage development on the agenda. Everyone seems to forget that children are the future," says Praphaiphun Phoomvuthisarn, a teen mental health expert. "Why not provide a place where they can do things together? The private sector offers singing contests, talent shows, dancing and beauty contests. It's good, but there's not enough variety." Amid a lack of pools, pitches and courts, Shma landscape architecture firm builds local recreational spaces in their WePark project. "Youth don't have many places to explore things they love. They want to express themselves, but parks close at 6 pm and clubs won't let them in," notes Amp. "That's why there are so many *dek waen* [motorbike racers] on our streets; they don't have anywhere else to go."

Due to an ageing population, nurturing the potential of youth is urgent. Thai education has among the world's highest budgets per head, yet among the worst results, mainly due to rote learning, and punishment of critical thinking. As most *wairoon* tend to be meek and unventuresome, onlookers wonder if the aim of education here is to raise little nationalists. Besides the fetish for uniforms, boys and girls must attend flag-raising and anthem singing at school assembly, which is effectively a parade ground. Children's Day, held each January, invites kids to try military equipment and most years its motto stresses duty.

Further education has expanded fast, with hip new universities and established ones like Silpakorn or Thammasat spawning extra campuses, but most are ranked low internationally. Graduation day is a jamboree of peer-group cheerleading and gifts of teddy bears in mortarboards, but also a choreographed ritual. The ceremony requires multiple dress rehearsals to perfect the correct posture to receive the degree certificate from the royal patron's hand. The photograph of that moment takes pride of place in any Thai home.

Rup nong (student initiation) involves rebuilding the personality through hazing. Rites-of-passage involve costumes, showmanship, group songwriting and bonding games, but often ordeals to instill hierarchy. I've witnessed seniors order three dozen male and female students to lie on top of each other in the rain, nose in crotch or crack, three bodies deep. Most years a *freshie* dies from hazing, but it persists as many deans support its slogan 'SOTUS': Seniority, Order, Tradition, Unity, Spirit.

Aping military initiations, SOTUS began at Chulalongkorn, where *rup nong* is mild: dress-up, stand-on-one-leg, sing saucy new lyrics to the freshie song 'Kai Yang' (Roast Chicken). "It can be heaven or hell," recalls Tay, an alumnus. "We were often told how to behave. If we do something wrong then Chula gets on the front page." The prestige of the institution requires all to uphold its position. The constructive result of *rup nong* gets showcased each January in the cheerleading at the annual Chulalongkorn vs Thammasat University Football Match.

left: **Dek waen rev their bikes while racing around on Loy Krathong night, with their dek sakoi (trophy girl) riding on the back.**

right: **Straight Outta Khlong Toei: A star of slum rap, 19TYGER, poses with bling rings on the Khlong Toei rooftops, so close to downtown, yet socially so far. "You said we're slum people, we're uneducated, but we're human as well," goes his trap hit** *Khlong Toei*. **"Don't look down on us for what we do." Photo courtesy of Cindy Gibier**

T-Rap

Youth subcultures revolve around clothes, hair and music. Many say Thais only adopt the look not the attitude, but music has fuelled young Thai rebels: country-blues in the 1970s October Generation, then alt rock in the 1990s Indie Movement, and now rap in the nihilistic era of social division.

In the US, hip-hop went mainstream from the alienated margins. The opposite happened here. Hip-hop spoke for alienated youth only after it was a pop fashion of back-turned caps, untied sneakers and outsize sportswear. Rap Thai's earliest stars won fame with humour, notably Da Jim and Joey Boy. The biggest rap act were Thaitanium, a US-raised trio with a polished gangsta stylee. Their anthem with Da of Endorphine, 'Mahanakorn' (Metropolis), extols Bangkokian exceptionalism in a lush riff on 'Empire State of Mind' by Jay-Z and Alicia Keys, which reveals a 'Bangkok State of Mind'. Here's a flava:

"It's Bangkok City. There is nowhere the same as our city. / ...Bangkok boy right here (yeah), born and raised. / Grew up at Phahonyothin 11, played at Saphan Kwai. / Studied at Raewadee, cycled around grandma's house. / On Saturday evenings we wai to Buddha. / Thainess cultivated in the heart of a small child. / My dad is class 8 from the Military Academy. / But I'm an artist living by song and dance in Bangkok city. / ...I represent for my city, I'm proud of my city..."

Hip-hop overtook Techno as the top music style in 2018. "Our lessons in school include writing poems," says DJ Kritsada Vadeesirisak of the Thonglor nightclub Beam. Rap chimes with old bantering song styles like *lamtad*. "So when there's a rap contest we are easily engaged, as writing rhymes clicks with the culture." Rap became the voice of the disaffected and spread into the chattering vocals of the Isaan folk music, *molam*, which tells of love amidst migrant labour struggles. Rap also inflected the death metal that provided catharsis to youth at festivals like Demonic. Goths in mascara and ripped black jeans headbang in the mosh pit to the thrash bands Killing Fields or Anarthipathai (Anarchy).

Corporate pop is inherently meek. It was punks and rappers who broke the taboo of criticising authority. First, punks let dissent rip at a concert where several were arrested, including the band BxSxSxSxD (Blood Soaked Street of Social Decay). "The Thai punk scene in the past has only cared about partying," said one of its managers. "I organised this event because I think punk should be rebellious. I care about freedom and rights."

That clarion call gained world fame in the 2018 hip-hop phenomenon, 'Prathet Ku Mee' (What My Country's Got), by the Rap Against Dictatorship collective. "The country where artists pretend to be rebels," zinged one of its lines, while most of the lyrics recounted a litany of political abuses as the camera spun round a recreation of the 1976 lynchings. The police threatened arrest, but as its video viewership sped to 100 million, the authorities relented. Its likes outnumbered dislikes by 10:1. Young protest rappers suddenly spoke for an angry mainstream.

Then emerged a posse of slum rappers with face tattoos, 'straight outta Khlong Toei', whose lives really are like gangsta homeboys:

"I'm the kid from Khlong Toei. If you think you're better than us, come here and fight to beat us," rap 19TYGER X H3NRI in their sombre 'trap' style hit 'Khlong Toei'. *"Don't look down on us for what we do. / Don't blame us as terrible people. / We were born in a slum – a land of waste water. / You think we're poor? You'd better watch yourself."*

Many Bangkokians wish slum rappers were less angry and spoke good things about the slum, but the rappers' anger is really about social attitudes:

"Khlong Toei people like to help each other, the opposite of snobbish rich kids. / You said we're slum people, we're uneducated, but we're human as well. / I'm sick of being looked down on like this. / I'm happy as the poor, at least we're not politicians with big corruption."

Their migrant parents had their hardship tales retold in *luuk thung* folk songs. Now their city-born kids rhyme their hardships through T-rap. "I feel like Khlong Toei is the equivalent to Compton [LA's hub of gangsta rap]; the area may look rough, people see it as the drug hub of Bangkok, but there are gems hidden inside," says Elevenfinger. At just 17, he founded the rap contest 'This Is Khlong Toey Compton', partly to track down his rap-loving half-brother, who was taken upcountry by his late mother's family. Elevenfinger also set up a 30-strong rap club at his slum school, where rap star Young Ohm was his senior. "There are a lot of talented kids in Khlong Toey who want to tell their life stories... things that are considered 'dangerous' to talk about. Things that people don't want to mention."

Heart 253

"If I didn't attend the cheering activity while my friends were being tortured, I would have felt selfish," says Tasinee Tantiwitthayanggoon, 18, of King Mongkut University of Technology. "I felt that I had developed closer relationships because we went through hardship together." People get referred to as "my senior who looked after me." Such bonds shape life choices, hiring and who holds power; several coups were plotted by academy classmates. *Rup nong* builds extrovert leadership, but it goes deeper than US fraternity and sorority clubs or British 'Rag Week' larks. SOTUS embodies the ethos of the National Culture in which *sen* (connections) spin a web of patronage.

Kids also owe *bun khun* (social debt) to their parents, which they repay through earnings and deference. Obligation extends to grandparents, and out to aunts, uncles, elders, doctors and teachers, then scales up to *phu yai* and monks, with abbots titled Luang Phor (holy father) and generals *mae tap* (mothers of the troops).

Inequality is hardwired into Thai language. No pronoun can be equal; one must be senior. The second twin to emerge must defer to the first as *phi* (elder) and forever be the *nong* (junior). Sibling terms also apply to friends, colleagues, peer groups and service staff: *nong* for a waiter, *phi* for an expert. Criticism is tantamount to ingratitude as the country is envisaged in familial terms rather than abstract law. The King is "Father of the Nation", with the birthdays of King Bhumibol and Queen Sirikit (on December 5 and August 12) still designated Father's Day and Mother's Day.

In 2019, pictures of parentless kids crying or putting a garland on an empty chair at prostrations in school on Mother's Day led to a change.org petition to end the decade-old practice. Many decried the trauma from such public regimentation of private life. "Thailand, especially the Ministry of Education, is holding on to the outdated ideal of a 'perfect family'," wrote columnist Atiya Achakulwisut. "This simplistic version of a mother-child relationship… may end up setting unrealistic expectations. The public worship of mothers is increasingly becoming irrelevant to growing numbers of people."

As conservatives see the state in terms of filial piety, they're alarmed by parenting trends. Some quote the proverb: "A mother can take care of ten children, but ten children can't take care of their mother." A UNFPA survey from 1987-2013 revealed that nuclear families have declined from 52% to just 26%, with only a third living in extended families, and 1.34 million single parents, plus LGBT parenting too. Around a third of Thai children aren't raised by parents, staying with friends or relatives during school, or being sent by Bangkok parents to a rural childhood with grandparents. Hence many kids get reared not with their parents' modern outlook, but by rural values dislocated from urban realities.

Waves of moral panic surge as Bangkok develops and goes *inter* (international). "Our youth are forced to stay a step behind the *farang*," noted the prime minister and literati MR Kukrit Pramoj, back in 1970. "Now some people are thinking of forbidding young women to wear mini-skirts – not realising that Thai women began to clad themselves in Western dress not by consent but by submission. I know it leads to feelings of despair and confusion." Skip to 2007: actress Chotiros Suriyawong was ordered to make a public apology and do community service for shaming her university by wearing a skimpy ball gown. Skip to 2017: police scoured the Songkran festival after a ban on skimpy outfits amid the water games.

The Ministry of Culture, nicknamed MiniCult for its sermonising against modernity, conducts

"teen-watching missions to internet cafés and Ratchada [nightlife zone]," revealed Ladda Thangsupachai, the first director of its Cultural Surveillance Bureau. She blamed "pernicious and toxic elements of adolescents." Its half-million volunteer informants include high schoolers recruited to "culture camp" with the aim of forming a school morality club.

This righteous rearguard reports offenders to police, writes policy and "disseminates information as a means of providing immunity against cultural mutation," Ladda told the *Bangkok Post*. Such mutation included computer game cafés, the now-banned video chat site Camfrog, and "tendencies to turn up at movie theaters in tank tops and to class in uniforms which are too short and too tight [that] can stifle breathing and lead to sex crimes."

MiniCult blacklisted 18 classic songs with titles like 'One Woman, Two Men', and 'A Step-Husband', including two by National Artists. The songwriters retorted that the lyrics were sarcastic realism rather than calls to promiscuity. "If not stopped, this attitude will infiltrate the whole of society without warning," admonished decency crusader Rabiabrat Pongpanich, whose first name means 'Regulations' and whose husband became Culture Minister in 2023. "Children and young people are especially vulnerable to the songs." Finally they banned three: 'I Fear No Sins', 'I Do Fear Sins' and 'Big Flabby Buttocks.'

Wairoon are now so aware of global norms that many shrug off the moralising as dated. "Many officials criticise youth culture, just like the media discourse that it's something bad or deviant," says pop culture expert Viriya Sawangchote. "It is the duty of the authorities to defend Thai values, but it does not affect the lifestyle of normal people."

In a breakthrough for realism, a 2013-15 TV series 'Hormones Wai Wawoon' (Agitated Generation) showed disaffected teens facing issues like gangs or coming out. It was the first Thai series shown on cable and online too – gaining it fans across Asia. "The characters are largely based on the lives and thoughts of my case as well as other teens we interviewed," says producer Songyos Sugmakanan. They smoke, they drink, they get pregnant. "Some adults will be shocked to find out what happens in our society. Many parents believe they can protect their children by prohibiting, but kids always find a way round the ban. I believe the best protection is understanding."

left: **Indie music includes few harsh styles, but there are small subcultures for hiphop, death metal and the occasional Thai punk.**

below: **Music at school means not rock bands, but military-style brass marching bands, for events like this ordination in Wat Benchamabophit.**

Conservatives counter new ideas by fostering so-called "immunity," through indoctrination and co-opting of youth media. A programme called MoSo – concocted as teen slang for "Moderation Society" – turned out to be psy-ops by the Internal Security Operations Command.

The 2014-23 junta decreed that kids must memorise '12 Core Values.' These include: 'Gratitude and obedience to parents, guardians and teachers' and 'Discipline, obey laws, respect elders and seniority.' The youth group Education for Liberation of Siam protested it as "thought control over students," said its leader Nathanan Warintharavej, 17. "Without pondering about diversity, they scornfully look at juveniles as an empty container into which they can press any ideologies."

Deferring to seniors does however seem to leaven the happy-go-lucky character of Thais – though *sanuk* declines with power. Lack of responsibility has other effects, too, notoriously in driving and safety. Much depends upon the few patrons taking wise decisions. It's been proven that more diverse input improves decision-making, but when the young or the masses voice their opinion, seniors seethe.

"The entrenched seniority system is our curse, invisible but omnipresent, and it exerts great power in preventing the young from saying an adult is wrong," wrote columnist Kong Rithdee, about how in 2018 an intern, Panida Yotpanya, exposed a cabal of officials stealing the welfare budget from the poor. Before the public lauded her courage she was initially punished. "That's exactly the nub

of our young-vs-old trouble… but it would be premature to believe that the young can actually bring about real change. The voice of the young is suddenly treated as naïve, inexperienced and 'manipulated' as soon as it's the progressive voice."

School rules on hair and uniform still rile. One teacher so furiously cut a girl's hair to ear level that she slashed off an earlobe. Even tying a bow got penalised by docking academic marks, revealing the educators' priority. A 10-point manifesto for a 'Student Hair Revolution' gained support in 2009 via the teen webboard Dek-D. Uniform reform was led by the secretary of Thai Students for the Thai Education Revolution Federation, Netiwit Chotipattanapaisan, who shocked many in 2013 by saying on TV that he was "sick of Thainess". While a freshman at Chulalongkorn in 2017, he was voted head of the student body, but after protesting seniority rites, he was deducted points and barred from office.

In response a 2019 amendment to the Child Protection Act criminalised dress code infringements like short schoolgirl skirts, punished by fines or imprisonment for parents. Also outlawed are students joining groups that cause "public commotion" and behaviour vaguely defined as "inappropriate."

Mocking that stereotype, the activist group Bad Student staged performances that go viral online, like tying a schoolgirl to a chair in public or wearing identical masks to recite the Thai alphabet, replacing its nationalist code words with critical or progressive words.

Media has made youth harder to ignore. "Teens dare to think and try new stuff," wrote Air in the print zine *You Are Here*. "Almost every teen magazine is stuck with the image of yesterday's teens, with the accent of adults who want to control and lecture, which is so darn wrong." Social media then accelerated a generational shift, giving a platform to creative youth, with influencers becoming the new role models. Those who grew up in the more open society of 1992-2014 don't have their elders' nostalgia for martial order and feel cheated by the patronage system. Aware of advances abroad, young netizens turn to entrepreneurs with a civic conscience, like architect Duangrit Bunnag or Ruangroj Poonpol, who founded Disrupt University. When Duangrit delivered his *Bangkok Manifesto* at BangkokEdge Festival in 2016, he was cheered by a hall full of young fans. It's the same at TCDC's symposia and workshops, when young creatives cram in and ask probing questions. Bangkok youth does have energy; it just hasn't been unleashed.

With the hashtag #youthofbangkok, images of 30 change-making Thais were fly-posted in the streets as well as in galleries and campuses in 2014. They weren't a guerrilla protest at the coup, but fashion ads for Greyhound's teen label Playhound by *Elle Men* magazine and the artist Napat Sutithon. He called them "silent leaders" who've awoken to the generational shift. Mandarins would be too staunch to admit it, but firms must be realists. "These individuals are representative of our hectic capital through their life choices and unspoken understandings of cultures," Playhound proclaimed. "They might be nonchalant about Bangkok, but, unknowingly, their combined energy is what makes the city throb and thrive."

Youth protest culture

Rebellion often comes from youthful idealism, yet Thai students had since 1992 been dismissed as apolitical – until the youth led protests of 2020-22 shocked the Establishment by broaching taboos.

The rival Red vs Yellow demos of 2005-14 were run by veterans of the 1970s *phuea chiwit* (For Life) student cause. Thai rebel style had got fixed in their hippy-era youth, blending Western counter-culture's long hair, blues, leftist poetry and agitprop art, with Thai farmer's indigo moh hom shirts and cowboy gear. Pubs like Raintree and Tawandang Saad Saen Duean (Red Sun Beneath Ten Thousand Stars) still feature revolutionary icons, converted cart furniture, buffalo skulls and defiant ballads.

When those Octobrists reached high positions in the 1992-2014 democratic era, their openness enabled the indie scene to emerge. Having few venues, alt culture flared at music festivals (Indie, FAT, Happening, Big Mountain), where the DIY arts and handmade books critiqued social issues.

Juniors raised under democracy felt anger at juntas taking their freedoms. Most protests against the 2014 coup were by youth, who got arrested for acts like reading George Orwell's *1984* in public or raising the three-finger salute from the *Hunger Games* movie, a gesture of defiance across the 'Milk Tea Alliance' – a camaraderie with youthful protestors in Hong Kong, Taiwan and Myanmar.

Music had been dissent-free for decades, then a burst of nihilistic punk and trap hip-hop vented the lack of hope. "The whole world is moving on, but we are still stuck," lamented Mhee, drummer of Blood Soaked Street of Social Decay (BxSxSxSxD), who saw the Internet as a space for youth. "Young people have always been interested in politics, but now they have a space to convey what they think, so other people can support their opinion."

The Rap Against Dictatorship (RAD) song 'Prathet Ku Mee' (What My Country's Got...) went viral in 2017, with lyrics scathing the system amid video images of the 1976 massacre. Censorship had the 'Streisand Effect' of boosting its online views past 100 million.

In 2020, mass protests erupted upon the abduction of a young exile and dissolution of the Future Forward party, which had voiced youth ideas. Covid rules and junta bans on dissent shifted protest culture from long occupations to flash mobs on specific topics that spread online as memes.

The students and young professionals were joined by many high schoolers. Their pop references let to rallies themed on Harry Potter or the manga hamster Hamtaro. The floating of inflatable rubber ducks on blue water-cannon sprays inspired other blow ups of aliens or dinosaurs, depending on the target of mockery. Their declared goal was to reform the system "within their generation."

Despite the crushing of protests through force and the courts, Thai youth had changed politics and society. Parties across the spectrum now court the youth vote that helped Move Forward to win the 2023 election, with young candidates and policies that youth Thais care about like jobs, facilities, LGBT rights and breaking the monopolies.

Two crucial changes underpin this generational divide. Young Thais can compare internationally online, while masses of them have travelled abroad and witnessed things that Thailand lacks. Many resent the mediocrity that stems from favouring connections, seniority or corruption over quality. Naturally those who've gained through those methods fear being measured by standards or popular consent. Yet the young have grown up amid the online norm of ratings, polling, reviewing, complaining and campaigning. The fact they can't do that freely offline fuels discontent.

Disillusionment got so high in 2022 that the top hashtag was #yaiprathetthaiganteu (leavethailand), with netizens posting their preferred countries. Some talented Thais have left for better prospects, though things became more optimistic under an elected government, despite the winning party being banned. The divisions have plainly not been healed by subordination to the past, which only widened the gulf, since the focus of the youth is so resolutely on the future – their future.

top left: **Mo-So was a faux psy-ops military program to 'immunise' youth.**

top: **Schoolgirls raise the *Hunger Games* salute.** Photo Vinai Dithajohn

left: **The activist group Bad Student performed readings of the Thai alphabet, swapping the letters' old code words for progressive words.** Photo Prachathipatype

Creative City
Arty citizens and bohemian scenes

Bangkok is a crossroads on 'The Bohemian International Highway' – a term coined by arts psychologist Eric Maisel for the flows of creatives linking hip hangouts like Lisbon and Medellin. Long a bolthole for misfits, Bangkok now beckons the trans-national ranks of designers and chefs. They encounter both international Thais and local Bohemians, who since the 1990s Indie Movement have transformed the cultural landscape. This creative class grapples with how to express the city's *genius loci* – the talent of this place.

Bangkok lacks a full sense of itself. Locals see it as a great city in terms of business, state power and landmarks. Anything cultural gets put in terms of Thainess, an ideology that's all about ancestral stuff rather than its own metropolitan brio. Such static values can't explain this *Bladerunner*-esque noirscape of tower-high LED billboards jostling ten-thousand stall markets.

Bangkok provides the stimulation required for creativity, but less of the calm needed for productivity. Noise pollution and visual incoherence bombard our senses. Formerly a cheap and freewheeling hideaway, Bangkok is getting pricier, prudish and ultra surveilled. Currently Bangkok is in a sweet spot between those extremes. All boats are rising as business wises up to the tide of creativity.

Into the tug between tradition and modernity, championing Bangkok's unsung qualities has for two decades been a mission of artists and designers. They've managed to eclipse the city's notoriety for sleaze, instability and fakes. Already by the mid-2000s, a London woman, when told I lived in Bangkok, didn't blurt out the usual lurid innuendo, but exclaimed: "Oh that's a design city, isn't it?" Indeed, Bangkok was among Asia's best for interior décor and quirky fashion, if not quite the mooted 'Milan of Asia.' An emergent presence in film and host of at least three art biennales, the city ranks among the global cream in advertising and hospitality, with Michelin-starred restaurants confirming its claim to be 'Kitchen of the World.'

Arising independently, this movement was given focus in 2005 by Thailand Creative and Design Centre (TCDC), a semi-public resource that relocated a decade later from Emporium to the heart of the Bangrak-Khlong San Creative District.' An independent initiative, the Creative District brings together galleries, urbanists, riverside businesses and local communities in a project that feels a bit contrived, but has brought keen international exposure that built on its momentum. Some accuse it of hyping gentrification, though it engages with locals and has a resident outreach scheme to solve local issues, called 'Co-Create.'

Having a 'Creative City' has been seen internationally to vault a country into the big league. Singapore researched in the 2000s on what it takes to attract innovative industries, but smarted at the results. It turned out you can't have Creative Cities without tolerating not just disruptive ideas, but the nightlife and sexual liberty demanded by arty provocateurs. Creative drive is an appetite, inextricable from sensuality, transgression and a thirst for ideas. In short, visionary seedbeds need to be open, cheap and naughty.

Singapore semi-loosened its prudery, and built the region's best theatres, galleries and museums, which host festivals of global calibre. Meanwhile, many Thais hope to emulate Singapore's controlled modernity, but their efforts have blunted their own existing competitive edge. Bangkok already led the region in sexual liberty and late-night allure, while its artistic ferment produced award-winning film and advertising. Plus it had other Bohemian draws: cheap rent; loose social control; ease with eccentrics; and an under-rated popular culture to explore. Yet the policy response was moralism to appear *siwilai*.

It's hard to measure a cultural value. In the 2015 Global Creativity Index, Thailand came a lowish 82nd out of 139, and behind Singapore, Philippines, Malaysia and Vietnam. It ranked middling in tech, education and LGBT freedom; but low for talent, tolerance, and ethnic openness. Yet within Asia, Thailand gets lauded for its creativity – more fun than China, more adaptable than Japan, more varied than Korea.

Creativity covers wildly differing things. Bangkok does excel at playful homewares, emotional soap operas and extrovert flair. Yet given the *mai pen rai* laxity, won't be devising 5G robotic gizmos. Quirky, impromptu charm nurtures fewer high achievers. And those who do gain global fame gain little acceptance back home. Bangkok's zing comes from its street-level cauldron of incompatible tastes.

Bangkok faces a 'Culture vs Creativity Dilemma.' Top-down centralised decisions preclude bottom-up consultation. Seniority trumps competence. Censorship and propaganda disable open communication. Patronage undermines partnership by denying individual initiative. Compulsory Thainess does forge a genteel national style, but smothers regional variation, indie subcultures and contrarian innovation.

The taboo against mixing status level – 'sky high, ground low' – crimps creativity. Just as temple murals show a hierarchy (with deities at the top and descending via angels, senior people, then low commoners to demons), media designers must layout social pages according to the status of who's depicted.

The arts have always been used here for moral instruction, where symbolism matters more than creative license. In that ancient cosmological order, artistic individualism feels impertinent. Protests greeted the prestigious

left: **At Art In Soi festival, this youth rode his 'horse' of garlands, inspired by King Taksin Monument near his home.**

above: **Creativity is a new buzzword. This mall contest invites new stories of how Bangkok could be.**

above: **Harnn** herbal products have Thai themes in their design.

right: The idea of multi-storey Bangkok stilt houses inspired this furniture by Rush Pleansuk, the 2019 Thai Designer of the Year.

below right: **IconSiam** has hundreds of installations by Thai designers, with QR codes that reveal the story behind each piece. The metal basket-like shelter by Pongsatat Auoyklang was inspired by farming life, from paddy fields to dappled shade.

annual Bangkok Bank art prize going in 2007 to Anupong Chantorn, for painting monks as tattooed crows, scavenging upon alms. There is a Cultural Surveillance Bureau patrolling such offences for the Ministry of Culture.

Tension between tradition and innovation exists worldwide, but here it affects all interaction. Deference is built into the language, and thus into books, drama, screenplays. The word for culture, *wattanatham*, means 'Dharma development' and implies righteous cultivation. So elevating streetlife as 'culture' is as déclassé as *wai*-ing a maid. Guardians of 'high' culture applauded Miss Thailand's novelty costume for Miss Universe resembling a warrior or white elephant, but dissed a tuk-tuk dress as too low to be the national face.

Amid the high/low rift, cinema is treated not as an art, but just as mass entertainment. Although film is a century old, it lacks ancient precedent as a Thai devotional art form. It was introduced as a pop culture novelty in fairs and youth hangouts. Indeed, most Thai features have indeed been genre capers, comedies and ghost stories with predictable plots and cheesy sound effects.

Once directors made art films with social messages, the mandarins sensed a threat. With the new wave of Thai film in the late 1990s, the state tried to turn it into a formal devotional art by using it as a channel for propaganda epics. Some funding now goes to auteur films, but the Culture Ministry spent vast sums on historical movies, directed by Prince Chatrichalerm 'Than Mui' Yukol. Like *khon* dance, Than Mui's *Suriyothai* and *Naresuan* were nuance-free epic serials with moralistic plots of good Thais versus bad Burmese. Their patriotic scripts were treated as if scholarly texts for pupils to view during school hours.

Age-based ratings finally came in, but film remained the only art censored, until a 2023 reform. *Insects in the Backyard*, which dissected a Bangkok family with realism and fantasy, was the first film banned under the ratings, due to a character who fantasised about killing their father. The film *Shakespeare Must Die* (a take on *Macbeth* alluding to the anti-Thaksin movement) was funded then banned by the same Culture Ministry, and only unbanned in 2024. The directors, Ing K and Manit Sriwanichpoom, documented their censorship struggle in the film *Censor Must Die*, which the censors didn't kill.

Access to provocative arts is one of the ways in which Bangkok lacks some common credentials for an aesthetic life. There's not much art education beyond learning traditional templates by rote. Absent are world-class art museums, cinematheques, or a supportive state theatre. Creatives lack sufficient spaces. In 2018 alone, the three leading stage companies each lost their theatres; the indie cinema Lido closed, though its replacement would be the multi-purpose Lido Connect; and the BMA threatened to turn the only arts hub, Bangkok Art & Culture Centre (BACC), into a co-working space. Thin readership keeps learned journals few.

The 1990s-2000s Indie Movement (at Phra Arthit) and today's Creative District (in Bangrak and Khlong San) both emerged at the riverside. Phra Arthit was near universities of the arts and humanities. In Khlong San, the neglected waterfront, shophouses and godowns offered cheap spaces to live, work, and open simpatico hangouts like Jam Factory.

Ports are by nature open-minded. A Montreal documentary series, *Ports d'attache* (Waterfront Cities of the World), berthed Bangkok in the same ribald slot as Barcelona, Miami and Marseilles. Ports have dodgy areas that inspire creatives. One Chinatown gallery opened beside a since-closed gambling den.

Thai society as a whole saw crafts driven by need, custom and devotion, rather than for creativity's sake. That left foreigners scope to explore aesthetic possibilities. It's a common story in the life of bohemian cities. Earlier, artists flocked to Paris and Amsterdam, where the indifference of the locals combined with the exciting environment allowed a freedom not necessarily available to the native. Few places were as buttoned up as Berlin, yet it hosted waves of the avant-garde. Interviewers habitually ask the novelist Lawrence Osborne why he made Bangkok home. "Living here is a place to be alone and concentrate," he says. "I feel the same when I am in Paris."

Bangkok has two kinds of bohemian, who partly straddle the political divide. The street-dressed "starving artists" hang out at the unsubsidised underground scene of shophouse studios and experimental garage galleries. Even if affluent, they identify with the marginalised, not the establishment. Conspicuously hippy-attired bohemians tend to be better resourced and connected. Their ethos of planet-saving reform is epitomised by Wonderfruit, a rising star on the global New Age music fest circuit, that "brings a slice of Thonglor to the Fields," with bamboo installations and "empathy engineering" in aid of causes like sustainable artisan incubators.

Bangkok's maker class are also a major part of their customer base, often buying from designers they know personally. Since income and arts education are so socially concentrated here, most creatives come from affluent circles, and themselves buy works from their peers, whether fashion, furniture or art. The social rituals of status – audiences, weddings, exclusive parties – invariably involve brandishing brands for face. So in art openings, product launches and especially fashion shows, creatives must not just please those taste-makers, but court their patronage and join entourages.

Many creatives pursue a professional focus on the international market, though that

requires uncommon education and resources. Among bylines of professional creatives recur many famous surnames of patrician dynasties. The heirs of Old Money, joined by scions of New Money tycoons, remain the most globalised class of Bangkokians and have the means to travel, study abroad, and launch ventures with minimal risk. While still enjoying imported brand names, they have become a crucial domestic market for Bangkok fashion, art and decor.

It's a peculiarly Bangkok thing that so many liberal outsiders are actually from insider families, having studied and worked overseas. Abroad they were genuine outsiders, frequenting arthouse cinemas that were absent from Bangkok until the early 2000s. Upon their return, many slip between the Thai and international scenes, depending on context.

A taste for foreign fashion has for centuries shaped traditional crafts, especially the high arts. This taste for imported luxury accelerated in the late 19th century among the aristocratic class. Only a tiny court faction had exposure to foreign arts, science and education. Their embrace of non-Thai forms like photography, film and plays showed the Thai enthusiasm for novelty. King Rama VI created the dramatic form *lakhon sangkeet* and is credited with writing over 2,000 literary works, earning the title 'Father of the Thai stage Play.' At each new palace, including Wang Phyathai in Dusit, he built a theatre. His uncle, Prince Naris, is hailed as the Father of Thai Design for his East-West painterly draftsmanship, seen in his museum at Ban Plainern, Wat Rachathiwat's baroque altar, and the 'Marble Temple' Wat Benchamabophit. Such legacies aren't bygone, but bolstered under an outlook that the 'who' and 'what' of creativity is ultimately a matter of national security.

Creativity helped save Siam from being colonised. The civilising mission of European imperialists was confronted in Siam by Greco-Roman porticos, Frenchified armchairs, and Gothic architecture like Wat Ratchabophit. Localising foreign design has been integral to making things Thai *siwilai*.

Grafting Thai and foreign elements onto each other had always been a Siamese technique since *wats* acquired Khmer prangs in the Sukhothai period, Persian windows and Versailles coffered ceilings. The prestige of those hybrids persists as a coded boast of independence. Visiting heads of state stay at a château in the Grand Palace, while Government House is a Venetian Byzantine palazzo. Much later, looking '*inter*' filtered down the social scale, especially since the 1980s boom. Corinthian pilasters grace many a shophouse. Nouveau riches erected cupolas atop the Greco-Roman skyscrapers like The Dome and The Mall Pinklao food court.

Creativity is integral to nation building. King Rama V drafted in foreign talent, whether to compose the anthem or architects from an Italy united under the Lombard monarchy to design institutional buildings in Turin style for the absolutist Siamese capital. King Rama VI continued to apply creativity to national identity, which was wrought through songs, literature, performance and design, such as the new flag.

The Florentine sculptor Corrado Feroci was hired to cast bronze monuments, but ended up the guiding spirit of Thai creativity. In founding the first art college (now Silpakorn Univeristy) and teaching art history, he's literally worshipped in ceremonies as Silpa Bhirasri, the 'Father of Modern Thai Art.'

Feroci's modernity made him a rare figure of continuity after 1932. The secular state took over the nation-building project and the 'Leader', Phibun, embarked upon a creative revolution in forging a new 'National Culture.' Many traditions were stopped, even banned, from sarongs to the *piphat* ensemble of Luang Pradit Pairoh, as dramatised in the film *Hom Rong* (The Overture). Luang Vichit-Vadhakan, wrote songs, plays and the ideology extolling

below left: **The 'Creative District' in Khlong San and Bangrak is a private community initiative that embraces many ventures, such as this light installation walk in Talad Noi during TCDC's Bangkok Design Week.**

above: **Tradition keeps things consistent. A banner at Soei restaurant by Vajiravudh College.**

right: **What could be more Thai than a swoosh logo? Spotted at The Street mall on Ratchadaphisek Road.**

State Thainess. Instead of copying masters, suddenly there was license to choreograph new dances, based not on sacred myths but on everyday acts like farming or courtship.

'National Culture' is still the lens through which conservatives view creativity as being in service of the state. Critical works like the Rap Against Dictatorship song get denounced as 'un-Thai.' Yet reinventing Siam's once static identity did open up a radical potential: it could be reinvented again. Revisionists keep broadening Thai identity from below by creating cultural 'facts-on-the-ground,' witness Sino-Thai soap operas, streetfood vlogs, or Isaan music going *inter*. Modern Bangkok history has been about finding a new voice.

Modernist architecture provided fresh kinds of social spaces like cinemas and department stores, with their designs stripped of most ornament, whether streamlined like Ratchadamnoen Avenue or deco like Sala Chalermkrung. The daringly abstract Democracy Monument has bas reliefs solely of ordinary people. While few physical traces survive from Phibun's era, his mechanisms persist though censorship and the militarist imposition of uniforms and uniformity.

An opposite legacy to Phibun's imposition of uniforms was his direction to hold fairs in communities and temples. Designed as a vehicle to spread modernity, fairs combined ritual, homewares and medicine with newfangled entertainment, like folk bands and outdoor movies. This 'temple fair' variety format suits the informal Thai way of grazing life's buffet. It remains the preferred mode to stage outdoor events.

Under royal revivalism since the city's Bicentennial in 1982, festivals have been infused with re-imagination. Nationalism and tourism fuel spectacles that are reverential yet fantastical expressions of Thai artistry.

In the face of top-down imposition of state creations, individual creativity from below has struggled for space, airtime and audience. Yet intervals of creative flowering became core strands that shape today's cultural terrain. Resistance to dictatorship in the 1960s and 70s sparked the anti-establishment 'For Life' movement, which revolutionised art and literature, film and music. Ageing 'For Life' figures can be identified by their long hair and farmers clothing, shoulders slung with a woven *yaam* bag. Still active from that radical phase are the singer Ad Carabao and his bluesy band, the Tawandang venues and anti-establishment artists like Vasan Sitthiket.

Amid that creative 1970s ferment, composers Somtow Sucharitkul and Bruce Gaston invented ingenious new ways to integrate Thai and western music. They were criticised at the time, but the neo-traditional music heard today, by the likes of Boy Thai, owes its sound to their discoveries.

Another reaction emerged with democracy after 1992: the Indie Movement. This novel generational shift began with alternative music, but transformed the arts through the

DIY trend. Making your own culture aligned artistry with improvised street inventiveness, and ushered in the trend of repurposing vintage objects. Mid-century retro remains a Bangkok motif through curated markets and bars like Tuba. At Tuba's immersive shop-cum-props-warehouse, Papaya, the outlandish collectables get rented out for events and films. DIY and re-purposing old things both became necessities after the pivotal event in Bangkok creativity: the 1997 economic crash.

The burst bubble, plus IMF restrictions, sparked an anti-materialism movement, which later merged into the anti-Thaksin protests. Its signature artist was Manit Sriwanichpoom of Kathmandu Gallery. A street photographer and film-maker, he devised the *Pink Man*, a photo series that put a fuchsia-suited businessman pushing a pink shopping trolley into commercialised sites like Wat Pho, classrooms and the Sathorn skyline – as depicted on the cover of Steven Pettifor's book *Flavours: Thai Contemporary Art*.

The 1997 crisis spawned creative industries by turning from imports to local resources. When the baht value fell, Anusorn 'Nong' Ngernyuang could no longer afford to import executive toys to his shop Reflections, nor Thai executives afford to buy them. Turning the tables, he sold his own designs to the Europeans he used to buy from. Nong led the trend of upcycling discards: rice-sack upholstery, bags woven from airport security straps. His Reflections art hotel (Thailand's first) showcased this Global Trash Chic – an impromptu kitsch aesthetic that's infused the city's 'contemporary vernacular' style.

Essential oils seem a Bangkok fixture, but before the crash herbalism was on the way out. Traditional medicine faced discrimination, while both the forest sources and oral healing knowledge were disappearing. After the crash, this local resource became a vital ingredient in Thais leading the global wellness trend. Spa interiors and Thai herbal products gained allure from the city's new design movement.

With construction stalled, architects and ad execs turned their skills to décor. The Bangkok design showcased at IconSiam owes many of its accents to post-crash inventors. Planet 2000 devised pod-like seating of wildly looping rattan, while Crafactor applied glass temple mosaic to fresh forms. Most influentially, Yothaka and Ayodhya discovered that water hyacinth clogging the Chao Phraya could be twisted into a spongy fibre that's now a staple of interior decor.

The city's design signature exudes *sanuk*, from Singh Intrachooto's 'walking bench' of re-used wood to Saran Yen Panya's 'Cheap Ass Elite' chair repurposing crates. Propaganda's cheeky goods depict a character Mr P, whose obliging penis corks bottles, acts as coat hook or the switch on a lamp.

We take for granted that contemporary objects quote traditional elements, but that had seemed innovative during its evolution. Modern buildings having clipped-on Thai details like gables began in the Phibun era in structures like the National Theatre. From the 1976 crackdown into the 1990s boom, a fantastical style of neo-Buddhist art reflected cultural exceptionalism. Then after the 1997 crash, creatives mined the trove of *lai thai* contours, flavours and sounds to lend their designs a sense of place. Their elegant hybrids became new classics, from Yothaka's pulpit-like chair to Fly Now's trouser-suits echoing the low-slung *jongkraben* leg-wrap. These pared-down accents are now used more than authentic forms to make Bangkok feel Thai.

All this creativity sprung from crises in society too. The old stasis – Sino-Thai monopolies under a patrician 'bureaucratic polity' – had to open up to transparent business, plural values and global cultural flows. Resident foreigners had ironically been freer to play with local forms than Thais inhibited by taboos, who have a lot more at stake in thinking different. Thai arts and crafts had historically been expressions of hierarchy, not originality. That's the devotional role of murals of the Buddha, carvings in pulpits, or *khon* danced as an offering at court. Neo-traditional artists adapted temple painting for boardrooms, public walls.

Areas of national life honour royal patrons as the Father or Mother of that particular field. King Bhumibol – a noted painter, musician, photographer – was the only monarch-inventor holding patents, and has been anointed the Father of Thai Creativity. Handicrafts and silk costume rose to refined levels under the promotion of Queen Sirikit. The fame of Bangkok fashion designers has been eclipsed by the catwalk collections of Princess Sirivannavari. She is also patron of the Royal Bangkok Symphony Orchestra.

Seniority is not just tradition but an ongoing dynamic across society. Master inducts apprentice, both in skills and into his retinue. Patron commissions anonymous artisan – and takes the credit. Craft is art that repeats, with only incremental adaptation down through generations. Traditional artists and even filmmakers hold *wai khru* ceremonies before performances or projects, then join in group gratitude upon their master's designated day.

At performers' altars in Joe Louis Puppet Theatre and The Artist's House in Khlong Bang Luang, masks from ancient epics gaze back immutably from their own hierarchy of nested stands. Their smoky patina accrues from repeated rounds of incense, candles, paste and gold leaf. Masks and puppets aren't mere dancers' props but sacred effigies that possess their human holders as a performed offering, animated through gestures and postures by a guiding creative spirit.

Siamese creativity was incremental adaptation by anonymous artisans, typically of forms that were sacred. So an indie kid inventing an original idea ruffles beliefs about the source of creativity itself. Designers have told me their originality got marked down as it didn't follow the university's instruction and so was wrong. Avoidance of experiment also plagues the professional world, lest it risk face loss for the boss or a patron.

Credit often goes to the one who commissions, and now that patron is often a firm that hogs the acclaim. One craftsman confided to me that credit for his work had been taken by the event where it happened to be shown. This opens to question whether those credited in the past really did the work.

left: **Catwalk shows during Bangkok Fashion Week are as much about seeing the audience.**

above: **Ever-theatrical runway designs by Tube Gallery, in the Portrait of a Lady collection.**

All this blunts ambition. Creatives must play the seniority game. Few dare vault to the top through sheer ability. Knowing sculptors or dancers by name – and celebrating the most brilliant as a genius– disturbs the Thai hierarchy. In modern times fine art gets signed by the artists, but people who buy top-level crafts like hand-loomed textiles or stone carvings still rarely know the name of the weaver or sculptor. Unlike in Western theatre or Japanese Kabuki, very few go to *khon* because of that particular cast. Upending the formula with above-title billing is one reason *khon* purists resent the global acclaim for the revisionist choreography by Pichet Klunchun.

My first week in Bangkok I sought out the most authentic traditional stage performance, of the kind scheduled at the Kraton in Jogja or the Kabuki-za in Tokyo. But the National Theatre, with no program publicised, was shut that day, and ever since only occasionally stages shows. Sala Chalerm Krung stages *khon* highlights for tourist bundled into the Grand Palace ticket. Most major productions – including royal *khon* revivals – are performed at the Thailand Cultural Centre.

Patronage is at the crux of Bangkok's 'Creative Contradiction.' World-renowned Thais struggle for acceptance at home of their challenging work. Although Thai soap operas play well in North Asia, what's popular domestically lacks global appeal, because it tends to be safe and derivative to please conservatives and mass taste. Apichatpong Weerasethakul has earned the top prizes at Cannes Film Festival, international honours for art, and a French knighthood. Among Bangkokians, he's a hero to indie types, but is otherwise known to few, and his films seen by fewer. Apichatpong's oeuvre is abstract, subversive and not *sanuk*. His slow, fixed camera meditations deal with spirits and sexuality, topics handled more excitingly in ladyboy ghost comedies with 'boing' noises.

The Neo-Traditional Movement has spawned both masterworks and schlock. Innovations can add to the canon, as with Panya Vijinthanasarn's fragmentation of Buddha contours. Tourists like the sense of exotic place imparted by *chofa* curves and gold leaf squares. Seen abroad, self-consciously Thai-style objects can have the air of a souvenir rather than contemporary design.

Deconstructing Thai things and reconstructing a modern work with the components has been a Bangkok thing ever since the late 1990s at Patravadi Theatre, when Manop Meejamrat choreographed how to dress in a six-metre red *jongkraben* leg wrap. Pichet Klunchun toured worldwide with his deconstructions of *khon*, like 'I am a Demon,' which reveal the martial arts energy behind the costume. This has precedent in the culture itself, in the making of ad hoc street furniture from repurposed parts, or Bangkok's floral art, whereby petals from various blooms recombine into symbolic flower shapes.

Cultural guardians resist loss of purity in traditional arts, but their resistance to change risks the arts' preservation by losing the interest of both artists and audience. Riffing creatively on heritage can keep tradition relevant, while infusing contemporary arts and design with a sense of place. Yet to a world market with so much choice, 'Thai style' is but one fleeting fashion. Bangkok design rose at the same time as the boom in cheap travel sparked a world fad for things with an ethnic twist. The rush to make goods that felt Thai found a niche in fairs at Milan. Then the style moved on. To influencers, things too

left: Blessing instruments at the Luang Pradit Pairoh Music School's *wai khru.*

right: A mural at Ratchathewi.

Graffiti

Before 2000 Bangkok had no graffiti. Now a city known for temple murals makes a show of its cute street art. Hip-hop lifestyle, like most creative imports here, went through a four-step Creative Arc, from outsider to under the thumb.

Hip-hop is a youth art, a way for rebels to express anxiety via expletive rhyme, daredevil tricks and public walls. Barred from internal dissent, disaffected Thais adopt outsider styles from abroad, whether punk, metal, or the gangsta flava of Snoop Dogg and Biggie Smalls. Thailand's first tagging was sprayed in the mid-1990s by a white American DJ spinning hip-hop in Bangkok's early rave parties. The late 1990s saw rap spread through Joey Boy's cheeky couplets, nu metal's nihilistic thrash and Da Jim's underground tape 'Hip Hop Against the Law'.

Early adopter can-artists evolved their own polite style, seeking permission to spray and creating cute characters like Alex Face's bunny-eared baby Mardi or Momofuku's hairy eyeball.

Trend-watchers launched an avant-garde project, 'Bukruk' (Trespass), a festival curated by French gallerist Myrtille Tibayranc that saw foreign cultural institutes pay for giant murals in first Ratchathewi's pocket park, then the Creative District. Acrobatic elephants and Rukkit's geometric tigers stayed long after the opening night, which featured rap bands and the city's first projection mapping. Influencers then riffed on ideas that cross-fertilised into other creative fields like clothing and graphics. Produce turned skateboards into canvases and Jam bar exhibited graffiti stickers, from the elusive BNE to a cockroach with the legend: "Hell my name is BKK."

Next, local private enterprise saw the potential, but sponsorship leeched the indie authenticity. Union Mall opened with live graffiti painting, bike stunts and amateur rap. Trendier and formalised, graffiti gravitated from abandoned lots to ongoing displays like the Khlong Saen Saeb footpath. Before long, stars like Alex Face exhibited in galleries abroad.

Once the state finally notices, it tries to co-opt trends and neutralise any edge. The first tax-funded graffiti went up on old town walls in Banglamphu Museum. A treasury official got residents and his bosses to accept his idea was not vandalism. Indeed, it's more like promotional street art, "designed to reflect an element of the neighbourhood: a craft they do, a feature of the place, or the kinds of food that are famous there," says painter Karma Srikogar. "Never would have happened five years ago. The government would have said 'hell no'."

Some creatives crave patronage, others steer clear. Talent gets corralled under career bureaucrats, a corporate board, titled patrons, instruction to conform. Once on the official radar, creatives can no longer outshine honoured seniors. It's like being put under cultural, or sometimes also literal, arrest. Graffiti became a tool of protest, often anonymous, but some by the satirical hand of Headache Stencil. When the Ital-Thai construction tycoon was caught in a cave with soup of a poached black leopard, graffiti of the big cat spread citywide. Now that graffiti is finally being used as a form of outsider protest, perhaps it's the start of a new creative arc.

left: **World renowned dancer, Pichet Klunchun, second left, deconstructs** *khon* **masked dance to find its inner energy, martial and cultural meanings, as seen in this publise streetside production at Noble Play, which has dancers in everyday clothes interact with a giant Ganesha.**

below right: **Saran Yen Panya's crate chairs, called Cheap Ass Elites.**

ethnic look dated. With old forms mined dry, Thais face a task to devise must-haves for the sustainable digital age.

Creativity is vital to escaping Thailand's middle income trap, and education is the key. Yet Thailand spends more per head than most nations, with among the worst results, in a 'credentialist culture' that puts titles and qualifications ahead of expertise and finding new knowledge. Learning often stops once the *ajarn* achieves a PhD, tenure or authorship of a textbook. As Thai universities slip in world rankings, new rules to publish research have upset academics swamped by paperwork.

Amid those predicaments, a decline in the teaching of Thai design and dance endangers traditions, both in future artistes and audience. Almost absent from school, TV or institutes is a fostering of art history and the aesthetics of the modernity present in Thai lives. Careers in the arts are seen as frivolous by parents and mentors. All this has sad effects.

Architects get paid a fraction of the global norm and employing foreign architects is banned by law, although 'starchitects' do 'consult' on landmarks (from Central Embassy to Mahanakorn), but without the discipline of instilling standards, practices and other perspectives. City-funded structures tend to be utilitarian given the ideal bid being the cheapest. Exceptions due to status end up florid with clip-on Thainess, like the gold trim cuffed around Sathorn's faux Victorian lamp posts and the Rama VIII suspension bridge.

Into that stasis, the Indie Movement took the initiative, learning and making things themselves. Handmade books platformed new magazines and writers. Home-recorded garage bands and young video makers made the leap into professional careers. The indie scene dovetailed with many strands in Thai informal culture: handmade, ad hoc, hawked in stalls. Due to the lack of steady venues, indie thrived through fairs and festivals like FAT.

Theatre is still quite itinerant and an entirely artist-led scene. Anyone into drama could learn their craft under workshop oriented troupes like Crescent Moon or B-Floor. Pradit Prasartthong was a key figure, leading the theatre-in-education group Makhampom and the Theatre Network that spawned the Bangkok Theatre Festival.

Before today's arthouse screening rooms and the era of downloads, Thai film buffs learned their art at sporadic film festivals, cramming five screenings into each baggy-eyed day. From that scene emerged eloquent critics like Kong Rithdee. The film discussion group Third Class Citizen spawned the director Nawapol Thamrongrattanarit, who made the first film ever scripted entirely of tweets, *Mary is Happy, Mary is Happy*.

In *The Master*, Nawapol filmed 20 devotees of Waen, a stall in Chatuchak Market that sold copied VHS tapes, later DVDs, of art films. Those clients became Bangkok's top directors, critics and film fans who couldn't otherwise have seen the oeuvres of Wenders, Tarkovsky or the Nouvelle Vague. Pen-Ek Ratanaruang reveals that Peter Greenaway liked the fact that piracy enabled his films to inspire enthusiasts in places starved of auteur provocateurs.

The circle around Chalida Uabumrungjit and the Short & Experimental Film Festival helped archivist Dome Sukwong in founding the Thai Film Archive, with its museum and restoration scheme, to acquaint Thais with their neglected celluloid heritage. Old films and their poster artwork also influenced the retro trend and even typography.

The Indie Movement spread the idea that young people could be creative, and that they could choose what to be creative about. It didn't have to be dictated by elders. This initiative had a huge impact on the creative industries that flowered in the early 2000s. After FAT Festival ended, this DIY spirit persists at periodic festivals like Museum Siam's Noise Market and Bangkok CityCity Gallery's Art Book Fair, where handmade volumes interpret the popular culture.

Under the seniority system, knowledge gets hoarded as a form of power, in which only approved selections passed down. With arts funding comes censorship and bias to the patron or sponsor. Access to alternative ideas was then liberated by both the Internet and a global trend to archive subcultures. After documenting Thailand for the Asia Art Archive, Narawan Pathomvat founded a meeting space, The Reading Room. She mapped the city's intellectual spaces, from bookstores to talk venues, such as the William Warren Library at Jim Thompson Art Centre, the Siam Society and Southeast Asia Junction. Meanwhile Neilson Hays Library stages the Bangkok Literature Festival, and Museum Siam hosts LIT Fest, and, with Chakrabongse Villas, the ideas festival BangkokEdge.

Trends go through a 'Creative Arc': artist originator; bohemian early adopters; expert niche showcases; corporate mass marketing; state regulation. Once it gets commercialised, the inventive scene has moved on to the next thing. This arc is the trajectory of many trends from graffiti to gourmet streetfood.

Creatives noticed that declining crafts were squandered sources of cultural and economic wealth. The creative industries that had emerged after the 1997 crash were leveraged under Thaksin inot a coherent industry to help lift Thailand out of the 'middle-income trap.' Inspired by Japan, Thaksin's One Tambon One Product (OTOP) scheme upgraded the quality and marketing of village crafts, enriching local economies and graduating the better brands to the twice-yearly Style trade fairs that showcase Thai designers for export. Bangkokians still flock to giant OTOP and Style fairs for their fix of herbal soaps, indigo shirts and fine basketry.

Institutions have begun to foster creativity. The National Museums had become dowdy, so the National Discovery Museum Institute (NDMI) network was set up to cultivate the public through sophisticated interactive exhibits. It began with Museum Siam, which filled gaps in the record, especially in popular culture. The National Museum then got an elegant refurbishment worthy of its exhibits.

As Thaksin's top advisor, Pansak Vinyaratn, devised new institutions that are both responsive and proactive: NDMI, TCDC and the children's library TK Park. These idea-germinating seedbeds were put beyond the mandarins' reach in a separate Office of Knowledge Management. All those schemes still thrive because their budget was spent on building high-quality capacity instead of face-showing and diversion to patronage.

TCDC continues to thrive, with libraries, exhibitions, workshops, and an annual Design Week. Its symposiums draw enthusiastic crowds of young Thais to hear insights from international design maestros. At the same time and with a similar budget, Bangkok Fashion City (BFC) was handled by an existing

ministry. BFC left no institution, library or ongoing events after two Fashion Weeks held on a specially-built island in Lake Rajada.

Pleasing superiors may be loyal, but a lack of standards results in mediocrity. Bureaucracy strives to scupper or take over successful independent projects. After the 2006 coup, three politically motivated audits found zero corruption in TCDC and it was saved from closure then and after the 2014 coup by the passionate support of the design industry.

The state has tried to control this independent upsurge. The Abhisit government started a 'Creative Thailand' scheme. The junta's policy to steer the 4th industrial revolution, 'Thailand 4.0,' claims to be driven by innovation and creativity. They also put TCDC under a new Creative Economy Agency (CEA). As if to bless all this repositioning, in 2019, UNESCO named Bangkok a 'Creative City' in the field of design.

When Thaksin revived the Culture Ministry in 2001, its brief was mostly to police tradition, but the country's renowned curator, Apinan Poshyananda, lobbied for an Office of Contemporary Arts and became a rare voice for creativity within officialdom. The meagre Ministry funding has part-financed art films, though most of the budget went to the jingoistic 'historical' movies.

Another reason to invest in the arts is to grow an audience. The city's main arts venue, BACC became "infrastructure for the brain" in the hub of Thai youth. It caters to all genres and hosts many festivals. Even its outlets support the mission: arts supply shops, bookstores, and Icedea – a conceptual ice cream parlour. Off its spiral atrium branch galleries that show emergent work, retrospectives and international-level shows. Several survey exhibitions have brought Thai art history to public awareness.

BACC only opened, in 2008, due to decade-long efforts by the Artists Network. Their highly visible campaign resulted in the centre, though many officials wanted another mall – and some still want its prime site for profit-making schemes. A magnet for social critics, BACC also has a plaza that attracts political protests. A decade later, the junta-appointed BMA governor withdrew BACC's annual funding, tried to turn it into a co-working space, and had the outspoken director sacked. While the city's sole art centre has an uncertain future, it has succeeded in building local audiences, attracting huge crowds for the Bangkok Art Biennale and Asia's biggest LGBT art exhibition, *Spectrosynthesis II*.

"Being creative is a fragile affair," explains Charles Landry, the guru of the Creative Cities movement. The necessary respect for authorship and authenticity, whether from tradition or innovation, require "management of fragility." Heritage crafts get just as little subsidy or consideration. Counter-intuitively, hip incubators and old communities can find common cause. The Creative District is a voluntary initiative between entrepreneurs, arts professionals and the neighbourhoods of Charoen Krung and Khlong San. Neither side have a place in the city plan, but now they made their presence an asset to the city.

Independents struggle for funding and secure, affordable space. In 2018 alone, while BACC (a home of Bangkok Theatre Festival) faced defunding, the three main alternative theatres – B-floor, Democrazy and Thonglor Art Space – all lost their venues. Indie music clubs don't last long either. This vulnerability shapes how Bangkokians encounter the arts. Itinerant scenes hop between short-term venues and gather intermittently in festivals. Bangkok arts get criticised for favouring 'festivalism' over institutions, though the lack of space requires temporary stagings and that suits the faddish Bangkokian taste. Besides, festivals have historically been the Thai format for arts and entertainment.

above: **At the first LIT festival in Museum Siam, writers type a text inspired by stories random people tell them at the table.**

right: **Bangkok Design Week stages events in unusual venues like the derelict New World department store.**

The arts are rarely considered in planning – nor are aesthetics a priority in development. Without subsidised public spaces, ventures that aren't self-funded either remain bohemian dives, or must conform to sponsorship by firms or the Thai Health Foundation, which curbs alcohol and transgressive topics. "Art is very underrated in Thailand," says Ou Baholyodhin, a designer who went from Jim Thompson Thai Silk to 'Chief Creative Officer' of property giant Sansiri. "We have a lot of talented Thai artists that still don't get any recognition. They can't make a living, so they give up and that's the real shame. They go into agencies, do things that they were not born to do, and throw away their talent. The future of business will need to be creativity-literate."

Investors with vision do exist, who've opened art film theatres at House Mitrtown, Cinema Oasis and Bangkok Screening Room. Music aficionados rescued the Lido arthouse cinema to create Lido Connect, the multiple arts venue that Siam Square had always lacked. The founder of the fashion house Fly Now, opened an indie art centre with art installations, a reconditioned airplane and a fine dining insect restaurant. With a nod to informal street design by non-designers, he calls it Chang Chui – untidy artisan.

Creative projects are becoming flagships for business. King Power runs Aksara Theatre and an insurer sponsors the Muang Thai Rachadalai musicals theatre. Central Embassy granted its entire top floor to Open House – a book-and-food venue with atrium-tall shelves that boosted the mall's traffic by half.

In fine art, the leading benefactor has been Eric Booth of Jim Thompson Art Centre to support traditional and contemporary arts. Now Thai tycoons are pouring in big money. ThaiBev sponsors the Bangkok Art Biennale (BAB), which carries its green livery, and hosts public art in One Bangkok complex. DTAC's Boonchai Bencharongkul displays his taste for surreal and neo-traditional art at MOCA (Museum of Contemporary Art). Central's Chirathivat family have set up DeCentral in Prakhanong, while CP's Chearavanont clan is turning a huge Chinatown print works into the Kunstahalle Bangkok art museum. Bangkok University and its BUG Gallery were founded by a magnate-cum-photographer, Surat Osothanugrah, whose ex-pop star son, Petch, died before the opening of Dib Bangkok, which houses his major collection of contemporary Thai and international art.

"Right now in Thailand, the main people who value art – apart from people in the industry – are brands. But they do it for their products," says Tap Kruavanichkit of design house Farmgroup. "Many in positions of high influence and power do not. In Thailand,

creativity will always take a back seat – it's the last priority. Then you have Europe or Japan, where creativity and design are industries that dominate and always come first." Mutual exchange is one reason Tap founded the Hotel Art Fair. Cooperation between galleries also marks other art fairs like Mango Art Festival.

Of all creative scenes, fine art is the greatest success, perhaps because it's the most flexible. Artists, curators and gallerists have joined with agencies and the French Embassy to show what can be achieved by setting up informal urban structures. The Creative District holds coordinated openings every few months and each February, the city-wide Galleries Night arranges its own signage and transportation to reach 59 galleries. Attendance has soared as venues coalesce around mass transit lines and the river, with galleries deep in *sois* being served by tuk-tuks installed with art.

Many Thai artists came to foreign notice though Visual Dharma gallery, followed by Numthong Gallery and a succession of contemporary spaces, such as Serindia, Tonson, Nova and H. During the 2010s, Thai art was elevated into the ambit of biennales, art fairs and museum collections.

Silpakorn remains the principal art school, but its status and lineages of alumni led to a non-Silpakorn graduates becoming a separate, less establishment tribe. It was a wake-up call to the ivory towers when international ranking placed Thailand's top university as King Mongkut University of Technology – a proving ground of architects and designers. Chulalongkorn responded with CommDe, an institute of design co-founded by the artist Takerng 'Be' Pattanopas. A lot of creative industry graduates also hail from the private Bangkok University, where BUG holds the annual young artists show Brand New.

In another legacy of the 1997 crash, a trio of spaces pioneered Thai conceptual art. Project 304 Tadu imported the white box template, above a car showroom. Gridthiya Gaweewong, now curator at Jim Thompson, launched Project 304, an experimental space that launched not just Apichatpong, but Michael Shaowanasai's gender-twisting performance art and Surasi Kosolwong's playfulness with pop culture. Recently reopened, About Café, was the first space to set up in Chinatown's Soi Nana, hosted the city's first poetry slams, and introduced locals to internationally famous Thai leaders in the 'Relational Aesthetics' genre: Navin Rawanchaikul and Rirkrit Tiravanija.

Soi Nana has again become a hub for edgy, critical art, which also clumps into counter-culture socialising scenes at the fringes, like

Phrakhanong and Bangrak Creative District. Some of the political shows at the N22 complex of converted garage galleries were censored by the junta. Less commercial, their art might end up getting grants from festivals and museums. Ultimately, these parallel scenes – professional, bohemian and state – led to parallel biennales in 2018.

When curator Apinan Poshyananda announced the big-money, big-name Bangkok Art Biennale (BAB), an underground Bangkok Biennial (BB) had already been planned in secret. The Culture Ministry then ran a roving Thailand Biennale (TB), held in Krabi, Khorat, Chiang Rai then Phuket. If you add Khon Kaen Manifesto in Isaan, the Ghost video art triennial, and the triennial Bangkok Photo expo, that was six periodic art fests in one year.

The BB drew global interest for its critique of biennials as a marketing tool for city place-making. Decentralised and experimental, BB was run anonymously using wiki crowd-contribution. It happened across the Creative District, but also upcountry and abroad, signalling that Bangkok is globally engaged.

BAB draws top international curators and artists to showpiece settings in temples, heritage sites, BACC and malls, which attract huge crowds. Bangkokians broke world attendance records for Marina Abramovic's MAI team. Her durational performance art resonated with Thai Buddhists.

The accessibility of Biennales helps narrow the gulf between Thai and international tastes, and shows the fruit of investing in aesthetics. They also bring rival Thai local art tribes onto the same stage – alongside the world's biggest names. For all the posing for selfies with Yayoi Kusama's pumpkins, many Thai artists steal the BAB show, like Kawita Vatanajyankur. Images of her body being used as a tool (mop, bobbin, plough, spade) to highlight labour rights were projected for three months across the 100-metre frontage of Central World.

Recent decades have seen Thai art's greatest flourishing since Sukhothai, yet the state has acquired few important pieces from that patrimony. The National Gallery holds rare exhibitions and has barely acquired major works since the 1980s – aside from donations by National Artists. Art owned by state agencies lacks a full inventory, while the new National Art Gallery, built to inadequate specification at the Thailand Cultural Centre, stands unused. The art bought for it languishes in storage, or on show at the Ratchadamnoen Contemporary Art Center. So Thais who want to see their own modern art history need to visit the peerless collection at the National Gallery… of Singapore.

Belatedly, the state is funding creativity as a source of 'soft power' income. But official instincts to control it like 'hard power' result in clumsy promotions for elephant pants or mango and sticky rice, whereas soft power is not their choice, but depends on the world liking Thai things. Thailand already has soft power in food, tourism and muaythai, but also in ways that discomfit conservatives, such as soap operas, BL (Boys' Love) dramas, and film, art or songs critical of the Thai establishment.

Insiders are advocating for an independent arts council tha could fund creatives, courses, collections, programming, fair artists' fees and quality venues. That requires an open attitude. Thailand has the talent; it just needs the platforms, funding and autonomy to flourish.

left: Faces of the artists in the first Bangkok Art Biennale in 2018, displayed at BACC.

right: A festival pairing rap and the old bantering song style of *lamtad*, beside a statue by Lolay.

Heart 273

left: **The Great Outdoor Market was first staged around and inside the dry dock, far below river level.**

below right: **Middle-class curated markets feature upscale vendors, such as the jeans tailor called Selvedgework.**

below far right: **Made By Legacy was the first curated market, charging entry for the right to browse second-hand stalls of vintage wares, seen here in the old Railway HQ.**

Bangkoklyn

Rumour has it that the *moo ping* vendor in Silom drives a Benz from selling pork-on-a-stick to bar-goers. Many hawkers struggle, but plenty do indeed build houses and send their kids to uni. Kerbside capitalism can lift hawkers into the middle class. It's a social sea-change that fuels the rise of populist politics. Despite the low image, some desk-bound Thais make the leap into street work as a non-conformist career path.

"The profile of Bangkok's street vendors has gone from uniformly poor to surprisingly diverse, with people from all walks of life," writes Witchaya Pruecksamars in Informal City Dialogues. "Well-educated entrepreneurs with prior experience in the white-collar world have been called Bangkok's 'new generation' of vendors, and they're shaking up the social dynamics."

Middle-class vendors are very evident at high-rent downtown sites, but can also be found at many *talad nat*. Night and weekend markets particularly suit stallholders with second jobs. Ae, who swapped insurance cubicle tedium for a jewellery booth, applies his MA in business from London: "Say you make 30,000 [Baht] of profit per month, per stall. What would you get if you can set up four stalls?" And he's as cagey about trade secrets as any streetfood cook. "Don't ask me where I sourced my products from or how much they cost. That'd be like asking for the recipe of my noodle."

Siam Square was where middle-class fashion designers first opened their own stalls in the 1980s boom. Labels like AB-Normal and Issue emerged from that warren of clothing racks. "The good thing about street trading is that you don't need to sign a contract" says Ae. "You can rent out your space [to other vendors] on certain days, you can set up your shop at multiple locations if you can afford to, and you don't need to come if you feel sick. It is a system that allows for trial and error."

Peddling had been the domain of Chinese and upcountry migrants, shut out of professions and without capital, land or access to loans. When the 1997 crash burst the Thai Dream, many professionals had to survive by hawking. One ex-tycoon self-publicised how he sold sandwiches to commuters. 'Car booth' second-hand sales and BMA-sponsored 'walking street' fairs changed attitudes towards flogging refined goods on the street. Those stopgap formats settled into urban lifestyle, with periodic pedestrianising of roads like Silom and the spread of retro markets using converted tuk-tuks and VW Combi vans.

The 1997 crash also initiated Bangkok's design industry. Many jobless architects turned to product design for homewares. Many opened booths at Chatuchak Weekend Market, which became a crucial source for stylists, buyers and copyists from across the world, spawning iconic pop brands like Karmakamet, Siamruay (now Chonabod) and Reflections. Their imaginatively styled booths evolved a vibrant market subculture: creative, articulate and plugged into music, media, fashion and the arts. "So many young designers open shops in JJ [aka Chatuchak]. You're bound to bump into a shop owner you know," said a product designer, Tom. Clothing and homewares flank the western side, artist-run galleries fill the northern corner. Traders and middle-class customers socialised in-market at Viva and after hours at pubs along Kamphaengphet Road. That scene dissipated other vintage markets, which all provide bars, food, live music and that bohemian JJ vibe.

Every success has its moment. Siam and Chatuchak peaked between 1997 and 2010, offering an open space to indie youth with fresh ideas. Vendors added the value to those locations that is starting to price them out. The fashion and design worlds have matured with that generation, whose boutiques migrated to malls.

The label Painkiller has inverted the trend by opening a pop-up shop in an increasingly upscale JJ. Young designer-vendors may now eye a start up in cheaper, trendier *talad nat*.

The new breed of arty retro bazaars began with Ratchada Night Market, where the Vespa subculture bought parts to customise their scooters. It occupied vacant ground, since redeveloped, because like street vendors, youth culture lacks space and has to operate in the margins. The scene shifted in 2011 to Talad Rot Fai, in abandoned train sheds near JJ. That, too, got demolished in 2013, but replicated the sheds in vast lots behind Seacon Square mall on Srinakharin and behind Esplanade mall on Ratchada.

Talad Rot Fai became the template, with its rough-edged mix of crafts, music and the vintage goods beloved of founder Pairod Roikaew. A former peddler of second-hand clothes, he sold classic cars and antiques, and worked as a props man on sets, so his retro market has a theatrical sense of discovery. A similar market, Siam Gypsy Junction, squeezes sheds of recycled wood under a SkyTrain beside a rail line. It suits cyclists, so *BK* suggests "if you happen to own a bike, bring it with you to avoid feeling left out."

Scooters, bicycles, classic cars are all hobbies of the well-to-do, who view running a stall as part of a lifestyle. Cyclists have their own fairs, as do artists with the Hotel Art Fair, musicians at Noise Market, and foodies at organic farmers' markets like Eat Responsibly Day. It seems that vending has gone bourgeois.

Bangkok retail is not just consolidating into malls. It's also diffusing, with dozens of community malls in residential areas and pop-up stores at events and plazas, like Pop X Haus at K-Village. A few years after shipping containers were used in pop-ups at Siam Discovery mall, the Art Box Exhibition Market utilised containers as part of the next stage in vending culture: curated markets.

Vuti Somboonkulavudhi caused a sensation in 2012 by charging 100 baht admission to enter Made By Legacy. In the courtyard of the picturesque Railway HQ, he placed hay bales and selected stalls, such as tailored denim by Selvedgework, hipster haircuts by Three Brothers, takeaways by a chef from El Bulli. It's a distillation of the vintage scene in New York says Vuti: "You can call it the Brooklyn of Bangkok." People dub the scene 'Bangkoklyn'.

Market-going used to be about either practicality or exploring diverse local cultures. Now that *yaan* have atomised, communities are forming around common pursuits. "It's a beautiful story of how like-minded people find their place together," says Vuti. "It's no longer about the items, it's the amazing network of people with shared interest, which leads to other amazing things."

Market curation reached the level of art through Gaem of The Great Outdoor Market. Her landscape architecture thesis on Bangkok's docklands sparked the idea of holding a non-branded, high-concept fair inside a working dry dock near Wat Yannawa. Thousands of Bangkokians descended the gantry, wove round the keel of a boat under repair and marvelled at how Bangkok vending has become such a charming art form.

Curated markets, like pop-ups, vintage fairs, art marts, food trucks and farmers markets, are a boutiquey combo of mall and stall. They appeal to the upwardly mobile because they are a high status import of concepts that Thailand already has, but which lack status. It's not that the market energy has declined, just that it's morphed as customers – and vendors – gain wealth and sophistication. Informal trading is not just the way of the flip-flop; now the bespoke boot is on the other pedicured foot.

A map of Bangkok selfies on Instagram. Warm colours show foreigners' photos, cool hues are Thai shots in very different areas of town. *Map by Eric Fischer*

Memory
Remembering to forget

The last Lao flute maker of Thonburi folds his wrinkled limbs under an anglepoise lamp and drills into a bamboo tube gripped by his feet.

The last smithy of Ban Bu hammers bronze alms bowls at a canalside shanty furnace, before aunties buff the sooty metal to a gleam.

Old Bangkok is down to the last of things. As urban folk *yaan* communities dwindle, crafts that made them distinct slip away. Soon many touchstones of Bangkokness will be just a memory. There may be no record left, no museum display of artefacts, or even a signboard. "There's only one engraver left alive," says a leader of Ban Bu, Pichit Boonjin. "He's leaving the craft to his son, but he's not even a craftsman yet."

Who and what gets to be remembered – and how – is not just a matter to settle over time, but urgent. As whole neighbourhoods get cleared of their historical buildings and ancient communities, old ways of life evaporate. Young Thais switch from time-honoured customs and trades to adopt modern lifestyles. And in a globalising digital economy, things lose material substance, leaving few keepsakes, and smaller homes to keep them in.

Memory is a sense under siege. What qualifies as heritage is opaquely decided and conforms to the harmonious official script. Evidence of awkward events gets removed. Minority stories go unrecorded. Contrasting views of how we got here now fuel the political divide.

Memory gaps are one cause of Bangkok's many mysteries, which get glossed over or spawn multiple theories. Why are there *two* city pillars? Victory Monument marks *what* victory? Where did Bangkok's many Muslims come from? National Day used to be which date? When asked about such conundrums, Bangkokians tend to shrug. Many don't know much about their city, weren't told, daren't ask, or think it not worth remembering.

Contrast Bangkok's auto-amnesia with other World Cities that are voluble on hometown history. Londoners prove their recall at pub quizzes, in a city of blue plaques marking where notables lived. Bangkokians claim a need for reconciliation, but haven't emulated how cities with trauma – post-partition Delhi, rainbow-nation Cape Town – weave pain into their reconciled tales. That's partly because Bangkok was never colonised, communist, segregated, or emptied like Phnom Penh. A recent surge in uncovering buried pasts discomfits the yearning for national harmony.

Memory depends on how much you know. Seeking knowledge for its own sake is a Western ideal. Researching Bangkok is a minority pursuit in a culture that values the incurious. *Khwam pen thai* (state of being Thai) implies a fixed character. The catch-all rejoinder *mai pen rai* (never mind) drops the subject. The admonishments *ya kit maak* (don't think too much) and *ya seriut* (don't be serious) deter looking deeper. And *guu na* (showing face) means getting your face back.

Thais take pride in being developed. "Fifty years ago, Bangkok was a city of wooden houses, squelchy bogs, rickety boardwalks and muddy *khlongs*, just like the rest of this very watery country," says the ACHR report on slums. "A little embarrassed of its humble, pre-urban past, the glitzy modern urban Thailand tends to stigmatise what is old, small and wooden, and glorify what is new, huge and concrete."

This improvised city lives in the moment; not keeping to plans, nor clinging to old things, blithe about legacy. Perhaps that springs from Buddhist thought. Thais seem remarkably forgiving, and that equanimity is partly about keeping composure. Laws of impermanence discourage attachment to the past. Our perception and recall are all just *maya*: illusion.

Guarding knowledge is a privilege of hierarchy, whether masters hoarding the secrets of their craft, or those with power burying information about decisions, incidents or an invisible 'Third Hand.' Blanks are often due to self-censorship, because questioning offends the seniority system, and gets punished. Holding someone accountable make them lose face, hence the urge to cover up scandal, bury reports or tamper with evidence.

Recall recedes with each generation gap. That's acute as analogue, manual ways become incomprehensible to the digital mindset. Sino-Thais are losing their ancestors' dialects in favour of Thai and Mandarin. Chinese opera survives, but often with players from Isaan.

The West had centuries to adapt its opera, literature and architecture into contemporary culture, but modernity hit Thais so fast that traditions like *likay* folk opera or *lamtad* team banter got dropped in favour of musicals. Huge forces have reshaped the city, rearranged its peoples, and displaced customs with consumerism. Identity rooted in location has waned, while incomers have no inkling of that history. Those raised in placeless condos are a blank sheet for a branded lifestyle.

Advertising and fashion need us to lose memory repeatedly. Fads get consumed with glee before being dropped abruptly for the next marketing lure, with locals queuing up for Rotiboy buns then hopping to new fads like salted egg ice cream. Innovation, branding and built-in obsolescence force us to discard the recently old – whatever its enduring quality.

Development has a 'fresh-start' aspect that separates people from inherited culture. Life now gets digitally tracked and recorded, with app algorithms nudging our decisions in what's termed 'Persuasive Technology.' As a relief, some crave sensations from genuine things. Retro is a partial retrieval from the

left: **An old house shows an early panorama of Rattanakosin taken from Wat Arun in the 1860s.**

above: **Corrado Feroci filmed sculpting this head of King Taksin, shown at BACC in** *Krungthep 226*.

Face 279

crashed hard-drive of early modernism, like teak deco chairs, hand-tinted postcards or vinyl records.

"The morphing of Bangkok is now nearly complete. The result is a strange mutation, a new environment garish and alien," Ing Kanchanavanit writes in *Bangkok in Technicolor*. "The people in this space and time surrender themselves and their city to the homogenous consumerist dream of imagined worldly joys… riveted to a tiny screen in the palm of their hands, like pinned butterflies with no memory of wings."

This disjoint is calamitous for Bangkok's intangible heritage – the ephemera of music and dance, crafts and ritual, food and vernacular design. Designers distill motifs from bygone arts, like basketry or *lai thai* patterns. Upcountry, tradition can survive more in tune with a now semi-agrarian lifestyle. Some masters can't bear to dilute or divulge their secrets to those deemed undeserving – an irretrievable loss of cultural memory. In town, expertise dwindles for want of recruits, even for skills in high demand with lucrative potential, like the Michelin-starred stall of Jay Fai, whose daughter may not inherit the sorcery of her wok.

Community legacies that are viable, can end up being destroyed by force. The last teak houses from the early Rattanakosin era were demolished in 2018 by the BMA, which refused to turn the houses behind Pom Mahakan fort into a museum, as every heritage body pleaded. *Likay* folk opera had been founded in that *yaan*, which was also known for songbirds, fireworks and the residents' self-made museum. The houses couldn't even be salvaged to re-erect elsewhere as their two-century-old timbers were intentionally bulldozed to splinters.

"The end of the Pom Mahakan community reflects the ignorance of the BMA and Thai society about preserving the history of normal townsfolk, especially when the Thai-style costume trend is on the rise," wrote Yiamyut Sutthichaya in the article: 'A living heritage is too good for a fake-preservist society.' "Unlike the state- and palace-centric history of schoolbooks, Pom Mahakan community's history and value lies in its tradition, history, community structure and architecture."

Pom Mahakan raised questions of what counts as heritage and who decides. The Rattanakosin Island Plan envisages a showcase of authorised heritage that omits ordinary residents and trades, that lauds Pom Mahakan fort as a symbol of national defence. Plans to 'save' historical houses often end up as empty monuments, without residents. "Tearing a community apart is an irreversible process in terms of physical and psychological space," Yiamyut adds. "It is also the eradication of the history of normal people in Bangkok. There are many other communities similar to Pom Mahakan. Where is the next domino for the BMA?"

Bangkok's streets are a gallery of architectural styles, ungazetted, under-appreciated – until a sudden demolition creates a hole in collective knowledge. National memory goes through a filter of Thainess. The texts instilled at kindergarten, school, university, and propaganda are often contradictory, with glaring omissions that few dare correct, so most people just repeat its stock phrases. That makes it hard to 'read' the evidence all around. "Thailand had to be created to meet the demands of a map," wrote historian Thongchai Winichakul about how the attributes of a 'nation state' were required in order to secure control over the 'geo-body' within the surrounding colonial borders.

left: **The oldest wooden houses of Rattanakosin, being demolished behind the City Wall at Pom Mahakan instead of being made into a living heritage museum.**

right: **The film *Paradoxocracy* by Pen-Ek Ratanaruang and Passakorn Pramunwong told recent history without the gaps. *Poster by Surat Tomornsak of try2benice***

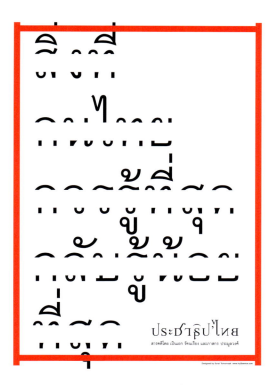

"Mapping did not passively reflect Siam. Rather it has actively structured 'Siam' in our minds as well as on earth… It was the space left over from direct colonialism. Whether Siam lost its territories to the imperialists or simply was the loser in the expansionist contest depends on one's perspective."

The idea of Thainess as one seamless culture has righteous goals to reject ethnic strife and join national rituals under an umbrella of seniority. Cutting the ethnic roots of this composite culture leads some to feel that the city's disconnected from their ancestral memory.

Traditionalists adapt bits of traditions into a coherent tale. To fend off Europeans colonialists, Siam had to legitimise Bangkok's civilised rule over a realm that was largely undemarcated jungle. Krungthep became capital at the dawn of nationalism, in the era of the French and American Revolutions. In tune with that, Siam's thinly chronicled history of entangled city-states and tributary kingdoms was retold as the modern nation with an ancient Thai presence in this land – a hindsight history. Publications still often project backwards the kingdoms of Sukhothai, Ayutthaya and Thonburi as "former capitals of Thailand," glossing over Lanna, Langkasuka, Si Thep and competing empires that don't fit the pattern.

That ideology underpins school texts, TAT guide manuals, books on Thai arts, and museum curating. The National Museum and its branches had long been stores of artefacts, arranged to an art history codified a century ago to fit the official sequence of civilisations. Only recently have its labels been updated in the light of discoveries about pre-Thai Thailand.

"Nations began at the end of the 18th century, but all nations imagine themselves ancient," said historian Benedict Anderson. "The function of nationalist memory is to create seamlessness, where in fact reality is extraordinary disjunctures, separations and dramatic changes in consciousness. Make it cosy for everybody." Tourism rides on the auto-exoticised image of Bangkok as angelic. To get a license, tour guides memorise an approved manual, which explains their reluctance to interpret the city off-script.

Bangkok's story is told as a chronicle of kings. To bolster the monarchy's continuity, pivotal Kings have been designated The Great, including Bangkok's Rama I, Rama IV, Rama V and, during his own reign, Rama IX. Before King Rama IV sat for portraits and photographs, looking at the king was a capital crime, so no likenesses existed. Since Field Marshal Sarit's royalist nationalism after 1957, portraits of the King and royal family have been displayed at homes, workplaces and public spaces, along with artistic impressions of past royals. Arts and architecture are labelled by reign more than by artistic style, while many advances are attributed to royally-initiated projects. Southeast Asia's biggest museum, the Rama IX Museum in Rangsit, showcases his scientific thinking. Other talented royals are revered as the 'father' of their interest, with Prince Damrong Rajanuphap commemorated on December 1 as the 'Father of Thai History.'

The inviolability of "the highest institution" is ensured by the royal defamation law, lese majeste. Section 112 of the constitution, deters full discussion of royalty on pain of 15-year prison sentences per charge. As the offence can't be reported, no one knows the limits of what's unsayable. The spurt in convictions since the yellow-red schism hampers documenting this pivotal era. Then in 2013, a man was prosecuted for criticising social conditions two centuries ago, and in 2014, the intellectual Sulak Sivaraksa was charged with Section 112 for pondering whether an ancient royal feat had been mythic, but escaped jail. "We have quite a limited

Face 281

knowledge of Thai history already," scholar Chanan Yodhong said of the Supreme Court extending protection of the king, queen, heir or regent to cover past monarchs. "There is no point in studying Thai history anymore."

News and media have the means to record and contextualise what happened, yet they omit anything deemed 'sensitive,' due to self-censorship and private warnings. Under criminal defamation laws, truth is no defence. So we get blanks. The ending of slavery is honoured, but there's silence on the slavery itself – and its legacies. Rattanakosin Exhibition Hall shows an animation of the Emerald Buddha's nomadic journey, but jumps from its stays in then-independent Lanna kingdoms to its arrival in Thonburi, without mention of its centuries in Laos. In the 1940s, Thailand annexed parts of Cambodia and The Shan States, which it had to give back after ending World War II on the losing side – the episode marked by the Victory Monument. In Bangkok history, memory is a zero-sum game.

Monuments imply permanence, but here they're impermanent. On 5 April 2017, the plaque in Royal Plaza marking the 1932 Revolution was removed, with no trace, culprit undisclosed. The plaque was anonymously replaced by one reading: "Long live Siam forever! Happy, fresh-faced citizens build up the power of the land. Loyalty and love for the Triple Gem, one's clan and having a honest heart for one's king is good. These are the tools to make one's state prosper."

Social media was abuzz on the night of 27 December 2018. Someone had spotted a crane lifting the Constitution Defence Monument off its pedestal, behind a barrier, under cover of dark, to media blackout. The art deco obelisk marked the defeat of the Boworadej Rebellion, which had tried to reinstate absolutism. It had faded into obscurity until Red and Yellow Shirts fought there in 2010. Authorities were uniformly tight-lipped about its fate. "This was the first monument erected after the revolution and it was dedicated to ordinary people," says conservation architect Chatri Prakitnonthakan, fearing for Democracy Monument. Earlier the modernist Justice Ministry building – erected beside Sanam Luang – had been demolished. "Removing these symbols of democracy is like erasing our political history."

To remind Bangkokians of that forgotten period, Chatri exhibited relics from the People's Party era in the exhibition 'Revolutionary Things' at Cartel Gallery. "While people tend to look at the 1932 Revolution as a power struggle involving a small group of elites, without consent or awareness of the people, most of the exhibits prove otherwise. These items were made by ordinary people for practical use, not the things that the state ordered them to make," he said, citing a lighter, lamp, ashtray, pen or water jar.

At that time, plays and dances about commoners replaced divine dramatic arts. Ancient rites like the Giant Swing Ritual gave way to secular festivals, with a National Day Fair on June 24. A National Culture was devised to occlude memory of old Siam. From that era came Bangkok's few commemorations of commoners, such as the bas reliefs on the Democracy Monument and the statue at Thammasat University, of its founder and People's Party premier Pridi Bhanomyong. Thainess ideology has since replaced that era's legacies with selected elements of tradition.

Forgetting is policy. Recent events dissolve before our very eyes, didn't happen here. A school history book issued by the NCPO omitted Thaksin, and media were asked not to cover him, yet whatever one's views of him, Thailand can't be understood without that pivotal figure. So journalists speak in code about such unmentionables. Columnist Alan

Dawson refered to "he who can't be named" as "Lord Voldemort na Dubai." Witnessing facts disappear today makes us doubt what we're told about yesteryear.

"Our history courses merely touch upon the national 'triumphant' pages of the past when the country conquered its neighbouring enemies," wrote journalist Surasak Glahan. "Teaching of history in school paints Thailand as a semi-utopian territory, instead of letting them learn from the country's past mistakes." So it can be daring to fill out a timeline. In the documentary *Paradoxocracy*, indie director Pen-Ek Ratanaruang simply put the events of Thai democracy in sequence, filling the holes and revealing who caused what.

Remembering approved things is also policy. Summoning of particular historical moments pervades Thai media, festivals, entertainment and public holidays. Most Bangkok commemorations relate to royalty. On Chakri Day, April 6, the monarch pays tribute at the Memorial Bridge statue of King Rama I, founder of Krungthep and the Chakri Dynasty, before conducting rites in the Pantheon of the Grand Palace, which enshrines figures of each Chakri king. October 13 is King Bhumibol Memorial Day, honoured by a yellow-clad public who lived most of their life under his reign. The middle class, lacking an urban deity, have since the 1980s worshipped King Chulalongkorn upon countless shrines and amulets as the 'Great Moderniser.' On Chulalongkorn Memorial Day, October 23, massed ranks of students, officials and devotees, dressed in the king's colour pink, all prostrate before the equestrian statue of King Rama V, the first statue of any Thai ruler. That Thais seek ongoing protection by past rulers shows wide belief in concepts of time as being both divine and simultaneous.

Krungthep recreated key temples and palaces to make itself a reincarnation of Ayutthaya, which was an avatar of the god Rama's city of Ayodhya in India. So Bangkok was built to embody both a physical memory and a metaphysical one. This City of Angels treats its past and future lives as contemporaneous, with a fortune that can be adjusted. Bangkokians make merit to improve their city's karma. King Rama IV added a second city pillar to improve the capital's horoscope. What was foretold at the installation of the original pillar remains unknowable.

Thai Buddhists share the Hindu belief that only intact images of a god can hold its spirit. Things rot fast in the tropics, and a local aversion to maintenance ends up with decayed sacred objects being either remade or refinished as new, to get rid of the weathered patina that so charms Westerners. UNESCO advocates that ruined artefacts and architecture be preserved with the original parts kept faithfully raw. In a rare case of that idea, Lhong 1919's restoration kept its eroded murals intact, showcasing the imperfections of age as the aesthetic of memory.

The Buddha image of Wat Trimitr shows how memory gaps get filled. Whilst being moved in 1955, the Sukhothai-era statue's stucco cladding cracked to reveal it as the world's largest gold object, weighing 5.5 tonnes and worth 250 million dollars. It had likely been disguised whilst at Ayutthaya to shield it from marauding Burmese, only the ruse got forgotten. This otherwise minor temple got a gleaming marble *mondop* to house the treasure

left: **The old East Asiatic Company building was a romantic mystery to most people until used as a venue for the Bangkok Art Biennale. It will be restored as a hotel.**

right: **Bangkhunprom Palace shows the art nouveau style used by its architect Mario Tamagno and other Italian designers hired by Kings Rama V and VI to show modernity.**

left: **Sumet Jumsai's 'Robot Building'** was literally defaced by owners UOB, who re-clad this unique, much-loved landmark in bland corporate anonymity.

below: **A nostalgic Winter Fair display** shows Khlong Prem Prachakorn, which King Rama V developed.

right: **Nai Lert's pillar.**

in 2010, when the statue was given pink-gold hair. The *mondop* also houses the Chinatown Heritage Centre, which is a long-awaited permanent exhibition that reinterprets the suppressed history of the Bangkok Chinese.

Many Thais dread being haunted by the past. Antiques might harbour ghosts. Belief in the spirits of buildings and objects moves Thais to make offerings and daub blessings to buy protection from a malevolent spirit. "One time I found an antique bed," recalls Chanchay 'Pook' Maleesuthikull, who founded the retro-style Hippie De Bar. "I really love it, but I wouldn't sleep in that bed of course. I'm afraid of ghosts!" Contrary criteria for heritage explain why Bangkok restores some patrimony, whilst neglecting or demolishing what foreigners or experts regard as treasures. Westerners loved that H Ernest Lee set up H Gallery in a vintage wooden house, while Thais were initially wary until it succeeded.

In a pivotal case, Blue Elephant restaurant occupies the former Bombay Department Store, which was saved from demolition by its owner, the Thai-Chinese Chamber of Commerce, only thanks to campaigners. "It's blocking the two stone lions in front of the new chamber," explained TCCC Chairman Boonsong Srifueng-

fung of the heritage building, adding: "This is not Thai style, but a mixture of Thai and Western architecture." Hybrids haven't been widely valued, despite being a dominant Bangkok style. Their preservation depends on owners gaining status from a new usage.

The main criterion for heritage is official Thainess. Many buildings are fusions, but get preserved due to high-status, while lower status puts the ethnic, commercial or popular culture at risk. The original Siam Commercial Bank HQ, bearing the prestige of royal ownership and Italian-style, has been restored, while the private Bangkok Bank's original office of local wooden Gothic design, languishes in disrepair. The Sala Chalermkrung Theatre was royally commissioned and got restored, while the Sala Chalerm Thai Cinema, an icon of Bangkok modernity and pop history built during the out-of-favour Phibun era, was demolished despite civic outcry.

What changed how the city perceived its legacies was the Bangkok Bicentennial in 1982. Pageantry and ritual that few saw in the absolute era were revived as spectacles for public participation and mass media audiences. The evocative highlight was King Bhumibol processing down the river in the longest of

Mind the Gaps

Artists can draw by outlining the negative space between what's visible. And Bangkok can be viewed via its memory gaps. Clues dot the map in discrepant sites of 'urban archaeology'. By Khlong San District Office lie ruins of a mid 19th-century star-shaped fort, from where a boat-stopping chain could be raised to a fort where River City now sits.

The concrete pillbox beside Central Embassy puzzles passersby. It was a boundary post of a vast estate that stretched from Soi Nai Lert to the Nai Lert Building in Nana, now severed by an expressway and railway. It was owned by Nai Lert Sreshthaputra, the pioneer Sino-Thaicoon investor-philanthropist who founded the first omnibus and taxi networks. His remarkable life can be traced at Nai Lert Heritage Home in Nai Lert Park.

Rails in tarmac by the City Pillar are remains of Bangkok's first mass transit, a tram network that was uprooted after 1957 by Field Marshal Sarit Thanarat under US-influenced car interests. Its length wasn't surpassed by the BTS/MRT until the 2010s.

Spaces found new uses. Rama IX Memorial Park was until 2018 the Royal Turf Club for horse racing. In the old town, Romaneenart Park retains the walls and watch tower from when this was the city jail. Its Corrections Museum notes that executioners used to dance before each beheading. Where people now tap *takraw* balls over a net, elephants once kicked a giant rattan ball lined with spikes to perforate the prisoner confined inside.

SECOND COURT
Phra Pinklao Bridge honours Phra Pinklao, who was a Second King, a Siamese rank bestowed upon the king's brother or son. The king ruled overall and managed the southern half of the city and country. This Viceroy ran a third of the forces and ministries, plus the half of Bangkok and Siam north from the Wang Na (Front Palace), which guarded the King's Grand Palace. When King Rama V abolished the rank in 1885 for a less powerful crown prince, part of the Front Palace was levelled to expand Sanam Luang. Its core became the National Museum, with its wooden Tamnak Daeng,

exquisitely muralled Buddhaisawan Chapel and model of the Wang Na.

People wonder why Bangkok has not one but many Chinatowns, Little Indias, Mon villages and other ethnic enclaves. It's because each group came (via war, trade or diplomacy) in separate entourages of the king, deputy king or nobles like the Bunnag family, who settled folk in areas they supervised. Varied groups in Baan Somdet Chao Phraya were brought by Chuang Bunnag, the regent of King Rama V.

SECOND FAMILY
The Bunnag family administered much of Siam for three centuries and became Siam's second most powerful clan. Bunnags still flourish, yet their golden age left few landmarks besides Wats Prayoon and Pichayat. In the book *Chariot of the Sun*, Shane Bunnag traced his origins and found that palatial Bunnag estates in Khlong San were lost to the city's first river bridge. Shaped auspiciously like an arrow, Memorial Bridge was erected on the capital's 150th anniversary to improve its fortune, just months before the 1932 Revolution ended absolutism.

CENTRAL MARKET
The heart of Phnom Penh or Yangon is its central market, but only fringe markets like Pahurat remain from when Talad Ming Meuang (City Treasures Market) filled a city block. Designed by Italian Mario Tamagno to mark Bangkok's 150th year in 1932, its lofty arcades were felled at a month's notice in 1978 to build the faux-colonial mall, Old Siam Plaza.

The area was named for Wang Burapha (Southeastern Palace), demolished in 1959, after which it became the city's first hub of pop and youth culture. Ming Meuang was ringed by milk bars, four cinemas (of which just Sala Chalermkrung stands) and early department stores, such as Merry Kings and Central. Bangkok's first fitness club was located in the Nightingale Olympic, the oldest extant department store, which preserves the 1966 Brutalist concrete frontage, while its dated stock seems frozen in a time-warp. In the top floor food court of Old Siam Plaza, dapper pensioners still croon nostalgic ballads of the Suntaraporn Band – nationalist songs of that 1960s heyday.

ONE BANGKOK, MANY HISTORIES
Sometimes, lost traces resurface. Sanam Chai MRT station, lined in trad Thai decor, displays artifacts unearthed during tunnelling. One Bangkok replaced Lumpini Stadium, Suan Lum Night Bazaar, the modernist Armed Forces Preparatory School and the site of Thailand's first radio broadcast in 1920, hence the name of Witthayu (Wireless) Road. But the arial and radio station have been rebuilt, as One Wireless Road, in nostalgic gingerbread style.

Face 285

fifty gilded royal barges, which then went on display. Queen Sirikit restored the golden teak Vimanmek Mansion for public view, though it has since been taken down for reassembly in the new palace district. Vimanmek sparked an ongoing revival of Bangkok's palaces, many of which had been requisitioned after 1932 for state agencies. The turreted Phyathai Palace (part of Phra Mongkutklao Hospital) and the Art Nouveau/Renaissance-style Bangkhunprom Palace (in the Bangkok of Thailand) are now showcases of royal lineage. To mark Bangkok's 250th Anniversary, official heritage is being broadened to include selected old communities like Tha Tien and Kudi Jeen.

Bangkok excels at the performance of memory through pageantry, in an ever-morphing rollcall of Songkran Parades, Anniversary Processions and son-et-lumière re-enactments like River of Kings or the Winter Fair. Whole industries have evolved to supply carved Styrofoam *nagas* and gilded leather crowns. The fantastical tableaux owe less to pre-modern Bangkok than to Cirque du Soleil and the Rose Bowl Parade. The past doesn't keep still in this city of novelty, which enacts evermore entertaining reminders.

Performing acts of memory is rooted in ritual. Thais believe that worship can animate effigies of spirits, statues of gods or shrines to ancestral leaders. They're activated not just on anniversaries, but through daily rites, scented by garlands and energised through costumed dance. In a survey of Thai landmarks, Ka F Wong noted that: "It is the memory or the story behind a monument that keeps the static object alive."

Tales of the past have often got passed on through the spoken word or imagery (murals, illustrated books, historical cartoons) more than by scholarly reading. This remains a heavily oral culture, with a thin literary crust. Writing used to deal primarily with religion, royal chronicles, governance, epics or manuals – and that still accounts for most Thai books. Proof of popular culture was limited to word-of-mouth and scenes painted low down in murals. Much pop non-fiction still takes the pictorial form of comics, travel diaries and social media posts.

Status limits what goes down in history. Some libraries may subscribe to the earnest magazine *Sarakadee* (Feature), which includes retrospectives on popular culture, but fail to collect indie monthlies like *a day*, *Way* or *Open* that track the contemporary scene as it unfolds. Future researchers – even today's researchers – face empty shelves in the archives of our times.

Delving deeper into hidden histories can reveal alternative readings of what we're told. It's not easy to cross-check. Bangkokians aren't diligent keepers of records. Access to documents isn't always granted in the few archives that do exist here, though researchers can see Thai records in libraries abroad. Many old inscribed palm-leaf folding books were burned in the sack of Ayutthaya. Prince Damrong collated the remnants with Rattanakosin documents into the National Archives in 1916, while his own palace, Wang Varadis, has an archival library. The Siam Society was founded in 1904 and still has a scholarly journal, a library and lectures on Siamology.

Bureaucracy gives the impression of elephantine memory. Bricks of paperwork, clasped by bulldog clips, stack into waist-high walls, never to be eyeballed again. Yet, state records have grown more scarce since the mid-20th century, as a rule change allowed officials to throw out government archives after several years. The excuse was cost of storage, though the ability to verify may not be relished by some

left: The artist Sutee Kunavichayanon dissects hyper-nationalism. In this performance at One Gallery, Sutee chalked, semi-erased, then redrew elements of Thai history that had got hidden, invented or re-interpreted, from revanchist borders to the now missing Constitutional Defence Monument.

far left: The Miss ACDC beauty pageant re-enacts a famous photograph of a 1940s beauty contest. Pageants were introduced here to spread the idea of a constitution, which is shown as a folding book on a pedestal tray.

keepers of secrets. A future public information act might yield less than expected. Computer archives take less space, but shifts in format may render many archives unreadable in a 'Digital Dark Age', with the loss of cultural memory including websites and public photographs, diaries, letters, the lot.

Bangkok offices suffer from a lack of institutional memory. Crucial info gets hoarded by key personnel, so it goes when they leave. Instead of being methodically filed, documents often go astray or get tossed without anticipation of future use. At a newspaper office I saw press releases dumped in a box for archiving, yet its separated sheets with photographs adrift from their captions would be unidentifiable. A music producer confided that one of the big two record companies hadn't kept many of its early press materials and even some master tapes, leaving just low-fi cassettes. When it came time to compile albums of greatest hits, they realised their greatest losses.

The accumulated knowledge of oral culture faced oblivion back in the 1990s boom. Herbalism was not just marginalised, but herbalists' expertise was disappearing as fast as the herbs were being lost from logged forests. What saved their lore was the 1997 economic crash. With imported medicine too pricy, herbalists revived their elixirs to renewed public interest, inadvertently sparking Thai leadership in the global rise of spas.

With anti-IMF anger rising, nationalist sentiment swung from modernity to the overlooked indigenous culture under the slogan *phum panya* – local wisdom. Other vanishing know-how was pulled back from the brink. Weaving found a future in the new Thai design industry. Old recipes dying out with grandma became must-try specialities at *phum panya* fairs and revived wooden markets. Those recovered histories became valuable branding.

In the nick of time, independent impulses to archive have swept Thai culture since the mid-2000s, from music to crafts to food. In 2004 Bangkok became the first project outside Finland for VernaDoc – an unusually aesthetic NGO that does high-quality technical drawings of vernacular buildings so that owners can see the value in saving them. Asia Art Archives and Thai Art Archives are documenting the full breadth of artists' work beyond finished pieces. The Dutch Protest Museum collected witty protest ephemera from the Red vs Yellow era. And historian Anake Nawigamune led a trend to print the stories of old *yaan*.

People who want to pore over the printed past, might think to try the National Library, but they won't find a state-of-the-art research service. Beyond its invaluable collection of rare tomes, this underfunded, understaffed institution is a depository of whatever's published in Thai. Countless volumes sit in boxes or piles unshelved, unindexed, unopened.

Retro and Nostalgia

Pining for lost Bangkok prompts two design revivals with contrasting psychological outlooks: nostalgia and retro. Revivalism – in fashion as much as religion – occurs at times of insecurity. Nostalgia is the yearning for a traditional past that never quite existed; retro is the wistful toying with pop relics of optimistic post-war development, which promised a future that never quite transpired.

Retro, named for 'retro rockets,' began as a wry take on a Jetson-style Space Age future that now seems quaintly naïve. The style sparked here during the 1990s boom, as an artists' critique on how consumerism eats itself. Thai Retro went mainstream after the 1997 crash derailed the Bangkok Dream.

Retro was an ironic way to process what went awry with Thai modernity. Artefacts from Bangkok's "mid-century moderne" are rapidly getting lost, but a liberal cognoscenti collects its design objects and treasures its gems of Brutalist architecture like the Narai Hotel, Srifuengfung Building or the sculptural branches of Bangkok Bank and Kasikorn Bank. Retro's stylists were the last generation raised with analogue not digital culture. Most of them grew up under democracy, so they're more comfortable with ambiguity.

Conservatives hark back to a mythical golden age – a maleable date that seems to match whenever their parents were young. Bangkok's elders were conditioned by dictatorship during the Cold War, when it was normalised for nostalgia to be deployed as a propaganda tool, trumpeting heroic history, untainted tradition and rustic idylls. New patriotic songs relayed over loudspeakers during festive periods – with rumpety-tump brass bands and trilling choirs – sound just like old patriotic songs that were written to propagate Thainess when that was a new concept. Nostalgia also romanticises ancient struggles through epic movies of battles against the Burmese.

Only since the 1997 crash has the capital begun to appreciate the disappearing life along the canals. A faux floating market held beside Government House in 2016 felt like an elegy more than a revival. What Thai nostalgia most harks back to is progress, specifically development under King Rama IX, and modernisation under King Rama V, when Siam turned into the second most advanced state in Asia. Thais take pride in how far they've come, but fret how they've been overtaken, with Vietnam gaining fast. Nostalgia basks in periods when Thais led the way.

Bangkok's new middle class lacked a talismanic deity, so during the 1980s boom, Rama V's image appeared in shrines and gilt-framed portraits, while his hybrid style pervaded fashion and décor. Doormen and wedding grooms donned the *jongkraben* leg wrap, with socks and shoes. His favoured brandy and cigars became

status markers in nightlife. Influenced by Queen Sirikit's restoration of his teak Vimanmek mansion, venues were decked in florid armchairs and tasselled curtains, under chandelier-fans of brass and cut glass. At restaurants like The Local, all can revel in bourgeois trappings that few Thais in the actual past could enjoy.

Retro also revels in the everyday trappings that most Thais could enjoy. Those products of industrial Bangkok were not handicrafted, but mass produced in cheap materials. That ephemera – '1 baht comics', tins of Hall's mints – hadn't been thought of as heritage, but became collectible at nightmarkets like Talad Rotfai, and displayed at venues like Shades of Retro bar or the boutique hotel Phranakorn-Nornlen, though not in museums. The best examples, like elliptical station benches, can be hired as movie props at the retro emporium Papaya, or sampled at its sister pub Tuba.

"I always wear retro clothes. Everything in my home is retro," says Chanchay 'Pook' Maleesuthikull, founder of Hippie De Bar in Khao San Road. "My bar plays retro songs and I design retro clothing for sale in my shop. I used to drive a vintage car, but it consumed a lot of petrol." Unfortunately others can be oblivious. "Mom got into my room, took all my favourite retro things, and sold them to a junk-dealer because she though they were all junk! I wanted to cry."

Retro showcases the mundane culture of mass taste and handpainted graphic advertising. As a hybrid culture infused by imports from Japan and the West, as well as Chinese shophouse culture, retro isn't deemed authentic Thai heritage. Vintage stuff is found in flea markets, so even many fans treat it as a throwaway fad. "Things from modern history are taken for granted," laments historian Anake Nawikamune. His pioneering Baan Pipitapan (House of Museums) reassembles urban objects of the modern era into themed displays: barbers, classrooms, pharmacies. "Many colleges collect folk items like baskets or fish traps, but everyday urban items don't even have storage space. People always think that these items must be easy to find. Most evidence I find is oral; few documents remain. State museums don't seem enthusiastic to collect or display retro things. The National Museum has only three cases on Thai toys. This is a gigantic problem that urgently needs to be solved, but still nobody takes it seriously."

In its medley of mismatched furniture, Retro collides eras and disrespects historical context, but that's part of its ironic stance. Nostalgia mixes eras and disrespects historical accuracy just as much, but is earnest in thinking it true, even moral. Yet nostalgia is more costume than conservation. While landmarks of yesteryear get demolished, MRT stations get dressed in décor that's Chinoiserie, faux shophouse and Rattanakosin-esque. At the Winter Fair held each December since 2017, thousands don mutton-sleeved blouses, monocles, bowler hats or *jongkraben* in neon hues. Amid much sentimental *sanuk*, they take selfies and group photos in front of painted cut-out backdrops evoking the Fifth and Sixth Reigns.

Over time, urban folk culture finds validation and favour with nostalgics, who regard retro as a sentimental throwback to a simpler, purer Thainess before globalisation embodied in the Kodachrome glow of the film *Faen Chan* (My Girl). In the absence of publicly-funded conservation, these banal collectibles may not be in museums, but the furnishings, fashions and artefacts of the Thai modern past are accessible in public venues. A city fretting about the future finds solace in orchestrating the past.

left: **Phranakhon Nornlen hotel was styled like a museum of mid-20th-century Thai retro.**

above: **The chequered *pha khao ma* loincloth has been turned into a retro fashion fabric.**

top: **People dressed in costumes resembling the Fifth Reign fashions walk to the nostalgic annual Winter Fair in Dusit.**

Despite the digitising of Thai life, the years since Y2K have spawned a boom in books. The TK Park reading centres draw children. Hordes of teens, students and adults cram the twice-yearly book fairs. Young professionals diligently research in libraries at Bangkok Art & Culture Centre (BACC) and Thailand Creative & Design Centre (TCDC). Bangkok's year as the UN World Book Capital spurred major new libraries, notably the specialist one at the Bank of Thailand Learning Center and the 24-hour City Library.

Renewed interest in books sprang from the indie revolution, which flourished during the liberal flowering of 1992-2010. Young Thais sought out new ideas and expression as 'independents.' Handmade books and small presses catered to an earnest readership keen to explore the world and to lift the lid on Bangkok's smothered past. *A day* magazine introduced young readers to in-depth social histories on anything from ads to comedy to corruption. Innovative intellectual hubs opened at Reading Room, the William Warren Library, Southeast-Asia Junction and Jim Thompson Art Centre – with archival exhibitions and provocative talks.

This new breed of independent researchers bridges the gulfs between the oral, printed and digital eras. Panel discussions (carefully) air dissenting views, with some recorded or webcast. Oral history projects preserve first-hand reminiscence of what's being lost. Exhibitions bring recognition to low-status patrimony, from streetfood to migrant traditions.

To raise expertise in handling such delicate 'intangible heritage,' Chulalongkorn and Thammasat Universities set up degrees in cultural management. Poor handling of heritage had often been down to a lack of skills; now a cadre of talented curators is broadening how the past gets put on display.

Before the 2000s, Bangkok museums carried little trace of ethnic diversity, artefacts of ordinary life, nor modern history after 1932, let alone contemporary culture. A few pioneers try to reassemble missing pieces. In House of Museums, historian Anake Nawikamune collates room-sets of everyday urban objects. His shophouse of curiosities triggers 'a-ha' moments in those who remember life before the Internet. It's an elegy for a lost era of analogue objects, each pre-used item invested with personal meanings we can only guess.

There is no tuk-tuk in the national museum, but there was one in the first room of the Museum Siam when it opened in 2008. Toying with the interactive displays in Museum Siam is like therapy to recover buried memories, asking reality-check questions like: "How real is true Thainess? What on earth does it mean?" and "Were the cavemen Thai?" It captioned political posters as propaganda and showcased voices from Bangkok's ethnic minorities, speaking of their centuries here: "Life was tough for us Khmers in early Bangkok. We were forced to work on the canals." It has since redesigned its galleries to focus on everyday objects under the tagline: 'Decoding Thainess.'

Official history has widened in recent decades to embrace a more plural identity, whether rural folk, Sino-Thais or religious minorities. But this has always been to submerse those other identities under generic Thainess, not to unearth their roots. Revisionist histories have surfaced through the rise of Thai Studies by both Thai and foreign scholars. Their findings are revealed warily here and candidly abroad.

What Craig Reynolds dubs 'Seditious Histories' probe contested local pasts. The findings of academics start off obscure, but loop back into general knowledge through guidebooks and web shares and exhibitions like the Chinatown Heritage Centre. Since the 2000s, some young indie Bangkokians have been keen to rediscovering the ethnic heritage – from Teochiu to Mon – that their parents and grandparents had suppressed in the nationalist era. Now the taboo is more about class than ethnicity; poor migrants are being

above: **A display at Siam Center urging young Bangkokians to explore the heritage of Kudi Jeen.**

top right: **A projected display about the multi-ethnic past in the Banglamphu Museum.**

Banglamphu was the heart of the city in term of entertain[ment]

expelled from the centre and the political schism cuts raw. Reconciliation remains elusive, because acceptance is possible only by addressing offences of the past.

Notable *yaan* have been turning remnants of what defined them into emblems of intangible heritage. They present their community to visitors with booklets and displays collating the memories of residents. Sam Phraeng, a grid of three intact row-house streets around a square, set the template by hosting fairs with tours, local wares and interviews with residents. BangkokEdge ideas festival also focuses on local stories, starting with its location in Tha Tien. The Urban Design & Development Centre (UddC) plans the conservation of *yaan* that play a role in the city's cultural and ethnic memory.

Back in 2000, elders led reporters through an abandoned lumber warehouse to view the last of the *lamphu* mangrove trees that gave Banglamphu its name. A riverside park on that site preserved the tree – until it withered. In an act of persistence, they planted new *lamphu* saplings. The area, famous for backpackers and uniform makers, has been home to court musicians as well as many kinds of artisans and ethnicities. Finally, after years of petitioning the Finance Ministry not to demolish the Khru Sapha printing building, it was turned into a community museum.

The BMA is now founding a local museum in all 50 districts, like Bangrak Museum, which makes vivid the mid-20th century prim lifestyle of the international quarter. Eventually, the City Hall will be vacated and the modernist edifice turned into something Bangkok has never had: a museum dedicated to this city.

A new breed of tourist is keen to get an 'authentic' urban experience. Cultural walks began with one-offs by the Siam Society and cultural expert Paothong Thongcheua, then by the Bangkok Tourist Bureau, high-end travel agencies and cycling tours that could penetrate narrow *sois*, which Thais have since embraced. The TAT responded with a domestic tourist campaign using the title: 'Unseen Bangkok.' It used to be nigh impossible to find out about important historical properties, as owners kept a low profile, suspecting questions as a prying threat from officials, developers or criminals. They're more at ease since realising that attention brings status as heritage; instead of old buildings losing them face, it gains face. Finally, walking tours and spotter's guides to architecture include modernist landmarks too.

Memory is good for business. Boutique hotels and restaurants often display their building's potted history. Period interiors make tangible the lost world of the patrician who built Phraya Palazzo, or the Indian doctor who lived in what's now the 1940s-era Bangkokian Museum. Fashion-conscious residents now treat nostalgia as a fad, whether Rama V era quaintness, mid-century modern retro.

Bangkokians have become invested in the past life of Bangkok. Partly that's nostalgia. Modernity appeals for its material status, but breakneck change leaves people disoriented, unmoored from time-honoured touchstones, rarely seeing elders. Community history and established ways were passed down because children in extended families were raised by seniors while the parents worked. Grandparents acted as a conservative brake on change by imparting stories, skills, and an affinity for tradition. Over two generations, Bangkok has become a city of nuclear families, trimming that lineage, but becoming curious about the last of things.

The present is a tussle over whose past will make it to the future. Discovering missing links about your ancestry carries a thrill. Finding out the cause of unexplained puzzles brings relief, perhaps sadness, but also confidence. Retrieving what's lost and saving what's precious clearly energises many of the young, the creative and the disaffected. No wonder Thai society feels traumatised, yet also giddily liberated – amnesiac Bangkok is recovering the gaps in its memory.

Protukate

Sorry Rome, Thais call Catholicism "the religion of the Portuguese." The first Christians to visit Siam (in 1511) they integrated better than any other *farang*. While their rival Catholic power, France, played hard but left little mark, soft power enabled Portugal's gentler presence to endure.

Rare among European imperialists, the Portuguese treated natives more like equals, albeit initially as idolaters. "The Portuguese had no idea what religious tolerance was, and so mistook Thai tolerance and interest as potential to convert," said Giacomo Mauri at a symposium on the 500th anniversary of Sino-Portuguese contact. Similarly, the Siamese couldn't imagine one monopoly god so intolerant of their multiple Buddhist-Hindu-Animist deities. "Unlike the French, the Portuguese realised very early that the Thais wouldn't convert. So they married locals, who became Catholic, sustaining the culture. They had the same strategy as the Muslims adopted; they became an indigenous community: the '*protukate*'."

You can still make out the olive skin, curly hair and rounder noses of their descendants in three *protukate yaan*, which show how deeply Europeans are part of this city. The grey square tower of the Church of the Immaculate Conception marks the Ayutthaya-era *yaan* of Samsen, Siam's second *bandel* (non-colonial settlement), granted in 1674 by King Narai. The Thonburi-era enclave of Kudi Jeen was settled in 1767 by Portuguese refugees floating on rafts from Siam's first *bandel* in ruined Ayutthaya. Today's domed Santa Cruz Church of 1913 was built by Italians working at the court. King Taksin had granted this prime land because they'd used their weaponry skills to help expel the Burmese. Long known as *farang man peun* (European gunmen), they were trusted to run the city's forts.

The area's name is disputed. Kudi is not from *kuti* (monk's residence), but a Mon word also applied to Thonburi's Shi'a mosques. Jeen likely means Chinese, but perhaps not from the nearby Hokkien shrine of Kian Un Keng, rather the Chinese roof on the second Santa Cruz chapel.

When Bangkok became the capital, a splinter group from Kudi Jeen were granted land at Talad Noi, where now stands the Gothic yellow spire of Holy Rosary Church of 1890. Thais dub it Wat Kalawar (after Calvary), and the church calls itself the "Temple of Death." In a rear chapel, a lacerated carving of Jesus eternally bleeds. In another show of trust, the Portuguese were granted the first European embassy, at Kalawar in 1820, closer to the power centre than the later British and French legations.

"Kudi Jeen seemed to be the most civilised village in [the mid-19th century]," says Narong Jaroensuk, 78. "So many new things appeared, such as a big department store named Morgan & Hunter, Siam's first photo studio of Frances Chit & Son on a house boat, Dr Bradley's clinic and printing press." Bangkokians went there by ferry for vaccinations, surgery, printing, tools, toiletries, homewares and portraits before Bangkok's new roads, shops and markets left Kudi Jeen in aspic.

So trusted were *protukate* that many rose to

left: **Bangkokians love Christmas, less so Easter, which gets a bit gruesome. Each Good Friday, Kudi Jeen reenacts the crucifixion of Jesus on the riverside, with Catholic Protukate locals playing roles in the Passion, some dressed up as Romans.**

below left: **Santa Cruz Church at Kudi Jeen's Protukate community.**

below: **Protukate devotees *wai* while touching the wounds of a wooden Christ, which was lowered from the crucifix, then draped under a Thai-style net of fragrant flowers.**

high titled rank. "This is the reason they remain a distinct group in Thai society," says Mauri. "Even today the *protukate* do the same professions: doctors, professors, soldiers. They're not good at business; they serve the state and so aren't very wealthy." However, during the Phibun dictatorship of the 1940s-50s, the suppression of minorities included the *protukate*. Discreet discussion of Protukate identity revived in the 2000s through interest in the multi-cultural *yaan* of Kudi Jeen, where a museum is planned for the wooden gingerbread mansion Windsor House.

The lantern-jawed great-grandson of a Captain Felipe, Narong hails from one of Kudi Jeen's 19 families who can trace Portuguese lineage, although only the Buptistas retain a non-Thai family name. "In 1965, I was in the national shooting team," he beams. "So I kept alive the term *farang man peun*!" Intermarriage, nationalism and modern lifestyle loosened such close-knit bonds, he laments. "Young people have forgotten. Some don't even know they descend from the Portuguese, because it's very mixed with Chinese, Thai, Mon."

Their greatest contribution was to transform Thai food, having introduced papaya, tomato and chilli, plus 'Thai' egg desserts. At Thai weddings, bride and groom exchange *foy thong*, *thong yod* and *thong yip*: golden sugar-and-egg strands, droplets and cups. These desserts were taught at court by Marie Guyomar de Pinha, the Goan-Japanese widow of Constantine Phaulkon, King Narai's Greek chief minister who was executed in a coup. Her story inspired *Golden Teardrops*, a sculpture of 6000 brass droplets by Arin Rungjang that debuted at the Thai Pavilion in the 2013 Venice Biennale. A version of that suspended sculpture hangs near Kudi Jeen at IconSiam.

Another iconic dessert is *khanom farang kudi jeen*, a cake of duck egg and candied fruit. Thanusingha Bakery House bakes a thousand cupcakes a day in a wooden filigree workshop. "I'm fifth generation *protukate*," says Pong, a baker who became Buddhist through his Thai mother. "I tried to investigate back, but I could manage only five generations. In Thailand we're not used to recording the past."

Ethnic amnesia and contextless history hides the reach and depth of Bangkok's diasporic communities. Like Chinese and Indian-Thais, the *protukate* shaped this city whilst also connecting it to a vast family of *bandels* and golden cultural threads around the globe.

Face **293**

Tourist Trappings
Branding Bangkok to the world

Bangkok is consistently the world's most visited city. Within five years of dethroning London in 2013, it could boast over 20 million arrivals, about twice the city's population. The Thai capital was also voted Best City by readers of *Travel + Leisure* four years running, and places at or near the top in other polls and charts. Bangkok loves being liked, but not all agree about what swelled this lackadaisical playground into the darling of those who love cities.

As the capital showcases so many prestigious sights, officialdom insists that visitors come for the high culture. To admit anything less noble would lose face, but that denial prompts eye-rolls among onlookers and tourists who've been coming, and coming back, due to Bangkok's allure to their senses. Bangkok's unique selling point is the exuberant mix of formal and informal attractions. The hifalutin side feels all the more fantastical because the seamier side lends such frisson. Visitors relish the feeling that all human life is here, and on display.

Thailand's presentation and appeal had for decades been largely non-urban: beach, pastoral and mountain settings. Historically, Bangkok was always a busy entrepôt and transit hub, but for tourists it had largely been a brief stopover for shopping, sights and a gawp at the saucy nightlife. Suddenly in the 2000s, Bangkok emerged as a prime destination in itself, and the draw was its unique kind of cityness.

Bangkok was ripe to benefit from a global shift in the zeitgeist. One factor was the international democratisation of luxury, which Bangkok served brilliantly through exquisite hotels, dining, spas and malls – all still at competitive prices. Another plus was the (since passed) trend for things ethnic, which again Bangkok was poised to provide, from festivals to herbalism and neo-tropical design.

As travellers' consumption shifted from packaged exoticism to authentic experiences, Bangkok again delivered. Trends for urban soft adventure – streetfood, cycling, homestays, community tours, engaging with local arts and music – found its epitome in Bangkok's chaotic popular culture. It has even drawn "extreme tourism": with daredevils exploring Bangkok's abandoned sites. Social media accentuated all this, with Bangkok claiming two of the most Instagrammed sites on earth.

The private sector easily adapted to trends like shabby chic and slum cycling tours, which jar with promoting national 'face.' The Tourism Authority of Thailand (TAT), which had led the world in country-marketing from 1987 till the mid-2000s, now played catch-up in adjusting to changing patterns in who comes and why.

Mention "Bangkok" to anyone and the response won't be neutral. But what trips peoples' triggers about Bangkok depends on the tourists themselves, whose origin and tastes keep shifting. Adventurers and misfits passed through between the mid-19th and 20th centuries. Their writings tell us much of what we know about the city's unofficial history. From these pioneers came the comparison 'Venice of the East' and the swooning fancy of Siam as the Land of Smiles.

The first mass tourists were US forces on leave from the American war in Indochina. Troops dubbed it R&R for 'rest and relaxation', though it was more like 'raunch and recreation'. Their antics colour Bangkok's notoriety and tourist services to this day (and night). By 2013, NGOs suspected that out of 26.74 million visitors, 11.23 million men were sex tourists.

Hippies had started coming in the 1970s, but the opening of guesthouses in Khao San Road for the Bangkok Bicentennial in 1982 turned that lane into a magnet for backpackers. At first the 'Dharma-Bums who went East' were mostly Western males. As taking a 'gap year' of shoestring travel became a norm in the West, they were joined by females and Khao San spawned an uninhibited party scene. While oft maligned for looking scruffy, backpackers pioneered many tourism innovations, from treks and community tours to courses in cooking, diving or massage.

Bangkok's visitorship had long settled into a 60:40 male:female imbalance. That masculine bias is still true among longtime Western and Japanese markets. So most of the sales pitches – shopping, food, spas, weddings, beauty clinics, culture – try to entice females, like TAT's Women Visit Thailand Year 1992 and 'Women's Journey' campaign.

What shifted the gender imbalance to 52% women was the influx of Chinese mass tourism.

"When Chinese men make a lot of money, they tend to take their wife, daughter and mother to travel, making the ratio heavier on the female side," says Virat Chatturaputpitak of the Thai Travel Agents Association. Among Bangkok's fans are city-loving single women, especially Western or Japanese, who rate the city as safer than it really is. Despite human trafficking and a spate of rapes that led to female zones in buses and trains, women rarely get accosted. Compared to Muslim, South Asian or Latin machismo, Thai men pester far less.

Selling the city as a precious spectacle began with the Bicentennial in 1982, just three years after TAT was founded. Ever since, print, TV and online promotion conjures a phantasmagoric pageantry of shimmering dancers, costumed natives, painted elephants, gilded barges, glittering temples and sumptuous banquets, spangled with shopping bags and superlative adjectives. Not just ads by TAT and Thai Airways, but commercial imagery too, revel in this majestic projection. One TAT slogan read: "Thailand: the Most Exotic Country in Asia." Bangkok became what I term 'Auto-Orientalist' – exoticising itself.

Visit Thailand Year in 1987-88 extended TAT's exotic theme to pull long-distance tourists from Japan and the West. Marking King Bhumibol's 5th cycle birthday, it ran until he became the longest reigning monarch in 1988. This template for promoting an entire country was copied worldwide. After the 1997 collapse of the baht, TAT went on to show how

top left: All of the Grand Palace surroundings have been given over to handling mass tourism.

right: **Wat Pho reflected in one of the many group tour buses outside.**

to rebrand a country re-emerging from crisis, using two brilliant strategies. The on-going Thailand Grand Sale, a twice-yearly discount campaign, has supported Bangkok's rise as an Asian retail magnet where even Singaporeans come to buy. The Grand Sale shopping bag appears on so many tourist ads it could stand as a mascot of this consumerist city. Then TAT used a much-copied idea: a single adjective to embody a destination. Risky reductionism, yes, but in "Amazing Thailand 1998" they picked the right word.

The genius of "amazing" is that it sums up the Thai extremes – all of them. When media and the public applied the epithet to "Amazing Traffic" or "Amazing Corruption", TAT was horrified. They'd assumed it meant only good, but as an expression of intensity, 'amazing' was unintentionally realist. The intensity of Bangkok is undeniably amazing. Whenever newer campaigns flop, TAT keep coming back to Amazing.

Every destination promotes itself, but in an act of auto-Orientalism TAT made 'Thainess' its prime selling point. The national narrative is enchanting, but tourists bore of hearing the same Thainess script in the airport, at their hotel, in the spa, from their tour guides, in museums, through advertising, and in every scene of the Siam Niramit tourist show. For visitors to stay longer, spend more and return, they need attractions of fresh interest.

There's world-class shopping and food, but few secondary sights. Bangkok hasn't developed a breadth of museums or art collections with blockbuster exhibitions. Unlike regional rivals, it lacks international-level arts and film festivals, theatrical shows, or sporting occasions. There's no must-see theme park, casino or cabaret. Even Thai culture lacks venues. While the National Theatre is mostly dark, Thai traditional music or dance-drama oddly lacks a permanent stage aside from *khon* at Chalerm Krung theatre.

With famous sights saturated and limited secondary ones, TAT directed foreign and domestic tourists to new areas of 'Unseen Bangkok.' This was already happening as tourist tastes shifted towards shopping and restaurants, focused in more downtown and residential areas like Sukhumvit. The BMA planned a museum of every district, and its Bangkok Tourist Bureau (BTB) encouraged community contact, walking tours, cycling routes and attention on little known treasures away from the main drag. This also focused on Thais. As a boom in Thai-language guidebooks, websites and travelogues testify, Thais filter their sightseeing through food and photography.

When a string of crises through the 2000s threatened the tourism industry, visitors kept coming, which sparked a new label: "Teflon Thailand." Bangkok's rise to top destination city came despite the post-2008 Great Recession, which hit established long-haul Western markets. New tourists more than took up the slack: North Asians, South Asians, Central Asians, Russians, Arabs, ASEAN. Bangkok had been a convenient hinge for intercontinental travel with long arms to Europe/Middle East, Japan/US, and Australasia; now it's also a central hub for East Asia with countless smaller spokes. As soon as budget airlines launched in Asia, Bangkok became the magnet for long weekenders, timid first-time holidaymakers and North Asians on their "Golden Week" national breaks.

Bangkok's "single hub" air policy – which saw Don Mueang shuttered when Suvarnabhumi Airport opened in 2006 – had to be abandoned when arrivals soared, reaching 60.8 million in 2017. Don Mueang reopened and by 2015 it became the world's busiest budget airline hub, with 38.3 million passengers by 2017. Even before the Airport Link reached Don Mueang, plans emerged to extend the train line from an expanding Suvarnabhumi to an upgraded U-Tapao Airport beyond Pattaya, creating a triple air hub.

left: **Guests at So/ Hotel get a pool view of Lumpini Park and the Srifuengfung Tower, a since demolished landmark.** *Courtesy So/ Hotel*

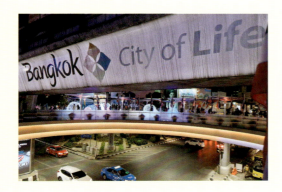

Slogans

Bangkok has been called a lot of things: romantically 'Venice of the East;' less romantically 'Big Durian,' 'Big Mango' or 'The Kok'. In taking charge of their international image, the authorities first applied national slogans to the capital: 'Land of Smiles', led to 'City of Smiles;' 'Amazing Thailand', spawned 'Amazing Bangkok', but the newly prominent city needed its own hip brand.

"The latest [city] to enter into the futility of a slogan competition is Bangkok," reported a city branding blog, noting the track-record that the whim of "silver bullet slogan" contests prevent a coherent branding strategy.

In 2012, BMA unveiled the chosen motto to demonstrate Bangkok's distinctiveness to locals and tourists in under 30 Thai letters. Mottos can evoke a city's less pristine aspects, as in London's 'The Big Smoke' or 'Whatever happens in Vegas stays in Vegas'. But the shortlist jury banned references to popular taste or informal streetlife in favour of prestige. 'World Class City with Historic Highlights' and 'Renowned Metropolis with Cultural Charm' lost the vote to a winner that safely avoided class and charm: "City of angels, built by angels, central city of governance, brilliant temples and palaces, the capital of Thailand." Reading like key words from its formal name plus generic Wikipedia data, the motto was due to adorn placards at 800 beauty spots, and doubtless attract crowds of governance tourists.

That contrasts with the analysis by an international branding agency that was commissioned a decade earlier to encapsulate the city's personality and identity. In marketing terms its profile for Bangkok's character matched that of a young woman, with attributes of being warm and generous, but insecure and overly sensitive. Matching these qualities with the populace's favourite symbol, the agency recommended that Bangkok be called 'The Big Heart'. Charming and in tune with the times, The Big Heart chimes with Thai, Asian and Western feelings about Bangkok – and even embraces the tourism professionals who embrace tourists. Yet the moment was lost. 'Heart of Asia' was soon taken by Taiwan, and Bangkok picked the equally apposite 'City of Life'.

Meanwhile, commerce came up with more memorable brands, like Emporium's souvenir range with the catchline: "Ich Bin Ein Bangkokian." Just as Bangkok gets a classy World City image, young Thai designers are embracing their former edginess as 'Sin City'. Urface launched a range of bags and clothes with pop imagery, labelled 'Bangcock'.

To similar mainstream marketing success, Adisak 'Beam' Jirasakkasem wanted to "find a new way to promote Bangkok, instead of the usual hook of temples or tuk-tuks." With Supakorn 'Grofe' Buaruan, he sprayed the graffiti 'I wanna Bangkok' on walls around town, before launching a range of clothing and bags bearing the slogan as "a naughty campaign promoting Bangkok and its current energy." This goes beyond portraying the city to inspiring its citizens and becoming a now-widespread souvenir brand. "We have our own philosophy. I want to remind the younger generation that they have a choice, and can be anyone they want to be. We are the future. We express ourselves freely."

above: **'City of Life'** is Bangkok's official and realistic slogan, seen here on the Skytrain line above the MBK/BACC Skywalk.

below: **'Bangcock'** is the slogan of Urface brand's bags and clothes.

bottom: **'I Wanna Bangkok'** slogan adorns bags, shirts and aprons.

Now that China, followed by Korea and Japan top the arrivals, the mystique of the exotic East has morphed into a different kind of 'other': the exotic South! Bangkok has become the Spain of China, which possessively calls this region Nanyang (Southern Ocean) and views Thailand as a quaint taste of tradition since lost from the Middle Kingdom. China's highest grossing movie, *Lost in Thailand*, was partly set in Bangkok and showed a trio's misadventures – no less objectifying of Thais than an American trio's misadventures here in Hollywood's *Hangover 2*.

When cool Northern Europe emerged from post-WWII austerity, it headed to Spain's warm Costa del Sol; now middle-class masses from cool Northern Asia (China, Korea, Japan, Kazakhstan, Russia) head to this tropical Spain. Bangkok's role is as gateway, market, buffet, masseur, karaoke companion and clinic. Asians seek a different holiday balance from the heritage and culture that dominates Western guidebooks. However, tourists from all origins are shifting towards the lifestyle tourism favoured by Asians, especially shopping, food, photo-ops, aesthetic ops, merry-making and merit-making at Ratchaprasong's shrines.

A city of minority networks, Bangkok attracts networks of minority tourists. In a tribute to Thai tolerance, these minorities might be mutually antagonistic and less welcome in certain lands – Arabs, Israelis, gays – yet all find succour in Bangkok. "We live in a country that is open and pretty liberal," said Wisoot Buachoom of TAT in a *New York Times* article called 'Thais cast a wide net for diverse tourists'. "I can't think of a market that we wouldn't welcome."

More than half of Thailand's tourists are return visitors, including regulars who come for the same period(s) each year. Perhaps the most loyal tourists of all are the gays. Bangkok is no paradise for gays, but few other places allow them so much unhassled space. "We've been to countries where it's illegal to be gay," said Australian Alex Cross at a Silom bar on a gaycation with his partner. "Here we can express ourselves… I feel there is no judgment here." Thais do judge, of course, but indirectly, mildly and without religious cruelty. The hospitality industry is hugely shaped by gays, but while that goes under the public radar, it bleeps on gaydar. TAT liked receiving the Pink Baht, but had tip-toed around how to acknowledge its source, until finally in 2013 launching a promo for gays and lesbians in scenes as touching as any honeymoon ad: "Go Thai – Be Free."

One of Bangkok's eye-popping juxtapositions is the way Muslim family tourism shares Nana with go-go sex tourism. Like other red-light districts of Patpong and Soi Cowboy, Nana is a hangover from the mostly Western expat and tourist era; now those go-go bars draw ogling tourists from harsher moral climates all over the world. Meanwhile, East Asian sex tourists pay hostesses at karaoke lounges and soap parlours in locales like Ratchada.

How people dress and behave matters much in Thai values. Many wince at the slovenly attire and boorish antics of 'ugly Americans' or Aussie 'bogans.' Now ire flares publicly over Chinese acting loud and brusque. In 2015 Thais published a manual on etiquette for Chinese, while a Chinese student here, Wei Yunmei, critiqued her crasser fellow Han in an e-book. "People who don't have these behaviours shouldn't be offended," she says of its title, *Pigs on the Loose*. "Chinese tourists who travel alone or as couples are the ones who want to explore and understand the culture, religion and people. But travelling in a group gives you a sort of protection so you don't have to change yourself." Tolerant hospitality versus "when in Rome" respect for local mores – it's travel's eternal tradeoff.

"It is just a significant difference between cultures, which we Thais are not accustomed to," said top official, Mongkol Suksai, of complaints

above: **One of Bangkok's many Arab tourists at a parade near Siam.**

about Chinese tourist rudeness. "That is why it is vital that we make them understand how Thai people are. It is our job to show them what is acceptable, and more importantly, what is inappropriate in Thai culture."

When tourism bigwigs talk of seeking "quality tourists," observers assume this must mean limits on mass tourism. Yet quality isn't incompatible with quantity given what's seemingly considered appropriate: manners and money. Bangkok places fifth in tourist spending (US$16.36 billion) but the tourist daily outlay (US$173) is just 60% of Singapore's and a third of Dubai's. Thailand Elite Card, was launched in 2003 as the world's first national loyalty scheme, offering golf, spa, valet-parking and long visas, marketing the country like a country club. "The definition of quality means those who have high spending around 4-5,000 baht each day," TAT Governor Thawatchai Arunyik explained. "Otherwise I do not know how to gauge if the industry is successful or not."

The true measure of quality tourism is not money, but quality: of attractions, of environment, of infrastructure, of treatment. Thailand didn't pursue the culturally sustainable route of France or Italy; it slid the way of Spain, Greece and Turkey, which undermined their beauty in the chase for volume, while treating tourists as an inexhaustible tap. "It doesn't take long for the so-called quality tourist to be driven out of town," notes blogger Ian Jack, whether in loss of heritage or the alienation of guests. "It is every baht-bus driver who pulled away without giving change. It is every chicken vendor who charged the foreigner more. It is every traffic ticket issued unfairly. It is every tour guide who refused to help a stranded tourist because 'he didn't pay for a guide.' And the Thai police do nothing about these people. Instead, the tourist is usually blamed in some way. Imagine those bad experiences being shared by social media in all corners of the world. As it is in China, right now."

As the flow of Europeans, Americans and Australians drained elsewhere, Central Asians arrived en masse, but now the Russians are departing. Chinese soared to ten million tourists, a third of the total. But then in 2018 – when an official punched a Chinese at immigration, and a junta leader blamed a mass boat drowning of Chinese on the Chinese – arrivals from China plummeted. Now the Arabs and Indians are being enticed. No market can be taken for

Urban Explorers

Bangkok feels like an adventure. The city nudges you out of your comfort zone, whether to leap into a canal boat, find a crocodile pond in Wat Chakkrawat, or marvel at Siriraj Hospital museum's preserved testicles the size of a backpack.

Urban explorers go further by venturing into abandoned spaces before they get closed off. You now need permission to do the dare of climbing the unfinished Sathorn Unique, which was known as the 'Ghost Tower' even before a foreigner suicided in its unfenced upper floors. But it's harder to see the carp farm in the flooded basement of the condemned New World Department Store at Banglamphu.

Some adventures go mainstream, like tracking the graffiti 'gallery' on the pillars of the aborted Hopewell train line. No sight is more arresting than the 'airplane graveyard' opposite Ramkhamhaeng Soi 62. You must pay admission to the caretaker family who live and raise fighting cocks in the broken fuselages of jets from the former airline Thai Smile.

top: **Climbing the Ghost Tower was a hip dare.**

above: **Scoping out the airplane graveyard.**

Face 299

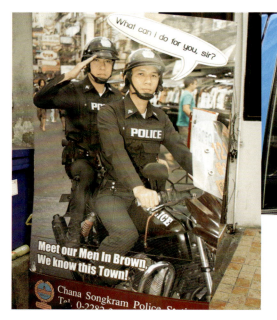

left: **The Tourist Police at your service. Just dial 191.**

above: **Taxi drivers love to try their English, asking passengers which football team they support.**

below right: **A *maneki-neko* cat beckons in customers from within the jaws of a *wai*-ing crocodile at a leather shop in Chatuchak Market.**

granted as structural problems roil the industry, from safety and shakedowns to double-charging and 'zero-baht tours.'

Petty hassles afflict cities worldwide, but despite an unthreatening ambiance, Thailand ranks low for tourist safety, and is the most lethal destination for Britons. "In 2014, there were train, bus, ferry, speedboat, motorbike and car accidents, murders, knifings, unexplained deaths, numerous suicides, diving accidents, robberies gone wrong, anonymous bodies washing up on the shores and a string of alcohol- and drug-related incidents," said Australian ex-correspondent John Stapleton, author of *Thailand: Deadly Destination*. "Thailand is still relatively safe to visit, …but tourists should be aware that this is a country where things can very suddenly go very wrong, and where there is no credible functioning justice system."

To cope with foreigners in trouble, there's the Tourist Police on 1155, a complaints line at 1111, and a Tourist Court for quick rulings. They face a lot of work. *CNN Go* listed things for travellers to watch out for. Top came the "Ciggy Police," who fine foreigners B2,000 for dropping a cigarette butt, ten times the rarely enforced Thai fine, reported Cattleya Jaruthavee, who noted "the well-documented sting operations set up to net hapless tourists and get them to hand over cash on the spot." She also listed "mafia-controlled beggars"; "red-light extortions," taxis not using the meter; tiered pricing; and touts who con tourists into taking a tuk-tuk to a gem scam, often facilitated by a spiked drink.

"The litany of troubles, frauds and crimes has grown as result of increasing greed," admitted TAT deputy governor Sugree Sithivanich. "Tourism won't be able to move forward if Thais don't improve their mindset." Often the first experience of Bangkok is an airport taxi overcharging. Media also reported an entrapment scam at Departures, whereby shoppers get falsely accused of theft to extort a bribe for their release. The wary now ask staff to take goods to the till. That's one hell of a hello and goodbye.

"The government claims to respect tourists as special guests. But it seems to be treating them as nothing more than walking ATMs," read a *Bangkok Post* editorial. "No topic sets a tourist's teeth on edge like double-pricing. The government knows this. When it sets different prices for Thai and foreign visitors, it prints the local price in Thai script. This merely compounds the sneaky intent, since tourists know full well about this trick. The amount of money shaken out of tourists' pockets is negligible, especially when put against the ill-will it causes."

Tourism is integral to Thailand's showing 'face,' but that's a social value more about self-image than how others truly view it. When unhappy situations occur, blame is invariably deflected onto a foreign scapegoat due to widespread xenophobia. "I walked the touristy bits of Bangkok pretending that I was a foreigner that couldn't speak Thai," said Australian expat Stuart Jay Raj on Facebook. "I was lied to, cheated, paid 180 Baht for a 40 Baht dish, laughed at and insulted… but all done with a smile of course. It takes a little bit of the euphoria out of the 'nice feelings' that Thailand leaves people with. It might have all been smoke and mirrors."

Efforts to stop bad news denting tourism end up fuelling the Streisand effect: inadvertently publicising the flaw. One bold response to the bad press was to roll with the critics, while pointing out that it's still amazing. In a viral video viewed 1.5 million times, 'I Hate Thailand,' a robbed backpacker yells "fuck" at police and throws rocks at a truck, but ultimately had an enriching time through the kindness of ordinary Thais and stayed on to live here. It was unmasked as a trolling campaign by TAT that won ad awards for 'Branded Content.' "The intention is to remind and educate the Thai people to always be a good host and not to take advantage of tourists," said Thawatchai of TAT, though tellingly the theft was by a monkey, with no blame on Thais.

Tourism affects a fifth of the country's economy, including indirect trades. The consequences reach so far that each sector wants to steer it in their direction. Commerce and corruption milk it dry, leaving almost no bench to sit without having to buy something. Creatives are generating new attractions in food and nightlife tourism. Bangkok Vanguards and Hivesters are among the social-enterprises supporting 'sustainable' community-based tourism. Yet all this can't help but diminish the quality of life under mass tourism, with overburdened transport the clearest blight.

Tourism can contribute much to a place, injecting energy and broadening its outlook, but sheer volume is flattening what makes Bangkok distinct. That blanding out has intensified through corporate domination, as travel shifts from seeking out difference to seeking out your lifestyle tastes in a new location. Social media treats anywhere primarily as a backdrop for selfies.

Tourism now reshapes the city. Ratchaprasong is geared to visitors, who've also displaced locals from Chatuchak Weekend Market. The old city of Rattanakosin has been purged of its communities and authentic occupations to make a historical park with vast crowds following flags held up by guides. Tha Maharaj pier mini-mall of chain outlets has transformed Tha Phra Chan, a still charming lane of students, amulet stalls, art supplies and indie music shops. Similarly, the flower market has been crimped by the characterless tourist trap Yodpiman River Walk. As long as mass-tourism is the aim, the hordes (and their coaches) must be accommodated somewhere.

Bangkok used to be known for its tailored tourism, but as sights have become more generic, indie entrepreneurs have revived personalised tours of non-obvious localities and niche interests. Inevitably, the mainstream now follows those cycle tours to slums, food tours of market stalls, art tours of galleries and craft workshops. With apps and online top-ten listicles replacing the curated style of guidebooks, the whole city is now exposed to tourism. As souvenirs, commodified crafts have almost all been replaced by mass-produced gewgaws. As a result, Bangkok feels more crowded, more generic, and more expensive, yet still amazing.

In a refreshing change from selling tourists a superlative adjective, TAT asked tourists what they truly want. The results were chastening. What visitors most cherished was not the high culture but its opposite – the liberating effect of the everyday chaos, which puts people at ease. Holidaymakers seek a respite from social pressure, not a lesson in propriety. Bangkok's gift to the world is its messy personal freedom. As it happens, the BMA's catchline already summed up that appeal: "Bangkok – City of Life."

Backpackers

Bangkok has a term for backpackers who grow blond dreadlocks, bargain too low, pair batik pantaloons with a tie-die vest, and reek of patchouli. They might be a Lord or a lawyer, but Thais still call them "*farang kii nok*" – bird shit Whitey.

Backpackers contribute a great deal to Bangkok, but go unappreciated due to offending Thai status values. Ostentatiously touring on a budget, and often unkempt, they lose face for seeming cheap. Independent by mission, they lack deference. Accessorised with ethnic crafts, backpackers tend to be curious, open and an "active participant in the world," notes Anita Mendiratta of travel news agency ETN. Yet Social Justice Wanderers' anti-hierarchy agenda can affront indigenous values, from negating social boundaries to baring too much skin. Hauling a backpack into the BTS prompts a visible recoil.

The 'packer tribe appears as a suspect 'other' to orderly Bangkokians. Conspicuously, four million of them a year collect in one main ghetto: Khao San (Milled Rice) Road in Banglamphu. Guesthouses opened there in 1982 to access the Bicentennial pageantry. Within a decade, this Freak Street magically mushroomed into a source of anything a 'seeker of experience' might consume, and entered the collective consciousness of the *Lonely Planet*.

Listed in *Lonely Planet*'s shoestring guides, Khao San flophouses spilled over into Rambuttri Road and Samsen's *sois*. In open fronted reception cafés, travellers swap tales, now spreading them via social media instead of the guestbooks of old. Upstairs, the tiny subdivided rooms had partitions so thin that in *The Beach* by Alex Garland, the protagonist overhears rumours of an idyll untouched by tourism.

Re-touched by tourism, Khao San rebuilt its dives into boutique hotels, starting with Buddy Beer, and swapped bookshops for stalls of digital music downloads. Mainstream Thais had been timid to visit until indie bars opened around 2000, founding a parallel Thai nightlife scene. But the Freak Street mayhem persists: hair-braiders, ID forgers, tribal bags, vegan *pad thai*, baggy 'elephant pants', and bars in converted VW vans flogging bucket cocktails of Saeng Som rum and Red Bull. "The sense of controlled madness is an integral part of the area, typifying the best and worst of mass tourism," Duangphat Sitthipat observes. "This is the Orient at its most laid back."

The BMA tries to tidy Khao San. After the 2014 coup, they banned vendors fully, then not, then partially, then by day, but not by night. Khao San vendors then united under an elected spokeswoman who has cut a fairer deal. "I believe the market stalls constitute the popular appeal of Khao San," said a BMA advisor to the "systemisation", Wichai Sangprapai. "But it's terrible that people cannot walk on the footpaths." Since the BMA had long ago made it Bangkok's first pedestrianised street, the oft-changing purges seem less about congestion than pandering to landowners. In 2018, the BMA announced a scheme to pave it all level under a Thai-style roof, like Singapore's anodyne tourist trap,

Clarke Quay. Such "systemisation" is what youths fly here to avoid. "I like Khao San the way it is," said New Zealander Rachel Read. "It is the spirit that everyone comes here for."

Officials' calls for 'quality tourists' fail to realise that 'scruffy bohemian' is often just a style affected by affluent, educated, discerning future leaders. They'll return with family or business, but only to places that treated them well. Thailand is a top stop for backpackers, who made a fifth of the world's billion tourist trips in 2011. They stay an average of 53 days, investing far more than five-day group tours from volume markets. Bangkok was a stop on the hippy trail known as KKKK: Kabul, Kathmandu, Khao San, Kuta. But reducing visa length at land borders (to punish visa runners) causes gap year kids to hop over Thailand via budget flights. As Khao San is already a world-famous hub, "bird-shit backpackers" might wisely be prized as a Golden Goose.

"Youth travellers opened many of today's most popular destinations and led the trend to independent travel," says David Jones of WYSE (World Youth, Student & Educational). "Destinations that work to build and maintain their appeal to the youth market are future proofing their brand." They sparked whole sectors: massage study, meditation retreats, trekking, diving, island-hopping, cultural courses, cooking schools, homestays, community contact, voluntourism. Tourism needs those who are "pollinating the future of the industry."

Middle-class Bangkokians are now slipping on backpacks in an Asia-wide trend that has tripled since 2010. Indie kids led with the first Thai backpacking zine, *Barefoot*. "My friends and I always go on a backpacking trip whenever we have time," says actress Archariya 'Nujah' Peeraputkunchaya, a regular at the hippy northern village of Pai. "It offers you more time to appreciate the nature, way of life and interactions. The locals and I are like family. I have more friends from backpacking also." Independent trips have become more normal. Sithikorn Wongwudthianun says of his

solo adventures: "My idea was to travel without a guidebook, making this an 'excuse me' trip."

Travellers spurning the label 'tourist' get mocked for actually being conformist in their non-conformist consumption along the well-trod 'Banana Pancake Trail'. There's also snobbery at today's easy, digitally monitored travel, compared to the veterans' trophy hassles in the storied past: risky borders, non-connecting transit, lack of familiar foods, international phone booths, and glee at getting post restante mail.

Older and wealthier travellers, who wheel their backpack to boutique inns, get labelled 'Flashpackers', a trend fostered at Buddy Beer in Khao San, that spread citywide. Many prefer the new wave of pop-coloured modern hostels located downtown.

"Tech-savvy customers are everywhere nowadays. If the WiFi is not good, they will certainly complain," says Lub-D hostel's Nalin Kalayanamitr. Otherwise ,reputation suffers through blogs, apps and Trip Advisor. As Bangkok room prices rise, solo and group backpackers relish the price and authentic locales of Airbnb digs, which offer more privacy than a dorm – but less camaraderie.

"At the heart of youth travel is a wonderfully personal, positively selfish, desire of the traveller to be a more active participant in the world," insists Anita Mendiratta. "A backpack is an overt statement of 'I am open'. They also possess an inner courage and curiosity. They want to go see, understand, and even help." If travellers and voluntourists encounter a blander, globalised Bangkok, they still encounter new ways of being.

"People are changing their concept of backpacking," says Nikki Scott, who founded a magazine called *South East Asia Backpacker*. "It's no longer a once-in-a-lifetime experience, but also a way to find job opportunities on the road." Co-working spaces like The Hive buzz with digital nomads, who are now granted nomad visas and can be found doing startups like writing apps.

Those finding a vocation abroad follow in the flip-flopsteps of earlier globetrotters, who travelled with the forces, imperial civil service or the Peace Corps. I was part of a gap-year influx to Bangkok in the 1990s, as were those who ran the backpacker magazine *Farang* (aka *Untamed Travel*) and the many who stayed and went into journalism, advertising, art, design, events, English-teaching, modelling and specialist travel. Many eventually go home a different person; some make Bangkok home.

top left: **Hair-braiding is the traditional craft of Khao San Road, and informally brands a tourist as being a backpacker.**

left: **Elephant pants have spread from being worn by backpackers to a staple of mainstream tourist wear.**

Face 303

Portrayals
Image, imagination, investigation

Courting attention, but hurt by scrutiny, Bangkok feels misunderstood. Understanding this place is hard, and many locals claim that's not possible by non-Thais. Yet there's a growing demand to know about what is now a major World City. More foreigners than ever are visiting, living and doing business here. There's been a huge increase in arts, books and media coverage about the city, both for foreigners as well as by and for Bangkok's residents. Bangkok had been a word-of-mouth city; now it's becoming a known city.

Reputation matters above all else in this 'face' society, with taboos against criticism and directness. That narrows the scope for diverse voices, with much propaganda and censorship. Reaction to sensationalist coverage of Bangkok's darker sides makes comment a minefield of things deemed 'sensitive.' That context of risk must be borne in mind with every portrayal.

There's also more going on to portray. For decades, guides and pictorial books re-trod the same obvious landmarks and left much unexplained until the past decade. Media, art and academia have grown in scale, access and insight, as noted in the side boxes and Bibliography. Thanks to inquiry and the Internet, we all know far more about the past and the present. Social media's crowdsourced views are even less filtered or restrained.

Between foreign and Thai takes yawns a chasm in tone. Values like *sanuk* and *kreng jai* (consideration of feelings) tilt local coverage way from realism towards praise, higher status topics, even fantasy. Thai non-fiction often smooths harsh topics by using cartoon characters and sentimental touches. Thai-style portrayals done by foreigners can be just as flattering, with flawless pictures captioned by gushy blurb. Upbeat curated guides like *We Love Bangkok* (2009) and *Bangkok City Scoops* (2009) frame the city as a quirky shopping spree, while hospitality media are compromised by accepting freebies.

As truth-telling can be risky, even many foreign books on the city tend towards the chic or exoticising, though there are exposés about topics like prison or politics. Comment on sensitive topics often lurks in fiction, especially Bangkok's genre of crime novels, with its cynicism drawn from real experience. Reports for abroad can get edgier, as in a YouTube report that contrasted streetfood cuisine with vendor evictions as its music track turns ominous. Whether glorifying or grim, Bangkok stories tend to be fatalist.

As modernity wrenches an ancient society, nostalgia raises demand for images of the old. The city's earliest photos appear in *Siam Through the Lens of John Thompson* and in shots by his contemporary, the first Thai lensman Francis Chit. Ben Davies documents *Vanishing Bangkok* in monochrome, while longtime resident Steve Van Beek compares key locations in *Bangkok Then and Now*.

A new aesthetic of Bangkok's urban chaos has emerged. As Big Things like politics are risky, indie culture dwells on the observation of Small Things, seen in the handmade books, street photography, and diary-like creations at the Art Book Fair. The youth magazine *a day* themes each edition on topics in everyday life. Bangkok gets shown with stylistic realism in indie films and albums like Daido Moriyama's *A City Aglow*, and Yanyong Boon-Long's affectionate *Bangkok: Handmade Transit*.

To launch Rattanakosin as a 'Cultural District', Museum Siam invited young Thai artists to depict the city. Amid some cutesy art, over half were critical. Comic book illustrator 3Puck made stickers of the marginalised, like garland sellers, glue sniffers and black magic gurus. Thanathip Jenthumrong generated a digital lottery draw for those who buy a ticket depicting problems, like unsafe bus driving, that are as unlikely to solve as winning a lottery. "I call my drawings not Bangkok city, but 'Bangkok Shitty,'" said Mayawee 'Benxblues' Thongsong, who drew intertwined urban problems with all the citizens' faces as black hollows. Their works illustrate this chapter's boxed text on 'Theories of Bangkok.'

In response to the alienated 'ugly aesthetic' of Thai urbanism, the mainstream has appropriated shophouse scenes as happy idylls rather than as hardscrabble realism. Neo-traditional arts project a pristine heritage. Bourgeois walls depict golden-era canalscapes of wooden houses, boat-noodle vendors and boys in topknots, jumping into water cleaner than the actual murk. To many locals, that is the warm Bangkok of the heart, and in Buddhist logic, it's reality that's the illusion.

Regardless, technology now portrays Bangkok digitally. Uploading words, sounds and pictures online is revolutionising public access to information and expression. Awkward facts and satire all get magnified via internet meme. This data can't be unlearned and feeds back into discourse. Digital devices also empower censors to spy and punish

left: **Modern city, ancient mindsets.** *Siam 2* by Teerawat Nutcharoenpol from the exhibition *Dramathais*.

above: **Digital mapping of the river, projected onto Magnolias Ratchadamri Boulevard at that condo's launch.**

Face 305

netizens for controversial posts. From all sides, accusations of fake portrayals swirl. In 2019, the state opened a monitoring centre to protect the public against 'fake news,' as if that couldn't emanate from the enforcers.

Even mild critiques may get condemned as "destroying the country." That's because face loss is felt as shaming one's entire social being, and underpins legitimacy of rank. Judging by foreign or universal standards undercuts the sense of Thai exceptionalism.

All countries have self-interested myths, but Thailand is one that proclaims its exceptionalism, despite sharing so much of its culture with neighbouring lands. The idea that Thailand is exempt from understanding or outside standards goes beyond mere exceptionalism, to what could be called 'Cultural Exemptionism.'

Foreign portrayals often get dismissed as biased or ignorant, but their main offence is not submitting to the official narrative or the system of deference. Hence the efforts to monopolise how Bangkok's perceived through censorship, law suits or social sanction.

Three past portrayals show the potential backlash. The publisher Longman has been banned since 1993 due to its dictionary definition of Bangkok: "It is famous for its temples and other beautiful buildings, and is also often mentioned as a place where there are a lot of prostitutes." Amid many protests, students burned the dictionary, which now just defines Bangkok as beautiful, matching the city's self image. The streetwise *Bangkok Inside Out* (2004) wasn't banned, but the Culture Ministry "asked shops not to stock it," because of sarcasm and one risqué photo. The most famous Orientalist tale of Bangkok – *The King and I* musical (1956) – was banned under the royal defamation law. Known as lese majeste, it ensures effusive coverage of regal Krungthep. Courts recently broadened it to cover past rulers, making city histories either incomplete or unpublishable.

Civil libel requires proof, so the offended reach for the criminal charge of defamation, in which truth is no defence. Whistleblowers, NGOs and even BBC reporters who expose a crime can face jail for damaging the reputation of a high-status perpetrator. So investigative reporting barely exists in what David Streckfuss, author of *Truth on Trial in Thailand*, dubs a "Defamation State."

Journalists and academics bump up against facts too risky to reveal. Investigations fall foul of 'influential figures.' Historians find gaps in archives that were lost, tossed, or never filed, with access barred to 'sensitive' documents. Filling those holes may provoke censure, so everyone, including world media, self-censors. If news crosses the ambiguous line, a private phone call can shut the reporting down. That's why news updates often omit crucial backstory – and thus so will history texts. But there are subtle ways of parking facts in public view.

Faced with this culture of indirectness, journalists and creatives resort to use of

left: **The annual Chula-Thammasat University student football match has a satirical parade, here critiquing the response to the 2011 flood.**

top right: **In *A Tale of Phantoms* by the group Nitimonster at WTF gallery, a loupe revealed tiny photos of rebellious Thais from history whose stories were suppressed.**

bottom right: **A T-shirt at FAT Festival about the blinding and silencing effects of nationalism.**

allusion, humour and coded language. Fictional Bangkok tends to be romans à clef that veil anecdotes too risky to state as fact. Initials or descriptions hint at unnamed culprits. In *BK* magazine, a spoof columnist, a teenage girl named Pancake, sends-up entitled *hi-sos*. It's risky to discuss the massacre in 1976, so it's often referred to as an 'incident' and by depictions of the folding chair used in one of the lynchings at Sanam Luang. Depicting the sex trade draws ire, so the pioneering artist Montien Boonma sculpted 'Venus of Bangkok' through an assemblage of re-used wood and twisted sheet metal propping up a red bucket and old sponge.

Bangkok (City of Plum Olives) is a realist description of place, but its nicknames are metaphoric: Venice of the East, City of Angels, Land of Smiles, Big Mango – the latter adopted by expat Jake Needham for his thriller. Its full Thai name is not literal either: Krungthep is short for a honorific claim that it's Rama's sacred city, commissioned by Indra and built by angels. Wags coin less-flattering metaphors, such as Americasia, Sin City, Big Durian or Thighlandia. Satirical cartoonist Kai Maew calls it Kala Land – 'under a coconut shell' – slang for people mistaking the shell's small interior for the universe.

Foreign coverage used to boil down to clichés: salacious scandal, political strife or orientalist exotica, like elephants begging in the infamous traffic. The boom and 1997 bust turned Bangkok into a business story, buoyed by features on its fashion, design and spas. Mass tourism then subjected Bangkok to the whims of social media reviewers. As more people see through what happens, censorship has the 'Streisand effect' of amplifying what it wants hidden.

Promoting the surface as superlative has a catch; what's beneath surely disappoints. "The magnificent image they have projected to millions has now started to backfire," writes researcher Flemming Winther Nielsen in 'Thailand's image tarnished by truth.' Many young Europeans he asked "were disgusted by much of what they saw, e.g. police arrogance, pompous officials, cheating." Singaporeans turned this same dissembling reputation into a catchphrase: "Don't Thai to me."

"We are rapidly becoming 'children of the globe' and not of national states," adds Nielsen, who notes that Millennials often join organisations with universal ideals, such as

Amnesty or Human Rights Watch. Cultural exemptionism in the name of "all Thais" must now contend with the interconnectedness of "all humans" on one planet.

"Those restating old truths are perhaps trying to reassure themselves that nothing has really changed. But it has," wrote Chang Noi (aka Chris Baker and Pasuk Phongpaichit). "The knowledge industry, both inside and outside the country, will continue trying to fill in the missing parts of the puzzle, because there is such a large audience that has so much at stake and a desire to understand." Thailand is under constant risk analysis by investors, NGOs and governments.

Bangkok touts its high ratings for most-visited city or best rooftop bar, but smarts when the self-declared Land of the Free ranks low in freedom. Foreign corruption cases that trail back here cause concern when implicating officials. Bangkok bigwigs were among those exposed by WikiLeaks and the Panama Papers, but Thai news dared not pursue it.

True Fiction

Bangkok isn't bookish, but Thai writers can be a companion to exploring its inner life though the filter of fiction. UNESCO found that Thais on average read eight lines a year, during which Vietnamese read five books and north Europeans 24 volumes. Bangkokians likely read much more than that, but all were incredulous when UNESCO named this World Book Capital 2013. It was more to foster than to honour a reading culture. It resulted in the 24-hour City Library, smaller libraries and a Museum of Thai Cartoons, although little of the budget went to stocking the shelves.

The BMA assigned a literary work (some translated in English) to each of its 50 districts. Saphanthawong (Chinatown) got Botan's *Letters from Thailand* about Sino-Thai migrants; Ratchathewi got *City People* by Krisana Asoksin, and Khlong Toei got Sri Burapha's much-filmed novel about family duty, *Behind the Painting*. *Prissana* by V na Pramuanmark is set in Jomthong, but its willful modern heroine, Miss Puzzle also faces snobbery in the Old Town district of Phra Nakhon. Most famous is *Si Phaendin* (Four Reigns) by Kukrit Pramoj, a saga set in Bangkok Yai about life through upheavals from Kings Rama V to VIII.

Peter Ackroyd and Dan Brown portray cities through historical clues in mystery novels. Now the award-winning detective novel *Kaholmahoratuek* (2014) by young author Chairat Pipitpattanaprap (aka Prapt), sparks readers to visit its settings in Phra Nakhon and Thonburi, like Kian Un Keng Shrine and a Protukate bakery in Kudi Jeen. "People don't really know much about these places. There is more to it than just the big Buddha and massages," he says. "There are also inscriptions of poems, and sculptures and rocks with stories." Cryptic words tattooed on the victims form a coded poem composed using the *kon kloeng* diagram as inscribed in Wat Pho.

Foreign writers made noir the non-Thai Bangkok Novel genre, but crime has been less popular than ghost tales among Thais, who prefer their novels romantic or righteous. "Thai literature had two pits," says Suchart Sawasdsri, a literary editor dubbed 'the encyclopedia of Thai literature'. "The first was the 'for life' pit and the second was the melodrama pit. And each side saw the other as no good."

Early Thai fiction had almost a magic realist subversiveness, but soon novels became an aristocratic hobby, then the preserve of bourgeois ladies penning prim love stories under noms de plume.

In the 1960s-70s the *Phuea Chiwit* 'For Life' movement brought idealistic politics into first literature, then art, music and film. Personal stories from experience fed into a genre of 'Literature for Life' by internal migrants, especially from Isaan, which bewails how the capital as a setting of woe.

"The artist as political activist was the paradigm for Thai writers, and that legacy still has some hold on Thai writing today," Suchart says. "It was didactic. Left or right, they were all that way. The right is still that way, even more so. A lot of morals. It has mutated... work that leaned on art, symbolism, and experimentation ended up talking about social problems more... the sentiment of being taken over by city folks, the problem of the gap between the city and the rural."

What the world knows about Bangkok literature has been distorted by the lack of translation, despite efforts in the 1990s by Marcel Barang. Literary expert Michael Barron noted that the "Five-Percent Problem" (of just 1 in 20 books being a translation) is in Thailand's case a "Zero Percent Problem." Even the 'Thai Shakespeare', Sunthorn Phu, who wrote inside and outside the court 200 years ago, has only recently gained literary justice in English, thanks to BKKLIT poetry prizewinner Noh Anothai's translation of *Poems from the Buddha's Footprint*. "Thais are very proud and rightfully so that Sunthorn Phu, their national poet, has been recognised as a representative world poet by UNESCO. Unfortunately, it's a rather superficial title," says Noh, noting the few translations. "Most were commissioned by the Thai government for his bicentennial in 1986, but are obscure and of questionable literary value."

Untranslated classics also got overlooked because some foreign-influenced Thais write in English.

above: A sculpture at BACC to mark Bangkok being UNESCO World Book Capital.

top right: Author Veeraporn Nitiprapha at LIT Fest.

right: A poster for the musical Si Phaendin.

Famed in the US for sci-fi, Somtow Sucharitkul evokes 1960s Sukhumvit in an erudite comedy of patrician manners, *Jasmine Nights*. Tew Bunnag gained repute for literary fiction like *Curtain of Rain*, in which Bangkok's wet season becomes a character and metaphor. Rattawut Lapcharoensap, gained fame abroad for *Sightseeing* (2006), with two of its short stories entwined in the film 'How to Win at Checkers Every Time.' Pitchaya Sudbanthad, a Bangkokian based in New York, earned international acclaim for *Bangkok Waits for Rain*. Penned in English, this epic threads vignettes of people connected to a wooden mansion, hopping between eras from its construction in the colonial era to a flooded future, including a love story set against the 1976 massacre. Post-Covid, a spate of fine Thai fiction in English included *Welcome Me to the Kingdom* by Mai Nardone, *A Good True Thai* by Sunisa Manning, and *Comrade Aeon's Field Guide to Bangkok* by Bangkok-born Emma Larkin.

One pioneer is Prabda Yoon, polymath son of *The Nation* newspaper founder, is also a publisher, screenwriter, filmmaker, graphic designer, editor, pundit, translator, founder of Bookmoby bookshop, and writer/producer of the bands Buahima and Typhoon. His experimental stories in *Probability* won the 2002 SEAwrite Award, the region's top literary prize, in which each country has a winner. His wordplay was so infused by Thai linguistics, that it didn't get translated until 2017, when Mui Poopoksakul won the PEN Translation Award for her brilliant rephrasing into English of his short story collection *The Sad Part Was*. They're tales of dark whimsy, whether guys holding a chilli-eating party to hail their late schoolyard crush, or a charismatic bully who goes daily to Lumpini Park just to judge strangers. A spoof on propriety sees a hi-so couple have sex on a rooftop in a storm uses haughty elocution to convey their posh affectations. Mui then translated Prabda's follow-up *Moving Parts*. One tale, of S 'n' M in a pink

suburban 'love hotel,' came from his movie *Motel Mist*.

The Thai-focused BKKLIT festival launched in 2018 and a year later a bilingual Bangkok Literature Festival. BKKLIT's first Translation Prize went to Wichayapat Piromsan for, 'The girl who was raped through her earholes' by Jidanun Lueangpiansamut, set aboard a minivan from Victory Monument to Rangsit. "A small plastic bucket is being passed from one passenger to the next," goes a metaphor for a rape survivor distressed by passenger banter.

Veeraporn Nitiprapha, founder of the indie mag *Hyper*, won the SEAwrite twice for her eccentric novels *The Blind Earthworm in a Labyrinth* and *Memories of the Memories of the Black Rose Cat*, which were both translated by Kong Rithdee for River Books. She uses a soap opera template to reveal Bangkok's ideological blindness. "If you can understand the myths of love then you can understand the myths of everything, of hatred and of conflicts," she says. "There has always been conflict in our country, but what struck me about the 2010 crackdown is how there were people who were glad about other people's deaths."

Some lament that the SEAwrite Award doesn't yet include literary non-fiction, but one benefit of its annual rotation between novels, short stories and poetry is that it motivates young Thais to attempt verse. Among Bangkok's literary lights is SEAwrite poet Zakariya Amataya, a Thai non-insider from the Muslim Deep South. "The disposition of the city is torture you done. Or is it my disposition that torments this city?" he muses in a poem about draconian punishment for sitting in an underground station. "I have the right to sit and the right to stand. Or have I have no right to sit and no right to stand?"

The rise of 'International Thai Studies' greatly extends foreign analysis and expertise. Professors, students and independent scholars trawl though sources here and beyond Thai restriction abroad. They probe case studies, develop theories and sidestep the sagas of Big Men to tell peoples' histories.

But many on the Yellow Shirt side don't accept Western media as fair or neutral. "Dear Foreign Friend, How do I write an academic study of my own lynching? How can the truth prevail against such apparent paragons of integrity and liberalism as Asian Studies academics, the BBC and *The New York Times*," wrote Ing K, director of *Bangkok Joyride*, a film about the Bangkok Shutdown protest. Referring to her writing: "The publisher is Western; can I trust them to edit something so sensitive? Won't they pass it by some Thai Studies expert who's had a grant from Thaksin perhaps through some foundation, who will say it's all lies?"

Every two years a International Thai Studies Conference alternates within Thailand and overseas. "Part of the excitement of these academic jamborees is the chemistry between the 'insiders' who have the intimacy of experiencing Thailand day by day, and the 'outsiders' who have the benefit of distance, detachment and a comparative perspective," writes Chang Noi. "Thailand can't avoid this attention. Inside there may be restrictions on debate. Outside, there are not. Academics, businessmen and journalists are all trying to understand what is truly going on."

The hyper-sensitivity of Thai portrayals seemed unusual, but the West has a taste of it now with 'identity politics,' which can prioritise hurt feelings over 'rationalist' facts and free expression.' Here, the offence felt is akin to religious blasphemy. The zeal partly derives from the Fascist era of nation building, but also from Buddhism. Whenever Thais admonish Western media, it's almost verbatim from the monastic code's 'Five Tests of False Speech,' namely is it: factual; harsh; motivated by profit; appropriately timed; or malicious?

Buddhism's precept for Right Thought leads to 'Right Speech' then 'Right Action.' In that light, propaganda, hagiography, and cleansed history might not be misinformation or denial, but positively righteous. Criticism gets decried as 'False Thought' becoming 'False Speech', which if not stifled leads to protest as 'False Action' – hence the junta deputy warning dissenters: "they have the right to think, but they cannot express that."

Often it's not what's said that's the issue, but the right to say it. Defenders of Thai Exemptionism hold the belief that knowledge is indivisible, and realised only by those with karmic wisdom. Thai people and law hold great store by intention, and that Good People with high merit have good intention, while holders of different opinions evidently have less karmic ability to comprehend. So we hear "foreigners can't understand" most from officials and conservative intellectuals who assume the role of arbiter. External views offend their claim of higher karmic position.

True believers judge iconoclasts as being easily misled, though globalised Thais are less dogmatic. "Thainess varies among Thai people. It's unconvincing to claim that what one thinks is totally correct," writes Saran Mahasupap, a Thai-language editor for Apple's Siri. "In the same way, foreigners also cannot claim that they know better than Thais." When asked if foreigners can't understand it, columnist Voranai Vanijaka retorts: "Don't be daft, even Thais don't understand Thainess! It's an issue of being self-aware."

Being objective can be just as hard for insiders as for outsiders, given their stake in a culture that punishes criticism. Tellingly, many commentators are from Bangkok's huge ranks of insider-outsiders: Thais who lived abroad, longtime expats, and *luk khrueng* with mixed parentage. Anthropology has a structure to minimise bias by declaring *emic* (insider) and *etic* (outsider) accounts. Locals are steeped in the culture, yet familiarity means they are biased and can miss patterns, quirks and comparisons. "Foreigners can't understand" is *emic* and only half the equation.

left: *Klongton, Bangkok*: A typical Bangkok moment caught by Dow Wasiksiri, a pioneer of Thai street photography.

below left: A panel at the Foreign Correspondents Club of Thailand about female motorcycle taxi drivers, with journalist Laure Siegel; writer Chris Baker; Chaloem Changthongmadn, president of the Motorcycle Taxi Association; Ussarin Kaewpradap, an expert in state enterprise workers; and FCCT President Gwen Robinson. *Photograph by Tom Vater*

The Indecisive Moment

The definitive art form of Bangkok is slices of urban life, as caught in street photography. No other medium comes close to capturing its quirkiness. Other arts interpret the city's juxtapositions, but only candid photography can capture the city's visual shocks by ambushing happenstance.

Thai street photography pioneers from the 1990s were Manit Sriwanichpoom of *Bangkok in Black and White*, and Dow Wasiksiri, who wryly snapped the unintended effects of tourism and development. The idea that affluent Thais would revel in low status streetlife rather than staged imagery had been preposterous until the mid-2000s zeitgeist for street aesthetics. Thais often label the look "Very Thai" after the as-found photos in the book, using the #verythai hashtag to post pics of popular culture online, which I feed through verythai.com.

That indie era saw DSLRs became affordable to the middle class, who roved parts of their own city they'd never cared about. Impromptu snaps of the human condition became not just the artform of Bangkok, but the artform most done by Bangkokians.

Lingering with a camera is a loner's pursuit, yet budding Thai Winogrands often shoot in groups. Posses with cameras descend on cafés, comparing shots and elaborately composing portrait shots, before stalking more subjects. Some submit images for approval to the Facebook feed of streetphotothailand.com, which was founded in 2008. The Street Photo Thailand club's shows in BACC helped spread the hobby. It proved that anyone with an eye could get wallspace.

This anti-style became a style, which permeates magazines and advertising. Cross-dressing online star Mae Ban Mee Nuad (Housewife With a Moustache) spoofed the genre by campily posing in gowns on *songtaews* and cement mixers. Yet spotting real begowned Bangkokians in unlikely settings is the kind of regular occurrence that keeps amateur lenses busy.

When anyone can be a smartphone photographer, ethics come into question. Street photography's legitimacy depends upon being free to depict anything in the public domain, though the Internet has spread ideas of privacy and that one's image is a kind of property. Yet Thais are leaders in uploading their personal photographs to Facebook, blurring privacy and personal brand. Bangkok street shooters run other risks if they photograph any illegalities in the street. A careless snap is unwelcome scrutiny to underworld traders, who can react violently, demanding to see that snap deleted. Conversely, designers suffer from pirates taking spy shots of their goods.

Thais seem happier than most to be photographed and often play up for the camera. They enjoy funny situations so long as they don't lose face. The downside is that some subjects instantly pose. Photographers wince as their artful composition morphs into cliché of practiced grins and victory-V gestures.

Bangkok street photographs often seem surreal, because the preoccupation of face-saving is a performance that can appear to observers as baffling or a futile denial of what's obvious. Such head-turning disjoints are common in an unstable city where efforts at control carry a tinge of hilarity. The originator of street photography, Frenchman Henri Cartier-Bresson, said it's all about capturing 'The Decisive Moment', the skill of freezing a moment to convey deep meaning. Given the way that Bangkok street photography can flummox the viewer with ambiguous juxtapositions, it could be said to capture 'The Indecisive Moment'.

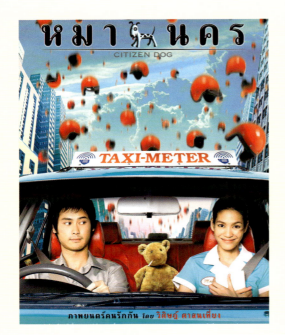

Cinematic Krungthep

Bangkok has a double-life acting as a film location for other cities, notably as Saigon in *Good Morning Vietnam*, *The Deer Hunter*, and *Tomorrow Never Dies*, with its James Bond tuk-tuk chase. It plays as an 'extra' in countless movies, but rarely does its sense of place drive the plot. Many directors began in advertising, and those values don't match the city's harsh urbanism, notes critic Robert Williams: "Films here need not appeal to the viewer's sense of self, consequently the way in which Bangkok's physical landscape may reflect something more internal."

The new wave of Thai cinema began with Nonzee Nimibutr's *Dang Bireley and Young Gangsters* (1997) set in the original pop culture scene of 1950s Wang Burapha. Its gentle paean to Siam Square, *Love of Siam* (2007), captured its youth culture bubble. In 2024, the Asia-wide hit *Lahn Mah (How to Make a Million Before Grandma Dies)* bathed Talad Phlu's Sino-Thai lifestyle in a similarly emotive glow.

Bangkok Love Story by Poj Arnon (2007) was a breakthrough movie twice over. Besides being Thailand's debut mainstream gay romantic thriller, its cinematography was the first to embrace urbanism as a character, with emotive shots of skyscrapers and abandoned buildings, while the Skytrain's rattling track felt as gnarly as a London films set beside railway arches. The BTS was romanticised (and initialised) in its acclaimed straight counterpart, *Bangkok Traffic (Love) Story* (2009) set mostly on the SkyTrain.

Cinematically, Bangkok is code for sin. *Bangkok Dangerous* (2000) had a deaf hitman causing mayhem, while Hollywood's less edgy remake (2008) reinforced the notoriety. Nicolas Winding Refn's well-researched *Only God Forgives* (2013) fit street life into a slick thriller, while *Four Kings 1 & 2* (2021 & 23) evoked the 1990s era of public student fights. The Sin City rep got sent up in *Hangover II* (2011), with stag night antics, savvy local insights, and a denouement that made Sirocco rooftop bar iconic. Its abandoned twin, Sathorn Unique (aka Ghost Tower), starred in one of many ghost movies shot at real-ife haunts, *The Promise* (2017). *Soi Cowboy* (2008) treated sex tourism with arty, stylised dark humour. The Thai-to-Thai flesh trade got overdue scrutiny in Prabda Yoon's *Motel Mist* (2016), about bondage in a suburban love motel.

It's telling that Bangkok simply doesn't have movies about corrupt cops, so familiar in Hollywood, Filipino slum dramas and Hong Kong chopsockies. Cinematically, things are tamer than in the 1990s, when *Sia Dai* (1996) had a single-parent policeman's daughter sniffing glue on the roof of his barracks, staring vacantly over the expressway.

As PR for the city, the BMA got Thai PBS TV to hire nine top directors for segments about urban lives in *Sawasdee Bangkok* (2010). The best four formed a movie: Wisit Sasanatieng (a blind lottery seller dossing under a bridge believes an angel acts as her eyes); Aditya Assarat (internationalised Thai guys try to fathom Thai women); Kongdej Jaturanrasamee (an artless migrant picks up a 'tamarind tree ghost', slang for a working girl of Sanam Luang); and Pen-Ek Ratanaruang (a young snob repels a hobo who's only wants to fix her broken-down car). *Ten Years Thailand* (2018) takes the same four-director format, but bleaker tone, Wisit, Aditya, Apichatpong Weerasthakul and Chulayarnon Siriphol reinterpret cultural suppression, re-staging a real military raid on Bangkok's N22 gallery enclave.

Pen-Ek has often depicted the capital, including the short, *Total Bangkok*, about kids footballing under the expressway at night. His early nihilistic thriller *6ixtynin9* (1999) was set in a typical suburban apartment, while *Ploy* (2007) had a *hi-so* Thai marriage unravelling in a condo. In Kongdej's *P-047* (2011), a pair of alienated Bangkokians break into empty homes to sample the lifestyles of others then leave them exactly as found.

A rare burst of realism infused *Tang Wong* (2013), which contrasted a youth having to learn traditional dance against the backdrop of his father's being shot at in a political protest crackdown. A dark fantasy take on informal Bangkok, *Mah Nakhon* (2004) is a pun on the name Krungthep Mahanakorn, translated as 'Citizen Dog'. Wisit Sasanatieng stars menial roles (maid, driver, guard) and lifts the city's everyday ways into an affecting fairytale of a brighter future.

above: ***Mah Nakhon* aka *Citizen Dog*. By Stadio for Five Star Entertainment**

top right: **A widely posted graffiti sticker displayed in the art-bar Jam.**

"I am not sure what the meaning of an outsider really is," mused Benedict Anderson, a late expert on Thai nationalism. "The implication is that *farang* who write about Siam think in a very different way from educated Thai. But *farang* journalists and scholars in fact are heavily dependent on their Thai opposite numbers. On the other hand, there is Chris Baker, very English, a longtime resident, in good command of Thai, who has penned the best modern books on Thai politics with Pasuk Phongphaichit. Is it right to call him an outsider? But aren't there millions of citizens of Siam who may be outsiders too?"

Bangkok's long history of contested opinion keeps resurfacing. "Why should we be compared against the Rama I era? Our society is governed by feelings, which override reason," says playwright Ornanong Thaisriwong. Her play *Banglamerd* (Violated Place) was restaged with a change in subtitle from 'My Wonderful Smiling City' to 'The Land I Do Not Own.' "There is no unity in this world. Everything is clashing and cultures are getting mixed up. You can't just deny someone because they don't think like you."

Thai media owes its origins to resident foreigners. After US missionary Dan Beach Bradley founded Siam's first newspaper, the *Bangkok Recorder*, in 1844-45, a lively press was sheltered by extraterritoriality treaties under the laws of their mostly missionary owners' home countries, including Sino-Thai papers under owners from European colonies. From researching the *Bangkok Times* (1887-1941), Steve Van Beek notes that it took some stands, but was largely deferential, and several papers closed due to libel suits. In the 1920s, because foreign-owned newspapers couldn't be shut, the elite had to respond in debate, though later dictatorships did suppress news. The *Bangkok Post* was founded by an officer of the OSS (now CIA) – and became a publication of record. Once among Asia's freest, the Bangkok press gets cowed after coups. Extreme computer crime laws now punish sharing, likes, and even viewing material deemed sensitive. The powers-that-be seem to prefer keeping Bangkok opaque.

Online, and especially offline, Bangkokians express divergent views. "The local media practice self-censorship because it would be dangerous not to. But in private space, Thais compensate for the gaps in public knowledge by exchanging opinions, relaying gossip,

comparing interpretations. This network of information sharing is very dense," wrote Baker and Pasuk. "Those consuming the international media do not have access to a similar network. Hence the gaps in their picture are glaringly obvious."

Access to such thinking is one of the many barriers due to language, although a growing minority of resident reporters and researchers speak Thai. "Let's consider the fact that there is pretty much nothing being explained in English," writes composer Somtow Sucharitkul, a polymath who often goes public during cross-cultural flare-ups like the 2010 protests. Schooled in Englishness like many Thai aristocrats, he became the "American sci-fi novellist" SP Somtow, before returning to found the Bangkok Opera and Bangkok Sinfonietta. Some of his classical scores feature Thai melodies and portray local culture, like the Buddha's lives and the Bangkok ghost *Mae Nak*. "Thai is a highly ambiguous language and is particularly well suited for seeming to say opposite things simultaneously. To get what is really being said takes total immersion."

Thais incensed at "helicopter journalists" allegedly misreporting the 2010 protests vented spleen at the Foreign Correspondents' Club of Thailand. Reporters bristled at Somtow's claim that reporting gets filtered through the Western literary tradition of linear progress. Rolling TV news – started by CNN coverage of the Philippines 'People Power' –

Messy Aesthetic

If there was a handover point in Bangkok's artistic depiction – from pre-modern to post-modern – it was the launch of The River condominium. Architecturally, its stream of shimmering glass soared vertically from the bank of the horizontal watercourse. Centrepiece of the event was an eight-panel mural of the contemporary city by Thai pop-art pioneer Navin Rawanchaikul. The actual painting was done by the restorers of the cloister mural of Wat Phra Kaew, the original river landmark upstream. Keeping the traditional brushwork, hues and perspective, it radically updated the content. Murals used to be idealised maps of the social and spiritual hierarchy. In Navin's realist murals, malls dwarf the temples, ads swamp the heritage while the 'low' vignettes of the kind confined to the bottom of old murals – blind lottery sellers, rival buses racing, skimpily dressed tourists parading drunk – are here found throughout, as in the city itself.

Teerawat Nutcharoenpol restyled murals another way. His paintings depict modern Bangkok populated by figures from ancient murals, showing the disjoint between traditional values and the modern city.

Murals evoke our experience of Bangkok. With few scenic vistas and centuries of dense living in a flat jungled plain, Bangkok couldn't be appraised at a distance until the advent of towers to look at and look from. Western visitors tend to think of cities in terms of panoramas or cityscapes, but Bangkok's congestion forces us to see it mostly as a city of close-ups, of curious details.

It's hard to get a handle on this city as a whole, so its depictions pick subjects that are physically local and scaled to the body. The mural format can encompass that variety; fussy from afar, without dominant focal elements, murals draw you closer to spy hidden action. Its conventions, like layering by status, enable artists to express change with continuity. Storyological paintings are effectively single mural panels with a visual narrative, like Kamin's scene of the 1992 massacre amid a hedonistic milieu, 'Sunrise Sunset in Thailand 1992'.

Traditionally, the arts were associated with being devotional, from temple and palace artefacts to ritual crafts like garlands or truck decorations. Most artists who depict modernity tend to present its haphazard development as alienating. Jaruwat Boonwaedlom paints the reflections of white-collar workers sliced and diced on glass panelled towers, implying their humanity's just as fragmented. Therdkiat Wangwatchakul paints the effects of this brutal development on lonely figures at bus stops or benches, with kids wearing masks of fastfood brands.

Consumer vulgarity is the target of Manit Sriwanichpoom, who pioneered street photography in the 1990s boom as a conduit for the city's absurdist serendipity, from classical domes over mall food courts to the elephants that used to beg on Bangkok's streets. His 'Pink Man' series, staged artist Sompong Thawee at city sights in a fuchsia suit, pushing a pink supermarket trolley.

left: **A collage by Pariwat 'Big' Anantachina.**

below left: **Gossamer silk metalwork by Christopher Wise at WTF.**

below: **Patipat Chaiwitesh augmented taxidermied creatures from the river to show the effect of pollution. Shown at Bangkok Art Biennale.**

Sculptor Rattana Salee depicts her hometown's urbanism by making its ugly infrastructure her muse. "The image of Bangkok has been changed radically," she says. "The lack of urban planning as new buildings are located unsystematically… leads to incredible loneliness. It is one of the consequences [of] the interaction between 'image' perceived through the eyes and 'form' perceived through five senses." Just as builders act oblivious to what they have wrought, her monumental sculptures of a "torn canal bridge" and distended stilt houses have a monumental heft, yet feel rough and spindly, showing the inhumane results of heedless sprawl. Rush Pleansuk showed this by stacking stilt houses like an indoor-outdoor skyscraper in 'Memory 6', showing the incompatibility of boxy modern condos with the values that stilt houses embodied.

The 2008 BACC show 'Krungthep 226: Art of Yesterday, Image of Tomorrow' surveyed Bangkok art history. It reified artefacts from tradition, waxed nostalgic with Vorasan Supap's pop paintings of houseboats, and delved into dystopias like bleak cementscapes by Julio Brujis and Navin's taxi robot. Its 2024 follow-up show, 'Bangkok 242' dwelt more on quality of life, with vibrating displays of everyday sound pollution.

Bangkok's informal culture wasn't considered worthy of artistic consideration until an appreciation of streetlife arose in the 2000s, appropriating the title of the book *Very Thai* as its generic label. That ugly-chic style spread into design, fashion, event organising and other creative fields. In counterpoint to formal Thainess, this way of representing informal culture morphed into Bangkok's 'Messy Pop' aesthetic.

That zeitgeist was led by Pariwat 'Big' Ananatachina, who found another way to represent the bittiness and juxtapositions of Bangkok streetlife: collage. He arranged close-up photo cutouts of those gritty details – signage, motorbikes, vendor umbrellas – into compositions that burst in all directions, epitomising the energy of this urban supernova.

Cogent details appear when cropped from the clutter. Sarawut Ngernpum turns impersonal urban spaces like Skytrain platforms into cold semi-abstracts, flush with synthetic colour. Foreign artists also warm to Bangkok's messy aesthetic. In 'Call Waiting', Frank Hallam Day photographed Bangkok's disappearing phone boxes, interpreting them as studies of urban light filtered through their decrepit stickers and stains. Fellow American, Christopher Wise of WTF, printed shots of shophouse balcony grilles onto silk that flutters in the breeze. In 'Bangkok Anytime', Catalan Daniel Monfort Gil paints urban scenes that that now adorn the Holiday Inn Express Bangkok. A decade earlier most hotels had been adorned with neo-traditional art. Today, the W Hotel has a stairwell chandelier with its LED lamps each moulded to resemble the drinks that vendors serve in a bag, complete with a straw.

Valuing everyday items has given artists a new subject matter that resonates with their lives. The winner of the UOB Thailand Painting of the Year 2018, artist and bar-owner Apiwat Banler, called his composition of tangled trains, expressways, and urban sprawl 'Persistent Problems'. "I have encountered all these issues they have frustrated me," he says. "Instead of complaining, I used them as my inspiration in creating my artwork."

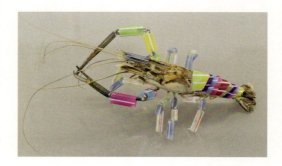

Face 315

emotionalised that mythical story arc. "It fulfilled a vision of history as a series of liberations. Finding another such story is a kind of Holy Grail for the international media." The ensuing Arab Spring got similar dramatisation. I've even heard a Thai say that Brexit and Trump are direct karma for Western criticism of Thailand.

That begs the question of what literary preconceptions shape how Thais frame news. The Western protocol of weighing evidence and balancing both sides affronts the patronage system, hence Bangkok's lack of news neutrality. As one Thai reporter confided to a foreign reporter: "If we didn't take sides then who would defend the nation?"

Historically this has been an oral culture that serially re-enacts epic morality poems like *Ramakien*. Similarly, Bangkok's slim modern canon of literature – from wartime occupation tragedy *Koo Gum* to the family business saga *Banlangmek* – keeps getting re-performed in films, soaps and musicals.

Oral traditions tend also to be image cultures, with fixed iconography. Portrayals of Bangkok's culture are often pictorial or performative, seen in all the festive costuming and processions. The limited visual expression that's found in statuary, puppetry or murals today recurs in the taste for cartoons and mascots. *Ramakien* masks are widely used in city branding and souvenirs.

Myths are metaphors taken literally. While Western dramatic heroes tend to be flawed, self-doubting personalities, the *Ramakien* is an epic with moral archetypes enacting a ritual script in order to prove political legitimacy. In *khon* masked dance, each semi-divine avatar fits into tableaux to show the hierarchy. Bangkok enacts this mode daily in the use of uniforms, positioning in group photos, and seniority dictating media layouts. No wonder this has been branded a "Theatre State."

This legacy of characters being generically righteous or evil still shapes *lakhon TV* (soap operas). Producers get criticised if they deviate from the stereotypes: wise elders, honorable hero, loyal younger brother, demure heroine, evil temptress, clowning servants. "You can find the sense of Bangkok in Channel 3 *lakhon*

316 Portrayals

drama," says editor Zcongklod Bangyikhan. "This is typical of the capital's lifestyle: well-dressed, beautiful office, condo or house. It represents the Bangkok dream."

That dream proves unreachable for many migrants, whose Bangkok tales of woe are a lyrical thread in *luk thung* and *molam* folk songs. In 'Bangkok Allergy,' by Pang Nakarin Kingsak (with Takkatan Chollada), a coughing city boy falls for a country girl in a metaphor for unhealthy urban life. It's typical of songs that portray the capital as a place of ambition and ailment. "The buildings are beautiful and impressive, but people here have no kindness," goes 'Goodbye Bangkok.' "Bangkok girls always cheat. These girls love big money. They don't care if you're old. They laugh with joy if you could buy a nice car, a diamond ring, and a house for them. If you see a ghost and get sick you can recover, but when someone cheats on you it hurts forever. Drinking toxin as if it's honey. Goodbye Bangkok."

Feisty, aggrieved migrant tales injected realism into Thai literature, most of which either fussed over propriety or sensationalised impropriety. "I don't care for books about Bangkok. All are a cliché to me," says Voranai. "They are either weepy, soapy Thai romance, or patriotic propaganda, or if written by Westerners, some adventure of a former CIA agent fighting against evil Thais or Asians, and saving his Patpong girlfriend." He exaggerates, since there have been classics in all genres, and indie novellists are finding fresh ways to tell the city's story. Yet it's true that sensationalist 'sexpat' noir thrillers lodged in the public mind as to the genre of 'The Bangkok Novel.'

It was the French philosophic-cum-erotic novel, *Emmanuelle*, that implanted the seed of Bangkok being a sybaritic fleshpot that seduces Westerners, who can't help but become debauched. Couched as memoir by Bangkok-born Marayat Bibidh, literally 'Ms Manners,' it was likely penned by her French diplomat husband Luis-Jacques Rollet-Andriane. "Here, idleness is an art form," pontificates the expat wife's bisexual mentor Mario. "One mustn't become resigned at any price. Here in Bangkok if you say that, everyone will agree."

Several resigned expats drift through the streetlife in *Bangkok Days* by Lawrence Osborne, a journalistically observed portrait of a seemingly impenetrable place that appeals to those seeking a detached urban existence. His follow-up, *The Glass Kingdom*, is an intrigue set among four women in a Bangkok condominium. In highbrow contrast, Asianologist Alex Kerr drew upon his heritage preservation projects in *Bangkok Found*, revealing traditional master keys that unlock this improbably graceful megalopolis.

"There are eight million stories in the Naked City" could be said of New York, yet few artists, writers or singers dare to bare the true stories of this buttoned-up city. The doyen of expatriate writers, William Warren, was famous for his biography of Jim Thompson, but his general book on the city, *Bangkok* revisited only familiar sights. With attention retreating to small details rather than the big issues, few writers tackle

top left: The BMA's new typeface by Farmgroup takes cues from Prince Naris' font, with pop hues and an official green, to unify city branding. *Photo Farmgroup*

left: Reebok's *Bangkok* **shoe, based on a tuk-tuk.**

above: At Cadson Demak type foundry, Anuthin Wongsunkakon designed this Bangkokean font to represent the Bangkok and Thonburi banks, Rama IX Bridge and other attributes of the city.

Face 317

Reality TV and Reality

Foreign television mostly takes a voyeur stance, treating Bangkok as a seducer, trap or backdrop to beach escapades like *Survivor*. Reality TV tends to be sensational, as in the 1990s UK series about expats and questers, *Bangkok Bound*, or the cheesy *The Airport of Smiles: Bangkok Airport*, which mocks passenger mishaps and the endearing staff. Bangkok tuk-tuk driver is one career in *Around the World in 80 Jobs*. *Travels With My Father* (Netflix, 2017) British comic Jack Whitehall and his cantankerous dad go to Khao San Road, Sirocco rooftop bar, elephant polo and the Chuchok Shrine – then adopt a *luuk thep* doll.

Among drama series, *Back in Bangkok* (2018-19) saw actor Byron Bishop direct his wife *luk khrueng* model Sirinya (Cindy) and Nophand Boonyai, in a comedy drama about not disclosing a lottery win. *Hormones* (2013-15), a realistic take on Bangkok youth issues, was an Asiawide hit. Netflix has got kudos for authentic Thai series, notably the gritty thriller *Bangkok Breaking* and the retro bio of serial killer Charles Sobraj, *The Serpent* (both 2021).

Thai-speaking foreigners who Thais watch online include Canadian travel host Daniel Fraser, Aussie English teaching guru Andrew Biggs, and a British chatterbox "with a Thai heart" Jack Brown (Jack Dek Farang). American Luke Cassady-Dorion presents *Farang Pok-Pok* and YouTube's Picnicly channel, wrote his autobiography *Yogi Boy* and documentary *Cheer Ambassadors* (2013) in Thai.

Documentaries often tackle issues fairly with insider pundits. *Bangkok: Megalopolis between Order and Chaos* (Swiss-German, NZZ, 2015) reflected on

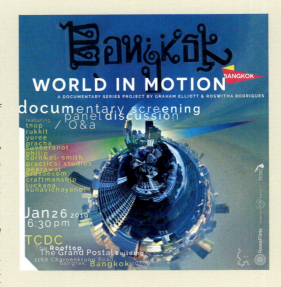

the contradictions and tensions. A French Canadian, series on port cities, *Ports d'attache* (*Riverfront Cities of the World*, TV5, 2010) had local experts guide a photographer around Bangkok in a sensitive take on its food, culture, pop and urbanism. *Welcome to Bangkok* (English, Deutsche Welle, 2017) was a tourist debrief with detours to the airplane graveyard and Lumpini's outside gym; gushy, but peppered with asides like "when money speaks, the truth is silent." *World in Motion: Bangkok* (English, 2019), in an international series on urban visual culture, probed creative themes from astral gemstones to ghost imagery and hybrid design.

a sweeping portrait. Canadian essayist and crime novelist Christopher G Moore, hints how foreign writers can solve Bangkok's "cultural mysteries" in *The Cultural Detective*. Perhaps no one can encapsulate this atomised city – what Lawrence Chua, in his novel, *Gold by the Inch*, called "a sloppy patchwork of unassimilable stories."

Other outsiders have done their detecting though past writings. For *Tales of Old Bangkok*, Chris Burslem compiled illustrated quirky vignettes from books, papers and postcards, spiced with urban legends. In a more rounded writerly portrait, *Bangkok: A Cultural & Literary History*, Maryvelma O'Neil is erudite and quotes some unheard voices amid the usual suspects.

More recent essays by long-stay expatriates often profile its personalities. James Eckhardt interviewed boom-era characters from vendors to tycoons in *Bangkok People*, while Jerry Hopkins dished on scandals with affectionate relish in *Bangkok Babylon* and *Thailand Confidential*. A veteran of Khao San's backpacker magazine *Farang*, Jim Algie profiles oddities in *Bizarre Thailand*, from a punk-dressed pathologist to the last executioner. While peculiar by Western standards, his tales of sex, crime and magic come from the regular news.

In *Bight of Bangkok* and *Gulfs of Thailand*, historian Michael Smithies based short stories on reported events. A guard impersonated a policeman and lived off the fake extortion fines until he was found out by saluting wrongly with his left hand. Another tale recounted a traffic policeman at Bangkok's Makkasan rail crossing. "I had a sixth sense that a grand procession of King Narai was approaching the crossroads," said the Ayutthaya-born officer. "So I pressed all the traffic lights to give the procession free passage." With each direction green, he danced *ramwong* through the resulting gridlock. Diagnosed with schizophrenia and lung damage, he was tranquilized and allowed back to work.

The scarcity of witty writing on Bangkok is unsurprising given the cascade of real-life absurdity. Headlines act as punchlines in this sample of true reports in *Bangkok Coconuts*, any of which could make short stories: 'Woman breaks into house to charge her phone.' 'Police catch thief using a fishing net.' 'Electricity Authority responds to viral pics of utility poles used in home construction.' 'Smelly instant noodles led to death and injuries in Bangkok housing complex.'

As making fun of Thais is anathema, 'Old Hands' – like Denis Segaller in his book series *Thai Ways* – often adopt a bemused stance at misadventures by foreigners, their mea culpas about committing cultural no-nos pleasing Thais as well as themselves. In *Mai Pen Rai Means Never Mind*, Carol Hollinger used the cloak of her subtitle, "*An American Housewife's Honest Love Affair with the Irrepressible People of Thailand*," to insert some home truths.

Travel blogger Janet Brown's *Tone Deaf in Bangkok* muses humanely on the 2000s, recounting a toyboy affair and various misadventures, from toilets without paper to sweating-out durian aroma on a *songtaew*. "It's unusual to see a Thai girl who isn't beautiful, and it's rare to see a woman over forty who is. What replaces it is power," Brown observes. "They are impeccable matrons, well-kempt and without the slightest trace of style. They dress in joyless pastel suits made of economical fabric, and their hair is styled in a way that no breeze could ever ruffle."

Satire flirts with danger. Combining caricature with parody, the French cartoonist Stephane 'Stephff' Peray (of *Metro*, *Gavroche*, *The Nation* and many international papers) sends up authority with glee. But most satire is wisely anonymous. *Phaic Tan*, a spoof 'Jetlag Travel Guide,' was inspired by the region, especially Thailand, in its jammed capital 'Bumpattabumpah' on the 'Pong River.' Most daringly, the website *Not The Nation* (2008-15), sent up not just news clichés, but named real names, except their own, in take-downs as raw as *The Onion*. Among its headlines: 'Rich Hi-So Girl Overcomes Advantages To Open Unprofitable Business;' 'Bar Staff, Sex Tourists Wait Patiently For White Woman To Get Off Go-Go Stage'; and 'Government Unveils Ministry Of Humor: New Cabinet position to strictly regulate and monitor what's funny.'

"Several comedy shows in the US and UK have made fun of Thailand over the years," wrote Pornchai Sereemongkonpol. He cited Sex Slaves (in *Family Guy*), Hellish Prisons (*American Dad*); Stolen Kidneys (*Saturday Night Live*) and Mail Order Brides and Ladyboys (*Little Britain*). "Their jokes aren't meant to be taken seriously, but they do reinforce stereotypes."

Just as the strongest critiques tend to come in theatre rather than print, jokes are safer said in comedy clubs. Stand-up stars from the London circuit had made periodic stops in Bangkok expat pubs as part of Asian tours, but in the 2010s the scene of local amateur comics went from occasional open-mic nights to almost nightly bills at venues like Raw Comedy, Thursday Night Fever or Bangkok Hilarious. Thai standups in English include Thai-Indian Sunanda Satchatrakul and the 'mentalist' Sarin 'Paco' Suriyakoon. Udom 'Note' Taepanich took Thai stand-up into surreal Thai realms. "Those stories I told really happened. I just tried to narrate them from a different angle," says Note. "Maybe making people laugh is another kind of virtue."

Thai 'Market talk' is ripe with sarcasm, but laughing at the establishment was rare in broadcasting until 2011, when satirist Winyu

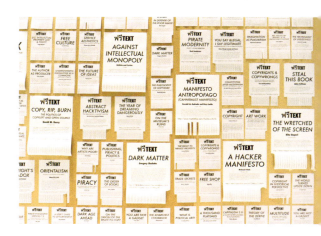

top left: **World in Motion: Bangkok documentary by Fovea Films.** *Logo by Graham Elliot*

above: *(=M/AK) / BKK – Work in progress*: A display of 'free-text' cultural critiques, with its name on tear-off tags so you can gain insight from the books. Installed at BACC.

Face **319**

'John' Wongsurawat launched *Jor Khao Tuen*: 'Shallow News in Depth.' Spurned by mass channels, it became Thailand's first ever online broadcast TV show. "The entertainment industry is open for expressing opinions, but only insofar as they support conservative ideas – the way things go, the authoritarian state or the action of demanding less," says Winyu. Dubbed 'John Stewart on crack,' he lampooned both sides in the colour-shirt protests by hosting a show bare chested. "*Jor Khao Tuen* is my mental therapy. I have my own space to speak my mind on topics and angles no one else wants to touch."

Hailed by *Time* magazine as "Thailand's Next Generation Leader whose weapon is laughter," Winyu inspired usually non-political young Thais to engage in public affairs. What the hosts call a "sugar-coated pill" ends up as a civics lesson never taught at Thai school. "*Shallow News* is a massive influence," says pop-culture blogger Jukapong Elmsaard. "I learned that by making my work funny, people find knowledge easier to absorb."

Others find power in anonymity. Khai Maew ('Cat Egg') is a wordless online comic strip that has satirised politics since 2014 via the gaze of a boy, Taa Sai ('Clear Eye'). "I think Thai society is maturing. People are questioning what's going on and not being castigated as aggressive contrarians," said Lalita Hanwong, co-curator of his 2018 show 'Kala Land' at Artist+Run gallery. "Everyone is Khai Maew. We all passed the stage from being naive to waking up politically."

Biting Thai wordplay has roots in a Bangkokian comedic form, *likay*, founded at Pom Mahakan. This folk opera grew out of local stagecraft and Muslim chanting. Agitprop troupes like Makhampom Theatre Group have used *likay* as a means to convey barbed commentary. The age-old plots matter less than the topical repartee between sparring players. "It is a verbal art bordering on verbosity, but this is contained within the rules of the game," says literary critic Chetana Nagavajara. "The public enjoy this verbal belligerence, which is at the same time a contest of intelligence, because they are fully conscious that they are engaged in a game, which is not real life."

By using anonymity and allusion, critics perpetuate that shadow game, making accountability harder. "We've been relying on metaphors, satire and comedy – not just in film but also in journalism and online," writes film expert Kong Rithdee. "The dilemma is painful: We speak in coded words and we risk being irrelevant, obscure, snobbish; but if we say it too directly, we risk a summons, or a mark on the forehead."

Intentionally vague cyber laws can quash any portrayal from circulation. In 2013, a writer got ten years for skirting a taboo using metaphor. "If even metaphors are executed – as in the firing squad sense – what do writers have left?" asks Kong. "The end of metaphor is the end of story."

left: **You know you've been in Bangkok too long when...** This series of cartoons is by French Cartoonist Stephff, who has been in Bangkok so long he can read beneath what's happening. His cartoons have appeared in *Gavroche*, *Metro*, *The Nation* and the *Bangkok Post*. This panel is from his book *Farang Affairs*.

Theories of Bangkok

Krungthep has always been a defined city. It was named and built to a mythic concept, yet that disconnects from its original character as an amphibious settlement of refugees and migrants. 'Great City of Angels' is inadequate to explain today's organic megalopolis. This ambiguous city flirts with multiple theories, leaving all foundering.

Early on, the city was coined in Western terms as the 'Venice of the East' – a category bestowed upon many 'water cities' like Suzhou, and earlier Ayutthaya. It emulated Imperial capitals as *siwilai* (civilised), without replicating their principles. Thai Studies is a growing academic field, and fascinates because this culture is often an outlier from ideological pigeonholes. Marxist notions of class, feudalism, Fascism or despotism don't quite fit what academic Sophorntavy Vorng calls a "Status City." Universalist philosophies, post-modern deconstruction and identity politics can only get so far, because Thai behaviours, beliefs and structures are so flexible and contradictory that they elude each logical premise.

Post-colonial theory struggles in a place self-defined as uncolonised, that some allege colonised itself. Author Alistair Shearer Shearer's encapsulated Bangkok as "Amerasia," but many places have been as Americanised. Meanwhile, Bangkok has cherry-picked systems from whichever power is in vogue, whether China, Europe or Japan.

Lately, observers treat the incoherence as a lesson, even an asset. Some allude to Bangkok's intangible cinematic quality, or it being a performative 'theatre state.' Writer Maurizio Peleggi called the city "the social space where Thai modernities unfolded." That's more than one modernity in a multifarious society that theorists have called a simultaneous simulation or "sometimes open, sometimes closed." A new concept of 'messy urbanism' tries to codify that chaos as an alternative model for resilient development. Any theory might at times apply, since adapting to context is the very nature of Bangkok the chameleon. "I think Bangkok is the city of variety," says Zcongklod Bangyikhan. "Its pattern is no pattern."

CAPITAL, CAPITALISM & COMMUNITIES

"Bangkok is the City of Big Cs: Capital, Capitalism and Communities," says Thai scholar Saran Mahasupap. Many of its icons are also state symbols and so not city-specific. "In addition to its status as the capital, Bangkok is shaped and driven by capitalism, so a serious search for the identity of Bangkok must find its last hope in its oldest communities."

All images in this box are from a project by Museum Siam to show young artists' views of Bangkok.

above: **Artist Mayawee Thongsong** draws not what ails "not Bangkok City, but Bangkok Shitty."

"In the dark side of progress, these old communities struggle to maintain their original way of life and professions. [They're] being invaded by an identity of Bangkok's own creation: streets full of life are being replaced by malls and skyscrapers, creating dead zones... shaped by a hidden hand," adds Saran, whose title puns on the mall chain Big C. "So it could be said that Bangkok's identities are diverse, but of very unequal value. Identity in Bangkok is easy to find, but it's not easy, so we should value it while it still exists."

CITY OF SELF-COLONISATION
Post-modern philosophers 'read' places for their symbolism. In 'Reading Bangkok', Ross King explores the meanings of key examples in the city and wedges the "incommensurate cultures" of Bangkok into elaborate philosophical constructs, like "City of Self-Colonisation," "Theatre State" or "Nation as Screen Against the Violent." He refers to different understandings of knowledge. For instance, in Thai cosmology, the capital is simply defined by the presence of King.

The book is ordered by kinds of space, referring to "A Landscape of Confrontations" (Ratchadamnoen); "Landscapes of Consumption" (Siam-Ploenchit-Sukhumvit); "Landscapes of Ruin" (slums and bankrupt constructions); "Libidinal Landscapes" (red light districts); "Landscapes of the Mind" (academia, planning, architecture) and "Subversive Landscapes" (protest). Each of these landscapes King calls a "Level of colonisation" in a city that invades itself.

LAK-KA-PID LAK-KA-PERD
Bangkok has an ephemeral, cinematic character. Glimpses of different ways of living pop in and out of view. Orthodox social mapping fails to explain this destabilised social structure, so film academic Sopawan Boonnimitra uses a metaphor, *lak-ka-pid-lak-ka-perd* (sometimes closed, sometimes open), which comes from the Thai slang for how homosexuality is visible only intermittently. LGBT are a microcosm of how Bangkokians fluctuate between concealment, controlled presentation and adaptation to the social context under the concept of *kala-tesa* (time and place). *Kala-tesa* implies 'appropriateness', in which the barriers are not physical but behavioural. Bangkokians must keep re-adjusting to the hierarchy of status, and to divisions of sacred, secular and supernatural space.

"*Lak-ka-pid-lak-ka-perd* conveys a rather ambiguous meaning that could be used in broader terms, such as to something that could not be decided one way or another." In a fickle city being so rapidly rebuilt, it could apply to identity, fads and taboos. We also see it on the street in temporary markets and informal transit. This open/closed switching even shapes the state through legal double standards and interventions by hidden hands.

LAYERS OF BANGKOK
A German design lecturer who took a Thai name, Christian Phongphit sought a fresh representation of Bangkok as 'An Urban Brands Study'. In an e-book in 2006 and exhibition at BACC in 2008, both called 'Layers of Bangkok,' he identified its interactions, classes, cultural divisions and accretion of new forms upon old. He calls it "a playful attempt to visually convey the structural discipline that evolves within a chaotic Asian metropolis."

"The cityscape is divided into a matrix of 61 urban 'brands' (i.e. filtered 'icons' that become a part of the numerous and contrasting layers that is often blind to the tourist as well as its inhabitants)," says Phongphit, who collated 2,500 photographs from banal snapshots to art-oriented abstracts. Viewing the city as an urban 'stage', he split the images into 'Performance' (acting) and 'Equipment' (the setting). "Within this urban mosaic, I tried to enhance even the most subtle of objects, and so began a process stripping the cityscape to its core; decoding it."

A CITY IN FLUX
"The degree of diversity and pluralism and how strongly they exist in Bangkok, start to become our peculiar quality, writes architect Kanika Rattanapridakul in *Asian Alterity*. "They make Bangkok a vivacious city."

"The same set of characteristics... also contributed to our ability and willingness to be flexible and adaptable. ...Quite significant to our chameleon-like behavior is that we do not strive to be original... that it is not part of our ethos. Furthermore, many Bangkokians find that an appropriate amount of

the disorder or chaotic conditions is something that Bangkok should be proud of."

The public and authorities have poor awareness of how the informal economy keeps the erratic system ticking. "Pockets of resistance" recognise the value of the city "as a 'self-organising structure' that is alive and should be allowed the freedom to grow more naturally, with minimal guidance, monitoring and maintenance, because nature has a way of balancing itself much more effectively than our best complex theory of urban planning ever could."

SIMULTOPIA

'Simultopia' is a wordplay by urbanist Brian McGrath on Bangkok's penchant for 'simulation' (fantasy), 'simulacra' (emulating foreign things but adding new meanings) and the 'simultaneous', whereby social layers, paradoxes and juxtapositions spark "multiple actions in one place." Simultopia also evokes "utopian modernisms" and the way that Bangkok invents new paradigms, multiple realities and changing perceptions.

'Simultopia' is one of three 'ecologies' in which McGrath places Bangkok in current debates about environment, urbanisation and psychology. Another is 'Liquid Perception,' which draws upon Bangkok's amphibious legacy as a water-culture and Deleuze's concept of cinema being a floating, non-solid, molecular condition that defies assimilation. McGrath adapts the Western 'metropolitan' idea into 'Transpolitanism' to show the Thai transformation of cityness. That involves the interplay of village-like urbanism, entrepôt history and foreign settlers, all under networks that are fluid, mobile and multiple.

JEK BON LAO

In the mid 1980s, two historians shocked Thais by rehabilitating the pejorative slang *jek* (chink) to label the Chinese-in-Thailand as a hybrid culture distinct from Chinese and omitted from the Thainess ideology. Nidhi Eosriwong argued in a book about King Taksin of Thonburi, a half-Teochiu, that Thai urbanism can't be understood without the crucial contribution by millions of *jek* immigrants.

"Nidhi implied that any version of Thainess which ignored the *jek* was incomplete, wrong, and offensive to a lot of people," wrote *Nation* columnist Chang Noi of a view that's spread through academia and popular culture. "The '*jek* tendency' was clearly dominant, and the attack on 'Thainess' very strong. Teochiu-Thai thinker Kasian Tejapira said he felt 'raped' by Thainess. Nidhi compared Thainess to 'a product that doesn't sell.'" Some brand that movement *neo-jek*.

"Sujit Wongthes described Thai culture as '*jek bon lao*', Chinese immigrant mixed with Laotian," Chang Noi continued. "He claimed he couldn't make head or tail of the official version of Thai society, history and culture. As far as he could see, the two biggest elements in the demography and the culture were Chinese immigrants and Laotian peasants."

HINDUISED CHINESE

Bangkok's divisions stem from contrary cultural outlooks, which are rooted in very different geography, organisation and tradition. "We were not a colony, but we were colonised; we colonised ourselves," says Vithi Phanichphant, an expert in the Middle Mekong civilisation. He distills the tribal Tai/Lao core of Lanna and Isaan as: matriarchal, sticky rice-eating folk of valley-based principalities run in a local way by approachable secular chieftains. That sensibility still infuses informal Bangkok.

Colonising that Tai/Lao culture was Krungthep, aggrandised by its Khmer and "Hinduised Chinese" inheritance: a patriarchal, wet rice growing state in the broad riverine/coastal plains with a centralised state under a Brahmanical hierarchy and a semi-divine ruler. As Vithi defines it, "Bangkok is the last fading light of the glorious Khmer Empire, performed by the Lao and operated by the Chinese."

left: **Comic book illustrator 3Puck made portraits of the marginalised, like garland sellers, glue sniffers and black magic gurus.**

above: **A digital lottery generated by artist Thanathip Jenthumrong. You win if it matches your ticket, which depicts one of many social problems.**

Futures
Plans, chaos and resilience

For years, I would board a pill-shaped ferry at Si Phraya Pier, and bob across the river to Khlong San, a rundown district of *fang thon*, the 'Thonburi side' of the city. I'd thread through Khlong San Market to a room above a 7-Eleven, via a door behind a shrine to every imaginable deity, from Kwan Im and Mary to Krishna and the Buddha. The venue offered a panorama across the busy river to the soaring towers and mouldering riverside of Bangrak.

This view was made public by some of Bangkok's most renowned masters of noticing things: the artist Rirkrit Tiravanija founded Ver Gallery here in 2006; then in 2012, World Photojournalist of the Year laureates James Nachtwey and Patrick Brown took it over as a casual drop-in venue called The Space. This vantage point offers a contrast to Wat Rakhang – two bends upstream and 316 pages ago in the Introduction – from which to reflect on the reincarnation of this cosmological water-town into a cosmopolitan world city.

Bangkok is returning its gaze to the river and canals – whether for transport, trade or leisure. Grand edifices like temples or the Oriental Hotel had always faced the water, until road-biased planning turned attention inland, which meant that old river buildings had to be accessed from the back. The sensory appeal of the river and its breezes led to hotels along the banks. Otherwise, aspirational investment neglected the old-fashioned waterfront, which decayed into what romantics cherish as a time capsule or, to many Thais, an unsightly mess to civilise. Now the river is trendy again, Space's building and Khlong San Market have been razed, so that a swish new develpment can have that view.

Nowhere was more neglected than Khlong San, a former mini-Chinatown that fell into decline with closure of the rice mills, whose chimneys used to dust the city in soot. Overgrown with trees, its riverbank retains disused warehouses, and a few Sino-Thai mansions of the kind demolished elsewhere. The district is a test-bed of possible futures, from fenced luxury to community heritage to alternative arts. In a rare case of sensitive redevelopment, the Wanglee family restored their ancestral house and converted its warehouses into Lhong 1919. The twisting lanes between there and Kudi Jeen community host installations, screenings or performances at festivals like Art in Soi.

Khlong San was a Shi'a enclave, too, with ancient mosque communities and estates of the aristocratic Bunnag clan, which converted to Buddhism. A Bunnag family temple, Wat

Phibunsongkhram regime built a Central Post Office in the *blockhaus* style of Albert Speer's Berlin Reich's Chancellery. Corniced by musclebound Garuda man-eagles, it was converted in 2017 into the permanent home of Thailand Creative and Design Centre, thus becoming the Creative District's hub.

Across a *soi* from TCDC, Duangrit converted a row of godowns into a mixed-use venue called Warehouse 30. It and TCDC both act as connecting links between dead-end lanes. Such hands-on cooperative urbanism works in simple, subtle ways that planners rarely can. During Bangkok Design Week and Galleries Nights, young crowds animate the whole District into a continuous strip of attractions along Charoen Krung Road, from the Oriental to Chinatown's Soi Nana. Just as the Tate Modern upgraded the image of London, the Creative District is a frequent, excited storyline in foreign coverage of Bangkok. Even before being fully realised, it is so effective as soft power that it was a must-see during a visit by Apple CEO Tim Cook.

Khlong San lies in the inner city and faces a rising tide of speculators. Commercialisation came via IconSiam, a mall so gilded that its own spur of the Skytrain is named the Gold Line. This 1.6 billion dollar landmark bills itself "The Icon of Eternal Prosperity." Golf carts swish around the marble concourses, past glitzy boutiques, palatial bathrooms and a suki restaurant growing hydroponic vegetables. The mall acts like a corporate balcony onto that same river panorama of Bangrak.

Prayoon, has joined the tourist circuit. Just as Wat Rakhang is branded the 'Temple of Bells,' Wat Prayoon is promoted under the tagline: 'Temple of the Iron Fence.' That red fence skirts a white-spired *chedi*, which won a UNESCO award for its restoration. The temple found unexpected kudos as a venue in the Bangkok Art Biennale, when Nino Sarabutra put 125,000 little ceramic skulls on the cloister floor encircling the *chedi*. Walking barefoot past the walled vaults of family ashes was an act of reflexology, bringing a rush of blood to the sole, and renewed vigour to address the work's title: 'What Will You Leave Behind?'

When artists move into a forgotten quarter like Khlong San, it often goes through tides of gentrification: artists, creative early adopters, mainstream commerce, and finally state re-engineering. Duangrit Bunnag – the city's highet profile architect – enjoyed that same riverscape of Bangrak from his Jam Factory arts complex in Khlong San. There in February 2015, he met under a tree with entrepreneurs, artists, gallerists, makers, chefs, landscape architects and people from riverfront communities. Together, in a re-imagining of the city, they co-founded an independent planning initiative: the Bangrak-Khlong San Creative District.

On the Bangrak riverside, the French and Portuguese embassies have sponsored many activities of the Creative District. Between them had stood the British legation before they moved out. On that site in 1940, the

top: **A new panorama of the Bangrak riverside opened up at IconSiam.**

above: **The mirror-tile mural by Sittivut Yavichai at IconSiam's folded glass frontage.**

Face   325

Project Singapore

Each time the BMA clears the streets of streetfood, it gets compared to Singapore, which confined its hawkers to bland, sanitary hawker centres – open-walled community food courts. Bourgeois Bangkokians yearn to match the order and *siwilai* cachet of Singapore, while others recoil that this city of surprises should become so predictable.

"Personally, I think Bangkok should look like Singapore," declared a Junta-era BMA chief advisor, Vallop Suwandee. "I would like to say on behalf of City Hall we'd like to benchmark with Singapore, with Tokyo." However, Bangkok doesn't yet benchmark with cities that have benches, let alone global standards. That aim may be futile in a land known for indiscipline. Post-junta, even the liberal elected governor Chadchart Sittipunt wants street hawkers regularised, and eventually all removed.

"Countries like Hong Kong and Singapore don't have street vendors because of strict law enforcement. The reason why we can't do it is because we turn a blind eye," said a BMA enforcer, former police chief Gen Vichai Sangprapai. "I actually want it to be that way [like Singapore], but Thais are still attached to the idea that some people will be affected." The people affected are the majority population who rely on streetfood and markets for affordable meals and goods – and the million or so who make their living from informal trade.

An old joke goes that Bangkok builds first and plans later, but it has always been highly planned. It began with Rattanakosin's sacred mandala. Ever since, there have been so many inconsistent plans that people of influence build what they want, while people with no influence build in the gaps.

Aspiring to Singapore is not new. That British colony was the first model emulated by King Chulalongkorn, seen on the first foreign trip by a Thai King. Inspired by its Sino-Portuguese shop-house, he built Na Phra Lan Road for court staff as a template for shophouse investment along the connective roads he commissioned. After visiting Europe, he laid out Dusit as a grid of leafy boulevards. King Rama VI, schooled in England, then created a miniature city at Phyathai Palace, dubbed Dusit Thani (Heavenly Town), which evoked the English 'garden city' of benevolent company towns like Bourneville.

After the 1932 revolution, Bangkok joined the global trend of statist plans. Pridi Bhanomyong's socialist plan was aborted by Field Marshal Phibunsongkhram's Fascist-era re-ordering. Then Field Marshal Sarit's 'Development State' instituted Five-Year Plans with an American bias for cars over canals. That style of suburbs outside ringroads peaked in a 1990s plan by Massachusetts Institute of Technology (MIT) that zoned land use in concentric bands. Zoning creates suburbs with long commutes to a downtown of corporate complexes, depopulated of its diverse *yaan*. The NCPO suspended city planning, then in 2018 enshrined its 20-year plan in its constitution, with penalties against flexibility.

Nowhere is more reordered than the Old Town. The Rattanakosin Island Plan consigned that living museum to tourism as a heritage park, with its human heritage evicted. Singapore pulled down most of its Chinatown, and refurbished what it kept behind old façades. Now the early shophouses of Rattanakosin have been sanitised like Singapore's Boat Quay. Authentic shophouses demolished to make way for the Wat Mangkon MRT station have been reconstituted in mock-Sino-frontages.

Plans imposed from alien models drain Bangkok of its intrinsic character, which inflames the proactive civil society. "The way we always implement design into the city is to say there's a problem, because the city is so untidy. So we tried to make it civilised by a thing called urban planning," says Thailand's top architect Duangrit Bunnag. "I say the city is just fine. The struggle of trying to portray the city as a problem is the real problem."

left: **The multiple towers of OneBangkok loom over the rebuilt site of Siam's first radio station, Wireless House, which is now a museum of the locale.**

top right: **Orderly planning, versus the loss of organic culture. This graphic protested the effect on the Old Town.** *Courtesy of Can Dan Isan*

Some reckon that planning might work better if it went with, not against, the grain of Thai ways. We see that order and chaos interplay, and that Thai organic nature can't be stifled. Clutter regrows as soon as the chance arises, just as after it rains, the moss rejuvenates and plants sprout on ledges. After the 2019 election, vendors crept back into Silom until the night market was half reconstituted. Informal streetlife is tidal; its influence ebbs and flows as authority's power waxes and wanes. Likewise, Bangkok's resilience depends on organic solutions.

Connecting dead-ends into networks is a quick, cheap, holistic way of improving flow while keeping the urban fabric intact. For instance, Bangkok needs more public access to the riverside, which is mostly private due to the past need for a jetty at each compound. Aside from paying to see the view from hotels or restaurants, the public has just a few parks or obstructed piers. To reach the next one, you must traipse back inland, go along the main road, then traipse down another *soi* to the water.

The simple fix is to join compounds to new and existing walkways like one that links the Bangkok Tourist Bureau with Santichaiprakan Park. Duangrit extended a path at Khlong San Pier through his Jam Factory venue to ease local access, though IconSiam didn't link that community path to the corporate plaza it calls a "riverside community space."

A new generation of landscape architects has taken several civic initiatives to show how more river paths could benefit both public and community. One of them, an urbanist doing her PhD, discovered the dry dock at Yannawa and co-founded the Great Outdoor Market there in 2014. It put the site on the map.

The second market there offered public consultation on an independent scheme by Urban Design & Development Centre (UddC) to include the dock in a Yannawa waterfront. The public would get benches and gardens along separate walking and cycle paths that weave in and out between viewpoints and interesting neighbourhoods, providing strollers with comfort, shade and variety.

Soon afterwards, the junta announced the 'Bangkok Landmark,' a river promenade decreed to stretch seven kilometres on each bank upstream from Phra Pinklao Bridge. Rather than test a bit first, officials evicted 29 *yaan* before the design was done, and before any claimed consultation. Critics noticed that this was the old planners' dream to line the river with a road and embankment, re-garnished as a cycle lane. At ten metres wide and flood wall height, the uniform structure would hide ground-level river views, block sunlight from 14 hectares of water, and disrupt currents, undermining the banks. From river-level, the narrowed waterway would be a boating hazard and block the sights from passengers, who'd instead see mile after mile of identical concrete pilings. Bangkok would finally be severed from its riverine history and water culture.

The Promenade was touted as akin to Seoul removing a road to restore a river, whereas it would be more like building that Korean road over the river. Skeptics ponder if the boondoggle might be more about the cleared land and the budget to pour 14 kilometers of concrete.

'Friends of the River' – an alliance of experts, hotels, communities, transit and architects – protested the scheme. One staggering reason why public facilities are often ugly and inappropriate is that the BMA had never employed landscape architects. It legally couldn't, because 'landscape architect' wasn't on its list of approved professional associations until 2019. So BMA schemes were previously done by engineers not steeped in aesthetics, ecology, heritage, social usage of other skills that landscape architects bring.

"The major obstacle against successful development is that Bangkok is being developed by people who lack real understanding about development," said an anonymous Thai resident cited in the book *Asian Alterity*. "Decision-makers never genuinely listen to the people, resulting in development which is without people participation and therefore ineffective and unsustainable."

The since-suspended Landmark Promenade project would have zoned a multi-use riverside into a monoculture. Zoning is for specialisation, whereby vast sectors get a 'single use,' quite unlike Bangkok's monohoods of single trades, which segregates some trades while everything else was wildly mixed. Thinning out the centre to the suburbs wastes space and requires travel to get basic needs, worsening gridlock.

This segregation mindset causes a vast megalopolis to have just three legal nightlife zones, because suddenly people think fun, temples and schools must have separate zones, when everyday life used to be intertwined.

"Our city plan has only 'single use' or 'mixed use', but in our life we have 'multiple' and 'differential' use," says Duangrit. "This is a huge problem. It means we plan without the full capacity of how we utilise the space. That is inauthentic." Planners bless 'mixed-use' in mall-condo mega-projects, but they don't recognise the mixed use found at market-bar-restaurant-transit nodes in public spaces like *pak soi*, which serve communities. Clearing street markets is efficient only for transit, whereas letting small bits of space host rotating stalls in shifts – to suit custom at each busy period – is space and time efficient. This 'differential' phasing of multiple uses is the basis of the shophouse and *talad nat* 'appointment markets' – yet planners miss that tides of vendors spread wealth, energy and social bonds.

The informal sector employs differential usage of space by nature, yet formal Bangkok is also phased. Each mall builds multi-function spaces, indoors and out, kept varied via food fairs, fashion weeks or cosplay conventions. Forecourts morph by season, too, with beer gardens, festive altars and themed settings for selfies. *Wats* and markets each hosted various functions. Bangkok is such a sensory experience because multiple things can go on in the same place.

Some residents chafe that vendors make money off public space. "Thais have little concept that streets, parks and so on, are common property, and that everyone has a responsibility to look after them," said a *Nation* editorial. "Thais have believed that public areas are not owned by anyone and are there only to be exploited. Such attitudes lead to filthy streets and parks. Those who engage in graft do not think they are violating anyone else's rights."

Nor do all want mixed neighbourhoods, as when affluent Soi Thonglor was the first area the NCPO cleared of streetfood. "Thonglor is the prime zone of the esidents, of the investors. We have to take care of those people as well," Vallop said. "Please do not come to Bangkok just to set up a food stall after harvest season. You have to care for the general public and the land value of the shop-house right behind you." Clearing a pristine downtown, within a messy greater metropolis, might not replicate Singapore, which doesn't have a vast hinterland like Thailand, but may instead resemble Manila.

This would be a historic break, as Bangkok was built upon refugees and migrants. Its economy grew from informal set-ups with minimal capital, stock or commitment. At whim, hawkers could switch location, timing or their entire trade, nurtured by malls and markets that let cheap booths. Fairs became an improvised circuit for music, contests and other entertainment. The over-planned West has brought

streetfood back to reinvigorate dulled downtowns, but here that spontaneity is integral to Bangkok's identity – and to its success.

"There are increasing 'pockets of resistance' – 'pockets of hope' – throughout the city," writes Kannika Ratanapridakul of New Urbanism. "They tend to... view [the city] as a 'self-organizing structure' that is alive and should be allowed the freedom to grow more naturally, with minimal guidance, monitoring and maintenance because nature has a way of balancing itself much more effectively than our best complex theory of urban planning ever could."

At BangkokEdge festival in 2016, Duangrit launched his 'Bangkok Manifesto' to an audience unexpectedly packed with young Thais. "Bangkok is the best city in the world. No seriously, I'm talking the truth," Duangrit said. "If you start from that, you become less problematic about what exists in the city. Getting to know the city as it is, you start to see new possibilities." His Manifesto proposes to make the city more 'fluent', creative and open to opportunities, and makes the case that diversity and density are assets that should be enfolded intact, like currants into dough, for a nourishing urban ecosystem. Instead of rigid top-down planning, he sees the city co-evolving through public-private initiatives through leadership that can come from anyone. The Manifesto itself is open-source. "Its not about authority, but about being socially responsible. Any of you can be a leader right away. Just take responsibility. The moment I feel responsible, I feel love for the city. If we love the city, we can be inspired by the city."

above: **A community-sensitive river walkway for Yannawa created by indie planners, shown at Great Outdoor Market in Bangkok's dry dock.**

right: **Landscape architect Yossapon Boonsom, from Shma SoEn and Friends of the River, invites public input into social enterprise initiatives.**

Thinking about cities matters hugely, especially since Thais and wider humanity both became majority urban in 2012. Books on urbanism have gone mainstream and are night-table reading for mayors from Berlin to Bogotá, and young Thai urbanists can find them in TCDC.

In the radical idea of 'Messy Urbanism', solutions to tropical megalopolises set aside perfectionism to work through informal mechanisms like slums, itinerant vending or handmade transit. Although Bangkok became the world's most visited city whilst being so chaotic, the notion that Bangkok could be a role model of 'messy urbanism' goes against received thinking. "Are you sure that the charm and the messy can go together?" Vallop responded when asked. "The City [Hall] could not equate the charm of Bangkok with untidiness."

Given official rigidity, many go ahead with their own plans. Corporations make mega-projects like OneBangkok, even redrawing roads. "We realised there was no hope to achieve proper planning, so we got together, businesses and communities by the river, and did it ourselves," Duangrit says of the Bangrak-Khlong San Creative District.

Its masterplan was drawn up by Thammasat University and Shma SoEn, the social enterprise offshoot of the youthful landscape architecture firm Shma. The plan and activities are done with the community and stakeholders, who get invited to 'Town Hall Meetings,' where socialpreneurs can propose ventures at a level of consultation that bypasses sclerotic procedures.

This has increased pockets of hope among officialdom too. The Creative District inspired Museum Siam to set up a 'Cultural District' in Rattanakosin. The City Plan has adopted Duangrit's urging for 'Incentive Planning' to allow higher density if builders provide a clinic, library or some wider benefit. However, some urbanists are aghast that more density would mar quality of life.

A pivot point is the BMA commissioning the young urbanists of UddC, a semi-independent organisation funded by alcohol and tobacco taxes and linked to Chulalongkorn University. Rather than top-down schemes to standardise local differences, they tailor specific interventions to enhance the sense of place, while consulting with residents for six months to jam solutions at 40 workshops. Their Good Walk scheme mapped the city's pavements using a 'Walkability Index', then rated each pavement for hazards, so selected sidewalks could be improved.

After decades of prioritising infrastructure, there's a shift towards smarter, targeted boosts to quality of life. The tangled cables slung from overloaded concrete poles were a symbol of modernity long after developed countries were burying cables, but Bangkok's now burying many of its cables, making those roads feel less constricted. More parks, both public and private, are enabling healthier activities. Most profoundly, new transit likes will complete one of the world's longest mass transit networks, with integration of boat services, cycle paths and Skywalks.

To mark Bangkok's 250th anniversary as capital in 2032, the BMA tasked UddC with upgrading the city. They seek incremental gains at 'intervention points,' such as conserving Kudi Jeen and other old *yaan* to benefit communities, not just tourism. A makeover of Victory Monument would integrate its hospitals into a 'Wellness District', while Thonglor-Ekamai would become walkable through landscaping of pavements and a disused canal. Active River Station would turn the BTS-connected pier at Saphan Taksin into a mass transit hub.

The centrepiece is Bangkok's answer to New York's HighLine, Phra Pokklao SkyPark, a garden bridge beside Saphan Phut upon unused pilings from an aborted train link. It connects Kudi Jeen to an upgrade of the old Rattanakosin moat. Shacks have been cleared to enable leafy pathways and markets along Khong Ong Ang, past Chinatown, Little India and Pom Mahakan, then extending beside Khlong Banglamphu to Pom Phra Sumen in Santichaiprakarn Park, linking with two new MRT lines. BMA landscaping has also brought shaded paving to each side of Khlong Padung Krung Kasem, Khlong Saen Saeb and other smaller canals. These become walkable ways to connect new and existing sights, with less exposure to traffic.

It's not Singapore's Gardens by the Bay, but in going step by achievable step, Bangkok should get tangible gifts in tune with its character for its Sestercentennial birthday. Such schemes upgrade Bangkok at human, sensory scale, and optimise the asset that the world treasures this messy city as the 'anti-Singapore'.

INCLUSIVE CITY.
YOSSAPON BOONSOM

right: **Tha Tien is named 'flattened pier' after a fight between the guardian giants of Wat Pho and Wat Arun. Sakarin Krue-On filmed this as today's fight over the Thai future. Screened at Wat Pho in Bangkok Art Biennale.**

below right: **Sea floods a Bang Khuntian temple.**

below far right: **The Great Flood of 2011 swamped the city.** *Photo by Can Dan Isan*

This book's Introduction considered the *krajok hok dan* – Luang Phor Toh's six-panel mirror – as a way to consider all sides of a topic, in this case competing visions of the river and the city's identity. The Creative District imagines a place of aesthetics and diverse communities. IconSiam engages with its setting more than most malls, and commodifies Thainess into a refined tourist souvenir, with installations by Thai designers and a 'Chief Visionary Director' who used to run TCDC.

IconSiam even looks like a box of mirrors. Instead of a six-panel mirror, six hundred glass panels, sixteen metres tall, zig-zag like the folded leaves of a *krathong* float – except they don't go all round. Its temple-style mirror mosaic by Sittivut Yavichai stretches sixty metres. Called 'The Light of Siam,' it depicts water, sky and temples in glass shards, which reflect the river, the skyline – and an all-glass temple: Icon's Apple Store.

Creative District and IconSiam are each contrasting approaches to urban goals through independent planning. Now the state plans to nationalise that Bangrak river vista by erecting a viewing tower beside IconSiam, a lookalike of Canton Tower in China, which in turn resembles Aspire Tower in Qatar. Meanwhile, the BMA pursues its vision for the city: emulating Singapore.

Bangkok life requires navigating a morass of rival agencies. To arrange an activity on the river could entail dealing with the Navy, Harbour Department, BMA, District Offices, landowners and boat operators. Bureaucracy multiplies obstacles due to overlapping jurisdictions in any city activity. 'Interchanges' of state and private stations like Mo Chit don't physically join, so passengers must brave rain and sun down narrow steps and paths, then switch ticketing systems, just to change platforms. For one operator to invite the other to share would imply the asker is subordinate, and nobody wants to lose face.

"The messy organisational structure of Bangkok fosters gross inefficiencies and allows for far too many hands in the cookie jar," wrote Voranai Vanijaka. "Vehicles could be regulated better, but that means fighting through the web of godfather interests. So the question of who's in charge is a funny one. The answer is: everyone and no one at the same time."

Bangkok seems chaotic, due to mess and surprise. Its hidden order becomes apparent in the interplay of two capricious kinds of power: 'Authority' that wields law or custom, vying with 'influence,' which is informal and indirect, often with impunity. "Influence is dangerous, and authority is dangerous, but survival is possible if both exist," wrote Nidhi Eoseewong of the Thai 'Cultural Constitution.' "The Thai common people... do not want either one to eliminate the other."

Note that 'authority' does not equate to 'order,' nor 'influence' to 'chaos.' Informal Bangkok looks messy due to ad hoc survival in public space. Yet it's ordered using village values and 'influential people' as a practical fix when unrealistic laws don't work. Formal authority appears serene, yet it too prompts chaos through corruption, bias and disregard for the law. Ultimately, any rules can be bent to enable the goal of order by status.

This ambiguity turns simple tasks into a power play. Nidhi points out that going public through media can curb influence, or spur authority to act. Now social media gives small folk a tool to sway big issues, which is why it's so penalised. Since no one player can dominate, plans aren't followed and give way to other plans that favour other interests. As Voranai adds: "The reality is the Bangkok governor and the BMA have very little power to effect real change in the capital."

Now influence is threatened by Thailand joining the OECD, a club of developed nations. Under its harmonised rules, both the *lo-so* masses and *hi-so* evaders are being forced into the declining tax base. Required regulation of the informal sector, which is half the Thai economy, would make Bangkok's life less characterful and far more corporate.

As the focus of Thai order is the hierarchy, everything else becomes structurally unstable. Bangkok has no consistent centre; it has several – and they keep moving. The political centre slipped northwards, the downtown eastwards, and the port downstream. Chinese junks docked at Tha Tien, then at Chinatown. Once Siam engaged with the colonial trading system after 1855, cutters and steamers docked in the *farang* quarter of Bangrak. The wharves moved to Khlong Toei in the 1960s, and now the Port Authority wants to move more container shipping out to the Eastern Seaboard. It plans to replace Khlong Toei's slum with a 'smart city' to rival IconSiam, but near upscale Sukhumvit. There's no strategy, just tactics, in this city of flow.

The city itself is on unstable ground, which is sinking and eroding. The river created the delta, provided the reason for settlement, and bore its early trade. But what water wrought, it can reclaim. Bangkok is one of the world cities most at risk from rising seas. Climate Central measured that by 2050 the high tide would flood most of the Central Plains. The coastline could retreat to where it was 1500 years ago, when today's inland towns of Ratchaburi, Suphanburi and Lopburi were sea ports.

To witness the future, go to Bangkok's seaside at Bang Khuntien. A marker with the border of Samut Prakan province now stands a kilometre out at sea from the eroded shore. You can see it while dining at Bangkok Seaview Seafood, which is itself now stranded on stilts in the Thai Gulf. At the water's edge, retention walls are being made by recycling concrete poles that used to carry Bangkok's infamously chaotic cables before some of them got buried in this geologically recent ground.

The implications for the city are apparent at nearby Wat Khun Samut Chin. The *bot* flooded twice daily, so the monks built a new concrete floor halfway up the window level,

Face   331

Bladerunneresque

When the present can't be discussed openly, and probing history is taboo, one path to truth is to project the future. A genre of sci-fi – call it Thai-fi – has emerged from Bangkok fiction. Part sci-fi, part noir, it's ironically a way to be realistic. Fantasy so dominates Thai imagery – and realism is so discouraged in film and fiction by those who won't be criticised – that writers and film-makers present today's reality as if tomorrow's.

Thai-fi is invariably, like noir, set at night. It's almost always raining. The advanced technology of Bangkok in the future is as grungy and inefficient as what we grapple with now – keeping its superficial look of modernity whilst still needing improvised solutions to function. Futurism began shiny and heroic, but realism made us see technology as something that also decays, while what remains are human foibles.

Thailand doesn't do dystopia as seamlessly as Beijing. Lackadaisical attitudes mean that attempts at a totalitarian panopticon like China's 'social credit', end up with surveillance being mired in haphazard paperwork like the TM30 form that foreigners must submit upon returning to their residence from even one night away. Bangkok monitors its 'aliens' in 2019 not through the tools of globalisation, but by using paperwork from a 1979 law. As Julian Evans put it in *Vanity Fair*: "Bangkok [is] more Dickensian and Langian than Orwellian – it'd be a perfect location to remake Fritz Lang's 1927 masterpiece, *Metropolis*."

Bangkok can seem like that movie's setting of vast gated towers encrusted by jury-rigged streetlife, but many reach for another film metaphor: "Bladerunneresque." In Ridley Scott's film, the bladerunner navigates a shabby-tech Amerasian city in seemingly perpetual twilight amid rumbling transit, its giant LED adboards gleaming from incessant rain. *Blade Runner* was set in a future 2019 in what might be Tokyo, but in actual 2019 it felt more like Bangkok.

The *Blade Runner* sequel seems directly influenced by Bangkok, specifically the Hugo-winning sci-fi novel by Paolo Bacigalupi, *The Windup Girl*, which combines the two main themes of Thai-fi: dysfunctional tech and cataclysmic flood. In the novel, from the wall around Bangkok you can view the sea over Thonburi. Advanced yet resource-short, the city gets powered by giant GMO elephants. Bangkok's black market is the only place left where humans still buy contraband natural seeds, appropriately of the alien-looking rambutan fruit with its rubbery red hairs.

In the year that climate change got renamed 'climate emergency', 2019, Bangkok became the go-to metaphor for the flooded coastal metropolis. In *Bangkok Drowning*, a noir thriller by Steven Palmer, roads had turned back into canals. Among three gangs dividing the deluged capital, the Itsaraphap "were popular with the poor as they gave away a lot of what they stole," while the Peripherals occupying downtown had the "demand that Bangkok be recognised by the UN as an independent city-state." Around what had been the river, the Black "swapped their motorbikes

332 Futures

for jet skis and maintained their former image as hard-riding badasses." While the city devolves back into being aquatic, its illicit trades stay afloat.

In a literary sensation the same year, Pitchaya Sudbantad's historical/futuristic novel *Bangkok Waits for Rain* hops between the mid-19th century arrival of modernity, the recent past, and the prospect of amphibious Bangkokians commuting to a barely functioning flooded Bangkok from refugee colonies in Kanchanaburi. The linking theme is a tropical European-style mansion that shapeshifts into neglect, restoration as a spa lobby and a hi-tech form of preservation.

A cyberpunk vibe infuses *Wayward Gods*, by Nate Pantumsinchai on YouTube. Set in a machine-like Bangkok circa 26XX. it pits a Yaksha in a Khon-mask helmet, against the evil Naga Corporation.

In *True Skin* by Stephan Zlotescu, we peer through a digital eye implant to track a man stalking a night market where vendors pull fake biotech gizmos from a plastic bag stash, dodging the touts, tempted by food stalls, scanned by figures in doorways. Bathed in disco blasts of neon, this science-fictional Bangkok style also infuses his five-part *Future Sex* and *AI Love You* (starring Mario Maurer) on implications of AI-intimacy.

Anakot: i+tomorrow (Netflix, 2024) – a darkly satirical Thai take on *Black Mirror* conceived by AI arts creative Pat Pataranutaporn – projects coming 'Paradystopias' with more varied aesthetics, from antiseptic to retro kitsch to techno-Buddhist.

Thai modernity is often seen as an impaired, cautionary tale. But as templates of progress – rationalist West, quirky Japan, panoptic China – either unravel or lurch to extremes, Bangkok appears as an unlikely role-model. If technology alienates rather than ameliorates urban living, Bangkok's ad hoc, piecemeal habits show how cities might cope with the onslaught.

'Bladerunneresque' was likely first coined of Bangkok in 1998 by its most famous fantasy writer, SP Somtow. The term appeared in an award-winning short story, *Dragon's Fin Soup*, along with *The Last Time I Died in Venice*, which he calls "a story about a place in a future Bangkok that offers virtual sex fantasies for the depraved, but to save costs the fantasies turn out not to be virtual." As ever, Bangkok's futurism needs ad hoc manual help. As Somtow sums it up: "Bangkok, the bastard daughter of feudalism and futurism."

above: **The lo-tech flooded Bangkok where Paolo Bacigalupi set his sci-fi novel** The Windup Girl **has inspired 'fan art,' like this by Canadian Julien Gauthier.**

left: **A biotech-adapted figure of the Bangkok night in the neurocinema film pilot** Dark Bridge Binaural Brainwaves. *Image courtesy of Stephan Zlotescu*

accessed from a boardwalk via planks over the temple precinct's muddy mangroves. The *wat* is being rebuilt, even though the villagers moved inland. Each October, when the river's highest, raised planking is common at Bangkok piers, but as at Wat Khun, that may become a year-round norm.

When Indonesia announced in 2019 that its capital would move from sinking Jakarta to Kalimantan, the Thai government floated the idea of moving the capital. That's not a new idea; Phibun had proposed Phetchabun in the 1940s and Thaksin suggested Nakhon Nayok in the 2000s. Even if juicy state contracts were awarded to build a Naypyidaw-style capital on higher ground, that would leave the hub of most national functions facing submersion. Millions worldwide live below sea level today, but could sea walls be made watertight in ad hoc Bangkok? Or might it revert to amphibious Thai ways of living with water?

When Absolut Vodka distilled Thainess in its famous ad series, the bottle shape was outlined by boats in a floating market. Bypassed by roads and malls, floating markets like the one at Taling Chan were left to tourists. Lately, Thais are rediscovering their water-culture roots by visiting resurgent old waterside markets in the Central Plains like Don Wai and Amphawa, or the retro Khwan Riam Floating Market created at Minburi.

Floating markets are now on weekends, but used to be held on a lunar calendar for higher tides. Bangkok is tidal. For eons, water washed into this delta from the sea twice a day and flooded annually from monsoon rains and runoff from the north. Now that water has less place to go. Embankments reduce flooding downtown, while watergates trap high water in the suburbs.

The Great Flood of 2011 inundated most of the outer city, even Don Mueang, the 'city heights.' The state planned giant walls topped by a promenade that would finally separate Bangkok's riverine communities from the river, and Bangkok's high-rise future from its floating past. It would turn the river – the city's historical lifeblood – into a concrete chute.

A decade before, the architect Sumet Jumsai, an expert in the water culture, avocated that embankments be built behind waterside communities to preserve their lifestyle and the riverscape. He also proposed a promenade that floats on pontoons, solving the need for river access using a solution from

Face   **333**

left: **The Bangrak/Khlong San Creative District's graphic (before IconSiam opened).**

right: **#riskeverything** A river expressboat surges between the bow of another expressboat and a barge tug. Given rising seas, is Bangkok risking everything?

Thai tradition that's flexible and sensitive to both ecology and community.

In the last roadless canalscapes of Bang Kruai, every stilt house has a canoe, and vendors, postmen, banks, fuel and the school run all still go by boat. Thai traits and informal lifestyle both grew from adapting to the water. Meanwhile, Bangkok's development has been about constraining nature to fit formal aspirations, treating tide, flood and messy stilt houses as problems to conquer.

In lists of 'Resilient Cities,' Bangkok scores low on measurable criteria like plans and technology that are brittle when systems fail, yet it withstands crises thanks to relationship factors, like flexibility, improvisation and reciprocity. 'Teflon Thailand' has deflected serial disasters, from SARS to smog, and reinvented itself after the 1997 crash. I arrived after the 1991/92 coup/massacre; and have seen two more coups (2006, 2014), protest occupations of downtown, periodic violence and another massacre in 2010. I needed to vacate my home three times: the live-fire crackdown on the Red Shirts in 2010, the Great Flood of 2011, and the whistle-blowing noise from the Bangkok Shutdown that blocked all roads to my home. Then in 2020, my tapwater turned brackish due to salt-water intrusion. All that isn't normal in most cities, but Bangkok copes thanks to its flexibility.

"If one starts to look at the 'degree' of diversity and pluralism and how strongly they exist in Bangkok, then they start to become our peculiar quality," says Kannika Ratanapridakul in *Asian Alterity*. "Many Bangkokians attribute it to [our] personalities, which we think consist of being loosely structured, highly tolerant, non-critical, non-judgmental, fun, friendly, generous and easy-going. But we also feel that all of these characteristics backfire on us."

Talk of Teflon Thailand risks complacency, given the rise of 'Urban Fragility.' Each new shock risks more, as systems grow complex, while regulation rigidifies the best proven shock absorber: the informal sector. As the 2011 flood was rising, hi-tech condos told residents they might have to evacuate due to vulnerabilities like lifts, card locks and pumping water up 50 floors. Simpler communities were more resilient with improvised solutions. The city needs a frank examination of what constitutes 'social order' and relate it to the city's true character, optimising its traits rather than denying them.

Clues to where all this leads may lie in the generational rift, with elders shocked by the progressive youth vote in 2019. There may not be major change until Cold War veterans, with their them-or-us ideologies, have been replaced. Generation X grew up with indie thinking during democracy in the 1990s-2000s, while Millennials are frank on social media and often become activists for causes. Individualistic, better educated and more globally aware, the coming generations have already revolutionised business to be more responsive and socially conscious.

Although traditionalists claim exemption from universal standards, Bangkok has long been a bellwether of modernity. Even by the 1980s, Procter & Gamble used this city as a test market for Western Europe as its tastes were so alike. Bangkokians still lead the curve in ageing demographics, female advances and Internet use. Lifestyle is radically altering through online work, dating and shopping, plus the rises of home delivery and convenience stores over malls. Social media can lead to vigilante netizens, but they're filling a void left by the waning of traditional legitimacy, whether through monk scandals, world-record inequality, or abuse of laws by the elite. The Internet can also be a six-panel mirror to improve quality of life, from hailing apps to pressure for cleaner air due to every smartphone being a monitor of PM2.5 smog. In the greatest transformation, mass transit is changing how Bangkokians experience their hometown. The time saved enables residents to do more beyond work – including reflect on how Bangkok could be.

Development doesn't have to be about making Bangkok like other places, dulling its edginess, or quelling its stimuli. Bangkok has accommodated contrary characters for centuries, with mixed communities and juxtapositions of trade and tradition, sacred and *sanuk*. That plurality, variety and sense of possibility has made this a magnet for migrants and visitors.

The city magazine *BK* asked residents: 'Why do you love Bangkok?' Responses included: "No rules;" "Differences;" "Happy hassles;" and "A hectic city, everything is right here." Bangkokians seem widely inured to the city's quirks, if not the traffic, and proud of their resilience. "I like the mess and extremes," says singer Leo Put. "The wires, the sidewalks, the bird shit, the noodle stalls are all amazing. But the most fascinating thing is how Thais learn to live with it all so easily."

The world prizes this city for its sensual excess, though many residents don't appreciate that reputation, seeing order as a moralistic calming of the senses. Those who prize the senses accept that chaos as realistic, even humane. People have senses, angels don't. In pairing six senses with his six mirrors, Luang Phor Toh treated the senses not as shallow, but as a rich way to consider all aspects of life.

Surveys find that Thais of all incomes are shifting some of their spending from products to having experiences – which depends utterly upon the senses. For instance, plans to standardise Thai recipes and purge streetfood fly in the face of public needs, the city's soft power reputation, and the relishing of street-side eating for its lively frisson. Writ large, Bangkok is loved and famed most for excelling as an experience.

In the battle for Bangkok's soul, symbols matter. The city insignia has its patron, Indra, riding Erawan, a flying elephant often depicted with three heads, but who in total has 33 heads. Bangkok isn't chaos; it is multiplicity. It is 33 heads looking 33 ways and using 33 senses. Those multiple facets have created a kaleidoscopic city through freewheeling adaptation at human scale. That is Bangkok's messy gift to the world.

Appendices
Including bibliography, notes and credits

Acknowledgements

Before all others I owe this book to my publisher, Narisa Chakrabongse, who persevered patiently and generously for so many years for the completion of *Very Bangkok*, in an act of trust, loyalty and friendship that I hope the finished book rewards. She also put in long hours proofing and indexing the book, in a huge team effort with production managed by Suparat Sudcharoen and the design completed by Ruetairat Nanta. Thanks also to the rest of the staff at River Books, BangkokEdge and Chakrabongse Villas, including Grissarin 'Yui' Chungsiriwat and Chris Shelley in London. Plus a hat-tip to Gee Thomson, Hugo Chakrabongse, Dominic Chakra Thomson and the rest of the Chakrabongse family.

This book is dedicated to my two editors, who are also great mentors. The late Marc Pachter edited my ideas over many years and has been an invaluable companion on the journey of this book. My editor on *Very Thai*, Alex Kerr, edited this text patiently in a drawn-out process, helping to sculpt enormous drafts into finished prose. Thank you both for your insights, endurance and friendship.

Xavier Comas of Cover Kitchen did the wonderful cover design. The text was transformed into a book when laid out by 1000 Ponies Co Ltd, with the calm, efficient designing by Peerapong Pongprapapan, Kad Krutharot and Neung, plus digital imaging by Daily Touch.

Although I'm a sponge for information and draw upon interviews and my library of reference sources, *Very Bangkok* could not have been compiled without research by others. A huge amount was done by my longtime assistant Saran Mahasupap, with contributions by Anirut Apidech, Mee Chanitra and Grissarin Chungsiriwat.

Some research was done on trips or visits made with, among others mentioned in the acknowledgments: Smiling Albino, Pop from Bangkok Tourist Board, Richard Barrow, Dow Wasiksiri, Pitch Pongsawat, Paothong Thongchua, Nilobol Panichkarn, TAT, Paolo Piazzardi, Spiceroads cycle tours, Exo tours, Public Relations Department, Indrawut 'Por' Jarat, Fovea Films, ZZF TV crew, *Ports d'attache* crew, Origin Cultural Programs, Zulkifli Mohamad,

Kwanchai Athikomrungsarit, Philip Sherwell, Roque Reymundo, Charlie's boat tour, Toby To, John Padorr, *a day*, Apichai Tragoolpadetgrai, *art4D*, Soroptomists, Marcus Tate, Jac Vidgen, EDM's *9 Days in the Kingdom*, Christine Kubisch, Daisann McLane, Ajarn Mill Baisri Ledominance with Ajarn Kiaow, Robert Carmack & Morrison Polkinghorne of Globetrotting Gourmet, and a group of Southeast Asian friends we call the 'Lotus Sect,' notably Tang Fu Kuen.

This book has taken so many years that it would be impossible to list here everyone who was mentioned, met or asked. People whose insights or help I have benefitted from include: Alka Puri; Andrew Biggs; Andrew Clark; Angrit Ajchariyasophon; Anucha Thirakanont; Anusorn Ngernyuang; Anuthin Wongsunkakorn; Apinan Pohyananda; Bob Halliday; Boony Narksakul; Brian Curtin; Brian Mertens; Carl Carthy; Chami Jotisalikorn; Charuwan Chanthop; Chatri Prakitnonthakan; Chris Coles; Christian Hogue; Christopher G Moore; Chuck Sutyla; Craig Knowles; Daniel Fraser; Darkle; Darren Hausler of Eat Me; David Mayer; David Robinson of Creative District; David Robinson; David Thompson; Disaphol Chansiri; DJ Seed Norasate Mudkong; Dominic Faulder; Dredge Byung'chu Käng-Nguyê; Duangrit Bunnag; Eric Bunnag Booth and Grithiya Gaweewong of Jim Thompson Art Centre; Gregory Galligan; Ing K; James Wise; Jarrett Wrisley; Jennifer Gampell; Jerry Hopkins; Jesper Haynes; Jin Ni; Jobe Nakcharoen; John Burdett; John Goss; John Twigg; Jonathan Head; Jorge Carrillo; Jureeporn Thaidumrong; Justin & Moni Mills; Kaewmala; Kage Mulvilai; Kamol 'Sukie' Sukosol Clapp; Kasin Dejcharoen; Kisnaphol Wattanawanyoo; Kompit Panasopon; Kong Rithdee; Kwanchai Athikomrungsarit; Laurie Osborne; Lawrence Osborne; Maitree Siriboon; Manit Sriwanichpoom; Marisa Marchitelli; Martin Rendel; Mason Florance; Nana Chen; Narawan Pathomvat; Nat Prakobsantisuk; Netiwit Chotiphatphaisal; Nick Nostiz; Nima Chandler; Oat Montien; Pangina Heals; Panu Boonpitattanapong; Parinot Kunakornwong; Patravadi Mejudhon; Philippe Laleu; Piboon Amornjiraporn; Pichet Klunchun;

Prabda Yoon; Pratarn Teeratada of Art4D; Rick Brown; Rirkrit Tiravanija; Ron Knapp; Rune Kippervik; Rush Pleansuk; Sakharin Krue-On; Saksith Saiyasombat; Sakul Intakul; Sanon Wangsrangboon; Saran Yen Panya; Saroj Kunatanad; Scott Coates; Shane Bunnag; Shane Suvikapakornkul; Somrak Sila; Somtow Sucharitkul; Sornchai Phongsa; Takerng 'Be' Pattanopas; Tawatchai Monda; Tay Pruecksamars; Tua Pradit Prasartthong; Vichien Chansevikul; Vinai Dithajohn; Vincent Vichit-Vadhakan; Viriya Sawangchot; Voranai Vanijaka; Wendy Goldman Rohm; Wit Pimkanchanpong; Worathep Akkabootara (Can Dan Isan); Yifan Singharaja; Yongtanit Pimonsathean; Yossapon Boonsom; Zcongklod Bangyikhan.

Also thanks to the staffs of: TCDC (including Albert Paravi Wongchirachai, Chaiyong Ratana-ankura, Pansak Vinyaratn, Nunnaree Panichkul, Jay Spencer, Kitt Pitipan, Chutayaves Sinthuphan, Inthapan Buakaew, Jeed Wichit, Songwad Sukmaungma); UddC, especially Daeng Niramon; *Bangkok Metro*, *Thailand Tatler*, *Art 4D*, *Way* and *a day* magazines; and all the people I've met and interviewed along the way.

I've also gleaned much from talks and exhibitions at: About Café, Art In Soi, BACC, Bangkok Design Festival, Bangkok Design Week, Bangkok Film Festival, BangkokEdge festival, Chulalongkorn University, Creativities Unfold, Foreign Correspondents Club of Thailand, Jim Thompson Art Centre, Mahidol University, Museum Siam, National Museum Volunteers' Lecture Series, Neilson Hays Library, Pecha Kucha, Reading Room, Siam Society, SEA Junction, TCDC, Thai Studies Conference, Thammasat University, The Space, Third Class Citizen, William Warren Library, World Film Festival of Thailand, and countless other events and venues.

In patient support of all my efforts and time spent on this book, I specially thank Anirut Apidech, Symon, all at Alas Sari, and my family.

Ultimately, thank you to the people of Bangkok, my neighbours and fellow residents, who've been endlessly friendly, funny and fascinating. The uniquely organic, surprising city of Bangkok is the best material a writer could wish for.

Bibliography

BANGKOK PORTRAITS

Askew, Marc, *Bangkok: Place, Practice & Representation* (Routledge, 2002).

Bell, Barry, *Bangkok: Angelic Allusions* (Reaktion, 2004).

Brown: Janet, *Tone Deaf in Bangkok and Other Places* (ThingsAsian, 2008).

Bunnag, Shane, *Chariot of the Sun* (River Books, 2022).

Hamilton, Annette, 'Wonderful, Terrible: Everyday Life in Bangkok' in *A Companion to the City* (Blackwell, 2003).

Kerr, Alex, *Bangkok Found* (River Books, 2010).

King, Ross, *Reading Bangkok* (NUS, 2011); *Heritage and Identity in Contemporary Thailand* (NUS, 2017).

Sriwanichpoom, Manit, (with Ing K), *Bangkok in Black & White* (Chang Phuak Nga Dum, 1999); *Bangkok in Technicolor*, Kathmandu Gallery, 2014).

Natayada na Songkhla, 'Bangkok: Colours of the Night' (Les Editions d'Indochine, 1994).

Osborne, Lawrence, *Bangkok Days: A Sojourn in the Capital of Pleasure* (North Point Press, 2009).

Osothanugroh, Surat, *Vanshing Bangkok* (Sawasdee, 2011).

Passenger, The, *Thailand* (Iperborea, 2025).

Smithies, Michael, *Old Bangkok* (OUP, 2006).

Van Beek, Steve, *Bangkok Then & Now* (AB Publications, 1999).

Warren, William, 'Bangkok' (Reaktion, 2002).

Wirasetthakul, Sasi, *Bangkok Stories* (fullstopbook.com).

Ziv, Daniel & Sharett, Guy, *Bangkok Inside Out* (Equinox2004).

ARCHITECTURE & CITIES

ASA Architectural Awards Bangkok Walking Guide (Association of Siamese Architects, 2012).

Bunnag, Duangrit, *Who Am I?* (ed Kisnaphol Wattanawanyoo) (ASA Forum Lecture Series).

Chua, Lawrence, *Bangkok Utopia: Modern Architecture and Buddhist Felicities* (U of Hawaii, 2021).

De Botton, Alain, *The Architecture of Happiness* (Vintage, 2008).

Gehl, Jan, *Cities for People* (Island Press, 2010).

Hoskin, John, *Bangkok By Design: Architectural Diversity in the City of Angels* (Post Books, 1995); *Bangkok Subways, SkyTrains and a City Redefined* (Curiosa, 2000).

Hughes, Rian, *Cult-ure: Ideas Can be Dangerous* (Carlton Books 2015).

Jumsai, Sumet, *Rattanakosin Chao Phraya Riverfront* (2009).

Landry, Charles, *The Creative City* (Routledge, 2008); *The Art of City Making* (Earthscan, 2006).

Lim, William SW (ed), *Asian Alterity* (World Scientific, 2007).

Manish, Chalana & Hou, Jeffrey, *Messy Urbanism: Understanding the 'Other' Cities of Asia* (Hong Kong Uni Press, 2016).

Mertens, Brian, *Architecture of Thailand* with Nithi Sthapitanonda, (Thames & Hudson, 2006).

Pongsawat, Pitch, *Meang Kin Khon* (The City is Eating Us: An Urban Manifesto) (FurD, 2017).

Small Talk Bangkok: What Makes a City a Good Place For Everyone? (Chulalongkorn Uni, Architecture Faculty, 2014).

Smith, PD, *City* (Bloomsbury, 2012).

Ward, Robin, *Exploring Bangkok: An Architectural and Historical Guidebook* (Li-Zenn, 2014).

Warren, William, *Heritage Homes of Thailand* (Siam Society, 1999).

ART & DESIGN

Anantachina, Pariwat, *The Big Street* (2016), Local Local (The Uni_Form Design Studio, 2019).

Boonpipattanapong, Panu, *Art Is Art, Art Is Not Art* (Salmonbooks, 2017).

Curtin, Brian, *Essential Desires: Contemporary Art in Thailand* (Reaktion, 2021).

Kisnaphol Wattanawanyoo, *Who Am I A lecture by Duangrit Bunnag* (ASA Forum Lecture Series, 2014).

Koditek, Walter, *Bangkok Modern* (River Books, 2025).

Kunavichayanont, Luckana & Spisak Sonjod, *Krungthep 226 catalogue* (BACC, 2008).

Mann, Rupert, *Bangkok Street Art & Graffiti* (River Books, 2022).

Mertens, Brian, *Bangkok Design*, (Cavendish Square Publishing, 2007).

Pettifor, Steven, *Flavours: Thai Contemporary Art* (Thavibu, 2005).

Phongphit, Christian, *Layers of Bangkok* (BACC, 2008).

Poshyananda, Apinan, *Modern Art in Thailand* (OUP, 1992); Bangkok Art Biennale catalogue (BAB, 2019, 2021, 2023).

Suksri, Naengnoi & Freeman, Michael, *Palaces of Bangkok* (River Books, 1996).

TCDC, *Always Prepare* (2014); *Isan Retrospective* (2006), Creativities Unfold Symposiums.

Teh, David, *Thai Art: Currencies of the Contemporary* (MIT Press, 2017).

BELIEF

Buddhadasa Bhikkhu, *Handbook for Mankind* (Mahachula Buddhist University Press, 1990).

Choo, Ricardo, *The Spirit & Voodoo World of Thailand* (Wang Ci Xuan, 2011).

Cummings, Joe, *Sacred Tattoos of Thailand* (Marshall Cavendish, 2012).

Guelden, Marlane, *Thailand into the Spirit World* (Asia Books, 1995).

Gilquin, Michel (translator Smithies, Michael), *The Muslims of Thailand* (Silkworm, 2005).

Hoskin, John, *The Supernatural in Thai Life* (Tamarind Press, 1993).

Majurpuria, Trilok, *Erawan Shrine & Brahma Worship in Thailand* (Techpress, 1993).

McDaniel, Justin, *The Lovelorn Ghost & the Magical Monk* (Columbia U Press, 2014).

Sanitsuda Ekachai, *Keeping the Faith: Thai Buddhism at the Crossroads* (Post, 2001).

Vater, Tom & Aroon Thaewchatturat, *Sacred Skin* (Visionary World, 2011).

Wongwaisayawan, Uthai, (ed) *Muslim Worship Sights in Thailand* (Foreign Ministry, 2001).

CULTURE & HISTORY

Baker, Chris & Pasuk Pongphaichit, *A History of Thailand* (Silkworm, 2005); *A History of Ayutthaya* (Silkworm, 2017); *The Tale of Khun Chang Khun Phaen* (Silkworm, 2012); see Chang Noi.

Bautze, Joachim K, *Unseen Siam: Early Photography 1860-1910* (River Books, 2016).

Chang Noi, *Jungle Book: Thailand's Politics, Moral Panic, and Plunder, 1996-2008* (Silkworm, 2009); see Baker & Pasuk

Davies, Ben, *Vanishing Bangkok* (River Books, 2020).

Grossman, Nicholas (ed), *Chronicle of Thailand* (Bangkok Post/EDM, 2009).

Harrison, Rachel & Jackson, Peter (co-ed), *The Ambiguous Allure of the West: Traces of the Colonial in Thailand* (Hong Kong Uni Press, 2010).

Hoskin, John, *The Thai World: Temples Tattoos and other Cultural Encounters* (Asia Books, 2012).

Jefcoate, Graham, ed, *In Bangkok: Siam's Capital through Foreign Eyes, 1895-1935* (River Books, 2024)

Kasemsiri, Charnvit, *Studies in Thai & Southast Asian Histories* (Foundation for the Promotion of Social Science & Humanities Textbooks Project, 2015).

Klausner, William, *Reflections on Thai Culture* (Siam Society, 1993); *Thai Culture in Transition* (Siam Society, 2002); *Transforming Thai Culture* (Siam Society, 1997-2004).

Landy, Simon, *The King and the Consul* (River Books, 2021).

La Torre, Farbrizio, *Bangkok That Was* (Serindia, 2018).

Museum Siam, *Phra Nakhon on the Move* catalogue (National Discovery Museum Institute, 2019).

O'Neil, Maryvelma, *Bangkok: A Cultural and Literary History'* (JSS, Vol. 98, 2010).

Palasthira, Teddy Spha, *The Last Siamese: Journeys in War & Peace* (Amarin, 2013).

Peleggi, Maurizio, *Thailand: The Worldly Kingdom* (Reaktion, 2007); *Lords of Things: The Fashioning of the Siamese Monarchy's Modern Image* (Hawaii U Press, 2002); *The Politics of Ruins & the Business of Nostalgia* (White Lotus, 2002).

Phra Ratcha Wang Derm Restoration Foundation, *The Legend of Thonburi* (2001).

Piemmettawat, Paisarn, *Siam: Through the lens of John Thomson* (River Books, 2015).

Redmond, Mont, *Wondering into Thai culture* (Redmondian Enterprises, 1998).

Reynolds, Craig, *National Identity and its Defenders: Thailand Today* (Silkworm, 2002).

Smith, Malcolm, *A physician at the court of Siam* (1919, Oxford in Asia, 1983).

Sumet Jumsai, *Naga* (Chalermnit Press, 1997).

Van Beek, Steve, *Chao Phraya: Thailand Reflected in a River* (Wind & Water, 2004); *News from the 90s: Bangkok 1890-1899* (Steve Van Beek, 2018).

Winichakul, Thongchai, *Siam Mapped* (Silkworm, 1994).

Wise, James, *Thailand: History, Politics and the Rule of Law* (Marshall Cavendish, 2019).

Wong, Ka F, *Visions of a Nation: Public Monuments in 20th-Century Thailand* (White Lotus, 2006).

Wyatt, David, *Thailand: A Short History* (Silkworm, 2002).

Yorsaengrat, Nithinand (ed), Kasetsiri, Charnvit, Wright, Michael, Sujit Wongthes, Srisakara Vallibotama, *Siam-Thai Millennia* (Nation, 2000).

ENTERTAINMENT

Ainslie, Mary J, *Thai Cinema: The Complete Guide* (I B Tauris, 2018).

Amranand, Pimsai (with Warren William), *Gardening in Bangkok* (Siam Society, 1996).

Clewley, John, *Rough Guide to World Music: Thailand* (Rough Guides, 2000).

Houton, Jody, *A Geek in Thailand* (Tuttle, 2016).

Jablon, Philip, *Thailand's Movie Theatres* (River Books, 2019).

Lockard, Craig A, *Dance of Life: Popular Music & Politics in SE Asia* (Silkworm, 1998)

Mitchell, James Leonard, *Luk Thung: The Culture and Politics of Thailand's Most Popular Music* (Silkworm, 2015).

Subyen, Sonthaya & Raden-Ahmad, Morimart, *Once Upon a Celluloid Planet: Hearts & Houses of Films in Thailand* (Film Virus, 2014).

Vick, Tom, *Asian Cinema: A Field Guide* (Harper Perennial, 2008).

Wenk, Klaus, *Thai Literature: An Introduction* (White Lotus, 2015).

ETHNICITY

Algie, Jim; Gray, Denis; Grossman, Nicholas; Hodson Jeff; Horn, Robert; Hsu, Wesley, *Americans in Thailand* (EDM, 2015).

Boccuzzi, Ellen, *Bangkok Bound* (Silkworm, 2012).

Disaphol Chansiri, *The Chinese Émigrés of Thailand in the 20th Century* (Cambria Press, 2008).

Ghosh, Lipi, *Connectivity and Beyond: Indo-Thai Relations through Ages* (The Asiatic Society, 2011).

Knapp, Ronald G, *Chinese Houses of Southeast Asia* (Tuttle, 2010).

Leo Suryadinata & Ang Cher Kiat, *Chinatowns in a Globalising Southeast Asia* (Chinatown Heritage Centre, 2009).

Lim, Su Chen Christine, *Hua Song: Stories of the Chinese Overseas* (Long River, 2005).

Pan, Lynn (ed), *The Encyclopedia of the Chinese Diaspora* (EDM, 1998, 2006).

Piazzardi, Paolo, *Italians at the Court of Siam* (Italasia Trading, 2010).

Rawanchaikul, Navin, *Khaek Pai Krai Ma* (Navin Productions, 2020).

Sachdev, Ramlal, *In the Footsteps of the Monsoon: A History of India's influence in Thailand* (City Media, 1996).

Sng, Jeffery & Pimpraphai Bisalputra, *A History of the Thai-Chinese* (EDM, 2015).

Brij v Lal (ed), *The Encyclopedia of the Indian Diaspora* (EDM, 2007).

Van Roy, Edward, *Siamese Melting Pot: Ethnic Minorities in the Making of Bangkok* (Silkworm, 2017); *Sampheng: Bangkok's Chinatown Inside Out* (Inst of Asian Studies, 2007).

Warren, William, *The House on the Khlong* (Archipelago Press, 2007).

Wasana Wongsurawat, *The Crown & the Capitalists: The Ethnic Chinese and the Founding of the Thai Nation* (Silkworm, 2020).

Yi Guangyan, *The Odyssey of the Overseas Chinese* (Modern Publishing, 1995).

FOOD

McDang, Chef, *The Principles of Thai Cookery* (McDang. com, 2010).

Nualkhair, Chawadee, *Bangkok's Top 50 Street Food Stalls* (Wordplay 2011).

Saiyuud Diwong, *Cooking with Poo* (UNOH, 2011).

Thompson, David, *Thai Food* (Ten Speed Press, 2002), *Thai Streetfood: Authentic Recipes, Vibrant Traditions* (Ten Speed Press, 2010).

Vandenberghe, Tom & Luk Thys, *Bangkok Street Food* (Lannoo, 2015)

Yasmeen, Gisèle, *Bangkok's Foodscape* (White Lotus, 2006).

GUIDEBOOKS

aLoud Bangkok (Fullstop, 2004).

Australia New Zealand Women's Group, *The Bangkok Guide* (ANZWG, 20th Edn, 2016).

Bangkok City Scoops (City Scoops, 2009).

Bangkok Tourist Bureau, *Must-see Sights of Bangkok* (BTB, 1999).

Bangkok: A Creative's Guide (Design Anthology, 2018).

Barrett, Ken, *22 Walks in Bangkok* (Tuttle, 2013).

Bracken, Greg Byrne, *A Walking Tour: Bangkok* (Times Editions, 2003).

Chakrabongse, Narisa, *Exploring Old Bangkok* (River Books, 2019).

Douglas, Andrew, *Undertow Guides: Bangkok: Off the Grid* (a.verse, 2012).

Intakul, Sakul, *Floral Journey: Bangkok* (Purple Press, 2013).

Lonely Planet: Bangkok (Lonely Planet, 2018).

Monocle Travel Guide: Bangkok (Gestalten, 2015).

Nancy Chandler's Map of Bangkok (Nancy Chandler Maps, 2019).

Rough Guide to Bangkok (Rough Guides, 2019).

Thailand: A Travellers' Companion (EDM, 2006).

Cornwel-Smith, Philip (ed), *Time Out Bangkok City Guide* (Time Out, 2010).

We Love Bangkok (Oom, 2009).

INFORMAL CULTURE

Algie, Jim, *Bizarre Thailand* (Marshall Cavendish, 2011).

Blenkinsop, Philip, *The Cars that Ate Bangkok* (White Lotus, 1996).

Coles, Chris, *Navigating the Bangkok Noir* (Marshall Cavendish, 2011).

Cornwel-Smith, Philip, *Very Thai: Everyday Popular Culture* (River Books, 2005, 2nd ed 2012); *Invisible Things* (TCDC, 2018).

Endo, Tamaki, *Living With Risk: Precarity & Bangkok's Urban Poor* (NUS, 2014).

Herzfeld, Michael, *Siege of the Spirits: Community and Polity in Bangkok* (Chicago Uni Press, 2016).

Kalak, Thomas, *Thailand: Same Same But Different* (Rupa, 2008).

Moore, Christopher, G, *Heart Talk* (Heaven Lake Press, 2013), *The Cultural Detective: An Insider's Look at Thai Culture* (Heaven Lake Press, 2013).

Nostitz, Nick, *Red vs Yellow Vol 1: Thailand's Crisis of Identity* (White Lotus, 2009); *Red vs Yellow Vol 2: Thailand's Political Awakening* (White Lotus, 2011).

Sopranzetti, Claudio, *Owners of the Map: Motorcycle Taxi Drivers, Mobility & Politics in Bangkok* (U of California Press, 2017).

Thamrongrattanarit, Nawaphol, *Made in Thailand* (A Book, 2012).

Yanyong Boon-Long, *Bangkok: Handmade Transit* (Afterword, 2016).

SEX & GENDER

Apisuk, Noi, Cameron, Liz & Pornpit Pukmai, *The Bad Girls Dictionary* (Empower, 2007).

Atkins, Gary, *Imagining Gay Paradise: Bali, Bangkok and Cyber-Singapore* (Hong Kong Uni Press,

2012).

Harris, Andrew, *Bangkok After Dark* (MB, 1968).

Jackson, Peter (ed), *Queer Bangkok* (Hong Kong Uni Press, Silkworm, 2011).

Law, Benjamin, *Gaysia: Adventures in the Queer East* (Cleis Press, 2014).

Loos, Tamara, *Subject Siam: Family, Law and Colonial Modernity in Thailand* (Silkworm, 2002).

Nostitz, Nick, Patpong: *Bangkok's Twilight Zone* (Westzone, 2001).

Odzer, Cleo, *Patpong Sisters* (Blue Moon, 1994).

Wilson, Ara, *The Intimate Economies of Bangkok, Tomboys, Tycoons and Avon Ladies in the Global City* (California, Uni Press, 2004).

SOCIETY

Daoruang, Panrit 'Gor', *Gor's Thailand Life* (Bamboo Sinfonia, 2007)

Eckhardt, James, *Bangkok People* (Asia Books, 1999).

Fellows, Warren, *The Damage Done* (Macmilan, 1999).

Hopkins, Jerry, *Bangkok Babylon* (Tuttle, 2005), *Thailand Confidential* (Tuttle, 2011).

Maier, Fr Joe, *The Slaughterhouse: True Stories from Bangkok's Khlong Toey Slum* (Post Books, 2002).

Mulder, Neils, *Thai Images: Thai Culture of the Public World* (Silkworm, 1997); *Inside Thai Society* (Silkworm, 2000).

Nisbett, Richard, *The Geography of Thought* (Free Press, 2003).

Persons, Larry S, *The Way Thais Lead: Face as Social Capital* (Silkworm, 2016).

Pimsai Svasti & Ping Amranand, *Siamese Memoirs: the Life & Times of Pimsai Svasti* (Amulet Productions, 2011).

Tinaphong, Adul, *Patpong Road: Untold Story* (Ghaowmai, 2005).

Vorng, Sophorntavy, *Status City: Consumption, Identity, and Middle Class Culture in Contemporary Bangkok* (U of Sydney, 2009); *A Meeting of Masks: Status, Power and Hierarchy in Bangkok* (Silkworm, 2016).

FICTION

Barrett, Dean, *Skytrain to Murder* (Kindle Edition, 2011); *The Go Go Dancer who Stole my Viagra & other Poetic Tragedies of Thailand* (Village East Books, 2013).

Botan, *Letters from Thailand*, transl Susan Falop Kepner (Silkworm, 1969/2002).

Bunnag, Tew, *Curtain of Rain* (River Books, 2014), *Fragile Days: Tales from Bangkok* (Mettavisions, 2010); *The Naga's Journey* (Orchid Press, 2007); *Slow Steps to Love* (River Books, 2023).

Burdett, John, *Bangkok 8* (Vintage, 2003); *Bangkok Tattoo* (Vintage, 2005); *Bangkok Haunts* (Vintage, 2007); *The Bangkok Asset* (Vintage, 2015).

Chua, Lawrence, *Gold by the Inch* (Grove Press, 1998).

Garland, Alex, *The Beach* (Penguin, 1996).

Jetlag Travel Guides, *Phaic Tan* (Hardie Grant, 2004).

Keefe-Fox, Claire, *Siamese Tears* (River Books, 2016).

Krisana Asokesin, *City People [Chao Krung]* (Saengdao, 1992).

Kukrit Pramoj, *Four Reigns* (Silkworm, 1998).

Lapcharoensap, Rattawut, *Sightseeing* (Picador, 2005).

Larkin, Emma, *Comrade Aeon's Field Guide to Bangkok* (Granta, 2021).

Manning, Sunisa, *A Good True Thai* (Epigram, 2020).

Moore, Christopher, G (ed), *Bangkok Noir* (Heaven Lake Press, 2011); Vincent Calvino novels (Heaven Lake Press, 17 spanning 1992-2020).

Naowarat Pongpaiboon, 'Krungthep Dvaravati' poem, (Silpawatthanatham Publishing House, 1986).

Nardone, Mai, *Welcome Me to the Kingdom* (Random House, 2023).

Nitiprapha, Veeraporn, *The Blind Earthworm in the Labyrinth* (River Books, 2018); *Memories of the Memories of the Black Rose Cat* (River Books, 2022).

Paiwarin Khao-Ngam, *Banana Tree Horse and Other Poems* (Amarin, 1995).

Palmer, Steven, *Bangkok Drowning* (Saraswati Press, 2019).

Smithies, Michael, *Gulfs of Thailand: A Collection of Short Stories* (Silkworm, 1999); *A Thai Boyhood* (Federal Publications, 1993).

Somtow, SP, *Jasmine Nights* (Diplodocus Press, 2013); *Dragon's Fin Soup: Eight Modern Siamese Fables* (Diplodocus Press, 1998).

Sopranzetti, Claudio, *The King of Bangkok* (UTP, 2021).

Sri Burapha, *Behind the Painting and Other Stories* (Silkworm, 2000).

Sudbanthad, Pitchaya, *Bangkok Wakes to Rain* (Riverhead Books, 2018).

Sunthorn Phu (transl. Noh Anothai), *Poems from the Buddha's Footprint* (Singing Bone Press, 2016).

V na Pramuanmark, *Prissana* (Chatra Books, 1938).

Vinicchayakul, V., *A Night full of Stars* (River Books, 2024); *A Passage to Siam* (River Books, 2024).

Yoon, Prabda, *The Sad Part Was* (Tilted Axis, 2017); *Moving Parts* (Tilted Axis, 2019).

Zakariya Amataya, 'Five-legged Chair' poem (1001 Nights Editions, 2010).

ONLINE SOURCES

ART & CULTURE

Art 4D & Creative Map (art4d.com)

Bangkok Art & Culture Centre (en.bacc.or.th)

Bangkok Literary Review (bkklit.com)

Creative District www.bangkokriver.com)

Journal of Urban Cultural Research, Chulalongkorn Uni (www.tci-thaijo.org)

Map of Living Local Cultural Sites of Bangkok (livingculturalsites.com; www.facebook.com/Bangkokculture/?fref=ts)

Mekong Review (mekongreview.com)

Museum of Contemporary Art (mocabangkok.com)

National Museum Volunteers (www.mynmv.com)

Siam Society (www.siam-society.org)

NEWS & WHAT'S ON

Bangkok Post (Bangkokpost.com)

BK magazine (bk.asia-city.com).

FCCT www.fccthai.com

Thai Enquirer (thaienquirer.com)

Khao Sod English (khaosodenglish.com)

The Nation (www.nationthailand.com)

ASEAN Now – formerly Thai Visa (ASEANnow.com)

Koktail (koktailmagazine.com)

Time Out Bangkok (www.timeout.com)

TRAVEL

Richard Barrow travel blog (www.richardbarrow.com)

Lonely Planet (www.lonelyplanet.com)

Migrationology food blog (migrationology.com)

Michelin Guide to Thailand (guide.michelin.com)

Bangkok Vanguards tours (bangkokvanguards.com)

Tourism Authority of Thailand (TAT) (www.tourismthailand.org)

Notes & References

ABBREVIATIONS

BK BK magazine
BM Bangkok Metro
BP Bangkok Post
CB Coconuts Bangkok
FB Facebook
JSS Journal of the Siam Society
KSE Khao Sod English
NYT New York Times
SCMP South China Morning Post
TN The Nation
TOB Time Out Bangkok
Notes listed by page number
Ibid pX refers to earlier note
Bib pX refers to Bibliography
'Interviews' were with author

INTRODUCTION

14 Mingkwan Charoennit-niyom, 'Translation Methods for Thai Cultural Words and Phrases in Non-Fiction. Case Study: Very Thai' (Chulalongkorn University, 2009).

TIME

Destiny

25 Fongsanan Chamornchan & cited by Teeranai Charuvastra, 'The Curse That Haunted Bangkok 150 Years – Until Now?' (*KSE*, 21/04/2017).

SMELL

26 Plunkett-Hogge, Kay Plunkett-Hogge, 'A Bangkok scented candle would smell of incense, grilled pork and tuk-tuk fumes' (*Guardian*, 17/03/2017).
27 Theroux, Paul, *The Great Railway Bazaar* (Houghton Mifflin, 1975).
27 Smell assessors, 'Nosy: Thai officials hire 167 people to smell bad stuff and report on it' (*CB*, 19/06/2017).
28 Green World Foundation, secretary general Saranarat Kanjanavanit cited in 'Apocalypse Now' (*BK*, 09/07/2010).
28 Rattawut Lapcharoensap, 'At the Café Lovely' in *Sightseeing*, Bib p339.
28-29 King Rama V cited by Chittawadi Chitrabongs, *The Politics of Defecation in Bangkok* (Journal of the Siam Society, Vol. 99, 2011).

29 Cameron Cooper (Facebook, 24/08/2015).

Flower Culture

28 Natayada, Bib p337.

TASTE

31 Suthorn Sukphisit, 'Local Wisdom: Bland Bangkok is most definitely not the food capital of the country' (*BP*, 23/12/2018).
31 Kasma Loha-unchit, '7 biggest misconceptions about Thai food' (CNN Travel, 22/08/2011).
32 Duangporn Songvisava, 'First Person' (*BK*, 22/02/2013).
32 Chef McDang, 'The Myth of "royal" Thai cuisine' (CNN Travel, 15/07/2011).
34 *Oxford Companion to Food*, Alan Davidson (OUP, 2014).
34 Thompson, David, in *Thai Food*, Bib p338.
34 Halliday, Bob, cited by Tom Fuller, 'Thais Bristle at Australian's Take on Thai Cuisine' (*NYT*, 23/09/10).
35 Thompson, David, about mandarin, cited by Tom Fuller, ibid p34.
35 Thaninthorn Chantrawan, cited by Oliver Irvine & Natcha Sanguankiattichai, 'Changes Up Top' (*BK*, 17/03/2015).
35 Napol Jantraget, interview, 2017).
35 Lime juice cited by Suthorn Sukphisit, 'Striking a Sour Note' (*BP*, 05/04/2015).
36 Thaweekiat Nimmalairatana, cited by Fuller, Tom, 'You call this Thai food? The robotic taster will be the judge' (*NYT*, 28/09/2014).
36 Bangkok Post editorial, 'Thai food, made bland' (*BP*, 07/09/16).

Streetfood

32 Vallop Suwandee cited in 'Bangkok to ban its famous street food stalls' (*Daily Telegraph*, 18/04/2017).
33 Chawadee Nualkhair cited by Dunlop, Nic, 'Will Bangkok's street food ban hold?' (*Guardian*, 27/08/2017).

Gastrothai

37 Krammy, Oliver, cited by

Gregoire Glachant & Pieng-or Mongkolkumnuankhet, 'Bon Apetit Bangkok' (*BK*, 07/06/2013).
37 Nan Bunyasaranand, cited by Pieng-or Mongkolkumnuankhet, 'The Rise of Thai Chefs: Why More Restaurants are Taking Pride in Local Talent' (*BK*, 06/05/2014).
37 Ian Kittichai, 'First Person' (*BK*, 12/02/2012).
38 Worathorn Udom-chalotorn, cited by Pieng-or, ibid p37.
38 'Tired Trends' (*BK*, 18/02/2011).
38 Ian Kittichai, ibid p37.
39 Chinn, Bobby, cited by Glachant, Gregoire, 'Is the Michelin Guide Coming to Bangkok?' (*BK*, 06/06/2013).
39 Anand, Gaggan, cited by Glachant, ibid p39.

HEAT & WATER

41 Tadsanawadee, *Wall*, cited by Boccuzzi, Bib p338.
41 Pariwarin Khao-Ngam, *Morning Song*, cited by Boccuzzi, Bib p338
41 Bunnag, Tew, *Curtain of Rain*, cited by Boccuzzi, Bib p339.
41 *Mekong Hotel* film.
43 Belgian advisor cited by O'Neil, Bib p337.
44 Scott, Trevor, 'All about aircon' (Postbag, *BP*, 22/04/2017).
45 Tarrin, 'Fake Beggar' cited by Boccuzzi, Bib p338
45 Public Works cited by Wassayos Ngamkham & Supoj Wancharoen, 'Pedestrians walk the bridges of fear' (*BP*, 23/08/2014).
45 Kaewta Ketbungkan, 'Society Of "Railway Sleepers" Resigned To Long, Uncomfortable Journey' (KSE, 15/04/2017
46 Temperature figures from Wikipedia.

SPACE

48 Size & population in 2010 census from Wikipedia.
49 Chittawadi Chitrabongs, 'The Politics of Defecation in Bangkok of the Fifth Reign' (*Journal of the Siam Society*, vol 99, 2011).
49 Cecilia Lindqvist cited by PD Smith, *City*, Bib p337.
49 PD Smith, *City*, Bib p337.
49 Theroux, Paul, ibid p27.
54 Sassen, Saskia 'Who owns our cities – and why this urban takeover should

concern us all' (*Guardian*, 24/11/2015).
54 Sopawan Boonnimitra, *Lak-ka-pid-lak-ka-perd* (Lunds Universitet, 2006).
56 Herzfeld, Michael 'Spatial Cleansing: Monumental Vacuity and the Idea of the West' (*Journal of Material Culture*, Vol. 11, 2006).

Third Places

55 Oldenburg, Ray, 'Character of Third Places' in *The Great Good Place* (Paragon House, 1989).

Green Space

57 Park area 3.3sqm, up to 4sqm, BMA park plan, 'Bangkok 1919' (*BK*, 07/10/2009).
57 Greenery per head & vegetated areas, Siemens Green City Index, cited in 'Makkasan Saving' (*BK*, 17/05/2013).
58 Santi Opaspakornkij, interview (FCCT, 30/10/2019).
59 Oraya Sutabutr, interview (FCCT, 30/10/2019).
59 Pok Kobkongsanti cited by Nutthachai Bunluthangthum, 'Bangkok Under Construction' (*BK*, 10/08/2012).

DIRECTION

64 Circular/linear experiments cited by Nisbett, Bib p339.

Feng Shui

64 Visit Techakasem, 'First Person' (*BK*, 28/01/2011).
65 City pillar Charoen Tanmaharan, interview (14/10/2008).

MOTION

67 'Bangkok ranked among world's top 10 cities with worst traffic', Thai PBS, http://englishnews.thaipbs.or.th/bangkok-ranked-among-worlds-top-10-cities-worst-traffic, 05/02/2015.
69 'Bangkok ranks top of the world for the most time wasted in traffic standstill for each trip' (Thai PBS, http://englishnews.thaipbs.or.th/bangkok-ranks-top-world-time-wasted-traffic-standstill-trip, 06/02/2015).
70 Accident figures, cited in 'Road casualties are wasting 6% of Thailand's GDP' (*Thailand Business News*, 06/10/2017).
70 Brands cited in 'The answer to road carnage - bottles of chicken extract and "sleep with the cops" '

340 Notes & References

(*Daily News*, 28/12/2017).

70 Groskopf, Christopher, 'Bad drivers are a good indicator of a corrupt government' (Quartz, 23/04/2016).

70 Soithip Trisuddhi, cited by Adam Janofsky, 'The (Real) Cost of Cars in Bangkok' (The Pulitzer Center, 14/08/2012).

71 Ploenpote Atthakor, '"Free riders" shouldn't spoil poor's travels' (*BP*, 06/02/2015).

74 Torpong Chantabubpha, 'First Person' (*BK*, 20/12/2013).

Walking

68 Zcongklod Bangyikhan, interview (2012).

68 Oraya Sutabutr cited in 'Walking on Hot Air' (*BK*, 22/04/2011).

69 Teerachon Manomai-phaibul, cited in 'Walking on Hot Air', ibid p68.

69 Khaisri Paksukcharern, cited in 'Walking on Hot Air', ibid p68.

Cycling

72 Zcongklod, ibid p68.

73 Aran Kamonchan, cited by Nutthachai Bunluthangthum, 'The Bicycle Gangs' (*BK*, 03/05/2013).

69 Wararat Puapairoj, cited by Nutthachai, ibid p 73.

73 Varin Somprasong, cited by Nutthachai, ibid p 73.

73 Peerawat Jariyasombat, 'Rush-hour Revelations' (*BP*, 27/03/2014).

73 Pongpet Mekloy, 'On the path close to home' (*BP*, 27/03/2014).

Custom Transit

76 Yanyong Boon-Long, *Handmade Transit*, Bib p338.

76 Rapeepat Inkasit in Yanyong, Bib p338.

76 Steersman cited by Rapeepat Inkasit in Yanyong, Bib p338.

76 Chaowalit Metayaprapas cited by Natthakarn Amatya-kul in Yanyong, Bib p338.

77 Sopranzetti, Claudio, *The Owners of the Map*, Bib p338.

77 Yanyong, Bib p338.

LOOKING

84 Sense research cited by Nisbett, Bib p339.

84 Chinese insights, Jin Ni, author interview (2018).

89 Condo styles, 'You are where you live' (Realist, 18/09/2017).

89 Zcongklod, ibid p68.

Vertical Living

82 Rangsan's "exultant post-

modernism", Waites, Dan, *Culture Shock: Thailand* (Marshall Cavendish, 2014).

82 24 Condo, 'On top of Bangkok' (*Tropical Living*, 11/2009).

83 Manit Sriwanchphoom, 'First Person' (*BK*, 21/11/2014).

83 Duangrit Bunnag, cited in 'Shophouse Redux' (*BK*, 19/11/2010).

Larkitecture

86 Hoskin (*Design*), Bib p337.

COLOUR

91 Instagram survey cited by M4tt, 'You are not a beautiful and unique snowflake, and neither is your Instagram' (The Verge, 04/07/2013).

94 Ploenpote Athakor, 'Thammasat, inequality and "colourism" ' (*BP*, 15/09/2013).

94 Atiya Achakulwisut, 'Confusion over colorus clouds future (*BP*, 31/10/2017).'

Blossom Season

95 Lumpini trees, Sakul Intakul, *Floral Journey Bangkok* (Purple Press, 2013).

95 Yongyuth Chanyarak, cited in 'University Under the Trees' (*BP*, 19/03/2009).

SACRED

99 Charoen Wongpiyachetchai, cited by Sanitsuda Ekachai, 'Return of the Goddess,' *Keeping the Faith* (Post Books, 2001).

100 Sanitsuda Ekachai, 'Dhammakaya is only a symptom' (*BP*, 25/02/2015).

100 Sanitsuda Ekachai, 'Making Thai Buddhism relevant again' (*BP*, 01/03/2017).

100 Nasa Saze, in forum 'Why is Thailand the most religious country in the world?' (Quora.com, 21/01/2016).

101 Suttichart Denpreuktham, in Quora, ibid p100.

101 Sophorntavy Vorng, 'Samsaric Salvation: Prosperity Cults, Political Crisis, and Middle Class Aspirations in Bangkok' (Max Planck Institute for the Study of Religious and Ethnic Diversity, 2010).

104 Monk numbers from *Bangkok Post*, cited by Anderson, Benedict, 'Outsider view of Thai politics' (*Prachathai English*, 05/08/2011).

104 McDaniel, Bib p337.

104 P. Payutto cited by Dhammacaro, 'Wisdom Begins With Simplicity' (http://www.buddhapadipa.org/dhamma-corner/wisdom-begins-with-simplicity/).

104 Buddhadasa, Bib p337.

105 Art, cited by Vorng, Bib p339.

105 Phra Kovit Khemananda, 'An Extemporaneous Talk to the Singapore Zen Group' (www.thaibuddhism.net).

105 Knowing Buddha, knowingbuddha.org

105 Ministry of Culture mission, cited by Gregoire Glachant (*BK*).

106 Chang Noi, 'Cultural Bureaucracy and Bureaucratic Culture' (*TN*, 12/11/2007).

106 Yok, Tom & TCH officials cited by Funahashi, Daena Aki, 'Rule by Good People: Health Governance and the Violence of Moral Authority in Thailand' (*Cultural Anthropology* 31/1, 2016).

106 Paisarn Likhit-preechakul, 'Karma confusion and the theology of Thai exceptionalism' (*TN*, 16/07/2011).

106 Thongchai Winichakul, 'Hyper Royalism: It's Spells and its Magic' (ISA, 25/05/2014).

Brahmins

98 Devasathan info, Dulyapak Preecharushh, 'Brahmin and Hindu Communities in Bangkok,' *Connectivity & Beyond: Indo-Thai Relations Through Ages*, ed Lipi Ghosh (The Asiatic Society, 2009).

98 Giant Swing source, Guelden, Bib p337.

98 Brahmin ritual, Hoskin (*Supernatural*) Bib p337.

99 Pakorn Wutthipram cited by Heamakarn Srichartatchanya, 'Mission to Minister' (*BP*, 25/01/2003).

99 Sisada Rangsibrahman-akul, cited by Heamakarn Srichartatchanya, 'Mission to Minister' (*BP*, 25/01/2003).

All in One

107 Lek Viriyahbhun, AncientCityGroup.net).

Muslim-Thais

108 8% cited by Islamic Committee Office of Thailand

108 12% cited by Thai embassy in Saudi Arabia

108 Muslim tourist numbers from TAT figures for 2016.

108 Fifth of city, cited by Askew, Bib p337.

109 Imtiyaz Yusuf, Celebrating the Prophet Muhammad's birthday in Thailand (*TN*, 07/03/2015).

109-110 Adis Idris Raksamani, 'Multicultural Aspects of the Mosques in Bangkok' (*Manusya*, Journal of Humanities No 16, 2008).

110 Gilquin, Bib p337.

110 Davud Lawang, cited by Anchalee Kongkrut, 'Reading Which changes Lives' (*BP*, 04/03/2007).

110 Farida cited by Anchalee Kongkrut, 'Reading Which changes Lives' (*BP*, 04/03/2007).

110 Kong Rithdee, 'The good, the bad, and the reality' (*BP*, 13/10/2007).

111 Don Pathan, 'The Authorities simply can't understand Southern angst' (*TN*, 10/02/2011).

111 70% halal, Globetrotting Goumet

111 Rattiya Salae, cited by Sanitsuda Ekachai, 'Finding unity in diversity' (*BP*, 26/06/2004).

SUPERNATURAL

113 Ajarn Kiaow from interview (14/05/2011).

113 & 115 Watcharapool 'Jack' Fukijdee, cited by Cohan Chew, 'Why Thailand Shrines offer Strawberry Fanta to Ghosts' (weareresonate.com, 14/04/2017).

113 Ghost Radio (youtube.com/theghostradioofficial).

115 Chatgew cited by Cohan Chew, 'Why Thailand Shrines offer Strawberry Fanta to Ghosts' (weareresonate.com, 14/04/2017).

115 Mill, interview (14/05/2011).

115 Neta Grill cited in 'Thai airline to issue child tickets to "spirit" dolls' (*Straits Times*, Bloomberg, 26/01/2016).

116 Wasant Techawongtham, 'The Bastardisation of Buddhism' (*BP*, 10/03/2017).

116 McDaniel, Bib p337.

119 Suwanna Satha-anand cited by Usnisa Sukhasvasti, 'Abode of the Gods' (*BP*, 29/09/2006).

Notes & References **341**

Animist Shrines
118 Kung Kannika, cited in 'Shakin' it with Chuchok in Bangkok: the Thai Shrine that has Sexy Dancers' (*Coconuts TV*, 29/12/2013).
119 Nark baby references, McDaniel, Bib p337.

TRANCE
121 Mill, interviews (14/05/2011, 24/03/2018).
121 Ajarn Kiaow, ibid p113.
123 devotee Max/Tintrinai, interview (2010).
123 Ton, interview (2010).
123 Mill, ibid p121.
Neo-Hindu
124 Komkrit Uitekkeng cited by Usnisa, ibid p119.
124 Max/Tintrinai, ibid p123.
124 Pok Chelsea, interview (2016).
125 Yanisa, interview (2010).
125 Manote Tripathi, 'The elephant god arises' (*TN*, 19/11/2006).
125 Mill, ibid p121.

NIGHT
126 Natayada, Bib p337.
127 Manta Klangboonkrong, 'The Night's Liveliest Nests' (*TN*, 05/09/2014).
128 Peerawat Jariyasombat, 'Rush-hour Revelations' (*BP*, 27/03/2014).
128 Natayada, Bib p337.
130 Zcongklod Bangyikhan, interview (2015).
130 Chanun Poomsawai, interview (2015).

SANUK
134 Beer, interview (2019).
135 Reindeer quote, interview (2019).
135 Kwanchai Atthikomprasit, interview (2015).

LIBIDO
136 King, Ross, *Reading Bangkok* (NUS, 2011).
136 Thitipol Panyalimpanan, 'Rape and romance: When will Thai soap operas stop trivialising sexual abuse?' (*Asian Correspondent*, 08/01/2016).
137 Chotiros Suriyawong cited by Alex Sehmer, 'Bangkok's battle of ethics' (Al Jazeera, 10/07/2008).
137 Tulsathit Taptim, 'Dirty Dancing Leaves Everyone in a Spin' (*TN*, 28/09/2011).
137 Usnisa Sukhsvasti 'Take Thainess with a grain of salt' (*BP*, 19/01/2015).
138 Chuvit Kamolvisit cited by Perry, Martin, 'Thai massage king prefers

"pimp" label to politician' (Reuters, 30/06/2011).
138 Kobkarn Wattanawarankul, cited by Marszal, Andrew, '"Thailand is closed to sex trade", says country's first female tourism minister' (*The Telegraph*, 17/072016).
138 Nostitz, Nick, Bib p339.
139 Sex worker cited in 'Thai sex industry under fire from tourism minister, police' (Reuters, 17/07/2016).
139 Feingold, David cited by Fenn, Mark, 'Thailand's Sex Trafficking Figures Suspect?' (Asia Sentinel, 05/01/2015).
139 Chantawipa Apisuk, cited by Subhatra Bhumiprabhas, 'Sex "trade", not "traffic".' (*BP*, 06/03/2012).
140 LaPalme, Michael (FB).
140 American visitor to Siam, cited by Atkins, Gary, *Imagining Gay Paradise: Bali, Bangkok & Cyber Singapore* (Silkworm, 2012).
141 Woolsey, Barbara, 'Night Prowl: the legendary lechery of Bernard "Night Owl" Trink' (*CB*, 26/08/2014).
141 Jiemin Bao, *Marital Acts: Gender, Sexuality, And Identity Among The Chinese Thai Diaspora* (Hawaii University Press, 2004).
142 AP: Jocelyn Gecker and Thanyarat Doksone, 'Thai soaps trigger outcry over romanticizing rape' (AP, 16/10/2014).
142 Nitipan Wiprawit, cited by Thitipol Panyalimpanan, 'Rape and romance: When will Thai soap operas stop trivialising sexual abuse?' (*Asian Correspondent*, 08/01/2016).
142 Arunosha cited by Jocelyn Gecker and Thanyarat Doksone, 'Thai soaps trigger outcry over romanticizing rape' (AP, 16/10/2014).
142 Napaporn Trivitwareegune, First Person (*BK*, 13/02/2015).
142 Sin Suesuan, cited in 'Our moral guardians need some lessons' (*BP*, 12/04/2015).
143 Kanokporn Chanasongkram, 'The Trouble with Love' (*BP*, 12/02/2015).
143 Kaewmala, cited by Saksith Saiyasombut,

'Only taboo when it's inconvenient!' – Interview with Thai author Kaewmala on the outrage at topless Songkran dancers (*Siam Voices*, 19/04/2011).
LGBT Paradise?
144 13th Legatum Propserity Index (2019).
144 Punnatha Pathikorn, '@me_me_me_bangkok' (*BK*, 14/06/2013).
145 Nuh Peace, cited in 'Nuh Peace preaches a punk-rock sermon of acceptance' (Luredby.com, 29/03/2019).

TOUCH
147 Research on authentic textures, Goldhagen, Sarah Williams, *Welcome to Your World* (Harper, 2017).
148 Osborne, Lawrence, *Bangkok Days* (North Point Press, 2009).

PAIN
150 Burdett, John, Workpoint News (FB).
150 Anucha Thirakanont, author interview (2006).
150 Buddhadasa Bikkhu, *Handbook for Mankind* (Mahachula Buddhist University Press, 1990).
151 Domestic violence figures, Frandsen, Louise Bihl, 'Bangkok has highest rate of domestic violence' (ScandAsia.com, 08/04/2015).
153 Awareness video, 'Ignored: Most Thais turn blind eye to domestic violence in Social experiment' (*CB*, 31/03/2016).
153 Jakkrit cited in 'Domestic violence blights society' (*BP*, 25/12/2016).
153 Kong Rithdee, 'Tabloid saga and our gang mentality' (*BP*, 19/01/2014).
153 Student brawls, Belford, Aubrey, 'Bangkok brawls, Jakarta rumbles' (*TN*, 08/01/08).
154 Abhisit Sa-in, cited by Chaiyot Yongcharoenchai, 'The school of hard knocks' (*BP Spectrum*, 21/12/2014).
154 Sittichai Chaivoraprug, cited in 'Bangkok hostel offers prison experience a la *The Shawshank Redemption*' (DPA, 20/01/2018).
Healing Hub
152 2.5m & 40% figures of 2013 cited by Finch, Steve, 'Thailand Top Destination for Medical Tourists'

(*CMAJ*, 07/01/2014).
152 Spurlock cited by Peltier, Dan, 'CNN Documentary Shows Medical Tourism in Thailand is a Serious Business' (Skift, 30/01/2015).

SOUND
157 Oraya Sutrabutr, from interview (20/02/2018).
157 Suchada Tangtongtavy, with Holmes, Henry & Tomizaway, Roy, *Working With The Thais* (White Lotus, 1995).
157 People Who Love Quiet Club, cited in 'Quiet Riot' (*BK*, 15/02/2007).
160 Museum of Endangered Sounds (mrgory.info/sm/#).
160 Westercamp, Hildegard, cited by Landry, Charles, *The Art of City Making* (Earthscan, 2006).
Birdsong
158 Bangkok Wild Watch 2014 figures, cited by Supoj Wancharoen, 'Lumpini Battles Urban Disaster' (*BP*, 17/01/2015).
158 Bangchak Birdwatching Club, *Must See Sights of Bangkok* (BTB, 1999).
158 Latkrabang Project 3, 0 2749 5259, *Must See Sights of Bangkok* (BTB, 1999).
158 Bangkok Wild Watch 2014 figures, cited by Supoj Wancharoen, 'Lumpini Battles Urban Disaster' (*BP*, 17/01/2015).
Bang-Pop!
162 Hugo, author interview (2015).
162 Norasete Mudkong, interviews & First Person (*BK*, 03/08/2012).
162 Jessada Theerapinan, First Person (*BK*, 23/03/2012).
162 Kamol Sukosol Clapp, author interviews & First Person (*BK*, 15/08/2014).
163 Vasu Sangsingkaew, First Person (*BK*, 19/09/2014).
163 Tul Waitoonkiat, author interview (2015).
163 Chanun Poomsawai, author interview (16/02/2015).

SENSORS
165 Panya Charusiri cited by Apinya Wipatayotin, 'Geologist warns of city quake risk' (*BP*, 08/05/2014).
165 Form reform cited by Nattaya Chetchotiros, 'Panel wants end to licensing nightmare' (*BP*,

342 Notes & References

165 Kobsak Pootrakul & index, 'Reformers push for simplified business licenses' (Thai embassy to US, 12/02/2017).
167 Nitipol Temprim, cited by Monruedee Jansuttipan, 'CCTVgate' (*BK*, 30/09/2011).
167 Christina Kubisch, interview (11/04/2016).

THAINESS & THE CITY
171 Ethical code cited by Peleggi, Maurizio, *Thailand: The Worldly Kingdom* (Reaktion, 2007).
171 Saksith Saiyasombat, interview (02/03/2015).
171 Ing K, interview (23/04/2016).
174 Voranai Vanijaka, interview (2015).
174 Riverside ribbon urbanism, coined by Baker & Phasuk, *A History of Thailand*, Bib 337.
175 Small City Branding Around the World http://citybranding.typepad.com/city-branding/2011/08/bangkok-joins-the-slogan-competition-club.html, 10/08/2011).
175 Askew, Bib p337.
175 Chittawadi, ibid p49.
175 Chiranan Pitpreecha, First Person (*BK*, 27/06/2014).
176 Prathet Krungthep (FB).
176 Saksith Saiyasombat, interview (02/03/2015).
176 Teng Terdterng, cited by Boccuzzi, Bib p338.
176 Pitch Pongsawat, interview (2015).
176 Ing K, introduction to *Bangkok in Black and White* by Manit Sriwanichpoom (Chang Puak Nga Dum, 1999).
177 Hamilton, Annette, 'Wonderful, Terrible: Everyday Life in Bangkok' in *A Companion to the City* (Blackwell, 2003).
177 Mercer rank, 'Bangkok City Performance, Brand Image and Reputation', (*Place Brand Observer*, 21/11/2013).
177 Tripuck Supawattana, cited by Nutthachai Bunluthangthum, 'Views of the City', (*BK*, 02/08/2013).
177 Zcongklod Bangyikhan, interview (2015).
177 Pachter, Marc, interview (2018).
178 Chadchart Sittipunt, 'Chadchart warns street

vendors of income checks & tax bills' (*BP*, 31/05/2024).
178 Voranai, Vanijaka, interview (2015).

Royal Presence
173 Yellow dust quote cited by Tulsathit Taptim, 'More than just specks of yellow dust' (*TN*, 12/12/2012).

Krungthep or Bangkok?
179 Charnvit Kasemsiri, interview at Siam Society (10/03/2015).
179 Askew, Bib p337.

INFLUENCE
182 Tulsathit Taptim, 'Thais arrive at a crucial juncture – again' (*TN*, 10/10/2007).
182 Mini, cited by Teeranai Charuvastra, 'TV host loses job, charged with assault in #graabmycar road rage incident' (*KSE*, 07/11/2016).
183 Nidhi Eoseewong, 'A Cultural Constitution' (1985).
184 Guide to Parliament (parliament.go.th, 2021).
184 Wise, David, Thailand: History, Politics & the Rule of Law (Marshall Cavendish 2019).
184 Military figures, 'Military largesse' (*BP*, 06/03/2024).
184 Army figs (Wikipedia, 2024)
184 Suan Dusit Poll cited by Pravit Rojanaphruk, 'The Real Influential Figure' (*KSE*, 19/03/2016).
186 Thitinan Pongsudhirak, 'Our custodial democracy on display' (*BP*, 21/07/2023).
186 Nidhi, ibid p183.

BECOMING BANGKOKIAN
189 Voranai Vanijaka, interview (2015).
189 Mono-ethnic figures, *CIA World Factbook* (2018).
189 Sujit Wongthes, 'Jek Bon Lao' (Sinlapa Watthanatham, 1987).
189 Vithi Phanichphant, interview (2004).
189 National ethnicities: 77.3% are Thai (32.2% Central, 26.6% Isaan, 10.6% Northern, 7.0% Southern), plus 10.5% Chinese, 6% Malay, and 3.4% Khmer.
189 77.3% survey by World Christian Database, cited by OMF Thailand (omf.org) 2010 census
190 2.2 million migrants cited in *World Population Review 2019*
191 *Siam According to Bangkokian* map,

by Rakchart Wong-arthichart, cited by Pravit Rojanaphruk, 'Politically Incorrect Map 'Ugly But True', Cartographer Says' (*KSE*, 22/03/2016)
192 Disaphol, Bib p338.
193 Skinner, William G, *Chinese Assimilation and Thai Politics* (Cambridge Uni Press, 1957), cited by http://absolutelybangkok.com/thailand-a-chinese-colony/
192 Botan, *Letters from Thailand* (Silkworm, 1969/2002).
193 *The Encyclopaedia of the Chinese Overseas*, Bib p337.
193 Sondhi Limthongkul, cited by Lim, Su Chen Christine, *Hua Song: Stories of the Chinese Diaspora* (Long River Press, 2005).
195 Ma Chongxian, cited by Shi Jiangtao, 'In Bangkok's Chinatown, grief and gratitude following Thai King's Death' (*SCMP*, 14/10/2016).
196 Headscarfed woman, Humans of Bangkok (FB, 17/11/2013).
196 Kamol Sukosol Clapp, author interview (2015).
198 MuseumSiam, 'Xenomania' exhibition (2011).

Mon
194-195 Thawatpong Monda, interview (2010).

Indian-Thais
199 Vorasa Srichaikul, cited in 'Crackdown on nut-selling Khaek article in newspaper is latest example of casual racism in Thai culture' (*CB*, 26/07/2016).
199 Maynica Sachdev, cited in 'Crackdown on nut-selling Kaek' article in newspaper is latest example of casual racism in Thai culture' (*CB*, 26/07/2016).

ROOTS
200 Boyce, Ralph, speech at US Embassy Bangkok (2007).
201 Tanyaporn Singchalee, interview (17/05/2011).
204 Prachuab Chaiyasarn, cited in 'Isan Retrospective' (TCDC, 2006).
204 Pitch Pongsawat, author interview (2015).
204 *World Values Survey*, cited by Peerasit Kamnuansilpa & Draper, John, 'Tackling trenchant discrimination' (*BP*, 21/03/2016).

204 Seri Wongmontha cited by Siripan Nogsuan Sawasdee, *Politics of Electoral Reform in Thailand* (Kyoto Uni, 2014).
205 Vithi Phanichphant, interview & cited by Farrell, James Austin, 'The Lanna Deception' (*City Life*, 12/12/2009).
205 National ethnicities survey by World Christian Database, cited by OMF Thailand (omf.org).
205 Charnvit Kasetsiri, author interview at Siam Society (30/06/2017).
205 Kong Rithdee, 'Serving up cruelty, a taste of 'Thainess' (*BP*, 20/08/2016).
206 Thongchai, Bib p338.
206 Peerasit Kamnuansilpa & Draper, John, 'Tackling trenchant discrimination' (*BP*, 21/03/2016).
206 Vithi Phanichphant, cited by Farrell, James Austin, 'The Lanna Deception' (*City Life*, 12/12/2009).

Isaan Travelogue
198 *Crying Tiger*, cited in Wise Kwai's Film Journal (18/07/2005).
198 Thongchai Prasongsanti, quoted by Kriangsak Suwanpantakul, 'Cracking up the Egg Emperor' (*TN*, 08/08/2005), cited by Mitchell, Bib p338
202 Pong Prida, cited by Waeng Phalangwan, 'Luuk Thung Isaan' (RP Books, 2002), translated by Mitchell, Bib p338.
202 Anderson, Benedict: 'Outsider view of Thai politics' (*Prachatai*, 05/08/2017).
202 Paiwarin Khao-Ngam, *Banana Tree Horse* (1995).
202 Boccuzzi, Bib p138.

Regional Rites
208 Takerng Pattanopas, interview (2015).
208 *khon pak tai* quote, interview (08/10/2010).
209 Tanyaporn Singchalee, interview (17/5/2011).
209 Worathep Akkabootra, interview (2012).
209 Wimonsiri Hemtanon, interview (2010).

STIR-FRY
211 Lee Hsien Loong, speech to Teochiu International Conference (22/11/2003).
211 Smith, Bib p338.
212 Smithies, Michael, 'Review of Maryvelma O'Neil's *Bangkok: A*

212 Chen Mingquan cited by Shi Jiangtao, 'In Bangkok's Chinatown, grief and gratitude following Thai king's Death' (*SCMP*, 14/10/2016).

213-214 Suppanut Jonjitaree posts in Quora.com, https://www.quora.com/What-effect-has-Confucianism-had-on-Thai-culture?.

215 Liang Chua Morita, *Religion & Family of the Chinese & Thai & influences* (Nagoya U, 2007).

216 Voranai Vanijaka, interview (15/01/2015).

216 Sam Po Kong reference: Charnvit Kasetsiri & Wright, Michael, *Discovering Ayutthaya* (Toyota Foundation, 2007).

216 @Honey_beigr cited by Asaree Thaitrakulpanich, 'Chinese god of wealth becomes unlikely meme on Thai internet' (*KSE*, 24/10/2019).

216 Warren, William, *Bangkok* (Talisman, 2002).

218 Liang, ibid 216.

From Jek to Thai-Jiin

214 Kasian Tejapira, 'Pigtail: A Pre-History of Chineseness in Siam' (*Sojourn*, vol 7:1, 1992).

Chinese Revival

219 Chang Noi, 'Cultural Revolution in Thailand, (*TN*, 29/08/96).

219 Visit Limprana cited by Yvonne Bohwongprasert, 'Bastion of his community' (*BP*, 17/09/09).

219 The Commemoration Gate Project, ed Prayudh Mahakitsiri (Copydesk, 2000).

220 Visit Limprana cited by Yvonne Bohwongprasert, 'Bastion of his community' (*BP*, 17/09/09).

220 Paisarn Piamettawat, interview (2019).

220 Sun Yat Sen cited by Pan, Bib p338.

220 Haiwai huaren, huayi and Xi Jinping cited by Frank Ching, 'China vies for hearts and minds of 'sons and daughters' overseas' (Ejinsight, 09/05/2016).

220 3rd World Chinese Entrepreneurs Convention & Kasian Tejapira cited by Vatikiotis, Michael, TEOTCO, P227 (2007).

221 Birthright programme,

Root Seeking Camp & patriotic education cited by Leah Liu, 'China has its own birthright tour' (*Foreign Policy*, 27/07/2016).

221 10 million tourists, 'Chinese Visitors to Thailand hit 10 million for first time' (Xinhua, 20/12/2018).

COMMUNITY

222 Pranee Sutdis cited by Matthew Strieb, AP, 'Thai bowlmakers survive via tourist trade?' (*San Francisco Chronicle*, 25/11/2007).

222 Hiran, interview (2008).

223 Surachai Sukson, cited in 'People of Kudee Jeen' (*Air Asia 360*, 07/2015).

223 Asian Coalition for Housing Rights, 'The Slums of Asia' in Housing People in Asia (http://www.asiasociety.org/policy-politics/human-rights/the-slums-asia).

224 Density decreased from 15,000 to 11,000 per sq km, 'Dynamics of urban structure in Bangkok' (Journal of the Eastern Asia Society for Transportation Studies, Vol. 7, 2007).

224 Slum figures, Nattha Thepbamrung, 'Tin Town: Just enough for the city' (BP, 01/09/2013).

224 Wimonrart Issarathumnoon, 'Cultural Heritage Places: the case of Yanaka district in Tokyo and Banglamphu district in Bangkok' (University of Tokyo, 11/11/2007).

224-225 Anirut Apidech, interview (2019).

226 *Mercer's Worldwide Quality of Living Survey* (Mercer.com, 13/03/2019).

226 Monruedee Jansuttipan, 'Save our streets' (*BK*, 21/01/2011).

227 Boonliang Koomklong & Auntie Jadd, cited by Korakot Punlopraksa (author interview & FB, 2010).

227 Empty homes figures, cited by Natnicha Chuwiruch, 'Want to Buy a Home in Thailand? You Have More Than 450,000 to Choose From' (Bloomberg, 16/05/2019).

228 Ploenpote Atthakor, 'Temples must support their communities' (*BP*, 22/08/2014).

228 Abbot boasting cited by Ploenpote Atthakor, 'Temples' ties with locals take turn for worse' (*BP*, 19/07/2013).

228 Supharat Pothisuwan & Prakij Thamniam, cited by Neon Boonyadhammakul, 'Voices from the River' (*BK*, 18/08/2017).

228 Inequality source, *Global Wealth Report* (Credit Suisse, 2016).

228 Grassroots ban cited in 'PM wants to ban word "grassroots"' (*BP*, 27/08/2015) & 'Why "Grassroots" is a phrase we're going through' (*BP*, 30/08/2015).

228 Askew, Marc, *Bangkok: Place, Practice & Representation* (Routledge, 2002).

229 Narisa Chakrabongse, interview (2019).

230 Amara cited by Sophorntavy Vorng, 'Status City' (U of Sydney, 2009).

230 Pen-Ek Ratanaruang, *Sawasdee Bangkok* (2010).

230 Oldenburg, Ray, 'Our Vanishing Third Places' (*Planning Commissioners Journal*, 1996-97).

232 Suwanna Walploy-ngam, cited by Teeranai Charuvastra, 'New Tourism Aims to Revive Bangkok's Dying Communities' (*KSE*, 26/11/2017).

232 Achariya Thamparipattra cited by Teeranai Charuvastra, 'New Tourism Aims to Revive Bangkok's Dying Communities' (*KSE*, 26/11/2017).

232 Supitcha Tovivich, cited by Ariane Kupferman-Sutthavong, Uprooted' (*BP*, 25/07/2017).

232 Walailak Songsiri of Lek-Prapai Viriyahpant Foundation, cited by Sasiwan Mokkhasen, 'Imagine Bangkok 2016: Better city, less life?' (*KSE*, 03/01/2016).

232 Gillison, Samantha, 'The way to kill a complex city is to chase out all the poor people – and their food' (*Guardian*, 01/10/2015).

233 Patama Roonrakwit, cited by Pichaya Svasti, 'Co-housing way of life' (BP, 08/07/2010).

Roofless

229 Samer Peerachai, cited by Prae Sakaowan, 'Homeless man on quest to scribble Illuminati conspiracies on

Ratchathewi bridge?' (*CB*, 23/09/2016).

229 Homeless figures, Issarachon Foundation, cited in 'Numbers of homeless and sex workers 'increasing in Bangkok' (*TN*, 14/07/2019).

Tin Town

234-235 Poo & Anji Barker, cited by Turtle, Michael, 'Trying to get out of the slum' (*Time Travel Turtle*, 15/01/2013).

235 Tui, from interview (22/12/2009).

235 Slum rehousing expert, from interview, (2010).

235 Business city cited in 'New mega-mall to occupy 400 rai at Khlong Toei port' (*BP*, 25/01/2019).

235 Slum figures, Nattha Thepbamrung, 'Tin Town: Just enough for the city' (*BP*, 01/09/2013).

MARKET

236 31 malls, cited in mall article in (*BP*, 30/06/2015).

237 Phibun market cited by Anchalee Kongrut, 'Under the bridge' (*BP*, 06/04/2015).

237 Chatuchak history, Amornrat Mahitthirook, 'Fate of market hangs in political balance' (*BP*, 11/03/2011).

237 Umpai Prommorn, cited by Patra Virasathienpornkul, 'Street Talk' (*BK*, 2/06/2012).

238 Charoen Rungreung, cited by Kangsadarn Suluomstarn, 'Street Talk' (*BK*, 25/09/2009).

238 Talad nat sources: 100talad.com, Supoj Wancharoen, 'Cheap chic at the talard nat' (*BP*, 16/06/2011).

238 Nuanla-or Sripila, cited by Kanyanun Sanglaw, 'Street Talk' (*BK*, 22/04/2011).

238 Chaivuth cited by Anchalee Kongrut, 'Under the bridge' (*BP*, 06/04/2015).

241 Siam Paragon, *Guru* magazine (*BP*, 11/2006).

241 Pitch Pongsawat, interview (2015).

241 Status code cited by Maurizio Peleggi, *Thailand: The Worldly Kingdom* (Reaktion, 2007).

241 McGrath, Brian, 'Bangkok: The Architecture of Three Ecologies' (*Prospecta*, 01/01/2007).

243 Inequality figures, 'Richest 0.1% Own Half of Nation's Assets' (*TN*, 23/11/2014).

243 Thanong Khantong, 'Planting the foreign media with a sinister plot' (*TN*, 27/04/2009).

243 Sophontavy Vorng, 'Status City: Consumption, Identity, and Middle Class Culture in Contemporary Bangkok' (University of Sydney, 2009) & *Meeting of Masks* (Silkworm, 2016).

243 Road rage cited by Teeranai Charuvastra, 'TV host loses job, charged with assault in #graabmycar road rage incident' (*KSE*, 07/11/2016).

243 Thai People Against Street Vendors cited by Natchanok Wonsamuth, 'Do we really want to be just like Singapore?' (*BP*, 12/07/2015).

244 Nuanla-or, ibid p238.

242 Wasant Techawongtham, 'Vendor culture can't be stamped out overnight' (*BP*, 22/08/2014

244 Nimit Kaewkrajang cited by Natchanok Wongsamuth, 'Do we really want to be just like Singapore?' (*BP*, 12/07/2015).

245 Wasant Techawongtham, 'Vendor culture can't be stamped out overnight' (*BP*, 22/08/2014).

Talad Nat

239 Talad nat sources: 100talad.com, Supoj Wancharoen, 'Cheap chic at the talard nat' (*BP*, 16/06/2011).

YOUTH

247 Population pyramid (https://www.populationpyramid.net/thailand/2070/).

247 Youth/elder figures (fopdev.or.th/situation-of-the-thai-elderly-population-situations/, 19/02/2015).

248 Kaewmala, 'Thailand: What has hair got to do with children's rights?' (*Siam Voices*, 13/01/2013).

248 Saran Mahasupap, interview (2018).

249 Suthita Chanachaisuwan cited by Asaree Thaitrakul-panich, 'Teen singer's critical tweets spark nationalist backlash' (*KSE*, 03/08/2017).

249 Winn, Patrick, 'Glitz and desperation in a Bangkok divided by income' (*Global Post*, 16/01/2013).

251 Pitch, ibid p241.

251 Nita 'Amp' Dickinson, 'First Person' (*BK*, 16/11/2012).

251 Saran, ibid p248.

252 Praphaiphun Phoomvuthisarn cited by Chaiyot Yongcharoenchai, 'Vanz Boys – illegal street racers riding for girls and glory' (*BP*, 09/12/2012).

252 Nita, ibid p251.

252 Tay, interview (2018).

254 Tasinee Tantiwitthayanggoon, cited by Suwicha Chanitnun & Rojana Maowalailao, 'Time to Bond, or excuse for abuse?' (*TN*, 4/8/04).

254 Atiya Achakulwisut, citing Education Ministry & UNFPA, 'Mother's Day should be a private affair' (*BP*, 20/08/2019).

254 UNFPA survey, 'Features of Thai Families in the Era of Low Fertility and Longevity' (UNFPA, 2013).

254 Kukrit Pramoj, *Kukrit Pramoj: His Wit & Wisdom* compiled by Vilas Manivat, edited by Steve Van Beek (DK, 1983).

254 Songkran sexy clothes ban, 'Thailand bans sexy dance moves, sexy clothes during Songkran holiday (*CB*, 11/04/2017).

255 Ladda Thangsupachai, cited by Fry, Erika, 'Here comes the culture brigade' (*BP*, 18/03/2007).

255 Song blacklist cited by 'Big Brother: You can't be serious!' (*TN*, 22/08/2003).

255 Rabriabrat Pongpanich cited by 'Blacklist cut down to 3 songs' (*TN*, 23/08/2003).

255 Viriya Sawangchote, interview (2018).

255 Songyos Sugmakanan cited by Kanokporn Chanasongkram, 'New Shot of Hormones' (*BP*, 10/07/2014).

255 Nathanan Warintharavej cited in 'Youths protest "12 core values" online' (*BP*, 21/10/2014).

255 Kong Rithdee, 'Youth start clock ticking on old guard' (*BP*, 03/03/2018).

256 Netiwit Chotipattana-paisan cited in '"Sick of Thainess" says high school student on Thai TV causing outrage across the country'

(*City News*, 28/06/2013).

256 Child Protection Act cited by Teirra Kamolvattanavith, 'It is now illegal for Thai schoolgirls to wear short skirts' (*CB*, 04/09/2019).

256 Air (*You Are Here*, issue 30, 05/2006, www.youareheremag.net).

256 Playhound & Napat Sutithon, 'Youth of Bangkok' (www.greyhound.co.th, 21/11/2014).

Siam Square

250 Premsiri Tarasantisuk, cited by Top Koaysomboon, 'Welcome Home' (*BK*, 17/06/2010).

250 Pim Sukhahuta, cited by Matt Gross, 'To be young and hip in Bangkok' (*NYT*, 20/11/2006

250 Pasaraporn Mongkolrueangrawa, cited by Top Koaysomboon, 'Welcome Home' (*BK*, 17/06/2010).

250 Air, ibid p256.

250 Saran, ibid p248.

T-Rap

253 DJ Kritsada Vadeesirisak, 'Techno Fades as Bangkok Loses Itself to Hip-hop' (*KSE*, 19/11/2018).

253 Punk organiser cited by Buchanan, James, '"This country has no freedom!": how Thailand's punks are railing against the junta' (*Guardian*, 30/05/2019).

253 19TYGER X H3NRI, cited by Gabriel Ernst, 'The Real Radical Cultural Force in Thai Society' (*New Bloom*, 28/08/2019).

253 Elevenfinger, cited by Choltanutkun Tun-atiruj, 'This 17-year-old rapper is uniting Klong Toey community through hip-hop' (*BK*, 19/07/2018).

Youth Protest Culture

257 Mhee cited by Buchanan, James, '"This country has no freedom!": how Thailand's punks are railing against the junta' (*Guardian*, 30/05/2019).

CREATIVE CITY

258 4.0, What is Thailand 4.0 (Royal Thai Embassy, Washington DC, 2018).

259 Global Creativity Index (Martin Prosperity Institute, 2015)

261 Osborne, Lawrence, cited by Curtin, Brian, 'The Freedom of the City' (*BP*, 11/04/2013).

268 Waen cited by Pimrapee Thungkasemvathana, 'Masterly delve into the video age' (*BP*, 05/12/2014).

270 Landry, Charles 'Creativity and the City: Thinking through the Steps (Comedia, 2005).

271 Ou Baholyodhin, cited in 'This is the future of city living according to one of Bangkok's most respected designers' (*BK*, 22/06/2018).

271 Tap Kruavanichkit cited by Mary Losmithgul, 'Why Farmgroup's Vorathit Kruavanichkit Started Hotel Art Fair' (*Thailand Tatler*, 07/06/2018).

Graffiti

267 Karma Srikogar, cited in 'Pipit Banglamphu Street Art project placed murals around old town with govt support' (*CB*, 17/10/2018).

Bangkoklyn

274 Ae cited by Witchaya Pruecksamars, 'The Middle Class Vendors Shaking up Bangkok's Street Trade' (*Informal City Dialogues*, 01/08/2013).

274 Tom cited by Clae Sea, 'Return to JJ' (*BK*, 02/12/2011).

275 bring a bike, cite in 'Siam Gypsy Junction' (*BK*, 27/02/2015).

275 Vuti Somboonkulavudhi, cited by Napamon Roongwitoo, 'Vying for Vintage' (*BP*, 19/12/2013).

MEMORY

278 Pichit Boonjin cited by Teeranai Charuvastra, 'New Tourism Aims to Revive Bangkok's Dying Communities' (*KSE*, 26/11/2017).

279 Slum report, 'The Slums of Asia' in *Housing People in Asia* (Asia Society).

280 Ing K, introduction to *Bangkok in Technicolor* by Manit Sriwanichpoom (Kathmandu Photo Gallery, 2014).

280 Yiamyut Sutthichaya, 'A living heritage is too good for a fake-preservist society' (*Prachatai*, 07/05/2019).

280-281 Thongchai Winichakul, *Siam Mapped* (Silkworm, 1995).

281 Anderson, Benedict, 'Imagined Communities: on (British) Nationalism' (*The World Today*, Bandung Films, 1991).

282 Chanan Yodhong &

Notes & References **345**

Thongchai Winichakul cited by Thaweeporn Kummetha, 'Academics condemn Supreme Court's ruling to have l_ese majest_e cover former kings' (*Prachathai*, 21/11/2013).

282 Plaque quote & Sinsawat Yodbangtoey cited by Todd Ruiz, '1932 Democratic Revolution Plaque Removed' (*KSE*, 14/04/2017).

282 Chatri Prakitnonthakan, cited by Phatarawadee Phataranawik, 'Disappearing democracy' (*TN*, 05/01/2019).

282 Chatri Prakitnonthakan on 'Revolutionary Things,' cited by Ploenpote Atthakor, 'The art of the people' (*BP*, 23/06/18).

283 Surasak Glahan, 'Kids not taught about horrific history' (*BP*, 31/01/2019).

284 Chanchay Maleesuthi-kull, interview (2008).

284 Boonsong Srifuengfung, cited by Philip Cornwel-Smith from *Bangkok Post* in 'SOS: Save Old Siam' (*BM*, 08/1996).

286 Wong, Bib p338.

Retro & Nostalgia

284 Chanchay, ibid p284.

289 Anake Nawikamune, interview (27/06/2007).

Protukate

292 Giacomo Mauri, International Colloquium: 500 years of Thai-Portugal Relations (Chulalongkorn U, 03-04/11/2011).

292 Narong Jaroensuk, International Colloquium: 500 years of Thai-Portugal Relations (Chulalongkorn U, 03-04/11/2011).

293 Pong, interview (2010).

TOURISM

294 Most visited city, MasterCard Global Destination Cities Index

295 Sex tourism figures cited by Lines, Lisa, 'Prostitution in Thailand: Representations in fiction and narrative non-fiction' (*Journal of International Women's Studies*, 07/2015).

295 Male/female tourist figures (56% of American, Australian and German, 58% of British, UK, US, Australian and German and 68% of Japanese) cited in 'Thailand slowly sheds sex tourism image as more women visit' (Travel Wire

Asia, 23/10/2017).

295 Virat Chatturaputpitak cited in 'Thailand slowly sheds sex tourism image as more women visit' (Travel Wire Asia, 23/10/2017).

298 Wisoot Buachoom, cited by Fuller, Thomas, } Thais cast a wide net for Diverse Tourists' (*NYT*, 03/08/2013).

298 Cross, Alex, cited by Fuller, Thomas, 'Thais cast a wide net for Diverse Tourists' (*NYT*, 03/08/2013).

298 Wei Yunmei, cited by Fernquest, Jon, 'Chinese tourists: Difficult to deal with?' (*BP*, 24/06/2013).

298 Mongkol Suksai, cited by Jack, Ian, 'How the Thais are killing their own tourist industry' (*The Jack Report*, 10/07/2018).

299 Tourist spending figures, Mastercard's 2018 Global Destination Cities Index (Mastercard, 2018).

299 Thawatchai Aranyik, cited by Karnchana Karnchanatawe, 'The power of positive thinking' (*BP*, 13/03/2014).

299 Jack, Ian, 'How the Thais are killing their own tourist industry' (*The Jack Report*, 10/07/2018).

300 Stapleton, John, 'Thailand is world's deadliest place to be a tourist, book claims' (*CB*, 14/11/2014).

300 Airport extortion scam, Cattleya Jaruthavee, '8 things travelers should watch out for in Bangkok', CNN Go (30/12/2010).

300 Sugree Sithivanich, cited by Chadamas Chinmaneevong & Sriwipa Siripunyawit, 'Greed in Hospitality' (*BP*, 06/10/2014).

300 'Double prices deter tourists' (BP, 09/02/2015).

301 Raj, Stuart Jay (Facebook, 06/02/2011).

301 Thawatchai Arunyik, cited in 'TAT viral sensation video "I Hate Thailand" wins Social Media Award at AdFest 2015' (*TAT News*, 31/03/2015).

301 Tourism 19.3% of economy, cited by Turner, Rochelle, *Travel & Tourism, Economic Impact 2015: Thailand* (World Travel & Tourism Council, 2015

301 TAT survey (2015).

Backpackers

302 Menditatta, Anita, 'Youth travel: building the future of tourism through backpacks' (ETN Global Travel Industry News, 01/03/2012).

302 Duangphat Sitthipat, 'The Circus at the end of the road' (*BP*, 15/10/2014).

302 Figures cited by Duangphat, ibid p302.

302 Wichai Sangprapai, cited by Duangphat, ibid p302.

303 Read, Rachel, cited by Duangphat, ibid p302.

303 WYSE/UNWTO, cited by Mendiratta, ibid p302.

303 Jones, David, cited by Mendiratta, ibid 302.

303 Archariya Peeraputkunchaya, cited by Pimchanok Phunbun na Ayutthaya, 'The backpacking actress' (*BK*, 29/11/2011).

303 Sithikorn Wongwudthianun, 'See more by going solo' (*BP*, 08/05/2012).

303 Nalin Kalayanamitr, cited by Nithi Kaweevivitchai, 'Backpacking's new look' (BP, 05/08/2013).

303 Mendiratta, ibid p302.

303 Scott, Nikki, cited by Nithi Kaweevivitchai, 'Backpacking's new look' (BP, 05/08/2013).

PORTRAYALS

305 Mayawee Thongsong, interview (2019)

307 Flemming Winther Nielsen, 'Thailand's image tarnished by truth' (*TN*, 11/03/2007).

307 Chang Noi, 'The international media and the missing parts of the puzzle' (*TN*, 05/01/2009).

310 Ing K, 'Bangkok Love Letter: Blacklisting Witch-hunt' (10/06/2016).

310 Chang Noi, 'Defining Balance in Thai academic studies' (*TN*, 02/04/2007).

310 Right to think, cited by Saksith Saiyasombat, 'Life under the Thai junta in 2014 – Part 2: The perils of 'different thoughts' (*Asian Correspondent*, 27/11/2014).

310 Saran Mahasupap, 'On the Battleground of Thai-ness' (FB, 01/12/2010)

310 Voranai Vanijaka, cited by Farrell, James Austin 'Interview with Outspoken Bangkok Journalist Voranai

Vanijaka' (*City Life*, 20/11/2012).

313 Anderson, ibid p202.

313 Ornanong Thaisriwong, cited by Kaona Pongpipat, 'B-Floor Theatre's Ornanong Thaisriwong: 'I stand for free speech' (*BP*, 22/01/2015).

313 Historical details, *The Chronicle of Thailand* (EDM/*BP*, 2009).

313 Baker & Pasuk, Chang Noi, 'Defining Balance in Thai academic studies' (*TN*, 02/04/2007).

313 Somtow Sucharitkul, 'Don't Blame Dan Rivers' (Somtow.org, 18/05/2010).

317 Zcongklod Bangyikhan, author interview (2015).

317 'Bangkok Allergy' song by Pan Nakarin Kingsak, cited by Bocuzzi, Bib p338.

317 Voranai Vanijaka from interview (2015).

317 Rollet-Andriane, Luis-Jacques, Emmanuelle.

318 Chua, Lawrence, *Gold by the Inch* (Grove, 1999).

318 Smithies, Bib p339.

319 Brown, Bib p337.

319 Pornchai Sereemongkon-pol, 'Are they laughing at us?' (*Guru*, 19/11/2010).

319 Note cited by Duangtawan Nilayon, 'Stand-up Comedian 'Note' Udom Taepanich' (*BK*, 01/12/2006).

319 Winyu 'John' Wongsurawat, cited by Paritta Wangkiat, 'Stars get struck for speaking out' (*BP*, 13/08/2017).

320 John Winyu, 'Shallow News in Depth's Winyu "John" Wongsurawat tackles Thailand's big topics' (*BK*, 27/03/2014).

320 Jukapong Elmsaard, cited by Campbell, Charlie, 'Laughing at the Establishment in Thailand' (*Time*, Nov. 13, 2014).

320 Lalita Hanwong, 'Secret "Khai Maew" Satirist Won't Make Exhibition Appearance' (*KSE*, 08/11/2018).

320 Chetana Nagavaraja, 'Criticism as an Intellectual Force in Contemporary Society' (Thailand Research Fund, 2003).

320 Kong Rithdee, 'In our special situation, hail the metaphors' (*BP*, 22/07/2017).

320 Kong Rithdee, 'In this saddest time, we mourn the metaphor' (*BP*, 26 Jan 2013).

True Fiction

308 Chairat Pipitpattanaprap (Prapt), cited by Melalin Mahavongtrakul, 'Dan Brown with a Thai voice' (*BP*, 05/03/2018).

308 Suchart Sawasdsri, cited by Mui Poopoksakul, 'Interview with Suchart Sawasdsri' (*Words Without Borders*, 11/2016).

308 Noh Anothai, interview (*BKKLIT*, 19/06/2018).

309 Barron, Michael, 'What's the Best Way to Promote Literature in Translation?' (*Medium*, 26/02/2018).

309 Veeraporn Nitiprapha, cited by Kaona Pongpipat, 'Myth, love and blind earth-worms' (*BP*, 09/11/2015).

309 Zakariya Amataya, *Five-Legged Chair* (1001 Nights Editions, 2010).

Cinematic Krungthep

312 Robert Williams, cited by O'Neil, Bib p337.

Messy Aesthetic

315 Rattana Salee, cited in 'Life in Parallel: The Relation Between Image and Form of Contemporary Cityscape' (*Videoart Asia*, 25/11/2015).

315 Apiwat Banler, 'Portrait of Bangkok chaos wins top art prize' (*TN*, 09/10/2018).

Theories of Bangkok

321 Shearer, Alistair, *Thailand: The Lotus Kingdom* (John Murray, 1989).

321 Peleggi (*Worldly Kingdom*) Bib p337.

321 Zcongklod, ibid p317.

322 Saran Mahasupap, 'In Search of Bangkok Identity' (Saran's blog, 10/02/2011).

322 King, Bib p337.

322 Sopawan Boonimitra, 'Lak-ka-pid-lak-ka-perd' (Lunds Universitet, 2006).

322 Phongphit, Christian, press release for 'Layers of Bangkok' (BACC, 14/10/2008).

322 Kanika Rattanapridakul, *Asian Alterity* ((World Scientific, 2007).

323 McGrath, ibid p 241.

323 Chang Noi, ibid p219.

323 Vithi Phanichphant, cited by James Austin Farrell, 'The Lanna Deception' (*City Life*, 12/12/2009).

323 Vithi Phanichpant definition of Bangkok, at launch of *Bangkok Found*, Chakrabongse House (River Books, 2009).

FUTURES

330 Voranai Vanijaka, 'Futility at finish line in race for governor' (*BP*, 17/02/2013).

330 Nidhi Eoseewong, 'Understanding the cultural constitution' (*Matichon*, 11/08/2014; *BP*, 13/08/2014).

331 Voranai, ibid p330.

334 Kanika, ibid p322.

335 'Why do you love Bangkok?' (*BK*, 29/03/2013).

335 Leo Put, 'First Person' (*BK*, 23/08/2013).

335 Experiences trend, 'Five Consumer Trends to Watch in Thailand (BCG, 02/10/2017).

Project Singapore

326 Vallop Suwandee on Singapore, cited by Nualkhair, 'What the street-food ban has really meant for Bangkok' (*BK*, 20/06/2018).

326 Vallop Suwandee on benchmarks, cited by Hutton, Mercedes, 'Is Bangkok the next Singapore or Tokyo?' (*SCMP*, 03/04/2018).

326 Vichai Sangprapa, cited in 'Crackdown on Bangkok street stalls as pedestrians vie for space' (*Japan Times/AFP*, 01/03/2015).

326 Duangrit Bunnag, 'Bangkok Manifesto' talk (BangkokEdge, 2016).

327 Anonymous source, cited by Kanika Rattana-pridakul, *Asian Alterity* (World Scientific, 2008).

328 Duangrit, ibid p326.

328 Vallop Suwandee, cited by Roberts, Amos, 'The social cost of Bangkok saying bye to Pad Thai' (SBS Dateline, 04/07/2017).

328 Vallop Suwandee on Thonglor, cited by Roberts, Amos, p328.

328 Kanika, ibid p322.

328 Duangrit, ibid p326.

329 Vallop, ibid p326.

329 Duangrit Bunnag, interview (2018).

Bladerunneresque

332 Evans, Julian, 'Babylon Revisited' (*Vanity Fair*, 11/2014).

332 Palmer, Steven, *Bangkok Drowning* (Saraswati Press, 2019).

333 Somtow, SP, 'The Last Time I Died in Venice,' in *Dragon's Fin Soup & Other Modern Siamese Fables* (Diplodocus Press, 1998).

BACK COVER FLAP

Naowarat Pongpaiboon, 'Krungthep' (translation author's own).

Photo Credits

Photographs by
© Philip Cornwel-Smith

Except for the following (also credited in captions): 19TYGER X H3NRI © Cindy Gibier; 3Puck; Anuthin Wonsunkakon of Cadson Demak; Bangsue Station clock © Tourism Promotion Department, State Railway of Thailand; BMA graphics © Farmgroup; Boony Narksakul; Cheap Ass Elites © Saran Yen Panya; Chris Coles; Christopher Wise; Chusak Srikwan; CJ Worx & AP; Climate Central; Country of Bangkok, artwork by Prakit Kobkijwattana, photo © Christopher Wise, WTF; Daniel Monfort Gil, courtesy Serindia Gallery; David Jacobson of Smalls; Depth Map © Apiradee Kasemsook; Dow Wasikasiri; Eric Fischer; Graham Elliott of Fovea Films; Jesper Haynes; Jim Thompson © Navin Rawanchaikul & Jim Thompson Art Center; Julien Gauthier; Landsat satellite image © Landsat; Mah Nakorn poster © Stadio for Five Star Entertainment; Mahanakorn lyrics ©Thaitanium & Da Endorphine; Mapbox; Mayawee Thongsong; Oriental Spa; Pairok Pittayamatee of Thai Tone; Paradoxocracy poster © Surat Tomornsak; Pangina Heals; Pariwat Anantachina; Pool party photo © So/ Hotel; Prachatipatype; R.Harn; Reebok; Rush Pleansuk sculpture © Rush Pleansuk; Sanya Suvarnaphouma; Siam 2 © Teerawat Nutcharoenpol; Sing Sing Theatre; Smalls photo © David Jacobson; So/ hotel; Somrak Sila; Space Syntax's Depth Map; Stefan Zlotescu; Stephff; Thanathip Jenthumrong; Tourist pool photo © So/ Hotel; Trasher photo © Yosakorn Saguansapayakorn; Tube Gallery © Tube Gallery; Vinai Dithajohn; Way Magazine poster © Way; Worathep Akkabootara (Can Dan Isan).

Index
with glossary and picture index

Pictures and themed groupings are in bold

1932 Revolution 23, 25, 51, 109, 173, 180, 183-4, 187, 191-3, 262, 282, 285-**6**, 290, 326
1997 Crash 17-8, 23, 26, 51, 68, 82, 92,147, 163, 171, 198, 200, 203, 219, 231, 241-2, 264-5, 269, 272, 274, 287-8, 295, 307, 312, 334
500 Tuktuks 256
7-Eleven **44**, 127, 160, 167, 212-3, 243, 324

Absolut Vodka 333
absolute monarchy 23, 25, 98, 125, 172, 227, 284
academics, see writers
ageism 247
AIDS 141
airports; see Don Meuang, Suvarnabhumi
Airport Link 296
air quality 23-5, 42-**3**, 158
algorithms 164, 279
Amazing Thailand 296-7
amulets 10, 23, 64, 66, 70, 97, 100, 104-5, 113-9, 121, 194, 221, 236, 282
Jatukam Ramathep 100, 115
Luang Phor Toh 10
ang yi (Chinese secret society) 192, 213, 215
Air Force, Royal Thai 184-5
animism 98, 107, 112-**20**, 122-3
Apple & Siri 248, 310, 313, 325, 330
apps 69, 71, 74, 132, 142, 145, 158, 164-6, 182, 212, 223, 236, **245**, 251, 279, 301, 303, 335; see also digitisation, Internet, social media
11 Street 245
Alibaba 221
Google Maps 14, 51
Google Street View 61
Grab 69, 71, 165
Lazada 243
Traffy Fondue 192
APEC Summit 9
Arab Spring 316
architects 56, 59, 82-3, 88, 135, 182, 185, 202, 262, 264, 268, 272, 274, 282, 322, 327
Boughey, Robert 88
Duangrit Bunnag 83, 256, 325-9
Krisda Arunwongse na Ayutthaya 82, 182
Lloyd Wright, Frank 87
Rangsan Torsuwan 82
Scheeren, Ole **83**
Speer, Albert 325
Sumet Jumsai **284**, 333

Tamagno, Mario **283**
Tri Devakul 88
Yossapon Boonsom & Shma 59, 233, 252, 256, 328-**9**
architecture 13, 17, 47, 52-3, 63, 66, 73, 77, 81-9, 92-4, 128, 158, 161, 171, 180, 198, 230, 252, 262-3, 275, 279-85, 288, 291, 314, 322, 329; see also Chinese places, shophouses
Association of Siamese Architects 232
Bauhaus 81
Brutalist 81, 87-8, 110, 285, 288
condos 52, 54, 71, 81-4, 89, 92, **161**, **190**, 224-**7**, **232**, 279, **305**, 314-5, 317, 328, 334
curtain walls 81, 83
Greco-Roman 86, 262
high-rise **82**-3, 79, 160, 333
Italian 85-6, 178, 197, **283**-5, 292
landscape 59, 233, 252, 275, 325, 327-**9**
Malay-Renaissance 109
Modernist 87-8, 183, 280, 323
neo-classical 38, 86-9, 92
neo-Gothic 86, 109, 262, 284, 292
neo-traditional Thai 86, 88, 265-6, 315
Sino-Portuguese 292, 326
vernacular wooden 28, 52, 54, 63, 66, 75, 81, 83, 85, 110, 121, 146, 175, 178, 194, **204**, 208, 222-4, 227-8, 231-3, 236, **278-80**, 284-5, 287, **292**-3, 305, 309
Western 47, 88
Army, Royal Thai 9, 23, 108, 144, 184-**6**, 187, 197
aromatherapy 26-9, 287
art & art world **6**, 13-**15**, 16, **19**, 22, **28**, 30, 39, **47**, **56**-**7**, **63**, **68**, **80**, 83-5, 90, 100, **103**, **105**, **115**, 123, 131, **133**, **135**, **140**, 145, 154, **161**, **167**-**8**, **171**, **183**, **188**, **196**, **199**, 202-**3**, 218, **229**-**31**, 232-3, 236, **242**, 249-50, **256**-**73**, 275, **279**, 281, **287**, 290, **293**, 296, 301, 303-**5**, **307**-8, **311**-**5**, **319**, **321**-25, **330**, **332**
Art Nouveau 283
Asia Art Archive 269, 287
neo-Buddhist 265
neo-classical 38, 89, 92
neo-Gothic 86
neo-traditional 86, 88,

263, 265-6, 271, 315
Relational Aesthetics 272
art curators 270, 272-3, 290, 320
Apinan Poshyananda 270, 273
Gridthiya Gaweewong 272
art exhibitions see also festivals
Bangkok Anytime 315
Bangkok Art Biennale **188**-**90**, 229, 259, w270-4, 283, **315**, 325, **330**
Bangkok Biennial **273**
Bangkok Objects 316
Bangkok Photo 273
Brand New 272
Gender Illumination **145**
Ghost 273
Hidden Sound of Bangkok **157**
Isaan Retrospective 203
Khaek Pai Krai Ma 199
Khon Kaen Manifesto 273
Krungthep 226 **279**, 315
Live the City 157
Our World 133
Revolutionary Things 282
Spectrosynthesis 145, 170
Thailand Biennale 273
Unseen Siam 216
UOB Painting of Year 315
Venice Biennale 7, 90, 293
Xenomania 197-8

art galleries
1Projects 105
100 Tonson 272
About Café 18, 272
Arsom Silp Institute 233
Artist+Run 320
ATT19 170
Bangkok Art & Culture Centre (BACC) 14, 19, 50, 51, 65, **109**, 145, **157**, 161, **167**, **184**, 187, **189**, 261, **249**, 270, **272**-3, **279**, 290, **297**, **308**, 311, 315, 319, 322
Bangkok CityCity 269
Bangkok University Gallery (BUG) 271-2
Cartel 282
Cho Why 231
DeCentral 231
Dib Bangkok 271
H Gallery 272, 284
Jam 267, 312-**3**
Jamjuree 95
Jim Thompson Art Centre **196**-7, 272, 269, 271, 290, **292**-3
Kathmandu Photo Gallery 83, 264
Kunsthalle Bangkok 271
Museum of Contemporary Art (MOCA) 271
N22 231, 273, 312
National Gallery 273
Noble Play 168
Numthong 272
One Gallery **287**
Project 304 18, 272
Pulse 145
Serindia **133**, 272
Speedy Grandma 55
Tadu 18, 272
Tentacles 231
Ver 324
Visual Dharma 272
WTF 55, **171**, 306-**307**, **314**-15

artists & photographers
3PUCK (Tripuck Supawattana) 305, **322**-3
Abramovic, Marina 273
Alex Face **80**, 267
Anuwat Apimukmongkhon 145
Apiwat Banler 315
Arin Rungjang 293
Ark Saroj 131, 145
Artists Network 270
Baphoboy 145
Blenkinsop, Philip 151
BNE 267
Boony Narksakul 181
Brown, Patrick 324
Brujis, Julio 315
Cartier-Bresson, Henri 311
Chakrabhand Posayakrit 83
Chardchakaj Waikawee 132
Christian Phongphit 322
Chulayarnon Siriphol 312
Chusak Srikwan **15**
Coles, Chris **140**
Davis, Ben 305
Day, Frank Hallam 315
Dow Wasiksiri **311**
Francis Chit 292, 305
Gil, Daniel Monfort **133**, 315
Harit Srikhao 145
Haynes, Jesper **230**-1
Headache Stencil 46-**7**, 267
Jakkai Siributr 173
Jaruwat Boonwaedlom 314
Kawita Vatanajyankur 273
Khrua In-khong 218
Komgrit Tepthian 219
Kubisch, Christina 166-**67**
LaPalme, Michael 140
Maitree Siriboon 145, **203**
Manit Sriwanichpoom 83, 260, 264, 311, 314
Michael Shaowanasai 272
Mit Jai-In 204
Moriyama Daido 305
Nachtwey, James 324
National Artists 83, 255, 273
Navin Rawanchaikul **19**, **190**, **199**, **272**, 314-5
Nino Sarabutra 325
Nitimonster 306, **307**
Nostitz, Nick 138
Oat Montien 145
Pangina Heals **144**-45
Pannaphan Yodmanee **105**
Panya Vijinthanasasrn 266
Pariwat 'Big' Ananatachina **315**
Patiwat Chaiwitesh **315**
Peray, Stephane 'Stephff' 319-**20**
Ping Amaranand 173
Prakit Kobkijwattana **171**
Rattana Salee 315
Rirkrit Tiravanija 272, 324
Rukkit Satapornvajana 267
Sakarin Krue-On 330
Sarawut Ngernpum 315

Silpa Bhirasri (Corrado Feroci) **192**-3, 262, **279**
Sittivut Yavichai **325**, 330
Somboon Hormtientong 90
Sornchai Phongsa **188**-90
Sompong Thawee 314
Surasi Kosolwong 272
Sutee Kunavichayanon **287**
Takerng 'Be' Pattanopas 208, 272
Teerawat Nutcharoenpol **304**-305, 314
Thompson, John 305
Tibayranc, Myrtille 267
van Schwarz, Marcelo 333
Vasan Sittiket 263
Vinai Dithajohn 186, 257
Vorasan Supap 315
Winograd, Garry 311
Wise, Christopher **173**, **314**, 315
Yayoi Kusama 273
Artificial Intelligence 61
ASEAN 14, 23, 61, 108, 138, 189, 196, 212, 219, 296
Asian Economic Crash (1997), see 1997
Asian Food Awards 39
Asian Games 23, 68
Asian Tiger boom 17, 39, 99, 231, 241
assimilation 61, 80, 110-1, 189-221, 232-3, 278-93, 318, 323
astrology 7, 22, 24-5, 92, 98, 113-**4**, **117**, 124, 198
Ayodhya (in *Ramayana*) 101, 172, 283

backpackers 7, 14, 16, 106, 155, 224, 237, 291, 295, 301, **302**-3, 318
Ballad of Lady Naga 98
Bangkok sites, see places
Bangkok Bank 28, 64, 88, 215, 223, 239, 284; Art Prize 260
Bangkok Bicentennial (1982) 56, 173, 228, 237, 263, 284, 295, 302, 308
Bangkok Dream **189**-90, **193**, 224, 229, 288, 317
Bangkok Governors 18, 69, 88, 98, 100, 138, 143, 173, 177-8, 181-**2**, 244, 270, 299-300, 326, 331; see also BMA
Apirak Kosayodhin 182
Aswin Kwanmuang 182
Bhichit Rattakul 18, 182
Chadchart Sittipunt 178, 182, 326
Chamlong Srimuang 182
Krisda Arunwongse na Ayutthaya 88, 182
Sukhumbhand Paribatra 173, 182, 244
Bangkok Landmark river promenade 327, 333
Bangkok Manifesto 256, 328-9
Bangkok Metropolitan Administration (BMA) 13, 18, 32-3, **41**, 57-9, **62**, 68-9, 72-3, 90, 142, 167, 175, 178, 181-**3**, 185, 201, 224, 228-9, 233, 238, 243-4, 261, 270, 274, 280, 291,

348 Index

296-7, 302, 308, 312, 326, 329-30
Bangkok name origin 8, 11, 24, 48-9, 53, 172, 174-9, 181-3, 225, 228-9
Bangkok Sabai Walk 68
Bangkok Shutdown (PDRC) 23, 94, 156, **160**-1, **176**, 182-**3**, 186-7, 205, 225, 310, 334
Bangkok Siege 61, 66, 117
Bangkok Swing Dance Club **135**
Bangkok Tourist Bureau 291, 296, 327
Bangkok Vegetarian Association 199
Bangkok Wild Watch 158
Bangkokians 8, 10-12, 22-5, 29, 31, 36, 42-7, 51, 53-8, 60-3, 66, 75, 78-85, 89, 92, 94-5, 97-136, 147-8, 152, 156, 158-60, 162-3, 167, 170, 176, 178-9, **187**, 189-245, 249, 253, 262, 266, 269-70, 273, 275, 278, 282-3, 286, 290-3, 302-3, 311-3, 322-3, 326, 333-5
'Bangkoklyn' 274-5
Bangkokness 11, 12, 170-1, 174-9, 278, 288-90, 294-7
Bangkrak-Khlong San Creative District, see Creative District
Bank of Thailand 161, 190
baramee (righteous charisma) 173, 182
bars, see restaurants
Batman 101
Baygon 29
Bhumibol, King, Memorial Day 283
'Big Durian' 297, 307
Big House shelter 225
'Big Mango' 297, 307
'Bike for Dad/Mom' 73
black economy 129, 185
'Bladerunneresque' 332-3
BMX bikes 73
Bohemians 55, 198, 231, 233, 241, 258-9, 261, 269, 271, 273-4, 303
books & literary culture 13, 16-**18**, 25, 30, 34, 39, 40, 43, 54-**5**, 63, 122, 125, 128, 130, 134, 137, 139-**41**, 177, 187, 193, 205, 218, 220, 230, 234, 257, 260, 264, 268-71, 280-2, 286-7, 290-1, 298, 301-5, **308-9**, 313, 317-**319**, **320**, 322-3, 327, 329; also: festivals, *Mahabharata, Ramakien*, writers
1984 257
aLoud Bangkok **242**
Art of War 218
Asian Alterity 322, 327, 334
Bad Girls Dictionary 139
Banana Tree Horse 203
Bangkok 8 140
Bangkok Babylon 318
Bangkok by Design 88
Bangkok City Scoops 305
Bangkok Days 148, 317
Bangkok Drowning 332
Bangkok Found 317
Bangkok in Black and

White 311
Bangkok in Technicolor 280
Bangkok Inside Out 306
Bangkok Noir **140**-1, 150
Bangkok People 318
Bangkok Tattoo 140
Bangkok Then & Now 305
Bangkok Waits for Rain 309, 333
Bangkok: A Cultural and Literary History 318
Bangkok: Handmade Transit 72, 305
Beach, The 302
Bible, The 103
Bight of Bangkok 318
Bizarre Thailand 318
Blind Earthworm in the Labyrinth, The 309
Cars That Ate Bangkok, The 151
Chinese Emigrés of Thailand, The 192
Cities 49
City Aglow, A 305
City People 308
Comrade Aeon's Field Guide to Bangkok 309
cookery books 34, 234
Cooking with Poo 234
Cultural Detective, The 318
Curtain of Rain, The 41, 260, 309
Damage Done, The 155
Dragon Fin's Soup 333
Encyclopedia of the Chinese Overseas 193
Farang Affairs **320**
Flavours: Thai Contemporary Art 264
funeral books 34
Glass Kingdom, The 317
Gold by the Inch 318
Good True Thai, A 309
Goodbye Bangkok 317
Gulfs of Thailand 318
Hamtaro 257
Harry Potter 257
How Buildings Learn 77
Hugo Award 332
Jasmine Nights 309
Kaholmaharatuek 308
Khun Chang Khun Paen 115, 214
Khai Maew 320
Koran, The 110
Layers of Bangkok 322
Letters from Thailand 193, 308
Lonely Planet 302
Longman 306
Mai Pen Rai Means Never Mind 319
Memories of the Memories of the Black Rose Cat, The 309
Meuang Gin Khon 176
Muslims of Thailand, The 110
noir 127, 138, **140**-1, 150, 258, 308, 317, 332
Owners of the Map 77
Oxford Companion to Food 34
PEN Award 309
Phaic Tan 319
Phrommachat 22, 113
Pigs on the Loose 298
Prissana 308
Railway Sleepers 46

Romance of the Three Kingdoms, The 218
Sam Kok 218
SEAwrite award 202-3, **309**
Si Phaendin (Four Reigns) 308-**9**
Siam Mapped 206
Siam Through the Lens of John Thomson 305
Sightseeing 309
Skytrain to Murder 140
Status City 230, 243, 321
Tales of Old Bangkok 318
Thai Food 34
Thai Streetfood 34
Thai Ways 319
Thailand Confidential 318
Thailand: Deadly Destination 300
The Last Time I Died in Venice 333
The Sad Part Was 309
Time Out Bangkok City Guide 16, **18**-9
Time Out London 16
Tone Deaf in Bangkok 319
Truth on Trial in Thailand 306
Vanishing Bangkok 305
Very Thai 6, 14, 16-7, **18**-9, 311, 315
We love Bangkok 305
Welcome Me to the Kingdom 309
Windup Girl, The 50, **332**
Wonderful, Terrible 177
Yogi Boy 318
Boworadej Rebellion 23, 282
Bowring Treaty 23, 214
Brahmins & Brahmanism 22, 49, 86, **98-9**, 101, 106-8, 112, 117, 118, 124-5, **159**, 174, 181, 183, 198, 206, 215, 247, 323
Braille sidewalk blocks 68
Brands Chicken Essence 70
Brexit 177, 316
British Woman's Club 155
BTS (Skytrain) 18, 23, 27, **42**, 45, **50**-**2**, 61-3, 66-72, **84**, 89, 102, 139-40, 158-9, 167, 173, 204, 229, 240, **245**, 249-50, 275, 285, **297**, 302, 312, 315, 325, 329; see also mass transit, MRT
Buddha images 41, 51, 53, 65, **96**-**7**, 99-100, **103**, **105**-**7**, 122, 133, 172, 208, 265, 283; also Emerald Buddha
Buddha relic 49
Buddha, The 65, 106, 118, 150, 216, 308, 313, 324
Buddhism 10, 12, 16, 22, 24, 28, 48, 63, 66, 78, 87-8, 95, 97-113, 116-25, 129, 134, 143-5, 150-56, 170-74, 179, 182-5, 191, 194-6, 198, 206-8, 210, 213, 116, 222-3, 241, 265, 273, 279, 283, 292-3, 305, 310, 324; see also meditation, monks
Buddhist theme park 155
Dhammakaya 100, 105
divination 22, 114, **117**, 216
Eightfold Path 171, 222
festivals 101
Four Noble Truths 171

knowingbuddha.org 105
Mahanikaya sect 103
Mahayana 99, 104, 112, 194, 213, 216
Santi Asoke sect 100
Thammayut sect 103
Theravada 9, 99, 103, 108, 112, 194, 215-6
Buddhist Era 24
Buddhist-Hindu cosmology 24, 48-49, 63, 65, 86-8, **91**, 102, 106, 112, 145, 155, 172, **174**-**5**, 178, 183, 185, 212, **226**-7, 240, 259, 292, 322, 324
bus, MRTA network 17, 45-6, 52, 59, **62**, 67, 69-72, 75-**77**, 80-1, 90, 127, 153, 160, 171, **189**, 201, 224, 237, 241, 248, **295**, 299-300, 305, 314
Bushido 170

Calypso Cabaret 144
canal boats **29**, 62, 66, 70, **76**-77, 299
canals, see *khlongs*
cannabis 14, 23, 132, 150, **154**
capitalism 183, 236, 274, 321; see also corporations
Cars 9, 25, 28, 40-1, 46, 61, **67**-9, **70**-**1**, 73, 75, 81, **91**, 104, 124, 127, 132, 151, 161, 177, 212, 240, 275, 326; see also driving, traffic
Alphard 53, **70**
BMW Mini 182
Car Free Day 73
Ferrari 70
Maserati 240
McLaren 240
Mercedes-Benz 18, 33, 104, 274
Wish 70
Catholicism & Catholics 34, 100, 191, 223, 235, **292-3**
CCTV **166**-7
censorship & self-censorship 17, 135, 137, 166, 180, 251, 257, 259-60, 263, 269, 273, 279-**80**, 282, 304, 306-**307**, 313
Chakri dynasty & Chakri Day 24, 174-5, 283
Chang Beer 212, 245
Chao Phraya River, see places: Bangkok
children 29, 34, 58, 78, 88, 99, 103, 104, 115-6, **119**, 132, 137, 143, 148, 153, 155, 158, 162, 167, 171, 193, 195-6, 199-200, 206, 208, 210, 215, 223-5, 229, 234-**5**, 242, **247**-**57**, 269, 290-1, 303, 307, 312, 314
Child Protection Act 255
Chinatown, see places
Chinese, see also Confucius, deities, feng shui, festivals, places & ethnicities: China, Thai-Chinese, shophouses
architecture 47, 63-**65**, 81-2, 87-8, 90, 159, 178, 189, 210, **212**, **214**-**5**, **218**-**20**, **222**, 292
assimilation 84, 103, 107, 142, 179, 189-3, 195-6, 202, 205,

210-21, 323
cemeteries 116, 151
ceramics 92, **214**
charities 151, 213
coolies 191, 197, 205, 214
food **32**-3, 42, 130, 134, 151, 190, 210, 213
general strike 23, 192
horoscope 114
immigration 23, 51, 99, 108, 140, 176, 192-3, 198-9, 202, 205, 210-21, 223, 232-3, 293
influence 48, 52, 63-5, 86, 91-2, 97, 99-100, 112-4, 122, 124, 141, 148-9, 156, 172, 175, 189-93, 195-98, 206, 210-221, 228, 233, 236-7, 242, 248-9, 274, 279, 284, 298-9, 323, 333
junk trade 23, 86, 88, 191, 212, 214, 221, 331
medicine 151
muslims 109, 111, 196
newspapers 193
Revolution of 1911 23, 140, 192, 215, 220
schools **64**-5, 193, 213, 215, 220
secret societies 189, 192, 213
style 62, 65, 74, 86, 88, 90-2, 134, 210-221, 289
surnames 64, 192
tourists 61, 84, 102, 215, 221, **294**-5, 298-9
Christian era 24
Christianity & Christians 63, 97, 99, 103, 116, 136, 145, 185, 195, **192-3**
missionaries 103, 116, 136, 313
Seventh Day Adventists 97, 199
Chula-Thammasat football match **94**, **306**
chumchon (community) definition 223-5
churches 97, 105, 108, 128, 185
Kalawar (Calvary) 86-7, 292-**3**
Holy Rosary **292**
Immaculate Conception 292
Santa Cruz 292
Churning of the Sea of Milk 7, 66, 97, **101**
CIA Worldbook 185
Cirque de Soleil 249, 286
cities 6-14, 17-9, 22, 37, 39, 43, 46-69, 83-85, 108, 130, 133, 150, 174-8, 198, 200, 204, 225, 233, 241, 243-4, 259, 261, 270, 278, 291, 300, 308, 312, 314, 318, 321-35; also: megalopolis, metropolis, urban, world cities
'City of Angels' 8, 78, 97, 104, 170, 174, 178, 283, 297, 307, 321
'City of Life' **297**
City Pillar; see *lak meuang*
class system 23, 27, 30, 33, 64-77, 81-9, 112, 114, 130, 138, 141, 176, 180, 187, 189, 214-15, 223-35, 236-45, 268, 290, 297-8, 303, 321-2

Index **349**

middle class 13, 18, 45, 52, 68, 71-2, 84-5, 100, 106, 114, 117, 120, 122, 128, 139, 142, 144, 152, 163, 171, 175, 182, 187, 204-5, 212-5, 218, 224-45, 274, 283, 288, 298, 303, 311
upper class 34, 128, 171-3, 213, 227, 240, 262, 308, 313, 324
working class 138, 141, 187, 234-5, 240
climate & climate change 12, 35, 40-7, 68, 78, 80, 158, 226, 232, 237, 331-2
Climate Central 331
Cold War 23, 67, 185-6, 198, 288, 333
colonialism & avoiding it 9, 23, 28, 48, 56, 81, 85, 110, 140, 146, 170, 176, 180, 193, 197-8, 204, 206, 214, 220, 262, 279, 280-1, 292, 309, 313, 321-3, 331
comedy 112, 133-5, 137, 144, 157, 176, 202, 260, 266, 290, 308, 318-20
Communism 186, 213, 279
Communities & sense of 9, 13-4, 17-8, 32-3, **48,** 50-2, 65, 67, 73, 75, **83**-90, 105-11, 115, 117, 135-45, 155, 161, 167, 176-9, 180-81, 185, 189-92, **195, 199, 200-38, 242-3,** 250, 254, 259, 263, 270, **275, 278-80,** 291-96, 301, **303,** 321-2, 324-30, 333-5
condominium life 13, 88, 104, 225-**6,** 240, 243, **305,** 314, 317, **327, 330**
Confucianism 63, 213, 215, 220
Confucius Institutes 215, 220
conscription 11, 23, 119, 144, 154-5, 180, 184, 247-8
Constitution Fair 206
constitution 23, 25, 66, 101, 103, 180-1, 183-7, 206, 281-2, **287,** 326, 330
Coronation Day **172**-3
corporations 18, 37, 56, 62, 67, 83, 90, 130, 163, 165, 175, 177, 182, 184, 186-7, 211-2, 225,231, 233, 235, 239, 245, 253, 267, 269, 284, 301, 325-7, 329, 331; see also malls, monopolies, shops & brands
CP (Charoen Pokphand) 212, 220, 271
CSR (corporate social responsibility) 73, 229
Grammy 163
Nescafe/Nestlé 62
Noble **161**
Pepsi 129
Procter & Gamble 334
Sansiri 271
ThaiBev 212, 271
corruption 16, 54, 138, 182-**4,** 213, 215, 253, 257, 270, 290, 296, 301, 307, 312, 330
cosplay 230, **246**-49, 328
coups 9, 3, 66, 117, 166,

171, 183, 180-3, **186**-7, 192, 230, 247, 254, 293, 313, 334; see also 1932 Revolution
1976 coup 23, 181, 183, 230
1991 coup 23, 334
2006 coup 17, 23, 108, 115, 173, **186,** 270, 334
2014 coup 17, 23, 94, 115, 161, 171, 173, 186-7, 201, 235, 247, 256, 257, 270, 302, 334
Covid-19 pandemic 14, 153, 155, 257, 309
Coyote dancers 114, 118, 137
crafts 34, **46,** 60, **72, 76, 79-80,** 85, **87,** 100-1, **129**-31, **146-8,** 188, 194-5, 198-9, **200, 204,** 218, 222, 231-4, 236, **242, 261**-2, 265-6, 269-70, 275, 278-80, 287, 301-**3,** 314
Creative Cities 13, 19, 258-73
Creative District 231-2, 259, 261-3, 267, 270-75, 325, 329, 330, **334**
Creative Economy Agency 270
Creative Thailand 19, 270
cremations 26, 28, 46, 51, 94, 98, 134, **150,** 173, 215, 234; also: funerals
crowd sourcing 61, 304
Crown Property Bureau 54, 58, 174, 227
cultural appropriation 85-6
Cultural District 305, 329
Cultural Surveillance Bureau 255, 260
Cyberia 199
cycling 57-8, 61, **72**-4, 127, 173, 234, 264, 275, 291, 294-6

dance & theatre 18, 36, 61, 78-**80,** 85, 87, 89, 92, 101-2, 109, 112, 114, 118, 121-3, 127, 131-**5, 137**-40, 149, 163, 171, 185, 187, 199, **206-10,** 218, 221, 225, 232, 234, 247, 249, 251, 253, 259-63, 265-6, **268,** 270-1, **273,** 280, 282, **285**-6, 295-6, 312, 316, 319
Aksara Theatre 271
B-floor 268, 270
Banglamerd 54, 313
Banlangmek 313
Calypso Cabaret 125, 127, 144
Crescent Moon 268
Democrazy Theatre 270
fon nan **207**
Joe Louis Thai Puppet Theatre 127, 265
kabuki 266
lakhon chatri 109, 232
lakhon sangkeet 262
lamtad 135, 253, **273,** 279
Lanna Dream **206**
likay 85, 92, 109, 156, 176, 222, 279-80, 320
Mahabharata 63
Makhampom 268, 320
Mambo cabaret 144
manohra dance 109, 209
Manop Meejamrat 266

nang talung 109
ngiew (Chinese opera) 215, **219**-21, 279
National Theatre 89, 265-6, 296
Nophand Boonyai 318
Ornanong Thaisriwong 313
Patravadi Theatre 18, 266
Pichet Klunchun 78, **80**-1, 266, **268**
Pradit Prasartthong 268
Rachadalai Theatre 271
Rajanikara Kaewdee 249
Ramakien 78-**9,** 101, 183, 316
Ramayana 78-**9,** 172, 179, 198
River of Kings 286
Sala Chalermkrung Royal Theatre 78, 263, 284-5, 296
Siam Niramit 179, 206, 296
Siam-Ganesha Theatre 250
Thonglor Art Space 270
Waewdao Sirisook **206**
Wayang Buku 16
deities 96-125; see also *phii,* shrines, temples
Ardhanarishvara 125, 144
bodhisattvas 99, 216
Brahma **97**-100, 102
Caishen 216
Chinese deities 97, 107, 210, 213, 215-6, **218**
Chuchok 114, 318
Daoist deities 99
Erawan 102, **181, 183,** 335
Ganesha 100, 102, 121, 124-5, 268
Garuda 101-2, 325
Guan Yin 99-100, 104-**5,** 120, 124, 151, 215-6, **220,** 324
Hanuman 9, 183
Hindu deities 102, 120, 122
Hok Lok Siew (The Three Sages) 210
Indra 6, 48, 90, 102, 115, 178-9, **181,** 183, 307, 335
Jesus **105,** 292-3
Kali 100, **125**
Krishna **105,** 125, 199, 324
Kumarn Thong **114**-5
Kwan Im, see Guan Yin
Lakshmana 179
Lakshmi 100, 102, 123, 125
Lao Tzu 218
Living Arahant 100
luk krok 115
luk thep 100, **114**-5
Mae Khongka 117
Mae Phosop 117
Mae Thoranee 100
Mae Tubtim 97, 114, 118
Mae Yanang 117
Maha Uma Devi 100, 102, 123-4, 199
Mara 100
Mazu 219
naga 9, 41, 88, 97, 98, **101**-2, 119, 123, 182, **199,** 203, 206, 208, 286
nang kwak 100, 111, 113, 115-6, 240

Parvati 125, 144
Phra Phum Jao Thii 112
Phra Seua Meuang 117
Phra Siam Devathiraj 117, 184
Phra Song Meuang 117
Pi Siew 100
Radha 125
Rahu 7, 92, 94, **106,** 129
Rama, Prince (*Ramakien*) 101, 142, 172, 179, 183, 283, 307
Ruessi **119-121,** 123, 149
Sam Po Kong 216
Shiva 64, 100, 102, 123, 125, 144, 199
Trimata **120,** 123
Trimurti & shrine 92, 100, **102, 120,** 123
Vishnu 100-102, 115, 120, 123, 125, 172, 178, 199
dek chang (vocational students) 153-4, 229
dek waen (boy racers) 128, 252
democracy 14, 18, 23, 175, 179, 181-4, 186-7, 205, 228, 235, 248, 257, 263, 282-3, 288, 334; see also places: Democracy Monument
design & designers 13-4, 16-8, 28, **35,** 49, 56, 59, 61-4, 72-3, **76, 85-9,** 90-2, 101, 109-11, 122, 128, 131, **146,** 159-60, **168-9,** 180-5, 203, 206, 218, 231, 237, 238-40, **258-74,** 280, **284-91,** 294, 303, 307, **315-8,** 322, **325**-7; see also fashion
Anusorn Ngernyuang 264
Anuthin Wongsunkakon, Cadson Demak **317**
Ayodhya 264
Bangkok Design Week, see festivals
CJ Worx **49**
Crafactor 264
Design City 18, 258
Farmgroup 272
Global Trash Chic 264
Jim Thompson Thai Silk 271
Ou Baholyodhin 271
Pairoj Pittayamatee **93**
Planet 2000 264
Propaganda 264
Reflections 250, 264
Rush Pleansuk **260,** 315
Sakul Intakul **28**
Saran Yen Panya 147, 264, 268-**9**
Siamruay 274
Singh Intrachooto 264
'Style' fair 269
Sutton, Ashley 131
Tap Kruavanichkit 271
Thai Tone **93**
Trop Design 59
universal design 69
Urface 297
Yothaka 264-5
Devaraja 85, 98, 101, 172
development 49, 57-9, 60, 63, 65, 67, 87, 100-1, 110, 119, 158, 171, 175, 178, 180-4, 201, 203, 212, 224, 229, 231-2, 244, 260, 271, 279, 288, 291, 311, 314, 321, 324,

327, 334-5
'Development State' 23, 45, 85, 177, 269, 326
Dhammaraja 101, 106, 172, 174
Dharma 12, 28, 97, 103-4, 121, 158, 184, 216, 260, 272, 295,
dictatorship 23, 24, 72, 101, 103, 170, 180, 186-7, 193-4, 205, 237, 252-3, 257, 263, 288, 293, 313
digital nomads 198, 303
digitisation 12, 52-**53,** **72,** 77, **89, 116,** 137, **164-**7, 198, 206, 220-1, 242, **245,** 268, 278-9, 287-8, 290, 302-03, **305, 323,** 333
disabled 56, **66,** 68-69, 235
DJs & party promoters 115, 131-2, 163, 199, 202, 236, 267
Jojo Goldenmountain 131
Kapol Thongphlub 129
Kritsada Vadeesirisak 253
Maft Sai **202**-3
Nakadia 202
Pongsuang 'Note' Kunprasop 131
Seed (Norasate Mudkong) 162
DNA 13, 189, 236
domestic violence 142
drinking age 129-30, 252
driving 18, 66, 70, 75-6, 80, 115, 132, 155, 166, **189,** 212, 255, 305
drugs 104, 129-32, 138, 152, **154,** 235, 253, 300; see also cannabis
Duang Meuang (city's fortune) 25
Dusit Thani (model city idea) 179, 326
Dvaravati 194
dystopia 13, 315, **323-33**

East Asiatic Company 127, **282**-3
Ease of Doing Business Index 165
economic crash, Asian; see 1997
education: 247-57; see also schools, universities
Education for Liberation of Siam 255
Education Ministry 254
Education Revolution Federation 256
Emerald Buddha 41, 90, 171, 174, 179, 182, 282; Robe Changing Rite 174
ethnicity 11, 13-4, 23, 26, 31-2, 48-9, 73, 84, 98, 108-11, 114, 122, 145, 172, 174-9, **189-**236, 238, 242, 266, 268, 281, 284, 290-3, 294, 302; see also places & ethnicities
expats 13, 16, 55, 131, 138, 140-1, 145, 155, 189, **190-99,** 216, 226, 230, 235, 298, 301, 307, 310, 317-19; see also places & ethnicities

family & famous clans 17, 27, 30-32, 34, 55, 62, 64, 71, 80, 97, 99, 101, 103-4, 108-9, 111, 126, 131, 134-53, 155, 157-8, 167, 173,

350 Index

176, 182, 184, 191-2, 198-9, 201, 207-35, 238, 240, 247-57, 260, 262, 271, 281, 291, 293, 298-99, 303, 308, 310, 312-7, 319, 324-25; see also generation, people
farang (Westerners) see places & ethnicities
Fascism 170, 198, 310, 321, 326
fashion
A Tale of Phantoms 306
AB-Normal 274
bad.outfit.today 250
Birkin bag 116, 243
Dior 243
Fly Now **244**, 265, 272
Greyhound 32, 37, 256
Issue 274
Jim Thompson Thai Silk 271
Karl Lagerfeld 199
Kinky for Homosapiens 250
Louis Vuitton 243
Painkiller 275
Playhound 256
Reebok **316**
Sretsis 250
Tube Gallery **265**
Versace 17
Father's Day 173, 254
feng shui 59, 63-**65**, 156, 212, 218-19, 240
festivals & events 24, 30, 38, 40-2, 51, 56-8, 63, 67, 72, 95, 101, 103, 105, 107, 109, 111, 122, 124-5, 128-9, 133-7, 139, 143, 171-2, 175, 185, 191, 202-9, 211, 215-19, 220-1, 225, 231-2, 239, 251, 255, 259, 263, 268-70, 273, 282-3, 288, 294, 296, 316, 324, 328; see also art, Thainess
Appear fair 232, 305
Art Book Fair 269
Art in Soi 63, **135**, 232, **258**, 324
Asalha Bucha 129
Bangkok Design Festival 72
Bangkok Design Week **35**, 61-**62**, **93**, **168-9**, **264**-5, 269-**271**, 325
Bangkok Fashion City 18, 269
Bangkok Food Fair 111
Bangkok Gourmet Festival 38
Bangkok International Festival of Dance and Music 199
Bangkok Literature Festival 269, 309
Bangkok Theatre Festival **81**, 268, 270
BangkokEdge Festival 229, 256, 269, 291, 328
Big Mountain 239, 257
Bukruk 58, 267
Chak Phra 208
Children's Day 252
Chinese New Year **65**, 134, 216, 219
Chinese Vegetarian festival **96**-7, 104, 122, 220
Ching Pret **208**-9
Christmas 42, 56, 105, **135**, 296

Culture One 251
Demonic festival 253
Divali 102, **198**-9
Easter crucifixion **293**
Eid 111
Epicurean Masters of the World 34
FAT festival 257, 268, 306-**7**
film festivals 268, 296
Galleries Night 272, 325
Hajj 109, 111
Halloween 134
hanami (blossom viewing) 95
Hotel Art Fair 272, 275
Indie 231, 236, 257
Japan Festa **247**
LIT Festival **141**, 269-**70**, 308-**9**
Kathin 209
Krungthep Thara Fairs 56
Low Fat Art Fest **218**
Loy Krathong **7**, 24, **129**, 142-3, 252
Lunar New Year 99, 176, 216
Makha Bucha 129
Mango Art Festival 272
Mawlid 109-10
Mon Songkran **194-5**
Navaratri 122, **124-5**, 199
New Year (Western) 24, 40, 56, 103, 105, 126-7, 133, 145, 166, 168, 242
Noise Market 269
Northern festivals 122, 201-6, **207**-9
Phansa 207, 209
Ploenchit Fair **197**
Pride **142**-3
Qing Ming 215, 220
Red Cross Fair 57
rocket festival 209
Rose Bowl Parade 286
Royal Ploughing Ceremony **98**, 101, 173-4
saba **194**-5
Sart Duen Sib 208
Sivaratri 125
Songkran (Thai New Year) 24, 40-2, 126, **133**, 143, 145, 157, 171, 176, 194-5, 207, 254, 286
Southern festivals **208**-9
Tattoo Festival 122
temple festivals/fairs 6, **7**, 67, 92, 105, **112**-3, **126**-9, 137, 143, 157, 208-10, 225, 227, 237, 239, 251, 263
Tham Guay Salak **92**-3, **207**-8
Valentine's Day 142
Vertical Marathon 82
Visakha Bucha 105, 129
walking streets 18, 68, 231, 274
Winter Fair **173**, **284**, 286, **289**
Wonderfruit 177, 239, 261
youth 220, **246**, 248-52
film 13-4, 18, 25, 41, 53, 90-1, 99, 110, 112, 114, 119, 127, 129, 137-8, 140, 144-5, 153, 157, 171, 173-4, 185, 191, 199, 202-3, 227, 230-1, 235, 250, 259-60, 262-5, 268-71, 273, 279-**81**, 289, 296,

305, 308-10, **312**-3, 316, **318**-20, 322, **330**, **332-3**
Bollywood 199
Cannes Film Festival 202-3, 266
Nouvelle Vague 268
Thai new wave 260, 321
films & shorts
AI Love You 333
6ixtynin9 312
Bangkok Dangerous 312
Bangkok Love Story 312
Bangkok Traffic (Love) Story 312
Blade Runner 332
Coyote Ugly 137
Cursed Land, The 111
Dang Bireley and Young Gangsters 312
Dark Bridge Binaural Brainwaves 333
Deer Hunter, The 138, 312
Emmanuelle 317
Faen Chan (My Girl) 289
Four Kings 1 & 2 312
Future Sex 333
ghost films 82, 116, 208
Good Morning Vietnam 312
Hangover 2 82, 127, 298, 312
Hom Rong 262
How to Win at Checkers Every Time 309
Hunger Games 186, **257**
Inception 90
Insects in the Backyard 144, 260
King and I, The 306
Lahn Mah (How to Make a Million Before Grandma Dies) 312
Lost in Thailand 221, 298
Love of Siam 250, 312
Mah Nakorn (Citizen Dog) 312
Malila 150
Mary is Happy... 268
Master, The 268
Mekong Hotel 41
Metropolis 332
Motel Mist 312
Nang Nak 119
Naresuan 312
Only God Forgives 312
P-047 312
Pee Mak Phra Kha Nong 119
Ploy 312
Promise, The 82, 312
Sawasdee Bangkok 312
Shakespeare Must Die 260
Shawshank Redemption, The 155
Shutter 116
Sia Dai 312
Soi Cowboy 312
Suriothai 260
Tang Wong 312
Tears of the Black Tiger 163
Ten Years Thailand 312
Tomorrow Never Dies 312
True Skin 333
Wayward Gods 333
film: cinemas 268, Bangkok Screening Room 271
Chalerm Thai 89, 284
Cinema Oasis 271
House Mitrtown 271
Lido, Lido Connect 250-1, 261, 271

Siam (cinema) 250
Scala Cinema 88, 250
Siam Theatre 250
film: directors
Aditya Assarat 312
Apichatpong Weerasethakul 41, 202, 204, 266, 272, 312
Chatrichalerm (Than Mui) Yukol, Prince 260
Greenaway, Peter 268
Hallacy, Jeanne 235
Ing K 171, 173, 176, 180, 260, 280, 310
Kongdej Jaturanrasamee 312
Lang, Fritz 83, 332
Nawapol Thamrongrattanarit 268
Nonzee Nimibutr 312
Panu Aree 111
Passakorn Pramunwong 280-**281**
Pen-ek Ratanaruang 230, 268, 280-**1**, 283, 312
Poj Arnon 312
Refn, Nicolas Winding 312
Santi Taepanich 63
Scott, Ridley 332
Sompot Chidgasornpongse 45
Songyos Sugmakanan 255
Tanwarin 'Golf' Sukkhapisit 144
Tarkovsky, Andrei 268
Wenders, Wim 268
Wisit Sasanatieng 312
Zlotescu, Stephan 333
film: documentaries
Around the World in 80 Jobs 318
Baby Arabia 111
Back in Bangkok 318
Bangkok Joyride 310
Bangkok: Megalopolis between Order and Chaos 318
Censor Must Die 260
Cheer Ambassadors 318
Crying Tiger 63, 202
In Between 111
Khaek: In Between 109
Mercy 235
Paradoxocracy 280-**281**, 283
Ports d'attache: Bangkok (Riverfront Cities of the World) 261, 318
Total Bangkok 312
Welcome to Bangkok 318
World in Motion: Bangkok 318
Fine Arts Department 125
First Effective Settlement Doctrine 190
floods 8, 13, 41-3, **46**-7, 49, 58, 66, 68, 78, 80, 87, 125, 164, 176, 181, 227, 237, 295, 309, 327, **331**-4
Great Flood of 2011 23, 41, 47, 164, 194, 225, **306**, 330-**1**, 333-4
flowers & floral culture 7, **25**-29, 88, 90, 92, **95**, 98, 111, 118, 266, **293**; see also markets
food, Thai & general 18, 26-**42**, **44**, 55-8, 63, 77, 98, 115, 123, 126, 131,149, 154, 175, 184, 191, 196, 201-14, 223,

227, **229**, **231**-3, 235, 237, **241-2**, 249, 262, 267, 271, 273-5, 280, 285, 287, 293, 295-6, 298, 301, 303, 314, 318, 328, 331
Chinese 210-**212**, **214**, 216, 219
delivery **245**
Eat Responsibly Day 275
halal 109, 111, 196
Indian 198
Isaan **37**, 202, 204, 209
khao chae 42, **195**
Mama noodles 35-**6**
Marmite 129
Mon 194-**5**, **224**
Northern 207
pad Thai 31, 210, 218, 302
ritual **98**, 104, **113**, 115, 123, **138**, 200, **208**-**9**, 216
somtam 31, 55, 135, 139, 140, 201-2, 204
Southern 11, 39, **208**-9, 242
streetfood 26, 30-39, 55, **74**, **92**, 126, **130**, **197**, 217, **238**, **245**-6, 250, 263, 269, 274-5, 290, 294, 305, **314**, 326, 328, 333, 335
Vietnamese 32
'For Life' (Pheua Chiwit) **163**, 257, 263, 308
fortune tellers (*mor doo*) 11, 64, 97, 113-**6**, 122, 124, 151, 242, 283
funeral books 34
funerals 22, 51, 65, 105, 134, 151, 173, 182, 213, 216, 224; also: cremations

galleries, see art
gambling 11, 129, 134, 213, 261; see also lottery
gap year kids 295, 303
Garuda Royal Warrant 102
gay 14, 39, 55, 57, 100, 118, 121, 125, 128, 136, **142**-5, 198, 229, 231, 240, 250, 298, 312; also: *katoey*, LGBT
generational bonds 54, 76, 105, 173, 176, 193, 201, 212, 215, 218-9, 222, 224-5, 228, 245-57, 265, 288, 291, 293
generation gap 16, 18, 87, 102-3, 110, 136, 162-3, 178, 180, 187, 220, 228, 230, 243, 245-57, 263, 274-5, 279, 297, 320, 327, 334
Millennials 122, 162, 195, 200, 227, 307, 334
gentrification 74, 130, 219, 223, 233, 259, 325
ghosts 7, 82, **112**-23, 128-9, 156, 208-9, 216, 260, 266, 284, 308, 312, 317, 318
Ghost Radio 113-4, 129
nang mai **119**, 312
Nang Nak 10, 11, **116**, **119**, 313
nang takian (wood nymph) 117, **119**
phii kraseu 114-**5**
phii pret **208**-9
gik (friend lover) 142
Global Creativity Index 259
global warming, see climate

Index **351**

globilisation 13, 18, 109, 116, 177-8, 190, 212, 220, 223, 230, 242, 262, 278-9, 289, 303, 310, 332
'Golden Land' 92
'Good People', see *khon dee*
Good Walk scheme 329
GPS 60, 164
graffiti & street art **13, 47**, 58, **68, 80**, 86, 90, **103, 229, 267**, 269, 297, 299, **313**
Great Depression 23
Guinness 129, 170
guns 119, 151, 153, **186**

Havocscope 139
hawkers see street vendors
health, see hospitals, ministries
herbalism 12, 16, 18, 26-30, 42, 113, 152, 204, 207, 213-**4**, 231, **260**, 264, 269, 287, 294
Hercules beetle wrestling **207**-8
heritage 13, 41, 52, 56, 73, 77, 85-89, 116, 127, 133, 149, 159, 163, 170, 174-5, 178-9, 190-233, 239, 250, 266, 269-70, 273, 278-93, 298-9, 305, 314, 317, 319
Hero Awards 143, 145
Hi Class massage 137
Himaphan Forest 87, 173
Hindus & Hinduism 11-2, 22, 24, 48, 63, 88, 91-2, 94, 97, 100-2, 106-7, 111-3, 120-5, 129, 143-5, 170-5, 179, 183, 189, 192, 195, 198-9, 206, 228, 283, 292, 323; cosmology see Buddhist Neo-Hindu 12, **124**-5, 143
hipsters 130, 178, 219, **230**-1, 239, **275**
hi-so ('new money' high society) 17, 37, 46, 52, 70-1, 82, 90, 105, 114, 116, 141, 153, 155, 167, 182, 199, 202, 204, 213, 230-1, 240, 243, 248, 251, 262, 307, 309, 312, 331
homeless 13, 51, **229**
hospitals & clinics 28, 105, 115, 131, 150-4, 173, 185-6, 292, 295, 329
Bumrungrad 111, 152
beauty clinics 105, 118, 295
Chinese medicine 151
Phra Mongkutklao 286
Police Hospital 102
Pulse 145
Samitivej 152
Siriraj **154**, 185, 209, 239, 299
Thantakit Dental Clinic 152
Tien Fah 151, 213, 216
Wellness District 329
hotels
Airbnb 232
Anantara 37
Banana State 145
Bangkok Tree House 57
Banyan Tree, The 37, 82
Chakrabongse Villas 269
Dusit Thani 49-50, 83, 87-8, 179, 326

Grand Pacific 88
Hilton 82
Holiday Inn Express 315
Lub-D hostel 303
Mandarin Oriental 9, 324
Manhattan 198
Marriott 82
Montien 113
Narai **86**, 88, 288
Peep Inn 2 143
Peninsula 37
Phranakorn-Nornlen **288**-9
Reflections 250, 264
Rosewood 50, 88-9
S31 Hotel 88
short-time 143, 202
Siam Intercontinental 87-8
Siam Kempinski 285
So/ 82, **132, 296**
Sook Station 155
Sukhothai 232
W Hotel 315

ILO 185
IMF 23, 198, 264, 287
immigration, see migrants, ministries
indie 11, 16-8, 53, 66-7, 72, 74, 95, 110, 130-1, 154, 156, 162-3, 220, **230-1**, 236, 248-9, 253-74, 283, 286, 290, 301-3, 305, 308, 311-5, 317, 328, 334; indie fairs 305
inequality 46, 50, 177, 151, 154, 334
informal sector 10-13, 16-8, **30, 32-4, 44, 46, 48**, 50-1, **53-6**, 62, 67, 69, **74-7**, 90, 105-6, 117, **131, 146-7**, 167, 171, 178-9, 200, 207, 209, 215, **222-45**, 247, 249-51, 263, 268, 271-2, 274-5, 294, 297, **302-4**, 312, **314-5, 321**-3, 326-8, 330-**2**, 334
Intangible Cultural Heritage 32, 133, 149, 195, 280, 290-1, 321
Interfaith Movement 106
Internal Security Oper-ations Command 255
Internet & websites 19, 136, 145, 152, 162, 164, 180, 185, 198-9, 251, 255, 257, 269, 290, 304-5, 311, 334-5; see also Apple, apps, social media
Dark Web 166
FuckGhost 117
Museum of Endangered Sounds 160
Quora 213
persuasive tech 279
Prathet Krungthep 176
Internet cafes 199, 251, 255
Saynostall 68
Thai Sex Talk blog 143
WikiLeaks 307
Wikipedia 297
YouTube 34, 37, 117, 137, 150, 305, 318, 333
Isaan; see food, music, places & ethnicity
Islam, see Muslims
Islamic Committee 108
Islamic Conference 108
Islamic State 177

Ja Choei **63**
jao choo (playboy) 142
jao sua (merchant lord) 214, 219
jek (coolie) 189, 193, 214-5, 323
Jinpanjara Katha 119
Juche 170
junta 12 core values 170, 229, 255

Kala Land 307, 320
Kalapapruk Tree of Life **15**
Karmic fundamentalism 106
katoeys 100, 118, 121-2, **125, 137**-45, 157, 231
khaek, meaning 109, 111, 189, 191, 198-9
khlongs (canals) 8, 11-2, 18, 23, 26, 28-**29**, 41, 47-**54**, 57-8, 62-3, 65-7, 69-**77**, 81, 89, 92, **95**, 103, 108, 112, 118-9, 141, 164, 171-3, 175, 191, 194, 204, 208, 223-4, 228, **233**-5, 324, 326, 329, 332, 334
Bangkok Noi 8, 23
Bangkok Yai 8, 23
Banglamphu 72, 329
Bang Luang 265
Lat Phrao 228, 235
Mahanak 12
Mon 194
Om **53**
Ong Ang 89, 329
Phadung Krung Kasem 49, 61, 73, **95**, 329
Prem Prachakorn 284
Prakhanong 12
Saen Saeb 66, **76**, 108, 111, 267, 329
khon (masked dance) 78-**9, 80**-1, 85, 92, 101, 183, 260, 265-6, **268**, 296, 316, 333
khon dee ('Good People') 106, 129, 155, 167, 174, 182-4, 186, 310
kings, see also royalty
Narai 23, 108, 292-3, 318
Taksin 9, 23, 49, 98, 120, 172, 177-8, 211, 214, 259, **279**, 292, 323
Phuttayotfa (Rama I) & Chao Phraya Chakri 23, 49, 51, 63, 102, 118, 172, 177, 179, 191, 199, 281, 283, 313
Phuttaloetla Naphalai (Rama II) 23, 88, 194, 214
Nangklao (Rama III) 23, 86, 214, 216
Mongkut (Rama IV) 23, 25, 98-9, 100-1, 103, 117, 281, 283
Chulalongkorn (Rama V) 23-4, 28, 43, 51, 64-5, 100, 108-9, 114, 117, 121, 170, 172-3, 175, 177, 179, 194, 197, 216, 221, 228, 232, 262, 281-**3**, 285, 288, 291, 308
Vajiravudh (Rama VI) 23-4, 94, 141, 170, 172, 179, 193, 262, 326
Prajadhipok (Rama VII) 23, 98, 183

Ananda Mahidol (Rama VIII) 23
Bhumibol Adulyadej (Rama IX) **23**, 51, 57-8, **65**, 73, 94-5, **101**, 110, 161, 171-3, 183, 187, 195, 254, 265, 281, 283-4, 288, 295, 317
Vajiralongkorn (Rama X) 23, **172**-4, 220
Deputy King 23, 49, 51, 179
K-Pop; see music
krajok hok dan (6-panel mirror) 10, 330

ladyboys 127, 136, 144, 266, 319; see also *katoey*
lai thai (Thai patterns) 28, 62, 87, 218, 265, 280
lak meuang (city pillar) **25**, 28, 51, 63-5, 72, 98, 102, 109, 117, 179, 212, 278, 283, 285
'Land of Smiles' 295, 297, 307
language 7, 14, 36, 48, 61, 101, 133, 156, 163, 172, 179, 193, 198-9, 204, 206, 211, 215, 220, 254, 260, 296, 307, 310, 313; see also places & ethnicities, Mandarin, Yawi
Landsat imaging **20**-1
landscape architects, see architects
LED signage 164-5, 332
Legatum Prosperity Index 219, 146
lesbians 142-5, 147, 231, 298; also: LGBT
lese majeste law 23, 173, 186, 281, 306
LGBT **143-5**, 187, 231, 250, 254, 257, 259, 270, 322; also: gay, *katoey*, ladyboys
lo-so (poor) 231, 251, 331
long khaek (reciprocity) 66
lottery 11, 24, 112, **117**-9, 213, 216, 248, 305, 312, 314, 318, **323**; also: gambling, fortune telling
love motels 143, 312
luk khrueng (half-Thai/ *farang*) **162**, **192**, 196, 310, 318
lunar calendar 24, 129, 216, 333; also see Moon

macho culture 142-3, 151, 157
mafia/gangsters (*nak leng*) 54, 113, 128, 184, 199, 213, 229, 235, 243, 247, 300, 312
magazines
a day 286, 290, 305
Attitude 144
Bangkok Metro 16, **18**, 19, 140, 201, 319, 320
Barefoot 303
BK 38, 68, 144, 178, 226, 275, 307, 335
BKKLIT 308-09
CHEEZE on Street 249
Da Jia Hao 220
Details 136, 142
Elle Men 256
Farang 29, 303
Guru 240

Image 173
Kinfolk 233
Marsala 195
Open 286
POP 162
Roti-Mataba 110
Sarakadee 286
South East Asia Backpacker 303
Thailand Tatler 91, 231
Tom-Act 144
Travel + Leisure 294
Vanity Fair 332
Way **177**, 286
You Are Here 250, 256
Magsaysay Prize 235
malls 13-4, 17, 24, 29, 30-5, 37, 42-5, 51-6, 67-9, 71, 91, 102, 107, 115, 127, 130, 135, 137, 145, **152**, 154, 157, **163**-7, 179, 185, **189**, 204, 213, 215, 225-30, **236-45**, 249-51, **259**, 262-3, 267, 270-1, 273, **275**, 285, 294, 296, 301, 314, 322, **325**, 328, 333-4
Amarin Plaza 102, **134**
Central 211, 213, 215, 238
Central Chidlom 240
Central Embassy **55**, 91, 130, 204, 240, 268, 271, 285
Central Rama IX 213
Central World 55-6, 58, 151, 241, 273
Commons, The 55-6
Dusit Central Park 54
Emporium **42**, 52, **67**, **152**-3, **179**, 240-**1**, 259, 297
EmQuartier **14**, 52, 59, 58, 91, **154**, 240
EmSphere 52
Esplanade 240, 275
Fashion Island 241
Fortune Town 242
Gaysorn Plaza 91, 102, 225
IconSiam 80, 82-3, 204, 213, 240, **260**, 264, 293, **325**, 327, 330-1
Imperial World 240
K-Village 275
Mall Group, The 213
Mall Pinklao, The 262
Market Mall, The **189**
MBK 69, 240, 245, **248**, 250, **297**
Mega Bangna 243
Pantip Plaza Ngamwongwan 115
Paradise Park 213
Platinum Mall 236
River City 11, 127, 285
Seacon Square 240-1, 275
Siam Center 148, 240-1, 250-**1, 273, 290**
Siam Discovery 69 240, 275
Siam Emporium 198
Siam Paragon 88, **240**-1, 251, 285
Samyan Mitrtown 143
Tawanna 250
Terminal 21 52, 88, 240-1
Tha Maharaj 56, 301
The Street 263
Union Mall 240, 250-1, 267
WestGate 243

352 Index

mandala 49, 60, 63-4, 110, 174, 181, 185, 211, 326

Mandarin 214-5, 220, 279

maps & mapping 14, **20-1**, 28, 38, **46**, **49**, 51-**53**, 60-4, 72-3, 102, 139, 145, 164, **168**-70, 190, 204-6, 267, 269, **276-77**, 280-1, **305**, 314, 322, 329; also media: Google *Bangkok Street Directory* 60

Depth Map **53**, 61

Mapbox 49

Nancy Chandler Map 60

OpenStreetMap 49

markets 11-4, 27, 33, 35, 60, 67-69, 76-7, 79, 104-6, 111, 113, 126, 135, 139, 147-**8**, 154, 160, 174, 185, 201, 207, 216, 221, 224, 227-8, 232-3, 239, 258, 251, 264, **274-5**, 285, 287, 289, 292, 298, 301-**3**, 322, 326, 328, 333; see also street vendors

Amulet 105, **114-5**

Asoke Market 52

Ban Mo 224, 236

Banglamphu 236

Bangrak 113, **117**

Chatuchak Weekend (JJ) 27, 51, 61, **110-1**, 115, 145, 158, 165, 185, 236-7, 239, 268, 274-5, **301**

Chokchai 4 239

farmers markets 35, 39

Flower Market Thailand 28; also Pak Khlong

Former Rich 18

Kao (Old) 64-5, 240

Khao San **302-3**

Khlong San 117, **119**, 324

Khlong Toei 35, 115, 231, 238, 325

Lang Krasuang 236

Loong Perm 239

Mai (New) 65, 240

Ming Meuang 285

Nang Loeng 199, 224, 232

Or Tor Gor (Markets Organisation) 35, 38, 238, 240

Pahurat 27, 187, 198-9, 237, 285, 329

Pak Khlong Talad flower market 25, 27-8, 114, 126, 128, 224, 227, 236-7, 240, 301

Prannok 239-40

Pratunam 79, 143, 161, 240

protest gear 182-**3**, 257

Sampeng Lane 89

Sathupradit **243**

Soi Lalaisap Silom 239

Talad Kon Lao 35

Talad Loong Perm 237

talad nat (set time markets) 238-41, 328

Talad Thai 240

Tha Tien (area & market) **27**, 29, 79, 85, 131, **150**, 220, 225, 236, 286, 291, 330

Thewes 27, 227

Wat Suan Kaew 239

markets: floating 24, 50, 57, 67, 126, 165, 206, 236, 239, 288, 333

Amphawa 31, 242, 333

Don Wai 333

Kwan Riam 333

Taling Chan 333

Wat Nampueng 57, 163

markets: night 33, 67, 72, 128, 130, 201, **204**, 239, 251, 289, 327, 332

Flashlight 244

Huai Khwang 128, 239, 243

Khlong Ong Ang 89

Na Ram 230, 239

Patpong 138, **238**

Ratchada 251, 275

Saphan Phut 2 239, 251

Suan Lum Night Bazaar 285

markets: night (curated) 74, 130, 230, 239, 245, 264, 274-5

Art Box 239, 275

Great Outdoor Market 239, **274-5**

Made by Legacy 275

Rot Fai (Train) 66, 239, 244, 251, 275, 289

Siam Gypsy Junction 275

marriage & weddings 53, 98-9, 111, 117, 141, 177, 182, 189, 196, 213, 215-6, 224, 247, 261, 288, 293, 295, 312

intermarriage 106, 177, 189, 192, 196, 293, mail order brides 319

marriage equality 143-5

mia noi (minor wife) 142

polygamy 141

mass transit 23, 47, 51, 66-7, 69-**71**, 72-5, **167**, 223, 227, 272, 285, 329, **334**-5; see also BTS, bus, canal boat, MRT, river expressboats, *songtaew*, tuk-tuk

Airport Link 296

Bus Rapid Transit 70

massacres of protestors 1973 23, 51, 61, 182, 187

1976 9, 23, 51, 61, 116, 182, 187, 253, 257, 265, **307**, 309

1992 16, 18, 23, 61, 182, 187, 257, 314

2008 23, 182, 187

2010 **17**, 23, 54, 176, 182, 187, 249-50, 282, 309, 334

massage: erotic 18, 128, 137-41, 149

massage: traditional Thai 12, **16**-7, 26-7, 147-50, 295, 303, 308

media, see internet, magazines, news, radio, social media, TV

medical tourism 111, 150-2, 185

meditation & retreats 6-7, 16, 99, 104-**7**, 113, 121, 123-4, 127, 150, 161, 216, 266, 303

Vipassana 16, 105-6

mediums 112, 115, 118 **120**-**5**, 234

megaprojects 54, 58, 227, 235, 285, 328-9

Memorial Days, Kings Bhumibol & Chula-longkorn 173, 283

Mercer Quality of Living Survey 177, 226

Meru concept 49, 51, 63-4, 87, 98, 173, **175**, 181, 184, 227

crematorium 51, 98, 173

'Messy Urbanism' 14, 44, 61, 57, 170, 180, 301, **314-15**, 321, 328-30, 335

metropolis/megalopolis 8-9, 14, 61, 66, 83, 99, 108, 147, 171, 174-5, 177-8, 181, 198, 223, 253, 297, 317-8, 321-2, 328-9, 332; also cities, urbanism, world cities

meuang (city) 25, 50, 174, 176, 179, 181; also: places *lak meuang, lan meuang*

Meuang Thai 174, 179

MICE facilities 185

Michelin stars **31**, 34-7, **38**-9, 202, 204, 259, 280

middle class, see class

middle income trap 164, 268-9

Middle Way 97, 107

migrants: foreign 23, 31-2, 65, 90, 99, 109, 139, 177, 180, **189-99**, **205-6**, **210**-25, 230-1, 274, 290, 299, 308, 313, 321-3, 328, 335

migrants: internal 11, 13, 31-2, 41, 45, 50, 63, 109, 119, 124, 139-40, **147**, 163, 171, 174-6, **189-209**, 222-5, 230-5, 253, 274, 290, 308, 317, 328, 335

'Milk Tea Alliance' 257

Millennials, see generation

Ministries

Culture 101, 105, 136, 143, 254-5, 260, 270, 273, 306

Education 254

Defence 111, 181, 237

Digital Economy & Society **164-5**

Finance 291

Fine Arts Dept 125

Foreign 108

Harbour Dept 330

Health 142

Immigration Dept 81, 166, 192, 214, 299

Interior 94, 108, 129-30

Justice 282

Office of Contemporary Arts 270

Office of Knowledge Management 269

Sanitation Dept 28

Miss ACDC **286**

Miss Thailand 260

missionaries, see Christian

'Moderation Society' (MoSo) 255-**6**

Mom Chao 173

Mom Luang 173

Mom Ratchawong 173

monks 9, 10, 16, 22, 24, 30, 53, 92, 97-**100**, 103-6, 109, 113-7, 119-23, 134, 143, 150, 156, 196, 207-10, 215, 222-4, 247-9, 254, 260, 292, 331, 334;

activist 103

Ajarn Chah 107

Buddhadasa Bhikkhu 16, 104, 107, 117, 150

charismatic 100, 116, 207

forest 107

Luang Phor Toh 9-12, 116, 119, 330, 335

ordination 98-**100**, 103-5, 247

scandals 104, 107

Phra Kovit Khemananda 105

Phra Maharajakhru Astacharya 98

Phra Prayuth Payutto 104

Sangha Council 103, 216

Thich Nhat Hanh 106

monuments, see places

moo baan (housing estates) 13, 52-3, 223-**5**, **233**, 243

monopolies 23, 58, 154, 180, 182, 186, 197, 211-2, 215, 257, 265

Moon 24-5, 41, 82, 86, 91-2, 94, 105, 129, 142-3, 184, 195, 239, 268

mor doo (soothsayer) 113

mor phii (shaman) 115-6, 121

morality 12, 66, 103-6, 112, 132, 134-6, 141-3, 171, 174, 182-4, 204, 213, 215, 243, 250, 255-6, 259-60, 289, 298, 308, 316, 335

Moral Promotion Centre 142

mosques 63, 97, 108-11, 185, 189, 292, 324

Bang Luang 109

Chakrabongse 110

Darul-Aeihasan 110

Haroon **108**-11

Islamic Centre 110

Jawa 108-9

Kudi Khao **107**

Mahanak **76**

Sai Kong Din 109

Seifi 109

Tonson 86-7, 108

most-visited city 8, 14, 23, 170, 185, 294, 329

Mother's Day 254

motorcycles 40, **42**, 45, 64, 68, 70-2, 74, 128, 148, 248

Harley-Davidsons 72

Vespas 72, 275

motorsai (motorcycle taxi) **24**, 45, 66-7, **69**, **74**, 76-7, 80, 148, 158, 225, **227**, 229, **310**

Mount Meru; see Meru

MRT (Mass Rapid Transit) 24, 28, 48, **52**, 61-2, 65, 67-8, **71**-2, 74, **137**, **148**, 166-8, 217, 236, 238, 285, 289, 329; see also BTS, mass transit

Sanam Chai MRT 74, 285, 289,

Wat Mangkorn MRT 62, 87, 221, 238, 242, 289, 326

MSG 35

Muang Thai Insurance 271

muaythai 27, 69, 78-9, 148, 151, 216, 218, 273, 285

muay Chaiya 79

muay Khorat 79

museums, see art & places

National Discovery Museum Institute 269

music

Bangkok Opera 313

Bangkok Sinfonietta 313

bhangra 199

buskers 68, 161, **203**, **247**

hip-hop 253, 257, 267

'Hotel California' 162

K-Pop 144, 163, 216, 249

'Khlong Toei' song 253

Luang Pradit Pairoh Music School 262

luk thung (folk music) 7, 90, 163, 203, 231, 317

luk krung (city kids genre) 162-3, 251

'Mahanakorn: Empire State of Mind' 253

Merseybeat 162

molam (Isan folk music) 163, **198**, 201-**3**, 206, 209, 253, 317

neo-traditional 86, 88, 263-6, 271, 315

patriotic 156, 171, 288; see national anthem

'Prathet Ku Mee' song 253, 257

protest rap 253, 257

Seattle grunge 162

ska music 162

Songs for Life; see *pheua chiwit*

T-rap 253

techno 57, 158, 163, 251, 253

ThaiNuMetal 162

musicians

19TYGER X H3NRI 234, 253

Anarthipathai 256

Apartment Khunpa 165

Asanee & Wasan Chotikul 163

Baby Arabia 111

Bakery Music 162, 196

Big Ass 162

Biggie Smalls 267

BlackPink 163, 216

Blood Soaked Street of Social Decay (BxSxSxSxD) 253, 257

BNK48 & AKB48 248

Bodyslam 162

Boy Thai 263

Buahima 309

Carabao 129, **163**, 263

Carreras, José 9

Da Jim 53, 267

Elevenfinger 253

Endorphine 253

G-Dragon 144

Gaston, Bruce 263

Green Music 159

Groove Riders 162

Hugo (Chulachak Chakrabongse) **162**-3

Jay-Z 162, 253

Jessada Teerapinan 162

JKT 48 248

Joey Boy 253, 267

Keys, Alicia 253

Killing Fields 253

Leo Put 335

Lisa Manoban 163, 216

Lo-So (band) 251

Mister Sister 144

Modern Dog 162

Paradise Bangkok Molam International Band **202**-3

Pradit Pairoh, Luang 262

Phrae (musician) 163

punk 248, 250, 253-**4**, 257, 267, 318

Rap Against Dictatorship 253, 257, 263
Royal Bangkok Symphony Orchestra 161, 265
Scrubb 74
Sek Lo-so 202, 251
Silly fools 162
Sinatra, Frank 45
SNH 48 248
Snoop Dogg 267
Sugree Sithivanich 300
Suntaraporn Band 163
T-Bone 162
Thaitanium 253
Thongchai 'Bird' Mcintyre 163
Tul Waitoonkiat 163
Typhoon 309
Vasu Sangsingkaew 163
Young Ohm 253
muslims & Islam 12-3, 103, 105, **108-111**, 124, 142-3, 145, 177, 192, 195-6, 199, 205-6, 295, **298**, 309, 320; see also Chinese, mosques
Dawoodi Bohras 109, 199
Hanafi 111
Shi'a 97, 108-9, 191, 292, 324
Sufi 109
Sunni 97, 109, 191

nakleng, see gangsters
National Anthem **22**, 79, 101, 111, 160, 172, 179, 193, 252, 262
National Anti-Corruption Commission 326
National Archives 286
National Culture 170-1, 179, 206, 218, 254, 262-3, 282
National Culture Commission 171
National Day 142, 206, 278, 282
National Defence College 184
National Identity Board 171
nationalism 23, 31, 35, 53, 87, 101, 110, 142, 160, 170-9, 187, 190, 192-3, 197, 199, 205-6, 214, 252, 256, 263, 281, 285, 287, 290, 293, 306, 312-3, 330
Navy, Royal Thai 9, 23, 184-5, 330
RTNS Sri Ayudhya 9
NCPO (National Council for Peace & Order) 23, 54, 105, 182, 228, 244, 282, 326, 328
Nelson Mandela Rules 155
news: print, TV, online, see also apps, social media
ASEAN Now (ThaiVisa) 138
Bangkok Coconuts 319
Bangkok Post 34, 36, 140, 153, 235, 255, 300, 313, 320
Bangkok Recorder 313
Bangkok Times 313
Chinese newspapers 193, 215, 220
CNN 32, 34, 36, 300, 313
ETN 302
fake news 306
Nation, The 47, 88, 309, 319-**20**
New York Times, The

298, 310
Nite Owl column 139-40
Not the Nation 319
Thai Rath 150, 199
New Year 2007 bomb 166
New Years, see festivals
nightlife **11**-12, 14, 33, 53, 61, 85, 105, **127-32**, 138-**9**, 158, 203-**5**, **230**, 239, 247, 251, 255, 259, 289, 294, 301-2, 328; see restaurants, bars & clubs
Nirvana 99
noir, see books: noir
Non-Governmental Organisations (NGOs)
Asian Coalition for Housing Rights (ACHR) 223, 279
Amnesty 317
Apcom 145
Big Trees 58-9
Duang Prateep 235
Empower 139
Friends of the River 327-8
Green World 28
Helping Hands 234
Human Rights Watch 307
Issarachon Foundation 229
Mercy Centre 235
Mirror Foundation **229**
Network of Thai Street Vendors 244
Oraya Sutabutr 59, 68
People Who Love Quiet Club 157
Poh Teck Tung 150-**1**, 213
Quiet Bangkok 156-7, 161
Ruam Duay Chuay Kan 225
Ruamkatanyu 151
Satarana 62
VernaDoc 287
nostalgia 163, 171, 203, 223, 256, 278-91, 305, 315
numerology 22, 25, 113, 187

'October generation' 163, 187, 253, 257
OECD 331
Om Santoshi 125
Om Shakti Om 124-5
OMOP (One Masayid One Product) 111
online, see apps, digital, Internet, shopping
oral history 206, 290
Orientalism 11, 13, 16, 81, 306-7
auto-Orientalism 171, 295-6
Orwellian 257, 332
OTOP (One Tambon One Product) 111, 289
Our Roots Right Now **201**

Paknam incident 9, 23
palad khik (penis charms) 114, 118, 240
Panama Papers 307
panya (wisdom) 106
parks 9, **45**, 54, **56-9**, 62, 69, 74, **79**, 82, **95**, 129, 158, 160-1, 173, 185, 201, **204**, 206, 227-8, 233, 237, 244, 250-2, 267, 285, 291, 296, 309, 327-9; listed in places
Parsuke Cohousing 233
Peace Corps 303
Pecha Kucha **93**

people, see also architects, artists & photographers, designers, DJs, film directors, governors, kings, monks, musicians, royalty, writers
Abhisit Sa-in 154
Abhisit Vejajiva 270
Acharanat Ariyarikwikol 241
Achariya Thamparipattra 232
Achmad Qomi 108
Achmadchula 108-9
Adis Idris Raksamani 109
Adisak 'Beam' Jirasakkasem 297
Adria, Fernand 39
Ajarn Kiaow 113, 121, **123**
Ajarn Mill 115, 120-**1**, 123
Ajarn Neng 120, 122
Ake Asapa 106
Alabaster, Henry 197
Ananada Rish 107
Anand Panyarachun 219
Anirut Apidech 224
Anon Chawalawan 186
Anucha Thirakanont 150
Anupong Chantorn 260
Apiradee Kasemsook **53**
Aran Kamonchan 73
Archariya 'Nujah' Peeraputkunchaya 303
Aristotle 12
Arunosha Bhanupan 142
Athip Nana 199
Banyat Sanguansittikul 244
Bao, Jiemin 141
Barker, Anji 234
Barnes, Jess 39
Barron, Michael 308
Beckham, David 101
Bishop, Byron 318
Boonchai Bencharongkul 271
Boonliang Koomklong 227
Boonsong Srifuengfung 288
Booth, Eric 271
Bout, Viktor 166
Boyce, Ralph 100
Bradley, Dan Beach 292, 313
Brown, Jack 318
Bunnag clan 108, 189, 191, 197, 285, 324; Chuang 86, 179, 285; Duangrit 83, 256, 325-6; Tew 41, 309
Butler, Tim 39
Canteen Malakanok 242
Cattleya Jaruthavee 300
Chakrarot Chitrabongs 83
Chalida Uabumrungjit 268
Chanan Yodhong 282
Chanchay 'Pook' Maleesuthikul 284, 289
Chantawipa Apisuk 139
Chao Phraya Mahayotha 191
Chaovalit Metayaprapas 76
Charoen 'Ang' Rungreung 238
Charoen Sirivadhanabhakdi 212, 245
Charoen Tanmaharan 65
Charoen

Wongpiyachetchai 99
Che Guevara 101
Chen Mingquan 212
Chinn, Bobby 39
Chiranan Pitpreecha 175
Chirathivat clan 211
Chittawadi Chitrabongs, M.L. 28-9, 49, 175
Chodoek Rachasetthi, Phraya 191
Chotiros 'Amy' Suriyawong 137, 254
Chularatchamontri 108-10, 191
Chuvit Kamolvisit 137
Cook, Tim 325
Cross, Alex 298
Dalai Lama 106
Deng Xiao Ping 211, 220
Deunchalerm Khiewpan 68
Dhanin Chearavanont 220
Dickinson, Nita 'Amp' 251
Direk Kulsiriwad 110
Disaphol Chansiri 192
Dome Sukwong 268
Duangporn 'Bo' Songvisava 38
Einstein, Albert 88
Ekkachai Jaruesilp 242
E Thi 117
Favro, Gianni 37
Fongsanan Chamornchan 25
Fraser, Daniel 318
Frerard, Hervé 37
Funahashi, Daena Aki 106
Gaggan Anand 39
Gauthier, Julian **333**
Gillison, Samantha 232
Goenka, S. N. 107
Groskopf, Christopher 70
Guimar, Marie 31, 293
Hausler, Darren 39
Jakkrit Panichpatikum 153
Jaruwat Boonwaedlom 314
Jiang Zemin 220
Jidanun Lueangpiansamut 309
Jit Malhotra 198
Jobs, Steve 100
Jolie, Angelina 122
Jones, David 303
Jones, Dylan 39
Jukapong Elmsaard 320
Kaewta Ketbungkan 45
Kalayanimit clan 216
Kamol 'Sukie' Clapp 162
Kamron Pramoj 173
Kanokporn Chanasongkram 142
Karma Srikogar 267
Kasma Loha-unchit 31
Kathawut 'Kot' Kangpiboon 145
Khaisri Paksukcharern 69
Kobkarn Wattanawarangul 138
Kobsak Pootrakool 165
Komkrit Uitekkeng 124
Korsak Chairasmisak 212
Krammy, Oliver 37
Krisadakorn Puangput 243
Krisana Asoksin 308
Kung Kannika 118
Kwan Khetpratum 251
Kwanchai Atthikom-

rungsarit 135
Ladda Thangsupachai 255
Lalita Hanwong 320
Lamyai Haithongkham 138-**9**, 251
Lee Kuan Yew 211
Lek Viriyahbhun 107
Luang Suwicharnpat 102
Ma Chongxian 195
Mae Baan Mee Nuad **135**
Maier, Father Joe 235
Manta Klangboonkrong 127
Mao Zedong 23, 84, 220
Marayat Bibidh 317
Maurer, Mario 248, 329
Mauri, Giacomo 292
McDang Svasti, Chef 32, 34, 173
Meechai Viravaidhya 141
Mongkol Suksai 298
Monruedee Jansuttipan 226
Montassier, Samuel **197**
Muhammed 109
Mussolini, Benito 56
na Ayutthaya name 173
Nadech Kugimiya **192**
Nai Lert Sreshthaputa (Bhakdi Noraset) 72, 95, 114, 118, **284**-5
Nakhon Sawan clan 173
Nalin Kalayanamitr 303
Nana clan 111, 199
Napaporn Trivitwareegune 142
Napat Sutithon 256
Napol Jantraget 35, 39
Narawan Pathomvat 269
Narong Jaroensuk 292
Narula clan, Rachvin, Surin 199
Nasa Saze 100
Nathinan Warintharavej 255
Netiwit Chotipattanapaisan 256
Nielsen, Flemming Winther 307
Nimit Kaewkrajang 244
Nithiphat Hoisangthong 157
Nitipan Wiprawit 142
Nitipol Temprim 167
Noo Kanphai 122
Nuanla-or Sripila 238, 244
Nuh Peace 145
Oberoi, J. S. 199
Pachter, Marc 19, 43, 177
Paetongtarn Shinawatra 23, 186
Pairod Roikaew 275
Pakorn Wutthipram 99
Pang Nakarin Kingsak 317
Pansak Vinyaratn 269
Panya Charusiri 1657
Paothong Thongcheua 291
Pasaraporn Mongkolrueangrawa 250
Patama Roonrakwit 233
Pat Pataraporn 333
Patpongpanich clan 211
Peerasit Kamnuansilpa 206
Petch Osathanugrah 271
Phaulkon, Constantine 31, 293
Phibunsongkhram Field Marsahal (Phibun),

23-4, 43, 101, 170, 177, 179, 193, 205, 210, 237, 262-3, 265, 284, 293, 325-6, 333
Phor Trimurti **120**, 123
Pichit Boonjin 278
Pim Sukhahuta 250
Pok Chelsea 124
Pok Kobkongsanti 59
Pong Prida 202
Pongsatat Auoyklang **261**
Pongtawat 'Chef Ian' Chalermkittichai 37
Poo (Saiyud Diwong) 234
Pornwipa Suriyakarn **105**
Prachuab Chaiyasan 204
Prakij Thamniam 228
Pramoj family 173
    Kamron 173
    Kukrit 171, 193, 220, 254, 308
    Prempreeda 145, 173
    Seni 173
Pranee Sutdis 222
Praphaiphun Phoomvuthisarn 252
Prem Tinsulanond, General 171, 173
Premsiri Tarasantisuk 250
Pridi Bhanomyong 282, 326
Punnatha Pathikorn 144
Purachai Piemsomboon 129-30
Rabiabrat Pongpanich 255
Raj, Stuart Jay 301
Rapeeat Ingkasit 76
Rattiya Salae 111
Read, Rachel 303
Ricker, Andy 34
Robuchon, Joel 39
Rojjana 'Yui' Phetkanha 202
Rollet-Andriane, Luis Jacques 317
Ruangroj Poonpol 256
Sachdev, Maynica 199
Sachdev, Varin 199
Samer Peerachai **229**
Santi Opaspakornkij 58
Sanya Souvarnaphouma 133
Sarit Thanarat, Field Marshal 23, 72, 85, 103, 171, 173, 177, 184, 282, 286
Savelberg, Henk 39
Schafer, R. Murray 160
Scott, Nikki 303
Scott, Trevor 40
Sehgal, Gaurav 199
Seri Wongmontha 205
Sheikul Islam 108
Sin Suesuan 142
Sirinya 'Cindy' Bishop 318
Sisada Rangsibrahman-akul 99
Sithikorn Wongwudthi-anun 303
Sittichai Chaivoraprug 155
Soithip Trisuddhi 70
Somkid Jarusripitak 215
Somram Teppitak 246
Sondhi Limthongkul 117, 193, 220
Sopawan Boonnimitra 53-4, 322

Stamm, Hanno 160
Suchart Sawadsri 308
Sühring Twins 39
Sun Yat Sen 65, 192, 211, 214-1, 220
Sunanda Satchatrakul 319
Sunanta Suapattakul 242
Supakorn Buaruan 297
Supaksorn Jongsiri 204
Supharat Pothisuwan 228
Supitcha Tovivich 232
Suppanut Jonjitaree 213
Surachai Sukson 223
Surat Tomornsak **280**
Suthita 'Image' Chanachaisuwan 248
Suttichart Denpreuktham 101
Suwanna Satha-anand 117
Suwanna Walploy-ngam 232
Svasti clan 34, 137, 173
Takkatan Chollada 317
Tanya Phonanan 60
Tanyaporn Singchalee 201, 209
Tasinee Tantiwitthay-anggoon 254
Tee Kachonklin 37
Teerachon Manomaiphaibal 69
Tejapaibul clan 151
Teng Terdterng 176
Thaksin Shinawatra 17, 23, 74, 100, 129-30, 151, 166, 175, 183-4, 186-7, 193, 211-3, 225, 241, 260, 264, 269-70, 282, 310, 333
Thaninthorn Chantrawan 35
Thawatchai Arunyik 299
Thawatpong Monda 194-**5**
Thaweekiat Nimmalairatana 36
Theeradej Wongpuapan 63
Therdkiat Wangwatchakul 314
Thitipol Panyalimpanun 136, 138
Thompson, David 34-5
Thompson, Jim 108, **194**-5, 242, 271, 317; see also art & places
Thongchai Prasongsanti 202
Tony Jaa 202
Torpong 'Ball' Chantabubpha 74
Tripak Supawattana 177
Trump, Donald 177, 259, 316
Tyson, Mike 127
Udom 'Note' Taepanich 319
Udom Patpongpanit 141
Umpai Promporn 237
Vallop Suwandee 32, 326, 328-9
Varin Somprasong 73
Vichit-Vadhakan, Luang 170, 193, 262
Virat Chatturaputpitak 295
Virilions, Paul 167
Visit Hirankitti 164
Visit Limprana 219
Visit Techakasem 64
Vithi Phanichphant

189, 205-6, 323
Vittaletti, Paulo 37
Vorasa Srichaikul 199
Vuti Somboonkulavudhi 275
Walailak Songsiri 232
Wanglee family 219, 324
Wararat Puaphairoj 73
Watcharapol 'Jack' Fukijdee 113
Wei Yunmei 298
Westerkamp, Hildegard 160
Whitehall, Jack 318
Wichai Sangprapai 302
Witchaya Prueccksamars 274
Wichayapat Piromsan 309
Williams, Hayden 19
Williams, Robert 312
Wimonrat Issarathumnoon 224
Wimonsiri Hemtanon 209
Winyu 'John' Wongsurawat 319-20
Wisoot Buachoom 298
Worathon 'Tae' Udomchalatorn 38
Wrisley, Jarrett 34
Wuthipol Ut 80
Xi Jinping 220
Yiamyut Sutthichaya 280
Yingluck Shinawatra 23, 161
Yongyuth Chanyarak 95
Yoovidhaya family 211
Yuphadee Wanich 242
Zelinsky, Wilbur 190
Zheng He 216
Phibunsongkram era; see people: Phibun
phii (spirits) 112-6, 121-2
photography 51, 91, 249, 262, 296; see artists & photographers
selfies **89**, 105, 206, 241, 249, 273, **276-7**, 289, 301, 328
street 234, 305, **311**, **314**
Street Photo Thailand 311
phudee ('old money' grandees) 240
phuea chiwit (For Life) Movement 163, 257, 263, 308
phum panya (local wisdom) 149, 287
piracy 16, 268
places & ethnicity: world
Africa & Africans 158, 189, 202
    Cape Town 279
    Marrakech 91
    Nigerian 110-1
    Tuareg 110
American, see USA
Arabs 27, 61, 97, 109-11, 189, 192, 198, 296, **298**-9, 316
    Qatar tower 330
Australia & Australian 16, 34, 39, 131, 184, 234, 296, 298-301
    Fitzroy 251
Austro-Hungarian Empire 190
Bangladesh 179
Belgium & Belgians 38, 43, 197
Colombia

Bogotá 177, 329
Burma: see Myanmar
Cambodia also: Khmer 23, 99, 191-2, 198, 282
    Angkor 85, 98, 172, 174
    Phnom Penh 232, 279, 285
Central Asia 30, 109, 296, 299
Chams 108, 110, 179, 191, 242
China 11, 23, 30, 42, 63, 74, 86-8, 146, 155, 176, 178, 189-90, 192-3, 196, 198-9, 206, 210-5, 218-21, 240, 249, 259, 298-9, 321, 330, 333; also places Thai: Sino-Thai
    Beijing 83, 174, 220, 232, 332
    Guangdong (Canton) & Cantonese 32, 48, 190, 211, 214, 219; viewing tower 330
    Fujian 128, 211, **214**
    Guangzhou 83
    Hainan (Hailam) **31**, 122, 193, 189, 211, 214-5, 221
    Hakka 191, 211, 214, 219
    Han 196, 210-1, 214
    Hokkien 23, 97, 111, 122, 189, 191, 211, **214**, 216, 220, **222**, 292
    Hong Kong 37, 48, 52, 95, 216, 219, 221, 257, 312, 326
    Kuomintang 195
    Pearl River Delta 48
    Ming dynasty 221
    Muslim 109, 196
    Shanghai 70, 131, 218, 248
    Straits Chinese 81, 218
    Suzhou 321
    Swatow 23, 211, 215
    Teochiu 8, 23, **32**, 51, 64-5, 191-2, 195, 211-**2**, 214, **216**, 219-21, 290, 323
    Uighur 102
    Xian 220-1
    Yunnan 205, 214
Denmark & Danish 197
Dubai 283, 299
Egypt & Egyptian 110-1
Europe & European 14, 23, 30, 49, 51-2, 69, 107, 109, 162, 172-4, 193, 197, 202, 206, 232, 240, 262, 264, 272, 281, 292, 296, 298-9, 307-8, 313, 321, 326, 333-4; also: *farang*
France & French 9, 23-4, 27, 39, 58, 84-5, 103, 109-10, 178, 191, **197**, 213, 266-7, 272, 281, 292, 311, 317-20, 325
    French Revolution 281
    Marseilles 261
    Paris 50, 67, 80, 85, 140, 170, 232, 261
    Versailles 262
Germany & German 32, 39, 60, 83, 88, 94, 133, 136, 162, 167, 170, 248, 318, 322;
    Berlin 39, 91, 136, 140, 177, 261, 325, 329

Kultur 170
    Munich 130, 251
    Prussian uniform 86
    Schwabing 130, 251
    Weimar 140
Greece & Greeks 31, 63, 86, 197, 293, 299
India & Indian 13, 23, 27-32, 63, 85-8, 98, 109-10, 114, 122-9, 149, 178, 189-94, 196, 198-9, 206, 213, 215; also: places: Thai-Indian
    Assam 205
    British Raj 199
    Chennai 199
    Delhi 199, 232, 279
    Goa 31, 293
    Ganges River 24
    Gujarat 109, 111, 199
    independence 193
    Kolkata 27, 39, 66
    Manipur 194
    Mughal 109, 124
    Mumbai (Bombay) 23, 138
    partition 191-2, 199, 279
    Punjab 191, 198-9
    Tamil 124, 199
    Uttar Pradesh 124, 199
    Varanasi 125
    Indian Cultural Ctr 199
Indian Ocean 42
Indochina 40, 140, 295
    Indo-Chinese 63, 218
Indian subcontinent 110
Indonesia & Indonesian 111, 176, 199, 333
    Bali 19
    Jakarta 111, 235, 248, 333
    Java & Javanese 25, 86, 108-9, 184, 218
    Jogjakarta 266
    Kalimantan 333
    Makassars 108
Israel & Israeli 298
Italy & Italian 31, 37, 81, 85-6, 170, 178, 197, 262, **284**-5, 292, 299
    Milan 258, 266
    Rome 56, 85, 206
    Venice & biennale 7, 90, 175, 293, 333
Japan & Japanese 23, 31, 39-40, 58, 62, 68, 71, 84, 86, 95, 141, 170, 189, 193, 197-8, 203, 241, 249, 259, 266, 269, 272, 289, 293, 295-6, 298, 321, 333
    Harajuku 249, 250
    Osaka 136
    Roppongi 138
    Shibuya 130, 250
    Tokyo 13, 70, 130, 138, 249-50, 266, 326, 332
Kazakhstan 148, 205, 298
Khmer era (802-1351) & influence 49, 63-4, 85, 98, 101, 178-9, 183, 189-90, 194, 205-6, 262, 290, 323; see also Cambodia
Korea, North 170
Korea, South & Korean 37, 84, 145, 186, 198, 249, 259, 298, 327
    Seoul 70, 198, 327
Laos & Lao 32, 35, 41, 48,

Index 355

64, 99, 140, 160, 189-91, 195, 201-3, 205-6, 216, 278, 282, 323
Vientiane 160, 191
Malay 32, 85, 103, 108-11, 158, 189, 195, 199, 201, 205-6, 209, 218
Malaysia 111, 195, 218, 259
  Kelantan 110
  Kuala Lumpur (KL) 57, 83, 110
  Malaya (colony) 205
  Penang 52, 221
Middle East 36, 109, 111, 296
Mongolia 205
Myanmar & Burmese 13, 23-4, 32, 85, 98-9, 104, 107, 109, 117, 174, 184, 190-2, 194, 212, 233, 257, 260, 283, 288, 292
  Mandalay 174
  Mon 194
  Naypyidaw 333
  Pagan 179
  Shan 192, 234, 282
  Yangon 55, 282
Netherlands/Holland 28
  Amsterdam 261
  Protest Museum 287
North Asian 296
Pakistani 110, 199
  Sindh 199
Persia (Iran) & Persians 23, 86, 108, 172, 189, 191, 197-8, 206, 262
Persian Gulf 27, 111, 198
Philippines 259, 313
  Manila 235, 328
Portuguese 13, 23, 31, 191, 195, 292-3, 325-6
Russia & Russian 86, 172, 296, 298-99
  Moscow 136
  Czarist uniform 172
Saudi Arabia 109
  Mecca 24, 63, 109
Silk Road, The 206
Singapore 12, 29, 33, 37, 43-4, 55, 57-8, 81, 87, 89-90, 101, 130, 138, 170, 178, 211, 215, 218-9, 236, 241, 251, 259, 273, 296, 299, 303, 307, 326-30
  Changi Airport 81
  Clarke Quay 303
  Marina Bay 130
  Orchard Road 241
Sino-Filipine 'Mestizo', Sino-Indian 'Chindian' & Sino-Malay 'Peranakan' 218
South Asians 295-6
Spain 298-9
  Barcelona 55, 130, 261
Sri Lanka 87, 99
Taiwan 145, 221, 257, 297
  Taipei 83
Turkey 299
  Istanbul 55, 136
  Ottoman 109-10
UK & British 23, 28, 86, 90, 106, 116, 144, 155, 193, **197**-9, 205, 250, 254, 292, 318, 325-6
  British Empire 106
  Edinburgh 91
  England 16, 236, 326
  Gherkin, The 87
  Greenwich Meridian

22
  London 16, 37-8, 70-1, 76, 87, 89-91, 138, 167, 173-4, 201, 241, 250, 258, 274, 278, 294, 297, 312, 319, 325
  Soho 138
USA & American 14, 23, 30-1, 37, 52, 62, 67, 85, 140-1, 151, 184-6, 196, 198, 235, 243, 249, 253, 267, 281, 295, 298-9, 307, 309, 313, 315, 318-9, 321, 326
  Brooklyn 275
  Central Park, NYC 54
  Chicago 81, 162, 202
  Disneyland 88
  High Line, NYC 52
  Hollywood 82, 116, 140, 298, 312
  Los Angeles 48
  Manhattan, NYC 54
  Miami 261
  Mississippi 202
  New York 34, 80, 90, 140, 151, 163, 174, 202, 275, 309, 317, 329
  Philadelphia 202
  Revolution 281
  Seattle 162
  Smithsonian Inst 19
  US forces 140, 295
  Washington DC 19
Vietnam 32, 192, 205, 213, 259, 288, 308, 312
  Hanoi 242
  Ho Chi Minh City (Saigon) 66, 178, 219, 312
West & Western 10, 13, 16-9, 23-5, 27-9, 34-5, 40, 43, 47-9, 52, 56-7, 61, 63-5, 78, 81, 84-6, 103, 105, 114, 116, 129-32, 135, 140-1, 145-6, 148, 151, 163, 171, 174, 177, 183, 189-93, 195-9, 202-3, 212, 216, 230, 240, 243, 247-54, 257, 262-3, 266, 274, 279, 283-4, 289, 292-3, 295-8, **300-3**, **310**, 313-4, 316-8, **320**-1, 323, 328, 331-4

places & ethnicity: Thai
see also Thainess
Ayutthaya & era (1351-1767) 9, 23, 31, 49, 63, 85-6, 98, 101, 103, 108, 172-5, 178, 183, 191, 197, 206, 211, 214, 222-4, 232, 281, 283, 286, 292, 318, 321
Baba-Nyonya 218
Central Plains 30, **46**, 66, 163, 171, 206, 224, 331, 333
Central Thais 31, 109, 189, 193, 205-5, 209
Chachoengsao 48, 51, 242
Chanthaburi 31, 204
Chao Phraya Basin 76
Chiang Mai 16, 95, 122, 174, 204-5
Chonburi 185
Deep South 110-1, 189, 205-6, 309

Eastern Seaboard 185, 331
Friendship Highway 202
Gulf of Thailand 158, 331
Had Yai 174
Hua Hin 200
Isaan 11, 31-2, 37, 41, 63, 124, 140, 156, 158, 163, 195, 200-7, 209, 211-2, 216, 234, 247, 253, 263, 268, 273, 279, 308, 323
Kalasin 201, 237
Kanchanaburi 333
Khao Yai 200
Khon Kaen 202, 209, 273-4
Khorat & Plateau 79, 174, 201-2, 273
Kra Canal 171
Krabi 118, 273
Laem Chabang Port 179
Langkasuka era (c200s-c1500s) 111, 281
Lanna (Northern Thai) 31, 122, 149, 179, 189-90, 200-9, 281-2, 303, 323
Lao; see places: global
Lopburi 241, 331
luk jiin 192, 215, 221
Mahachai 192, 194, 242
Malay; see places: global
Mekong River & Basin 23, 41, 174, 179, 323
Mon 13, 23, 32, 42, 57, 73, 122, 178, **188-95**, 200, 205, **224**, 290, 292-3
Nakhon Chaisi 122
Nakhon Nayok 333
Nakhon Si Thammarat 208
Nan 207-8
Narathiwat 202
Nong Bua Lamphu 204
Northern Thai, see Lanna
Ongkarak fault 165
Pai 303
Pattani **110**-1, 191, 205
Pattaya 107, 140, 296,
Phattalung 208
Phrae 163, 206
protukate (Portuguese) see places: global
Ramanayadesa 194
Ratchaburi 194, 331
Roi-et 201
Saraburi 95
Satun 189, 242
Siam & Siamese 9, 11, 23-5, 28, 30, 56, 63-4, 86-8, 98, 101, 103, 109, 134, 141, 146, 149, 151, 170-5, 179, 184, 190-4, 197-8, 204-6, 211-6, 262-3, 265, 281-2, 285-6, 288, 292, 305, 313, 331
Si Thep 281
Southern Thai 11, 39, 109, 111, 115, 190, 196-7, 200-06, **208-9**, 242
Sukhothai & era (1328-1438) 101, 108, 172-4, 185, 206, 214, 262, 273, 281, 283
Sungai Kolok 16
Suphanburi 331
Surat Thani 208
Tai tribes 63, 114, 172, 174, 179, 189, **201**, 205-6, 323
Thai-Chinese (jek, Thai

Jiin, Sino-Thai) 13, 42, 64-**5**, 84, **96**, 99, 104, 107, **109**, 134, 141, 144, **151**, 156, 170, 175, 182, 184, 187, 189, **192**-3, 195-7, 199, 202, 205, **210-21**, 231, **237**, 240, 263, 265, 279, 284-5, 290, 308-**9**, 312-3, 324; see also Chinese
Thai-Indian (khaek) 13, 23, 27-32, 109-10, 124, 189-92, **195-6**, 199, 218, 237, 291, 293, 319; see also Sikhs
Thai-Islam, see Muslims
  U-Tapao airport 296
Ubon Ratchathani 201
Udon Thani 174, 201

places: Bangkok, see also art galleries, dance, film, hotels, khlongs, malls, markets, restaurants, shops, schools, shrines, universities, wats
6 October 1976 Memorial 187, 282
14 October 1973 Memorial 187
Alliance française 220
Amorn Sathan Palace 185
Ananta Samakhom Throne Hall 86, 128, **173**, 184
Aree 153, 233
Asiatique 56, 87, 127
Asoke 32, 52, 69, 166, 199
Aspire condo 224
Baiyoke Towers I & II **57**, **83**
Bamrungmeuang Rd 49
Ban Baat 222-**3**
Ban Bu 278
Ban Khrua 108, 110, 191, 242
Ban Mangkon 235
Ban Nai Lert 72
Ban Plainern 172, 262
Ban Khaek 189, 191, 198-9
Ban Somdet Chao Phraya 179, 189, 195
Bang Bu 232, 235, 242
Bang Bua Thong 232, 242
Bang Khuntian 28, 33, 57, 73, 330-**1**
Bang Kra Jao 57, 158
Bang Kradee 57, **194-5**, **224**
Bang Kruai 334
Bang Kwang Prison 155
Bang Makok 178, 236
Bang Or 109
Bang Phlad 47, 110
Bang Phra 112, 122
Bang Pu 251
Bangchak 158
Bangkhunprom, Wang 172, **283**, 286
Bangkok Bank HQ 28, 64, 83, 88, 215, 223, 239, 260, 284, 288
Bangkok Noi 8, 23, 178-9, 201, 229
Bangkokian Museum 175, 179, 291
Bangkok Pearl **88**-9
Banglamphu 72, 77, 91, 111, 224, 236, 242, 267, 290-1, 299, 302
Banglamphu Museum 267, 290-**1**
Bangna 28, 59, 201, 243

Bangna-Trad highway 69
Bangrak 53, 61, 97, **117**, 198-9, 259, 261, 263, 273, **324**-5, 329-31, **324**
Bangrak Museum 291
Bangsue Station **23**
Bangyai 243
Banthad Thong 33
Benjasiri Park 57
Benjakitti Park **58**
Bhumibol Bridge 57
BITEC 185
Bon Kai 226
British Club 116
British Council 250
Buddhaisawan Chapel 285
Bunditpattanasilpa Hall 89
CAT Building 81
CBD (Central Business District) 61, 116, 223
Center Point Silom 113
Central Post Office 325
Chaengwattana 61, 185, 203
Chaiyaphum, Trok 65
Chakri Bongkot Palace 185
Chakri Maha Prasat Throne Room 86
Chang Chui **38**-9, **101**, 271
Chao Phraya River **8**-9, **11**, 13, 18, 23, 25, 27, 41, 47-9, 57, 63-4, **73**-7, 80-3, **8**, 87, 89, 97, 108, 126-8, 130, 158, 160-1, 165, 173-**5**, 179, 181, 184-5, 189, 191, 194, 208-9, 219, 223, 228, 235, 238, 240, 259, 261, 264, 272, 274, 284-6, 291, 293, 301, **305**, 314-5, 319, 323-5, 327, **328**-31, 333-**5**
Charansanitwong **60**, 159
Charoen Krung Rd 27, 49, 61, 65, **93**, 113, 160, 162, 193, 229-30, 232-3, 270-1, 325
Charoen Chai area 65
Charoenrat Rd 95
Chatuchak Park **44**, 58, 95, **107**; also: Markets
China Cultural Centre 215
Chinatown, see also Sampeng, Yaowarat 8, 13, 14, **32**-3, 49, 53, 60-2, **64-5**, 83, 87, 130, 141, 151, 175, 185, 193, 198, **210**-12, 231, 236, **237**-44, 261, 271-2, 284, **290**, 308, 324, 329, 331
  Gates 60, **65**, 215, 219-20
  Heritage Centre 175, 215, 221, 284, 290
  'new Chinatown' 215
Chitralada Palace 285
Chokchai 4 53, 99, 215-6, 239
Chong Nonsi 108, 192, 221
Chokchai Tower 81, 83
City Library 161, 290, 308
Constitution Defence Monument 282, **287**
Convent Road 238, 244
Corrections Museum 285

356   Index

CU Centenary Park 58
Customs House 109
Democracy Monument 25, 61, 63, 128, **181**, 187, 263, 282
Din Daeng 158, 181, 226
Don Mueang & airport 31, 50, 61, 184-5, 296, 333
Dumnam 214
Dusit 28, 51, 54, 61, 63, 122, 127, 184, 200-1, 207, 262, 289, 326
Dusit Central Park 54
Dusit Palace 172, 187
East Asiatic Company building 127, **282**
East Thonburi 51, 178, 211
Eastern Bus Station 71
Ekamai 18, 32, 44, 61-2, 71, 83, 119, 130, 242, 329
Elephant Building 88
Empire Tower 81
Erawan Musem 88, **107**
Foreign Correspondents' Club of Thailand (FCCT) 311, 313
Forestia 59
French Embassy 109, 272
Front Palace, see Wang Na
Giant Swing 98-**9**, 158, 181, 199, 282
Goethe Institute 220
'Ghost Tower' 18, 51, 82, **299**, 312
Golden Mount **7**, 12, 27, 49, 83, 128, **159**, 222
Government House 61, 64, 109, 117, 143, **186**-7, 262, 288
Grand Palace **8**, 28, **41**, 49, 51, 63, 86, 89, 128, **170**, **172**, 179, 185, 187, 211, 262, 266, 283, 285, **295**
Greater Bangkok 14, **20**-**1**, 48-9, 107-8
'Green Lung' 57, 161
'Green Route' 50
Gurdwara 97, 199
Haroon area **108**-11
Hive, The 303
Hopewell graffitti 299
Hopewell train 51, 299
House of Museums, The 289-90
Hua Chang Bridge 229
Hua Lamphong Railway Station 138-**9**, **201**
Huai Khwang 128, 215, 233, 239, 243
Hindu Shrine 94, 124, 129
Impact Arena 185
Itsaranupharp, Trok 64
Jambu Dvipa 63
Jamjuree Building 95
Jim Thompson House 193, 249
Jomthong 308
JUSMAG 179
Kamphaengphet Rd 274
Kasikorn Bank 288
Khao San Rd 69, 168, **234**-5, 289, 318
Khlong Samwa 233
Khlong San **113**, **213**, 215, 259, 261, 271, 285, 324-25, **334**
Khlong Tan **108**-9, 200
Khlong Toei 197, 308;

port 53, 57, 331; slum 25, **44**, 220, **231**-3, 257
Khru Sapha 291
Kiakkai 179, 224
Kit Mai Buddhist Centre **155**
Ko Kret **69**, 190
Korea Town 194
Krung Thep Aphiwat Central Terminal (train) **23**, 72
Krungthep 7, 8, 11, 44-5, 52, 62, 87-8, 126-7, **172**-83, 225, 279, 281, 283, 306-7, 314-5, 321, 323
Kudi Jeen 79, 107, 137, 191, 210, 219, 227, 286, 290, 308
Lak Meaung 59-60, 100, 183, 208
Lan Meuang (City Hall Plaza 73, 187, 229
Lamlukka 160
Lamsalee 160
Landmark river promenade 69
Langsuan, Soi 197, **223**
Lao-Isaan 28, 37
Lassalle, Soi 201
Lat Krabang Industrial Estate 160
Lat Phrao 57, 65, 133, 145, 159, 217, 220
Lhong 1919 130, **209**, 215, 218-9, 283, 324
Lido Connect 272
Line, The **52**, 71
Link, The 71
Little Arabia 23, 109
Little India 185, 187, 194, 235, 329
Luan Rit community 221
Lumlukka 160
Lumpini Park 50, 54-55, **75**, 78, 121, 160, 173, **200**, 202, 285, 309
Lumpini Stadium 285
Lumpini Stadium, New 79
Mahachak 61
Magnolia condo **305**
Mahanak 160
Mahanakhon Tower **50**, **78**-9, **324**, **330**
Maitreechit 140
Makkasan 106, 160, 232
Makkasan depot 54, 57
Material Connexion Library 149
Minburi 50, 53, 106, 333
Mini Myanmars 192
Mo Chit 57, 67, 330
Mo Chit bus station 201
Muang Boran 107
Museum of Floral Culture 28, **98**
Museum of Popular History 186
Museum of Thai Cartoons 308
Museum of Thai Corruption **184**
Museum Siam 18, 111, **141**, **145**, **174**, 197, 221, 229, 269-**70**, 290, 305, **321**-3, 329
Na Phra Lan Rd 326
Nai Lert Heritage Home 285
Nakhon Pathom 48, 57, 95, 194

Nana (Chinatown) 130, 199, 214, 231, 272, 325
Nana (Sukhumvit) 27, 61, 84, 97, 111, 127-8, **130**-1, **137**-9, 148, 166, 191, 198-9, 223, 285, 298
National Library 287
National Museum 51, 269, 281, 285, 289-90
National Stadium **149**, 201, 242
Neilson Hays Library 269
New Phetchaburi Rd 138, 140
Noble Ploenchit 89
Nong Chok 57, **59**, 108, 229
Nonthaburi 47-8, 57, 74, 76, 100, 111, 122, 139, 155, 164
Odeon Circle 60, **65**, 219
Old Siam Plaza 285
Old Town 34, 61-2, 73, 83-4, 86, 89, 93, 105, 108, 112, 115, **128**-30, 160, 170, 179, 181, 185, 228, 237, 242, 267, 285, 308, **327**; also: Rattankosin
On Nut **46**, 120, 199
One Bangkok 54, 58, 185, 271, 285, **328**
One Wireless Rd 185
Oriental Spa, The **149**
Park Ventures 88
Pan Rd 83, **125**
Parliament House 61, 108, 110, 143, **180**-85
Pathum Thani 48, 115, 158
Pathumvanarak Park 58
Pathumwan 54, 227
Patpong 18, 61, 131, **138**-41, 145, 147, 158, 211, 213, **238**, 298, 317
Patpong Museum 141
Phahonyothin 61, 88, 253
Phanu Rangsi, Soi 64
Phetchaburi Rd 50, 139, **147**, 239
Phiphat, Soi 223
Phlabphlachai 151, 213
Phra Chan Rd 94
Phra Nakhon 11, 34, **104**, 179, 229, 308
Phra Pinklao Bridge **9**, 285, 327
Phra Pradaeng 194
Phrakhanong 11-**2**, 32, 53, 61, 76-**7**, 110, **116**, **119**, 271, 273
Phutthamonthon Dhamma Park 77, 185
Phyathai 184
Phyathai Palace 179, 262, 286, 326
Pinklao 163, 201, 203, 244, 262
Plaeng Nam, Soi 242
Ploenchit **42**, **50**, **56**, 66, **69**, 88-9, 102, 118, 322
Pom Mahakan 48, 109, **174**-5, 228, 232, **280**, 320, 329
Pom Phra Sumen 48-**9**, 58, 329
Portuguese embassy 325
Prachanaruemit 233, 242
Praditmanutham 61

Q House Lumpini 92
Raffiné Jambu Dvipa, Le 82, **226**-7
Rajini Pier 74
Rama I Rd 102
Rama II Rd 57, 118-9, 194
Rama III Rd 61
Rama IV Rd 81, 83, 226
Rama IX Bridge 317
Rama IX Museum 281
Rama IX Park 58
Rama IX Memorial Park 58, 185
Rama IX Rd 83, 201, 213
Rama V Statue 117, 283
Rama VII Statue 183
Rama VIII Bridge 9, **50**, 58, 123, 127, 268
Rambuttri, Soi 302
Ramintra Rd 73, 224
Ramkhamhaeng Rd 17, 61, 76, 145, 149, 200-1, 230, 239, 251, 299
Rangnam, Soi 197, 200
Ratchadaphisek Rd (Ratchada) 18, 49, 61, 127-8, 131, 137-8, 141, 145, 158, 192, 213, 221, 239, 251, 255, 263, 275, 298
Ratchadamnoen Avenue 49, 54, 79, 86, 128, 161, 187, 263, 273, 322
Ratchadamnoen Boxing Stadium 79
Ratchadamri Rd 95, 102, 241, **305**
Ratchaprasong **17**, **42**, 54, 61, 69, 97, **102**, 117, 166, 187, 241, 250, 285, 298, 301
Ratchapruek Rd 95, **232**
Ratchathewi **50**, **74**, 192, 201, **229**, 233, **267**, 308
Ratchawong 65
Rattanakosin **8**-**9**, 31, 48, 53, 56, 61, 63, 65, 83, 85, 87, 89, 92, 98, 108-9, 118, 172-3, 179, 197, 199, 211-2, 236, 238, 279-80, 301, 305, 326, 329
Rattanakosin Exhibition Hall 111, 175, 282
Rattanakosin Island Plan 83, 89, 229, 280-2, 326
Rattanakosin View Mansion 83
Reading Room 269, 290
Rich, The 224-**5**
river; see Chao Phraya
River, The condo 314
River City 11, 127, 285
'Robot Building' **284**
Romaneenart Park 58, 285
Royal Bangkok Sports Club **59**, 229
Royal City Avenue (RCA) 18, 61, 131, 158, 201
Royal Turf Club 58, 285
Saladaeng 47, 52, 154
Sam Phraeng 291
Sampeng 8, 27, **61**, 64-5, 89, 109, 128, 141, 191-3, 198, **208**, 211-4, 216, 219, 221, 236, 242; see also Chinatown, Yaowarat
Samphanthawong 53 District Office 81

Samsen 23, 34, 49, 191, 208, 227, 233, 292, 302
Samut Prakan 48, 57, 73, 154, 331
Samut Sakhon 48
Samyan 58, 227, 250
Sanam Luang **51**, 61, 89, 98, 105-6, 130, 173, 187, 237, 282, 285, 307, 312
Santichaiprakarn Park 58, 95, 329
Saphan Kwai 115, 138, 159, 200, 213, 253
Saphan Phan Fah 66
Saphan Phut (Memorial Bridge) 25, 185, 251, 329
Saphan Taksin 61, 76, 329
Saranrom Park 237
Sathorn 34, 47, 51, 61-2, 85, 88, 114, 127, 129-30, 185, 264, 268, 299, 312
Sathorn City Tower 88
Sathorn Unique, see Ghost Tower
SCB Plaza 92
SEAMEO-SPAFA 185
Sena Nikhom, Soi 224
Sex Museum 139
Si Yaek Jaidee 115
Si Yaek Roy Sop 115
Siam Commercial Bank HQ 88, 284
Siam Society 269, 286, 291
Siam Square ('Siam') **36**, 56, 58, 61, 69, 87, 90, **113**, 130, 144, 148, 179, **187**, 240-1, **247**, **249**-51, 271, 274, 285, **290**, **298**, 312
Silom 18, 26, 34, **44**, 57, 61-2, 64, 83, 116, **122**, **124**-**5**, 127-8, 131, **142**-45, 148, 158-9, 199, 203, 238-9, 274, 298, 327
Silom Soi 4 131, 145, 158, 203
Sindhorn Village 54, 227
Singha Estate 59
Sino-Thai, see Thai
Siri Wireless **232**
Siriraj Hospital **154**, 185, 209, 299
Siriraj Pier 239
SkyBridge 329
So Heng Tai 128, **214**
Soho House 130
'Soi Arab' 97, 198
'Soi Cowboy' **127**, 138, 298, 312
Songwad Rd 215
Southeast Asia Junction 269, 290
Sra Pathum Palace 185
Srifuengfung Building 77, 81, 288, **296**
Srinakharin 251, 275
Suan Luang Square 33, 251
Suan Mokkh retreat **107**
Suan Plu, Soi 53, **119**, 130, 235
Suan Rot Fai Park 95
Suan Si Nakhon Keun Kan (Middle Park) 57
Suan Santhiphap (Peace Park) 56-**7**
Sukhapibal Rd 29

Index   357

Sukhothai Palace 32, 185
Sukhumvit Rd & Sois
26, 34, 50, 57, 62, 83,
97, 111, 117, 125, 137,
144, 148, 154, 159, 198-
9, 201, 203, 208, 234,
244, 296, 309, 322, 331
SuperTower 82
Surawong/Suriwong Rd
41, 61, 145, 179
Suvarnabhumi Airport
23, 58, 72, 81, 92, 97,
101, 108, 158, 296
Tai Wah Tower II 82
Talad Noi 27, **45**, 128,
191, 199, **214**, **222**,
263, 292
Taling Chan 103, 333
Tamnak Daeng 285
Tha Phra **52**, 61, 105, 121
Tha Phra Chan 68, 94,
105, 115, 232, 301
Thai Art Archives 287
Thai Film Archive 268
Thailand Creative &
Design Centre (TCDC)
18-9, **35**, 55, 93, 116,
147, 161, 203, 238, 259,
269-70, 290, 325, 329-30
Thailand Cultural
Centre 74, 266, 273
Thaniya, Soi 138, 198
Thantawan, Soi 138
Thewes 27, 242
Thonburi & era (1767-
1782) 8-9, 23, 28,
47, 49, 51, 53, 63, 77,
83, 107-10, 155, 160,
172, 178-9, 189, 191,
194, 198-9, 211, 214,
239, 251, **278**, 281-2,
292, 308, **317**, 323,
324, 332
Thonglor, Soi 18, 32,
55-**6**, 61-2, 127, 130,
154, 162, 198, 253,
261, 270, 328
TK Park 18, 269, 290
Tobacco Monopoly 58
Tridhos City Marina 88
Vertic 82
Vertical, The 82
Vertiq 82
Victory Monument 60,
62, 184, 187, 201, 278,
282, 309, 329
Vimanmek Mansion
286, 289
Viphavadi Rangsit
Highway 73
Wang Burapha 61, 241,
285, 312
Wang Dek 88
Wang Derm 214
Wang Lang 11, 49
Wang Na (Front Palace)
49, 51, 285
Wang Varadis 172, 286
Wanglee, Soi 228
Wanit Soi 1 193
William Warren Library
269, 290
Windsor House 293
Witthayu (Wireless) Rd
95, 285
Woeng Nakhon Kasem
221
Wong Wien Yai 35, 120
Wutthakat 70-**1**
Yannawa 88, 192, 199,
214, 228, 275, 327-**8**
Yaowaphanit Rd 65
Yaowarat 39, 53, 61,

65, 92, 175, 195, **197**,
213-**7**, 219-21; see also
Chinatown, Sampeng
Yodpiman River Walk
238, 301
plans: see urban planning
Five Year Plans 326
planet day colours **91**-2
plastic bags 33, 182,
239, 333
Police, Royal Thai 53, **63**,
70, 102, 129, 131-3, 140,
142-3, 153-4, 157, 164-
6, 181-2, 187, 212, 243,
253-5, 270, 299-0**1**, 307,
319, 326
political parties 23, 177,
182, 186, 257
Bhumjai Thai 154
Democrat 100
Love Thailand 138
Muan Chon 144
People's Party (1932)
87, 183, 187, 282
People's Party (Future/
Move Forward) 23,
144, 186, 257
Pheu Thai 23, 186
politics 51, 53-4, 88, 101,
140-1, 143, 170, 172,
180-6, 215, 257, 273-4,
282, 290-1, 305, 307-8,
310, 313, 316, 320-1, 331;
see also people, protests
divisions 91, 94, 110,
171, 176, 278, 189,
202, 205, 222, 225, 261
geopolitics 197
pollution 16, 27, 41, 46-
7, 83, 146, 156-8, **167**,
315, 335
noise 156-7, 161, 258
PM2.5 27, 41, 46, 335
Port Authority 235, 331
Prathet Thai (Thailand) 193
'pretties' 137, **244**
primate city 48, 170, 185
prisons 23, 48, 58, 115,
155, 182, 185-6, 201, 242,
256, 281, 285, 305, 319
PromptPay 165
prostitution 16, 136-45,
148, 213, 260, 306-7
protests 13-4, 16-7, 23,
54, 56, 61, 66, 94, 100-1,
117, 155-6, **160**-1, 167,
176, 180, 181-2, **183**-**7**,
192, 205, 215, 225-6,
228, 247, 250, 253-**7**,
259, 264, 267, 270, 287,
306, 310, 312-3, 320,
322, 326-7, 334; see also
Bangkok Shutdown,
Ratsadorn, Red Shirts,
Yellow Shirts
public transport 52, 70-1,
136, 225; see also bus,
mass transit, BTS, MRT,
Airport Link
Purachai Curfew 129-30

queens, see royalty
Queensberry Rules 218

raang song (mediums) 120
radio 156-7, 160, 163, 184-
5, 203, 225, 250, 285
FAT FM 257, 268-9, 306
Ruam Duay Chuay
Kan 225
The Shock 113, 115, 129
rain 26-7, **40-1**, **43**, 45,
47, 72, 75, 81, 155, 158,

237, 252, 309, 330, 332-3
Rains Retreat 104, 143, 207
Rainbow Archives 145
Ramadan 105, 109-10, 176
Ramkhamhaeng Stele 174
Rattanakosin era (1782-
1932) 31, 48, 63, 65, 92,
108-9, 118, 171-2, 175,
178-9, 191, 197, 199,
211-2, 228, 236, **278-80**,
286, 289, 301, 326
Ratsadorn & youth protest
13, 23, 186-**7**, 247-8,
252, 255-**7**
Raw Comedy 319
Red Bull 130, 155, 211, 302
Red Shirts 17, 23, 43, 51,
54, 94, 117, **160**-1, 167,
176, 186-7, 205, 225,
247, 250, 282, 287, 334
refugees 23, 108, 166,
190-4, 223, 232, 292,
321, 328, 333
'resilient city' 176, 321,
327, 334
restaurants, bars & clubs,
see also food, nightlife
80/20 35
Beam 253
100 Mahaseth 37
Adhere 162
Appia 33
Aran Bicicletta Cicli 73
Asia Today 130
Ba Hao 214
Baan Ice 204
Bangkok Island 127
Bangkok Seaview
Seafood 331
Bearbie 145
Beef 145
Beaulieu, Le 37
Bed Supperclub 90, 131
Big Mama 32
Biscotti 37
Blue Elephant 38, 215,
284
Bo.lan 32, 38
Brit Pub 131
Broccoli Revolution 37
Buddha Bar 105
Buddy Beer 302-3
Café Chilli 204
Café Democ 251
Chandrphen 215
Check Inn 99 140
Club Culture 251
Club Soma 131
Dalat, Le 37
Death Café **153**
Din Tai Fung 37
DJ Station 145
Dome, The 38, 82, 86,
92, 262
Dudesweet 131
Eat Me! **39**
Eat Thai! 204
El Bulli 39, 275
Fake Club 145
G-Circuit parties 145
Gaggan 39
Gedhawa 204
Gianni's 37
Gig Groceries **230-1**
go-go bars **127**, 130-1,
138-41, 145, 298, 319
G.O.D. 145
Greyhound 32, 37, 256
Hard Rock Café 250
Have a Zeed 204
Heals 145
Hi-so bar 82
Hippie De Bar 284, 289

Holland Beer House 118
Hyde & Seek 38
Ia Sae coffee shop **212**
Indus 199
Insects in the Backyard
38-9
Inter 250
Iron Balls 131
Iron Fairies 131
Isaan Tawandang **204**
Isaan Terd Terng 203
Issaya Siamese Club 34
Jam 267, 312-**3**
Jam Factory 130, 161,
325, 327
Jay Fai 34, 39, 280
Jesters 37
Junker 130
Kalapapruek 34, 37
Khrua Apsorn 34
Khrua Aroy Aroy 34
Kiin-Kiin 37
Klang Soi 34
La Maison 88
La Table de Tee 37
Le Banyan 37
Le Du 38
Little Beast 37
Local, The 30, **38**-9, 289
Maggie Choo's 131,
144-5
Mississippi Queen 138
MK Suki 133, 243
ML Terb 34
Moon Bar 82
Moose **230-1**
Munjai Café 234
My Grandparents'
House **213**, 219
Nahm 35, 37, 38
Namsaah Bottling Trust 38
Never Ending Summer,
The 334
No-Hands 148
Normandie, Le 37
Opposite 39
Osha 35
Paste 37
Peppina 37
Phoebus 131
Phraya Palazzo 291
Pok Pok 34
Pulse 145
Q Bar 18
R-Harn **31**
Raintree Pub 163, 257
rooftop bars 37, 51, 80,
82-**3**, 126, 128, 130,
307, 312, 318
Route 66 131
Saxophone Pub 60
Shades of Retro 289
Sing Sing Theatre **131**
Sirocco 312, 318
Smalls 55, 130, **132**
Somtam Der 202
Sorn 39, 204
Soul Bar 164, 200
Soul Food 34
Space, The 324
Starbucks 250
Stranger 145
Studio Lam bar 203
Supanniga 34, 204
Tawandang German
Brewery 32, 88, 133,
156, 162-3, 263
Tawandang Saad Saen
Duean 163, 257, 263
Teens of Thailand 130
Tep Bar 130, 159, **161**
Thai Heaven 139
Thanusingha Bakery

House 293
Thanying 34
Third Place, The 55
Ton Krueng 34
Trasher 131-**2**
Tuba 264, 289
Vertigo 37, 82
Viva 237, 274
Water Library 37
Wimpy 241
Wine Republic 55
Wong's Place 55, 132
retro 34, 72, 88, 146-7,
163, 178, 203, 226, 231,
239, 264, 269, 274-**5**,
279, **288-91**, 318, 333
Revolution, see 1932
River, Chao Phraya, see
places: Bangkok
River Books 309
river expressboats 8, 68,
72-7, 127, 156, 334-**5**
rooftop farms 35, 59,
178, 233
Royal Barge Procession 9,
92, 101, **173**, 185, 286
Royal Projects 35, 173
royalty, see also kings
Chumporn, Prince 185
Damrong Rajanuphap,
Prince 170-2, 281,
286
Deputy King (Viceroy)
23, 49, 51, 179, 285
Marsi Chumbhot-
Pantip, Princess 173
Mongkut, Prince 103
Naris, Prince 172, 262,
317
Narisa Chakrabongse 229
Paribatra, Prince 172-3
Saovabha, Queen 211
Sirikit, Queen 73, 173,
254, 265, 286, 289
Sirindhorn, Princess
Maha Chakri 65, 195,
216, 219
Sirivannavari, Princess
265
Suthida, Queen 173

sabai (ease) 68, 170
saduak (convenience) 85,
170, 237
sae (clan) 192, 211-2
saeb (intense flavour) 170
Saeng Som 302
safe sex promotion **142**-3
sai sin (magic strings) 99,
113, 207
sakdina (feudal ranking)
64, 197, 204-5
samlor (three-wheeler) 77
Sanskrit 114, 179
sanuk (fun) 55, 93, 127,
129-35, 144, 156-7, 163,
170, 250, 255, 264, 266,
289, 304, 335
Sarit dictatorship 23, 72,
85, 103, 171, 173, 177,
184, 281, 285, 326
sayasaat (black magic) 112
schools 247-57; see also
Chinese schools
Bangkok Christian
College 103, 185
Brain, The 250
DaVance 250
Debsirin 185
Khru Lily 144, 250
Lanna Cultural 204
Mater Dei 103, 185
Pei-ing **64**-5

358 Index

Saint Gabriel's 103
Satree Witthaya 2 95
Triam Udom 250
Vajiravudh College 185, **263**
sci-fi 177, 309, 313, **332-3**
selfies, see photography
Seri Negara 111
Seri Patani 111
Seven Dangerous Days 70
sex tourism 140, 145, 213, 295, 298, 312, 319
sex trade, see prostitution
Shaktism 125
shamans 100, 113, **120-2**
Shark energy drink **244**
shophouses **10**, **13**, **32-3**, **44-5**,47, **50-5**, 60, 65, 77, **81**, 83, **85-90**, 120, **128**, 131, 158-9, 171, 178, 189, 210, **212**, 220, **222**-23, 228, 230-2, 236, 243-5, 250, 261-2, 289-90, 305, **314-5**, 326, 328
shops & brands, see also 7-Eleven, apps, malls
Apple Store 330
Big C 102, 240-1, 251, 322
Bombay Dept Store 284
Bookmoby 309
Burger Queen 250
Central Group 213
Central Chidlom 240
Chaps 199
Daeng Kan Chang 242
DJ Siam 250
DoReMi 250
Erb 26
Fuji film 7, 91
Harnn 26, **260**
I Wanna Bangkok 197
Jaspal 199
Karmakamet 26
King Power Duty Free 271
Kodak film 7, 91, 289
Merry Kings 285
Morgan & Hunter 292
New World 270, 299
Nightingale-Olympic 88, 241, 285
online shopping 13, 61, 139, 164-5, 236, 243-5, 334
Open House **55**, 130
Panpuri 26
Papaya design & studio 264, 289
Parrot Sporting 242
Pony Stone 250
Pop X Haus 275
pop-ups 275
Rajawongse Tailors 198
Robinson 240
Rolex 18
Selvedgework **274**-5
Tesco-Lotus 240
Thai Daimaru 251
Thai Pefume Runway 27, **29**
Thann 26
Uniqlo 42
Velayenn bike shop 73
Waen 268
Warehouse 30 **93**, **114**, **199**, 325
Zen **17**, 117, 240
shrines 60, 63, 91-2, 94, 97, 100-2, **113**-25, 172-3, 198, 216, 222-**3**, 225, 283, 286, 288, 298; see also *phii*, spirit houses
Chao Mae Tubtim Shrine 97, 114, 118
Chinese Shrines 60, 63, 91, 105, 216, 206-217
Chokchai 4 Kwan Im Shrine 215-6
Chuchok shrine 114, 318
Dev Mandir temple 199
Devasathan **97-9**, 199, 247
Erawan Shrine **102**, 109, 112, 167
Ganesha Shrine 102, 124-5
Hainanese Shrine 122
Hindu shrines and temples 94, **97**, **102**, 113, **120-5**, 129, 198
Indra Shrine 102
Jao Pho Lak Muang 65
Jao Por Seua Shrine 105
Kian Un Keng Shrine 214, 292, 308
Lakshmi Shrine 102
Lao Pun Thao Kong shrine **64**-5, 211-2
Leng Buay la Shrine 64
Nang Nak Shrine 10-11, **116**-7, 119
Por Lao Eia Shrine 65, 212
Sanctuary of Truth 107
Sia Ung Kong Shrine 65
Sikh Shrine 189
Snake Shrine 118-9
Uma Thevi Shrine 102
Vishnu Shrine 102, 199
Madonna Shrine 86-7, 324
Nai Lert Shrine 114
Siam (state) see places: Thai
Siam (Siam Square) see places: Bangkok
signage 28-9, 57-58, 60-4, 69-72, 89-90, 94, 115, 128, 149, 164, 183, 205, 166, 250, 272, **315**
Sikhs 97, 111, 189, 198-**9**; Namdhari 199
'Simultopia' 323
Sin City image 104, 127, 130-2, 136, 215, 297, 307, 312
siwilai (being civilised) 43, 56, 71, 85, 116, 130, 136, 170, 179, 198, 218, 230, 259, 262, 281, 321, 323-4, 326
skateboarding 58, 247, 250, 267
Skytrain, see BTS
Skywalks **36**, 45, 51-2, 69, 71, **82**-3, 89, 102, 159, 230, **248**, **297**, 329
slums 11, 13, 17, 29, 50, 53, 65-6, 79, 83, 220, **223**, 228, **234-5**, 250, **253**, 279, 295, 301, 312, 322, 329, 331
social justice 106, 302
social media 16, 34, 68, 94, 104, 116, 129, 133, 143, 156, 166, 182, 204, 215, 225, 241, 245, 251, 256, 282, 286, 294, 299, 301, 304-7, 331, 334; see also apps, Internet
Baidu 212, 221
Blued 145, 221
Facebook 14, 68, 94, 117, 164, 166, 176, 228, 243, 245, 301, 311
Grindr 145
Instagram 14, 42, **89**-91, 133, 165, 221, 230, 241,
245, 251, **276-7**, 294
LINE 164, 245
Tinder 136, 142
Trip Advisor 16, 303
X (Twitter) 241, 245
Social Order Campaign 106, 127, 129, 144, 334
songtaew (pick-up bus) 45, 75, **77**, 90, 319
SOTUS (Security, Order, Tradition, Unity, Spirit) 252-4
Southerner Association 209
Space Syntax 53
spas 26, 137, 147-**9**, 264, 296, 299, 333
spirit houses 97, 102, 112-5, 117, 179, 216; see also *phii*, shrines
sports 56, 73, 79, 105, 110, 122, 156, 185, 201, 229-30, 242, 248, 296
street vendors & stalls 24, 32-33, 36-7, **44**, 53, 55-6, 66-8, **74**, 77, 83, 85, 90, 111, 114-5, 128, **130**-1, 133, 137-**8**, 154, 158, 160, 164, 166-7, **183**, **197**, 199, 201, 203-4, **208**, 212, 226, 229, 234-8, **238**-45, 248-50, 258, 268, **274-5**, 280, 299, 301-2, 305, 326, 328, 333, 335; see also markets
streetfood, see food
streetlife 11-12, 16, 51, 55, 82, 85, 90, 105, 159, 178, 201, 222, 232-3, 238, 243, 247, 260, 297, **311**, **315**, 317, 327, 332
Streisand effect 257, 301, 307
Sufficiency Economy 183, 241
Sun, The 18, 24, 40-7, 63, 75, 80, 82, 84, 86, 90-92, 128-9, 184, 235, 237, 257, 330
supernatural; see black magic, mediums, *phii*, shrines, shamans
Supreme Court 51, 282, surnames 64, 192, 202, 243, 262

taew (locality) 49, 53, 160, 75, 190, 201, 223, 230
takraw 77, 285
tamnak (shaman den) **120-5**
Taoism 103, 213, 216, TAT, see tourism
tattoos (*sakyant*) 64, 97, 105, 113, 120-**3**, 129, 257, 260, 308
taxis, see also motorcycle taxis 6-7, 18, 45-6, 53, **60**, 64, 66, 70-1, 74, 76, 90-**1**, 97, 148, 156-7, 164, 189-90, 201, 212, 235, 285, **300**, **312**, 315
'Teflon Thailand' 296, 334
television & shows 22, 31, 37, **69**, 116, 119, 129, 134, 144, 156, 158, 182, 184-5, 187, 199, 204, 218, 221, 227, 240, 243, 255-6, 268, 295, 312-3, 318, 320; see also news
Academy Fantasia 163
American Dad 319
Anakot (Future): Tomorrow+i 333
Bangkok Bound 318
Bangkok Breaking 318
Bangkok Hilarious 319
BBC 306
Big Brother 81, 165
Black Mirror 333
Channel 3 204, 316
Channel 7 204
Family Guy 319
Dae Jang Geum 37
Farang Pok-Pok 318
Hormones Wai Wawoon 255, 318
Iron Chef 31, 37
Jor Khao Tuen (Shallow News in Depth) 320
Koo Kam 316
Little Britain 319
Netflix 318, 333
Power of Shadows 142
Reality TV 31, 163, 249, 318
RuPaul's DragRace 145
Saturday Night Live 319
Serpent, The 318
soap operas 85, 142, 151, 204, 251, 259, 263, 266, 273, 309, 316
Thai PBS 312
Thailand's Got Talent 137, 249
Travels with My Father 318
Voice, The 249
Work Point 125
temples, see *wat*
TEN House 233
Thai Airways 28, 239, 295
Thai exceptionalism & exemptionism 306, 310
Thai Gaze, the 84
Thai Go Association 212
Thai Health Foundation (TCH) 106, 271
Thai Smile airline 115, 299
Thai Studies 290, 310, 321
Thai Travel Agents Association 295
Thai-Bharat Lodge 193, 199
Thai-Chinese Chamber of Commerce 195, 220, 284
Thai-Chinese Traders Association 212
Thailand 4.0 165, 270
Thailand Elite Card 299
Thailand Grand Sale 241
Thainess 7, 10-3, 17, 19, 23, 57, 63, **79**, 87-8, 101, 106, **109**, 111, 117, 135-7, 141, **170-9**, 180, 190, 196, **200**-1, **204**-6, 212-3, 218-9, 223, 230, 241, 247-8, 253, 256, 258-63, 268, 280-4, 288-90, 296, 306, 310-6, 323, 330, 333; also places Thai
Thainess Festival/Fair/ Parade 57, **79**, 137, 171, **196**-7, **201**, **204**, 206
theatre: see dance & theatre
Third Class Citizen 268
third places 55-6, 136, 178, 223
third sex/gender 118, 121, 125, 143
Thotsakan 101, 183
top-knots **97**, **195**, 200, 234
tourism 9, 13, 16, 18, 33, 37, 70, 89, 101, 111, 128, 138-40, 150-1, 154, 171, 177, 185, 187, 195, 200, 206, 213, 215, 232, 235, 250, 263, 273, 281, **294-303**, 307, 311-2, 326, 329
Bangkok Vanguards 301
Best Bangkok Tours 128
Co van Kessel 73
community tours 294-5
cultural walks 291
Expique 80
Hivesters 232, 301
Nature Trails 158
Spice Roads 73, 158
Tourism Authority of Thailand (TAT) 31, 33, 145, 219, 281, 291, 295-6, 298-301
Tourist Police **300**
tradition 11, 13, 34, 36-9, 49, 86-7, 92-4, 97-125, 141-5, 147-9, 170-80, 200-35, 241, 247-70, 280-2, 288-91, 298, 313-5, 323, 334-5
traditional arts 28, 34, 36, 63, **79**, **80**, 86-7, 90-3, 97-111, 121-2, **129**, **147-8**, **159**, **165**, **172-3**, **195**, **200**, **202-9**, 222-4, 242, 258-73, 278-91, **293**, 296, 303-**4**, 312, 314-5
see also architecture: neo-traditional
traditional medicine 211, 264; see herbs, massage
traffic 8-9, 16, 18, 22, **24**, 28, **42**, 45, 47, 57, **61**-3, 66-7, 69-70, **74**, 77, 80-1, 115, 127, 156-7, 159-60, 164-7, 176-7, 185, 223, 225, 232, 237, 242, 245, 271, 296, 299, 307, 312, 318-9, 335
trafficking, human 139, 166, 190, 213, 295
trains 22-3, 45, 49, 51, 53, 60-1, 67, 71-2, **74**-7, 81, 89, 95, 157, 171, 185, **201**, 223, 227, 236, 241, 275, 295-6, 299-300, 315, 318, 329, **334**; see also Airport Link, BTS, MRT, places
trams 67, 71-2, 192, 285
trance **120-5**, 199, 208
transsexuals **125**, 136, 246
Treaty of Amity & Commerce 23
Treaty, Bowring 23, 214
Tri Bhumi Katha 63
Triple Gem 216, 282
tuk-tuks 26, **43**, 66, 69, **74**, 80, 86, 139, **156**, **179**, 238, 260, 290, 300, 312, **316**-7
Twelve Core Values 171, 229, 255

UN ESCAP 185
UNESCO 133, 139, 149, 185, 270, 283, 308, 325
UNFPA 254
uniforms 43, 45, 86, 89, **100**, **104**, 136-6, 154-5, 172, 180, 187, 237-8, **244**, **249**, 252-6, 263, 291, 316
universities
Assumption U 103
Bangkok U 110, 179, 271-2
Buddhist univesities 185
Chulalongkorn U 16, 36, 58, **94**-5, 185, 242, 250-2, 256, 272, 290, 329
CommDe 272

Index   359

Deem U 99
'Disrupt University' 256
Harvard Business
   School 135
Kasetsart U 95, 164
King Mongkut U of
   Technology 254, 272
Ramkhamhaeng U 201,
   239
Sheffield U 18
Silpakorn U 115, 125,
   185, **196**-7, **249**, 252,
   262, 272
Srinakharinwirot U 185
Thammasat U 9, 59, 94,
   116, 137, 145, 150, 185,
   187, 211, 248, 252, 282,
   290, **306**, 329
upper class, see class
Urban Design & Develop-
   ment Centre (UddC)
   231, 291, 327, 329
urban planning 8, 13-4,
   16-8, 25, 28, 33, 47-65,
   69-77, 80, 83-5, 89, 130,
   142, 161, 166, 174-5,
   179, 181, 221, 228-9,
   235, 270-1, 279-80, 291,
   296, 315; 322-34
urbanism & urbanists 14,
   17, 54, 56, 61, 67, 69,
   76, 171-8, 214, 212, 230,
   241, 251, 259, 305, 312,
   315, 318, 321-9, 333-4;
   see also messy urbanism

Vedas/Vedic 7, 92, 98, 198
vegetarianism **96**-7, 100,
   104, 122, 199, 220
vendors, see street vendors
'Venice of the East' 16, 41,
   175, 295, 297, 307, 321
Very Thai 6, 14, 16, 17-**19**,
   311, 315
Vessandorn, Prince 118
Viagra 140, 237
vintage; see retro
Vipassana; see meditation

wai khru (guru worship)
   78-**9**, 100, **122**-3, 222,
   265-**6**
wai khru rum muay 79
wairoon (youth) 247-57
Walkability Index 329
walking 6, 18, 53, 68-9,
   74, 76, 79, 107, 126, 158,
   182, 231, 241, 291, 296,
   325, 327, 329
War on Dark Influence 128
wat (**monasteries &**
   temples) 2, 8-9, 11, **27**,
   49, 53-4, 60, 63-5, 67,
   83, 86-8, 91-2, 97, **101**,
   104-7, 113-6, 122, 124,
   126-7, 129, 137, 139,
   143, 149, 150, **155**, 157,
   161, 171-**2**, **175**, 179,
   181, 185, 199, 201, **204**,
   207-**9**, 213, 216, 218,
   224-5, 227-8, 236-7,
   239, 247, 251, 259, 262-
   7, 273, 283, 292, 295,
   297, 306, 314, 324-5,
   328, **330**, 333
Wat Arun 9, 49, 64,
   83, 88, 92, **175**, **278**-
   9, **330**
Wat Baan Nampueng
   57, **163**
Wat Bang Phra 122
Wat Benchamabophit **2**,
   93, 201, **207**, **255**, 262

Wat Borom Niwat 218
Wat Bowonniwet 218, 172
Wat Chakkrawat 299
Wat Chong Nonsi 108
Wat Dusitaram 208-**9**
Wat Hualumphong 151
Wat In **112**-3, **126**, 129
Wat Kalawar 292-**3**
Wat Kalayanimit **79**,
   216, 228
Wat Khaek (Maha Uma
   Devi) 124-**5**, 199
Wat Khlong Toei Nai **150**
Wat Khun (Khun Samut
   Chin) **331**, 333
Wat Khun Chan **106**
Wat Kor **103**
Wat Mahabutr **12**, 113,
   116, **119**
Wat Mahathat **40**, 49,
   51, 106
Wat Mangkon (Leng
   Noi Yi) 65
Wat Pailom 158
Wat Pariwat **6**, 88, 100
Wat Pathumwan 100
Wat Pho 7, 27, **41**, 88-9,
   92, **128**, 149, 172, 264,
   295, 308, **330**
Wat Phra Kaew **170**,
   172, 179, 314
Wat Phut Udom **155**
Wat Pichayat 185
Wat Prayoon 185, 325
Wat Rachathiwat 201,
   208, 262
Wat Rakhang 8, 9, 11,
   324-5
Wat Ratchabophit 103,
   172, 262
Wat Ratchanadda 89
Wat Soi Thong 228
Wat Suan Kaew 239
Wat Suan Mokkh 16, **107**
Wat Suthat 24, 45, 59
Wat Takian 100
Wat Trimitr 221, 283
Wat Wachiratham Sathit
   2, **207**-8
Wat Wisanu 124
Wat Yannawa 88, 214,
   228, 275
Water Culture 41, 47, 66,
   323, 327, 333
websites, see Internet
Westernisation, see
   colonialism, places: West
win; see *motorsai*
women 28, 45, 49, 78,
   100, 104, 111, 118-9,
   121, 125, 136-45, 150-1,
   153, 192, 215, 235, 251,
   254, 295, 312, 317
working class, see class
World Bank 165
World Book Capital 2013
   290, 308
World Cities 13, 38, 47,
   185, 190, 229, 236, 278,
   297, 304, 331
World Happiness Report
   226
World Heritage Site 174
World Trade Center 241
World Values Survey 204
World War II 23, 107,
   170, 282
writers & academics
   7, 19, 30, 142, 180, 223,
   228, 264, **270**, **308**-**9**,
   317-8, 320, 332; see also
   books
Ackroyd, Peter 308

Algie, Jim 318
Anake Nawigamune
   287, 289-90
Anek Laothamatas 180
Anderson, Benedict
   202, 281, 313
Askew, Marc 175,
   179, 228
Atiya Achakulwisut
   94, 254
Bacigalupi, Paolo 50,
   332
Baker, Chris 174, 307,
   310-1, 313
Barang, Marcel 308
Barrett, Dean 140
Biggs, Andrew 318
Boccuzzi, Ellen 45, 203
Botan (Supha
   Sirisingh) 193, 308
Bourdain, Anthony 34
Brand, Stuart 77
Brown, Dan 308
Brown, Janet 319
Bunnag, Shane 285
Burdett, John 140, 150
Burslem, Chris 318
Bush, Austin 34
Cassady-Dorion, Luke
   318
Chanun Poomsawai
   130, 163
Chang Noi 106, 219,
   307, 310, 323
Charnvit Kasemsiri
   179, 205
Chatri Prakitnonthakan
   282
Chawadee Nualkhair 33
Chetana Nagavajara 320
Chua, Lawrence 318
Cooper, Cameron 29
Cotterill, Colin 140
Dawson, Alan 283
Draper, John 206
Duangphat Sitthipat 302
Eckhardt, James 318
Evans, Julian 322
Feingold, David 139
Fellows, Warren 151
Garland, Alex 302
Gehl, Jan 177
Gilquin, Michel 110
Gillison, Samantha 232
Halliday, Bob 34-35
Hamilton, Annette 177
Herzfeld, Michael 56
Hollinger, Carol 319
Hopkins, Jerry 318
Hoskin, John 88
Jack, Ian 299
Jacobs, Jane 225
Ka F Wong 286
Kaewmala 143, 248
Kannika Ratanaprida-
   kul 328, 334
Kasian Tejapira 214,
   220, 323
Kerr, Alex 19, 317
Khamsing Srinawk 202
King, Ross 136, 322
Kong Rithdee 100-1,
   153, 205, 255, 268,
   309, 320
Korakot 'Nym'
   Punlopraksa 34, 227
Kukrit Pramoj, M. R.
   171, 173, 193, 220,
   254, 308
Landry, Charles 19, 270
Lao Khamhom 202
Larkin, Emma 309
Lawang, Davud 110

Liang Chua Morita
   215, 218
Main Nardone 309
Maisel, Eric 258
Manote Tripathi 125
McDaniel, Justin 104,
   112, 116
McGrath, Brian 241, 323
Mendiratta, Anita 302-3
Moore, Christopher G
   140, 318
Mui Poopoksakul 309
Natayada na Songkhla
   28, 126
Needham, Jake 307
Newman, James 138,
   140
Nidhi Eoseewong 183,
   186, 323, 330-31
Noh Anothai 308
Nostitz, Nick 138
Oldenburg, Ray 55, 230
Osborne, Lawrence 7,
   148, 261, 317
Paisarn Likhit-
   preechakul 106
Paiwarin Khao-Ngam
   41, 203
Palmer, Stephen 332
Pasuk Phongpaichit
   174, 307, 313
Pathan, Don 111
Peerawat Jariyasombat
   73, 128
Pelegri, Maurizio 321
Pettifor, Steven 264
Pimsai Amaranand 173
Pitch Pongsawat 176,
   204, 232, 241, 251
Pitchaya Sudbantad
   309, 333
Ploenpote Atthakor
   71, 94, 228
Plunkett-Hogge, Kay 26
Pongpet Mekloy 73
Pornchai Seree-
   mongkonpol 319
Prabda Yoon 309, 312
Prapt (Chairat Pipit-
   pattanaprap) 308
Rattawut Lapcharoen-
   sap 28, 309
Reynolds, Craig 290
Saksith Saiyasombut
   171, 176
Sanitsuda Ekachai
   100, 104
Saran Mahasupap 248,
   250-51, 310, 321-2
Saskia Sassen 54
Segaller, Denis 319
Shakespeare, William 88
Shearer, Alistair 321
Skinner, William 193
Smith, Malcolm 211
Smith, P. D. 49
Smithies, Michael 212,
   318
Somerset Maugham,
   William 88
Somtow Sucharitkul
   (SP Somtow) 263,
   309, 313, 333
Sophorntavy Vorng
   101, 241, 321
Sopranzetti, Claudio 77
Spurlock, Morgan 152
Sri Burapha 308
Streckfuss, David 306
Suchada Tangtongtavy
   157
Sujit Wongthes 189, 323
Sulak Sivaraksa 281

Sunisa Manning 309
Sunthorn Phu 308
Surasak Glahan 283
Stapleton, John 300
Suthorn Sukphisit 31,
   34, 204
Tadsanawadee 41
Tew Bunnag 41, 309
Thanadsri Svasti 34
Thanong Khanthong 243
Theroux, Paul 27, 49
Thitinan Pongsudhirak
   186
Thongchai Winichakul
   106, 206, 280
Trink, Bernard 139
Tulsathit Taptim 137,
   182
Ung Ang Talay 34
Usnisa Sukhsvasti 137
V na Pramuanmark 308
Van Beek, Steve 305, 313
Vasit Dejkhunjorn 140
Vater, Tom 140
Vatikiotis, Michael 220
Veeraporn Nitiprapha
   308, **309**
Voranai Vanijaka 174,
   178, 189, 216, 310,
   317, 330-31
Warren, William 216,
   269, 290, 317
Wasant Techawong-
   tham 116, 244-5
Wise, David 184
Wolfe, Tom 38
Woolsey, Barbara 139
Worathep Akkabootra
   (Can Dan Isan) 209,
   326-**7**, 330-**1**
Wyatt, David 118
Yanyong Boon-Long
   69, 305
Zakariya Amataya 309
Zcongklod Bangyikhan
   68, 72, 87, 89, 130,
   177, 317, 321

yaan (neighbourhood)
   49, 53, 56, 73-4, 110, 151,
   158, 175-9, 191, 195,
   201, 222-35, 238, 240,
   242, 275, 278, 280, 287,
   291-3, 327, 329
Yakult 114
Yawi 110
Yellow Shirts 17, 23, 47,
   94, 100, 117, 125, **160**,
   167, 176, 183, **186**-7,
   193, 225, 247, 250, 282,
   287, 310
youth culture 12, 14, 18,
   53, 55-6, 61, 102, 106,
   110, 128-32, 142-5, 153,
   161, 186-7, **194**, 199,
   204, 220, 224, 239, 240-
   1, **247**-**58**, 260, 267, 270,
   274-5, 285, **302**-**3**, 305,
   312, 318, 329, 334

360 Index